금융·증권·보험 용어 사전

월드사이언스
worldscience.co.kr

금융·증권·보험
용어 사전

월드사이언스
worldscience.co.kr

金融・證券・保險 用語 辭典

금융・증권・보험 용어 사전

(The Dictionary of Securities Insurance & Financial Terms)

인　쇄 | 2013년 4월 1일
발　행 | 2013년 4월 10일

원저자 | 주식회사 アイ・エス・エス
감수자 | 정혜진
발행인 | 박선진
발행처 | 도서출판 월드사이언스

주　소 | 서울특별시 서초구 방배4동 864-31 월드빌딩 1층
등록일자 | 1988년 2월 12일
등록번호 | 제 16-1601호
대표전화 | (02) 581-5811~3
팩스 | (02) 521-6418

E-mail | worldscience@hanmail.net
URL | http://www.worldscience.co.kr

정가 | 20,000원
ISBN | 978-89-5881-215-9

이 도서의 국립중앙도서관 출판시도서목록(CIP)은 e-CIP홈페이지(http://seoji.nl.go.kr)와 국가자료공동목록시스템(http://www.nl.go.kr/kolisnet)에서 이용하실 수 있습니다.
(CIP제어번호: CIP2013001812)

신판 발행의 인사말

금융·증권·보험 거래의 국제화는 멈출 줄을 모르며 자유화, 다양화, IT화에 따라 많은 새로운 상품이 생겨나고 거래방법도 나날이 새로워지고 있다.

따라서 금융·증권·보험 분야의 전문용어도 대폭 증가하여 영어와 우리말 사이의 확인과 통일이 불가피한 상황이 되었다. 또한 금융 빅뱅의 영향으로 은행·신탁·생명보험·손해보험 각 업계간의 상호참가가 가속화됨에 따라 여러 분야를 포괄하는 전문용어를 간편한 한 권에 집약할 필요성이 대두되었다.

1995년에 초판을 발행한 본 사전은 이러한 인식하에 은행·증권·생명손해보험업계에서 활약하는 국제비즈니스맨은 물론 일반기업의 재무부, 국제부, 변호사, 공인회계사, 세무사, 대학관계자, 통역사, 번역사 등을 위한 휴대 간편한 전문용어사전으로 편찬되었다.

본 사전은 편자가 오랫동안 통, 번역 업무에 종사하는 과정에서 축적한 영한 두 언어의 정보를 데이터베이스화하고 중요한 용어를 엄선하여 수록하였다. 그러나 새로운 용어는 매일같이 생겨나므로 초판 발행 이후에도 계속해서 신어정보를 축적한 끝에, 마침내 전면적인 개정, 추가 작업을 거쳐 더욱 독자의 수요에 부응하는 신판으로 재편찬하였다. 방대한 편집 작업에는 만전의 주의를 기울였으나 누락이 없다고 단언할 수는 없으므로 독자 여러분의 질책과 조언을 간절히 바라는 바이다.

마지막으로 본 사전의 신판 편찬에는 도쿄증권거래소 파생상품부 · 파생상품총무실장인 아다치 세이지(安達精司) 씨의 감수도움을 받았다. 이 자리를 빌어 깊은 감사를 드리는 바이다.

2001년 3월

편저자

목차

[범례]

I 이 사전은 금융·증권·보험 분야에서 날로 증가하는 새로운 전문용어에 중점을 두고 편집하였다. 또 영어에 대한 기초지식을 갖춘 이용자를 대상으로 하였으므로 일반적인 영한사전의 품조와 발음기호는 생략하였다.

II 용어의 배열은 영한의 경우에는 알파벳순으로 배열하고 복수를 나타내는 s, 또는 es는 무시하였다. 한영의 경우는 가나다순으로 배열하였다.

III 동일한 용어라 할지라도 사용방법이 다르면 두 종류의 번역어를 모두 게재하였다.

[ENGLISH–KOREAN]

영한편

AAA class AAA등급
abandon 철회하다
abandonment 방기
abandonment clause 위탁조항
abandonment of action 소송방기
abandonment of right 권리방기
abandonment value 방기가치
abate 줄이다
abatement 감액
abatement claim 감액청구
abide by 준수하다
abiding sense 고정관념
ability 능력
ability theory of taxation 담세능력설
ability to generate favorable cash flows 바람직한 자금흐름을 만들어내는 능력
ability to pay 지불능력
ability to pay basis 지불능력기준
ability to pay dividend 배당능력
ability to pay principle 응능원칙
abnormal cost 이상원가
abnormal growth model 이상원가모델
abnormal item 이상항목
abnormal returns 이상수익
abnormal settlement of accounts 이상결산
abnormal shrinkage 이상감모
abode 거주
abolition 폐지
above market 시장에 맞추어
above par 평가이상
above the line 경상비 이상의
above-normal earning 초과이익
abridgment 적요
abrogation 폐지
absconding debtor 실종된 채무자
absence 부재
absentee 부재자
absentee owner 부재소유자
absentee ownership 부재소유권
absolute 절대적인
absolute advantage 절대우위
absolute conveyance 절대적 양도
absolute cost 저대원가
absolute delivery 무조건인도
absolute difference 절대차액
absolute error 절대오차
absolute fixed capital 절대적 고정자산
absolute income hypothesis 절대소유가설
absolute level 절대수준
absolute liability 결과책임
absolute performance 절대적 퍼포먼스
absolute probability 절대확률
absolute profit 순익
absolute sales 무조건매매
absolute total loss 절대전손
absolute value 절대치
absolutism 절대주의
absorbed bond 매매채권
absorbed burden 배부를 마친 제조간접비
absorbed corporation 흡수합병된 회사
absorbed cost 회수를 마친 원가
absorption 매매;흡수합병

absorption account 배부계정
absorption approach 흡수적 접근방법
absorption cost 전부원가
absorption costing 전부원가계산
absorption rate 배부율
abstract 요약
abstract of accounts 발췌계산서
abstract of financial statements 재무제표적요서
abstract of register 초본
abstract of title 권리서
absurdity 불합리
abuse 활용
abuse of rights 권리남용
accelerated amortization 가속상각
accelerated benefIts 진불한 시망보험금
accelerated cost recovery system 가속상각법
accelerated depreciation 가속감가상각
accelerated depreciation methods 가속상각법
accelerated land purchase 공유지선행취득
accelerated method 상각법
accelerated redemption 조기상각
acceleration 기한이익상실
acceleration claims 촉진클레임
acceleration clause 기한이익상실조건
acceleration coefficient 가속도계수
acceleration demand 기한전 반제요구
acceleration of registration 조기등록
acceleration principle 가속도원리
accept 수리하다, 받아들이다
acceptable level 용인할 만한 수준
acceptance 인수
acceptance commission 인수수수료
acceptance credit 인수조건부 신용장
acceptance line 인수한도
acceptance notice 인수통지
acceptance of bill 어음인수
acceptance of order 수탁
acceptance on security 담보부 인수
acceptance outstanding 어음인수
acceptance payable 지불어음
acceptance price of net assets 순자산인수액
acceptance rate 수입어음결제상장
acceptance receivable 수취어음
acceptance system 인수방식
accepting bank 어음인수은행
accepting house 어음인수회사
accepting rate of exchange 환인수상장
acceptor 인수자
access card 억세스카드
access to capital market 금융시장에 억세스함
accession 권리취득
accessory 보조
accessory product 부산물
accessory to tax evasion 탈세방조범
accident and health insurance 상해 및 건강보험
accident error 우연오차
accident insurance 사고보험
accidental cost 우발경비
accommodation 융통
accommodation bill 융통어음
accommodation endorsement 융통이서
accommodation lands 가격이 상승한 토지
accommodation marker 융통어음발행인
accommodation note 융통어음
accommodation trades 담합거래
accommodation works 편의공작물
accompanying document 첨부서류
accord 협정
accord and satisfaction 대물변제
accordance 일치
accordant 일치하는
account 계정;계좌;고객
account analysis 계정분석
account balance 계정잔고
account book 출납부;장부
account chart 계정과목일람표
account closing procedure 결산절차
account code 계정과목코드
account current 당좌계정
account day 회계일

account debtor 외상채권채무자
account due from sales on approval 시용판매미수금
account due on consignment-out 위탁판매미수금
account executive 광고기획자
account form 계정식
account form income statement 계정식손익계산서
account from profit and loss statement 계정식손익계산서
account headings 계정과목
account in transit 미달계정
account method 장부방식
account number 계좌번호
account number plan 계정과목번호표시법
account of business 영업보고서
account of credit sales 외상매출금계정
account of sales 매상계산서
account owed to employees 종업원에 대한 채무
account paid 지불필 계정
account payable 외상채무
account receivable 수취계정;외상매출금;미수금계정
account receivable discounted 할인수취계정
account receivable due from affiliated company 관계회사외상매출금
account receivable insurance 외상보험
account record 보고서
account rendered 확정계정
account report service 어카운트레포트서비스
account stated 확정계정
account statement 계정서
account system 계정시스템
account termination 계좌해약
account title 계정과목
account transfer 계좌대체
account year basis 어카운트이어베이시스
accountability 설명할 책임
accountability unit 책임단위
accountable 책임있는
accountable event 회계사상
accountable officer 회계담당자
accountable person 책임자
accountable receipt 수령증
accountable warrant 회계워런트
accountancy 회계학
accountancy service 회계감사업무
accountant 회계사
accountant business 경리사무
accountant in bankruptcy 파산청산인
accountant in charge 주임회계사
accountant report 감사보고서
accountant's inspection 회계감사
accountant's office 회계사사무소
accountant's report 회계상의 보고서
accountant's responsibility 회계사책임
accounting 회계
accounting adjustment 회계수정처리
Accounting and Auditing Enforcement Release 회계감사실시발표
accounting audit 회계감사
accounting axiom 회계공리
accounting base 회계기준
accounting based on legal requirements 회계법규에 따른 규제
accounting beta 회계베타
accounting beta value 회계베타수치
accounting book 회계장부
accounting by month 월할계산
accounting control 회계관리
accounting convention 회계원칙
accounting currency 회계통화
accounting data 회계자료
accounting data process 회계사무처리
accounting department 경리과
accounting division 회계과
accounting earnings 회계이익
accounting entity 회계실체
accounting evidence 회계증거
accounting firm 회계사무소

accounting for branch office 지점회계
accounting for business combinations 기업결합회계
accounting for changing prices 화폐가치변동회계
accounting for compensated absences 유급휴가회계
accounting for contingencies 우발사건회계
accounting for control 통제회계
accounting for future cost 미래원가계산
accounting for income tax allocation 세금배포회계
accounting for income taxes 세효과회계
accounting for internal reporting 내부보고회계
accounting for inventories 재고자산회계
accounting for ownership equity 자본회계
accounting for pension plan 연금회계
accounting for price-level change 가격수준변동회계
accounting for tax allocation 세금배분회계
accounting for the cost of pension plans 연금제도상의 연금회계
accounting function 회계직능
accounting identity 회계등식
accounting information system 회계조직
accounting issues 회계상의 문제점
accounting machine 회계기
accounting manual 회계매뉴얼
accounting model 회계모델
accounting objectives 회계목적
accounting organization 회계조직
accounting period 사업연도
accounting period in case of merger 합병사업연도
accounting policy 회계방침
accounting postulate 회계공준
accounting practice 회계실무
accounting principle 회계원칙
Accounting Principles Board 회계원칙심의회
accounting principles for business enterprise 기업회계원칙
accounting procedures 회계절차
accounting profession 회계사업
accounting rate 산정레이트
accounting rate of return 회계이익
accounting ratio 재무비율
accounting ratio of profits to net worth 회계자기자본이익률
accounting recognition 회계상의 인식
accounting records 회계기록
accounting regulation 회계규정
accounting regulations 경리규정
accounting report 회계보고
Accounting Research Bulletin 회계연구공보
accounting return on equity 주주자본이익률
accounting rules 회계통칙
accounting section 회계과
Accounting Series Release 회계연속통첩
accounting sheet of collected amount 징수액계산서
Accounting Standard Board 회계기준심의회
Accounting Standard Division 회계기준부서회
accounting standards 회계기준
accounting system 회계제도
accounting terminology 회계용어
Accounting Terminology Bulletin 회계용어공보
accounting theory 회계이론
accounting transactions 회계거래
accounting treatment 회계처리
accounting unit 회계단위
accounting valuation 회계평가
accounting year 회계연도
accounts due 미수금
accounts of margin transaction 신용거래계정
accounts of the Bank of Japan 일본은행계정
accounts receivable insurance 인수계정보험
accounts to receive 인수계정
accounts-receivable aging 미수금경과기간

A B

accredited buyer 신용장상의 매주
accredited investor 적격투자가
accredited party 신용장발행의뢰인
accreting swap 원금증가형 스와프
accretion 재산증가
accretion bond 어크리에이션본드
accrual 발생
accrual account 자연증식계정
accrual accounting 발생주의회계
accrual basis 발생주의
accrual basis accounting 발생주의회계
accrual method 발생주의
accrual of cause of action 소송원인발생
accrual of discount 할인기간대응할부
accrual of interest 이자미불
accrual period 발생기간
accrual rate 경과이자
accruals 미수지계정
accrued account 미불계정
accrued assets 자연증식자산
accrued benefit 급부수령권
accrued bonuses 상여수당금
accrued charge 미불비용
accrued commission 미불수수료
accrued depreciation 감가상각발생액
accrued dividend 미불배당액
accrued donation 미불기부금
accrued employees retirement benefit 퇴직급여준비금
accrued expenses 미불비용
accrued expenses payable 미불비용
accrued income 미수이익
accrued income taxes 납세준비금
accrued interest 경과이자;미불이자
accrued interest on loan 대부미수이자
accrued item 경과항목
accrued liabilities 예상채무
accrued liability 미불채무
accrued payroll 미불급여
accrued premium 계상보험료
accrued rent 미불임차금
accrued revenue 미수이익
accrued salaries 미수급료
accrued severance indemnities 퇴직급여예비금
accrued taxes on income 납세예비금
accrued wages 미불공임
accumulated amount 누적액
accumulated assets 적립자산
accumulated benefit obligation 누적급부채무
accumulated capital 축적
accumulated debt 누적채무
accumulated deficit 누적적자
accumulated depreciation 감가상각누적액
accumulated dividend 누적배당
accumulated earning tax 유보수익세
accumulated earnings 이익잉여금
accumulated earnings credit 유보이익공제액
accumulated fund 적립금
accumulated income 누적이익
accumulated income tax prepayment 장기전불세금
accumulated interest 누적이자
accumulated investment 누적투자
accumulated investment plan benefits 연금급부누적액
accumulated preferred stock 누적배당우선주식
accumulation 누적
accumulation of basis reserve 기본준비금을 적립함
accumulation of capital 자본축적
accumulation of default compensation reserve 위약손실보상준비금을 적립함
accumulation plan 적립플랜
accumulation system 누적시스템
accumulation trust 수익을 원본에 편입하는 형태의 투자신탁
accumulation unit 누적유닛
accumulations 이자적립
accumulative 누적적인
accumulative investment period 누적투자기간

accumulative investment plan 누적투자플랜
accumulative investment unit 누적투자유닛
accumulative judgment 누적판결
accumulative rate 누적비율
accumulative stock 누적배당형 주식
accuracy 정확성
accusation 고발
accusatory part 기소부분
accused 피고인
accuser 기소자
achievement 업적
acid ratio 당좌비율
acid test ratio 산성시험비율
acknowledgment 승인
acknowledgment of order 응낙
acquiescence 묵인
acquired company 피매수회사
acquired right 기득권
acquired surplus 취득잉여금
acquirement of properties 자산취득
acquirer 애콰이어
acquiring member 가맹점획득회원
acquisition 취득
acquisition accounting 매수회사
acquisition adjustment 취득원가조정
acquisition by subsides 보조금으로 취득함
acquisition cost 취득원가
acquisition cost adjustment 취득원가조정
acquisition cost method 취득원가법
acquisition cos of assets 자산취득가액
acquisition cost of depreciable assets
감가상각자산취득가액
acquisition cost of inventory
재고자산취득가액
acquisition cost of leasehold 차지권취득원가
acquisition cos of property 자산취득가액
acquisition cost of securities
유가증권취득가액
acquisition cost price 조달가격
acquisition cost theory 취득원가주의
acquisition date 취득일
acquisition for value 유상취득
acquisition of concessions 이권획득
acquisition of debenture 사채취득
acquisition of membership 가입
acquisition of qualification 자격취득
acquisition of right 권리수록
acquisition of stock 주식취득
acquisition of the application right
출원권 취득
acquisition strategy 매수전략
acquisition value 취득가격
acquisitive prescription 취득시효
acquit 면소되다
acquittal of debt 채무면제
acquittance 채무완제
acreage 지적
across the board 모든 종류를 포함하는; 일괄의
act of bankruptcy 파산행위
act of God 불가항력
act of honor 참가인수
act of incorporation 설립법
act of indemnity 면책법
act of insolvency 지불불능행위
act of law 법의 행위
act of parliament 국회제정법
act of state 국가의 행위
act tax 행위세
action 행위
action program 액션프로그램
actionable fraud 사기
actionable negligence
소송대상이 될 만한 과실
active account 활동계정
active balance 활동잔고
active bond 이자부 채권
active buying 적극적인 매입
active cardholder
실제로 카드를 사용하는 고객
active conduct of business 사업활동
active dealer 적극적인 딜러
active debt 채권

active investment management theory 적극투자이론
active life fund 현직자기금
active management 적극적인 운용
active market 호황시장
active partner 액티브파트너
active portfolio 액티브포트폴리오
active return 액티브리턴
active risk 액티브리스크
active risk aversion 액티브리스크 회피도
active stock 인기주
active trust 적극신탁
activity accounting 활동회계
activity analysis 액티비티분석
activity level 조업률
activity rates 활동률
actual 현실의
actual absorption costing 실제전부원가계산
actual acquisition cost basis 실제취득원가주의
actual annual percentage rate 실질연리
actual assets 실가자산
actual balance 직물보유고
actual basis accounting 실제주의회계
actual burden rate 실제배부율
actual cash value 현금환가가치
actual cost 실제원가
actual cost accounting system 실제원가계산제도
actual cost method 실제원가계산
actual costing 실제원가계산
actual delivery 현물인도
actual delivery of stock sold 현물인도
actual demand 실수요
actual demand rule 실수원칙
actual exchange rate 직물레이트
actual expenses 실비
actual index price 실제지수
actual interest rate 실효금리
actual inventory 실지재고
actual number of days elapsed 경과실수
actual position 액추얼포지션
actual price 실제가격
actual production 생산실적
actual purchase price 실제구입가액
actual rate of growth 현실성장률
actual receipt of stock purchased 현실거래
actual results of recent stock transactions 주식거래실적
actual return on plan assets 연금자산실제운용수익
actual state of business 영업상황
actual state of property 자산상황
actual surplus 순잉여금
actual total loss 현실전손
actual trading behavior 실제거래행위
actual transfer price 실제양도가액
actual useful life 실제내용연수
actual value 실가
actual value method 실가법
actual volume 실제조업도
actually expected standard cost 현실표준원가
actuals 현물
actuarial asset value 보험수리에 따른 자산가치
actuarial cost method 연금수리비용계산방식
actuarial expectation 보험수리상의 기대치
actuarial gains or losses 수리손익
actuarial hours 평균실제노동시간
actuarial method 연금이율법
actuarial yield 보험수리이율
actuary 보험계리인
ACU 아시아결제동맹 (이란, 파키스탄, 스리랑카, 인도, 네팔, 방글라데시 6개국의 지역청산지불기구)
ad hoc arbitration 개별중재
ad valorem 종가
ad valorem duty 종가세
ad valorem storage 종가보관료
ad valorem tariff 종가세율
ad valorem tax 종가세
add on system 애드온방식

add-on rate 애드온금리
added float 추가발행
added or deducted 가감하다
added value 부가가치
added value statement 부가가치계산서
addenda 추가문서
adding back the credited reserve amount in full to the income in the following period 기전에 계상한 대손준비금을 기말에 전부 잔액을 환산해서 새로 대손준비금을 적립하는 방법
adding to holdings 추가소유
addition of scale 규모확대
addition to reserve 준비금이월
addition to retained earnings 이익잉여금으로 대체함
additional allowance 할증수당
additional amount to a refund of national tax 국세환부가산액
additional amount to refundment 환부가산금
additional arrearage charge 연체가산금
additional budget 보정예산
additional capex 설비투자증가
additional capital 증가자본
additional charge 추가비용
additional charge for deficient return 과소신고가산금
additional collateral 증가담보
additional conditions 추가조항
additional deposit 증가상각
additional depreciation deduction 할증상각
additional depreciation on fire-proof buildings 내화건축물을 증가상각함
additional depreciation ratio 할증상각률
additional equity 증자
additional establishment 추가설정
additional expenses 추가비용
additional freight 할증운임
additional investment 추가출자
additional issue 추가설정
additional listing 추가상장
additional margin 추가이익
additional minimum liability 최저추가채무
additional paid-in capital 추가자본준비금
additional premium 할증보험료
additional tax 가산세
additional tax due to failure to file a return 무신고가산세
additional tax for deficient returns 과소신고가산세
additional tax on nonpayment 불납부가산세
additional-type investment trust 추가형 투자신탁
additions and betterment reserve 증개축적립금
additions and omissions 추가 및 생략
additions to plant and equipment 설비신규구입액
additions to reserves 적립금편입
additions to tax 부대세
additive substruction 가법감산
addressee 수신인
adduce 인증하다
adequate 상당한
adequate liquidity 적정유동성
adequate profit 적절한 이익
adequate protection 충분한 보호
adjacent 인근의
adjective law 절차법
adjoining 근접의
adjournment 연기
adjudge 사법적인 판단을 내리다
adjudication 재판
adjudication of bankruptcy 파산선고
adjudication order 파산명령
adjunct account 부가계정
adjustable basket technique 비대칭바스켓방식
Adjustable Life Insurance 어드저스터블보험
adjustable mortgage 변동금리모기지
adjustable peg 어드저스터블페그
adjustable peg system 조정가능고정상장

adjustable rate mortgage 변동금리모기지
adjustable rate mortgage loan 조정금리저당론
adjustable rate notes 조정가능이부어음
adjustable rate preferred stock 변동이율우선주
adjusted 조정필
adjusted basis 조정기준
adjusted beta value 수정베타수치
adjusted capital gain 조정후 양도소득
adjusted central bank money stock 조정 후 중앙은행통화스톡
adjusted cost basis 수정원가주의
adjusted debit balance 신용거래융자잔고
adjusted dividend increase 조정 후 배당증가율
adjusted EPS increase 조정 후 EPS 증가율
adjusted equity 수정주주자본
adjusted gross income 수정총소득
adjusted historical cost 수정취득원가
adjusted income 조정소득금액
adjusted net minimum tax 수정순미니멈세
adjusted net profit 수정후 순이익
adjusted regression analysis 수정회귀분석
adjusted to seasonal variations 계절변동 조정필
adjusted trial balance 정리 후 시산표
adjusting entry 수정기입
adjusting journal entry 수정분개
adjustment 체제구축;조정
adjustment account 조회계정
adjustment at term-end 기말정리
adjustment bond 정리사채
adjustment entry 정리기입
adjustment factor 조정지수
adjustment for price fluctuations 가격변동수정
adjustment for taxable income 세무조정
adjustment in filing a final tax return 신고조정
adjustment in settling accounts 결산조정
adjustment inflation 조정인플레이션
adjustment item 조정항목
adjustment of accounts 장부정리
adjustment of business income 기업이익조정
adjustment of capital 자본수정
adjustment of cost variance 원가차액조정
adjustment of debts 채무조정
adjustment of surplus 잉여금조정
adjustment of the carrying amount 부가수정
adjustment of the debts of a municipality 지방공공단체의 채무조정
adjustment pressure 조정압력
adjustment premium 조정보험료
adjustment process of balance of payments 국제수지조정과정
adjustment securities 조정증권
admeasurement 배분
administered price 관리가격
administered-price inflation 관리가격인플레이션
administered rate liabilities 규제금리부채
administration 사무관리
administration estate 유산관리
administration in bankruptcy 파산관재
administration order 관재명령
administration accounting 관리회계
administrative act 행정행위
administrative and maintenance expenses 유지관리비용
administrative audit 관리감사
administrative discretion 행정재량
administrative disposition 행정처분
administrative dispute 행정쟁소
administrative expense 일반관리비
administrative expenses variance 일반관리비차이
administrative fees 국채사무취급비
administrative guidance 행정지도
administrative interpretation 행정해석
administrative litigation 행정소송
administrative officer 행정직원
administrative order 행정명령

administrative power 행정권
administrative protest 불복신청
administrative reform 행정개혁
administrative remedy 행정구제
administrative review 불복심사
administrator 관재인
administrator in bankruptcy 파산관재인
administrator of bequest 유산관리인
administrator of tax payment 납세관리인
admission 허가
admission fee 가입금
admission to membership 회원가입
admitted assets 미승적격자산
admonition 훈계, 경고
adopted concept 차용개념
adoption 채용
adoptive act 임의법
adoptive provisions 임의규정
adulteration 조악화
advance 대부금;상승;입체금
advance account 대부계정
advance by customers 고객전수금
advance collection 사전징수
advance demand 사전청구
advance for purchase 구매대전도금
advance freight 선불운임
advance from controlled companies 자회사선수금
advance funding method 사전적립방식
advance made on contract 계약전도금
advance made to salesmen 판매원전도금
advance money 입체금
advance of salary 급료선불
advance on a promissory note 어음대부
advance on account of sellers 구입선불대금
advance on consignment-in 수탁판매입체금
advance on indent 매부위탁입체금
advance on subscription 신청증거금
advance payment 선금
advance payment bond 선불금반환보증증권
advance preservative seizure 사전보전차압
advance pricing agreement 사전가격확인제도
advance received 선수금
advance received on contract 계약선수금
advance received on indents 수탁매부전도금
advance received profit 선수수익
advance refunding 사전조달
advance salary 선불급여
advance sale 선매
advance seizure 사전차압
advance wages 선불임금
advance-decline line 등락선
advanced accounting 상급회계학
advanced collection on sale contracts 매매계약선수금
advanced countries 선진국
advanced depreciation 압축기록
advanced depreciation deduction 압축손
advanced depreciation limit 압축한도액
advanced money 전도금
advanced processing 소매부문
advanced redemption 사전상환
adventure 모험
adversary party 상대방당사자
adverse claim 이의신청
adverse effects 악영향
adverse element 마이너스요인
adverse possession 시효취득
adverse selection 역선택
advertisement 광고
advertisement for bid 입찰공고
advertisement tax 광고세
advertising and general publicity expenses 광고선전비
advertising expenses 광고비
advertising media 광고매체
advertising rate 광고료
advertising regulation 광고규제
advertising tax 광고세
advice note 발송통지서
advice of credit 입금통지
advice of debit 출금통지

advice of subrogation 대위통지서
advice payment 통지지불
advice slip 통지전표
advice and pay 통지를 받고 빚을 갚음
advising bank 통지은행
advisor 고문
advisory 조언적인
advisory board 어드바이저리보드
advisory committee 자문위원회
advisory opinion 조언의견
advisory service 투자고문업
advisory tax board 세무자문위원회
advocate 변호사
affairs 업무
affect 영향을 주다
affidavit 선서공술서
affiliate 관계자
affiliated card 제휴카드
affiliated company 관계회사
affiliated family corporations 동족관계회사
affiliated financial institute 계열금융기관
affiliated group 제휴그룹
affiliated loan 제휴론
affiliation 계열화
affiliation procedure 회원가입절차
affinity card 어피니티카드
affirm 확인하다(액수를)
affirmation 확약
affirmative covenants 긍정적인 약인
affix 서명하다
affordable 부담할 수 있는
affranchise 개방하다
affreightment 용선계약
affreightment contract 해상대물운송계약
African Development Bank 아프리카개발은행
Afro-Asian Common Market 아시아-아프리카 공동시장
after cost 후비용
after effective tax 실효세공제후
after loss 애프터로스
after market 신규발행 후 시장
after maturity endorsement 만기 후 이서
after sight 일람 후
after tax 세금공제 후
after tax profit rate 세금공제 후 이익률
after tax yield 세금공제 후 이익
after-acquired clause 사후취득조항
after-acquired property 사후취득재산
after-session undertone 공제후의 상황
after-tax gain 세금공제 후 실수령액
after-tax income 세금공제 후 이익
after-tax yield 세금공제 후 이익
afternoon session 후장
afternoon trading session 후장
against all risks 전위험담보
against the will 뜻에 반하여
age at entry 가입연령
age of discretion 분별연령
age of retirement 퇴직연령
aged dependent 노인부양친족
aged person 노령자
AGEF Index 프랑스 AGEF 지수
agency 대리점
agency account 대리점계정
agency account receivable 대리점대출
agency agreement 대리점계약서
agency arrangement 거래약정서
agency bookkeeping 대리인부기
agency commission 대리점수수료
agency contract 대리점계약
agency cost 대리점경비
agency fee 대리점수수료
agency fund 대리인자금
agency ledger 대리점원장
agency loan 대리대부
agency margin 중개증거금
agency market 에이전시마켓
agency theory 에이전시이론
agency to receive tax 수납기관
agency transaction 위탁거래
agenda 협의사항

agendum 의사일정
agent 대리인;중개인
agent account 대리점계정
agent bank 대행은행
agent commission 대리수수료
agent development era 외무원개발시대
agent handling payment of the dividends 배당금을 지불할 법인
agent replacement deposit 중개인차환예금
aggravation 가중사요
aggregate 총계
aggregate active risk 총액티브리스크
aggregate amount 총액
aggregate average 총평균
aggregate basis 일괄기준
aggregate corporation 사단법인
aggregate demand 총수요
aggregate demand function 총수요기능
aggregate face amount 액면통액
aggregate gross margin 조이익총계
aggregate limit 총액규제
aggregate managed portfolio 총운용 포트폴리오
aggregate market value 시가총액
aggregate net sales 순매상고총계
aggregate normal 총노말포트폴리오
aggregate of depreciation deduction 감가상각비누계
aggregate social capital 사회총자본
aggregate supply 총공급량
aggregate supply function 총공급함수
aggregate theory 집합이론
aggregated shipment 일괄운송
aggregation 합산
aggregation of income amount 소득금액합산
aggregation of profit and loss 손익통산
aggregation problem 집계의 문제
aggressive investment 공격적인 투자
aggressive portfolio 적극적인 운용
aggressive securities 공격적인 증권
aggressively held up 다소 높은 유도
aggressiveness 공격적인 정도
aggressor 공격자
aggrieved party 피해자
aging 경과연수; 연령조사
agreed cut 합의하에 이율을 내림
agreed insured value 협정보험가액
agreed interest 약정금리
agreed order 합의명령
agreed price 협정가격
agreed statement of facts 합의사실진술서
agreed yield to maturity 약정만기이익
agreed-upon interest rate 약정금리
agreed-upon price 약정단계
agreement 계약;약정
agreement among underwriters 인수업자간 계약
agreement for overdraft 당좌대월약정서
agreement for the account for financial futures transaction 금융선물거래계좌설정약정서
agreement jurisdiction 합의관할
agreement jurisdictional court 합의관할법원
agreement of articles 기본약정
agreement of IMF IMF 협정
agreement of special liquidation 특별청산에 동의함
Agreement of the International Bank for Reconstruction and Development 국제개발부흥은행협정
Agreement of the International Monetary Fund 국제통화기금협정
agreement on commerce 통화협정
agricultural bank 농업은행
agricultural bookkeeping 농업부기
agricultural credit 농업금융
agricultural economics 농업경제학
agricultural expenditure 농업경영비
agricultural income 농업소득
agricultural insurance 농업보험
agricultural lien 농업선취특권
agricultural production corporation

농업생산법인
agricultural society 농업조합
agricultural tariff 농산물관세
Ahlers model 어레즈주가모델
aid and comfort 도움
aid bond 보조공채
aid package 지원책
aid prayer 원조청원
aid recipients 원조를 바라는 쪽
aid societies 공제조합
aids 원조금
ailing 업적부진의
air fare 항공요금
air transport industry 항공운송업
air transportation industry 항공운송업
aircraft financing 항공기파이낸스
aircraft hull insurance 항공기보험
airway bill 항공화물운송장
airway freight 항공운임
alias 별명
alien 외국인
alien corporation 외국법인
alien insurer 외국보험회사
alien property 외국인재산
alienable 이전가능한
alienation 양도
alienation clause 양도무효조항
alienator 양도인
alienee 양수인
all amounts invested in capital 총출자금액
all and singular 예외없이 모두
all buyers 모든 소비자
all gone 품절
all in cost 올인코스트
all issued stocks 발행필 총주식수
all or none(AON) 올오어논
All Ordinaries Index
오스트레일리아 종합주가지수
all purpose card 범용카드
all risks clause 올리스크담보약관
all sold 품절
all time now 사상최저치
all totaled 총계로
all-inclusive basis 포괄주의
all-inclusive concept 포괄주의
all-inclusive income concept
포괄주의이익약관
all-inclusive income statement
포괄손익계산서
all-inclusive principle 포괄주의
all-or-none order 일괄매매주문
all-purpose balance sheet 만능대차대조표
all-purpose financial statement
다목적재무재표
all-time high 신고치
alliance 동맹
allied company 동맹회사
allied members 증권거래소 준회원
allocator spread 앨리게이터스프레드
allocated funding instrument 할당적립방식
allocation 배분
allocation and execution of budget
예산배부와 집행
allocation model 배분모델
allocation of cost 원가배당
allocation of new shares to a third party
제삼자할당
allocation ratio 배분비율
allot 분할하다
allotment 할당
allotment certificate 주식할당증
allotment ledger 할당예산원장
allotment letter 할당서
allotment of share 주식할당
allotment system 토지배분제도
allotment to shareholders 주주할당
allotment warden 배분지관리인
allotted amount in constructing public facility
공공시설건설부담액
allow 허용하다
allowable limit for depreciation amount
상각한도액

allowable maximum amount 허용한도액
allowance 준비금
allowance account 준비금계정
allowance for bad debt 대손예비금
allowance for bad loan 대손준비금
allowance for dependent 부양공제
allowance for depreciation 감가상각예비금
allowance for doubtful accounts 대손준비금
allowance for old person 노령자공제
allowance for promotion of employment 취직촉진수당
allowance for repairs 수선수당금
allowance for uncollectable accounts 대손예비금
allowance for undistributed profits 유보공제액
allowance for widow 미망인공제
allowance for working student 근로학생공제
allowance in kind 현물지급
allowance method 예비금설정법
allowed amortizable limit 상각한도액
allowed cost 허용원가
allowed depreciation 상각범위
allowed depreciation limit 상각한도액
allowed limit chargeable to the bonus payment reserve 상여준비금편입한도액
allowed limit of accumulation 적립한도액
allowed limit of retirement allowance reserve 퇴직급여준비금편입한도액
allowed retirement income deduction 퇴직소득공제
alongside delivery 자가배달;자가인도
alpha value 알파수치
alphabet fund 알파벳펀드
already-issued bond 이미 발행한 채권
alteration 변경;변조
alteration demand 변경요청
alteration of species 성질이 상실됨
alteration liquidity 대체유동성
alternate product 대체제품
alternation 교체
alternative accounting principles 대체회계원칙
alternative contract 선택계약
alternative costs 대체비용
alternative duties 선택세
alternative fund 대체자금
alternative liquidity 대체유동성
alternative minimum tax 대체미니멈세
alternative obligation 선택채무
alternative order 선택주문
alternative pricing 선택형 가격결정
alternative remedy 선택적인 구제
alternative withholding tax on dividends 배당원천선택과세
alternatives 대체안
altruism 이타주의
amalgamated company 합병회사
amalgamation 합병
amalgamation on an equal basis 대등합병
amalgamation procedures 합병절차
amalgamation process 합병과정
amalgamation surplus 합병잉여금
ambiguity 모호;불명료함
ambit 권한범위
ambulatory 변경할 수 있는
amelioration 개선
amend 수정하다
amended budget 수정예산
amended return 수정신고
amended shelf registration statement 수정발행신고서
amended usury lax 개정대금업법
amendment 수정;변경
amendment of articles of corporation 정관변경
amerce 벌금을 부과하다
amercement 벌금
American Accounting Association 미국회계학회
American Bankers Association 미국은행협회
American Bar Association 미국법조협회

American clause 중복보험의 순위주의약관
American College 외무원대학
American Depositary Receipts 미국예탁증권
American depositary share 미국예탁주식
American Institute of Accountants 미국회계사협회
American Institute of Certified Public Accountants 미국공인회계사협회
American Law Institute 미국법률협회
American Management Association 미국경영자협회
American option 미국형 옵션
American Society of C. L. U. 미국인정생명보험사회
American Stock Exchange 미국증권거래소
American type 미국형
Americus Trust Scores 아메리카트러스트스코어
Amex Commodity Exchange 아메리카증권거래소
AMEX Index 아메리카증권거래소 주가지수
amortisation period 분할상환기간
amortisation structure 상환구조
amortising cap 상각캡
amortization 채무상환
amortization cost 상각비용
amortization effect 상각효과
amortization event 상각사유
amortization fund 부채상각준비금
amortization loan 분할반제형 대부
amortization of bond premium 사채발행차금상각
amortization of deferred assets 이연자산상각
amortization of goodwill 영업권상각
amortization of initial expenses 창업비상각
amortization of intangibles 무형자산감가상각
amortization of principle 원금반제
amortization of prior service cost 과거근로채무의 상각액
amortization of taxes 세금환급
amortization period 원본상환기간
amortization rate 상각률
amortization schedule 채무상환계획
amortize 상각하다
amortized cost 상각원가
amortizing cap 상각캡
amortizing diffusion model 절대확산모델
amortizing swap 약정반제부 스와프
amortizing term loan 분할반제형 텀론
amount 금액
amount added to capital 증자
amount advanced 대부금액
amount allowable 손금산입한도액
amount appraised 평가액
amount assessed 평가액
amount billed 청구액
amount carried forward 차기이월고
amount claimed 청구액
amount covered 보험금액
amount credited to capital stock 자본금편입액
amount deducted 공제액
amount due 만기지불고
amount equivalent to 상당액
amount financed 대출액
amount imposed 부과액
amount in arrears 미불금
amount in hand 현재수량, 재고
amount insured 보험금액
amount invested 출자액
amount issued 발행고
amount issued by types of straight bonds 상장보통채권의 종류별 발행액
amount listed by types of straight bonds 상장보통채권의 종류별 상장총액
amount matched within each member 회원사내 상당금액
amount of bill 어음금액
amount of capital 자본액
amount of capital investment 설비투자액
amount of claim 구상액
amount of clearing 어음교환고

amount of consumption 소비고
amount of damage 손해액
amount of dividends paid 배당금총액
amount of goods purchased 구입액
amount of income 총수득액
amount of income for each taxable year 각사업연도의 소득액
amount of investment 출자액
amount of loss 결손액
amount of loss carried forward 이월결손액
amount of money delivered due to merger 합병교부금
amount of proceeds 수취고
amount of profit 이익금액
amount of sales 매상고
amount of tax 세액
amount of tax payment 총세액
amount of taxable purchase 과세매상고
amount of the first payment 초회금
amount of the offset 상쇄액
amount trade receivable 외상매출금
amount on hand 현재고
amount outstanding 잔고
amount overbought 과잉구매고
amount oversold 과잉매출고
amount paid 지불고
amount paid per new share 신주일주당 지불가액
amount raised 자금조달액
amount raised by stock 주식을 통한 자본조액
amount realized 현실금액
amount receivable 수취금
amount received 수입금액
amount regarded as dividend 배당액으로 간주하는 금액
amount subscribed 응모금액
amount to be written off as depreciation 감가상각고
amount withheld 원천예금
analysis 분석
analysis of budget variance 예산차이분석
analysis of cost variances 원가차이분석
analysis of credit 신용분석
analysis of financial statement 재무제표분석
analysis of income statement 손익계산서분석
analysis of lender's preference 대출자의 우선권분석
analysis of securities 증권분석
analysis of the affairs of a business 경영분석
analysis of variance 분산분석
analysis of variance from budget 예산차이분석
analyst 분석가
analytical accounting 분석회계
analytical data 분석데이터
analytical reports 분석보고서
ancient rent 임료
ancillary 보조의
ancillary attachment 가차압
Andean Common Market 안데스공동시장
anglers' insurance 낚시보험
animal insurance 동물보험
annex 부속서류
annexation 병합
annexed letter 부속서류
annexed structure 부속설비
anniversary of the foundation of a corporation 회사창립기념
annotation 주석
announcement 공시
announcement effect 고지효과
announcement of bids and offers 호가를 주지함
annual accounting 연차결산
annual audit 연도감사
annual audited financial statement 감사필 연차재무보고서
annual basis 연환산
annual business report 사업보고서
annual capacity 연간생산능력
annual closing 연도마감
annual compounding 유럽식 복리이율

annual coupon 연불쿠폰
annual dues 연회비
annual earnings 연간소득
annual economic review 경제연보
annual expenditure 세출
annual fees 연부과세
annual financial statements 연차재무제표
annual income 연간수입
annual installment 연간할부
annual interest rate 연이율
annual meeting 연차총회
annual member 연회원
annual payment 연 1회후불
annual percentage rate 연율의 퍼센테이지
annual profit disposition amount 연간이익처분액
annual rate of returns 연수익률
annual report 연차보고서
annual report to stockholders 주주를 위한 연차보고서
annual revenue 세입
annual securities statistics 증권통계연보
annual value method 연가법
annualised basis 연율환산
annualised yield 연이율
annuity bond 원리균등불채
annuity certain 확정연금
annuity insurance 연금보험
annuity loan 연리형 론
annuity method 연금법
annuity purchase fund 연금구입기금
annuity purchase rates 연금구입요율
annuity regarded as salaries and wages 급여로 간주하는 연금
annuity repayment method 원리균등상환방식
annuity rider 연금특약
annuity unit 연금유닛
annul 취소하다
annulment 무효화
annulment of a contract 계약해제
annulment right 취소권
annunciator board 호출게시판
anonymous 익명의
anonymous association 익명조합
ANP/CBS General Index 네덜란드의 ANP-CBS 종합주가지수
antedated check 전일부 수표
antedating 전일부의
anti-dilution clause 희박화 방지조항
anti-dumping code 안티덤핑코드
anti-monopoly law 독점금지법
anti-social power 반사회세력
anticipated acceptance 만기전 인수
anticipated cost 예상원가
anticipated profit 예상수익
anticipation of falling market 염가예상
anticipation of low interest rate 저금리예상
anticipation tax bill 납세준비증권
anticipatory breach of contract 기한 전의 계약위반
antithetic variable 대칭변수
apartment dwellers' comprehensive insurance 단지보험
apparent 명백한; 외견의
apparent agency 표면상의 대리
apparent danger 명백한 위험
appendix 첨부서류
appetite 흥미
appliance 설비
applicable 적용할 수 있는
applicable law 준거법
applicable statutory useful life 적용법정내용연수
applicable useful life 적용내용연수
applicant 신청인
applicant for intial listing 신규상장신청서
applicant for original listing 신규상장신청서
applicant member 신청회원
application date base 신청일기준
application for approval 승인신청

application for financial futures transaction account 금융선물거래계좌개설신청서
application for listing 상장신청서
application for listing of security 유가증권상장신청서
application for membership 회원가입신청
application for withdrawal 탈퇴신청
application form for stock 주식신청서
application money 신청금
application money for stock 주식신청금
application of fund 자금운용
application of funds statement 자금운용표
application of overhead 간접비할부
application rate of overhead cost 간접비할부표
application right 출원권
application to list 상장신청서
application of working capital 운전자본운용
applied cost 적용원가
applied factory burden 제조간접비배부액
applied manufacturing expenses account 제조간접비배부계정
apply correspondingly to 기준에 따라 운용하다
appointed day 기일
appointed goods 지정상품
appointee 피임명자
appointing authority 중재인선정기관
appointment 지정
appointment of depreciation 상각비배부
appointment sales 어포인트상법
appointor 지정권자
apportion 분할
apportioned tax 배부세
apportionment 분할(계약의)
apportionment base 배부기준
apportionment of loss 손해분담
apportionment of cost valuation 원가차액조정
appraisal 평가
appraisal loss 평가손
appraisal method 평가법
appraisal of assets 자산감정
appraisal of dutiable value 과세액평가
appraisal of securities 유가증권평가
appraisal of shares 주식평가
appraisal profit 평가익
appraisal profit or loss 평가손익
appraisal rights of shareholder 주식매취청구권
appraisal standard 평가기준
appraisal surplus 재평가적립금
appraisal value 평가액
appraised price 산정가격
appraisement 평가사정
appraisement method of securities 유가증권평가법
appraiser 평가인
appreciated market price 시가상승
appreciation 등귀
appreciation surplus 재평가잉여금
appreciation swap 어프리시에이션스와프
approach 수법
appropriate 계상하다
appropriate interest rate 적정이율
appropriated earned surplus 처분필 이익잉여금
appropriated surplus 처분필 이익잉여금
appropriation 충당
appropriation account 이익처분계정
appropriation for the deposit 예탁금에 편입함
appropriation of fiscal resources for redemption 상환재원편입
appropriation of net income 순익처분
appropriation of profit 이익처분
appropriation of refund 환부금충당
appropriation section 이익처분부서
appropriation surplus 잉여금처분
approval 승인
approval of decrease of income tax 소득세감액승인

approval of export license 수출승인
approval of extension of time to file 신고시간연장승인
approval of filing a blue return 청색신고승인
approval of special liquidation 특별청산승인
approval sales 시용판매
approved bidder 지정입찰자
approved expenses to be carried over to the following tear 이월을 허가받은 예산
approved list of investment 투자승인리스트
approved pension contract 적격퇴직연금계약
approved pension funds 적격퇴직연금적립금
approved retirement annuity 적격퇴직연금
approved retirement annuity contract 적격퇴직연금계약
approved retirement annuity plan 적격퇴직연금제도
approved superannuation fund 적격퇴직연금
approved tender 지정입찰
approximate amount 개산액
approximate cost 개산원가
approximate market price 시가개산액
approximate price 개산가격
approximate value 개산가격
appurtenance 재산에 부속되는 권리
apt time 적기
Arab League 아랍연맹
arbitrage 중재;재정거래;차익매매
arbitrage business 재정거래
arbitage date 재정데이터
arbitrage house 중재소
arbitrage margin 재정마진
arbitrage operation 재정거래
arbitrage opportunity 재정기회
arbitrage position 재정포지션
arbitrage possibility 재정기회
arbitrate pricing theory 재정가격결정이론
arbitrage trader 중재업자
arbitrage transaction 재정거래
arbitrageur 재정거래자
arbitrary 독단적인
arbitrated exchange rate 재정환상장
arbitrated rate 재정상장
arbitrated rate of exchange 재정환율
arbitration 중재
arbitration award 중재재정
arbitration clause 중재조항
arbitration of exchange 환재정
arbitration proceeding 중재절차
arbitrator 중재인
arena 입회장
arithmetic average 산술평균;단순평균
arithmetic dividend yield average 단순평균이율
arithmetic mean 산술평균
arithmetic stock price average 단순평균주가
arm's length price 독립기업간 가격
arm's length principle 독립기업원칙
arm's length transaction 일반적인 제삼자거래
arrangement 회사정리;채무정리
arrangement of unsettled transaction 미결제거래를 조정함
arranger 알선인
arrears swap 어리어스와프
arrearages 연체
arrears 연체채권
arrears of local tax 지방세연체금
arrival draft 도착후 일람불어음
arrival of shipment 착하
article 조항
article in custody 보관품
article of the peace 안전보증신청
article on the free list 관세면제품
article subject to taxation 과세품
articled clerk 실무수습생
articles of agreement 계약각서
articles of association 통상정관
articles of confederation 연합규약
articles of incorporation 회사정관
articles of partnership 조합정관
artificial person 법인

artificial presumptions 법률적인 추정
artificial statement 다행식 시산서
artificially 전문적으로
as at ~일 현재
as occasion demands 임시필요에 따라
as per specifications attached 첨부명세서대로
ascending 상승
ascending curve 상승커브
ascending order 오름차순
ascending patterns triangle 상승트라이앵글
ascending tops 어센딩톱스
Asia Pacific Economic Cooperation 아시아태평양경제협력회의
Asian Clearing Union 아시아결제동맹
Asian Currency Unit 아시아동화단위
Asian Development Bank 아시아개발은행
Asian Development Fund 아시아개발기금
Asian dollar 아시아달러
Asian dollar bond 아시아달러채
Asian dollar market 아시아달러시장
Asian Monetary Unit 아시아통화단위
Asian Payment Union 아시아지불동맹
Asian Reserve Bank 아시아준비은행
asked price 매호치
asked quotation 판매자가 부르는 가격
asked rate 판매가레이트
aspiration 열망
aspiration level 요구수준
assay office 순분검정소
assent 수락
assent claims 항변하다
assess 평가하다
assessable income 과세소득
assessed amount 사정액
assessed income 사정소득액
assessed market value 시가평가액
assessed tax 과세금
assessed valuation 평가가치
assessed value 사정가액
assessing organ 사정기관
assessment 평가액
assessment and collection 부과징수
assessment and decision 부과결정
assessment by estimation on the basis of the size of business 외형과세
assessment of income tax 신고소득세
assessment of market timing 시장타이밍평가
assessment of taxes 신고납세
assessment plan 부과식 보험
assessment rate of collateral 담보물건을 가격보다 낮게 평가할 때의 비율
assessment roll 과세원부
assessor 감정인
asset accounting 자산회계
asset acquisition 자산매입
asset allocation 자산분배
asset allocation technique 자산분배법
asset allocation and equities 자산과 지분
asset and liability management 자산부채종합관리
asset approach 어셋어프로치
asset backed securities 자산담보증권
asset basis 자산기준
asset book value 장부상의 자산가격
asset base swap 어셋베이스 스와프
asset bubble 자산거품
asset capitalization 자산계상
asset class 자산클래스
asset class target 자산클래스타겟
asset coverage 자산담보율
asset deterioration 자산악화
asset devaluation 자산평가절하
asset differentials 자산격차
asset distribution 자산분배
asset diversification 자산분산
asset efficiency 자산효율
asset finance 어셋파이낸스
asset freeze 자산동결
asset gap 자산격차
asset income 자산소득
asset life 자산내용연수

asset management 자산운용
asset mix 자산구성
asset out of books 장부외자산
asset outflow 자산유출
asset period guidelines 자산내용연수지침
asset pool 자산가격
asset pricing model 자산가격평가모델
asset quality 자산의 질
asset register 자산대장
asset reserves 자산준비금
asset reshuffling 자산이체
asset return 자산수익률
asset revaluation 자산재평가
asset revaluation tax 자산재평가세
asset sales 자산매각
asset securitization 자산증권화
asset selection 자산결제
asset shift 자산시프트
asset structure 자산구성
asset swap 어셋스와프
asset swap transaction 어셋스와프거래
asset turnover ratio 자산회전율
asset utilization 자산활용
asset valuation reserve 자산평가준비금
asset value 자산가치
asset write down 자산평가감
asset-backed bond 자산담보증권
asset-backed commercial paper 어셋백커머셜페이퍼
asset-backed stock 포함자산주
asset-management 자산관리
asset-pass-through certificate 어셋패스스루증권
asset-utilization ratios 자산활용률
assets 자산
assets and liabilities 자산과 부채
assets effect 자산효과
assets money 자산화폐
assets off the book 장부외자산
assets revaluation law 자산재평가법
assets revaluation tax 자산재평가세
assets subject to lien 담보차입자산
assign 양도하다
assigned accounts 담보계정
assigned accounts receivable 할당채권
assigned amount 담보제공액
assigned surplus 특별적립잉여금
assignee 수탁자
assignment 양도
assignment and transfer 양도 및 이전
assignment charge 양도수수료
assignment clause 양도조건
assignment expense 할당비용
assignment fee 양도수수료
assignment in blank 백지양도
assignment of business 영업권양도
assignment of claim 채권양도
assignment of exercise 권리행사할당
assignment of receivable 채권양도
assignment of rights 권리양도
assignment of sales contract 매매계약양도
assignment of stock 주식양도
assignor 양도자
assimilation 동화
assist 원조하다
assistance 원조
assistant certified public accountant 회계사보조
assisted acquisition 구제합병방식
associate 조합원
associate company 관련회사
associate member 어소시에이트멤버
associated person 특수관계인
association 협회
Association Cambiste Internationale 상공회의소
Association of Average Adjusters 해손인협회
Association of Call Loan and Discount Companies 단자협회
Association of Insurance and Financial Analysts 보험재무분석가협회
Association of International Accountants

국제회계전문가협회
Association of International Bond Dealer 국제채무딜러협회
Association of Life Insurance Medicine of Japan 일본보험의학회
Association of South-East Asian Nations 동남아시아국가연합
assortment of goods 상품구성
assume 인계하다
assumed bond 보증사채
assumed liability 인계부채
assumed rate of interest 예정이율
assumed settling day 가결산일
assumption of accounting 회계상의 가정
assumption of risk 위험부담인수
assumptions 가정
assurance 보험
assurance of bill 어음보험
assured 피보험자
asymmetry 불균형
at a decrease in price 가격하향국면에서
at a discount 액면이하
at a premium 액면이상
at an increase in price 가격상승국면에서
at arm's length 대등한 입장에서
at cost 원가로
at issue 쟁점에 달한
at low ebb 몹시 차가와지다
at one's own discretion 임의의
at par 액면대로
at risk 앳리스크
at sight bill 일람불어음
at sight buying rate 일람불어음매입률
at sight buying rate with credit 신용장부 일람불어음매입률
at sight rate 일람불상장
at the close of the market 종장무렵
at the market 시장동향
at the money 앳더머니
at-closing price transaction 종장거래
at-market 앳마켓
attach 압류하다
attached document 첨부서류
attached goods 차압물건
attachment 차압
attachment of the risk 리스크어태치
attain 달성하다
attainable 달성가능한
attendance 입회
attest 증명하다
attestation 증명
attested copy 승인등본
attested witness 증명증인
attitude 태도
attorney 변호사
attorney in fact 대리인
attorney's lien 변호사리엔
attractive 묘미가 있는
attractive trading opportunity 절호의 매장
attributable income principle 귀속주의
attributable interest 귀속지분
attributable profit 귀속이익
attribute 속성
attribution analysis 요인분석
attribute of income 소득귀속
attribute of income of business office 사업소소득의 귀속
auction 경쟁매장
auction date 입찰일
auction market 경매시장
auction of government bond 국채입찰
auction period 입찰기간
auction sale 경매
auction system 옥션시스템
auctioneer 경매인
audit 감사
audit certificate 감사증명서
audit certification 감사증명
audit evidence 감사증거
audit fee 감사보수
audit file 감사조사서
audit of banks 은행감사

audit on bank account 은행조사
audit on property 재산조사
audit opinion 감사의견
audit procedure 감사절차
audit report 감사보고서
audit report of certified public accountant 공인회계사가 작성한 감사보고서
audit representation 감사표명
audit time 감사시기
audit timing 감사타이밍
audit year 감사연도
audited amount 감사필 금액
auditing 회계감사
auditing corporation 감사법인
auditing procedure 감사절차
auditing standards 감사기준
Auditing Standards Board 감사기준심의회
auditing theory 감사이론
auditor 감사역;감사
auditor's opinion 감사인의 의견
auditor's report 감사보고서
auditors' independence 감사인의 독립성
auditors' liability 감사인의 책임
augmentation 수입증가
augmentation of earnings 수익증가
Aussie bond 오스트레일리아달러채
Aussie dollar 오스트레일리아달러
austere budget 긴축예산
austere fiscal policy 긴축재정
Australian Accounting Research Foundation 오스트레일리아회계연구재단
authentic 진정한
authentic act 인증행위
authentication 인증
authorities 당국
authority 권한
authority bond 공사공단채
authority to inquire and inspect 질문검사권
authority to pay 절차수권서
authority to purchase 어음매입수권서
authorization 승인
authorization by law 법률위임
authorization criteria 증거기준
authorization number 인증번호
authorize 권한을 부여하다
authorized agency 공인기관
authorized bank 공인은행
authorized bond 수권사채
authorized capital 수권자본
authorized dealer 승인딜러
authorized deferred payment 연납
authorized foreign exchange bank 외국환공인은행
authorized investment list 투자허가리스트
authorized shares 수권주식
auto sales 자동차판매대수
auto-regressive model 자기회전모델
automated clearing 자동어음교환
automated teller machine 자동예금수납기
automatic account transfer 자동계좌이체
automatic approval system 자동인가방식
automatic collection service 자동집금(集金)서비스
automatic fund transfer 계좌이체
automatic increase in tax revenue 세수자연증가
automatic premium loan 자동이체대부
automatic reinstatement 자동복원
automatic renewal 자동갱신
automatic renewal time deposit 자동계속정기예금
automatic settlement 자동결제
automatic stay 자동정지
automatic transfer service 자동대체서비스
automaticity 자동성
automobile bodily injury liability insurance 대인배상보험
automobile drivers' liability insurance 자동차운전자 손해배상책임보험;드라이버보험
automobile insurance 자동차보험
automobile Insurance rating association of japan (일본)자동차보험요율산정회

automobile liability insurance 자동차손해배상책임보험
automobile passengers' personal accident insurance 탑승자상해보험
automobile physical damage insurance 차량보험
automobile property damage liability insurance 대물배상보험
automobile receivables 자동차론채권
automobile sales finance 자동차판매금융
automobile tax 자동차세
automobile tonnage tax 자동차중량세
autonomous investment 독립투자
autonomous item 자발적 항목
autonomous recovery 자립회복
autonomous tariff 자수관세
autonomously strong 자율반등
autonomy 자치
auxiliary book 보조부
auxiliary journal 보조장부
auxiliary ledger 보조원장
auxiliary rules 보조규제
availability 입수가능성
availability clause 가능성조항
availability of bank 은행의 어베이러빌러티
availability period 자금인출가능기관
availability risk 어베이러빌러티리스크
available 환금성이 높은
available assets 이용가능자산
available bond 이용가능채권
available capital 이용가능자본
available profit 가처분이익
average absolute deviation 평균절대편차
average age of inventory 재고자산회전기간
average balance outstanding 평균발행잔고
average bond 공동해손맹약서
average clause 분손담보조항
average collection 평균회수기간
average collection period 매상채권회수기간
average consumer price index 평균소비자물가지수
average contracted interest rates on loans and discounts of all banks 전국은행대출약정평균금리
average contractual interest rate on bank loan 대출약정평균금리
average cost 평균원가
average cost method 평균원가법
average cost of capital 평균자본코스트
average cost of debt 평균채무코스트
average dividend of paying companies 유배당회사평균배당금
average dividend paid 평균배당금
average down 평균 가격을 낮추다
average earnings 평균수익
average exchange rate 중간수치
average growth rate 평균신장률
average income 평균소득
average index monthly earnings 평균표준보수월액
average interest rate 평균금리
average interest rate cap 평균금리캡
average inventory 평균재고
average issued 평균발행고
average life 평균잔존연수
average margin buying price 신용구매의 평균단위
average maturity of debts 평균부채기간
average method 평균법
average of daily figures 평균잔고
average outstanding 평균잔고
average over period 기간평균
average period of production 평균생산기간
average profit 평균이익
average propensity to consume 평균소비성향
average provision rate 평균준비율
average rate of dividend 평균배당률
average return on investment 평균투자수익
average spot rate option 평균스폿레이트옵션
average strike price option 평균행사가격옵션
average tax rate 평균세율
average taxation 평균과세

average term to maturity 평균상환연한
average trading value 평균매가대금
average up 평균 가격을 올리다
average value 대금평균
average volatility 평균변동율
average yield 평균이율
average yield by types of industry 업종별 이율
average yield of listed stocks 상장주식평균이율
averaged type forward contract 애버리지타입 선물환예약
averaging 평균가격
averaging taxation on fluctuating income 변동소득평균과세
aversion 회피
aviation hull insurance 항공기보험
aviation insurance 항공보험
avoidable cost 회피가능원가
avoidable risk 배제가능리스크
axiom 공리
axis 축선

B

BA rate BA 레이트
baby bond 소액채권
baby fund 베이비펀드
back bond 손실보상증서
back dating 실제보다 전날일자로 하다
back dividend 파급불배낭금
back door listing 정규가 아닌 상장
back money 연체금
back office 백오피스;배후부문;비영업부문
back pay 파급급여
back rent 체납임차금
back spread 시중은행의 할인율상회
back tax 체납세
back to back loan 백투백론
back to back transaction 백투백거래
back-up facility 백업퍼실리티
back-up line 백업라인
backdrop 배경
background information 배경사항
backing 이서
backlog 체화
backlog of orders 주문잔액
backward countries 후진국
backward difference 후방차분근사치
backward difference approximation 후방차분지불인
backward integration 후방통합
backward needs 과거의 수요
backwardation market 시중은행의 할인율상회시장
backwardation rate 역일변
bad account 대손계정
bad debt 대손금;불량채권
bad debt account 대손계정
bad debt caused by insolvency 지불불능으로 인한 대손
bad debt caused by the legal effect 법률적인 소멸에 따른 대손
bad debt loss 대손금
bad debt provision 대손준비금
bad debt ratio 불량채권율
bad debt recovery 상각필 채권회수
bad debt written-off 불량채권상각
bad debt written-off 대손금상각 (대손상각)
bad delivery 불완전인도
bad faith 불성실
bad loan 대손
bad member 불량회원
bad news 악재료
baht 바트(타이의 화폐단위)
bail out 구제하다
bail-piece 보석계약서
bailee's liability insurance 수탁자배상책임보험
bailment 수탁
bailor 수탁자
bailout 구제조치
bailout clause 구제조항
bailout market 구제상장
bailout plan 구제계획
balance 차액;잔고
balance account 잔고계정

balance at the bank 은행예금잔고
balance at the beginning of the period 기초잔고
balance at the end of the term 기말잔고
balance book 잔고장
balance brought forward 이월잔고
balance carried forward to the next term 차기이월
balance certificate 잔고증명서
balance due 부족액
balance form 잔고식
balance in hand 생계잔고
balance of accounts 수지계정
balance of clearing 결제수지
balance of current account 경상계정수지
balance of international indebtedness 국제대차
balance of international payments 국제수지
balance of invisible trade 무역외수지
balance of loans 융자잔고
balance of monetary movements 금융계정
balance of payments statistics 국제수지통계
balance of revenue account 수익잔고계정
balance of stock loans 차주잔고
balance of stores 현재고
balance of the amount charged to special account 특별계정잔고
balance of trade 무역수지
balance of transfer account 이전수지
balance on ledger 원장잔고
balance order 주금불입명령
balance renewal 론갱신
balance sheet 대차대조표
balance sheet analysis 대차대조표분석
balance sheet approach 밸런스시트어프로치
balance sheet formula 대차대조표등식
balance sheet items 대차대조표항목
balanced budget 균형예산
balanced budget theorem 균형예산정리
balanced finance 균형재정
balanced form 계정식
balanced fund 밸런스펀드
balanced fund portfolio 밸런스펀드포트폴리오
balanced growth 균형세력
balanced manager 밸런스형 매니저
balances 잔채
balancing adjustment 평균공제
baling charges 포장비
ballon maturity 벌룬상환
ballon mortgage 벌룬모기지
balloon payment 차입잔고를 일괄지불함
ballot 투표
ban 금지
ban call 밴콜
band 변동폭
band and crawl 밴드앤드크롤
band wagon effect 밴드왜건효과
bank 은행
bank acceptance 은행인수
bank account 은행계좌
bank act 은행법
bank activities 은행업무
bank affiliated securities firm 은행계증권회사
bank balance 은행예금잔고
bank basis 뱅크베이시스
bank bill 은행어음
bank bookkeeping 은행부기
bank bookkeeping machine 은행부기회계기
bank capital requirements 은행자기자본규제
bank card 은행카드
bank cashier's check 예금수표
bank check 은행수표
bank clearing 어음교환결제
bank credit agreement 은행융자한도
bank credit card 은행계신용카드
bank creditor 채권은행
bank crisis 은행공황
bank dealer 은행딜러
bank debenture 금융채
bank debit card 은행데빗카드

bank debt 은행차입
bank deposit 은행예금
bank discount method 은행할인방법
bank discount rate 은행할인료
bank draft 은행어음
bank examination 은행검사
bank financing 은행융자
Bank for International Settlements 국제결제은행
bank full dealing 은행풀딜링
bank fund position 은행자금포지션
bank guarantee 은행보증
bank holding company 은행주주회사
Bank Holding Company Act 은행주주회사법
bank holiday 은행휴업일
bank identification number BIN
bank insurance fund 은행보험기금
bank interest 은행이자
bank law 은행법
bank lending 은행대부
bank letter of credit 은행신용장
bank license 은행면허
bank line 뱅크라인
bank liquidity 은행유동성
bank loans 단기차입금
bank loans-deposit ratio 예대율
bank loans payable 은행차입금
bank loans secured by mortgage 담보를 통한 은행차입
bank mandate 은행위임장
bank note 은행권
bank of issue 발권은행
Bank of Japan 일본은행
Bank of Japan Act 일본은행법
Bank of Japan credit 일은신용
Bank of Japan discount rate 공정할인
Bank of Japan financial network system 일본은행금융 네트워크시스템
Bank of Japan loans 일은대출
Bank of Japan note 일본은행권
Bank of Japan note issue tax 일본은행권발행세
Bank of New York 뉴욕은행
Bank of Spain Circular 스페인은행안내장
bank paper 은행권
bank point-of-sales 은행 **POS**
bank rate 은행이율
bank reference 은행조회
bank refinancing 은행차환
bank remittance 은행송금
bank reserve 은행준비
bank senior obligation 은행채무
bank usance 뱅크유전스
bank's automatic accounts transfer system 은행자동납부시스템
banker's acceptance bill 은행인수어음
banker's blanket bond 은행포괄보증
banker's credit 은행신용장
bankers syndicate 은행금융단
banking accounts of all banks 전국은행계정
banking business 은행업무
banking circular 은행공보
banking day 은행거래일
banking facilities 금융기관
banking principle 은행주의
banking regulation 은행규제
banking service 은행서비스
banking syndicate 은행단
banking transaction contract 은행거래약정서
bankrupt 파산자
bankrupt equity 파산기업
bankrupt's estate 파산재단
bankruptcy 파산
bankruptcy administrator 파산관재인
bankruptcy and composition 화의
bankruptcy court 파산법원
bankruptcy debtor 파산채무자
bankruptcy filing 파산신청
bankruptcy law 파산법
bankruptcy notice 파산고지
bankruptcy proceedings 파산절차
Bankruptcy Reform Act of 1978 신파산법

bankruptcy remote 뱅크럽시리모트
bankruptcy rules 파산규칙
bankruptcy trustee 파산관재인
banks futures 은행업선물
bankwire 뱅크와이어
bar chart 막대그래프
bar code 바코드
barbell strategy 바벨전략
bare body 드러난 본문
bare trustee 수동적인 수탁자
bargain 매매
bargain buying 일시적으로 하락할 때 구매함
bargain counter
본래의 가격을 밑돌다가 매각된 증권
bargain purchase option 염가구입권
bargain stock 할인주
bargainee 사는 쪽
bargainer 파는 쪽
bargaining power 교섭력
barometer stock 표준주
barrier 장벽
barriers to entry 진입장벽
barter 물물교환
barter terms of trade 교역조건
barter trade 바터무역
base cost estimate 기초비용견적
base currency 기준통화
base date 기준일
base date for assessment 부과기일
base date for clearing margin calculation
거래증거금액산정기준일
base earnings 기초수익
base EPS 표준 EPS
base free 제한부동산권
base market value 기준시간총액
base money 베이스머니
base of taxation 과세표준
base pay 기본급
base period 기준기간
base price 기준가격
base rate 기준레이트
base standard cost 기준표준원가
base year 기준연도
base-stock method 기준재고법
based on round lots 단주분을 포함하지 않음
Basel agreement 바젤합의
Basel Committee 바젤위원회
baseline budget 기본예산
basement 저가
basic administration policy 운영기본방침
basic allowance 기초공제
basic assumption 기초상정
basic automobile policy 일반자동차보험
basic balance of payments 기초수지
basic capital 최저자본
basic convention 기초공준
basic cost 기초원가
basic deduction 기초공제
basic discount rate 기준할인레이트
basic exchange rate 기준환상장
basic exemption 기초공제
basic financial statements 기초재무제표
basic industry 소재산업
basic period 기본기간
basic principle 기본원칙
basic rate 기준상장
basic rate of foreign exchange
기준외국환상장
basic regulations 기초법규
basic research 기초연구
basic reserve 기초적립금
basic retirement funds 기초퇴직연금기금
basic salary 기본급
basic statistics 기초통계
basic stockholder 판정의 기초가 되는 주주
basic tax rate 기초세율
basic value 기본가격
basic year 기초연도
basis 기초
basis for conclusions 결론의 근거
basis for recording sales 매상계산기준
basis gap 베이시스갭

basis market 베이시스마켓
basis of the calculation 계산기초
basis on the amount of salary 급여기준
basis point 베이시스포인트
basis risk 베이시스리스크
basis swap 베이시스스와프
basis to prorate local tax 분할기준
basis trading 베이시스거래
basis transaction 베이시스거래
basket 바스켓
basket cost trading 바스켓대당거래
basket purchase 일괄구입
basket system 바스켓방식
basket trading 바스켓거래
basket transaction 바스켓서래
basket warrant 바스켓워런트
batch processing 일괄처리
batch trading system 배치거래시스템
battle of the brands 브랜드경쟁
bear 낳다
bear bond 베어본드
bear bull bond 베어불본드
bear call spread 베어콜스프레드
bear hug 베어허그(강한 포옹)
bear index bond 베어인덱스채
bear market 하락시세
bear raiding 시장을 어지럽히다
bear spread trading 베어스프레드거래
bear squeeze market 시세하락을 예견하고 팔았는데 반대로 시세가 상승하여 손해를 감수하고 환매한 탓에 일시적으로 시세가 상승함
bear the market 마구 팔기
bearer 지참인
bearer bond 무기명채권
bearer check 무기명식수표
bearer debenture 무기명사채
Bearer Depositary Receipts 무기명예탁증권
bearer securities 무기명증권
bearer share 무기명주식
bearer stock 무기명주
bearing date 일정기일이 있는
bearish 약세의;내림시세의
bearish channel 약한 채널
bearish consolidation patterns 약세 콘솔리데이션패턴
bearish market 약세시장
bearish mood 약세시장
bearish resistance line 약세저항선
bearish reversal patterns 하락전환패턴
bearish sentiment 약세시장
bearish support line 약세지지선
bearish tone 약세시세
bears over 매출우세
become due 기한이 오다
beef up 강화하다
before due endorsement 만기전이서
before fees 수수료공제전
before refund of fees 수수료환급전
before tax 세금포함
beggar-my-neighbor policy 근린궁지화정책
beginning balance 기초잔고
beginning day of the taxable year 사업연도개시일
beginning of the fiscal year 연도초
beginning of the period 기초
behavior 동향
behavior of inflation 인플레동향
behavioral theory 행동이론
bellwether issue 지표상품
belongings 재산
below cost 원가이하로
below market 벨로우마켓
below par 액면이하;평가이하
below par issue 액면이하상품
below the line 벨로우더라인
benchmark 표준
benchmark bond 채권지표상품
benchmark portfolio 벤치마크포트폴리오
benchmark rate 표준가격권
benchmark securities 지표증권
benchmark yield 지표상품이율

beneficial association 상호부조단체
beneficial duty 편익관세
beneficial investors 실질투자주
beneficial owner 실질소유자
beneficiary 수익자
beneficiary certificate 수익증권
beneficiary certificate of investment trust 투자신탁수익증권
beneficiary company 수익기업
beneficiary holders of preferred equity securities 실질우선출자사원
beneficiary interest 수익권
beneficiary interest certificate 수익증권
beneficiary of the retirement annuity 퇴직연금수취인
beneficiary principle 수익자부담원칙
beneficiary right 수익권
beneficiary securities 수익증권
beneficiary shareholder 실질주주
benefit 급부
benefit analysis 편익분석
benefit association 공제단체
benefit cost analysis 편익비용분석
benefit eligibility 수급자격
benefit formula 연금급부액산정방식
benefit plan expense 연금비용
benefit principle 응익부담원칙
benefit security 부급보증
benefit society 공제조합
benefit taxation 부조료과세
benefits for survivor 유족급부금
benign 우호적인
bequest 동산유증
best efforts basis 최선노력원칙
best efforts issue 매출발행
best efforts selling 위탁판매
best evidence 최량증거
beta 베타
beta coefficient 베타계수
beta service 베타서비스
beta value 베타수치
beta value prediction equation 베타예측방정식
betterment 개선
betterment expense 개량비
bias 바이어스
biased 편향된
bid and ask 호가
bid and ask quotation 시황가격
bid and asked price 호가
bid and offer 호가
bid and offer situation 호가상황
bid ask spread 호가스프레드
bid bond 입찰보증증권
bid by advertising 경쟁입찰
bid guarantee insurance 입찰보증보험
bid price 판매가;입찰가격
bid quotation 매수시황
bid rate 매수율
bid-offer spread 호가스프레드
bidder 입찰자
bidding 입찰
bidding for public offering 공모입찰
bidding up 값을 끌어올림
Big Bang 대폭발
Big Board 뉴욕증권거래소
big push in the downward move 하락촉진
big shareholder 대주주
big ticket goods 고가상품
biggest single day advances and declines 등락순위
bilateral agreement 양국간 협정
bilateral contract 쌍무계약
bilateral loan 상대론
bilateral trade 쌍무무역
bilateral trade agreement 상호무역협정
bilge 선저침수
bill 청구서;법안
bill accepted 인수필 환어음
bill bearer 어음소지자
bill book 어음계정장부
bill bought 환매입

bill broker 어음브로커
bill buying and selling rate 어음매매레이트
bill buying system 어음매입제도
bill clearing 어음교환
bill collection 외상매출금회수
bill discount 어음할인
bill discounted account 할인어음계정
bill drawn for sale 매출어음
bill for foreclosure 권리상실소장
bill in domestic currency 방화어음
bill in foreign currency 외화어음
bill obligatory 강제채무증서
bill of credit 신용증권
bill of debt 채무증서
bill of dishonor 부도어음
bill of exchange 환어음
bill of lading 선하증권
bill of material 재료명세서
bill of mortality 사망기록
bill of others 타행인수
bill of particulars 청구명세서
bill of quantities 수량표
bill of rights 권리장전
bill of sale 양도담보증서
bill pass 빌패스
bill payable 지불어음
bill payable at a fixed date 확정일지불어음
bill payable to bearer 지참인지불어음
bill payable to order 지정인지불어음
bill rate 어음매매레이트
bill receivable 수금환;역환
bill sale 빌세일
bill sent 발송송금환
bill sold 환매출
bill to order 지도증권
bills market average outstanding 어음매매시장평균잔고
bimetallism 복본위제
binding 구속력이 있는
binding clause 구속조항
binomial distribution 이항분포
binomial model 이항분포모델
BIS standards BIS 기준
black box auction 블랙박스옥션
black market dealing 암딜링
Black Monday 블랙먼데이
Black-Scholes formula on option valuation 블랙숄즈의 옵션평가식
Black-Scholes method 블랙숄즈방식
Black-Scholes model 블랙숄즈모델
blacklist 블랙리스트
blame 책임
blank acceptance 백지인수
blank bill 백지어음
blank book 미기입장부
blank endorsement 백지이서
blank stock 백지주식
blanket bond 포괄저당권부 채권
blanket mortgage 포괄저당권
blanket order 일괄주문
blanket policy 포괄보험계약
blanket system 포괄담보설정방식
blazing a trail 신기원을 열다
bloc economy 블록경제
block exemption 집단적용면제
block flow 블록플로
block offer 일괄매출;블록오퍼
block positioner 블록포지셔너
block sales 대량매매거래
block trader 블록트레이더
block trading 블록거래
block transaction 대량거래
blockade 봉쇄
blotter 일계표
blue chip 우량주
blue chip company 일류기업
blue chip stock 우량상품
blue collar 블루칼라
blue form return 청색신고
Blue Return Association 청색신고회
blue return system 청색신고제도
blue return taxpayer 청색신고자

blue sky law 창공법
blunder 실책
board broker 보드브로커
board member 이사회구성원
Board of Governors 이사회
Board of Governors of the Federal Reserve System 연방준비제도이사회
Board of Review 과세평가심사위원회
board of supervisors 감리위원회
board of trustees 평의회
board trading 보드거래
body 본문
body of an instrument 문서의 본문
bogus dividend 배당이익이 없는데도 배당함
bogus stock 위조주
boiler room 보일러룸
boilerplate 공통기사;틀에 박힌 문구
BOJ net 일본은행넷
bona fide 성실한
bona fide contracts 선의계약
bona fide cost 진정한 원가
bona fide creditor 선의채권자
bona fide holder 선의소지자
bonanza 노다지;대성공
bond account 채권계정
bond analyst 채권분석가
bond and debenture 채권
bond anticipation notes 장기채차환예정증권
bond attribute 채권속성
bond authorized 사채최고발행한도
bond broker 채권브로커
bond buying operation 채권구매오퍼
bond call provision 채권의 임의상환조항
bond certificate 사채권
bond collateral loans 공사채담보금융
bond conversion 채권전환
bond credit rating 채권의 등급을 매김
bond creditor 채권권리자
bond cross holding 채권보합
bond dealer 채권딜러
bond demand 채권수요
bond discount 채권할인
bond dividend 사채배당
bond equivalent yield 채권환산이율
bond flotation 기채
bond flotation market 기채시장
bond for public offering 공모채
bond form 보증증권주식
bond fund 채권펀드
bond futures 채권선물
bond futures transaction 채권선물거래
bond held 보유채권
bond holder 사채권자
bond holding 채권보유
bond in a pipeline 발행예정채권
bond in portfolio 수중에 있는 채권
bond in won issued by nonresidents 비거주자가 발행한 원기준채권
bond index 채권지수
bond inventory 재고채권
bond investment trust 공사채투자신탁
bond issuance 채권발행
bond issue 채권발행
bond issue costs 채권발행비용
bond issued 발행필 채권
bond issued and purchase by offshore parties 외국-외국 채권
bond issued at a discount 외채디스카운트발행
bond issued at a premium 사채프리미엄발행
bond issued by government related agency 정부계 기간채권
bond issuing bank 채권발행은행
bond issuing expense 사채발행비
bond issuing market 기채시장
bond lending 채권대차
bond lending market 채권대차시장
bond linked to stock price index 주가지수연동채권
bond loan transaction 채권대차거래
bond market 채권시장
bond market equilibrium 채권시장균형

bond of affiliated company 관계회사사채
bond of international agency 국제기관채권
bond on tap 탭채
bond option 채권옵션
bond option at over-the-counter 채권장외옵션
bond outstanding 미상환채권
bond portfolio 채권포트폴리오
bond premium 채권상승액
bond price 채권가격
bond price index 채권가격지표
bond pricing model 채권가격모델
bond purchase 채권구입
bond rating 채권등급을 매김
bond redemption 채권상환
bond refunding 채권차환
bond register 사채원부
bond return 채권이율
bond selection option 채권선택옵션
bond sinking fund 사채감채기금
bond stock mixes 채권주식조합
bond subscription 채권응모
bond swap 채권스와프
bond switching 채권입체거래
bond trader 본드트레이더
bond transaction by investor types 투자가별 공사채매매상황
bond transaction with repurchase agreement 채권현선거래
bond transfer 채권전이
bond trust 공사채투신
bond trust indenture 채권신탁증서
bond trustee 채권수탁자
bond underwriter 채권인수업자
Bond Underwriters Association 공사채인수협회
bond underwriting 채권인수
bond unissued 사채미발행고
bond unit trust 단위형 채권투자신탁
bond valuation 사채평가
bond with debt warrant 데트워런트채
bond with stock purchase warrant 주식매취권부 사채
bond with subscription warrant 신주인수권부 사채
bond with voting right 의결권부 사채
bond with warrant 워런트채
bond with warrant attached 신주인수권부 사채
bond yield 채권이율
bonded area 보세지역
bonded debt 채권발행차입금
bonds issued for daily fund raising of the national treasury 융통채
bonds issued to substitute for government cash payment 이연채
bonds transaction with repurchase agreement 공사채현선매매
bonds used to finance government expenditure 재정지출을 충당하기 위한 국채
bonds with warrants to new shares 신주인수권보 사채권
bonds-cum-warrants 신주인수권부 사채권
bonus dividend 특별배당
bonus issues 무상주식
bonus paid per employee 일인당 상여
bonus payment entered into expenses 손금산입상여
bonus payment reserve 상여준비금
bonus stock 특별배당주
bonus to directors 임원상여
book account 당좌계정
book balance 장부잔고
book building 북빌딩
book building method 북빌딩방식
book closing period 결산기
book credit 외상매출금
book entry 장부기입
book keeper 부기계
book loss 장부에 계상되지 않은 손실
book money 장부화폐
book of account 계정장부

book of final entry 최종기입부
book of original entry 원시기입부
book of regulations 규정집
book runner 사무간사회사
book to bill ratio BB 레이쇼
book value 장부가격
book value method 장부가격방식
book value of assets 장부상의 자산가격
book value of bond 장부상의 채권가격
book value per old stock 장부상의 구주 1주의 가격
book value per share 일주당 순자산
book value stock purchase plan 장부가격주식구입제도
book yield 장부가격이율
book-entry clearing system 대체결제제도
book-entry system for bond 채권보관대체결제제도
book-entry transfer 대체
book-entry transfer fee 대체수수료
book-entry transfer of stock certificates 주권대체
book-keeper 장부계
book-keeping institution 계좌관리기관
book-keeping machine 기장기
book-value 장부가격
booking center 기장장소
bookkeeping 부기
bookkeeping by double entry 복식기장법
bookkeeping by single entry 단식부기
books of account 회계장부
boom 호황
boom and bust 어지러운 시황
boom town 신흥도시
boomerang effect 부메랑효과
boost 경기증대
boosting 자극하다
booth 부스
border tax adjustment 국경세조정
borrowed capital 차입자본
borrowed money 차입금
borrowed reserves 대출준비금
borrowed securities 차입유가증권
borrowed share 차입주식
borrowed stock 차입주식
borrower 차입자
borrower's credit worthiness 차입자의 신용도
borrowing 차입금
borrowing account 차입금계정
borrowing arrangement 차입계정
borrowing cost 차입코스트
borrowing demand 차입수요
borrowing facility 차입한도
borrowing fund 차입자금
borrowing in advance 가불
borrowing rate 조달금리
borrowing limit 차입한도
borrowing requirements 차입필요액
borrowing short 단기차입
Boston Stock Exchange 보스턴증권거래소
both days included 양일포함
bottle-neck inflation 애로인플레이션
bottom 바닥
bottom line 당기이익
bottom price 바닥값
bottom reversal day 버텀리버설데이
bottom straddle 하향제한스트래들
bottom vertical combination 수직적 컴비네이션
bottom-up budget 축적예산
bottom-up forecasting 버텀업형 예측
bottom-up process 버텀업형
bottoming out 최저시세까지 내려감
bought and sold note 매매보고서
bought deal 매입인수
bought for cash 현금구입
bought ledger 구입대장
bounce 부도반각
boundary 경계선
bounds 경계
bounty 격려금
bourse 거래소
bourse tax 거래소세

bourse transaction tax 거래소거래세
boutique 전문적인 증권회사
box 보관상자
box office revenue 흥행수입
box spread 박스스프레드
Box-Jenkins method 박스젠킨스모형
bp 베이시스포인트
bracket creep 요율단계변경
Brady plan 브래디구상
brain drain 두뇌유출
branch 지점
branch account 지점계정
branch accounting 지점회계
branch banking system 지점은행제도
branch handling foreign exchange business 외국환취급지점
branch ledger 지점원장
branch office 지점
branch system 지사제도
brand item 브랜드상품
brass-plate office 간판뿐인 가게
breach 위반
breach of contract 계약위반
breach of covenant 날인증서계약을 위반함
breach of duty 의무위반
breach of law 법률위반
breach of privilege 특권남용
breach of trust 신의위반
breadth 넓이
break-down 내역
break-even analysis 손익분기분석
break-even bond price 손익분기채권가격
break-even chart 손익분기도표
break-even line 채산수준
break-even point 손익분기점
break-even point analysis 손익분기점분석
break-even price 손익분기가격
break-even repo rate 브레이크이븐레포레이트
break-even time 손익분기시기
break-even yield 손익분기이율
break-up value 청산가치
breakage 파손
breakdown 붕괴
breakdown of revenue and expenditure of general account 일반회계세입세출내역
breakthrough 브레이크스루;돌파구
Bretton Woods 브레턴우즈
Bretton Woods Agreement 브레턴우즈협정
bribery 뇌물;뇌물을 줌
bridge finance 입금예정의 공백을 메우기 위해 받는 융자
bridge loan 브리지론;연결융자
bridging exchange 브리지환
brief 준비서면
brief rally 일시적인 반등
briefing 설명회
bring forward 이월하다
bring over 인도하다
brisk market 활황시장
brisk recovery 순조로운 회복
British Accounting Association 영국회계협회
British Banker's Association 영국은행협회
British Export Trade Research Organization 영국무역진흥회
broad based stock index 종합주가지수
broad market 대상;큰장사
broad market index 광범위한 시장지표
broad money 브로드머니
broad tape 전광정보판
broader employee stock ownership 확대종업원지주제도
broadly-defined liquidity 광의유동성
broken term 특정기간인도
broker 중개업자
broker agent 주식거래원
broker's market 업자에 의한 투기상장
broker's business 브로커업무
broker's call loan 브로커의 콜론
broker's loan 브로커론
broker's loan interest 브로커론금리
broker's market 업자의 투자상장
brokerage 브로커업무

Brokerage Agreement Standards 수탁계약준칙
brokerage commission 위탁수수료
brokerage margin 수탁증거금
broking 수탁매매
brought forward account 이월계정
brought-in capital 지입자본
bubble economy 버블경제
buck 달러지폐
bucket shop 장외거래점
bucketeer 거래소, 경마장에서 부당이익을 얻는 사람
budget 예산
budget agreement 예산합의
budget allotment 예산배분
budget audit 예산감사
budget balance 재정수지
Budget Committee 예산위원회
budget deficit 재정적자
budget draft by Ministry of Finance 재무부원안
budget outlay 예산지출
budget principle 예산원칙
budget system 예산제도
budget variance 예산차이
budgetary account 예산계정
budgetary control 예산통제
budgetary expenditure 예산지출
budgetary procedure 예산절차
budgetary process 예산편성
budgeted balance sheet 견적대차대조표
budgeted cost 예산원가
buffer stock 완충재고
buffer stock financing facility 완충재고융자
builders' risks insurance 선박건조보험
building account 건축계정
building and loan association 건축대부조합
building block 구성부분
building expenses 건축비
building lease 건축대차권
building societies 건축조합
building tax 건축세
building under construction 건설 중인 건물
buildup 누적
built-in flexibility 빌트인플렉서빌러티
built-in stabilizer 자동안정장치
bulk buying 생산전량구입
bulk cargo 벌크카고
bulk purchase 대량구입
bull and bear 강세, 약세
bull and bear index 강약지수
bull bear bond 강약세
bull buying 강세매입
bull clique 강세근성
bull market 강세시장
bull speculation 투기매입
bull spread transaction 강세스프레드거래
bull the market 시세에 파동을 일으키다
bullet 일시불형
bullet bond 만기일괄상환채
bullet issue 만기일괄상환상품
bullet loan 일괄반제론
bullet maturity 만기일괄상환
bullet repayment 일괄반제
bullet swap 불릿스와프
bullion 금괴
bullish 희망적;낙관적
bullish channel 강한 채널
bullish consolidation pattern 강세 콘솔리데이션 패턴
bullish factor 강한 재료
bullish resistance line 강한 저항선
bullish reversal patterns 강세 리버설 패턴
bullish support line 강한 지지선
bullish tone 강세
bunched cost 일괄원가
Bund 동맹; 연맹
Bundesbank 독일연방은행
buoyant market 활황
burden 부담
burden charge 부담금
burden of paying tax 납세부담

burden of payment of entrance fees 입회금부담
burden of proof 입증책임
burden of tax 조세부담
burden of tax liability 납세의무부담
burden on cost 간접비(원재료와 노무비 이외)
bureau 국 (국(局))
Bureau of Internal Revenue 내국세입국
bureaucracy 관료
burglary insurance 도난보험
burst 파열
business 사업
business accountability 독립채산제
business accounting 기업회계
Business Accounting Council 기업회계심의회
business accounting principle 기업회계원칙
business activities 기업활동
business activities bring profit 수익을 얻기 위한 경제활동
business adjustment 경기조정
business analysis 경상분석
business annuity 기업연금
business assets suffering from disaster 재난사무용 자산
business audit 업무감사
business barometer 경기지수
business circle 업계
business climate 경기
business combinations 기업결합
business commencement expenses 간접비
business company 사무법인
business concern 기업
business conditions 경기
business continuously carried on 지속적으로 운영되는 사업
business corporation 사업회사
business cycle 경기순환
business cyclical company 경기순환형 기업
business cyclical stock 경기순환주
business day 영업일
business entity 기업실체
business environment risk index 사업환경리스크지수
business establishment 사업소
business event 기업사상
business excution 사무집행
business expansion 사업확장
business expectation 사업전망
business expenses 영업비
business finance 기업금융
business finance company 사업금융회사
business finder 사업 아이디어를 발견하는 사람
business fluctuation 경기변동
business forecast 경기예측
business fund 사업자금
business hours 영업시간
business income 사업소득
business indicator 경기지표
business information 경제정보
business information service 경제정보서비스
business insurance 사업보험
business inventory 기업재고
business investment 기업투자
business judgment principle 경상판단의 원칙
business law 사업법
business loan 사업금융
business meeting 영업회의
business of renting property 부동산대부업
business office tax 사업소세
business opportunity 사업기회
business place 사업소
business plan 경상계획
business practice 사업습관
business profit 영업이익
business profit tax 영업이익세
business proprietor 사업주
business regulations 사업규모
business report 영업보고
business results 영업성적
business secret 사업상의 비밀

business statistics 경상통계
business stimulating measure 경기자극책
business survey 경기동향조사
business tax 사업세
business terms 거래조건
business transaction 기업거래
business trust 사업신탁
business unit 사업단위
business with fluctuating profit 이익이 변동하는 사업
business worth 기업가치
business year 사업연도
but-for income 가정이익
butterfly spread 버터플라이스프레드
butterfly spread trading 버터플라이스프레드거래
buy and hold strategy 장기보유전략
buy and write strategy 바이앤드라이트전략
buy back 되사다
buy high 비싸게 사다
buy on close 싸게 사다
buy on dip 일시적으로 하락할 때 매입함
buy on opening 오전장의 최초 가격으로 매입하다
buy on reaction 시세가 내릴 때 매입하다
buy on scale 세분화하여 매입하다
buy out 매수하다
buy recommendation 매수추천
buy side 바이사이드
buy signal 매신호
buy-in 처분매수
buy-out arrangement 지주매입협정
buyer 사는 쪽
buyer's credit 바이어즈크레디트
buyer's guide 구매자차관
buyer's market 매수시장
buyer's over 신용거래에서 매출잔고가 매수잔고를 웃도는 상황
buyer's risk 매수부담
buying 매입;처분매입
buying agent 구입대리점
buying and selling 매매
buying and selling of securities 유가증권매매
buying at top price 비싼 값으로 구입
buying balance 매수잔고
buying by institutional investors 기관구입
buying commission 매입수수료
buying cost 구입원가
buying energy 구입에너지
buying exchange 환구입
buying hedge 구매헤지
buying offer 구매신청
buying on an yield basis 이익구매
buying on commission 위탁매입
buying on credit 외상구입
buying operation 구매오퍼레이션
buying opportunity 구매장
buying order 구입주문
buying over 매수
buying power 구매력
buying price 구입가격
buying rate 매입률
buying rate without credit 신용장 없는 어음매입률
buying side 구입측
buying support 구입지원
buying terms 구입조건
buying title 권원(權原)구입
buying up 매점
by default 계약서에 씌어있지 않더라도
by measurement 증권중개회사를 통해서
by proxy 대리인을 통해서
by record 기록에 의한
by representation 표시에 의한
by silence 침묵에 의한
by types of industry 업종별
by types of licenses 면허세
by types of trading 거래종류별
by-product 부차적인 결과
bylaws for the election of officers 임원선거세칙
bystander 방관자

C

Cabinet Office 내각부
Cabinet Order of the Securities and Exchange Law 증권거래법시행령
cable 펀드 대 미달러율
cable address 해외전보수신인
cable credit 전신신용장
cable transfer 전신송금
CAC 40 CAC 40종 주가지수
CAC General Index 프랑스 CAC 공업주가지수
calculate 계산하다
calculated tax amount 산출세액
caculating table 속산표
calculation 산정
calculation of compounded interest 복리계산
calculation of theoretical price 이론가격산출
calculator 계산조견표
calendar day 자정에서 자정까지의 24시간
calendar month 1년의 12분의 1; 역월
calendar month delivery 역월인도
calendar month delivery rate 역월제선물상장
calendar spread 캘린더스프레드
calendar spread transaction 캘린더스프레드 거래
calendar year 역년
call 콜; 소집하다
call and bill market 콜어음시장
call bond 콜옵션부 채권
call date 조기상환일
call loan 콜론; 단자; 당좌차입금
call loan dealer 단자회사
call loan market 단자시장
call market 콜시장
call market average outstanding 콜시장평균잔고
call money 콜머니
call money and discount market 단자시장
call money market 단자시장
call money rate 콜금리
call option 콜옵션
call option contract 콜옵션계약
call option premium 콜옵션의 옵션료
call option valuation and dividend 콜옵션 평가와 배당
call premium 콜옵션의 옵션료
call price 기전상환가격
call provision 임의상환조항
call rate 콜금리
call ratio back spread transaction 콜 레이쇼 백 스프레드 거래
call risk 조기상환리스크
call spread 콜 스프레드
call swaption 콜 스왑션
call trigger 콜 트리거
call warrant 콜 워런트
call-sales merchant 방문판매업자
callable bond 임의상환채권
callable debt 즉시상환가능한 채권
callable loan 콜러블 론
callable obligation 임의상환채무
callable preferred stock 상환가능주식
callable securities 임의상환가능채권

callable shares 상환주식;상각가능주식
callable stock 상환주식
callable swap 콜러블스와프
callable swaption 콜러블스왑션
cambist 환어음업자
Canadian-dollar long-term bond 캐나다달러장기국채
cancel money 위약금
cancel order 취소주문
cancelable 해약가능한
cancelable swap 캔슬러블스와프
canceled order 캔슬드오더
canceling date 해약기일
cancellation 해약
cancellation before maturity 중도해약
cancellation before the maturity 기한전 해약
cancellation money 해약금
cancellation of a contract 중도해약
cancellation of debts of directors 임원채무면제
cancellation of designation 지시를 취소함
cancellation of filing a blue return 청색신고취소
cancellation of register 등록말소
cancellation of shares 주식소각
cancellation of when-issued transaction 발행일거래취소
cancellation request 해약청구
cancelled check 지불필 수표
cap and floor 캡 & 플로어
cap interest rate 상한금리
cap loan 캡론
capacity 행위능력
capacity cost plan 고정비회수계획
capacity to contract 계약능력
capacity utilization rate 설비가동률
capital 자본
capital account 자본계정
capital account balance 자본수지
capital accumulation 자본축적
capital adequacy 자본충실
capital adequacy requirements 자기자본비율규제
capital adequacy standards 자기자본기준
capital adjustment 자본수정
capital and liabilities ratio 자본부담비율
capital appreciation 값이 오른 이익
capital arrangement 고정성 배열법
capital asset pricing model 자본자산가격모델; 자본자산평가모델
capital assets 자본자산; 자본재산
capital base 자산기반
capital budget 자본예산
capital budgeting 설비투자계획
capital certainty 원본확실성
capital change 자본변동
capital coefficient 자본계수
capital committed 수탁자산
capital composition 자본구성
capital consolidation 자본연결
capital consumption 자본소비
capital consumption adjustment 자본소비를 조정함
capital consumption allowance 자본감모준비
capital contribution 자본거출
capital control 자본통제
capital cost 자본비용
capital debenture 열후채
capital decrease 감자
capital demand curve 자본수유곡선
capital disposition 자본지출
capital distribution 자본분배
capital duty 자본세
capital equipment 자본설비
capital expenditure 자본지출
capital export 자본수출
capital flight 자본도피
capital flow 캐피탈플로
capital formation 자본형성
capital formation account 자본형성계정
capital formula 자본등식
capital gain 캐피탈게인; 매매이익

capital gain free of taxation 비과세양도소득
capital gain fund 캐피탈게인펀드
capital gain tax 캐피탈게인세
capital gain taxation 캐피탈게인과세
capital gain from sales of securities 유가증권판매익
capital gearing 캐피탈기어링
capital goods 자본재
capital goods export 자본재수출
capital immediately after the specified merger 특정합병 직후의 자본
capital import 자본수입
capital improvement 자본지출로 처리하는 개선
capital in excess of par or stated value 자본준비금
capital in excess of par value 액면초과금
capital income 자본소득
capital increase 증자
capital increase by new shares at market price 시가발행증자
capital inflow 자본유입
capital intensity 자본집약
capital interest 자본이자
capital interest tax 자본이자세
capital investment 설비투자
capital investment intention 설비투자의욕
capital lease 캐피탈리스
capital leverage 재무레버리지
capital levy 자본과세
capital liabilities 자본부채
capital liberalization 자본자유화
capital loan 캐피탈론
capital loss 캐피탈로스
capital market 자본시장
capital market line 자본시장선
capital outflow 자본유출
capital outlay 자본지출
capital paid in 불입자본
capital paid in excess of par value 액면초과지불자본
capital participation 자본참가
capital position 자본포지션
capital productivity 자본생산성
capital profit 자본이윤
capital ratio 자기자본비율
capital receipt 자본수입
capital recovery 자본회복
capital redemption 자금환급;자본보상
capital reduction 감자
capital requirement 자기자본규제
capital reserve 자본준비금
capital risk 캐피탈리스크
capital saving industry 자본절약산업
capital saving technical progress 자본절약을 위한 기술진보
capital spending 자본투자
capital stock 자본금
capital stock account 자본계정
capital stock adjustment 자본스톡조정
capital stock adjustment principle 자본스톡조정원리
capital stock issued 발행필 자본금
capital stock paid in 불입자본금
capital stock preferred 우선주자본금
capital stock registered 공칭자본금
capital stock subscribed 인수필 자본금
capital stock tax 자본세
capital stock unpaid 미불입액
capital structure 자본구성
capital subscription 출자
capital sum 자본액
capital supplier nation 자본공급국
capital surplus 자본준비금
capital tax 자본세
capital theory 자본이론
capital transaction 자본거래
capital transfer 자본이전
capital turnover 자본회전율
capital utilization 설비가동률
capital working rate 자본가동률
capital-intensive merchandise

자본집약적인 상품
capital-output ratio 자본 대 산출고비율
capital-reconciliation statement 자본조정표
capitalism 자본주의
capitalism market economy
자본주의시장경제
capitalist 자본가
capitalist bracket 자본가계급
capitalization 자본편입
capitalization issue 신주발행
capitalization of accumulated earnings
이익적립금을 자본에 편입함
capitalization of interest 이익을 자산화함
capitalization of interest cost
차입이자를 자산계상함
capitalization of revaluation reserve of joint stock company
주식회사의 재평가적립금을 자본편입함
capitalization of revaluation surplus reserve
재평가적립금을 자본편입함
capitalization unit 자산화 단위
capitalization weighted 시장가치가중
capitalization weighted indices
시가총액 가중 인덱스
capitalized interest 자산화이익
capitalized surplus 자본금편입잉여금
capitalized value 자본가치
capitalized value of stock 배당환원가액
capitation tax 인두세
capped floating rate note 캡부채
capped loan 캡부론
capped swap 캡스와프
capping 캐핑
capsized 배가 뒤집힌;전복된
captive finance company 금융자회사
captive insurance company 자가보험회사
capture 수집
car loan backed securities 자동차론담보증권
car tax 자동차세
card counterfeiting 카드위조
card criminal fraud 카드범죄
card discrimination code 카드식별코드
card issuer 카드회사
card loan 카드론
card member 카드회원
card merchant 카드가맹점
card of accounts 계정과목표
card renewal 카드갱신
card replacement 카드재발행
card shopping 카드쇼핑
card standardization 카드표준화
card system 카드시스템
card system of bookkeeping 카드식 기장법
card-holic 다중채무
care 주의
care and custody 관리책임
care of works 공사관리
career agency system 전속외무원제도
careless business system 부주의한 사무처리
cargo insurance 화물해상보험
carriage 운송비
carriage and insurance paid to
운송비와 보험료를 포함해서
carriage paid to 운송비포함
carried forward 이월
carried interest 이월지분
carry back 환급
carry back of deficit 결손금환급
carry back of loss 손실환급
carry back of losses 결손금환금공제
carry back of net loss 순손실환급
carry forward 이월하다
carry forward of casualty loss 재해손실이월
carry forward of net operating loss
순손실이월
carry income 캐리인컴
carry on 경영하다
carry out compensation 보상하다
carry over of casualty loss
잡손실을 이월공제함
carry over of deficit 결손금이월
carry over of foreign tax

외국세액을 이월공제함
carry over of foreign tax credit limit
외국세액의 공제한도액을 이월함
carry over of net loss 순손실이월
carrying amount 장부상의 자산가격
carrying broker 고객계정을 확보한 브로커
carrying charge 재산보유비용
carrying cost 재고비용
carrying value 이월가액
carrying-over contract 이연계약
cartage 운임
carte blanche 백지위임
cartel 카르텔
cartel tariffs 카르텔관세
Carter bond 카디본드
cascade tax 누적세
cascade type turnover tax 누적형 거래고세
case 준비서면
case administration 파산관리
case law 판례법
case stated 사실기재서
case study 케이스스터디
cash 캐시;현금
cash account 금융계정
cash advance 캐싱
cash and carry 현금지불
cash and carry system 현금지불방식
cash and carry trade 현금지불거래
cash and cash equivalents 현금 및 현금등가물
cash and deposits 현금예금
cash and deposits banks accounts
현금예금계정
cash and deposits with banks 현금예금자산
cash asset value 현금자산가치
cash assets 현금자산
cash at bank 당좌예금
cash audit 현금감사
cash balance 현금잔고
cash basis 현금주의
cash basis accounting 현금주의회계
cash basket 현물바스켓
cash bond 현물채권
cash book 현금출납장
cash break-even point 수지분기점
cash buying rate 현금매상장
cash capital 현금자본
cash card 현금카드
cash collection 현금회수
cash contribution 현금공여
cash control 현금관리
cash credit 당좌대출
cash currency 현금통화
cash delivery 즉일인도
cash deposit 현금예금
cash deposited for bond interest
사채이자지불금
cash disbursed 지출
cash disbursement 현금지불
cash disbursement book 지불장부
cash discount 현금할인
cash dispenser 현금지불기
cash dividend 현금배당
cash dividend declared 현금배당결의액
cash earnings 현금수입
cash equity 현물주
cash equivalent 현예금
cash flow 캐시플로
cash flow analysis 수지분석
cash flow coverage ratio 캐시플로부담배율
cash flow crisis 캐시플로위기
cash flow from financial activities
재무활동으로 인한 캐시플로
cash flow from investing activities
투자활동으로 인한 캐시플로
cash flow from operating activities
영업활동으로 인한 캐시플로
cash flow interest 캐시플로이율
cash flow projection 캐시플로예측
cash flow ratio 캐시플로비율
cash flow ratio to capital expenditures
설비투자 캐시플로비율
cash flow ratio to long-term liabilities

장기부채 캐시플로비율
cash flow return 캐시플로리턴
cash flow statement 자금운용표
cash flow to current liabilities
캐시플로 대 유동부채
cash forecasts 수지예측
cash forward contract 캐시플로계약
cash forward transaction 현물선도거래
cash forward handling clerk 금전취급자
cash in advance 선불로
cash in bank 은행예금
cash in banks and hand 예금현금
cash in hand 생계현금보유고
cash in transit 미달현금
cash income 현금수입
cash index 현물지수
cash issue 현물상품
cash items 현금항목
cash journal 현금분개장
cash letters 현금송장
cash letter of credit 현금신용장
cash liabilities 현금부채
cash loan 현금대부
cash management 현금관리
cash management bills 캐시매니지먼트빌
cash management service
캐시매니지먼트서비스
cash market 현물시장
cash matching 현물대당
cash multiplier 현물승수
cash on delivery 대금교환인도
cash on hand 생계현금
cash on shipment 선적지불
cash option 현물옵션
cash outlays 현금지출
cash over and short 현금과부족
cash over and short account 현금과부족계정
cash payment 현금지불
cash payment journal 현금지불장
cash position 현금상태
cash price 현금가격
cash purchase 현금구매
cash ratio 현금비율
cash receipt 현금수령
cash receipt book 현금수납장
cash receipt journal 현금수납장
cash received 수입현금
cash records 현금기록
cash redemption 현금상환
cash remittance 현금반송
cash reserve ratio 예금지불준비율
cash reserves 현금준비고
cash sale 현금매매
cash selling rate 현금매상장
cash settlement 현금결제
cash slips 출납전표
cash statement 현금계산서
cash stock 현물주
cash surrender value 해약반환금
cash tender offer 현금공개매부
cash to be payed or received for settlement
결제를 위해 수수하는 금전
cash to current liabilities ratio
현금유동부채비율
cash trading 현물거래
cash transactions 현물거래;당일거래
cash value 운용부분
cash value insurance 저축형 보험
cash-book 출납부
cash-management bills 캐시매니지먼트빌
cashable goods 환금성 상품
cashier 현금출납계
cashier's check 은행수표
cashier's department 현금출납과
casting vote 결정권
casual expenses 임시지출
casual loss 우발손실
casual profit 우발이익
casualty and surety insurance
신종보험;손해보증보험
casualty insurance 재해보험
casualty loss 잡손

casually loss deduction 잡손공제
casualty losses carried over 이월재해손실
catalog 영업안내
catalog sales 카탈로그판매
catch-up adjustments 파급수정
categories of members 회원종류
category killer 카테고리킬러
category of business 업종
cats and dogs stock 투기주
causal analysis 인과분석
causal credit 원인채권
causal relationship 인과관계
causality 인과관계
cause 원인
cause inducement 동기
cause list 사건목록
cause of action 소송원인
cause of bankruptcy 파산원인
cause proximate 근인주의
cause sine qua non 필수조건
cause-books 사건부
caution 등기변경예고
caution money 보증금
cautionary 보증채무의
cautious stance 경계하는 자세
caveat 절차중지예고
CD market CD 시장
CD outstanding CD 발행잔고
cease to exist 소멸하다
ceded premium 재보험료
cedel 세델
ceding 상한
ceiling price 최고액
ceiling rate 상한금리
ceiling system 실링방식
cellular approach 셀룰러어프로치
cellular operation 휴대전화사무
census bureau 상업통계
Central American Common Market 중미공동시장
central bank 중앙은행
central bank intervention 평형개입
central bank note 중앙은행권
central bank rate 중앙은행할인율
Central Co-operative Bank for Commerce and Industry 상업조합중앙금고
central custody and book-entry transfer services 보관대체제도
central government 중앙정부
central government transfers to local governments 지방교부금
central market 중앙시장
central party 중심레이트
central rate 중심상장;중심레이트
central securities depository 보험대체기관
central tendency 중심경향
centralization of capital 자본집중
centralized economy 집중경제
certain assets 확실성 자산
certainty 명백성
certificate 증명서
certificate holder 증서보유자
certificate number 증서번호
certificate of a seal-impresstion 인감증명
certificate of analysis 분석증명서
certificate of bank balances 은행예금잔고증명서
certificate of compliance 납세필 증서
certificate of incorporation 회사설립면허
certificate of incumbency 재직증명
certificate of indebtedness 채무증서
certificate of insurance 보험인수증
certificate of origin 원산지증명
certificate of preemptive rights 신주인수권증서
certificate of tax payment 납세증명서
certificate of time deposit 정기예금증서
certificate of weight and measurement 중량용적증명서
certificated financial statement 감사필 재무제표
certificated share 주권이 있는 주식

certification of subscription rights 신주인수권증서
certification of payment 지불보증
certified check 지불인수수표
certified copy 인증등본
certified copy of commercial registration 상업등기부등본
certified copy of real estate register 부동산등기부등본
certified public accountant 공인회계사
Certified Public Accountant Law 공인회계사법
certified tax accountant 세무사
certified tax accountant association 세무사회
Certified Tax Accountant Law 세무사법
certifying bank 지불보증은행
cession 양도
cession of a credit 채권양도
cession of an obligation 채무양도
chain banking 체인뱅킹
chairman emeritus 명예회장
Chakuchi transaction 착지거래
chamber of commerce 상업회의소
chamber of commerce and industry 상공회의소
chance to sell 매장
Chancellor of the Exchequer 영국재무부장관
change 변화
change claims 변경클레임
change date 변경일
change in employment 전적
change in growth rate 성장률변화
change in par value 액면변경
change in valuation method 평가방법변경
change in business 사업전환
change of depreciation method 상각방법변경
change of risk 위험변동
change of tax computation basis 세액계산기준변경
change of taxable year 사업연도변경
change of the place of tax payment 납세지변경
change of venue 관할이전
change over 체인지오버
changes in accounting principles 회계원칙변경
changes in earning per share 일주당 이익변동
changes in estimates 견적금액변경
changes in gross margin 조이익증감
changes of owners of the principal 원본소유자이동
channel line 채널라인
channeling back 환류
characteristic line 특성선
characteristics 특징
charge 수수료;비용
charge account 외상매출금계정
charge against revenues 손금
charge and commission 지불수수료
charge back 입금취소
charge extra 부대비용
charge for call 독촉료
charge for collection 수금수수료
charge for collection of bill 어음수금수수료
charge for custody 보관료
charge for demand for tax in arrears 체납독촉수수료
charge for development 개발부담금
charge for installment payment 할부수수료
charges for remittance 환수수료
charge off 대손상각
charge on the declining balance 잔채방식
charges forward 입체지불
charitable donation 자선기부
charitable trust 공익신탁
charities and donations 자선기부금
chart 차트
chart analysis 차트분석
chart of accounts 계정과목표
chart pattern 차트패턴

C D

chart reading 차트분석
charter 기본정관
charter contract 용선계약
charter party B/L 차터파티 B /L
charter provision 회사설립허가서
charter-land 특허보유지
chartered 공인의
chartered accountant 칙령으로 허가된 회계사
chartered company 특허회사
chartered financial analyst
공인증권분석전문가
chartered public accountant 공인회계사
charterparty 용선계약
chartist 차티스트
chattel 동산
chattel loan 동산대부
chattel mortgage 동산저당
chattel paper 동산저당증권
cheap money 저금리자산
cheapest-to-deliver 최염가저당
cheapest-to-deliver bond 최염가저당채권
cheat 사기
check act 수표법
check and bill clearing 어음교환
check book 수표장
check drawee 수표지불인
check drawer 수표발행지
check guarantee card 체크개런티카드
check holder 수표지정인
check mark 조회필 기호
check register 수표기입장
check to bearer 지참인지불수표
check to order 지정수표
check writer 체크라이터
check-out counter 계정구
checkable deposit 결제성 예금
checkbook stub 수표장원부
checking 조회
checking account 당좌계정
checking deposits 당좌예금
checking inventory 재고조회
checking system 수표제도
chemicals industry 화공업계
Chicago Board of Trade 시카고상품거래소
Chicago Board Options Exchange
시카고옵션거래소
Chicago Mercantile Exchange
시카고싱공회의소
Chicago school 시카고학파
chief 주석
chief accountant 회계주임
chief examiner 통괄국세조사관
chief executive officer 최고경영책임자
chief financial officer 재무담당임원
chief insurance regulators 보험규제책임자
chief investigator 통괄국세사찰관
chief operating officer 최고업무책임자
chief revenue officer 통괄국세징수관
child tax credit 부양공제
children allowance 아동수당
Chinese wall 만리장성;큰 방해물
chit 전표
chit book 송달부
chit system 전표지불제도
chose in action 무체동산
chose in possession 유체동산
chronic 만성적인
chronic absenteeism 만성적인 태업
chronic deflation 만성적인 디플레이션
chronic inflation 만성적인 인플레이션
chronological 연대순으로
CIF price 원가·보험료·운임포함 가격
Cincinnati Stock Exchange
신시내티증권거래소
circuit breaker 동시거래정지
circuit court 순회재판소
circular flow of economic system 경제순환
circular letter 회람판
circulating assets 유동자산
circulating capital 유동자본
circulating fund 운임자금
circulation 유통

circulation of capital 자본유통
circulation of national income 국민소득순환
circulation tax 유통세
circumstances 환경
circumstantial evidence 정황증거
circus swap 서커스스와프
City 도시
city bank 도시은행
city planning tax 도시계획세
civil 민사의
civil action 민사의 (민사소송)
civil code 민법
civil execution 민사집행
civil group 시민단체
civil law 민법
civil remedy 민사상의 구제조치
civil service 공무
civil suit 민사소송
civilian demand 민수
civilian enterprise 민간사업
claim and delivery 동산회복소송
claim cost 보험비용
claim for a refund 환부청구
claim for compensation 구상
claim for correction 갱정청구
claim for damage 손해배상청구
claim for examination 심사청구
claim for guarantee 미수보증금
claim for reimbursement 상환청구
claim for tax refunds 조세환부청구권
claim in bankruptcy 파산채권
claim in foreign currency 외화기준채권
claim notice clause 손해통지조항
claim of prepayment of income tax 예정납세액독촉
claim of redemption 상환청구권
claim of the fund of taxes 세금환급청구
claim paid or payable 보상액;보험금
claim payable to a specific person 지명채권
claim payment 보험금지불
claim period 구상기간
claim processing 보험금지불업무
claim receivable 채권
claim similar to account receivable and loan 외상매출금이나 대부금에 준하는 채권
claim the refund 반환청구하다
claim to cash 현금청구
claiming bank 구상은행
claims 배상금
clarification 설명
class action 집단소송
class cost 조별원가
class cost system 조별원가계산
class of the stock 주식의 종류
classes of stocks 주식등급
classification of a taxpayer 납세의무자분류
classification of accounts 계정과목일람표
classification of securities 유가증권의 분류
classification of shares 주식구분
classification of tax 세금분류
classified income 각종소득
classified income tax 분류소득세
classified stock 분류된 주식
classified trial balance 구분식 시산표
clause 조항
clause "touch and stay" 기항지체류조항
clause as to the binding effect of policy 보험증권의 구속력에 대한 조항
claused bill of lading 조건부 서하증권
clean bill of lading 클린 B/L
clean float 클린플로트;자유변동시세제도
clean letter of credit 클린신용장
clean loan 클린론;무담보론
clean opinion 클린오피니언
clear band 클리어밴드
clear days 순일수
clearance fee 출항수수료
clearance goods 재고품
clearance of bills 어음교환
clearing 청산
clearing account 어음교환계정
clearing agency 청산기관

clearing agreement 청산협정
clearing balance 어음교환차액
clearing bank 어음교환소가맹은행
clearing business 결제사무
clearing contract 청산거래
clearing corporation 청산회사
clearing for nonmember 대리교환
clearing function 청산기능
clearing fund 클리어링펀드; 결제기금
Clearing House Inter-Bank Payment System 뉴욕어음교환소의 은행간 자금이체지급제도; CHIPS
clearing margin 거래증거금
clearing margin for customer's account 수탁거래증거금
clearing margin for proprietary account 자기거래증거금
clearing member 청산회원
clearing organization 청산기관
clearing price 청산가격
clearing procedure 청산절차
clearing system 어음교환제도
clearing time 결제시
clearing transaction 청산거래
clearing-house balance 교환잔고표
clearinghouse 어음교환소
clearinghouse for commodity futures 상품선물거래청산소
clearinghouse proof 어음교환결산표
clerical error 오기
clients 거래처
clientele effect 고객효과
climbing angle 상승각
climbing power 상승력
clique 파벌
clone fund 복제펀드
close down 종가가 전일의 종가보다 쌈
close of the market 인출
close of the session 인출
close one's position 거래관계를 청산하다
close up 종가가 전일의 종가보다 비쌈
closed account 마감필 계정
closed corporation 동족회사
closed economy 봉쇄경제
closed market 폐쇄시장
closed period 클로즈드기간
closed-end dual fund 폐쇄형 듀얼펀드
closed-end fund 폐쇄형 펀드
closed-end mortgage 폐쇄식 담보
closed-end mortgage bond 폐쇄식 담보부사채
closed-end trust 폐쇄식 신탁
closed-end type 폐쇄식
closely-held company 비공개회사
closing 계약내용을 실행함; 인출
closing adjustment 결산정리
closing all accounts in the ledger 원장의 각 계정을 마감함
closing balance 기말잔고
closing balance a /c 기말잔고계정
closing business 사업폐쇄
closing date 결산일
closing entries 결산분개
closing high 시세가 높을 때 물러남
closing inventories 기말재고고
closing lower 시세가 낮을 때 물러남
closing meeting 최종회의
closing of accounts 결산
closing of the ledger 원장체결
closing of the morning session 오전장에서 물러남
closing out 청산
closing price (거래소의) 종가
closing the book 결산
closing the ledger 원장마감
closing tone (거래소의)최종분위기
closing transaction 반대매매
closing trial balance 마감시산표
closure 폐쇄
club deal 공동인수
club dues 회비
co-branded card 제휴카드

co-finance 공동융자
co-heir 공동법정상속인
co-insurance 공동보험
co-lead-manager 공동주간사
co-maker 공동발행인
co-manager 부간사
co-movement of corporate earnings 기업이익의 공변동
co-movement of earnings 이익의 공변동
co-owner 공유자
co-ownership 공유
coastwise cargo insurance 내항화물해상보험
cobweb cycle 거미집순환
cocktail swap 칵테일스와프; 복합스와프
code 규정
code of conduct 행동규범
Code of Procedure for Handling Trade · Practice Complain 전미증권업협회 분쟁처리규칙
coefficient 계수
coefficient of determination 결정계수
coefficient of variation 변동계수
coercive 강제적인
cognitive 인지적인
cognizance 승인
coincident indicator 일치지수
coincident series 일치계수
cold call 전화를 통한 거래권유
collaboration 제휴
collapse 폭락
collapse in oil prices 유가하락
collar 칼라
collared swap 칼라스와프
collateral 담보
collateral bond 부대증서
collateral commodity 상품담보
collateral condition 부대조건
collateral consanguinity 방계혈족
collateral deposit 담보부 예금
collateral export 반제수출
collateral import 담보부 수입
collateral loan 담보대부
collateral note 담보부 약속어음
collateral on loans on bills 어음대부담보
collateral on property 물적담보
collateral security 대용증권
collateral shares 담보주
collateral trust bond 담보부 신탁채권
collateral value 담보가치
collateral value of substitute security 대용증권담보율
collateralized 유담보
collateralized mortgage obligations 저당부 모기지증서
collateralized overnight 유담보익일물
collation 조회
collation of seals 날인의 인장을 조회함
collect 징수하다
collected amount 징수액
collectible 회수가능한
collecting agent 징수업자
collecting tax 징수
collection 회수
collection bank 징수은행
collection basis 회수기준
collection bill 징수어음
collection charge 징수경비
collection cycle 회수순환
collection expenses 징수비용
collection fee 징수료
collection floater 수집물포괄보험
collection letter 독촉장
collection management technique 회수기술
collection measure 징수조치
collection of bad debts deducted 상각필 대손금 회수
collection of bill 외상매출금회수
collection of claim 채권회수
collection of loans 대부금회수
collection of rates 조세징수
collection of securities by purchase 유가증권매출집금

C D

collection period 회수기간
collection practices 회수업무
collection rate 회수율
collection term 회수기간
collection bargaining 단체교섭
collection bargaining agreement 단체협약
collective investment fund 합동운용형 펀드
College Retirement Equities Fund 미국대학교직원퇴직변액연금기금
collision 충돌
color 표견상의 권리
combination 컴비네이션
combination of securities 유가증권을 조합함
combination sale 공동판매
combine 합동
combined 총계의
combined account 합동계정
combined balance sheet 결합대차대조표
combined depreciation 결합상각법
combined financial statement 결합재무제표
combined income statement 합병손익계산서
combined profit and loss statement 결합손익계산서
combined ratio 합산비율
combined single limit 사고 1건당 보상한도액
combined transport documents 복합운송서류
comfort letter (비공식)감사의견서;각서
commemorative dividend 기념배당
commencement date 개시일
commencement of reorganization proceedings 갱생절차개시
commendation system 표창제도
commerce and industry finance company 상공업금융회사
commerce clause 통상조항
Commerce Department 상무부
commercial accounting 상업회계
commercial and industrial loan 상공론
commercial arbitration 상사중재
commercial bank 시중은행;상업은행
commercial bank credit 민간은행대출
commercial bank discount and loan 시중대출
commercial banker 상업은행가
commercial bill 상업어음
commercial bill eligible for rediscounting with the Bank of Japan 일본은행재할인적격어음
commercial bookkeeping 상업부기
commercial business 영리사업
Commercial Code 상법
commercial company 영리회사
commercial court 상업재판소
commercial credit 상업신용
commercial credit insurance 상업신용보험
commercial customs 상습관
commercial discount 상업할인
commercial enterprise 영리사업
commercial expenses 영업비
commercial finance 상업금융
commercial invoice 상업송장
commercial L/C 상업신용장
commercial law 상법
commercial lending 상업대부
commercial loan 상업대출
commercial mortgage 상업용 모기지
commercial mortgage backed securities 상업용 모기지담보증권
commercial mortgage pool 상업용 모기지풀
commercial paper 상업어음
commercial paper outstanding 상업어음발행잔고
commercial real estate 상업용 부동산
commercial real estate loan 상업부동산론
commercial registration 상업등기
commercial risk 신용위험
commercial statistics 상업통계
commercial trader 상업트레이더
commercial tranche 민간트란시
commercial transaction 상행위
Commercial Union Assurance Co. 커머셜유니온
commercialization 상품화

Commerzbank 코메르츠은행
Commerzbank-Index 코메르츠지수
commingled custody 혼성보관
commingled fund 합동운용펀드
commingled investment account 혼합투자계정
commission 위탁매매인; 수수료
commission account 수수료계정
commission agent 위탁매매인
commission broker 거래소중매인
commission del credere 보증부 위임
commission earned 수취수수료
commission for purchase 매입수수료
commission income 수수료수입
commission of authority 위탁계약서
commission on consignment 위탁수수료
commission payable 미불수수료
commission rate 수수료요율
commission receivable 미수수수료
commission received 수입수수료
commission sale 수수료매매
commission schedule 수수료명세서
commission system 커미션제
commission to consignee 위탁판매수수료
Commission's White Paper EC 위원회 백서
commissioners for oaths 서약관리인
commitment 약속
commitment base 커미트먼트베이스
commitment fee 약정수수료
commitments 계약채무
committed line of credit 신용공여한도
committee 위원회
committee of inspection 검사위원회
Committee on Accounting Procedure 회계절차위원회
committee on auditing procedure 감사절차위원회
Committee on Uniform Securities Identification Procedures CUSIP
committee regulations 위원회규칙
commodities exchange commission 상품거래소위원회
commodities investment trust 상품투자신탁
commoditization 상품성
commodity 상품
commodity account 상품거래계좌
commodity backed bond 상품담보채권
commodity customers agreement 상품고객계약
commodity demand 상품수요
commodity exchange 상품거래소
commodity exchange act 상품거래법
commodity exchange responsibility reserve 상품거래책임준비금
commodity excise 물품세
commodity flow method 커머디티플로법
commodity futures 상품선물
commodity futures index 상품선물지수
commodity futures price 상품선물거래가격
Commodity Futures Trading Commission 미국상품선물거래위원회
commodity index 상품지수
commodity market 상품시장
commodity money 물품화폐
commodity option 상품옵션
commodity pool 커머디티풀
commodity pool operator 상품 펀드 풀 운영자
commodity price 물가
commodity price index 상품가격지수
commodity statistics 상품통계
commodity swap 커머디티스와프
commodity tax 물품세
commodity tax law 물품세법
commodity trading adviser 상품거래고문
commodity transaction 상품거래
commodity transaction responsibility reserve 상품거래책임준비금
common 입회권
common account 공동계정
common agriculture policy 공통농업정책
common assurance 양도증서

C D

common background 공통기반
common carrier 일반통신사업자
common collateral 공통담보
common cost 공통원가
common counts 일반항목
common dividend 보통배당
common dollar statements 안정가치로 수정한 재무제표
common factor risk 공통요인리스크
common gap 커먼갭
common goods 공통재
common informer 정보제공자
common injunction 일반금지명령
common law 관습법
common law action 민사소송
common law corporation 보통법주식회사
common law trust 공통법신탁
common liquidation 통상해산
common logarithm 공통대수
common market 공동시장
common nuisance 공적불법방해
common property 공유자산
common stock 보통주식
common stock book value 보통주의 장부가격
common stock for treasury 자기주식
common stock outstanding 사외발행보통주식
common stock ownership statistics 보통주보유에 관한 통계
common stock preemptive right 신주인수권
common tariff 공통관세
common-size balance sheet 백분율대차대조표
common-size financial statements 백분율재무제표
common-size income statements 백분율손익계산서
communication charges 통신비
communications industry 통신업계
community 공동체
community credit 커뮤니티크레디트
community of interest 이해가 일치함
community reinvestment 지역재투자
commutation 환산
companies act 회사법
companies changing the amount of dividend 배당금이동회사
companies having changed their fiscal terms 변칙결산회사
companies previously paying dividend 무배전락기업
companies with employee stock ownership plan 지주제도실시회사
company 회사
company law 회사법
company leverage 기업부채비율
company limited 주식회사
company limited by guarantee 유한책임보증회사
company limited by shares 주식회사
company of lower equity rank 자본하위회사
company organization 회사조직
company rehabilitation law 회사갱생법
company representative 회사대리인
company union 어용조합
company with reduced capital 감자회사
company-specific 개별기업 고유의
company's own stock 자사주
comparability 비교가능성
comparative advantage 비교우위
comparative advantage theory 비교우위이론
comparative analysis 비교분석
comparative balance sheet 비교대차대조표
comparative cost 비교원가
comparative cost studies 비교원가조사
comparative financial statement 비교재무제표
comparative income statement 비교손익계산서
comparative profit and loss statement 비교손익계산서
comparative statement 비교계산서
comparative statement of cash flows 비교수지계산서

comparative statistics 비교통계학
comparison 비교
comparison of beta values of funds 펀드베타수치를 비교함
comparison slip 조회표
comparison table 비교표
compatible 호환성이 있는
compensated absence 유급휴가
compensating balance 구속잔고
compensating error 상쇄오차
compensating interest 상쇄이자
compensating trade or transactions 구상무역
compensation 보수
compensation bond 교부공채
compensation duties 상쇄관세
compensation for damage 손해배상
compensation for expense and loss 경비보상금
compensation for expropriation 수용보상금
compensation for fixed costs during the suspension of business 휴업기간중의 고정비를 보상함
compensation for injuries and deaths 부상사망보상금
compensation for moving expenses 입퇴비용을 보상함
compensation for profit from business 업무상의 수익을 보상함
compensation for residual land 잔지보상금
compensation for revenue 수익보상금
compensation for the failure to settle 결제불이행에 대한 반제
compensation for transfer of property 이전보상금
compensation of the damage 손해변제
compensation paid to directors 임원보수
compensation plans based on assets 운용자산액비례보수방식
compensation principle of taxation 조세의 수익자부담원칙
compensation trade 구상무역
compensatory budget policy 보정예산정책
compensatory deposit 보상예금
compensatory effect 보정효과
compensatory financing facility 보상융자
compensatory fiscal policy 보정재정정책
compensatory item 보정항목
compensatory surplus 보정여잉
compete 경합하다
competence 직권
competency 능력이 있음
competent 자격이 있는; 관할권이 있는
competent authority 권한이 있는 당국
competent minister 주무대신
competent parties 능력이 있는 당사자
competent interest 대립하는 이해
competition among markets 시장간 경쟁
competition pressure 경쟁압력
competitive auction 경쟁매매
competitive bid 경쟁입찰
competitive depreciation 경쟁적인 평가절하
competitive edge 경쟁력
competitive market maker system 투자기관경합시스템
competitive price 경쟁가격
competitive sale 경쟁판매
competitive tender 경쟁입찰
competitiveness 경쟁력
competitor 경합기업
compilation 조정
compilation of the budget 예산편성
complainant 원고
complaint procedures 고충처리절차
complementary goods 보완재
complementary loan 보완론
complete audit 완전감사
complete specialization 완전특화
complete stripping between interest and principal 원본금리를 완전분리함
completed audit 기말감사
completed contract method 완성기준
completeness fund 보완펀드

C D

completion bonus 완공보너스
completion guarantee 완성보증
completion of unsettled transaction 미결제거래를 조정함
complex 복잡한
compliance 준수
compliance test 준수테스트
component analysis 구성비율분석
component percentages 구성비율
components of cost 원가구성요소
composite depreciation 종합감가상각
composite depreciation assets 종합상각자산
composite index 종합경기지수
composite index of leading indicators 경기선행지수
composite insurer 복수보험자
composite price 컴포지트프라이스
composite quotation system 종합거래정보시스템
composite stock price index 종합주가지수
composite stock price tables 종합주가표
composite useful life 종합내용연수
composition 구성;시담
composition of inventory 재고자산의 범위
composition of working capital 운전자본구성
composition ratio 구성비
composition requirements 구성요건
compound annual rate 복리연율
compound annual return 연복리수익률
compound discount 복리할인
compound entry 복합기입
compound interest 복리
compound interest method 복리방식
compound interest yield 복리이율
compound multiplier 복합승수
compound option 복합옵션
compound transaction 복합거래
comprehensive bonded area 종합보세지역
comprehensive budget 포괄예산
comprehensive general liability insurance 제삼자배상개별보험
comprehensive general liability insurance coverage part 종합배상책임보험
comprehensive income 포괄이익
comprehensive income taxation 종합과세
comprehensive insurance 종합보험
comprehensive opinion 종합의견
comprehensive system model 코스모모델
comprehensive trade bill 포괄통상법안
compromise 타협
compromise method 절충방식
comptroller 감사역
comptroller in bankruptcy 파산감사관
compulsory 강제적인
compulsory audit 강제감사
compulsory cancellation 강제해약
compulsory composition 강제화의
compulsory conversion into money 강제환가
compulsory deposit as a condition for loans 상환준비예금
compulsory execution 강제집행
compulsory insurance 강제보험
compulsory liquidation 강제청산
compulsory sale by auction 강제경매
compulsory transfer of property 강제자산양도
compulsory winding-up 강제청산
compulsory withdrawal 강제철수
computation 산정
computation of business income 사업소득계산
computation of tax amount 세액계산
computation of useful years 내용연수계산
computation on a per diem basis 일할계산
computation period 산정기간
computation procedure 계산절차
computed price 계산가격
computer assisted execution system 딜링거래시스템
computer audit 컴퓨터감사
computer center 컴퓨터센터

Computer-assisted Order Routine and Execution System CORES
computerization 컴퓨터화
concealment 은닉
concentrated investment 집중투자
concentration effect 집중효과
concentration of enterprise 기업집중
concentration of resources 자원집중
concept 개념
concerned 해당하는
concerned activities 협조행동
concerned intervention 협조개입
concession 수수료
concession contract 양허계약
concession hunter 중개인
concessionaire 영업권소유자
conciliation 조정
conclusion 결론
conclusion of a contract 계약체결
conclusive presumption 결정적인 추정
concord 화해
concurrent cause 병존원인
concurrent jurisdiction 경쟁관할권
concurrent lease 변존임차권
concurrent liens 동순위선취특권
condemnation of land 토지수용
condensed account form 요약계정식
condensed balance sheet 요약대차대조표
condensed income statement 요약손익계산서
condensed report form 요약보고식
condition 조건
condition collateral 부대조건
condition of the transfer of the property 양도상태
condition precedent 정지조건
condition subsequent 해제조건
conditional 조건부
conditional acceptance 조건부 인수
conditional approval 조건부 승인
conditional contract 조건부 계약
conditional liquidity 조건부 유동성
conditional loan 조건부 융자
conditional loss 기회손실
conditional regression analysis 조건부 회귀분석
conditional sales 조건부 매매
conditional subsidy from the national treasury 조건부 국고보조금
conditions for payment 지불조건
conditions of issuance 발행조건
conditions of sale 경매조건
conditions of the national economy 경제사정
condolence money 조위금; 부조금
condor type spread transaction 콘도르스프레드거래
conference 협의
Conference on International Economic Cooperation 국제경제협력회의
confidence 신뢰
confidence building 신뢰조건
confidence coefficient 신뢰계수
confidence interval 신뢰구간
confidence level 신뢰도
confidential operation 은밀오퍼
confidential relation 신뢰관계
confidentiality 기밀성
confidentiality agreement 비밀유지계약
confidentiality of information 비밀유지의무
confirmation 확인
confirmation document 확인서류
confirmation fee 확인수수료
confirmation for financial futures transaction 금융선물거래에 관한 확인서
confirmation letter 확인장
confirmation note 확인통지서
confirmation of transaction 거래확인
confirmation request 확인청구
confirmed letter of credit 확인필 신용장
confirming bank 확인은행
confirming charge 신용장확인수수료
confirming house 컨퍼밍하우스
confiscation 몰수

C D

conflict of interest 이해충돌
conflict of laws 법률에 저촉됨
conflict of risk 이해대립
conformity 적합성
confrontation 대면
confusion 혼동
conglomerate 콘글로머리트;거대복합기업
connivance 묵인
consecutive advances 연등
consecutive declines 연락
consecutive dividend 안정배당
consecutive dividend increase 연속증배
consecutive quarters 연속사반기
consensual contract 낙성계약
consensus 일치
consensus on earnings estimate 수익예측컨센서스
consent 동의
consent dividend 간주배당
consequential damage 간접손해
conservatism 보수주의
conservative accounting 보수적인 회계
conservative management 견실한 경영
conservative view 보수적인 견해
conservator 후견인
considerable investment 거액의 투자
considerable rise 급증
considerable low price 굉장히 낮은 가격
consideration 대가;약인
consideration clause 약인조항
consigned goods 수탁품
consignee 수하인
consignment 위탁
consignment contract 위탁계약
consignment fee 위탁수수료
consignment goods 위탁품
consignment guarantee money 위탁증거금
consignment invoice 위탁품송장
consignment ledger 납세위탁
consignment of tax liability 납세위탁
consignment of tax payment 납부위탁
consignment sale 위탁판매
consignment sales and purchases 위탁매매
consignment sales contract 위탁판매계약
consignor 위탁인
consistency 일관성
console market 콘솔시장
consolidate 경합하다
consolidated 연결의
consolidated account 연결계정
consolidated annuities 콘솔공채
consolidated assets 연결자산
consolidated balance sheet 연결대차대조표
consolidated base 연결베이스
consolidated bond 연결사채
consolidated capital 연결자본
consolidated current profit 연결경상이익
consolidated financial statements 연결재무제표
consolidated financial statistics 연결재무통계
consolidated goodwill 연결된 선의
consolidated income 연결이익
consolidated income statement 연결손익계산표
consolidated income tax 종합소득세
consolidated net loss 연결순손실
consolidated profit and loss statement 연결손익계산서
consolidated quotation system 통합시황정보시스템
consolidated recurring profit 연결경상이익
consolidated retained earnings 연결잉여금
consolidated return 연결납세신고
consolidated sales 연결매상
consolidated statement of cash flow 연결캐시플로시산서
consolidated stock ticker 종합주식티커
consolidated subsidiary 연결자회사
consolidated surplus 연결잉여금
consolidated tape 종합테이프
consolidated tax return system 그룹과세
consolidated working capital 연결운전자금

consolidation 연결
consolidation date 연결일
consolidation excess 연결초과액
consolidation group 연결집단
consolidation ledger 연결원장
consolidation loan 콘솔리데이션론
consolidation of corporations 기업의 신규합병
consolidation of mortgages 양도저당병합
consolidation of operation 사무결합
consolidation of public loans 공채정리
consolidation pattern 조정패턴
consolidation policy 연결방침
consolidation statement of income statement 연결손익계산서
consolidation take-over 흡수합병
Consols 콘솔공채
consortium 국채모집인수단' 컨소시엄
consortium bank 컨소시엄뱅크
constant capital 불변자본
constant continuously compounded 일정한 연속복리
constant cost 고정비
constant divisor 항상제수(恒常除數)
constant dollar base 항상달러베이스
constant dollar net income 안정가치로 수정한 순이익
constant dollar plan 정액법
constant dollars 항상달러
constant elasticity of variance model 정탄성 분산모델
constant expenses 고정비
constant percentage method 정율법
constant power purchasing accounting 안정구매력회계
constant purchasing power 안정구매력
constant risk tolerance 불변리스크
constant variance 등분산
constant-dollar accounting 안정가치회계
constant-growth rate model 정율성장모델
constant-growth rate valuation model 정율성장평가모델
constraint 제약
construct 구축하다
construction 해석
construction account 건설비계정
construction bond 건설국채
construction expenditure 건설지출
construction in process account 건설가계정
construction industry 건설업
construction of completion 완성공사고
construction revenue 공사수입
construction subsidy 건설조성금
construction work 건설공사
construction work account receivable 공사미수금
construction work revenue 건설공사수입
constructive bonus 인정상여
constructive delivery 의제인도
constructive dividends 간주배당
constructive eviction 의제퇴거
constructive ownership 간주소유
constructive receipt 인정수입
constructive service 간접송달
constructive taxable year 인정사업연도
constructive total loss 해석전손(全損); 추정전손(全損)
constructive trust 법정신탁
consuetude 관습
consular invoice 영사송장
consulting sales 컨설팅세일즈
consumables 소모품
consumer advocate 소비자단체
consumer confidence 소비자신뢰
consumer credit 소비자신용
consumer credit company 소비자금융회사
Consumer Credit Protection Act 소비자신용보호법
consumer credit rate 소비자금리
consumer credit report 소비자신용정보
consumer demand 실수요
consumer electronics 가전제품

C D

consumer expenditure 소비자지출
consumer finance company 소비자금융회사
consumer goods 소비재
consumer group 소비자단체
consumer leasing 소비자리스
consumer loan 소비자금융
consumer price index 소비자물가지수
consumer sector stock 소비자관련주
consumer spending 소비자지출
consumer's behavior 소비자행동
consumer's cooperative society 소비생활협동조합
consumer's credit file 개인신용정보
consumer's union 소비자단체
consumers' durables 내구소비재
consumption demand 소비수요
consumption entry 소비세신고
consumption function 소비함수
consumption growth 소비신장
consumption lag 소비래그
consumption level 소비수준
consumption multiplier 소비승수
consumption quota 소비할당
consumption tax 소비세
Consumption Tax Law 소비세법
consumption transfer tax 소비양여세
consumption trend 소비동향
consumption unit 소비단위
contango 주식결제예비금
contemplation of bankruptcy 파산예기
comtemporary capitalism 현대자본주의
content-certified mail 내용증명우편
Continental Depositary Receipts 유럽주식예탁증서
continental form of closing the ledger 대륙식 원장마감수속
continental law 대륙법
contingency 우발사상
contingency fund 위험준비금
contingency insurance 우연손실보험
contingency reserve 이상위험준비금
contingency risk 우발적인 위험
contingent 파생적인
contingent assets 우발자산
contingent beneficiary 차순위보험금수취인
contingent charge 우발비용
contingent claim 파생상품
contingent credit swap 우발신용스와프
contingent debt 우발채무
contingent estate 불확정재산권
contingent fund 우발자금
contingent interest 불확정이자
contingent liabilities 우발채무
contingent liabilities on bill endorsed 이서의무
contingent loss 우발손실
contingent outlay 임시비
contingent profit 우발이익
contingent reserve 우발채무적립금
contingent transaction 우발거래
contingent warrant 우발성 워런트
continuation 지속
continuation clause 지속약관
continuation pattern 지속패턴
continued deficit 적자지속
continued expenses 계속비
continued no dividend 무배당지속
continuing account 지속계정
continuing contract 지속계약
continuing expenditure 지속비
continuing guaranty 무기한보증
continuing operations 지속사업
continuous audit 지속회계감사
continuous buying and selling 지속적인 매매
continuous compound interest rate 연속복리
continuous compounding calculation 연속복리계산
continuous disclosure 계속개시
continuous dividend 연속배당
continuous inventory 지속재고
continuous market 계속시장;연속거래
continuous probability distribution

연속확률분포
continuous reinsurance cover 지속적인 재보험
continuous session 연속회기
continuous time 연속시간
continuous trading 연속매매
continuous transaction of securities 주식 등의 지속적인 거래
continuous transaction of entered into for profit 영리를 목적으로 한 지속적인 행위
continuous variable 연속변수
contra account 대조계정
contra entry 상대기입
contra-cyclical 반순환적인
contraband 수입금지품
contraband of export 수출금지품
contraband of import 수입금지품
contract 계약
contract balance 계약잔고
contract bond 계약보증
contract charge 계약수수료
contract curve 계약곡선
contract deposit paid 계약전도금
contract deposit received 계약전수금
contract entered into by mutual consensus 낙성계약
contract for service 역무계약
contract formation 매매계약체결
contract in bulk 일괄계약
contract in kind 요물(要物)계약
contract index 약정지수
contract market 계약시장
contract money 계약금
contract month 한월(限月)
contract notice 약정통지
contract of commission 위임계약
contract of guarantee 보증계약
contract of indemnity 보상계약
contract of merger 합병계약서
contract party 계약당사자
contract position 계약포지션
contract price 협정가격
contract rate system 계약운임제
contract ratio 계약률
contract size 계약규모
contract slip 매매확인서
contract system 청부제도
contract term 계약기간
contract terms 계약조건
contract type 계약형
contract type accumulative investment plan 계약형 계속투자플랜
contract type investment trust 계약형 투자신탁
contract value 계약금액;거래금액
contract work 청부공사
contract work account receivable 청부공사미수금
contract work system 청부제도
contract works condition of deferred payment attached 연불조건부 청부
contracted interest rate 약정금리
contracted out 적용제외
contracted rate 약정이율
contraction 수축
contractors' all risks insurance 건설공사보험
contractual accumulation plan 이익누적형 투신
contractual documents 계약서
contractual wage 협정임금
contrarian 역발상에 능한 주식투자가
contrary opinion 반대의견
contravention 위반
contravention of listing agreement 상장계약위반
contributed capital 거출자본
contributed surplus 거출잉여금
contribution 거출금;분담금
contribution deduction 기부금공제
contribution defined 거출형의
contribution for social insurance 사회보험분담금

contribution in aid of construction 공사부담금
contribution margin 공헌이익
contribution margin form 공헌이익식
contribution plan 거출제도
contribution to equity capital 불입출자금
contribution to the equity capital 회원출자금
contribution to welfare facilities 복지시설부담액
contributions to affiliated company 관계회사출자금
contributory 출자의무자
contributory infringement 기여침해
contributory negligence 기여과실
contributory shares of estate 기여분
control budget 통제예산
control limit 관리한계
control market 지배시장
control measure 억제조치
control mechanism 관리기구
control of inflation 인플레억제
control stock 지배주
controllable expenses 관리가능원가
controlled account 피통괄계정
controlled company 피지배회사
controlled currency 관리통화
controlled discretion 법규재량
controlled economy 통제경제
controlled trade 통제무역
controller 회계검사관
controlling account 통괄계정
controlling company 지배회사
controlling equity 지배주주소유분
controlling interest 경영지배권
controlling relationship 지배관계
controlling stake 지배소유분
convenience 편의
convenience of tax collection 징세상의 편의
convention expense 회의비
convention for the avoidance of double taxation 이중과세방지조약
conventional auction 컨벤셔널방식
conventional commodity market 전통적인 상품시장
conventional loan 일반대출
conventional method 컨벤셔널방식
conventional mortgage loan 통상형 모기지론
conventional tariff 협정관세
converge 수렴하다
convergence 수렴
convergence analysis 집중분석
convergent fluctuation 수검성변동
converse preference 역특혜
conversion 횡령;환산
conversion agent 전환대리인
conversion at market price 시가전환
conversion at par 액면전환
conversion conditions 전환조건
conversion date 전환일
conversion discount 전환 디스카운트
conversion factor 변환계수
conversion into cash 환가처분
conversion into cash of seized property 차압재산환가
conversion issue 차환발행
conversion of building for productive use 건물을 생산적인 사용변경함
conversion of items in foreign currencies 외화기준계정항목을 환산함
conversion parity 전환비율
conversion period 전환청구기간
conversion premium 전환프리미엄
conversion price 전환가격
conversion price formula 전환가격방식
conversion privilege 보험종류변경청구권
conversion ratio 전환비율
conversion to gold 금태환
conversion value 전환가치
convertible assets 전환자산
convertible bond 전환사채
convertible bond index 전환사채이율
convertible bond with redemption request right

기중상환청구권부 전환사채
convertible bond with warrant
워런트부 전환사채
convertible bonds with option
옵션부 전환사채
convertible contract 중도전환계약
convertible currency 태환통화
convertible exchangeable preferred stock
교환가능전환우선주
convertible loan 주식전환대부
convertible mortgage 전환모기지
convertible note 태환지폐
convertible preferred stock 전환우선주
convertible ratio 교환비율
convertible reserve 태환준비
convertible securities 전환증권
convertible stock 전환주식
convexity 볼록한 모양
conveyance of estate 재산양도
convict 유죄판결을 받은 자
conviction 유죄결정
convincing proof 확신적인 입증
convocation 소집
convocation of general meetings 기회소집
cooling time 냉각기간
cooling-off 쿨링오프
cooling-off period 쿨링오프기간
cooperative association 협동조합
cooperative association on indirect taxes
간접세협력단체
cooperative bank 신용조합
cooperative business association
사업협동조합
Cooperative Credit Purchase Corporation
공동채권매입기구
cooperative financing facility
수출변동보상융자제도
cooperative marketing 공동판매
cooperative society 협동조합
coordinated cut 협조가격하락
coordinated intervention 협조개입
Coordinating Committee for Multilateral Strategic Export Controls
코콤(COCOM; 대공산권 수출통제위원회)
copyright 저작권
core 중핵
core business 중핵사업
core business division 주력부문
core holding 코어홀딩
core market 핵심시장
core stock 핵심주
corn hog cycle 콘허그순환
cornering 매점
corporate accounting 기업회계
corporate accounting principles
기업회계원칙
corporate action 회사행위
corporate average tax rate 평균법인세율
corporate banking 기업금융
corporate bankruptcy 기업도산
corporate body 법인단체
corporate bond 사채
corporate business 법인기업
corporate card 법인카드
corporate charter 인가장
corporate culture 기업문화
corporate customer 법인고객
corporate debenture 사채
corporate debt 기업채무
corporate deposit 법인예금
corporate executive 회사중역
corporate finance 사업금융
corporate franchise 회사특권
corporate governance 기업통합
corporate guarantee 기업보증
corporate identity 기업이미지통합전략; CI
corporate image 기업이미지
corporate income 법인소득
corporate income tax 법인세
corporate income tax rate 법인소득세율
corporate income taxes expenses
법인소득세비용

C D

corporate inhabitant tax 법인주민세
corporate insurance 기업보험
corporate investor 법인투자가
corporate juridical person 사단법인
corporate management 기업경영
corporate name 상호
corporate pension insurance 기업연금보험
corporate profile 기업프로필
corporate profit 기업이익
corporate profitability 기업수익성
corporate raider 기업매수자
corporate registration 법인등록부
corporate reorganization 회사갱생
corporate resolution 이사회결의
corporate right 법인권
corporate savings 법인저축
corporate seal 법인인감
corporate securities 사채
corporate separation 회사분할
corporate settlement 기업안정
corporate shareholder 법인주주
corporate size 기업규모
corporate strategy 기업전략
corporate tax 법인세
corporate treasurer 기업재무담당자
corporate trust 법인신탁
corporate vitality 기업활력
corporate-type investment trust 회사형 신탁
corporation 법인
corporation aggregate 집합법인
corporation amalgamated 피합병법인
corporation carrying on foreign trade 외국과 거래하는 기업
corporation ceased to exist after merger 합병으로 소멸한 회사
corporation filing a blue return 청색신고법인
corporation finance 기업금융
corporation free from taxation 비과세법인
corporation in need of reorganization 갱생회사
corporation in public interest 공익법인
corporation in the course of liquidation 청산중인 법인
corporation law 회사법
corporation levy 법인세할주민세
corporation liable to taxation 납세의무가 있는 법인
corporation member 법인회원
corporation of public utility 공익법인
corporation profit tax 법인이득세
corporation qualifying for filing a blue return 청색신고를 할 수 있는 법인
corporation reorganization law 회사갱생법
corporation report 회사레포트
corporation sector 기업부문
corporation settling accounts twice a year 연 2회 결산회사
corporation subject to filing return 신고의무가 있는 법인
corporation subject to taxation 납세의무가 있는 법인
corporation tax 법인세
corporation tax credit 법인세공제
corporation tax law 법인세법
corporation tax rate 법인세율
corporation type 기업형
corporation type investment trust 기업형 투자신탁
corporation under liquidation 청산절차중인 법인
corporation 's equity 기업지분
corporation's own stock 자사주
correction 갱정;조정
correction of errors 오진을 정정함
correction of prior periods 전기수정항목
correction of prior years earnings 전기손익수정
corrective market 정정상장
corrective selling 정정매출
correlation 상관관계
correlation analysis 상관분석

correlation coefficient 상관계수
correlation diagram 상관도
correlation of return 수익률의 상관관계
correlation ratio 상관비율
correlation table 상관표
correlative adjustment 대응조정
correlative industry 관련산업
correspondent account 코레스계정
correspondent agreement 코레스계약
correspondent bank 코레스은행
correspondent charge 코레스비용
correspondent relation 코레스관계
corresponding account 상대계좌
corresponding day 응당일
corresponding deposit 상대예금
corresponding period of last year 전년동기
corroborate 보강하다
corroborating evidence 보강증거
corruption 뇌물수수; 부패
cost 원가
cost absorption 원가흡수
cost account 원가계정
cost accounting 원가계산
cost accounting by department 부문별 원가계산
cost accounting by product 제품별 원가계산
cost accounting period 원가계산기간
cost accounting standards 원가계산기준
cost accounting system 원가계산제도
cost analysis 원가분석
cost and expenses 원가 및 비용
cost and freight 운임포함
cost at the margin 한계비용
cost audit 원가감사
cost basis 원가주의
cost behavior 비용동향
cost card 원가계산서
cost classification 비용분류
cost competitiveness 가격경쟁력
cost consciousness 원가의식
cost control 원가관리
cost curve 비용곡선
cost cutting 비용소멸
cost data 비용데이터
cost depletion method 취득잔고비례법
cost distribution 원가배분
cost effective 비용효율이 좋은
cost effectiveness analysis 비용대비효과분석
cost element 원가요소
cost estimate 비용견적
cost finding 원가산정
cost flow assumption 재고자산평가방법
cost function 비용함수
cost ledger 원가원장
cost matching income principle 비용수익대응의 원칙
cost method 원가법
cost method of depletion 감모상각원가법
cost object 원가대상
cost of assets 자산취득원가
cost of borrowing 조달비용
cost of carry 자산소유비용
cost of completed work 완성공사원가
cost of construction 공사비
cost of disposal 처분비용
cost of entry 참가비용
cost of finished goods 제품원가
cost of goods purchased 구입원가
cost of goods sold 매상원가
cost of insurance 보험비용
cost of issuing stocks 주식발행비용
cost of manufactured goods 제조원가
cost of processing 가공비
cost of production 제조원가
cost of production budget 제조비예산
cost of purchase 구입원가
cost of raising funds 자금조달코스트
cost of sales 판매원가
cost of short-term funds 단기자금조달비용
cost of tax collection 징세비용
cost of temporary repair 가수선비
cost of transferred properties

양도자신취득비용
cost of work performed 생산고원가
cost or market whichever is lower basis 분리저가법
cost overrun 예산초과
cost performance 가격대비성능비
cost plus 원가(이윤)가산방식
cost plus contract 실비정산계약
cost plus fixed fee contract 정액보수실비지불계약
cost plus method 원가기준법
cost price 구입가격
cost principle 원가주의
cost rate 원가율
cost recovery 원가회수
cost reduction 코스트삭감
cost report 원가보고서
cost savings 원가삭감
cost sharing 비용분담
cost sheet 원가계산표
cost standard 원가기준
cost statement 원가계산서
cost structure 원가구조
cost system 원가시스템
cost unit 원가단위
cost utility 비용효과
cost value 원가가치
cost variance 원가차액
cost; insurance and freight 운임과 보험료 포함
cost-of-living index 생활비지수
cost-or-less principle 원가이하주의
cost-push inflation 코스트푸시인플레이션
cost-reduction programs 원가저감계획
cost-volume-profit analysis 비용; 조업도; 이익 분석
cost-volume-profit relationship 원가; 조업도; 이익 관계
costing 원가계산
costing period 원가계산기간
costing unit 원가계산단위
cosureties 공동보증인
cotenancy 부동산공동보유
council 평의회
council on alcoholic beverages 주류심의회
counselor 법률고문
count out 정족수를 채우지 못했다고 인정하여 유회하다
countercyclical 반순환적인
countercyclical policy 반순환정책
counterdeed 반대증서
counterfeit 위조
counterfeit card 위조카드
countermand 취소하다
countermeasure 조치;대책
counteroffer 반대오퍼
counterpart 상대방
counterparty (계약의)한쪽 당사자
counterparty rating 카운터파트레이팅
counterparty risk 카운터파트리스크
counterpurchase 대가구입
countersecurity 역담보
countersign 부서하다
countersignature 연서(連署)
countervailing duty 상쇄관세
countervailing power 대항력
country exposure 컨트리익스포저
country fund 컨트리펀드
country having deficit in cap transaction 자본수출국
country limit 국별한도
country risk 국가신용도
county borough 특별시
coupon 이자표
coupon bank debenture 이부금융채
coupon bearing bond 이부채
coupon bond 이표채; 이자부채권
coupon curve 이자부채권이율곡선
coupon fund 아부자금
coupon income 쿠폰수입
coupon interest 쿠폰금리
coupon off 이자표가 떨어진

coupon on 이자표가 붙은
coupon pass 쿠폰패스
coupon payment 이자지불
coupon payment date 이불기일
coupon payment period 쿠폰지불기간
coupon rate 채권의 표면이자율
coupon sale 쿠폰세일
coupon swap 쿠폰스와프
coupon-bearing government bond 이자부국채
coupon-only currency swap 쿠폰만의 통화스와프
course of employment 직무집행과정
court of equity 에퀴티재판소
covariance 공분산
covariance analysis 공분산분석
covenant 특약조항;약인
covenant for title 권한담보조항
covenant of seisin 권리담보조항
covenants 약인
cover 보험을 통한 담보
cover dealing 커버딜링
cover note 가증서; 보험인수증
coverage 담보범위
covered call 커버드콜
covered call option 커버드콜옵션
covered option 커버드옵션
covered position 커버드포지션
covered straddle 커버드스트래들
covered warrant 커버드워런트
covering entry 분개기입
CP market CP 시장
craft union 동업조합
crash 붕락
crawling peg 크롤링페그; 단계적인 평가변동방식
crawling peg system 단계적인 평가변동방식
craze for speculation 투기열
cream skimming 크림스키밍
creation 창립
credibility 신용도
credible 신용할 수 있는
credit accommodation 신용공여
credit account 외상거래계정
credit against corporation tax 법인세공제
credit against tax 세액공제
credit among corporations 기업간 신용
credit analysis 여신분석
credit and suretyship insurance 신용 및 보증보험
credit approval 여신승인
credit assessment 신용평가
credit association 신용조합
credit audit 신용감사
credit authorization terminal 신용조합단말
credit availability 여신공여량
credit balance 대변잔고
credit bill 신용어음
credit bureau 신용정보센터
credit business 여신업무
credit buying rate 기한부 어음매상장
credit capability 신용력
credit card 신용카드
credit card burglary insurance 카드도난보험
credit card business 신용카드업무
credit card company 신용카드회사
credit cards issued by bank or its subsidiary 은행계 카드
credit cards issued by the agent 대행카드
credit ceiling 신용한도
credit ceiling application system 대출한도액 적용제도
credit concern 신용불안
credit control 여신관리
credit conversion factor 신용환산계수
credit creation 신용창조
credit crisis 신용공황
credit crunch 신용제한
credit customer 신용외상거래처
credit decision 신용판단
credit decline 신용저하
credit default swap 크레디트디폴트스와프

credit demand 자금수요
credit derivatives 신용파생상품
credit ease 신용완화
credit enhancement 신용보완
credit exposure 신용리스크
credit exposure management 여신관리
credit facility 크레디트퍼실리티; 신용편의
credit for dividend 배당공제
credit for experimental and research expense 시험연구비특별공제
credit for foreign taxes 외국세액공제
credit for handicapped person 장애인공제
credit for income tax 소득세액공제
credit guarantee 신용보증
credit guarantee company 신용보증회사
credit history 크레디트히스토리
credit inquiry 신용조회
credit instruments 신용증권
credit insurance 신용보험
credit investigation 신용조사
credit life insurance 신용생명보험
credit limit 신용한도
credit line 대출한도액;신용한도
credit line system 신용한도제도
credit loan 신용대출
credit losses 대손
credit margin 신용증거금
credit memorandum 대출메모
credit money 신용화폐
credit note 대변전표
credit option 크레디트옵션
credit past due date 기일도래원본
credit policy 신용정책
credit price 외상거래가격
credit purchase 외상구입
credit quality 신용도
credit rate 대부금리
credit rating 신용등급부여
credit ratio 신용비율
credit rationing 신용제한
credit records 신용정보
credit reference 신용조회
credit risk 여신리스크
credit risk analysis 여신리스크분석
credit risk weight 여신리스크웨이트
credit sale 외상판매
credit sales 외상거래
credit scoring 크레디트스코어링
credit slip 입금표
credit spread 신용격차
credit squeeze 금융긴축
credit standing 신용상태
credit standing condition 신용상태
credit strength 신용력
Credit Suisse Index Generals 크레디스위스지수
credit support 신용보강
credit swap 크레디트스왑
credit system 신용제도
credit terms 신용조건
credit tightening 금융긴축
credit tranche 크레디트트란시
credit union 신용조합
credit union exchange 신용조합환
credit watch system 신용감시시스템
credit worthiness 신용력
credit-linked note 크레디트링크채
creditable amount of foreign taxes 외국세액공제한도액
creditor 채권자
creditor account 대출계정
creditor bank 대출은행
creditor country 채권국
creditor side 대출란
creditor's equity 채권자지분
creditor's voluntary winding-up 채권자에 의한 임의청산
creditors ledger 구입처원장
creditors' meeting 채권자회의
creditworthiness 신용도
creditworthy 신용력이 있는
creep back upwards 시세가 조금씩 오르는 경향

creeping deflation 크리핑디플레이션
creeping inflation 크리핑인플레이션; 잠행성 인플레이션
creeping nationalization 점진적인 국유화
Criminal Code 형법
criminal suit 형사소송
crisis 공황
crisis at maturity 일괄반제리스크
crisis management 위기관리
crisis of liquidity 유동성위험
criteria 표준
criteria for delisting 상장폐지기준
criteria for examination 심사기준
criteria for listing 상장기준
critical function 비판기능
criteria issue 심각한 문제
critical mass 임계량
criteria path accounting 크리티컬패스회계
critical path method 크리티컬패스메소드
critical point 임계치
criticism 비판
crop 생산고
crop basis 수확기준
cross 크로스매매
cross action 반대소송
cross arbitration 크로스재정
cross border 크로스보더
cross border information 국경없는 정보
cross border listing 국외상장
cross border market 국제시장
cross claim 강제소송참가
cross currency swap 통화간 채무교환거래
cross debt 상대채무
cross default 크로스디폴트
cross default clause 크로스디폴트조항
cross elasticity 교차탄력성
cross entry 대체기입
cross hedge 크로스헤지
cross liabilities basis 교차책임주의
cross license contract 특허권교환계약
cross margin 크로스마진
cross offer 교차신청
cross order 크로스오더
cross rate 크로스레이트
cross sectional analysis 타기업 비교
cross slip 대체전표
cross trading 크로스거래
cross transaction 대당거래
cross-currency interest rate swap 교차통화금리스와프
cross-demand 반대청구
cross-holding 복수기업이 주식을 소유함
cross-sectional analysis 횡단분석
cross-sectional valuation approach 크로스섹셔널평가법
crossed check 횡선수표
crossing for the purpose of financing 금융크로스
crowd 군중;대중;동아리
crowd trading 크라우드거래
crowding out 크라우딩아웃;구축
crowding out effect 크라우딩아웃효과; 구축효과
crown jewel 중요부문
crude oil futures option 원유선물옵션
crunch 재정제한
crystallization of floating charge 유동담보결정화
culpa 과실
cum call 불입부
cum coupon 이자표부
cum dividend 배당부
cum new 신주부
cum right 신주인수권부
cum warrant 컴워런트
cum-dividend 배당포함
cum-drawing 추첨포함
cum-interest 이자포함
cum-profit distribution 이익분배금포함
cumulative amount of depreciation 감가상각누계액
cumulative deficit 누적적자

cumulative dividend 누적배당
cumulative effect of accounting change 회계방침변경에 따른 누적영향액
cumulative fiscal deficit 국가예산누적적자
cumulative investment 누적투자
cumulative legacy 누적유증
cumulative limit 누적한도액기준
cumulative limitation 누적제한
cumulative loss 누적
cumulative maximum amount 누적한도액
cumulative method 누가법
cumulative preferred stock 누적우선주
cumulative surplus 누적흑자
cumulative taxation 누적과세
cumulative voting 누적투표
Curacao Depositary Receipts 유럽예탁증서
curator 후견인
curb market 장외시장
currency 통화
currency adjustment 통화조정
currency appreciation 통화등귀
currency basket 통화바스켓
currency bloc 통화블록
currency commodity 통화상품
currency conversion 통화환산
currency conversion bond 커런시컨버전채
currency convertible in fact 사실상 교환가능한 통화
currency crisis 통화위기
currency deflation 통화디플레이션
currency deposit 통화성 예금
currency depreciation 통화가치하락
currency devaluation 통화절하
currency fluctuation 통화변동
currency futures 통화선물
currency futures price movement 통화선물가격동향
currency futures trading 통화선물거래
currency hedging 환헤지
currency in circulation 통화유통고
currency indemnity 통화보상
currency inflation 통화인플레
currency movement 환동향
currency note 정부통화
currency option trading 통화옵션거래
currency principle 통화주의
currency swap 통화스와프
currency swap bond 통화스와프채
currency system 통화체계
currency translation adjustments 외화환산조정액
currency unit 통화단위
currency upvaluation 통화절상
currency value 통화가치
current account 당좌계정
current account balance 경상수지
current account cheek 당좌수표
current account deficit 경상적자
current amount 현재치
current arrangement 유동성 배열법
current assets 유동자산
current balance 경상수지
current budget 경상예산
current cost 현재원가
current cost accounting 취득원가주의회계
current cost method 시가방식
current cost / constant dollar accounting 시가주의 안정가치회계
current cost / nominal dollar accounting 시가주의 명목가치회계
current coupon 기간지표
current credit accounts with agencies 대리점대출
current deposit 당좌예금
current disbursement approach 부과방식
current dollar 경상달러
current exchange rate 실세환상장
current expenditure 경상지출
current expenses 경상비용
current exposure 커런트익스포저
current fiscal year 현회계연도
current fund 당좌자금

current income 당기이익
current interest rate 현행이자율
current investment 단기투자
current level of stock price 현재의 주가수준
current liabilities 유동부채
current market value 현행시장가액
current market yield spread 실제시장이율폭
current maturity 당기만기부분
current maturity of long-term debt 장기부채의 당기반제액
current money 유통화폐
current operating performance income statement 당기업적주의에 따른 손익계산서
current operating performance theory 당기업적주의
current operating profit 당기영업이익
current payment 경상지불
current period 당기
current period of long-term debt 단기차입금(장기차입의 1년 내 반제분)
current premium value 현행프리미엄
current price 시가
current profit 경상이익
current rate 결산일레이트
current ratio 유동비율
current replacement cost 재취득가격
current report 임시보고서
current taxable year 당기
current taxes 당기세액
current term 당기
current term net income 당기순익
current term net loss 당기순손실
current term net profit 당기순이익
current term net profit or loss 당기순손익
current term settlement 당기결산
current transaction 경상거래
current transfer 경상이전
current transfers 경상이익수지
current value 현재가치
current value accounting 시가회계
current year 당기
current yield 직접이익
current-asset cycle 유동자산회전기간
current-assumption whole life insurance 커런트어섬션종신보험
current-first order 유동성 배열
current-outlay cost 당기지출원가
curtailed operation 조업단축
curtailment of expenditure 경비소멸
curtailment of operation 조업단축
curve 곡선
curve flattening 장단기이율격차축소
curving trend line 비선형 추세선
cushion bond 쿠션채
cushion of cash flow 캐시플로의 여력
custodial account 보관계정
custodian 주식보관인
custodian bank 보관은행
custody 보관
custody account 보관계좌
custody and transfer institution 대체보관기관
custody fee 보관료
custom index 커스텀인덱스
customary practice 관행
customary tenure estates 관습상의 보유권
customer 고객
customer base 고객기반
customer relations 고객관계
customer repos 고객보고
customer transaction 고객단가
customer's account 고객계정
customer's agreement and consent 거래약정서
customer's deposits 거래처수입보증금
customer's ledger 거래처원장
customer's loan 신용거래대출
customer's margin 수탁증거금
customer's order 고객주문
customers mobilizing power 고객동원력
customers' deposits 예금보증금
customers' ledger 외상매출금원장

customers' liabilities on guaranties 보증채무담보
customers' securities 보관유가증권
customized performance standards 커스텀 퍼포먼스 스탠다드
customs 관세
customs autonomy 관세자주권
customs basis 통관베이스
customs clearance 통관
customs debenture 세환급증명서
customs duty 관세
customs duty refund system 관세환부제도
customs house 세관
customs invoice 통관용 송장
customs law 관세법
customs of merchant 상관습법
customs procedures 통관절차
customs tariff law 관세정율법
customs tariff table 관세율표
customs union 관세동맹
cutback 단축
cutoff date 마감일
cuttings 이자표
cycle 주기
cyclical depression 순환불황
cyclical fluctuation 순환변동
cyclical growth 순환성장
cyclical peak 경기의 고점
cyclical stock 순환주
cyclical trough 경기의 저점
cyclical upturn 경기회복
cyclicals 순환주
cylinder 실린더

D

daily allowance 일당
daily average 일일평균
daily balance 일일잔고
daily chart 일일차트
daily interest for arrearage 연체이자
Daily Life Security Law 생활보호법
daily price limit 가격폭제한
daily rate 하루이자
daily stock price index 일별주가지수
daily trial balance 일계표
daimyo bond 다이묘본드
damage 손해
damage insurance 손해보험
damaged property 피해자산
damaged payment 손해배상액
damping effect 억제효과
dangers of navigation 해상위험
data bank 데이터뱅크
data base 데이터베이스
data capture 데이터수집
data communications 데이터통신
data processing business 데이터가공업무
date 기일
date of acquisition 취득일
date of delivery 인도일
date of enforcement 시행일
date of execution 집행기일
date of maturity 만기일
date of record 기준일
date of tax to be levied 과세고지일
date proved by notary 확정일부
dating backward 후일부의
dating forward 선일부의
date count basis 일할베이스
day of admission 회원가입일
day order 당일만 유효한 주문
day trader 데이트레이더
day trading 일계매매
day-to-day management 항상 운영함
day-to-day trader 단기투자가
daylight trading 일계매매
days after sight 일람후 지불
days in arrears 연체일수
days of grace 지불유예기간
days to run 할인일수
de facto 사실상
de facto existing company 사실상의 존속회사
de jure 법률상
dead freight 공하(空荷)운임
dead loan 대손금
dead stock 불량재고
dead weight loss of customs duty 관세사중손실
deadline for filing 신고마감일
deal between speculators 투기전
dealer 딜러
dealer commission 딜러수수료
dealer loan 딜러론
dealer market 딜러시장
dealer paper 딜러어음

dealer participation 딜러참가
dealer's fee 딜러수수료
dealer's option 딜러옵션
dealer's position 딜러포지션
dealers' market 업자간 상장
dealing 자기매매
dealing account 거래계정
dealing cost 거래비용
dealing in transit 미달거래
dealing market 업자간 상장
dealing risk 딜링리스크
dear money policy 고금리정책
dearth 부족
death duty 상속세
death rate 사망률
debenture 채권
debenture account 채권계정
debenture assignment 사채권양도
debenture bond 사채권
debenture convertible at par 액면전환사채
debenture holder 채권보유자
debenture interest 사채이자
debenture issuing expenses 사채발행비
debenture redemption 사채상환
debenture redemption reserve 감가적립금
debenture stock 무상환사채
debenture trust 사채권신탁
debenture with lump-sum payment at maturity 이자일괄불 이자부금융채
debenture with warrant 워런트채
debit 차변
debit account 차변계정
debit advice 차기(借記)통지서
debit authorization 차변승인
debit balance 차변잔고
debit card 지불카드
debit memorandum 차변메모
debit note 차변표
debit note for premium 보험금청구서
debit side 차변
debit slip 지불전표
debt 채무;부채
debt account 차금계정
debt accumulation 누적채무
debt agreement 차입계약
debt asset ratio 부채자산비율
debt assumption 채무인수
debt balance 채무잔고
debt bond swap 채무의 채권화
debt capital 타인자본
debt capital market 채권시장
debt ceiling 차입한도액
debt collection 채권회수
debt collector 회수업자
debt covenant 부채조항
debt coverage 채무반제능력
debt cross 데트크로스
debt discount and expenses 사채발행차금
debt equity rate 부채비율
debt equity swap 데트에퀴티스와프
debt expense 사채발행비용
debt exposure 대출리스크
debt factoring 채권매입
debt financing 차입으로 자금을 조달함
debt for collection 수금채무
debt in foreign currency 외화기준채무
debt in U. S. dollar 달러기준채무
debt instrument 채무수단
debt leverage 채무레버레지
debt loan 차입금
debt management policy 공채관리정책
debt maturity 부채기간
debt ratio 부채비율
debt reduction 채무삭감
debt relief 채무면제
debt retirement 채무반제
debt securities 채무증권
debt securities market 채무증권시장
debt service 미불금
debt service payment 국채비
debt service ratio 채무반제비율
debt servicing 원리지불

debt warrant 데트워런트채
debt-credit transaction 대차거래
debtor 채무자
debtor account 차변계정
debtor and creditor accounts 대차계정
debtor and estate 채무자 및 파산재단
debtor balance 차변잔고
debtor bank 대차은행
debtor country 채무국
debtor in possession 점유채무자
debtor side 대차란
debtor's deposit 채무자예금
debts accelerated 기한의 이익을 상실한 채무
debts and credits 채권채무
decelerating trend 감속경향
deceleration 둔화
decentralization 집중배제;분권
decision 결정
decision making 의사결정
decision of a general meeting of stockholders 주주총회결의
decision of a reorganization scheme 재건계획결정
decision of the general meeting 총회의 결정
decision on request for reinvestigation 이의결정
decision support system 의사결정지원시스템
decision-making body 의사결정기관
declaration 신고
declaration against interest 이익에 반하는 공술
declaration form 신고용지
declaration of bankruptcy 파산선고
declaration of change of land category 지목변환계
declaration of import 수입신고
declaration of income 소득신고
declaration of non-payment 지불거절선언
declaration policy 통지보험
declaratory 확인하다
declared capital 공시자본
declared profit 계상이익
decline 하락하다
decline in prices of inventories 재고자산평가하락
declining balance depreciation 정율감가상각법
declining balance method 정율법
declining industry 쇠퇴산업
decrease in book value 장부가격감소
decrease of income tax 소득세감액
decreased earnings 감익
decreased receipts 감수
decreasing rate 저하율
decree 판결
decree of distribution 배분판결
decree of insolvency 지불불능판결
decree of nullity 무효판결
decrement 저감;감소
dedicated bond portfolio 채권에 대한 데디케이트포트폴리오
dedicated portfolio 데디케이트포트폴리오
deductible 공제조건부 보험
deductible amount for donation 기부금의 손금산입한도액
deductible clause 공제조항
deductible expenses 손금
deductible liabilities 공제해야 하는 채무
deductible reserve 손금산입할 수 있는 준비금
deduction 공제
deduction for casualty losses 잡손공제
deduction for damage insurance 손해보험공제
deduction for dependents 부양공제
deduction for dividends 배당공제
deduction for donation 기부금공제
deduction for employment income 급여소득공제
deduction for foreign taxes 외국세액손금산입
deduction for housing savings 주택저축공제

deduction for insurance proceeds 보험금공제
deduction for life insurance premiums 생명보험료공제
deduction for medical expenses 의료비공제
deduction for old-age person 노령자공제
deduction for physically handicapped person 장애인공제
deduction for public pension 공적연금공제
deduction for retirement income 퇴직소득공제
deduction for small enterprise mutual aid premiums 소규모기업공제 외상금공제
deduction for spouse 배우자공제
deduction for tax reduction 감면세액공제
deduction from property 유형고정자산에서 공제함
deduction limit applicable to donation 기부금손금산입한도액
deduction of entertainment expenses 교제비공제
deduction of estimated expenses 개산경비공제
deduction of foreign corporation tax carried forward 이월외국세액공제
deduction of interest on borrowed fund 부채이자공제
deduction of liabilities 채무공제
deductions 이익에서 공제하는 항목
deductions from income 소득공제
deductions from working capital 운전자본감소
deductive method 연역법
deed 날인증서
deed of arrangement 채무정리증서
deed of conveyance 양도증서
deed of title 권리증서
deed of trust 신탁증서
deemed accounting period 간주사업연도
deemed bounty 간주교부금
deemed corporation 간주법인
deemed dividend 간주배당
deemed donations 간주기부금
deemed inherited property 간주상속재산
deemed request for reconsideration 간주심사청구
deemed transfer 간주양도
deep discount 대폭할인
deep discount bond 디프디스카운트채
deep in the money 디프인더머니
deep rock doctrine 디프록주의
deep-rooted inflation 만성적인 인플레
Default Compensation Fund 위약손실보상기금
default compensation reserve 위약손실준비금; 위약손실보상준비금
default free 디폴트리스크가 없음
default interest 연체이자
default loss 디폴트손실
default of obligation 채무불이행
default on clearing obligation 결제불이행
default receivable 디폴트채권
default risk 채무불이행리스크
default risk premium 채무불이행 프리미엄
defaulter 불이행자
defeasance 권리소멸조항
defeasance clause 해제조항
defeasible 무효로 할 수 있는
defeasible title 취소할 수 있는 권원
defective 불완전한
defective check 부정수표
defective goods 결함품;하자품
defective random variables 불완전확률변수
defective title 하자가 있는 권원
Defense Agency 방위청
defense bond 방위채
defense expenditure 방위비
defense of the dollar 달러방위
defensive investment 방위투자
defensive purchase 방위매입
defensive securities 방위증권
defensive stock 방위주
deferment 연기; 거치

deferment of investment 투자연기
deferment of payment 연납
deferment of taxation 과세연기
deferred account 이연계정
deferred and accrued accounts 경과계정
deferred annuity 거치형 연금
deferred assets 이연자산
deferred bond 이연채권
deferred charge 이연비용
deferred charge account 이연비용계정
deferred charge before amortization 상각전의 이연자산
deferred compensation 이연보수비용
deferred coupon 이연지불
deterred credit 이연대변항목
deferred debit 이연대변항목
deferred delivery 이연
deferred depreciation 이연상각
deferred expenditure 이연지출
deferred expenses 이연비용
deferred income 이연수익
deferred income tax liability 이연법인채무
deferred income taxes 연체세
deferred interest 연체이자
deferred interest account 전수이자계정
deferred item 이연계정
deferred liabilities 이연부채
deferred life annuity 거치종신연금
deferred payment basis 연불기준
deferred payment credit 후일불신용장
deferred payment of income tax 소득세연납
deferred payment sales 연불조건부 판매
deferred premium 미수보험료
deferred rebate system 운임환불제
deferred repairs 이연수선비
deferred revenue 이연수익
deferred savings 거치저금
deferred share 후배주
deferred stock 후배주
deferred swap 디퍼드스와프
deferred tax 연납세
deferred tax account 연납세계정
deficiency 결손
deficiency account 결손계정
deficiency bill 일시차입어음
deficiency guarantee 부족액보증
deficit 적자
deficit account 결손금계정
deficit amount 결손금액
deficit at the beginning of a period 전기이월차손금
deficit budget 적자예산
deficit carried forward 이월결손금
deficit covered by directors 임원이 보상한 결손금
deficit disposition statement 결손금처리계산서
deficit finance 적자재정
deficit financing 적자융자
deficit for the current term 당기손실금
deficit in aggregate amount 총액 중의 부족액
deficit in cash 현금부족액
deficit of fiscal balance 재정적자
deficit reconciliation statement 결손금처리계산서
deficit reduction 적자소멸
deficit statement 결손금계산서
deficit-covering bond 적자국채
deficit-covering finance 적자금융
defined benefit 확정급부
defined benefit plan 확정급부형 연금플랜
defined contribution annuity plan 확정거출형 연금플랜
defined contribution plan 확정거출제도
definite insurance 확정보험
definite policy 확정보험증권
definite settlement of accounts 확정결산
definition 정의
definition of characteristic line 특성선의 정의
definitive bond 정식본권
deflation 디플레이션

deflation caused by won appreciation 원고 디플레
deflation expectation 디플레기대
deflation gap 디플레이션갭
deflation policy 디플레정책
deflationary effect 디플레효과
deflationary gap 디플레갭
deflationary period 디플레기간
deflationary pressure 디플레압력
deflator 디플레이터;가격수정인자
defunct company 주식소멸회사
degradation 악화
degree 등급
degree of concentration 집중도
degree of concentration of control 지배집중도
degree of consanguinity 촌수
degree of dependence 의존도
degree of dependence upon exports 수출의존도
degree of dependence upon imports 수입의존도
degree of financial leverage 재무면의 증익효과도
degree of monopoly 독점도
degree of operating leverage 영업면의 증익효과도
degressive cost 체감원가
deindustrialization 탈공업화
del credere agent 매주지불보증대리인
del credere commission 지불수수료
delay 지체
delay claims 지체클레임
delay of evacuation 명도지체
delayed interest 연체이자
delaying settlement 지연결제
delegate 위임하다
delegation 권한부여
delegation of authority 권한위임
delegation of authority to rules 규칙에 대한 위임
deletion of exclusion 면책조항삭제
delinquency 체납
delinquency amount 연체금
delinquency tax 연체세
delinquent charge 지연손해금
delinquent tax 체납세
delinquent taxpayer 체납자
delisting 상장폐지
deliverable bonds 인도적격채
deliverable grade 인도적격의
deliverable issue 인도적격상품
delivered 인도필
delivered at frontier 국경인도
delivered at frontier price 국경인도가격
delivered duty paid 발송지지입인도(관세입)
delivered duty unpaid 발송지지입인도(관세제외)
delivered ex quay 부두지입인도
delivered ex ship 본선지입인도
delivered price 인도가격
delivered stock due to merger 합병교부주식
delivery 인도
delivery against payment 지불인도
delivery basis 인도기준
delivery bond 교부국채
delivery date 결제일
delivery day 인도일
delivery expenses 발송비
delivery of articles 물품납부
delivery of dividends 배당금지불
delivery of due bill 유가증권인도표를 교부함
delivery of long-term contract work 장기공사를 인도함
delivery of subsidies 보조금교부
delivery order 하도지시서
delivery price 인도가격
delivery settlement 인도결제
delivery system by calendar month 역월도제
delivery to order 지도인도
delivery versus payment DVP
delivery versus payment settlement DVP 결제

delivery with option 옵션인도
delivery-certified mail 배달증명우편
delta 델타
delta hedge 델타헤지
delta value 델타수치
demand account 요구불계정
demand analysis 수요분석
demand and supply 수급
demand bill 일람불어음
demand curve 수요곡선
demand debt 요구불채무
demand deficiency 수요부족
demand deposit 요구불예금
demand deposits 통화성 예저금
demand draft 송금환수표
demand elasticity 수요탄력성
demand for capital 자본수요
demand for conversion 전환청구
demand for fund 자금수요
demand for investing fund
투자를 위한 자금수요
demand for money 화폐수요
demand for name registration 명의변경청구
demand for tax payment 납부독촉
demand for withdrawal 교부청구
demand for withdrawal of stock certificates
주식교부청구
demand forecasting 수요예측
demand function 수요함수
demand function for money 화폐수요함수
demand in reconvention 반소(反訴)
demand index 수요지수
demand loan 당좌대부
demand note 요구불어음
demand pressure 수요압력
demand pull inflation
디맨드풀인플레; 초과수요인플레
demand to hold securities 증권보유수요
demand-and-supply balance 수급밸런스
dematerialization 증서를 발행하지 않음
dematerialized 증서발행을 수반하지 않음
dematerialized securities
증서발행을 수반하지 않는 증권
demerit 결점
demises 지소(地所)
democratization 민주화
demographic analysis 데모그라픽분석
demographic change 인구구성변화
demographic scoring 데모그라픽스코어링
demographic statistics 인구통계
demolition expenses 해체비
demonstration effect 데몬스트레이션효과
demurrage 체선료;하차유치료
denial 부인
denial of opinion 의견보류
denominated in each currency 각국통화단위
denominated in foreign currency 외화기준
denominated in U. S. dollar 달러기준
denominated in won 원기준
denomination 권면;디노미네이션
denomination reduction 디노미네이션
denomination related stocks
디노미네이션관련주
denominator level 기준조업도
dental expense insurance 치과치료비보험
department audit 부문감사
Department of Commerce 미국상무부
Department of Justice 사법부
Department of State 미국국무부
Department of Trade and Industry
무역산업부
Department of Treasury 재무부
department store sales 백화점매상고
department variance on overhead
부문간접비차이
departmental burden 부문부담비
departmental charge 부문비
departmental cost 부문원가
departmental cost accounting
부문별 원가계산
departmental costing 부문별 원가계산
departmental expenses 부문비

departmental expenses budget 부문비예산
departmental overhead 부문간접비
departmental process cost system 공정별 종합원가계산
departmental profit 부문별 이익
departure 이탈
dependence 의존
dependence effect 의존효과
dependency 종속
dependent allowance 가족수당
dependent family member 부양가족
depleted cost 상각후 원가
depletion 감모상각
depletion allowance 감가수당금
depletion assets 감모상각
depletion of natural resources 천연자원감모상각비
depletive 감모가능한
deployment 전개
deposit 예탁
deposit account 예탁계정
deposit administration fund 예탁관리기금
deposit and saving 예저금
deposit as collateral 담보예금
deposit at financial institutions 금융기관예금
deposit at notice 통지예금
deposit by the Ministry of Finance 재무부예탁금
deposit certificate 예금증서
deposit company 기탁회사
deposit currency 예금통화
deposit diary 예금기입장
deposit due from bank 은행예금
deposit due to bank 은행예금
deposit fee 예금수수료
deposit float 플로트예금
deposit for public auction 공매보증금
deposit for tax 납세준비예금
deposit for tax payment 납세준비금
deposit from employees 종업원예금
deposit in a fictitious name 비실명예금
deposit in current account 당좌예금
deposit in trust 신탁예금
deposit insurance bailout 예금보험구제
deposit insurance system 예금보험제도
deposit interest rate 예금금리
deposit law 공탁법
deposit ledger 예금원장
deposit liability 예금채무
deposit loan 예금대부
deposit market 예금시장
deposit minus checks and bills on hand 실세예금
deposit money 예금통화
deposit of margin 증거금예탁
deposit of nondebtor 비채무자예금
deposit of public money 예금통화
deposit of securities on contracts 보증차입유가증권
deposit of stock certificates 주권예탁
deposit of title-deeds 권리서기탁
deposit office 공탁소
deposit on a net basis 실세예금
deposit on contract 예보증금
deposit on long-term leases 장기임대계약예금
deposit paid on construction work 공사전도금
deposit paid to trade creditors 구입전불대금
deposit payoff 예금정산불방식
deposit rate 예금이율
deposit received 보증금
deposit received for guarantee 예보증금
deposit received on sale 예보증금
deposit share 예금쉐어
deposit slip 예금전표
deposit taking business 수신업무
deposit through deduction from monthly pay 공제저금
deposit to be relent to a third party 도입예금
deposit transfer 예금대체방식

deposit war 예금전쟁
deposit window 예금창구
deposit with depository 대체보관기관에 예탁함
deposit with landlord 전세보증금; 거래보증금
deposit with other bank 예금
deposit with public utility corporation 공익사업회사예금
deposit with the Bank of Japan 일본은행예금
deposit-to-loan ratio 예금율
deposited article 공탁물
deposited money 예탁금
deposited securities 예탁유가증권
deposited stock certificate 예탁주권
deposition 증언기록
depositor 공탁자
depositor protection 예금자보호
depository assets 예탁자산
depository bank 예탁은행
depository correspondent 디포지터리코러스폰던트; 예치환거래은행
depository institution 예금수입금융기관
depository period 예탁기한
depository receipts 예탁증서
Depository Receipts of Singapore 싱가폴예탁증서
depository shares 예탁주식
depository trust company 예탁신탁회사
deposits of funds of national annuities 국민연금예탁금
deposits with Trust Fund Bureau 자금운용부예탁금
depreciable 감가상각가능한
depreciable amount 상각액
depreciable assets 감가상각자산
depreciable cost 감사상각원가
depreciable limit 상각한도액
depreciable property 상각자산
depreciable property for nonbusiness 비영업용 상각자산
depreciable used in business 영업비상각자산
depreciated cost 감가상각후 원가
depreciated original cost 감가상각후 원시원가
depreciated value 감가상각후 가액
depreciation 감가상각
depreciation account 상각계정
depreciation accounting 감가상각회계
depreciation adequacy 감가상각타당성
depreciation and amortization 상각
depreciation assets 상각자산
depreciation base 감가상각기초액
depreciation burden 감가상각부담
depreciation by depreciation rate 감가율에 따른 상각
depreciation expense 감가상각비
depreciation fund 감가상각기금
depreciation in excess of the limit 초과상각
depreciation in won 원저
depreciation method 감가상각법
depreciation of building 건물감가상각
depreciation of currency 통화가치저하
depreciation of deposit by inflation 예금감소
depreciation of dollar 달러저
depreciation of ship costs 선가(船價)상각
depreciation of time value 시간가치감가
depreciation on obsolete assets 진부화 자산상각
depreciation on property 자산감가상각
depreciation period 감가상각연수
depreciation rate 감가상각률
depreciation ratio 상각률
depreciation reserve 감가상각준비금
depreciation reserve ratio 감가상각준비금비율
depreciation unit 감가상각단위
depression 불황
depression cartel 불황카르텔
depression of business 불경기
depth of market 시장의 두터움
deputy 대리

C D

deregulated interest rate 자유금리
deregulated interest rate product 자유금리상품
deregulation 규제완화
deregulation of finance 금융자유화
deregulation of financial and capital market 금융자본시장자유화
derivative deposit 파생예금
derivative income 파생취득
derivative market 파생상품시장
derivative pass-through securities market 파생패스스루증권시장
derivative portfolio 파생상품포트폴리오
derivative product 파생상품
derivative security 파생증권
derivative suit 파생소송
derivative transaction 파생거래
derivatives market 금융파생상품시장
derived demand 간접수요;파생수요
derived function 도함수
derived income 파생소득
descending 하강
descending curve 하강곡선
descending order 내림차순
descending tops 최저점
descending triangle 하락삼각형
descending triangle pattern 하락삼각형
description of business 영업과목
descriptive data 기술데이터
descriptive financial statement 설명부 재무제표
descriptive function 설명기능
descriptive statistics 설명을 위한 통계
design 의장
designated account 지정계좌
designated bind 지명입찰
designated city 지정도시
designated currency 지정통화
designated deposit 지정예금
designated exchange 지정거래소
designated money in trust 지정금전신탁
designated nominee 지정명의인
designated statistics 지정통계
designated stock 지정상품
designated trading 지정거래
designation for transfer 불입지정
designation of accounting period 사업연도지정
designation of place for tax payment 납세지지정
designation of security 유가증권상품
desired profit 목표이익
destination 발송지
destruction of environment 환경파괴
destructive disposition 파괴처분
detachable 분리형의
detachable warrant 분리가능워런트
detached employees 파견사원
detail 상세
detailed account form 세목계정식
detailed audit report 장문식 감사보고서
detailed check 자세히 조사함
detailed enforcement regulations 시행세칙
detailed statement 내역서
details of distribution 분매요령
deteriorate 저하시키다
deteriorated assets 열화자산
deterioration 악화
determination by estimate 추계를 통한 갱정
determination of dividend 배당결정
determination of taxable year 사업연도결정
determination of the necessary adjustments 수정사항결정
deterrent 억지력
Deutch mark 독일마르크
devaluation 절하
devaluation risk 절하리스크
devalue 절하하다
develop and import scheme 개발수입
developed countries 선진국
developer 개발업자
developing countries 개발도상국

development assistance 해외원조
Development Bank of Japan 일본정책은행
development capital 개발자본
development cost 개발비
development cost of residential site 택지조성비
development expenses 개발비
development fund 개발자금
development gap 개발격차
development of distribution channel 판로개척
development regulation 개발규제
deviation 특별요율적용;편차
device 장치; 설비
diagonal spread 대각스프레드
diagram 도형
dialogue 회화
diamond formation 다이아몬드포메이션
diary on securities market 증권경제일지
dichotomy 이분법
difference 차이
difference among issues 상품간 격차
difference by renewal 갱신차금
difference from exchange of property 교환차금
difference in yield 이익격차
difference resulting from offsetting futures contracts 선물거래차금
different account 다른 계좌
differential account 차액계정
differential analysis 차분분석
differential coefficient 미분계수
differential cost 차액원가
differential costing 차액원가계산
differential equation 미분방정식
differential of return 수익률교차
differentiation 차별화
diffusion index 경기동향지표
diffusion of risks 위험분산
diffusion rate 보급률
digest 소화하다; 요약하다; 침지하다
dilemma 딜레마
diligence 주의
dilution 희박화
dilution factor 희박화율
dimension 차원
diminishing balance depreciation 정율상각
diminishing balance method 체감원가법
dip 침하; 후퇴
diplomacy 외교
direct aid 직접원조
direct attack 직접공격
direct banking 다이랙트뱅킹
direct budget transfer 예산편입
direct capital 직접자본
direct deal 직거래
direct dealing 직접환거래
direct debit 계좌에서 대리납부함
direct department 직접부문
direct department cost 부문개별비
direct deposit 직접예금
direct evidence 직접증거
direct exchange arbitrage 직접환재정
direct exercise 직접행사
direct expense 직접경비
direct financing 직접금융
direct financing tax credit 외국환직접공제
direct financing lease 직접금융형 리스
direct foreign tax credit 외국세액직접공제
direct insurance 원수보험
direct insurer 원수회사
direct interest 직접이해관계
direct intervention 직접개입
direct investment 직접투자
direct issue paper 직접매출페이퍼
direct labor 직접노동
direct labor cost 직접노무비
direct liabilities 확정부채
direct loan 직접금융
direct material cost 직접재료비
direct method 직접법
direct method of depreciation 직접상각

direct national tax 직접국세
direct or equity investment 직접투자
direct overhead 직접경비
direct paper 다이렉트어음
direct payment 완전변제
direct placement 직접모집
direct premium 원수보험료
direct presentation 직접표시
direct pricing 직접정산법
direct rated deposit administration contract 직접참가예탁관리계약
direct selling 직판
direct tax 직접세
direct tax credit 세액직접공제
direct transaction 직접거래
direct valuation 직접평가
direct yield 직접이익
direction 지도
direction of interest rate 금리방향
directional index 방향성지수
directional movement 방향성
directive 통달
director 이사; 임원
director having duties in an employee's capacity 겸무임원
director's retirement allowance 임원퇴직급여금
director's salaries and remuneration 임원보수
directors and officers liability insurance 임원배상책임보험
directory statute 지시적인 법률
directory trust 지시신탁
dirty float 더티플로트;관리변동환율제도
disability 고도장애
disability income insurance 취업불능소득보상보험
disability insurance 소득보상보험
disablement benefit 장애보상
disabling statutes 재산이전금지법
disagreement 동의하지 않음
disappointing 낙담
disappointing export 수출부조
disarray 혼란
disbursement 지불
disbursement book 현금지불장
disbursement cycle 지불순환
disbursement slip 출금전표
disbursements insurance 선비(船費)보험
discarded equipment 폐잔설비
discharge 방출;면책
discharge of debt 채무면제
discharge of delinquent tax 연체세면제
discharge of officers 임원해임
discharge of repayment 상환면제
discharge of reponsibility 책임이행
disciplinary action 징계처분
discipline 징벌
discipline on members 회원처분
disclaimer 거절
disclaimer clause 발주자면책조항
disclaimer of opinion 의견거절
disclosed capital stock 공표자본금
disclosing function 공시기능
disclosure 개시
disclosure of terms and conditions of loans 대출조건명시
disclosure philosophy 개시원칙
disclosure system 공시제도
discontinuance of accounts 계좌폐지
discontinuance of business 폐업
discontinued business 비계속사업
discontinued operations 폐지부문
discontinuity 거절
discount 현재가치로 환원하다; 디스카운트
discount bank 할인은행
discount bank debenture 할인금융채
discount bond 할인채
discount bond amortization 채권발행차금상각
discount broker 어음할인중개인
discount charge 할인율
discount commission 할인수수료

discount earned 수취할인료
discount expenses 할인료
discount factor 할인계수
discount function 할인함수
discount government bond 할인국채
discount house 할인상사
discount issue 할인발행
discount ledger 할인어음원장
discount market 할인시장
discount on banker's acceptances 은행인수어음할인
discount on bill 어음할인
discount on bills sold on condition of repurchase 환매조건부 매각어음
discount on note 어음할인료
discount or premium on bond 사채발행차금
discount policy 할인정책
discount rate 할인율
discount rate cut 공정할인율인하
discount rate policy 공정할인율조작
discount register 할인어음기입장
discount value 할인가격
discount window 할인창구
discount yield 할인이익
discounted bill 할인어음
discounted cash flow 할인수익
discounters 수수료할인업자
discounting 할인
discredit 신용하지 않다
discrepancy 차이
discrete time 이산(離散)시간형
discrete-variable 이산변수형
discretion 자유재량
discretion of law 법의 재량
discretional act 재량행위
discretionary account 매매일임계정
discretionary account transaction 매매일임계정거래
discretionary cost 재량원가
discretionary expenses 임의비용
discretionary loan 재량대출
discretionary order 일임주문
discretionary trust 일임신탁
discriminant 차별요인
discriminating duty 차별관세
discrimination 차별
discriminative price 차별가격
discriminative tariff 차별세율
diseconomy 불경제; 경제적이지 못함
disequilibrium 불균형
disequilibrium growth 불균형성장
disfranchise 공권을 박탈하다
disguised act 가장행위
disguised transaction 위장거래
disguised conduct 불신행위
dishonor 인수거절
dishonor notice 부도통지
dishonored bill 부도어음
dishonored check 부도수표
disinflation 디스인플레이션
disintegration 해체
disinterested 이해관계가 없는
disintermediation 비중개
disintermediation of bank 탈은행
disinvestment 투자해제
disjunctive allegation 흑백논리
dismissal 면직; 각하
disparate ratio 괴리율
disparity 불일치
dispatch 급파하다; 급파
displaced diffusion model 확산변환모델
disposable income 가처분소득
disposable personal income 개인가처분소득
disposable profit 가처분이익
disposal 처분
disposal date 처분일
disposal of fixed assets 고정자산처분
disposal price 처분가격
disposal value 처분가치
disposing capacity 재산처분능력
disposition 처분

C D

disposition by public sale 공매처분
disposition by suspension of bank credit 은행거래정지
disposition by suspension of business 거래정지처분
disposition for failure to pay 체납처분
disposition of a member 회원처분
disposition of assets 자산처분
disposition of cost variance 원가차액조정
disposition of failure to pay income tax in advance 예정납세액체납처분
disposition of net income 순익처분
dispossession 불법점유
dispute 분쟁
dispute settlement 분쟁해결
disqualified 부적절한
disqualified substance 부적절한 내용
disqualify 자격을 빼앗다
disregard of decimal places 소수점이하 버림
disregard of tax rule 세법을 무시함
disruption 중단
disruption claims 방해클레임
disseminate 공표하다
dissemination 공표
dissemination of transaction price 약정가격을 공표함
dissent 반대하다
dissenting opinion 반대의견
dissolution 해산
dissolution and extinction due to merger 합병을 통한 해산; 소멸
dissolution of corporation 법인해산
distor 왜곡
distrain 차압하다
distress 차압
distress infinite 무기한차압
distress sale 차압물건매각
distress selling 투매; 출혈판매
distribution 분배
distribution channel 유통경로
distribution cost 판매비
distribution date 분매집행일
distribution industry 유통업계
distribution of local allocation tax 지방교부세교부금
distribution of net assets of investment trusts 투자신탁운용상황
distribution of net profit 이익처분
distribution of overhead cost 간접비분배
distribution of ownership of shares 주식분포상황
distribution of PBR PBR 분포
distribution of profits 이익배당
distribution of property 재산분여
distribution of residual assets 잔여재산분여
distribution of residual property 잔여재산분배
distribution of shares 주식분포
distribution of single day advances and declines 전일대비변동률분포
distribution of stock prices 주가수준분포
distribution of surplus 익금처분
distribution rate of overhead cost 간접비배부율
distribution ratio 구성비율
distribution revolution 유통혁명
distribution structure 유통기구
distribution tax 배부세
divergence 괴리
divergence indicator 괴리지표
divergence threshold 괴리한도
diverse 다양한
diversification 분산화
diversification investment 분산화 투자
diversification of risks 리스크분산
diversification strategy 다각화전략
diversified investment 분산투자
diversified portfolio on stock investment 분산주식투자포트폴리오
diversified type common stock fund 분산형 보통주펀드
diversified type investment company

분산형 투자회사
diversified type portfolio 분산형 포트폴리오
diversify 분산하다
divest 주식을 매각하다
divestiture of assets 자사매각
dividend 배당
dividend account 배당계정
dividend credit 배당공제
dividend cut 감배
dividend decrease 감배
dividend discount 배당할인
dividend discount method 배당환원방식
dividend discount model 배당환원모델
dividend discount rate 배당할인율
dividend distribution 배당
dividend earned 수취배당금
dividend equalization fund 배당평균준비금
dividend equalization reserve 배당평균적립금
dividend excluded from income 수취배당금익금불산입
dividend exclusion 배당공제
dividend extra 특별배당
dividend flow 배당플로
dividend for the second half 후기배당
dividend from capital 자본배당
dividend from stocks owned 주식소유와 관련 있는 배당
dividend growth rate 배당률
dividend in arrears 연체배당금
dividend in kind 현물배당
dividend income 배당소득
dividend increase 증배
dividend off 배당락
dividend on 배당부
dividend on common stock 보통주배당금
dividend on dummy stock 명의주배당
dividend on interest 이자배당
dividend on preferred stock 우선주배당금
dividend on stock 주식배당
dividend payable 미불배당금
dividend paying company 배당회사
dividend payment 배당지불
dividend payment bank 배당지불은행
dividend payment despite deficit 적자임에도 배당함
dividend payout ratio 배당성향
dividend per share 일주당 배당금
dividend preferred stock 배당우선주식
dividend rate 배당률
dividend receivable 미수배당
dividend received 수취배당금
dividend reinvestment plan 배당금재투자
dividend reserve 배당적립금
dividend schedule 배당예정
dividend stock 배당주
dividend to policyholders 보험계약자배당
dividend yield 배당이익
dividend-included stock price indices 배당포함주가지수
dividend-paid deduction method 배당손금법
dividend-paying stock 유배주
dividends of listed companies 사장회사배당상황
divisible claim 가분채권
divisible obligation 가분채무
divisible surplus 배당가능잉여금
division 구분; 부문
Division of Corporate Finance (SEC) 기업재무국(SEC)
Division of Enforcement (SEC) 법률시행국(SEC)
Division of Investment Management (SEC) 투자관리국(SEC)
division of margin 증거금구분
Division of Market Regulation (SEC) 시장규제국(SEC)
division of succession 분할상속제
division of trading sessions 매매입회구분
divisional breakdown of profit and loss 부문별 손익
divisional sales 부문매상

divisional sales breakdown 부문별 매상내역
dockage 부두사용료
doctrine of discovered peril 발견위험의 원칙
document 서류
document against acceptance 인수도
document of seizure 차압서
document of title 권리증권
documentary bill 화환어음
documentary clean credit 무담보신용장
documentary credit 화환신용장
documentary evidence 증거서류
documentary letter of credit 화환신용장
documentary stamp tax 인지세
documentation bank 계약서류작성은행
documented discount note 신용장보증부 할인어음
documents for opening a U. S. dollar account 달러계좌개설서류
Dodge Line 다지라인
Doi Moi 도이머이정책(베트남의 개혁정책)
doing business 영업행위
dollar account 달러계정
dollar average method 달러평균법
dollar averaging 달러평균
dollar bloc 달러블록
dollar call option 달러콜옵션
dollar convertible bond 달러기준전환사채
dollar crisis 달러위기
dollar denominated 달러기준의
dollar overhung 과잉달러
dollar parity 달러평가
dollar pool 달러풀
dollar preference 달러선호
dollar put option 달러풋옵션
dollar shift 달러시프트
dollar shortage 달러불황
dollar-weighted rate of return 달러가중수익률
dollar-weighted return 금액가중수익율
domain 활동영역
domestic capital 국내자본
domestic corporation 내국법인
domestic credit 국내신용
domestic currency 자국통화
domestic demand 내수
domestic demand expansion 내수확대
domestic demand oriented industry 내수산업
domestic demand related stock 내수관련주
domestic demand stimulation 내수진흥
domestic equilibrium 국내균형
domestic expenditure 국내지출
domestic factor 국내요인
domestic income 국내소득
domestic institutional investor 국내기관투자가
domestic investment 국내투자
domestic loan system 국내론방식
domestic market 국내시장
domestic operations 국내사업
domestic price 국내가격
domestic share 내국주식
domestic source 국내원천
domestic source income 국내원천소득
domestic stock 국내주
domiciled bill 지불지정어음
dominate the market 시장의 대부분을 점유하다
domino effect 도미노효과
donated property 증여재산
donated stock 증여주
donated surplus 증여잉여금
donation 증여
donation of property 재산증여
donation tax 증여세
donation to designated organization 지정기부금
donator 기증자
done 계약성립
dormant account 휴지계정
dormant balance 휴지잔고
double account interests 이중이자

double accounting 복식부기
double attachment 이중차압
double bottom 이중바닥
double check 재확인
double counting 이중계산
double crossover 더블크로스오버
double dated 이중만기
double declining balance method 배액정율법
double distribution 이중분배
double entry book keeping 복식부기
double insurance 중복보험
double jeopardy 이중위험
double leverage 더블레버리지
double liability 이중부채
double listing 중복상장
double name paper 복명(複名)어음
double option 더블옵션
double peak 이중천장
double price 이중가격
double seizure 이중차압
double settlement 삼일후 인도
double tariff 이중관세
double taxation 이중과세
double top 더블톱
double-digit recurring profit growth 두자리수성장기조
double-up 더블업
doubtful account 불량채권
doubtful loan 불량대출
Dow Jones 15 Public Utility Average 다우공공주 15종 평균
Dow Jones 20 Bond Index 다우 20종 채권지수
Dow Jones 20 Transportation Average 다우운송주 20종 평균
Dow Jones 30 Industrial Average 다우공업주 30종 평균
Dow Jones Average 다우평균
Dow Jones Industrial 다우공업주
Dow Jones Industrial Average 다우평균
Dow Theory 다우이론
Dow-Jones Commodity Index 다우식 상품지수
down and out call option 다운앤드아웃콜옵션
down payment 전도금
down spread 매매차익금
downfall 하락
downhill course 하강선
downside potential 하향탄력성
downside risk 가격인하여지
downsizing 가격인하불안
downstairs merger 역흡수합병
downswing phase 하강국면
downtick 전날 종가보다 싼 거래
downturn 악화
downward movement 시세가 내리는 상태
downward phase of the business cycle 하강국면
downward revision 하향수정
downward revision on business results 실적을 예상한 하향수정
draft at sight 일람불어음
draft bill of exchange 환어음
draft payable 지불어음
draft receivable 수취어음
dragon bond 드래곤채
dramatic surge 대상(大商)
draw 발행하다
draw down 자금인출
drawback 관세환불
drawback allowance 환불세급부
drawdown period 자금인출가능기간
drawee 어음수신인
drawer 발행인
drawer of bill 어음발행인
drawing 발행
drawing account 인출금계정
drawing bank 발행은행
drawing of bill 어음발행
drawing of number 추첨
drawing right 발행권

drawn bill 발행어음
drifting mix 표류믹스
drop 하강
drop below par 액면하락
drop-lock bond 드롭록채
dropout option 드롭아웃옵션
dry weight 건조중량
dual banking system 이중은행제도
dual capacity 이중용량
dual character of investment 투자의 이중성
dual closed-end fund 듀얼클로즈드엔드형 펀드
dual convertible bonds 듀얼전환사채
dual currency bond 이중통화기준채
dual currency bonds 듀얼커런시채
dual economy 이중경제
dual exchange market 이중환시장
dual fund 듀얼펀드
dual interest policy 이중금리정책
dual rate system 이중운임제
dual structure 이중구조
dual structure of the economy 경제의 이중구조
dual tariff 복관세
dual trading 이중계정거래
dual-purpose bond 듀얼펀드
duality 이중성
due and deferred premiums 미수보험료
due bill 금전채무인증서
due care 정당한 주의
due date 만기일
due date coming basis 회수기한도래기준
due date for payment 지불기한
due date for tax payment 납기한
due date of bills 어음만기
due date of filing return 신고기한
due date of payment 불입일
due date of property tax payment 고정자산납세기한
due date of the tax return 신고기한
due diligence 자세히 조사함
due from foreign banks(our a/c) 외국지점예금
due process of law 적법절차
due to foreign banks 외국타점예금
duet bond 듀엣채
dull 별로 마음이 내키지 않음
dumbbell portfolio 덤벨포트폴리오
dummy account 더미계정
dummy company 더미회사
dummy stock 명의주
dumping 덤핑
dumping petition 덤핑제소
duplex system 이중계약주의
duplicate 부(副)의
duplicate taxation 이중과세
duplicate tenor 등본
duplication 중복
durable consumer goods 내구소비재
durable goods order 내구재수주
durable years 내용연수
duration 계속기간
duration gap 듀레이션갭
duration method 듀레이션법
duration of bond 채권평균만기
duration of risk 위험기간
duration of risk clause 보험기간조항
duration-matching 듀레이션매칭
duration-weighted yield 듀레이션가중이익
Durbin-Watson ratio 더빈-왓슨비
Dutch auction 값을 깎아 내려가는 경매
Dutch guilder bond 더치길더채
Dutch system 더치방식
dutiable goods 세금이 붙는 상품
dutiable value 과세가격
duty 직무
duty exemption 면세
duty free 면세의
duty free imports 면세수입품
duty of care 주의의무
duty of disclosure 고지의무
duty to sue and labor 손해방지의무

duty-paid 납세필
dwelling house 주거
dynamic analysis 동태분석
dynamic credit swap 다이나믹크레디트스와프
dynamic hedge scheme 다이나믹헤지
dynamic input-output analysis 동학적인 산업연관분석
dynamic multiplier 다이나믹승수
dynamic portfolio 다이나믹포트폴리오
dynamic programming 다이나믹프로그램
dynamic risks 동태적인 위험
dynamic statistics 동태통계
dynamic strategies 다이나믹전략

E

each way 수수료 각자지불
early amortization 기한전 상환
early redemption 조기상환
early redemption option 조기상환옵션
early repayment 조기반제
early termination 기한전 해약
earmark 자금 등을 모아둠
earmarked tax 목적세
earned income 소득기준
earned income allowance 근로소득공제
earned income tax 근로소득세
earned premium 경과보험료
earned reserve 이익준비금
earned surplus 이익잉여금
earned surplus carried forward to the following term 이월이익잉여금
earned surplus reserve 이익준비금
earned surplus statement 이익잉여금계산금
earnest money 계약증거금
earnest money received 예금수부금
earning assets 수익자산
earning capacity 수익력
earning coverage 수익력 커버리지
earning coverage ratios 부담이익배율
earning power 수익력
earning rate 수익률
earning statement 손익계산서
earning tax 수익세
earnings 수익
earnings before extraordinary items 특별손익전 이익
earnings before interest and taxes 금리세금공제전 이익
earnings before tax 세금공제전 이익
earnings from continuing operations 계속사업부문이익
earnings model 수익모델
earnings multiplier 주가수익률
earnings on equity 자기자본이익률
earnings outlook 수익예측
earnings per share 일주당 이익
earnings per share of common stock 보통주식일주당 순이익
earnings performance 업적
earnings recovery 수익회복
earnings reinvested 재투자이익
earnings retained in business 이익잉여금
earnings retention rate 수익유보율
earnings risk 수익리스크
earnings stability 수익안정성
earnings target 이익목표
earnings yield 이율
earthquake insurance 지진보험
easement 지역권
easement appurtenant 부속지역권
easement holder 지역권자
easing 완화
easing of credit 금융완화
easing of yield 이율저하
East African Community 동아프리카공동체
East Asian Insurance Congress 동아시아보험회의

easy 완만한 약세인(물가)
easy monetary policy 금융완화정책
easy payment 분할불
EC joint floating system EC 공동플로팅
echo effect 반향효과
echo principle 반향원리
econometric analysis 계량분석
econometric model 계량경제모델
economic accounting 경제회계
economic activity 경제활동
economic activity stimulating measure 경제활동자극책
economic aid 경제원조
economic analysis 경제분석
Economic and Development Review Committee 경제개발검토위원회
Economic and Social Commission for Asia and the Pacific 아시아태평양경제사회위원회
economic assistance 경제협력
economic barometer 경제지표
economic benefits 경제적인 편익
economic big power 경제대국
economic bloc 경제권
economic blockade 경제봉쇄
economic boom 호경기
economic center 경제센터
economic circles 경제계
economic conditions 경제상황
economic continuity 경제의 연속성
economic cooperation 경제협력
economic cost 경제원가
economic crisis 경제공황
economic cycle 경기순환
economic diplomacy 경제외교
economic dualism 이중경제구조
economic earnings 경제적 이익
economic earnings beta 경제적 이익의 베타수치
economic engineering 경제성 공학
economic entity 경제실체
economic environment 경기
economic ethics 경제윤리
economic event 경제논리, 경제사상
economic exchange 경제교류
economic figure 경제지표
economic fluctuation 경기변동
economic forecast 경제예측
economic friction 경제마찰
economic goods 경제재
economic growth 경제성장
economic growth model 경제성장모델
economic growth policy 경제성장정책
economic growth rate 경제성장률
economic index 경제지수
economic indexes 경제지표
economic indicator 경제지표
economic integration 경제통합
economic interpretation 경제해석
economic life 경제생활
economic malaise 경제질병
economic maturity 경제적인 성숙
economic model 경제모델
economic number effect 경제지표효과
economic obsolescence 경제적인 진부화
economic order 경제질서
economic organization 경제조직
economic outlook 경제예측
economic path 경제경과
economic philosophy 경제철학
economic plan 경제계획
Economic Planning Agency 경제기획청
economic policy 경제정책
economic power 경제대국
economic prediction 경제예측
economic progress 경제진보
economic prospect 경제전망
economic reality 경제의 실체
economic recession 경기후퇴
economic recovery 경기회복
economic reform 경제개혁
economic regime 경제체제

economic risk 경제리스크
economic sanction 경제제재
economic security 경제안전보장
economic size 경제규모
economic slump 경기후퇴
economic statistics 경제통계
economic stimulus package 경기자극책
economic structural adjustment 경제구조조정
Economic Summit 선진국수뇌회의
economic superpower 경제대국
economic system 경제체제
economic table 경제표
economic tide 경제의 흐름
economic union 경제동맹
economic value qualifying for investment in kind 현물출자가 될 수 있는 경제적 가치
economic war 경제전쟁
economic welfare 경제적 후생
economic white paper 경제백서
economics 경제학
economies of scope 다각화의 경제성
economist 경제학자
economy of scale 규모의 경제
ECU bond ECU 채
ECU market ECU 시장
EDGAR 에드가
edge down 우위
edge up 소폭상승
Edge-Act company 에지액트법인
education expense 교육비
education industry 교육산업
education loan 교육론
effect 효과
effect of discount 할인효과
effect of exchange rate changes 환환산수정
effect of limiting risk 위험한정효과
effective aggregate tax rate 종합효과세율
effective competition 유효경쟁
effective date 발효일
effective demand 유효수요
effective exchange rate 실효환상장
effective income 실질소득
effective interest rate 실효금리
effective period of order 주문유효기간
effective price 실효가격
effective rate 실세레이트
effective rate of interest 실효금리
effective rate of discount 어음할인율
effective rate of protection 실효보호율
effective tariff 실효세율
effective tax rate 실효세율
effective volatility 실제가격변동율
effective yield 실효이율
effectiveness of diversified investment 분산투자의 유효성
efficacy 실효성
efficiency audit 능률감사
efficiency variance 능률차이
efficient allocation 실효적 지배
efficient cause 주요원인
efficient frontier 유효프론티어
efficient market 효율적인 시장
efficient market hypothesis 효율적인 시장 가설
efficient portfolio 효율적인 포트폴리오
efficient spread 실효스프레드
efficient statistics 유효통계
eight column work sheet 팔행식 정산표
either or facility 이더오어퍼실리티
elaborate 교묘한
elapse of the time 기간경과
elapsed years 경과연수
elastic demand 탄력적인 수요
elastic limit system 굴신제한제도
elastic tariff 탄력관세
elasticity approach 탄력성 어프로치
elasticity clause 탄력조항
elasticity of demand 수요탄성치
elasticity of substitution 대체탄력성
elasticity of supply 공급탄성치
elasticity of the balance of payments

국제수지탄력성
elasticity optimism 탄력성 낙관
elasticity pessimism 탄력성 비관
elder title 선권원(先權原)
electric appliances futures 전기제품선물
electric appliances industry 전기제품업계
electric industry 전기업계
electric power and gas industry 전기가스공업
electric power bonds 전력채
Electric Power Development Co, Ltd. 전력개발주식회사
electric power expense 전력비
electricity and gas tax 전기가스세
electricity tax 전기세
electronic banking 전자금융
electronic commerce 전자상거래
electronic data gathering analysis and retrieval system EDGAR 시스템
electronic engineering 전자공학
electronic fund transfer 전신송금
electronic market 전자시장
electronic money 전자화폐
electronic order transfer system 전자주문전달시스템
electronic trading market 전자거래시장
electronic cost accounting 요소별 원가계산
eligibility 적격성
eligibility for syndicate membership 신디케이트참가자격
eligible bill 할인적격어음
eligible investment 적격투자
eligible securities 적격유가증권
eligible security 적격담보
eliminating entry 소거분개
elimination 소거
elimination of intercompany indebtedness 회사상호간 대차소법
elimination of intercompany ownership 회사상호간 지분소법
elimination of intercompany profits 회사상호간 이익소법
elite card 엘리트카드
Elliot Wave Theory 엘리어트파동이론
emancipation 해방
embargo 수출금지
embarrassing 곤란함
embedded loss 포함손
embedded profit 포함익
embezzlement 횡령
emergency 출현
emergency amortization 긴급상각
emergency duty 긴급관세
emergency funds 임시비
emergency import 긴급수입
emergency legislation 긴급입법
emergency loan 긴급융자
emergency measure 비상조치
emergency tariff 긴급관세
emergent financial disposition 재정상 긴급처분
emerging corporation 신흥기업
emerging market 신흥경제지역
emerging markets 신흥마켓
eminent domain 토지수용
empirical analysis 실증분석
empirical approach 경험적 어프로치
empirical study 실증연구
employee 종업원
employee benefit plan 종업원급부제도
employee bonus 상여
employee compensation 미불급여
employee deposits 사원예금
employee pension benefit plan 종업원연금제도
Employee Retirement Income Security Act 엘리사법
Employee Retirement Income Security Act of 1974 종업원퇴직소득보증법
employee stock ownership plan 종업원지주제도
employee stock purchase plan 종업원주식구입계획

E F

employee welfare benefit plan 종업원복지급여제도
employees bonus and allowance 종업원급여수당
employees pension fund 종업원연금기금적립금
employees relief fund 부조기금
employees retirement allowance 종업원퇴직급여금
employees retirement benefit 퇴직급여준비금
employees union 종업원조합
employer 사용자
employer's contribution 기업부담
employer's liability insurance 사용자배상책임보험
employment 고용
employment adjustment 고용조정
employment contract 고용계약
employment cost 인건비
employment data 고용데이터
employment growth 고용신장
employment income 급여소득
employment income deduction 급여소득공제
employment income earner 급여소득자
employment income exemption 급여소득공제
employment index 고용지수
employment insurance 고용보험
employment multiplier 고용승수
employment prospectus 고용예측
employment statistics 고용통계
empowerment 임파워먼트
emulate 모방하다
enactment 현금화
enclosure 담;울타리
encouragement 격려
encumbrance 토지부담
end goal 최종목표
end of the fiscal year 연말
end of the month 월말
end of the period 기말
end result 최종결과
end-user 최종수요자
ending balance 기말잔고
endogenous change 내생변화
endogenous variable 내생변수
endorsed bill 이서어음
endorsed bills exchanged between two parties 회전어음
endorsed bond 이서채권
endorsed note 이서어음
endorsee 피이서인
endorsement 이서
endorsement for option contract 옵션계약의 이서
endorsement for transfer 이서양도
endorsement in blank 백지식 이서
endorsement to order 지도식 이서
endorsement to transfer 양도이서
endorsement without recourse 소급의무면제이서
endorser 이서인
endowment annuity 연금부 보험
endowment insurance 양로보험
endowment mortgage 양로모기지
energy conservation 에너지탄성
energy risk 에너지리스크
energy sector stock 에너지주
energy stockpiling 에너지비축
energy tax 에너지세
enforce 강제하다
enforceable 강행할 수 있는
enforcement 시행
enforcement day 시행일
enforcement regulations 시행규칙
enforcement right 실시권
enfranchisement 공권부여
engage in 종사하다
engagement 계약
Engel coefficient 엥겔지수
English auction 영국식 경매
English law 영국법

enhance 가치를 높이다
enjoin 명령하다
enlarged European Communities 확대 EC
enlighteening activities 계몽활동
enrichment 충실
enrollment 등록
ensuing account 차기계정
enter 기입하다
enterprise 기업
enterprise accounting 기업회계
enterprise approach 기업전체의 리스크를 평가함
enterprise cost 기업원가
enterprise mortgage 기업담보권
enterprise tax 사업세
enterprise tax on corporation 법인사업세
enterprise value 기업가치
entertainment 오락
entertainment and social expenses 교제비
entertainment expenses not qualifying for deduction 손금불산입교제비
entire agreement clause 완전합의조항
entire tenancy 단독보유
entitle 권리를 부여하다
entitlement 권리확보
entity 실체
entity accounting 실체회계
entity theory 법인이론
entrance fee 입회금
entrepreneur 기업가
entrepreneurship 기업가정신
entropy 엔트로피
entrust of collection 징수촉탁
entrusted business commission 위탁업무수수료
entrustment 위탁
entrustment clearing business 결제사무를 위임함
entry 기입
entry age cost method 가입연령방식
entry cost 가입코스트
entry of judgment 판결등록
entry system of a candidate 후보자신고제도
enumerate 열거하다
environmental assessment 환경평가
environmental audit 환경감사
environmental data 환경데이터
environmental impairment liability insurance 환경오염배상책임보험
environmental protection 환경보호
environmental tax 환경세
equal annual payment method 연간정액지불
equal cost curve 동비용곡선
equal credit opportunity 신용기회균등
equal employment opportunities 고용기회균등
equal footing 공정한 경쟁
equal installment repayment method 원본균등불방식
equal monthly payment 월액균등지불
equal monthly payments with interest 원리균등반제
equal payment method 원리균등불방식
equal weighted portfolio 등금액 포트폴리오
equal-weighted average 균등가중평균
equaled time of payment 평균지불기일
equalization of tax burden 세부담의 평준화
equalization of tax collection 공평한 징수
equalization of tax payment 공평한 납세
equalization reserve 평준화준비금
equalizing divergences 격차균등화
equally divided 균분
equation of exchange 교환방정식
equilibrium analysis 균형분석
equilibrium basis 적정베이시스
equilibrium point 균형점
equilibrium price 균형가격
equilibrium rate of exchange 균형환상장
equilibrium rate of interest 균형이자율
equipment 설비
equipment fair value 설비적정가격
equipment fund 설비자금
equipment investment 설비투자

equipment trust 설비신탁
equitable assignment 형평법상의 양도
equitable lien 형평법상의 리엔
equitable mortgage 형평법상의 모기지
equitable obligation 형평법상의 채무
equities insurance 에퀴티보험
equity account 지분계정
equity accounting 기분회계
equity at book value 자기자본부가
equity at market value 자기자본시가
equity boom 주식붐
equity call option 주식콜옵션
equity capital 자기자본;자본금;출자금
equity capital cycle 자기자본사이클
equity capital ratio 자기자본규제비율
equity capital ratio to fixed assets 고정자산자기자본율
equity capital ratio to long-term capital 장기부채자기자본율
equity capital ratio to total debt 총부채자기자본율
equity capital ratio to total liabilities 총부채자기자본비율
equity contribution 출자
equity derivatives 주식파생상품
equity finance 에퀴티파이낸스
equity financing 주식을 통한 자금조달
equity flotation 주식공개
equity fund 주식펀드
equity growth rate 자기자본성장률
equity holder 주주
equity in earnings 순이익에 대한 지분
equity income 지분이익
equity index 지분지수
equity instrument 지분증권
equity investment 주식투자
equity investor 주식투자가
equity margin 공정한 이익
equity market 주식시장
equity method 지분법
equity options 주식옵션
equity options trading 주식옵션거래
equity participant 출자자
equity participation 자본참가
equity partner 출자가
equity position 출자비율
equity purchases by institutions 기관구매
equity put option 주식풋옵션
equity ratio 자기자본비율
equity receiver 회사갱생절차관재인
equity redemption bond 주식상환채
equity repurchase 주식환매
equity risk premium 주식리스크프리미엄
equity securities dealer 주식딜러
equity share 지분주식
equity stake 주식지분
equity structure 자본구성
equity warrant 주식워런트
equity weighting 주식편입률
equity write-off 주식평가손
equivalence 등가
equivalent bond yield 채권상응이율
equivalent coefficient 등가계수
equivalent exchangee 등가교환
equivalent level annual dividend 균등평준연차배당
equivalent taxable yield 조세채권상당이율
equivalent yield 등가이율
era of high interest rate 고금리시대
erection insurance 조립보험
erode 저감하다
erosion in purchasing power 구매력침식
erosion in stock price 주가하락
erratic fluctuation 불안정한 동요
errors and omissions 오차탈루
errors in calculation 계산차이
errors in posting 전달 과정에서 발생한 차이
escalator clause 에스컬레이터조항
escapable cost 회피가능원가
escape clause 면책조항
escrow 조건부 날인증서
escrow account 에스크로계정

escrow agreement 에스크로계약
escrow and trust agreement 에스크로신탁계약
escrow credit 에스크로신용장
escrow fund 기탁자금
escrow letter of credit 기탁신용장
essential condition 필수조건
establishment expenses 사업소비
establishment of corporation 법인설립
establishment of hypothec 저당권설정
establishment of leasehold 차지권설정
establishment of tax liability 납세의무확정
establishment of the right of pledge 질권설정
estate agent 부동산업자
estate contract 부동산계약
estate duty 상속세
estate in possession 소유부동산
estate income 유산소득
estate planning 자산계획
estate tax 상속세
estate upon condition 조건부 부동산권
estate upon limitation 제한부 부동산권
estimate cost 견적원가
estimate of budget requests 개산요구
estimate of sales 예상매상고
estimated appropriation 경비예산
estimated balance sheet 견적대차대조표
estimated cost 개산원가
estimated cost accounting 견적원가계산
estimated cost accounting system 견적원가계산제도
estimated cost of construction work 견적공사원가
estimated exit value 견적매각가격
estimated expenses 견적비용
estimated future income taxes 이연소득세채무
estimated holding period return 예상보유기간수익률
estimated liabilities 견적채무
estimated profit 견적이익
estimated profit and loss statement 견적손익계산서
estimated sales 예상매상고
estimated tax 견적세액
estimated tax prepayment 예정납세
estimated uncollectable amount 수금불능예상액
estimated usable period 사용가능기간
estimated useful life 견적내용연수
estimated useful life of used property 중고자산의 견적내용연수
estimated value 평가가격
estimating-cost system 견적원가제도
estimation error 추정오차
estimation sampling 추정샘플링
estoppel 금반언(禁反言)
estovers 필요물
ethics 윤리
Eurobond 유러채
Eurobond market 유러채시장
Euroclear 유럽시장의 어음교환소
Eurocommercial paper 유러기업어음
Eurocredit market 유러대부시장
Eurocurrency banking market 유러금융시장
Eurocurrency market 유러통화시장
Eurocurrency syndicated loan market 유러통화신디케이트론시장
Eurodollar 유러달러
Eurodollar deposit 유러달러예금
Eurodollar depositary interest futures 유러달러예금금리선물
Eurodollar futures option 유러달러선물옵션
Eurodollar market 유러달러자금시장
Eurodollar time deposit 유러달러정기예금
Euromark futures 유러마크선물
Euromarket 유러시장
Euromoney 유러머니
Euronote 중기유러채
Euronote facility 유러노트퍼실리티
European Atomic Energy Community

유럽원자력공동체
European bond market 유러채시장
European Coal and Steel Community 유럽석탄철강공동체
European Commission 유럽위원회
European Common Market 유럽공동시장
European Community 유럽공동체
European Currency Unit 유럽통화단위
European Depositary Receipts 유럽예탁증권
European Economic Community 유럽경제공동체
European Free Trade Association 유럽자유무역연합
European Fund 유럽펀드
European Investment Bank 유럽투자은행
European Investment Trust 유럽투자신탁기관
European Monetary Agreement 유럽통화협정
European Monetary Cooperation Fund 유럽통화협력기금
European Monetary Fund 유럽통화기금
European Monetary System 유럽통화제도
European option 유러피언옵션
European Options Exchange 유러피언옵션거래소
European Parliament 유럽의회
European Payment Union 유럽지불동맹
European term 유럽방식
European type 유럽타입
European Union 유럽연합
European Unit of Account 유럽계산단위
Europound bond 유러펀드채
Eurosecurity 유러증권
Eurosyndicate loan 유러신디케이트론
Eurotrack 유러트랙
Euroyen 유러엔
Euroyen bond for resident 거주자유러엔채
Euroyen bond issue 유러엔채발행
Euroyen floater 유러엔변동이부채
Euroyen interest rate 유러엔금리
Euroyen market 유러엔시장
evade 회피하다
evaluation of market mechanism 시장기구를 평가함
evaluation of solvency 지불능력평가
evasion of income tax 소득세탈세
even lot 단위주
evening session 이브닝세션
evening up (신용거래나 선물거래에서) 전매나 환매를 마치고 거래관계를 청산함
event insured against 보험사고
event of default 기한이익의 상실사유
event risk 이벤트리스크
event subsequent to balance sheet date 대차대조표일후의 발생사항
evergreen credit 계속적인 신용공여
eviction 퇴거시킴
eviction order 퇴거명령
evidence 증거
evidenced document 증거서류
evidences of indebtedness 채무증서
evidentiary facts 증거사실
evil practice 악용
evolution 진화
ex facto 행위에 바탕을 둔
ex post facto 사후(事後)의
ex works 공장인도
ex-allotment 신주분배; 할당
ex-ante analysis 사전분석
ex-ante test 사전테스트
ex-coupon 이표락
ex-coupon price of bond 채권원가
ex-dividend 배당락
ex-dividend date 배당락일
ex-interest 이자락
ex-interest bond 이락채권
ex-interest for interest-bearing bond 이자부채권의 원가
ex-interest period 이락기간
ex-new 권리락;신주락으로(의)
ex-post alpha value 사후수치

ex-post analysis 사후분석
ex-post assessment 사후평가
ex-post beta 사후베타수치
ex-post characteristic line 사후특성선
ex-post investment 사후투자
ex-post optimum analysis 사후최적분석
ex-post saving 사후저축
ex-post variance 사후차이
ex-rights 권리락
ex-rights of capital increase 증자권리락
ex-stock-dividends 주식배당락
ex-warrant 엑스워런트
ex-warrant bond 순수채권
exaggerated final return 과대신고
examination 심사
examination and decision 심사재결
examination by reference 조사
examination fee 심사료
examination for listing 상장심사
examination of entrance qualification 입회심사
examination of loan application 대출심사
examination of witness 증인심문
examined copy 대조한 등본
except for ~을 제외하고는
excepted perils 면책위험
excepted risks 제외위험
exception principle 예외의 원칙
exception to amortization of deferred charge 이연자산상각특례
exception to depreciation deduction 감가상각특례
exception to the Commercial Code 상법특례
exceptional item 예외사항
exceptional participant 특례참여자
exceptional rates of tax 예외세율
exceptional tax treatment 세무상의 특례
excess 소손해면책
excess and deficiency 과부족
excess burden 초과부담
excess capacity 과잉설비;과잉능력
excess demand 초과수요
excess disbursement 초과지불
excess fund 초과펀드
excess income 초과소득
excess liquidity 과잉유동성
excess margin 초과증거금
excess of debt 채무초과
excess of loss 초과손해액
excess of loss reinsurance 초과손해재보험
excess of loss treaty reinsurance 초과손해액특약재보험
excess over par 자본준비금편입액
excess payment 초과지불
excess profits 초과이윤
excess profits credit 초과이윤공제
excess profits tax 초과이윤
excess receipt over contract price 계약초과금액
excess reserves 초과준비
excess spread 여잉스프레드
excess supply 초과공급
excessive competition 과당경쟁
excessive consumption 과잉소비
excessive depreciation deduction 초과상각
excessive lending 과잉융자
excessive liquidity 과잉유동성
excessive profit 부당이득
excessive savings 과잉저축
excessive seizure 초과차압
excessive service 초과서비스
excessive trading 과잉거래
exchange acquisition 거래소매입
exchange act 거래소법
exchange arbitrage transaction 환재정거래
exchange at night 야간교환
exchange bank 환은행
exchange bill payable 병위채
exchange bought 매환
exchange broker 환브로커
exchange business 환업무
exchange cambist 환딜러

exchange check for money 금전의 인환권
exchange clause 환율문언
exchange clearing 환결제청산
exchange clearing agreement 환청산협정
exchange contract 환예약
exchange contract with option 선택권부 환예약
exchange control 환관리
exchange cover 커버거래
exchange cover rate 환은행이 환보유고를 조정하기 위해 다른 은행과 조건이 일치할 때 하는 거래
exchange dealer 환딜러
exchange dealing 환거래
exchange distribution 거래소분배
exchange dumping 환덤핑
exchange economy 교화경제
exchange equalization account 환평형계정
exchange equalization fund 환평형기금
exchange equalization operation 환평형조작
exchange fluctuation 환변동
exchange fluctuation reserve 환변동준비금
exchange for collection 수금환
exchange for means of foreign payment 대외지불을 위한 환
exchange forward contract 선물환예약
exchange fund cover 자금조정거래
exchange fund cover operation 환자금조정거래
exchange funds operation 자금조작
exchange gain 환차익
exchange gain from the won appreciation 원고차익
exchange gain or loss 환환산차손익
exchange intervention 환개입
exchange law 거래소법
exchange link 외국환의 링크
exchange loss 환차손
exchange loss and profit 환차손익
exchange manipulation 환조작
exchange market 거래소시장
exchange marriage profit 환매리이익
exchange marry 환매리
exchange member 거래소회원
exchange of equivalents 등가교환
exchange of machinery and equipment owned by the government 국유기계설비교환
exchange of money 환전
exchange of notes 교환공문
exchange of property 자산교환
exchange of shares 주식교환
exchange operation 환조작
exchange parity 환평가
exchange position 환보유고
exchange premium 환프리미엄
exchange profit 환차익
exchange quotation 대고객환상장
exchange rate 환율
exchange rate against dollar 대달러환상장
exchange rate at break-even point 손익분기환상장
exchange rate band 환상장권
exchange rate basket 통화바스켓
exchange rate in favor of won 원고
exchange rate in foreign currency 외화기준상장
exchange rate per dollar 달러환율
exchange rate policy 환율정책
exchange reservation 환예약
exchange risk cover 환보유고조정조작
exchange risk insurance 환변동보험
exchange settlement 환결제
exchange sold 매환
exchange speculation 환투기
exchange stabilization fund 환안정기금
exchange tax 거래소별세
exchange ticket 주문집행확인서
exchange trade 거래소거래
exchange value 교환가격
exchange-traded issue 상장상품
exchangeable bond 타사주식교환가능채권
Exchequer 영국재무부

exchequer bills 영국재무부증권
excise duty 물품세
exclusion clause 제외조항;면책조항
exclusion from capital gain 캐피탈게인에서 공제함
exclusion from expenses 손금불산입
exclusion from expenses of corporation tax 법인세액손금불산입
exclusion from expenses of entertainment and social expenses 교환비손금불산입
exclusion from expenses of remuneration of director 임원보수손금불산입
exclusion from gross revenue 익금불산입
exclusion from taxation 비과세
exclusion of dividends from gross revenue 수취배당손금불산입
exclusion of loss 손실제외
exclusion of profit accrued from valuation profit 평가익의 익금불산입
exclusion of refund from gross revenue 환부금의 익금불산입
exclusive agent 독점대리점
exclusive dealing 경쟁품취급금지계약
exclusive distributor 독점판매업자
exclusive distributorship 독점판매권
exclusive jurisdiction 전속관할권
exclusive privilege 독점권
exclusive right 독점권
exclusive selling agent 독점판매대리점
exclusive use 전용
exclusive use of a new production 신생산방식을 독점함
exclusive use of property 자산을 전속적으로 이용함
exclusive-occupation house 전용주택
exculpate 죄를 면하게 하다
excuse 변명;면책사유
executed 이미 이행한
executed contract of sale 완성매매계약
execution creditor 집행채권자
execution of order 주문집행
execution organ 실행기관
executive committee 집행위원회
executive compensation option 임원보장을 위한 옵션
executive debtor 집행채무자
executive directors 대표이사
executive measure 집행처분
executive officer 집행관리
executive organ 집행기관
executive pension 경영자연금
executive power 집행권
executive proceedings 집행절차
executive salaries 임원보수
executive summary 개요
executive vice president 부이사장
executory contract 미확정의 계약 (미확정계약)
executory interest 장래권
exemplar company 모범기업
exemplification 인증등본
exempt corporation 비과세법인
exempt from taxation 면세의
exempt gift 비과세증여
exempt income 비과세소득
exempt private company 면제사회사(私會社)
exempt property 비과세재산
exempt stock exchange 등록면제거래소
exempted amount 공제액
exempted securities 적용제외증권
exemption agreement 면책약관
exemption and deduction from income 소득공제
exemption clause 면책조항
exemption for aged person 노령자공제
exemption for handicapped person 장애자공제
exemption for spouse 배우자공제
exemption for working student 근로학생공제
exemption from return of subsidy 보조금반환면제

exemption from taxation 면세
exemption method 외국소득면제방식
exemption of debt 채무면제
exemption of gift tax 증여세면제
exemption of inheritance tax 상속세면제
exemption of real estate acquisition tax 부동산취득세비과세
exemption of taxes 조세면제
exemption point 면세점
exemption regime 적용제외범위
exemptions 차압금지채권
exercise day 권리행사일
exercise limit 권리행사가 인정된 거래량
exercise notice 권리행사통지
exercise of claim on clearing margin 증거금에 대한 권리행사
exercise of preemptive rights 신주인수권 행사
exercise of right 권리행사
exercise of security right 담보권 행사
exercise of stock option 스톡옵션행사
exercise of voting rights 의결권행사
exercise period 권리행사기간
exercise price 행사가격
exercise volume 권리행사수량
exercised value 권리행사가격
exhaustion 소모
exhibit 증거서류; 첨부서류
EXIM bank 수출입은행
existing assets 기존자산
existing debt 기존채무
existing exposure 여신잔고
existing issue 이미 발행한 상품
existing preferential duties 기존특혜
exit bond 졸업채
exit price 발매가격
exit value 발매가액
exogenous change 외생변화
exogenous demand 외생수요
exogenous variables 외생변수
exoneration 면책
exorbitant profit 법외이익
exotic bond 엑조틱본드
exotic currency 엑조틱커런시
exotic derivatives 엑조틱파생상품
exotic option 엑조틱옵션
expanded EC 확대EC
expanded lead manager 확대주간사
expansion of a new market 신시장개척
expansion of currency 통화팽창
expansion path 확대경로
expansion period 경기확대기간
expansionary budget 적극예산
expansive economy 확대경제
expectant heir 기대상속인
expectation gap 기대갭
expectation hypothesis 기대가설
expectation of life 평균여명
expectation theory 기대이론
expected annual volume 기대연간조업도
expected earnings 기대수익
expected earnings growth rate 기대이익성장률
expected holding-period rate of return 기대보유기간수익률
expected income 예정수입
expected life 견적내용연수
expected loss 예상손실
expected mortality rate 예정사망률
expected profit 기대이윤
expected return ratio of loan trust 대부신탁예상배당률
expected value 기대치
expected volatility 예상변동률
expected wealth effect 기대자금효과
expected yield 기대이율
expected yield-to-maturity 기대만기이율
expendable fund 지출가능자금
expenditure 지출
expenditure curtailment 지출삭감
expenditure for public bond 공채비
expenditure for public works 공공사업비

expenditure incurred for the restoring to its original state 원장을 회복하기 위한 지출
expenditure on capital accounts 자본계정지출
expenditure on unemployment benefit 실업보험지출
expenditure rate 지출율
expenditure tax 지출세
expenditure unaccounted for 사용용도불명금
expense account balance 경비계정잔고
expense budget 경비예산
expense distribution 비용배부
expense item 비목
expense ledger 경비원장
expense ratio 경비율
expense reduction 경비소멸
expense report 경비보고
expenses for education and culture 교양비
expenses incurred for having the user remove 이전료
expenses incurred for maintaining household 가사관련비
expenses incurred for opening of business 개업비
expenses incurred for the fire 화재로 인해 발생한 비용
expenses incurred for the transfer 양도비용
expenses of bringing up children 양육비
expenses of entering port 입항비용
expenses paid in advance 미경과비용
expenses quota 경비할당
experience assumptions 기초율
experienced judgment 경험상의 판단
experimental and research expense 시험연구비
experimental and research expense tax credit 시험연구비세액공제
experimental manufacturing cost 시작비
expert system 익스퍼트시스템
expiration date 만기일
expiration date of the credit card 카드유효기한
expiration day of the exercise 권리행사일
expiration of obligation 채무소멸
expiration of option 옵션소멸
expired card 기한이 끝난 카드
expired cost 소멸원가
expiry 기한만료
explanatory leaflet for financial futures transaction 금융선물거래설명서
explanatory note 주석
explanatory notes to the financial statements 재무제표각주
explicit cost 명시적 비용
explicit model 명시모델
exploitation 착취
exploitation of new resources 신자원개발
explosive growth 폭발적인 신장
exponential curve 지수곡선
exponential distribution 지수분포
export account 환당좌대
export advance 수출전도금
export advance loan 수출전대금융
export advanced account 수출전대계정
export and import price index 수출입물가지수
export and import statistics 외국무역통계
export bill 수출어음
export bounty 수출장려금
export cartel 수출카르텔
export competition 수출경쟁
export credit 수출신용
export credit guarantee 수출신용보증
export declaration 수출신고
export dependence 수출의존
export drive 수출드라이브
export duties 수출세
export earnings 수출이익
export exemption 수출면세
export financing 수출금융
export function 수출함수
export growth 수출신장

export import loan 수출입론
export industry 수출산업
export letter of credit 수출신용장
export license 수출승인증
export mix 수출구성
export of capital 자본수출
export of goods purchased 구입한 물품을 수출함
export on consignment 위탁판매수출
export permission 수출허가
export price index 수출물가지수
export proceeds 수출대금
export profitability 수출의 수익성
export stocks 수출관련주
export subsidy 수출보조금
export supplier credit 수출업자신용
export tax 수출세
export to an overseas territory 이출(移出)
export usance 수출유전스
export-import bank 수출입은행
Export-Import Bank of Japan 일본수출입은행
Export-Import Bank of USA 미국수출입은행
exposure draft 공개초안
exposure profile 리스크프로파일
exposure to counterpary 카운터파티리스크
exposure to interest rate 금리리스크
exposure to risk 리스크부담
express contract 명시계약
express trust 명시신탁
express warranty 명시담보
expropriation 공용징수
expropriation loss 접수로 인한 손실
expulsion 제명
expulsion from membership 제명
extel card 익스텔카드
extended benefit 확장급부
extended bill 연기어음
extended coverage 확장담보특약
extended fund facility 확대신용공여제도
extended insurance 연장보험
extendible maturity 연장가능만기
extensible swap 연장가능형 스와프
extension 확장
extension effect 기간효과
extension of credit 신용공여
extension of due date 납기연장
extension of loan 융자실행
extension of the maturity 상환연장
extension of time claims 연장클레임
extension of time for completion 공기연장
extension of time to file 제출연기
extension of disclosure 개시범위
extenuation 경감
external account 대외수지
external audit 외부감사
external auditor 외부감사인
external bond 외채
external capital 외부자본
external consistency 외부정합성
external debt 외채
external demand 외수
external diseconomy 외부불경제
external economy 외부경제
external equilibrium 대외균형
external financing 외부금융
external fund 외부자금
external hazard 외부위험
external liabilities 외부부채
external liquidity 외부유동성
external loan 외채
external pressure 외압
external purchasing power of money 화폐의 대외가치
external rate of return 외부수익률
external reserves 외화준비
external resources 외부자원
external transaction 외부거래
external transactions account 해외계정거래
external user 사외이용자
external valuation 외부평가

extinction 소멸
extinction of hypothec 저당권소멸
extinctive prescription 소멸시효
extinguishment of property 자산의 소실
extra charges 부대비용
extra cost 추가비용
extra depreciation 할증상각
extra dividend 특별배당
extra expenditure 임시비
extra item 이상항목
extra premium 할증보험료
extra wage 할증임금
extra work claims 여분공사클레임
extramural 구역외의
extraneous risk 부가위험
extraordinary average 비상해손(海損)
extraordinary depreciation 특별상각
extraordinary expenditure 임시경비지출
extraordinary expenses 임시비
extraordinary gain 특별이익
extraordinary gain or loss 특별손익
extraordinary general meeting 임시총회
extraordinary income 임시소득
extraordinary item 특별손익항목
extraordinary loss 특별손실
extraordinary measures 비상조치
extraordinary profit and loss 특별손익
extraordinary profit and loss item 특별손익항목
extraordinary repairs 임시수선비
extraordinary resolution 임시결의
extraterritorial application 역외적용
extraterritoriality 치외법권
extraterritoriality on tax laws 면세특권
extrinsic evidence 외부증거

F

fabless 제조부문이 없는 개발메이커
fabricating cost 제조원가
fabrication 위조
face amount 액면금액
face of instrument 증서의 문면
face of note 할부가격
face value 액면가액
facilities 설비
facilities for buying and selling 매매를 위한 시설
facilities fee 퍼실리티요금
fact book 팩트북
fact finding 사실조사
fact in issue 주요사실
factor beta 팩터베타
factor cost 요소원가
factor income 요소소득
factor price 요소가격
factor return 요소수익률
factor risk 팩터리스크
factor technology 요소기술
factorage 팩터수수료
factoral 제조요소의
factoring 외상채권매입업무;팩터링
factors of production 생산요소
factory 공장
factory account 공장계정
factory accounting 공장회계
factory bookkeeping 공업부기
factory burden 공장간접비
factory cost 공장원가
factory cost report 제조원가보고서
factory expenses 제조간접비
factory expenses variance 경비차액
factory fitting 공장비품
factory furniture 공장용 집기
factory furnitures and fixtures 공장비품
factory ledger 공장원장
factory ledger account 공장원계정
factory overhead 제조간접비
factory supplies 공장용 소모품
facultative reinsurance 임의재보험
facultative reinsurance agreement 임의재보험협정
faculty theory of taxation 지불능력과세설
fade-out formula 페이드아웃방식
fade-out policy 외자비율소멸정책
fail position 불이행포지션
failed financial institution 파탄금융기관
failing company 파탄기업
failing of record 기록미제출
failure 불이행
failure of consideration 약인멸실
failure to consider dividend policy 배당에 배려가 결핍됨
failure to file a return 무신고
failure to pay 지불불능
failure to settle 결제불이행
fair 공평한
fair and equitable 공정과 형평
fair and orderly market 공평하고 질서 있는 시장

fair average quality 평균품질
fair leasehold value 차지권가격
fair market value 공정시장가격;시가
fair price 공정가격
fair price formation 공정한 가격형성
fair trade bureau 공정거래국
Fair Trade Commission 공정거래위원회
fair value 공정가치
fair value accounting 시가주의회계
fair wage 적정임금
fairness 공평성
fairy and impartially 공평하게
fall 하강
fall of gold standard 금본위제도붕괴
fall under 해당하다
falling in price 가격하락
falling in stock price 주가하락
falling interest rate 금리하락
falling market 하락기조상장
falling off 주가폭락
false declaration 부정신고
false demonstration 오류표시
false missing 위장분실
false personation 성명사기
false rally 반등
false report 허위보고
false representation 허위표시
false return 허위신고
false statement 허위진술
false trade description 허위상품표시
faltering economies 경기냉각
family allowance 가족수당
family bookkeeping 가계부
family company 동족회사
family fund 패밀리펀드
family income and expenditure survey 가계조사(家計調査)
family partnership 동족조합
family personal accident policy 가족상해보험
family policy 가족보험
family saving survey 저축동향조사
family taxation of assets income 자산소득의 세대합산과세
family-register 호적
fan line 팬라인
fan theory 팬이론
fancy stocks 저가주
Fannie Mae 패니메이;저당증권
fare 운임
farm accounting 농업회계
farm subsidy 농업보조금
Farmer MAC 연방농업금융저당금고
fast growth 급성장
fault 과실
favorable 순조
favorable balance of overall 종합수지흑자
favorable balance of payments 국제수지흑자
favorable balance of trade 무역수지흑자
favorable balance on current account 경상수지흑자
favorable cash flows 바람직한 현금의 흐름
favorable factor 호재
favorable leverage effect 긍정적인 증익효과
favorable news 호재
favorable treatment 우대조치
favorable variance 유리차이
favored stock 인기주
fear 경계
feasibility study 타당성조사
feasible 실행가능한
features 특징
Fed 연방준비제도이사회
Fed fund rate **FF** 금리
Fed fund target **FF** 금리유도목표
Fed watcher **FRB** 전문가
Fed wire 연방전신이체
Federal Advisory Committee 연방자문위원회
federal agency 연방기관
federal agency securities 연방기관증권
Federal Banking Commission 연방은행위원회

Federal Bankruptcy Act 연방파산법
Federal Communication Commission 연방통신위원회
federal court 연방법원
Federal Credit Union Act of 1934 연방신용조합법
federal deposit insurance 연방예금보험
Federal Deposit Insurance Corporation 연방예금보험공사
federal financing bank 연방금융은행
federal fund 연방자금
federal fund market 연방자금시장
federal fund rate 연방자금금리
Federal Home Loan Bank 연방주택대부은행
Federal Home Loan Bank Board 연방주택대부은행이사회
Federal Home Loan Bank System 연방주택대부은행제도
Federal Home Loan Mortgage Corporation 연방주택금융저당금고
Federal Housing Administration 연방주택국
federal income tax 연방소득세
federal intermediate credit banks 연방중개신용은행
Federal Land Bank 연방토지은행
federal loan guarantee 연방정부론보증
Federal National Mortgage Association 연방저당금고
Federal Open Market Commission 연방공개시장위원회
Federal Reserve Act 연방준비법
Federal Reserve Bank 연방준비은행
Federal Reserve Bank of New York 뉴욕연방준비은행
Federal Reserve Board 연방준비제도이사회
Federal Reserve District 연방준비지구
Federal Reserve membership of state banks 주법은행이 연방준비제도에 가맹함
Federal Reserve Notes 연방준비증서
Federal Reserve open market operation 연방공개시장조작
Federal Reserve Reform Act 연방준비개혁법
Federal Reserve System 연방준비제도
Federal Savings and Loan Insurance Corporation 연방저축대부보험회사
Federal spending 연방정부지출
Federal Trade Commission 연방거래위원회
Federal of Bankers Associations of Japan 일본은행협회연합회
Federal of Economic Organizations 경제단체연합회
Federal of Tax Accountants 세리사연합회
fee and commission 수수료
fee business 수수료사업
fee for book-entry transfer 대체결제수수료
fee for legal advice 법률상담료
fee for settlement 결제에 필요한 수수료
fee income 수수료수입
fee on loans 대출수수료
fee simple 단순부동산권
fee simple absolute 절대적인 부동산보유권
feedback 피드백
fees after listing 상장후 비용
fees and permits 면허료
fees for custody 보관수수료
fees for off-floor distribution 입회외 분매취급료
fees for original listing 신규상장수수료
fees for stock name transfers 명의변경수수료
fees for withdrawals of stock certificates 교부수수료
fellowship grant 연구보조금
feneration 고리대
feverish market 과열장세
Fibonacci sequence 피보나치수열
fictitious account 가공계좌
fictitious assets 의제자산
fictitious capital 의제자본
fictitious coupon 간주이자
fictitious demand 가수요
fictitious dividend 회사신용을 유지하기 위한 배당

fictitious name deposit 가공명의예금
fictitious price 에누리
fictitious profit 가공이익
fictitious sales slip 가공매상전표
fictitious transaction 가공거래
fidelity bond 신용보험
fidelity guarantee insurance 신원신용보험
fiduciary 수탁자
fiduciary accounting 신탁회계
fiduciary business 신탁업무
fiduciary contract 신탁계약
fiduciary duty 신탁의무
fiduciary estate 신탁재산
fiduciary fund 신탁기금
fiduciary issue 보증발행
fiduciary power 신탁권한
fiduciary responsibility 수탁자책임
field audit 실지감사
field examinations 임점검사
field inspection 현장감사
field inspector 현장감사인
field-work audit standards 감사실시기준
fifty percent depreciation 이분의 일 상각법
fifty percent owned company 이분의 일 소유회사
file 제출하다
file and use 신고후 사용제
file income tax return 소득액을 신고하다
filing 파일링
filing date 제출일
filing of a seal-impression 인감신고
filing of claims 채권신고
filing of final return of merger 합병확정신고
filing of final return on corporation tax 법인세확정신고서제출
fill or kill 즉시집행
fill-or-kill order 즉시 또는 취소주문
filling of orders 주문집행
filing up of a deficit 적자보전
filing accounts 최종결산
final audit 기말감사
final balance 기말잔고;최종잔고
final balance method 최종잔고방식
final beneficiary 최종수익자
final bid-asked quotation 최종특별시세
final cash settlement 최종결제
final claim 본클레임
final demand 최종수요
final depreciable limit 상각가능한도액
final maturity 만기
final payment 확정신고에 따른 납부
final phase 최종국면
final products 최종생산물
final prospectus 최종설립취지서
final quarter 사사분기
final rate of return 최종수익률
final return 확정신고
final return in the case of loss 손실신고서
final return of liquidation 청산확정신고서
final return of loss 확정손실신고서
final return of merger 합병확정신고서
final session of a month 납회
final session of a year 대납회
final settlement of accounts 확정한 결산
final tax return 확정신고
final trading day 최종거래일
final value 종가
final yield 최종이익
final yield on investment 최종투자이익
finally settled financial statements 최종적으로 확정한 재무제표
finance accounting 금융어음
finance bill 정부단기증권
finance capital 금융자본
finance charge 금융비용
finance company 금융회사
finance for deficit 적자금융
finance for prepaid installment sales 전불식 할부판매금융
finance law 재정법
finance lease 파이낸스리스
Finance Ministry note 재무부증권

E F

Finance Ministry Ordinance 재무부령
finance receivable 대출채권
finance receivables as collateral 채권담보
Finance System Council 재정제도심의회
financial accommodation 재무회계
financial accounting 재무회계
Financial Accounting Foundation 재무회계재단
Financial Accounting Standards Advisory Council 재무회계기준자문위원회
Financial Accounting Standards Board 재무회계기준심의회
financial accounting standards for business enterprise 기업회계원칙
financial accounts 금융계정
financial activities 금융활동
financial advisor 재무고문
financial affairs 재무
financial agreement 금융협정
financial aid 금융원조
financial analysis 재무분석
Financial Analysts Federation 전미증권분석가연합회
financial arrangement 파이낸스중개
financial asset value 금융자산가치
financial assets 금융자산
financial assets and liabilities account 금융자산부채잔고표
financial assets of individuals 개인금융자산
financial audit 재무감사
financial balance 재무밸런스
financial books 회계장부
financial budget 재무예산
financial capital 금융자본
financial center 금융중심지
financial claim 금융채권
financial clique 재벌
financial collapse 금융붕괴
financial community 금융업계
financial condition 재무내용
financial conditions 재정상태
financial consultant 재무컨설턴트
financial contribution 자금협력
financial cost 재무코스트
financial crisis 금융공황
financial decision 금융면의 결단
financial deficit 자금부족
financial democracy 재정민주주의
financial difficulty 금융난
financial disclosure 재무내용개시
financial documents 계산서류
financial engineering 재테크
financial environment 금융환경
Financial Executive Institute 재무담당경영자협회
financial expenses 금융비용
financial exposure 금융담보
financial facilities 금융서비스
financial flow 재무플로
financial forward contract 금융선도계약
financial futures 금융선물
financial futures contract 금융선물계약
financial futures exchange 금융선물거래소
financial futures instrument 금융선물상품
financial futures market 금융선물시장
financial futures option 금융선물옵션
financial futures transaction 금융선물거래
financial gearing 재무레버리지
financial guarantee 자력보증
financial guarantor 신용보증회사
financial guaranty insurance 금융보증보험
financial highlights 경리의 하이라이트
financial holding company 금융지주회사
financial income 금융수익
financial indexes 금융지표
financial innovation 금융혁신
financial institution 금융기관
financial institution for agriculture forestry and fisheries 농림어업금융기관
financial institution for foreign exchange 외국환금융기관

financial institutions for long-term credit 장기신용금융기관
financial institutions for small business 중소기업금융기관
financial instrument 금융상품
financial intermediaries or brokers 금융중개기관
Financial Investment and Loan Program 재정투융자계획
financial item 금융항목
financial lease 금융리스
financial leverage 재무레버리지
financial leverage effect 재무면의 증익효과
financial leverage ratio 재무레버리지비율
financial liability 금융부채
financial liberalization 금융자유화
Financial Liberalization Fund 금융자유화대책자금
financial liberalization policy 금융자유화정책
financial management 재무관리
financial margin 금융수익
financial market 금융시장
financial market analysis 금융시장분석
financial market globalization 금융시장 글로벌화
financial market liberalization 금융시장자유화
financial measurement 재무지표
financial model 금융모델
Financial News index option 파이낸셜뉴스지수옵션
financial obligation 금융채무
financial operations 금융업
financial option contract 금융옵션
financial option market 금융옵션시장
financial panic 금융공황
financial planner 파이낸셜플래너
financial planning 재무계획
financial policy 금융정책
financial position 재정상태
financial position statement 대차대조표
financial product 금융상품
financial profit 금융수익
financial ratio 재무비율
financial recession 금융불황
financial regulation 금융규제
financial report 유가증권보고서
financial reporting 재무보고
financial reporting accounting 재무보고회계
financial research center 금융연구소
financial resources 재원
financial retrenchment 경비절감
financial revenue 재무수익
financial review 재무개황
financial revolution 금융혁명
financial risk 재무리스크
financial sector 금융섹터
financial sector stocks 금융주
financial service 금융서비스
Financial Services Act 금융서비스법
financial slack 재무상의 슬랙
financial statement 재무제표
financial statement analysis 재무제표분석
financial statement audit 재무제표감사
financial statistics 금융통계
financial status 재정상태
financial strain and stress 금융긴박
financial strength 재무건전성
financial structure 재무체질
financial surplus 자금여잉
financial surplus or deficit 자금과부족
financial synergy 재무상의 상승효과
financial system 금융제도
Financial system Research Council 금융제도조사회
financial target 재무목표
Financial Times Index of Industrial Ordinary Shares 파이낸셜타임즈공업주가지수
Financial Times Index of Industrial Sensitive World Commodity Prices 파이낸셜타임즈공업주가지수

financial transaction 금융거래
financial variables 재무지표;재무수치
financial year 회계연도
financier 출자자
financing 자금조달
financing activities 재무활동
financing adjustment law 자금조정법
financing bills 금융단기증권
financing burden 금융부담
financing business industry 금융업계
financing by public institutions for implementing policies 제도금융
financing charge 금융비용
financing corporation 금융회사
financing cost 자금조달비용
financing for carrying unsold inventories 체화금융
financing for deficit-covering 적자융자
financing for sales by installment payment 월부판매금융
financing for stocks 주식자금조달
financing from brokers' own capital 자기융자
financing lease 파이낸스리스
financing method 자금조달방법
financing policy 금융조달방침
financing regulation 융자준칙
financing vehicle 금융수단
finder 파인더
fine 과태료
finished goods 완성품
finished goods ledger 제품원장
finished goods on hand 소유제품
finished product ledger 제품금융
finished products 완성품
finished products account 제품계정
finished products inventory 제품재고액
finished products on hand 제품소지액
finite difference 유한차분
fire and casualty insurance 화재손해보험
Fire and Marine Insurance Rating Association of Japan 일본손해보험요율산정회
fire and other casualty insurance premiums deduction 손해보험공제
fire clause 화재보험약관
fire insurance 화재보험
fire insurance on dwelling houses 주택화재보험
fire insurance premium 화재보험료
fire insurance proceeds 화재보험금
fire loss 화재손실
fire loss suspense account 화재손실미결산계정
fire mutual insurance 화재상호보험
fire policy 화재보험증권
fire wall 방화벽
fire-insurance for mortgagee interest 채권보전화재보험
firm 사업법인
firm banking 펌뱅킹
firm bid 확정매호수치
firm commitment 확약;전액인수
firm commitment underwriting 매입인수
firm contract 확정계약
firm offer 확정가격제시
firm order 확정주문
firm price 확정가격
firm tone of the U. S. dollar 달러고기조
firmer 강보합
firmer tone 시세가 오를듯한 기세
first bottom 가장 아래
first check 초감
first cost 구입원가
first demand bond 퍼스트디맨드본드
first exchange 제 1권
first generation on-line system 일차온라인
first instance 제 1심
first lien mortgage 제 1순위 모기지
first mortgage 제 1저당
first mortgage bond 제 1순위 저당권부 사채
first mortgage loan 제 1순위 모기지론

first peak 첫 천정
first preferred stock 제일우선주식
first priority 최우선
first purchaser 최초취득자
first refusal 제 1거부권
first section market 일부상장
first session of a month 발회
first session of a year 대발회
first surplus treaty 일차초과액특약
first year commission 초년도수수료
first-in first-out method 선입선출법
first-loss insurance 실손전보
fiscal agency 재무대리인
fiscal agenda 재무정책
fiscal agent 재무대리인
fiscal agent agreement 재무대리인계약
fiscal agent for treasury fund 국고재무대리인
fiscal and monetary policy 재정금융정책
fiscal balance 재정수지
fiscal boost 재정자극
fiscal consolidation 재정통합
fiscal deficit 재정적자
fiscal drug 재정팽창억제
fiscal expenditure 재정지출
fiscal illusion 재정착각
fiscal inflation 재정인플레이션
fiscal inflexibility 재정경직화
fiscal investment 재정투자
fiscal investment and loan 재정투융자
fiscal outlook 재정예견
fiscal period 회계기간
fiscal policy 재정정책
fiscal privileges of diplomat 외교관과세특권
fiscal reform 재정개혁
fiscal reserve 재정준비
fiscal resources for redemption 상환재원
fiscal stimulus package 재정자극책
fiscal structure 재정본질
fiscal surplus 재정흑자
fiscal target 재정목표
fiscal tightness 재정핍박
fiscal year 회계연도
fiscal year closed 결산기
Fisher effect 피셔효과
fishery; agriculture and forestry industry 농림수산업
5 year government bond futures 중기국채선물거래
5-year discount government bonds 5년할인국채
5-year Japanese government bond 중기일본국채
fixed amount 정액
fixed amount method 정액법
fixed amount minimum payment 최저한도지불의무액
fixed amount taxation 정액과세
fixed annuity 정액연금
fixed arrangement 고정성 배열법
fixed asset ledger 고정자산대장
fixed asset ratio 고정자산비율
fixed asset register 고정자산대장
fixed asset schedule 고정자산명세표
fixed asset tax 고정자산세
fixed asset to net worth ratio 고정비율
fixed asset turnover ratio 고정자산회전율
Fixed Asset Valuation Council 고정자산평가심의회
fixed assets 고정자산
fixed assets acquired as contribution in kind to capital 현물출자로 취득한 고정자산
fixed assets acquired through merger 합병으로 취득한 고정자산
fixed budget 고정예산
fixed capital 고정자본
fixed capital investment 고정자본투자
fixed cash flow 고정금리캐시플로
fixed charge 특정담보
fixed charge coverage 금융비용커버리지
fixed collateral 근저당
fixed costs and expenses 고정비

fixed coupon bond 확정이부채
fixed date 확정일부
fixed date delivery 확정일인도
fixed debt 고정차입금
fixed deposit 정기예금
fixed difference 확정차액
fixed exchange rate 고정환율
fixed exchange rate system 고정환율제도
fixed expenses 고정비
fixed fee 정율보수
fixed gain 확정이익
fixed general tariff 고정세율
fixed income 고정수입
fixed income assets 확정이자부 자산
fixed income benchmark 채권지표상품
fixed income debt 채권
fixed income market 고정채시장; 채권시장
fixed income securities 확정소득증권
fixed income warrant 데트워런트
fixed installment method 정액법
fixed interest 확정이자
fixed interest-bearing bond 확정이자부 채권
fixed liabilities 고정부채
fixed liquidity reserve requirements 고정유동비율제도
fixed loan 고정대부금
fixed maturity 확정기일
fixed mortgage 근저당권
fixed obligations 확정채무
fixed overhead 고정비
fixed parity system 고정평가제
fixed payment bond 확정기일 상환채
fixed percentage depreciation 정율감가상각법
fixed percentage method 감가정율법
fixed percentage on declining balance method 감가정율법
fixed price 고정가격
fixed price contract 고정가격계약
fixed property 부동산
fixed rate 고정금리
fixed rate annuity 정액연금
fixed rate assets 고정금리자산
fixed rate bond 고정이자부 채권
fixed rate liability 고정금리부채
fixed rate payer 고정금리지불인
fixed rate swap 고정금리스와프
fixed rate tax reduction 정율감세
fixed ratio 고정비율
fixed return insurance 정액보험
fixed return securities 고정이율증권
fixed salary 고정급
fixed share 고정쉐어
fixed tax rate 일정세율
fixed unit investment trust 고정단위형 투자신탁
fixed wages 고정급
fixed weight index 고정웨이트지수
fixed-amount membership fee 정액회비
fixed-rate membership fee 정율회비
fixed-rate transfer 정율편입
fixtures 부대설비
flag 깃발
flat 균일의;배당락의
flat curve 플랫커브
flat exchange contract 균일환예약
flat fee 일률적인 수수료
flat growth 동일한 성장률
flat loan 플랫론
flat market 플랫마켓
flat price 균일요금
flat rate 균일요율;균일레이트
flattening of curve 장단이율격차평준화
flattening of the yield curve 이율곡선평준화
flaw 결점
flea market 도떼기(고물, 벼룩)시장
fleet insured 플리트계약자
flexible budget 탄력예상
flexible exchange rate 변동환율제
flexible forward contract 렌지포워드거래
flexible tariff 신축세율
flexible-premium variable life insurance

변액유니버설보험
flier 광고쪽지; 등귀
flight money 도피자금
flight to quality 질로 도피함
flip-flop FRN 플립플롭채권
floatation cost 기채비용
floater 변동이자부 채권
floating assets 유동자산
floating basis 플로팅베이시스
floating capital 유동자본
floating charge 유동담보
floating debt 유동채무
floating exchange rate 변동환율
floating exchange rate system 변동환율제
floating interest rate 변동이율
floating interest rate account with ceiling 변동상한금리부 계정
floating liability 유동부채
floating policy 유동보험증권
floating prime rate 시장연동형 우대금리
floating property 포괄재산
floating rate 변동금리
floating rate bond 변동이자부 채권
floating rate certificate of deposit 변동금리 CD
floating rate index 변동금리지표
floating rate lending 변동금리대출
floating rate market 변동이자부 채권시장
floating rate mortgage 변동이자부 모기지
floating rate note 변동이자부 채권
floating shareholder 유동주주
floating shares 유동주
floating stock 유동주
floating supply 매매수요
floating system 변동상장
floating-rate payer 변동금리지불인
floor broker 중매인
floor clerk 증권업자의 대리인으로서 거래소에 나와 거래하는 사람
floor issue 입회장상품
floor member 입회장회원
floor middleman 입회장종업원
Floor Order Routing and Execution System 입회장사무합리화시스템
floor price 바닥시세
floor rate 하한금리
floor representative 증권업자의 대리인으로서 거래소에 나와 거래하는 사람
floor trader 플로어트레이더; 룸트레이더
floor trading 입회장거래
floored swap 플로어드스와프
flotation of external loan 외채모집
flotation of government bond 공채발행
flotation of loan 기채
flotsam 표류물
flow chart 플로차트
flow diagram 플로다이아그램
flow of fund accounts 자금순환계정
flow of funds analysis 자금순환분석
flow through method 플로스루법
flower bond 플라워본드
fluctuate 변동하다
fluctuating and extraordinary income 변동소득 및 임시소득
fluctuating income 변동소득
fluctuation analysis 변동분석
fluctuation clause 변동조항
fluctuation limit 가격변동폭제한
fluctuation of stock prices 주가동향
follow-up selling 권유장을 내어 판매함
food bill 식량증권
Food Management Special Account 식량관리특별회계
Food Securities 식량증권
foods industry 식료품업계
footing 계산다툼
footnote 각주
for customer's account 위탁분의
for one's proprietary account 자기분의
force majeure 불가항력
force majeure clause 불가효력조항
forced auction 강제경매

forced conversion 강제전환
forced exchange 강제교환
forced liquidation 강제청산
forced sale 강제매각
forced saving 강제저축
forced-sale value 강제처분가치
forcible disposition 강제처분
forcible execution 강제집행
forcible provisions 강행규정
forecast by the econometric model 계량모델예측
forecast for market tendency 상장관
forecast of performance results 실적예상
forecast of sales 예상매상고
forecasting model 예측모델
foreclosed assets 담보권행사자금
foreclosure 담보권행사
foreclosure sales 담보권행사에 따른 매각
foregift 권리금
forehand rent 전불지대
foreign affiliate 외자계 기업
foreign agents accounts 외국대리점계정
foreign assets 해외자본
foreign banks in Japan 재일외은
foreign bill 외국어음
foreign bill of exchange 외국환어음
foreign bond 외국채권
foreign branch 해외지점
foreign branch account 해외지점계정
foreign branch-our account 외국지점발송계정
foreign branch-their account 외국지점피발송계정
foreign buying 외국인구매
foreign capital 외자
foreign capital consumer finance company 외자계 소비자금융
foreign capital inducement 외자흡수
foreign claims and debt 대외채권채무
foreign company 외국기업
foreign corporation 외국법인
foreign corporation tax 외국법인세
foreign corporation tax credit 외국법인세액공제
Foreign Credit Insurance Association 외국신용보험협회
foreign currency 외화
foreign currency account 외화계정
foreign currency bill receivable 외화징수외국환
foreign currency bond 외화채
foreign currency borrowing 외화차입
foreign currency denominated 외화기준
foreign currency denominated bond 외화기준외국채
foreign currency deposit 외화예금
foreign currency deposit account 외화예금계정
foreign currency deposit with exchange bank 외화예탁
foreign currency deposits 외화예금
foreign currency forward 환선물계약
foreign currency futures 외국통화선물
foreign currency futures contracts 외국통화선물계약
foreign currency holdings 외화보유고
foreign currency inflow 외화유입
foreign currency reserves 외화준비
foreign currency securities 외화증권
foreign currency series securities 외화기준증권
foreign currency statements 외화표시재무제표
foreign currency transactions 외화거래
foreign currency translation gain or loss 환차손
foreign currency-denominated bond 외화기준채권
foreign debt 대외채권
foreign debt servicing 대외채무반제
foreign demand 외수
foreign direct investment 해외직접투자

foreign direct investment regulation 직접투자규제
foreign exchange 외국환
foreign exchange account 외국환계정
foreign exchange allocation system 외화할당제
Foreign Exchange and Foreign Trade Control Law 외국환관리법
foreign exchange bank 외국환은행
foreign exchange bill 외국환어음
foreign exchange bills bought 매입외국환
foreign exchange broker 외국환브로커
foreign exchange budget 외화예산
foreign exchange centralization system 외화집중제도
foreign exchange contract 외국환예약
foreign exchange control 외국환관리
foreign exchange conversion rate 외국환환산율
foreign exchange conversion table 외국환환산표
foreign exchange fund bill 외국환자금증권
Foreign Exchange Fund Securities 외국환자금증권
Foreign Exchange Fund Special Account 외국환자금특별회계
foreign exchange futures 외국환선물
foreign exchange gains and losses 외국환차손익
foreign exchange holding restriction system 외화집중제도
foreign exchange law 외환법
foreign exchange market 외국환시장
foreign exchange market intervention 외국환시장개입
foreign exchange market operation 외국환시장조작
foreign exchange operation 외국환조작
foreign exchange position 외국환포지션
foreign exchange position sheet 외국환포지션표
foreign exchange quotation 외국환상장
foreign exchange rate 외국환율
foreign exchange reserves 외화준비고
foreign exchange risk 환리스크
foreign exchange speculation 외국환투기
foreign exchange transaction 환거래
foreign financial futures exchange 해외금융선물거래소
foreign government bonds 외국국채증권
foreign government securities 외국채증권
foreign income tax 외국소득세
foreign institution 외국기관
foreign investment 해외투자
foreign investment in Korean securities 대내증권투자
Foreign Investment Law 외자법
foreign investment in Korean stocks 대내증권투자
foreign investors 외국인투자가
foreign judgment 외국의 판결
foreign juridical person 외국법인
foreign loan 외채
foreign market 외국시장
foreign marketable securities 외국투자증권
foreign means of payment 대외지불수단
foreign money bill 외화어음
foreign money order 외국송금환
foreign operations 해외사업
foreign reserves 외화준비
Foreign Section 외국주식시장
foreign securities 외국증권
foreign securities company 외국증권회사
foreign securities exchange 외국증권거래소
foreign service allowance 해외근무수당
foreign source income 해외원천소득
foreign stock holding ratio 외국인지주비율
foreign stock market 외국주식시장
foreign stocks unlisted 외국비상장주
foreign subsidiary corporation 외국자회사
foreign tax 외국세액
foreign tax credit method 외국세액공제방식

foreign tax credit system 외국세액공제제도
foreign tax deductible as expenses 손금산입외국세
foreign tax exemption method 외국세액면제방식
foreign trade credit 무역신용
foreign trade deficit 무역적자
foreign trade finance 무역금융
foreign trade multiplier 외국무역승수
foreign trade policy 무역정책
foreign trade statistics 무역통계
foreign transactions 외국거래
foreign won denominated bond 원기준 외국채
foreigner's investment 외국인투자
forerunner stock 선구주
forest fire insurance 삼림화재보험
forestalling the market 시장방해
forestry income 산림소득
forestry income deduction 산림소득특별공제
forex club 포렉스클럽
forex risk 환리스크
forfeit 위약금
forfeited share 실권주
forfeiture 몰수
forfeiture of bail 보석금상실
forged bill 위조어음
forged cards 변조카드
forged check 위조수표
forged note 위조지폐
forged stock 위조주권
forgery 문서위조
forgiveness of debt 채무면제
forgiveness of repayment 상환면제
form 형식
form of action 소송방식
form of bid 입찰서
form of stock certificate 주권양식
form required by law 법률에서 요구하는 형식
formal 형식적인
formal capitalization of reserves 자본구성
formal contract 정식계약
formal lawsuits 본소(本訴)
formalities of incorporation 설립절차
formation expenses 창업비
formation of secondary market 유통시장형성
forms control 장표관리
forms of enterprise 기업형태
formula 공식
formula additions 정식편입액
formula fund 포뮬러펀드
formula investing 포뮬러투자
formula plan 포뮬러플랜
formula timing 포뮬러타이밍
forum 법원
forward agreement 선도거래
forward bid rate 선물환매상장
forward calendar 포워드캘린더
forward commitment 대부예약
forward contract 선도계약
forward delivery 선도
forward deposit 선도예금
forward difference 전방차분
forward discount 선물디스카운트
forward discount of U.S. dollar 달러화약세
forward exchange 선도환
forward exchange market 선물환시장
forward exchange rate 선물환상장
forward exchange transaction 선물환거래
forward foreign exchange rate 선물환예약레이트
forward integration 전방통합
forward interest rate 장래이자율
forward margin 선물마진
forward market 선물시장
forward offer rate 선물환매상장
forward operation 선물환거래
forward premium 선물환프리미엄
forward price 선도가격
forward quotation 선물환상장
forward rate 선도금리
forward rate agreement 금리선도거래

forward rate spread 선물환스프레드
forward settlement 선도결제
forward swap 선스타트스와프
forward transaction 선도거래
forward-forward rate 선-선레이트
foul B/L 파울 B/L
foul bill 고장어음
foul means 부정한 수단
foundation 재단
foundation collateral 재단저당
founder 창립자
founder's profit 창업자이익
fourth market 기관투자가간 시장
fractional figure 단수
fractional interest 단수이자
fractional lot 단주
fractional order 단주주문
fractional share 단위미만주
fractional shares 단위미만주식
fractional sum 단수금융
fractional year 일년이 안 되는 해
franchise clause 면책율조항
franchise tax 영업세
franked income 과세면제소득
Frankfurter Allgemeine Zeitung Index 독일 FAZ지수
fraternal society 공제조합
fraudulent act 부정행위
fraudulent action 사기행위
fraudulent bankruptcy 사기파산
fraudulent card 부정카드
fraudulent conduct 사기행위
fraudulent conveyance 사기양도
fraudulent creditor 사기채권자
fraudulent gains 부정이득
fraudulent misrepresentation 사기표시
fraudulent transfer 사기양도
Freddie Mac 프레디맥
free alongside ship 선측인도
free article 면세품
free capital 자유자본
free carrier 운송인인도
free cash flow 프리캐시로
free economy 자유경제
free financial fund 프리파이낸셜펀드
free floating exchange rates system 자유변동상장제
free from capture and seizure clause 포획나포부담보조항
free from particular average 분담부담보
free from strikers; riots and civil commotion clause 파업폭동부담보조항
free goods 면세품
free issue 무채발행
free list 무세품표
free loan 프리론
free market 자유시장;제삼시장
free market economy 자유시장경제
free market price 시중상장
free of charge 비용포함
free of tax 비과세
free of taxation 무세
free offer 자유오퍼
free on board 본선인도
free on rail 철도인도
free payment 임의인도
free payment system 자유반제시스템
free period 프리기간
free price 자유가격
free rate 자유요율
free reserves 자유준비
free ride period 우대조치기간
free rider 프리라이더
free riding 프리라이딩; 달러로 신주를 일부 유지함
free share 무상주
free trade zone 자유무역지대
free won account 자유원계정
free won deposit 자유원예금
freedom from encumbrance 무담보
freehold 자유보유의
freehold property 자유보유재산

E F

freight 화물
freight and cartage outward 발송운임
freight collect 착불
freight earnings 화물수입
freight insurance 운임보험
freight inward 구입운임
freight out 판매운임
freight prepaid 운임전불
freight rates 화물운임
freight receipts 운임수입
freight revenue 운임수입
freight tariff 화물운임
freight to collect 운임착불
freight usance 운임유전스
freight-in 구입운임
French Institute Index 파리종합주가지수
frequency distribution 도수분포
fresh capital 신규자본
fresh pursuit 즉시속행
fresh start 재출발
fresh water damage 담수에 젖음
frictional unemployment 마찰로 인한 실업
friendly society 우애조합
fringe banking 프린지뱅킹
fringe benefits 부가급부
front loaded 예정; 예산 따위를 앞당겨 씀
front running 앞서감;프런트러닝
front-end fee 프런트엔드피
front-foot rule 전회규칙
frontier delivery 국경인도
frontier tax 국경세
fronting 프런팅
frozen account 동결계정
frozen assets 동결자산
frozen credit 회수불능
frozen stock 잔품;팔다 남은 물건
fruit 성과
frustration 계약의 목적을 달성하지 못함
FT Actuaries All-share Index FT 전종목지수
FT Industrial Ordinary Stock Index 파이낸셜타임즈주가지수
FT Stock Exchange 100 Index FT 100종 지수
FT Stock Index FT 주가지수
FT-SE 100 FT-SE 100종 주가지수
FT-SE Actuaries AllShare FT-SE 액추어리즈 종합지수
fuel account 연료계정
fuel cost 연료비
fulfillment 이행
fulfillment of a contract 계약이행
fulfillment of procedures 절차이행
fulfillment settlement 결제이행
full age 성년
full amortization 완전상각
full banking service 풀뱅킹서비스
full bodied money 완전화폐
full capacity 완전조업
full capacity output 완전이용산출량
full compensation 충분한 보상
full consolidation 완전연결
full cost 전부원가
full cost principle 풀코스트원칙
full costing 전부원가계산
full coupon bond 풀쿠폰본드
full disclosure 완전개시
full eligibility dat e 완전수급자격일
full employment 완전고용
full employment policy 완전고용정책
full employment surplus 완전고용재정여잉
full equilibrium 완전균형
full hedge 풀헤지
full insurance 전액보험
full legal tender 완전법정통화
full paid capital stock 전액불입필 주식
full payment 전액지불
full pension 완전연금
full proof 완전증명
full repayment before maturity 조기완제
full scale local production 현지일관생산
full time 상근
full year 평년도

full year business result 본결산
full-faith-and-credit debt 신의신용채무
full-fledged secondary market 본격적인 유통시장
fully covered option 완전한 커버드옵션
fully depreciated 감가상각필
fully diluted 희석필
fully owned subsidiary 전액출자한 자회사
fully paid-up 전액불입
function 기능
functional analysis 기능분석
functional accounting 기능별 회계
functional cost 기능별 원가
functional currency method 기능통화법
functional depreciation 기능적인 감가
functional organization 기능별 조직
functional pricing 기능적인 가격설정
functional statement 기능별 계산서
fund absorption 자금흡수력
fund account 자금계정
fund accounting 자금회계
fund and trust 펀드앤드트러스트
fund balance sheet 자금대차대조표
fund budget 자금예산
fund demand 자금수요
fund equity 자금지분
fund for operation of foreign exchange 외국환운영자금
fund management 자금운용
fund management method 자금운용수단
fund manager 펀드매니저
fund obligation 자금부채
fund of funds 자금 중의 자금
fund position 자금포지션
fund raising business 자금조달업무
fund raising capacity 자금조달력
fund settlement 자금결제
fund shortage 자금부족
fund statement 자금운용표
fund surplus 자금잉여금
fund swap 자금관련 스와프
fund transfer 자금이전
fund transfer service 자금대체서비스
fund trust 펀드트러스트
fund unit account 기금단위계정
fund's mission 연금기금의 역할
fundamental analysis 펀드멘털분석
fundamental directives of income tax 소득세기본통달
fundamental disequilibrium 기초불균형
fundamental financial approach 기초금융상품 어프로치
fundamental market 경제기초조건을 바탕으로 움직이는 상장
fundamental rights 기본권리
fundamental rules 기본규제
fundamental statistics 경기통계
fundamental tax 기간세
fundamental theorem 기초정리
fundamental value 기초가치
fundamentalism 원리주의
fundamentalist 경제기초조건 중시파
fundamentals 경제기초조건; 펀드멘털즈
fundamentals deterioration 펀드멘털즈가 악화됨
funded debt 장기채무
funding 자금조달
funding agency 연금기금적립기관
funding cost 조달코스트
funding gap 자금부족
funding instrument 연금기금적립계약
funding method 적립방식
funding policy 차환정책
funding side 자금조달사이드
funding source 자금원
funds for purchase 매입자금
funds from operations 영업수입
funds lent by members 자기금융
funds statement 펀드스테이트먼트
fungibility 대체가능성
fungible 대용할 수 있는
fungible goods 대체가능성

fungible securities 대체증권
further advance 재대부
further directions 속행
future cash flows 장래자금흐름
future cost 미래원가
future risk 미래리스크
future specific risk 장래의 고유리스크
future value 장래가치
futures 선물(先物)
futures and option trading account 선물옵션거래계좌
futures brockerage business 선물위탁거래업무
futures commission merchant 선물중개업자
futures contract 선물계약
futures dealer 선물딜러
futures industry 선물업계
Futures Industry Association 미국선물업자협회
futures instrument 선물상품
futures margin 선물마진
futures market 선물시장
futures option 선물옵션
futures option market 선물옵션시장
futures position 선물포지션
futures price 선물가격
futures product 선물상품
futures quotation 선물상장
futures rate 선물레이트
futures trading 선물거래
futures trading based on government securities 국채증권선물거래
futures trading based on securities price index 유가증권지수선물거래
futures trading based on stocks 주권선물거래
futures trading based on the stock price index 주가지수선물거래
futures transaction 선물거래
futures valuation 선물평가
fuzzy theory 퍼지이론

G

GAAP 갭(일반적으로 사용되는 회계원칙)
gain from operation 영업이익
gain or loss 손익
gaining 강보합
gains derived from dealings in property
자산거래에서 발생한 이득
gains from appreciation of securities
유가증권평가익
gains from capital stock reduction 감자차익
gains from exchange of properties 교환차익
gains from forgiveness of debt 채무면제익
gains from revaluation off fixed assets
고정자산평가익
gains from sale of fixed assets
고정자산매각익
gains from stock retirement 감자차익
gains from the transfer of property
자산양도익
gains in sales 매상증가
gains on bond retirement 사채상환차금
gains on foreign exchange 외환차익
gains on insurance claim 보험차익
gains or losses from sales of fixed asset
고정자산매각손익
galloping inflation 악성인플레이션
gambling 도박
game plan 게임플랜
game theory 게임이론
gamma 감마
gamma distribution 감마분포
gamma exposure 감마익스포저
gap analysis 갭분석
gap between supply and demand 수급갭
gap management technology 갭법
gapping horizon 갭기간
garnishee 제 3채무자
garnisher 채권차압인
garnishment 채권차압통지
gather steam 활황
GDP deflator GDP 디플레이터
GDP growth rate GDP 신장률
gearing 기어전동장치;기어링
gearing effect 기어링효과
gearing ratio 기어링비율
gearing acceptance 일반인수
general account 일반회계
general account expenditure 일반회계세출
General Accounting Office 회계검사원
general accounting principles 일반회계원칙
general administration expenses 관리비
general administrative and selling expenses
일반관리비 및 판매비
general administrative cost 일반관리비
general administrative expenses budget
일반관리비예산
general agency system 총대리점 제도
general agent 총대리점
General Agreement on Tariffs and Trade
가트; 관세와 무역에 관한 일반협정
general assembly 총회
general assembly meeting of members
회원총회

general audit 일반감사
general audit standards 감사기준
general authority 포괄적인 권한
general average 공동해손
general average contribution 공동해손분담액
general average expenditure 공동해손비용
general average sacrifice 공동해손희생손해
general balance sheet 일반대차대조표
general binded-debt fund 일반공채자금
general building scheme 일반주택지 분양계획
general business 일반사업
general cargo 일반화물
general cash 일반현금
general closing 통상결산
general conditions and terms of the contract 일반조건서
general consumer goods 일반소비재
general contingency reserve 일반우발채무준비금
general corporate assets 전반자산
general corporate bond 일반사업채
general corporate revenues and expenses 일반손익
general cost 일반비
general credit 제너럴크레디트
general creditor 일반채무자
general crossed check 일반횡선수표
general election 총선거
general equilibrium 일반균형
general expenses 일반경비
general fixed-assets fund 일반고정자산자금
general fund 일반자금
general government section 일반정부부문
general grant 일반보조금
general index 종합지수
general indirect cost 일반간접비
general insurance 손해전종목보험
general insurance clause 보통보험약관
general insurance law 보험법
general inventory 재산목록
general journal 보통분개장
general ledger 총계정원장
general ledger account 총계정원장계정
general lending rate 일반대출금리
general letter of credit 매입은행무지정신용장
general liability insurance 일반배상책임보험
general lien 일반적인 리엔
general liquidity 일반유동성
general market 일반시장
general means of payment 일반적인 지불수단
general meeting 총회
general meeting of investors 투자주총회
general meeting of shareholders 주주총회
general meeting of stockholders 주주총회
general meeting of substitutional members 사원총대회
general merchandise 잡비
general mortgage 제너럴모기지
general mortgage bond 제너럴모기지사채
general obligation bond 일반재원채
general operating expenses 일반영업활동비
general overhead 일반간접비
general partner 무한책임사원
general partnership 무한책임파트너십
general place of tax payment 원칙적인 납세지
general price level 일반물가수준
general price-level accounting 일반물가수준회계
general profit and loss account 손익계정
general property tax 일반재산세
general provisions 총칙
general provisions of budget 예산총칙
general provisions of the budget 예산총칙
general public investment 일반자산
general public work 일반공공사업
general purchasing power 일반구매력
general purpose card 범용카드
general purpose financial statements 일반목적재무제표
general realignment 일반조정
general security agreement 일반담보계약

general successor 일반승계인
general tax 보통세
general tax not stipulated in Local Tax Law 법정외 보통세
general taxation 종합과세
general terms and conditions of trade 일반무역조건
general transfer 일반대체
general words 일반문언
generally accepted accounting principle 일반적으로 사용되는 회계기준
generational accounting 세대간 회계
generic swap 제네릭스와프
generous coupon 고이율쿠폰
gensaki 겐사키시장
geographic control 지역별 관리
geometric average 기하평균
geometric model 기하모델
German bearer certificate 독일무기명증서
getting ashore 싸게 매입한 주를 시세가 올랐을 때 매각함
Gibson paradox 깁슨의 역설
gift 증여
gift tax 증여세
gift tax credit 상속세공제
gilt auction 길드채입찰
gilt yield 길트채이율
gilt-edged bond 길트에지채
gilt-edged securities 길트에지채;금연증권
Gini coefficient 지니지수
Ginnie Mae 지니메이
gist 취지;요령
glamor stock 매력주
glass and ceramics products industry 유리세라믹제품업계
Glass-Steagall Act 글래스스티걸법
global bearer certificate 글로벌 무기명 예탁증서
global bond 글로벌본드
global certificate 글로벌증권
global credit market 국제금융시장
global custody 글로벌커스터디
global depository certificate 글로벌예탁증권
global economy 글로벌경제
global long-term bond 글로벌장기채권
global market 세계적인 시장
global marketing 글로벌마케팅
global note facilities 글로벌노트퍼실리티
global portfolio 글로벌포트폴리오
global trading 글로벌트레이딩
globalization 세계화
GNMA 지니메이
GNMA debenture 미국정부주택저당금고증권
GNMA pass-through securities 지니메이 패스 스루 증권
gnomes of Zurich 취리히의 난쟁이; 스위스 금융계의 실력자
GNP deflator GNP 디플레이터
GNP gap GNP 갭
GNP growth rate GNP 성장률
God's penny 계약금
going concern 지속기업
going concern value 지속기업가치
going long 시세가 오를 것을 예상하고 증권을 매입함
going private 기업의 비공개화
going public 주식공개화
going short 시세가 내릴 것을 예상하고 증권을 매각함
going value 지속기업가치
gold accounts 금투자계좌
gold and dollar reserve 금달러준비
sold and foreign exchange reserves 외화준비고
gold and silver bimetallism 금은복본위제도
gold bond 금채권
gold bullion futures contract 금선물계약
gold bullion standard 금지금본위제
gold center 골드센터
gold clause 금약관
gold coin standard 금화본위제
gold collateral 금담보

gold convertible securities 금전환증권
gold exchange 금환
Gold Exchange of Singapore 싱가폴금거래소
gold exchange reserve 금환준비
gold exchange standard 금환본위제
gold export point 금수출점
gold fixing 금기준치결정
gold futurues 금선물
gold futures option 금선물옵션
gold holdings 금보유고
gold import point 금수입점
gold par value 금평가
gold parity 금평가
gold points 금현송점(金現送點)
gold pool 금풀
gold purchase warrant 금구입워런트
gold reserve 금준비
Gold Reserve Act 금준비법
gold rush 골드러시
gold standard 금본위제
gold sterilization policy 금불태화정책
gold tranche 골드트란시
gold warrant 금워런트
golden cross 골든크로스
golden hand cuffs 골든핸드커프스
golden parachute 골든패러슈트
golden rule 황금률
golden section 황금분할
golfers' insurance 골퍼보험
good and collectible 확실히 회수할 수 있는
good and lawful men 유자격자
good behavior 선행
good consideration 선량약인
good debt 확실히 회수할 수 있는 대금
good delivery 적격인도
good faith 성실
good merchantable quality 판매적성품질
good news 호재
good offices of banking facilities
금융기관의 알선
good results 호성적
good this month order
당월에 한해 유효한 주문
good value 자금화 자금
good yield 호이율
good-till-canceled orders
취소할 때까지 유효한 주문
goods account 상품계정
goods and products 상품 또는 제품
goods carried over 보유품
goods for sale 판매용 상품
goods in process 제작중인 물건
goods in process at the end of period
기말에 제작중인 물건
goods in process ledger 제작 중인 물건원장
goods in transit 미착품
goods left 잔품
goods on approval 시송품
goods on consignment-in 수탁품
goods on hands 소유재고품
goods returned to vendor 반품
goods sold on credit 외상으로 판 상품
goodwill 영업권
governed market 관리시장
governing clause 준거법조항
governing law 준거법
government account 정부계정
government agency 정부계 기관
government agency bond 정부계 기관채권
government agency securities 정부기관증권
government appraisal of land price
지가공시제도
government audit 정부감사
government bill 단기국채
government bond 국채
government bond administration
국채에 대한 사무
government bond agency 국채대리점
government bond auction system
국채입찰제도
government bond book-entry system
국채대체결제제도

government bond for tax reduction 감세국채
government bond futures 국채선물거래
government bond futures option 채권선물옵션
government bond in foreign currency 외화국채
government bond issuance 국채발행
government bond management policy 국채관리정책
government bond redemption 국채상환
government bond system 국채제도
government bond yield 국채이율
government bonds and corporate debentures 공사채
government bonds in domestic currency 국내국채
government bookkeeping 관청부기
government broker 정부브로커
government compensation bond 교부공채
government credit 정부차관
government current deposit 정부당좌예금
government current surplus 정부경상여잉
government debt 공채
Government Debt Consolidation Fund 국채정리기금
government debt redemption cost 채무상환비
government enterprise 정부기업
government expenditure 정부지출
government finance 재정
government financial agency 정부금융기관
government financial corporation 공고
government fund 정부자금
government fund transactions 국고수지
government fund transactions with the public 국고 대 민간수지
government grant 정부보조금
government guaranteed bond 정부보증채
government guaranteed bonds 정부보증채
government intervention 정부개입
Government National Mortgage Association 정부저당금고
Government National Mortgage Association debenture 지니메이채
government note 정부지폐
government obligation 정부보증채
government ordinance 정령(政令)
government procurement 정부조달
government purchases 정부구입
government related deposit 정부관계예금
government saving 정부저축
government saving certificate 정부저축증권
government securities 정부증권
government subsidy 정부보조금
government subsidy for capital expenditure 건설조성금
government to government trade 정부간 무역
government trade 정부무역
government transaction 정부거래
government transfers 정부이전수지
Government Trust Fund Law 자금운용부자금법
government-guaranteed public corporation bond 정부보증공영기업증권
governmental and municipal accounting 관청회계
governor 총재
Governor of the Bank of Japan 일본은행총재
grace of payment 지불유예
grace period 거치기간
graded tariff 차등세율
gradual devaluation 서서히 절하
graduated payment mortgage 고정금리기준모기지
graduated taxation 누진과세
graduation clause 졸업조항
Gramm-Rudman-Hollings Law 그람러드만법
grand distress 전부차압
grand total 총계
grandfather provision 기득권조항
grant anticipation note 보조금전망채

grant element 그랜트엘리먼트
grant in aid 조성금
grant loan 무상론
granting credit 신용공여
granting of trading qualification 거래자격을 부여함
grantor 양여자
Granville theory 그랜빌의 법칙
gratis 무상
gratuitous bailment 무상기탁
gratuitous contract 무상계약
gratuitous use of property 재산을 무상으로 사용함
gray market 발행전 유통시장
great depression 대공황
greater fool theory 그레이터풀이론
green card system 그린카드제도
green field business 신규참가사업
green goods 위조지폐
green mail 그린메일
greenback 미달러지폐
Gresham's law 그레샴의 법칙
grid 그리드
grievance committee 고충처리위원회
gross amount 총액
gross amount principle 총액주의
gross assets 총자산
gross base 총액베이스
gross book value 총장부가격
gross capital 총자본
gross cost 총원가
gross cost of merchandise sold 총매상원가
gross debt 총채무
gross domestic capital formation 국내총자본형성
gross domestic product 국내총생산
gross earnings 총수익
gross error 과실
gross expenditure 총지출
gross fund position 그로스펀드포지션
gross gains 총수익
gross income 총소득
gross income of corporation 법인이익금
gross investment 총투자
gross loss 총과실
gross loss on sales 매상총손실
gross margin 매상총이익
gross margin rate 조이익률
gross merchandise margin 총상품매매차익
gross national demand 국민총수요
gross national expenditure 국민총지출
gross national product 국민총생산
gross national supply 국민총공급
gross national wealth 국민총자산
gross negligence 중과실
gross of 총(總)
gross operating spread 총영업이폭
gross output 총지출
gross premium 총보험료
gross product 총생산
gross profit 총이익
gross profit analysis 총이익분석
gross profit margin 매상총이익률
gross profit margin rate 조이익률
gross profit method 총이익
gross profit on sales 매상총이익
gross profit ratio 총이익률
gross profit test 총이익테스트
gross purchase 구입총액
gross redemption 그로스상환
gross revenue 총수익
gross sales 총매상고
gross spread 인수모집수수료
gross trading volume 그로스거래고
gross transaction 총거래
gross up method 그로스업방식
gross working capital 총운전자본
ground price 공장원가
ground-making expenses 토지조성비
groundage 정박료
grounding clause 근거 있는 조항
group accident insurance 단체상해보험

group annuity insurance 단체연금보험
group auction 일괄경매;집단경쟁매매
group cost system 등급별 원가계산
group credit insurance association 단체신용생명보험조합
group credit life insurance 단체신용생명보험
group deferred annuity contract 단체거치연금계약
group deposit administration contract 단체예탁관리계약
group depreciation 조별상각
group endowment insurance 단체양로보험
group financial statements 기업집단재무제표
group gearing 연결부채비율표
group health insurance 단체건강보험
group insurance 단체보험
group life insurance 단체생명보험
group method 조별법
group mortgage insurance 단체모기지보상생명보험
Group of 5 G 5
group pension 단체연금
group permanent insurance contract 단체장기보험계약
group relief 그룹세액공제
group term insurance 단체정기보험
growing at a moderate speed 적절하게 성장하는
growing currency 성장통화
growing economy 성장경제
growing equity mortgage 지분체증모기지
growing leverage 채무비율증대
growth curve 성장곡선
growth fund 그로스펀드
growth of industrial structure 산업구조고도화
growth of investment 성장신장
growth potential 성장성
growth rate 성장률
Growth Section 그로스섹션
growth stock 성장주
growth strategy 성장전략
growth theory 성장이론
guarantee 보증
guarantee business 보증업무
guarantee by endorsement 이서보증
guarantee charge 보증료
guarantee deposits 보증금
guarantee facility 채무보증
guarantee fee received 수입보증료
guarantee in favor of the primary guarantor 이보증(裏保證)
guarantee insurance 보증보험
guarantee loan 보증론
guarantee money 보증금
guarantee money received 수입보증금
guarantee of debt 채권보증
guarantee of repayment 차입반제보증
guaranteed amount 보증액
guaranteed bond 보증사채
guaranteed cost contract 비용보증계약
guaranteed dividend 확정배당
guaranteed interest contract 이율보증계약
guaranteed investment contract 보증투자계약
guaranteed securities 보증증권
guaranteed stock 보증주
guaranteed warrant 보증부 워런트
guarantees outstanding 보증잔고
guarantor 보증인
guarantor bank 보증은행
guarantor's right of indemnity 구상권
guaranty 담보물건
guaranty insurance 손해담보계약
guaranty money deposited 차입보증금
guaranty of liabilities 채무보증
guardianship 후견
guideline 가이드라인
guideline service life 가이드라인 내생연수
guild 동업조합
guild bond 길더채
Gulf Cooperation Council 페르시아만협력회의
gun jumping 정보공개전의 증권거래

H

habit persistence hypothesis 관습가설
half-finished goods 반제품
half-yearly report 반기보고서
half-yearly 매번 반기마다
hammering the market 해머링마켓; 값을 몹시 깎는 시장
hand-to-mouth buying 꼭 필요한 만큼만 구입함
handling cost 취급비
handling expenses 취급비
Hang Seng Index 홍콩한센지수
harakiri swap 하라키리스와프
harbor 감추다
harbor dues 입항세
hard currency 경화
hard labor 중노동
hard landing 하드랜딩
hard loan 하드론
harden 굳히다;경화하다
hardware market 하드웨어시장
harmless error 무해한 오진
harmless warrant 함리스워런트채
haulage 선박여객운송비
hazard 위험
hazard function 하자드함수
head 주석
head and shoulder 헤드앤드숄더
head book 주요장부
head office 본점
head office account 본사계정
head tax 인두세
heading 표제
health benefit 보건급부
health care 헬스케어
health care obligation 의료급부채무
health care plan 의료보건제도
health insurance 건강보험
health insurance premium 건강보험료
Health Maintenance Organization 건강유지기구
health service 보건
healthy demand 견실한 수요
healthy revenue growth 순조로운 매상신장
healthy trend 고수준
hearing 심문
heated up economy 고열경제
heavy additional charge imposed 중가산금
heavy electrical stocks 중전(重電)상품
heavy market 둔조(鈍調)시장
heavy penalty tax 중가산세
heavy share 주가수준이 높은 주
heavy taxation 중세
heavy users 헤비유저
hedge 헤지
hedge account representation letter 헤지계산대행서
hedge accounting 헤지회계
hedge accounting treatment 헤지회계처리
hedge buying 헤지구매
hedge clause 면책조항
hedge fund 헤지펀드
hedge gains 헤지이익

hedge instrument 헤지상품
hedge margin 헤지증거금
hedge operation 헤지조작
hedge period 헤지기간
hedge ratio 헤지비율
hedge selling 시세하락을 예상하고 매각함
hedge trading 헤지거래
hedge transaction 헤지거래
hedged bond 헤지채
hedged portfolio 헤지드포트폴리오
hedged position 헤지포지션
hedger 헤저
hedging 헤징;연계매매
hedging against inflation 인플레이션헤징
hedging cost 헤지코스트
hedging function 헤지기능
hedging on commodity futures 상품선물거래헤징
hedging on option 옵션헤징
hedging scheme 헤지스킴
hedging technique 헤지수법
hedging vehicle 헤지수단
hegemony 주도권;헤게모니
heir 상속인
heir apparent 법정상속인
heir presumptive 추정상속인
heir-looms 법정상속동산
held to maturity 상환기간까지 보유함
hell or high water clause 헬오어하이워터조항
hereditaments 상속재산
hereinafter 이하
heterogeneous market 이질시장
hidden assets 비밀자산
hidden assets stock 비밀적립자산주
hidden cost 보이지 않는 비용
hidden profit distributions 비밀리에 이익을 처분함
hidden reserves 은닉한 적립금
hierarchy of responsibilities 책임서열
high grade investment 유리한 투자
high income brackets 고액납세자
high interest rate 고금리
high interest rate policy 고금리정책
high level of business activity 고수준의 경기
high liquidity 높은 유동성
high possibility 높은 가능성
high powered money 하이파워드머니
high price 고가
high rise 급등
high seas 공해(公海)
high taxpayers 고액납세자
high yield bond 고이율채
high-coupon bond 하이쿠폰채
high-interest-bearing debenture 고리부 사채
high-leveraged 효과가 높은
high-low method 고저법
high-priced stock 고가주
high-risk high-return 하이리스크하이리턴
high-tech stock 하이테크주식
higher in quotation 고가
higher interest rates application system 고율적용제도
higher order goods 고차재(高次財)
higher quotation 고가
higher quotation at the close 마감장의 고가
higher quotations 상장상승
highest-in first-out method 최고가격선출법
highly traded stock 집중적으로 거래되는 주
hike in official rate 정책금리인상
hindrance to business 정책방해
hire purchase 분할불구입
histogram method 히스토그램법
historical analysis 실적분석
historical beta 히스토리컬베타
historical cost 취득원가
historical cost accounting 취득원가주의회계
historical cost basis 취득원가기준
historical cost financial statements 취득원가주의재무제표
historical data 히스토리컬데이터
historical earning 과거실적
historical peak 과거최고치

G H

historical rate 발생시레이트
historical trading range 과거의 수치폭
historical volatility 누적변동성
history-dependent derivative 경로의존형 파생상품
Hoffmann's law 호프만의 법칙
hold-to-maturity 만기까지 보유함
holder 소지인
holder for value 유상소지인
holder in bad faith 악의의 제삼자
holder in due course 선의의 제삼자
holder in good faith 선의의 소지인
holder of lien 리엔보유자
holder of record 주주명부상의 주주
holders of preferred equity securities 특정사원
holding company 지주회사
holding gain or loss 보유손익
holding high 고보합
holding of assets 자산보유
holding period return 보유기간수익률
holding period value-relative 보유기간상대가치
holding the market 매입을 촉진하여 급격한 시세 변동을 막음
holdings of Special Drawing Rights 특별인출권보유액
home banking 홈뱅킹
home country 본국
home country control 원적국주의;본점감독주의
home currency 자국통화
home currency bill bought 자국환매입외국환
home equity loan 홈에퀴티론
home improvement loan 증개축론
home made inflation 홈메이드인플레
home mortgage 주택모기지
home office account 본점계정
home port 선적항
home rule 자치
home service 내지근무
home service agent 지구외무원
home state 출신주
homestead right 가산
homogeneity 동질성
homogeneous market 동질시장
homogeneous security group 동류증권그룹
homologation 결재하여 허가함
Hong Kong depositary receipts 홍콩예탁증권
Hong Kong dollar 홍콩달러
Hong Kong inter-bank offered rate 홍콩은행간 오퍼레이트
honor 인수
honorarium 사례금
hook damage 갈고리손
hooked 갈고리모양의
horizon analysis 투자계획기간분석
horizon return 소유기간이율
horizontal 수평적
horizontal analysis 수평분석
horizontal audit 수평적인 감사
horizontal integration 수평형 통합
horizontal international specialization 수평적인 국제분업
horizontal M&A 수평적인 M&A
horizontal merger 수평합병
horizontal multiplier 수평승수
horizontal specialization 수평분업
horizontal split 수평분단
horizontal spread 수평스프레드
horizontal trade 수평무역
hospital expense insurance 입원비보험
hostile acquisition 적대적인 매수
hostile possession 자주점유
hostile takeover 적대적인 매수
hot issue 인기증권
hot money 국제단기부동자금;핫머니
hot money market 핫머니시장
hours worked 가동시간
hours-of-service method 사용시간비례법
house agency 하우스에이전시

house bill 하우스빌
house margin rule 증거금내부규제
house organ 사내보
house rent income 가임료
house rent received 수취가임
household 가계
household consumption expenditure 가계소비지출
household debt 가계채무
household expenses 가계비
household goods 가재도구
household sector 가계부문
household taxation 세대과세
householders' comprehensive insurance 주택종합보험
housekeeping expenses 가계비
housing allowance 주거수당
Housing and Urban Development Corporation 주택도시정비공단
housing credit 주택신용
housing expenses 주거비
housing loan 주택금융
housing loan claim 주택론채무
housing loan corporation 주택금융회사
housing loan guarantee 주택론보험
housing market 주택시장
housing permits 주택착공허가건수
housing renewal program 하우징리뉴얼프로그램
housing savings tax credit 주택저축공제
housing starts 주택건축착공수
housing stocks 주택관련주
hull insurance 선박보험
human capital 인적자본
human engineering 인간공학
human life value 인간의 생명가치
human resources 인적자원
human resources accounting 인적자원회계
humped curve 험프드커브
hung up 정서가 불안정한; 걱정하는
hunters' insurance 헌터보험
hurdle rate 최저목표수익률
hush-money 입막음돈; 무마비
hybrid 혼합
hybrid cap 혼합캡
hybrid capital 복합자본
hybrid instrument 하이브리드상품
hybrid model 혼합형
hybrid securities 복합증권
hybrid stocks 혼합주식
hybrid trading system 하이브리드트레이딩시스템
hybrid trust 혼합신탁
hyper inflation 초인플레이션
hypothec 저당권
hypothecated assets 담보자산
hypothecation agreement 담보차입동의서
hypothesis 가정
hypothetical assumption 가설상의 상정

IAS 국제회계기준
IASC 국제회계기준위원회
IATA 국제항공운송협회
IBRD special law 국제부흥개발은행특별조치
iceberg theory 빙산이론
ideal standard cost 이상표준원가
identical with 동일한
identifiable assets 인식할 수 있는
identification card 신분증명서
identified cost method 개별법
identity 동일성
idle assets 유휴자산
idle balance 이상적인 밸런스
idle capacity cost 저조업도원가
idle cash 여잉현금
idle cost 부동비
idle equipment 유휴설비
idle facilities 유휴시설
idle money 행방이 정해지지 않은
idle plant 유휴설비
idle time 한가한 시간
if-converted method 전환가정법
ignore 각하하다
illegal 불법의
illegal act 위법행위
illegal employment 불법취로
illegal lending 위법대부
illegality 불법
illiquid 비유동적
illiquid assets 유동성이 낮은 자산
illiquid issues 유동성이 낮은 상품
illiquidity 비유동성
imbalance 불균형
imbalance of orders 주문의 불균형
IMF Board of Directors IMF 이사회
IMF gold tranche IMF 골드트란시
IMF loan IMF 차관
IMF par value IMF 평가
IMF stand-by IMF 스탠드바이
IMF subscription IMF 출자
imitation 유사물제작
immaterial capital 무형자본
immaterial evidence 중요하지 않은 증거
immaterial issue 중요하지 않은 쟁점
immaterial property 무형재산
immediate annuity 즉시개시연금
immediate cause 직근원인
immediate future 당장
immediate liquidity 당면의 유동성
immediate order 지급주문
immediate participation guarantee contract 직접참가방식단체연금계약
immediate-or-cancel order 이미디어트오어캔슬오더
immediately available fund 즉시 이용가능한 자금
immediately proceeding 직전의
immediately proceeding business year 직전사업연도
immovable property 부동산
immovables 부동산
immovables account 부동산계정

immunity 면제
immunization 면역화
immunization fund 이뮤니제이션펀드
impact claims 파급효과클레임
impact loan 임팩트론
impact on business 사업에 주는 영향
impaired capital 자본결손
impairment of contract 계약상의 권리를 침해함
impairment of value 과세의 공평
impediment 장애
imperfect competition 불완전경쟁
imperfect competition market 불완전경쟁시장
imperfect hedge 불완전한 헤지
imperfect obligation 불완전의무
imperfect trust 불완전신탁
impersonal account 물적계정
impersonal deduction 물적공제
impersonal exclusion from taxation 물적과세제외
impersonal security 대물담보
impersonal tax 물세
impertinent 무관계한
impignoration 저당잡힘
impignorative contract 저당계약
implementation 실시
implementation stage 실시단계
implication 미루어 판단함
implicit assumption 암묵적인 전제
implicit call price 내재적인 콜가격
implicit cost 명시하지 않은 비용
implicit deflator 암묵적인 디플레이터
implicit interest 내포금리
implied 암묵적인
implied contract 준계약
implied forward rates 임플라이드선도금리
implied license 묵시허용
implied repo rate 이론상의 환매수익률; IRR
implied spread 임플라이드스프레드
implied trust 묵시신탁
implied volatility 임플라이드볼라틸리티
implied warranty 묵시담보
implied yield 임플라이드일드
import bill 수입어음
import cartel 수입카르텔
import clearance 수입통관
import control 수입무역관리
import country 수입국
import credit 수입신용
import duties tariff 수입세표
import duty 수입세
import financing 수입금융
import financing system 수입자금대부제도
import for manufacturing 이입
import function 수입함수
import guarantee money 수입보증금
import inflation 수입인플레이션
import license 수입승인증
import on consignment 위탁판매수입
import permit 수입허가
import price index 수입물가지수
import quota 수입할당
import ratio 수입비율
import restriction 수입규제
import settlement bill system 수입결제어음제도
import substitute 수입대체
import surcharge 수입과징금
import tax 수입세
import usance 수입유전스
import volume 수입량
important factor 중요한 요소
important part of business 중요한 업무
importation of foreign capital 외자수입
importation of income tax 소득세를 과세함
importation of tax 과세
impossibility of performance 이행불능
impossible contract 불능한 계약
impost 수입세
impoverishing theory 곤궁화 정책
imprest cash 전도금

imprest cash fund 소액전불준비금
imprest fund 정액전도자금
imprest system 정액전도제
improvement 개량
improvement cost 개량비
improvement expense 개량비
improvement from no dividend 복배
improvement of the property 자산개량
improvement patent 개량특허
improvement trade 가공무역
impulse buying 충동구매
imputation 귀속
imputation method 임퓨테이션방식
impute 귀속시키다
imputed cost 귀속원가; 부가원가
imputed income 귀속소득
imputed interest 귀속이자
imputed negligence 귀책과실
imputed price 귀속가격
imputed value 귀속가치
in a lump sum 일시금으로
in all 총계로
in black 흑자
in blank 백지로
in bond 보세
in dollar terms 달러기준으로
in good faith 성실하게
in good standing 우량인
in kind 동종의
in line with 연동하여
in number 숫자상으로
in real terms 실질베이스로
in red 적자
in red ink 적자의
in return 그 자체
ill specie 특정의
in terms of revenue 수익면에서
in the light of 거울삼아
in the money 인더머니
in the near term 목전
in transit 미달의
in up trend 상승하는 경향인
in violation of 반하는
in-and-out trading 단기로 매매하는
in-and-put dealer 인앤드풋딜러
in-cycle work 기계운전시작업
in-house exchange 행내교환
in-house product 자사제품
in-kind 현물로
in-port duty 항만세
inactive 한산한; 활발하지 않은
inactive account 미활동계정
inactive bond 비인기채권
inactive market 한산시장
inadequate capital 과소자본
inadmissible 허용할 수 없는
inadmitted assets 승인되지 않은 자산
inalienable rights 양도할 수 없는 권리
inappropriate merger 부적절한 합병
inappropriate substance 부적절한 내용
inaugural meeting 창립총회
incentive 장려
incentive effect 장려효과
incentive fee 성공보수
incentive stock option 자사주저가격구입권
inception 개시
incidence 일어난 일; 사건
incidence of taxation 조세부담
incidental 부수적인
incidental appeal 부대소송
incidental condition 부대조건
incidental expenses 부대비용
incidental gains 부수적인 수입
incidental increase payment 일부증액반제
incidental suit 부대소송
including tax 세포함
inclusion in expenses 손금산입
inclusion in gross revenue 익금산입
income account 손익계정
income accrued from domestic sources 국내원천소득
income accrued from foreign sources

외국원천소득
income after tax audit 조사후 소득
income analysis 소득분석
income and expenditure equation 수지방정식
income and expenses 손익
income approach 소득접근법
income arising as a result of exemption of debts 채무면제익
income at liquidation 청산소득
income basis 소득베이시스
income before employee bonus 상여전 소득
income before extraordinary items 경상손익
income before income taxes 세금공제전 이익
income bond 배당사채
income bracket 소득층
income by coupon reinvestment 쿠폰재투자수입
income compensation insurance 소득보상보험
income consumption curve 소득소비곡선
income deposit 소득예금
income derived from business 사업에서 생기는 소득
income distribution 소득분포
income earned 가동이익
income effect 소득효과
income effect of exchange adjustments 환조정의 소득효과
income elasticity 소득탄력성
income endowment 연금부 보험
income enhancer 인컴인헨서
income factor 소득요인
income from appreciation of assets 재산평가익
income from assets 자산소득
income from collection of securities by purchase 주식매집에 따른 소득
income from continuing operations 지속사업부문의 이익
income from discharge of indebtedness 채무면제익
income from discontinued operations 폐지부문의 이익
income from fees 수수료수입
income from Korean sources 국내원천소득
income from life insurances and endowment contract 생명보험 및 양로보험계약의 소득
income from real estate 부동산수입
income from transfer of securities 유가증권양도소득
income from trust deposits 금전신탁이익
income fund 인컴펀드
income gain 인컴게인;배당소득
income gearing 인컴기어링
income generating effect 소득창출효과
income in advance 전수수익
income in respect of a decedents 피상속인의 소득
income indemnity insurance 소득보상보험
income inflation 소득인플레이션
income level 소득수준
income leveling 이익평준화
income manipulation 소득조작
income policy 소득정책
income realization 이익실현
income received but unearned 이연수익
income redistribution effect 소득재분배효과
income return 소득신고
income return blank 소득신고용지
income share 채산주
income share note 이익분배채
income statement 손익계산서
income statement account 손익계산서계정
income statement approach 손익계산서어프로치
income statement audit 손익계산서감사
income statement principles 손익계산서원칙
income statement ratio 손익계산서비율
income stock 자산주
income summary 손익
income tax 소득세

income tax allocations 소득과세배분
income tax collected at the source 원천소득세
income tax credit 소득세공제
income tax deferred 이연법인세
income tax law 소득세법
income tax on bond interest 사채이자에 부과되는 소득세
income tax prepayment system 예정납세제도
income tax rapid calculation table 소득세속산표
income tax rate 소득세율
income tax rates table 소득세율표
income tax return 소득세신고
income tax return form 소득세신고서
income tax self-assessed 신고납세액
income tax withheld at source 원천공제소득세
income taxes payable 미불법인세
income terms of trade 소득교역조건
income warrant 인컴워런트
income yield 직접이율
incompetency 금치산
incompetency person 금치산자
incomplete transaction 미완료거래
inconvertible bank note 불환은행권
inconvertible paper money 불환지폐
incorporated school 학교법인
incorporation 법인화
incorporation of enterprise 법인설립
incorporation procedures 회사설립수속
incorporator 발기인
incorporeal chattel 무휴동산
incorporeal property 무체재산
Incoterms 인코텀스
increase and decrease method 증감법
increase and decrease ratio 등락레이쇼
increase in capital at the market price 주식을 시가발행함
increase in capital stock 증자
increase in dividend 증배
increase in PER PER 상승
increase of revenue 증수
increase of sales 매상증가
increased earnings 증익
increased income tax 증가소득세
increased tax 증세
increased value insurance 증식보험
increasing domestic demand 내수확대
increasing working capital 증가운전자본
increment card 인크리먼트카드
incremental analysis 증분분석
incremental budget 누적증가예산
incremental cost 증분원가
incremental profit 증분원가
incremental rate of return 증분수익률
incremental return 증가수익
incumbency 현직
incurred 이미 발생한
indebtedness 채무
indebtedness of affiliates 관계회사채권
indefeasible 무효라 할 수 없는
indemnification 변상
indemnify 보상의 약속을 하다
indemnity 면책
indemnity agreement 보증위탁계약
indemnity allowance 보상금
indemnity right 구상권
indent 주문서;매입위탁서
indenture trustee 인덴처수탁인
independent accountant 독립회계사
independent audit 독립감사
independent auditor 회계감사인
independent contract 독립계약
independent contractor 청부인
Independent Insurance Agents of Japan 일본손해보험대리업협회
independent intermediary 독립책임액비례주의
independent marketing organization 독립판매조직
independent tax 독립세

index 지수
index arbitrage trading 지수재정거래
index arbitrager 지수재정거래자
index bond 인덱스채권
index fund 인덱스펀드
index holding 지수보유
index linked bond 인덱스채
index linked products 지수링크채
index number by aggregative method 총화법지수
index number of production 생산지수
index number trend series 경향지수
index of financial condition 재정력지수
index of net terms of trade 순교역조건지수
index of producers' inventory of finished goods 생산자제품재고지수
index of producers' shipments 생산자출하지수
index of productivity 생산성지수
index of terms of trade 교역조건지수
index of trade 무역지수
index of urban land prices 전국시가지가격지수
index option 인덱스옵션
index participation 인덱스파티시페이션
index risk 지수리스크
index transaction 지수거래
indexation 지수화
indicated bid-asked quotation 시세표시
indicated price 시세가격
indication at a store counter 장외표시
indication method 인디케이션방식
indication of interest 인디케이션오브인터레스트
indicative price 시세가격
indicator 지표
indifference curve 무차별곡선
indigenous capital 토착자본
indirect business tax 간접사업세
indirect cost 간접비
indirect credit 간접공제
indirect department cost 간접부문비
indirect deposit 간접예금
indirect evidence 간접증거
indirect exchange arbitrage 간접재정
indirect expenses 간접비
indirect financing 간접금융
indirect foreign tax credit 간접외국세액공제
indirect guarantee 간접보증
indirect incidental expenses 간접부수비용
indirect investment 간접투자
indirect inward investment 대내간접투자
indirect issue 간접발행
indirect labor cost 간접노무비
indirect liability 간접부채
indirect material cost 간접재료비
indirect method 간접법
indirect method of depreciation 간접상각
indirect presentation 간접표시
indirect production 간접생산
indirect sales 간접매매
indirect securities 간접증권
indirect tax 간접세
indirect trade 간접무역
indirect wage 간접임금
indirect yield 간접이익
individual annuity 개인연금
individual auction 개별경쟁매매
individual basis 개별기준
individual dealing system 개별매매방식
individual depreciation 개별상각
individual exclusion 개인공제
individual health insurance 개인건강보험
individual income tax 개인소득세
individual inhabitant tax 개인주민세
individual investor 일반투자가
individual issue 개별상품
individual life insurance 개인생명보험
individual production 개별생산
individual proprietor 자영업자
Individual Retirement Account 개인퇴직적립계정

individual retirement account 개인퇴직연금제도
individual separate account 단일고객분리계정
individual stockholder 개인주주
individual taxation 개별과세
individual useful life 개별내용연수
individual variable annuity 개인변액연금
individual with regular income 고정수입이 있는 개인
indivisible credit 불가분채권
indorsed note 이서어음
indorsement 이서
indorsement in blank 백지식이서
indorsement of address 주소이서
indoser 이서인
induced investment 유발투자
inducement 유인
inducement to invest 투자유인
inductive statistics 귀납적 통계
industrial accounting 공업회계
industrial bank 노동자나 소매상의 저축; 융자를 담당하는 금융기관
industrial banking 인더스트리얼뱅킹
industrial bill 공업어음
industrial bond 사업채
industrial bookkeeping 공업부기
industrial capital 산업자본
industrial classification 산업분류
industrial composition 산업구조
industrial cooperation method 산업협력방식
industrial corporation 사업법인
industrial debenture 사업채
industrial development bond 상업개발채권
industrial dispute 노동쟁의
industrial engineering 생산공학
industrial foundation 공업재단
industrial fund 산업자금
industrial injury 노동재해
industrial insurance 간이보험
industrial law 노동법
industrial loan 사업대부
industrial new design 실용신안
Industrial Ordinary Shares Index 공업주가지수
industrial origin of net national product 산업별 국민순생산
industrial output 노동생산
industrial policy 산업정책
industrial production 공업생산
industrial production index 광공업생산지수
industrial property 공업소유권
industrial rationalization 산업합리화
industrial revenue bond 산업특정재원채
industrial right 공업소유권
industrial stock 공업주
industrial structure 산업구조
industrial structure policy 산업구조정책
industrial-accident reserve 산업사고준비금
industrialized countries 공업국
industry 산업
industry average 업계평균
industry beta value 산업의 베타수치
industry concentration 산업집중
industry effect 산업효과
industry information 산업정보
Industry Investment Special Account 산업투자특별회계
industry practice 업계관행
industry realignment 업계재편
industry segments 업계
industry specialist 업계스페셜리스트
industry standard 업계기준
industry weighting ratio 업종별 편입률
inefficient 비효율적인
ineligible 적합하지 않은
ineligible bill 비적격채
inertia effect 관성효과
inescapable cost 회피불능비용
inevitable accident 불가피한 사고
inference 추리
inferior assets 열등자산

inflation 인플레이션
inflation accounting 인플레회계
inflation adjusted 인플레조정필
inflation caused by yen depreciation
엔저인플레
inflation differential 인플레격차
inflation fear 인플레우려
inflation forecast 인플레예측
inflation gap 인플레갭
inflation hedge 인플레헤지
inflation indication 인플레지표
inflation led by import 수입인플레
inflation pressure 인플레압력
inflation psychology 인플레심리
inflation rate 인플레율
inflation sensitivity factor 인플레감응도
inflation spiral 인플레스파이럴
inflationary demand curve 인플레수요곡선
inflationary expectation 인플레기대
inflationary money supply 인플레머니
inflationary supply curve 인플레공급곡선
inflict a loss 손해를 끼치다
inflow of foreign capital 외자유입
influx 유입
influx of foreign capital 외자유입
informal acceptance 약식승인
informal organization 비공식조직
informal sector 비공식부문
information accounting 정보회계
information audit 정보감사
information economics 정보경제학
information highway 정보고속도로
information industry 정보산업
information network system
고도정보통신시스템
information pollution 정보공해
information ratio 정보지수
information retrieval 정보검색
information risk 정보리스크
information service 정보서비스
information society 정보화사회
information sources on beta value
베타수치에 기반을 둔 정보원
information system 정보시스템
information system business 정보시스템사업
information technology 정보기술
information value 정보가치
information vendors 정보벤더
information-motivated trader
정보동기로 인한 거래자
information-motivated transaction
정보동기에 따른 매매
infrastructure 인프라스트럭처
infrastructure cost 인프라비용
infrastructure improvement 인프라정비
infrastructure stock 인프라관련주
infrastructure work 인프라사업
infringement 권리침해
infringement of copyright 판권침해
infringement of ownership 소유권침해
infringement of patent right 특허권침해
infusion 투입
inhabitant tax 주민세
inheritance tax 상속세
Inheritance Tax Law 상속세법
inheritance tax on undivided bequest
미분할 유산의 상속세
inheritance tax paid in kind 상속세물납
inherited property 상속재산
initial 기초
initial balance 기초잔고
initial capital 기초자본
initial cost 원가
initial cost of business 개업비
initial date in reckoning 기산일
initial delivery 최초인도
initial depreciation 초기상각
initial down payment 내입금
initial establishment 초기설정
initial expenses 창업비
initial goods in process 기초제작중인 물건
initial installment 내입금

initial inventories 기초재고자산
initial listing 신규상장
initial margin 기본증거금
initial margin requirement 초기증거금비율
initial margin requirements 위탁보증금비율
initial measurements 당초측정
initial par value 일차평가
initial payment 내입금
initial public offering 신규주식공모
initial reserve 초회준비금
initial special depreciation 초연도특별상각
initial work in process account 기초제작품계정
initiation fee 입회금
injection of public pund 공적자금주입
injunction 금지명령
injunction proceedings 금지절차
inland bill 국내어음
inland bill of exchange 내국환어음
inland exchange 내국환
Inland Revenue 영국국내세입청
innocent misrepresentation 선의의 부실 표시
innocent purchaser 선의의 매주
innovation 혁신;갱정
innovative 혁신적인
input coefficient 투입계수
input-output analysis 투입산출분석
input-output table 투입산출표
inquiry 조회
inquiry agency 신용조사기관
inquiry for the balances 잔고조회
inscribed bond 기명채권
inscribed securities 기명증권
inscribed stock 기명주
inscribed stock certificate 기명주권
insecurity clause 저당약관
inside build-up 책임준비금증가액
inside information 내부정보
inside market 인사이드마켓
inside the room 장내
insider 인사이더
insider information 인사이더정보
insider trading 인사이더거래
Insider Trading and Securities Fraud Enforcement Act of 1988 내부자거래와 증권사기에 대한 규제법
insolvency 채무초과
insolvency of debtors 채무자의 반제불능
insolvency proceedings 파산절차
insolvent corporation 지불불능회사
insolvent debtor 파산자
insolvent liquidation 채무불이행에 따른 청산
inspection 검사
inspection certificate 검사증명서
inspection of corporate record 회사기록을 검사함
inspection of documents 문서열람
inspection of property 재산검사
installation 설치
installation work 설치공사
installment 할부
installment basis 할부기준
installment bond 연속상환채
installment credit 할부채권
installment method 할부기준
installment payable 할부미불금
installment payment 분할지불
installment payment of tax 불할납세
installment plan 할부판매법
installment purchase 할부구매
installment receivable 할부외상금
installment sales 월부판매
installment savings 정기예금
installment settlement 분할지불
installment time deposit 적립정기예금
instance 신청
Instance Court 해사사건법원
Institute Cargo Clauses 협회화물약관
institute clauses 협회약관
Institute of Chartered Financial Analyst 미국공인증권분석가협회
Institute of Internal Auditors

미국내부감사인협회
Institute of London Underwriters 런던보험업자협회
institute strikes; riots and civil commotion clauses 협회파업폭동담보약관
institute theft; pilferage and non-delivery clauses 협회도난불도착담보약관
institute war clauses 협회전쟁위기담보약관
institution 기관
institution buying 법인매입
Institution of Chartered Accountants in English and Wales 영국특허회계사협회
institution of law suits 소송
institutional 제도상의
institutional accounting 제도회계
institutional approach 제도연구
institutional arbitration 기관중재
institutional buying 기관매입
institutional factor 제도상의 요인
institutional investors 기관투자가
institutional investors' index option 기관투자가지수옵션
institutional postulate 제도공준
institutional school 제도학파
institutional selling 기관매출
institutional stockholder 법인주주
instruction 지시
instruction of exercise 권리행사를 지시함
instruction to bidders 입찰자에 대한 지시서
instructions at entrustment 위탁시의 지시사항
instrument 상품
instrument payable to bearer 지참인지불증권
instruments for buying operation 매입대상채권
insufficient funds 잔고부족
insurable interest 피보험이익
insurable risk 보험대상이 되는 리스크
insurable value 보험가액
insurance 보험
insurance accounting 보험회계
insurance against death 사망보험
insurance agent 보험대리점
insurance amount 보험금액
insurance broker 보험브로커
insurance brokers act 보험브로커법
Insurance Brokers Registration Council 보험브로커등록평의회
insurance business 보험업
insurance business law 보험업법
insurance claim 미수보험금
insurance claims unsettled 미결산보험금
insurance clause 보험약관
insurance company 보험회사
insurance contract 보험계약
insurance council 보험심의회
insurance expense 보험료
insurance for account to whom it may concern 불특정타인을 위한 보험
insurance holding company 보험지주회사
insurance industry 보험업계
insurance law 보험감독법
insurance leverage 보험레버리지
insurance management 보험관리
insurance of medical expenses 의료보험
insurance of substandard lives 표준하체보험계약
insurance payable at death 사망보험
insurance policy 보험증권
insurance pool 보험풀
insurance premium 보험료
insurance premium deduction 보험료공제
insurance prepaid 전불보험료
insurance principle 보험원리
insurance product firm 보험상품취급업자
insurance proposal form 보험계약신청서
insurance scheme 보험형 연금
insurance sector 보험업계
insurance tax 보험세
insurance value 보험가액
insurance with annuity 연금부 보험

insurance without medical examination 고지서취급(감수자 의견 확인 요망)
insurance year 연금가입연수
insured 피보험자
insured amount 보험금액
insured pension plan 보험형 연금
insured peril 피보험위험
insured property 피보험물
insured unemployment 보험수급실업
insurer 보험자
insurmountable difficulty 쉽게 회복되지 않는 상태
intake of foreign capital 외자도입
intangible assets 무형자산
intangible capital 무형자본
intangible depreciable assets 무형감가상각자산
intangible depreciable property 무형상각자산
intangible effects 무형효과
intangible fixed assets 무형고정자산
intangible property 무형재산
intangible right 무체권
intangibles 무형고정자산
integral part 중요한 부분
integrated circuit card IC 카드
integrated economy 통치경제
integrated production 일관생산
integration 통산
integrity 통합
intellectual property right 지적소유권
intensification 격화
intensive investment 집중투자
intention 의사
intention to purchase 구입의사
intentional 고의의
inter industry analysis 산업연관분석
Inter-American Development Bank 미주개발은행
inter-bank 은행간의
inter-bank deposit 은행간 예금
inter-bank exchange transaction 인터뱅크 환거래
inter-bank loan 인터뱅크론
inter-bank market 인터뱅크장
inter-bank rate 은행간 상장
inter-bank spot rate 은행간 스포트레이트
inter-branch account 지점상호계정
inter-branch loss 지점상호간 손실
inter-branch profit 지점상호간 이익
inter-company account 회사간 계정
inter-company elimination 회사간 제거
inter-company loss 회사상호간 손실
inter-company profit 회사간 이익
inter-company transfer variance 내부대체차액
inter-government 정부간의
inter-industry 산업간의
inter-industry-relation table 산업관련법
inter-market 시장간
inter-market spread 시장간 스프레드
inter-market trading system 시장간 거래시스템
inter-office account 본지점계정
inter-office exchange adjustment account 환끝환산차금
inter-office rate 본지점레이트
inter-period tax allocation 연도간 세배분
interaction 쌍방향성
interbank money market 은행간 시장
intercommon 상호입회하다
intercontract month spread trading 한월간 스프레드거래
interdepartment account 부문간 계정
interdepartmental 부문간의
interdepartmental profit 내부대체이익
interest 지분;이해관계;이권
interest advance 선불이자
interest after the maturity 기한후 이자
interest and amortization 원리반제액
interest and dividends received 수입이자 및 배당금

interest arbitrage 금리재정
interest arrears 지연이자
interest bearing 이자부
interest bearing bank debenture 이자부 금융채
interest bearing issuance 유리발행
interest bill 이자부 어음
interest burden 이자부담
interest cap trading 금리캡거래
interest capitalization 이자자산화
interest capitalization method 원가방식
interest charge 이자비용
interest claims 이자클레임
interest component 금리부문
interest cost 이자비용
interest coupon 이권
interest cover 이자비용
interest coverage ratio 금리부담율
interest earned 수취이자
interest equalization tax 금리평형세
interest exposure 금리리스크
interest for arrears 지연이자
interest for delinquency 연체이자
interest futures 금리선물
interest group 압력단체
interest in arrears 연체이자
interest included 원리합계
interest income 이자소득
interest incurred during construction 건설이자
interest margin 이자마진
interest method 이자법
interest of shareholder 주주이해
interest on bond 사채이자
interest on borrowed 차입금이자
interest on borrowed fund 부채이자
interest on call loans 콜론이자
interest on call money 콜머니이자
interest on deposit 예금금리
interest on external bond 외채이자
interest on foreign currency deposits 외화예금이자
interest on funded debt 장기채이자
interest on government bond 공채이자
interest on government securities 국채이자
interest on guaranty capital 기금이자
interest on loans 대부금이자
interest on loans and discount 대출금이자
interest on loans on bills 어음대부이자
interest on loans rebated 대부금이자반려
interest on overdrafts for export bills 환당좌대이자
interest on postal savings 우편예금이자
interest on Special Drawing Rights 특별인출권이자
interest only 금리만
interest option transaction 금리옵션거래
interest outlay 이자지불
interest parity 금리평가
interest payable 미불이자
interest payment 이자지불
interest payment method 이자지불방법
interest payments on foreign debt 대외채무이자지불
interest per annum 연리
interest per diem 일변
interest prepaid 선불이자
interest rate 금리
interest rate abroad 해외금리
interest rate adjustment 금리조정
interest rate arbitrage 금리재정
interest rate arbitrage transaction 금리재정거래
interest rate change 이자율변화
interest rate collar 금리칼라
interest rate control 금리조작
interest rate differential 금리차
interest rate floor 금리플로어
interest rate fluctuation 금리변동
interest rate futures 금리선물
interest rate futures contracts 금리선물계약
interest rate futures option trading

금리선물옵션거래
interest rate level 금리수준
interest rate minded 금리마인드
interest rate movement 금리동향
interest rate on borrowing 차입금금리
interest rate on inter-bank deposit
은행 간 예금 금리
interest rate on loans 대출금리
interest rate on loans secured by time deposit
정기예금담보대출금리
interest rate on the Eurocurrecy market
유로 금리
interest rate on time deposit 정기예금금리
interest rate option 금리옵션
interest rate payable by buyer 매수자금리
interest rate policy 금리정책
interest rate raise 금리인상
interest rate receivable by seller 매수자금리
interest rate risk 금리리스크
interest rate sensitive items 금리감응항목
interest rate sensitive stock 금리민감주
interest rate sensitivity 금리감응도
interest rate spread 금리마진
interest rate swap 금리스와프
interest receivable 수취이자
interest receivable on bank deposits
미수은행예금이자
interest received 수취이자
interest sensitive policy 변액보험
Interest Sensitive Whole Life
금리감응형 종신보험
interest sensitivity of the pension surplus
연금잉여의 금리감응도
interest skimming 인터레스트스키밍
interest spread 금리차
interest strips 금리스트리프채
interest surplus 금리차익
interest swap 금리스와프
interest swap bond 금리스와프채
interest tax 이자세
interest tax on authorized deferred payment of income tax
소득세의 연납에 수반되는 이자세
interest tax on delayed payment
연납과 관련된 이자세
interest volatility risk 금리변동리스크
interest-bearing bank debenture 이자금융채
interest-bearing bond 이자부채
interest-bearing debt 이자부부채
interest-bearing security 이자부증권
interest-rate risk 이자율에 관한 리스크
interest-sensitive products 금리감응형 상품
interested party 이해관계자
interference 간섭
interference with trade 영업에 대한 간섭
interfirm analysis 기업간 분석
intergenerational 세대간의
intergenerational altruism 세대간 이타주의
interim 임시의;중간의
interim account 중간계정
interim audit 기중감사
interim closing 중간결산
interim contract 가계약
interim dividend 중간배당
interim financial statements 중간재무제표
interim interest payment 중간지불이자
interim loan 입금예정의 공백을 메우기 위해서 받는 융자
interim measure 경과조치
interim measures 경과조치
interim receipt 가영수증
interim report 중간보고
interim results 중간결산
interim return 중간보고
interim return form 중간보고서
interim sales 중간매상
interim statement 중간계산서
interim tax return 중간신고
interlocking 운동
interlocking directors 겸임중역
interlocking stockholding 주식비율
intermarket spread 시장간 스프레드

intermediary 중개자
intermediary agents 중개기관
intermediary bank 중개은행
intermediary trade 삼국간 무역
intermediate accounting 중급회계학
intermediate goods 중간재
intermediate improvement trade 중계가공무역
intermediate lag 중간래그
intermediate product 중간제품
intermediate securities 중기증권
intermediate target 운영목표
intermediate tariff 중간세율
intermediate term market outlook 중기예상
intermediate tranche 중기트란시
intermediate-term loan 중기론
intermediating financial institution 금융중개기관
intermediation fee 중개수수료
intermediation of a third party 제삼자의 개입
intermediation of trading 거래를 중개함
internal accounting control 내부회계통제
internal analysis 내부분석
internal audit 내부감사
internal audit report 내부감사보고서
internal audit standard 내부감사기준
internal audit system 내부감사제도
internal auditor 내부감사인
internal bond 내국채
internal business analysis 내부경영분석
internal capital 내부자본
internal cash flow 내부캐시플로
internal check 내부견제
internal check system 내부견제제도
internal consistency 내부정합성
internal control 내부통제
internal credit enhancement 내부신용보완
internal debt 내채
internal document 내부자료
internal evidence 내부증거
internal financing 내부금융
internal fund 내부자금
internal investment management 자가운용
internal labor market 내부노동시장
internal liability 내부부채
internal profit 내부이익
internal rate of interest rate 내부이자율
internal rate of return 내부수익률
internal regulations 내부규정
internal reporting 내부보고
internal reporting system 내부보고제도
internal reserve 내부유보금
Internal Revenue Code 미국내국세입법
Internal Revenue Service 미국내국세입청
internal rule 사내규정
internal structure 내부구조
internal tax 내국세
internal trade 국내무역
internal transaction 내부거래
internal transfer profit 사내대체이익
internalization 내재화
internalized order 내부화주문
international accounting 국제기업회계
international accounting standards 국제회계기준
International Accounting Standards Committee 국제회계기준위원회
international affairs 대외관계
international agency bond 국제기관채권
international agreed specialization 합의에 따른 국제분업
international aid 외국의 원조
International Air Transport Association 국제항공운송협회
international asset management 국제자산운용
International Auditing Practices Committee 국제감사실무위원회
international balance of accounts 국제수지
international balance of payment 국제수지
International Bank for Economic Cooperation 국제경제협력은행

I J

international bank for investment 국제투자은행
International Bank for Reconstruction and Development 국제부흥개발은행
international banking 국제은행업무
International Banking 국제은행법
international banking facilities account IBF 계정(국제은행업무계정)
international banking facility 국제은행업무
international banking operation 국제은행업무
international bond 국제채권
international bond trading 국제채권 트레이딩
international borrowing 대외차입
international broking 국제브로킹
international business 국제사업
international capital 국제자본
international capital market 국제자본이동
international capital movement 국제자본이동
international cartel 국제카르텔
international cash management service 국제 CMS
International Center for Settlement of Investment Disputes 투자분쟁해결국제센터
International Chamber of Commerce 국제상공회의소
International Civil Aviation Organization 국제민간항공기관
International Clearing Union 국제청산동맹
international commercial arbitration 국제상업중재
International Commercial Terms 인터컴즈
international commodity agreement 국제상품협정
international comparables 국제비교
international comparison 국제비교
international competitiveness 국제경쟁력
international consortium 국제인수단
international contribution 국제공헌
international conventions 국제조약
international crisis 국제위기
international currency 국제통화
international currency system 국제통화제도
international custody 국제보호
international custom 국제관습법
international debts 대외채무
international depositary receipts 국제예탁증서
International Development Association 국제개발협회
international diversified investment 국제분산투자
international division of roles 국제분업
international double taxation 국제이중과세
international economics 국제경제학
international economist 국제이코노미스트
international equilibrium 국제균형
international equity market 국제주식시장
international equity placement 주식해외매출
international exchange 국제환
International Federation of Stock Exchanges 국제증권거래소연합
international finance 국제금융
International Finance Corporation 국제금융공사
international financial institution 국제금융기관
international financial market 국제금융시장
international financial system 국제금융제도
international fund 국제자금
International Fund for Agricultural Development 국제농업개발기금
international indebtedness 국제대차
international interest-spread 내외금리차
international investment 국제투자
international investment bank 국제투자은행
international investment trust 국제투자신탁
International Labor Organization 국제노동기관
international law 국제법

international lease 국제리스
international liquidity 국제유동성
international loan portfolio 국제론포트폴리오
international long-term capital movement 국제장기자본이동
international managed currency system 국제관리통화제도
International Maritime Organization 국제해사기관
international market 국제시장
international market price 국제시장가격
international marketing 국제마케팅
international marketing research 국제시장조사
international merchandise 국제상품
International Monetary Exchanges 국제금융거래소
International Monetary Fund 국제통화기금
International Monetary Market 국제통화시장
international monetary system 국제통화제도
international monetary turmoil 국제통화불안
international money management 국제적인 금융관리
international money market 국제금융시장
international movements of funds 국제자금이동
international offerings 국제공모
international oil plays 국제적인 석유주
international operation 국제업무
International Organization of Consumer's Unions 국제소비자기구
International Organization of Securities Commissions 국제증권거래위원회기구
international portfolio 인터내셔널포트폴리오
international portfolio diversification 국제분산투자
international portfolio investment 국제증권투자
international public law 국제공법
international reserves 대외준비고
International Resources Bank 국제자원은행
international securities 국제증권
International Securities Clearing Corporation 국제결제기관
international settlement 국제결제
international settlement currency 국제결제통화
international short-term capital transaction 국제단기자본거래
international short-term money market 국제단기금융시장
International Standardization Organization 국제표준화기구
International standards 국제기준
international stock 국제주권
International Swap Dealers Association 국제스와프딜러
international syndicate 국제신디케이트
international tax law 국제조세법
International Telecommunication Union 국제전기통신연합
international trade 국제무역
International Trade Commission 국제무역위원회
international tranche 국제트란시
international transaction currency 국제거래통화
international underwriting group 국제인수단
International Union of Credit and Investment Insurers 국제수출신용보험기구
International Union of Marine Insurance 국제해상보험연합
international unit 국제단위
internationalization 국제화
interperiod income tax allocation 소득과세를 기간상호배분함
interpolated rate 기간안분이율
interpretation 취급
interpretation clause 해석조항
interpretation for special rule 특례취급

interpretation of cash flows 캐시플로해석
interregional analysis 지역연관분석
interruption of business 영업정지
intersegment sales 사업부문간 매상
Interstate Commerce 주제(州際) 통상
Interstate Commerce Commission 주제(州際)통상위원회
interunit pricing 부문간의 대체가격을 결정함
interunit transfer 부문간 대체
intervention 개입
intervention against market 역풍개입
intervention by selling dollars 달러매출개입
intervention currency 개입통화
intervention following market 순풍개입
intervention level 개입수준
intervention operation 개입조작
intervention point 개입점
intervention purchase 개입구입
intervention rate 개입금리
intra vires 권한내에서
intracompany transfer 내부대체
intracompany transfer price 내부대체가격
intracontract spread 상품간 스프레드
intraday 하루 중에
intraday deviations 당일변동상황
intraday fluctuation margin 당일중의 변동폭
intraday fluctuation rate 당일중의 변동율
intraday high and low 일중고저치
intrafirm analysis 기업내 분석
intramarginal intervention 허용변동폭내 개입
intramarket 시장내
intraperiod income tax 기간 내의 소득과세배분
intraperiod tax allocation 기간 내의 세금배분
interregional trade 지역 내 무역
intrinsic deposit 본원예금
intrinsic value 본원적인 가치
introduced mortgage business 제휴론에 따른 모기지조건
introduced stock 공개주
introducing 중개
introducing firm 주문중개업자
introduction 소개
introduction of technology 기술도입
invalid card 무효카드
invalid coupon 효력이 없는 쿠폰
inventories acquired by merger 합병으로 취득한 재고자산
inventories of merchandise and supplies 저장품
inventory 재고자산
inventory accounting 재고자산회계
inventory accounts 재고자산계정
inventory adjustment 재고조정
inventory assets 재고자산
inventory at the beginning of the period 기초재고자산
inventory at the end of period 기말재고자산
inventory audit 재고자산감사
inventory budget 재고예산
inventory capital 재고자산
inventory carrying cost 보관비
inventory certificate 재고증명서
inventory change 재고변동
inventory control 재고정리
inventory cycles 재고순환
inventory excess 과잉재고
inventory financing 재고금융
inventory fluctuation account 재고자산가격변동계정
inventory indexes 재고지수
inventory investment 재고투자
inventory loss 재고손
inventory management 재고관리
inventory method 재고자산계산법
inventory of security 담보목록
inventory of work in process at the beginning of period 제작중인 물건의 이월고
inventory profit 재고자산이익

inventory ration 재고율
inventory recession 인벤토리리세션
inventory reserve 재고자산평가준비금
inventory sales ratio 재고율
inventory sheet 재고표
inventory shipments ratio 재고율
inventory tag 재고표
inventory turnover 재고자산회전율
inventory unit 재고단위
inventory valuation 재고자산평가
inventory valuation adjustment 재고평가조정
inventory valuation method 재고자산평가방법
inventory valuation-reserves 재고자산평가준비금
inventory value 재고평가액
inventory variation 재고자산증감
inverse floater 역플로터채
inverse matrix table 역행렬표
inverse yield 역이익
inverted market 시중은행의 할인율상회시장
inverted yield curve 역이율
inverted yield curve phenomena 역이율현상
invested assets 운용자산
invested capital 투하자본
investing activities 투자활동
investing public 대중투자가
investment 출자
investment abroad 해외투자
investment account 투자계정부문
investment advisor 투자고문
investment advisory industry 투자고문업계
investment advisory law 투자고문법
investment analysis 투자분석
investment analyst 투자분석가
investment and loan 투융자
investment approvals 투자승인액
investment assets 투자자산
investment bank 투자은행
investment banking business 투자은행업법
Investment Banking Financing Company 투자은행금융기관
investment boom 투자경기
investment budget 투자예산
investment business 투자업
investment buying 투자매
investment by foreign investors 외국인투자
investment capital 투자자금
investment choice 투자처
investment climate 투자환경
investment club 투자클럽
investment committee 투자위원회
investment company 투자회사
Investment Company Act of 1940 1940년의 투자회사법
Investment Company Amendments Act of 1970 1970년의 개정투자회사법
Investment contracts 직접투자총액(계약베이시스)
investment counselor 투자카운셀러
investment credit 투자공제
investment criteria 투자척도
investment currency 투자통화
investment curve 투자곡선
investment decision 투자결정
investment demand 투자수요
investment dollar 투자달러
investment environment 투자환경
investment expenditure 투자지출
investment flexibility 투자유연성
Investment friction 투자마찰
investment function 투자함수
investment function of profit principle type 이윤원리형 투자함수
investment fund 투자신탁
Investment goods 투자재
investment grade 투자적격
investment grade bond 투자적격채권
investment grade corporate 투자대상기업
investment grade rate 투자적격레이팅
investment grade securities 투자적격채
investment holding period 투자기간

I
J

investment horizon 소유기간
investment in affiliates 관계회사출자금
investment in bonds 사채투자
investment in capital 출자금
investment in kind 현물출자
investment in kind theory of merger 현물출자설
investment in long-term financial instruments 장기금융상품에 투자함
investment in money 현금출자
investment in plant and machinery 설비투자
investment in securities 투자유가증권
investment in stocks 주식투자
investment income 투자소득
investment information sources 투자정보원
investment judgment 투자판단
investment ledger 유가증권원장
investment letter 투자목적확인서
investment management 투자운용
investment management company 투자고문회사
investment manager 투자매니저
investment manager structure 투자매니저구성
investment market 투자시장
investment merit 투자메리트
investment multiplier 투자승수
investment objectives 투자목표
investment opportunities 투자기회
investment overseas 해외투자
investment performance 운용실적
investment period 투자기간
investment philosophy 투자철학
investment policy 투자정책
investment policy of personal investor 개인투자가의 투자방침
investment portfolio 투자포트폴리오
investment products 투자상품
investment profit 자기계정매매익
investment program 투자계획
investment propensity 투자성향
investment property 투자부동산
investment purchased register 유가증권매입기입장
investment rate 투자율
investment real estate 투자부동산
investment recovery 투자회수
investment result 투자성과
investment return 이익
investment revaluation reserve 투자재평가적립금
investment risk 투자리스크
investment securities 투자유가증권
investment securities gains 투자유가증권수익
investment securities markets 투자유가증권시장
investment securities portfolio 투자유가증권포트폴리오
investment securities transaction 투자유가증권거래
investment security 투자증권
investment selection summary 투자선택개괄
investment sold register 유가증권매각기입장
investment stock 투자주
investment strategy 투자전략
investment tax credit 투자세액공제
investment trust 투자신탁
Investment Trust Association of Japan 증권투자신탁협회
investment trust management company 투자신탁위탁회사
investment trust on securities 증권투자신탁
investment value 투자가치
investment vehicle 투자자회사
investment year method 투자연도별 방식
investor 출자자
investor briefings 투자가를 위한 세미나
investor buying 투자가의 구매
investor interest 투자가의 관심
investor perceptions 투자가의 견해
investors relations 인베스터즈릴레이션즈
invisible account 무역외수지

invisible assets 무형자산
invisible hand 보이지 않는 손
invisible trade 무역외
invisible trade balance 무역외수지
invitation 유인
invitation telex 권유텔렉스
invoice 송장;청구서
invoice amount 운송장가격
invoice book 청구서
invoice method 인보이스방식
invoice-book inward 상품구입장
invoice-book outward 상품발송장
involuntary 자발적이 아닌
involuntary bankruptcy 강제파산
involuntary conversion 강제교환
involuntary exchange 교환처분
involuntary insolvency 강제지불불능
involuntary loss or gain 비자연적인 손익
involuntary transfer 강제적인 양도
involuntary unemployment 비자발적인 실업
inward direct investment 대내직접투자
inward exchange 타발환
inward investment 대내투자
IOU 차용증권
iron and steel industry 철강업계
irrational tax 악세
irrecoverable cost 회수불능원가
irredeemable bond 불상환채
irregular installment payment 불균등지불
irregular practices 부정행위
irrelevant 관련성이 없는
irreparable injury 회복불가능한 침해
irretrievable deprivation 가망이 없는 상실
irrevocable 철회할 수 없는
irrevocable commitment 취소불가능한 위임
irrevocable L/C 취소불능신용장
irrevocable license 취소할 수 없는 허가
I-S curve · L-M curve IS 곡선, LM 곡선
island reversal pattern 아일랜드리버설패턴
issuance guidelines 적채기준
issuance of bond 채권발행
issuance of capital stock for non-cash assets 현물출자
issuance of new debt 신규발행채권을 발행함
issuance of stock 주식을 발행함
issuance purpose 발행목적
issuance volume 발행액
issue at face value 액면발행
issue at intermediate price 중간발행
issue at market price 시가발행
issue at par 액멸발행;퍼발행
issue by tender 입찰발행
issue date 발행일
issue market 발행시장
issue of bond 기채
issue of public bonds 공공채발행
issue of shares 주식발행
issue of shares at market price 주식시가발행
issue of the wall between banking and security business 은행 증권 간의 담장논쟁
issue on a tap basis 탭채로 발행하다
issue price 매출가격
issue standards 적채기준
issue tax 발행세
issue terms 발행조건
issue used in the average 평균주가채용문제
issue value 발행가격
issued at a discount 할인발행된
issued at par 액면발행된
issued capital stock 발행필 주식자본금
issued share 발행필 주식
issued shares 발행필 주식
issued stocks 발행필 주식
issuer 발행회사
issuer defaults 발행채채권불이행
issuer's cost 발행자비용
issuer's own stock repurchase 자기주권매입
issues listed on the over-the-counter market 장외등록상품
issues paper 토의보고서
issues to shareholders 주주할당

issuing bank 발행은행
issuing corporation 발행회사
issuing house 발행상사
issuing yields 발행이율
item 항목
item depreciation 개별상각
item in transit 미달항목
item of account 계정항목
itemized account 분개계정; 명세계정
itemized bill 내역계정서
itemized deduction 개별공제
items not affecting cash flows
캐시플로에 영향을 받지 않는 항목
items of business 영업종목
items of payment 지불항목
items on income statement 손익계산서항목
itinerant merchants 행상인

J

J curve J 커브
J curve effect J 커브 효과
J-NET J-NET 시장
Jacobson & Ponsbach General Index 스웨덴 J&P 종합지수
JASDAQ 자스닥
jeopardy 위험
job analysis 직무분석
job application 유효구직자수
job availability 고용기회
job cost 개별원가
job cost system 개별원가계산
job lot 싸구려물건
job opportunities 고용기회
job order cost system 개별원가계산법
job order costing 개별원가계산
job slip 작업전표
jobber 중매인
jobbing 중매행위
joint 공동의
joint account 공통계정
joint agreement 연합협약
joint and several 연대
joint and several bond 연대증서
joint and several guarantee 연대보증
joint and several guarantor 연대보증
joint and several liability 연대책임
joint and several obligation 연대채무
joint and several obligation of tax liability 연대납세의무
joint and several obligation of tax payment 연대납부책임
joint audit 공동감사
joint bond 합동사채
joint cost 결합비용
joint currency float 공동변동상장
joint development 공동개발
joint enterprise cooperative 기업조합
joint financing 공동융자
joint floating exchange rate 공동변동상장
joint guarantee 공동보증
joint inspection 합동검사
joint intervention 협조개입
joint investment 합병
joint lead 조인트리드
joint liability 공동책임
joint life insurance 연생보험
joint marketing 공동판매
joint obligation 합유채권
joint ownership 공유
joint partners 공동파트너
joint product 연산품
joint purchase 공동구매
joint relationship 공동관계
joint return 공동신고
joint right 합유
joint sales 공동판매
joint stock company 주식회사
joint submission of return 신고서를 공동제출함
joint surety 연대보증인
joint tenancy 합유부동산권

joint trust 합동운용신탁
Joint venture 합작투자
joint-and-several liability 연대보증채무
joint-floating market system 공동변동장
journal 분개장
journal book 분개장
journal entry 분개기입
journal ledger 대체원장
journal slip 대체전표
journal voucher 대체영수증
journalizing 분개
judge 판사
judgment creditor 판결채권자
judgment debtor 판결채무자
judgment of definite liabilities 채권확정판결
judgment of exclusion on shareholders rights 주권제권판결
judgment set-off 판결채권이 상쇄됨
judicial act 법률행위
judicial definition 판례
judicial proceedings 사법절차
judicial valuation 법정평가
jumbo issue 대형발행
jump process 점프과정
junior accountant 회계사보
junior bond 후순위채권
junior claim 열후청구권
junior creditor 후순위채권자
junior debt 열후채권
junior encumbrance 토지에 대한 후순위권리
junior issue 하위증권
junior lien bond 후순위선취특권부 사채
junior mortgage 후순위저당
junior securities 열후증권
junior security 후순위담보
junior subordinated 하위열후
junior tranche 하위트란시
junk bond 정크본드
junk issue 정크채
Juridical person 법인
juridical person for public interest 공익법인
juridical person in a public law 특수법인
juridical personality 법인격
juridical sale 강제매매
jurisdiction 관할
jurisdiction of the person 인적관할권
jurisdiction of the res 대물관할권
jurisdictional defect 관할차이
jurisprudence 법률학
juristic act 법률행위
Just after the opening 시작하자마자
just and equitable principle 신의성실의 원칙
just and equitable principle of transactions 거래의 신의칙
just compensation 정당한 보상
justifiable act 정당행위
justifiable reason to apply 적용하는 정당한 이유
justification 정당화
juvenile comprehensive insurance 어린이종합보험

K

Kansas City Board of Trade 캔자스시티상품거래소
keep-well agreement 건전성유지계약
Keogh Plan 자영업자 퇴직연금
key currency 기축통화
key executive insurance 경영자보험
key factor 주요원인
key industry 기간산업
key rate 정책금리
key rate cut 공정금리인하
key reversal day 상장의 대전환일
key statistics 통계총괄표
keymoney 권리금
Keynes effect 케인즈효과
Keynesian 케인스학파
Keynesian economics 케인즈경제학
Keynesian revolution 케인스혁명
keystone bond funds 키스톤채권
kick back 킥백
killing 큰 벌이
kinds of transaction 거래의 종류
Kingston Regime 킹스턴체제
kinked demand curve 굴절수요곡선
Kitchen cycles 단기파동; 키친사이클
kite bill 융통어음
knock out 담합경매
knock-down price 크게 깎은 가격
knock-down product 녹다운제품
knock-on effect 파급효과
knock-out option 정지조건부 옵션
knock-out option trading 정지조건부 옵션거래
knowledge 인식
knowledge and discernment 견식
knowledge engineering 지식공학
knowledge industry 지식산업
knowledge intensive industry 지식집약산업
Kondratieff wave 콘드라티에프파(주기)

L

labeled price 매가
labor & material payment bond
임금하청대금지불보증증권
labor account 임금계정
labor agreement 노동협약
labor audit 노무감사
labor coefficient 노동계수
labor cost 노임
labor credit associations 노동금고
labor dispute 노동쟁의
labor economics 노동경제학
labor efficiency 작업효율
labor force 노동력
labor income 노동소득
labor laws 노동법
labor legislation 노동입법
labor market 노동시장
labor market data 고용통계
labor rate standard 임률표준
labor rate variance 임률차이
labor regulations 노동법규
labor relation 노사관계
labor share 노동분배율
labor time variance 작업시간차이
labor trouble 노동분쟁
labor turnover 노동자이동
labor union 노동조합
labor variance 노동비차이
labor-intensive industry 노동집약적 산업
lackluster 활기가 없는
Latter curve 래터곡선
lag 뒤떨어지다
lag analysis 래그분석
lag effect 래그효과
lagging 지연
lagging indicator 지행지수
lagging series 지행계수
lagging stock 지연주식
laid-down cost 도착원가
laissez-faire 무간섭주의
lame duck 제명회원
land 토지
land account 토지계정
land and building 토지건물
land category 지목
land charges 토지부담
land cost 용지비
land development tax 택지개발세
land expropriation 토지수용
land expropriation law 토지수용법
land expropriation right 토지수용권
land for residence 주택용 토지
land for sale in lots 분양권
land improvement 토지개량
land improvement enterprise 토지개량사업
land improvement expenses 토지개량비
land ledger 토지대장
land lot 토지
land lot without construction
건물 등이 들어서지 않은 택지
land ownership 토지소유
land price 지가

land proprietor 토지소유자
land purchase for specified business 특정사업의 용지매수
land quality terms 용지품질조건
land reform 토지개량
land registration 토지등기
land registry 토지등기소
land required for 용지
land tax 지조(地租)
land tax register book 토지과세대장
land taxation 토지세제
land tenant 토지보유자
land tenure 토지보유
land transportation industry 육운업
land trust 토지신탁
land value tax 토지가격세
Land Value Tax Law 토지세법
landed estate 부동산;토지
landing tax 입국세
landowner 토지소유자
languish 활기를 잃다
laps 집행
lapse 보험계약에 실패함
lapse of the leasehold 차지권의 기간이 경과함
lapsed contract 실효계약
lapsed days 경과일수
lapsed share 실효주
lapsed time 경과시간
lapsing schedule of fixed assets 고정자산증감명세표
large acquisition 대형매수
large amount deposit interest 고액예금금리
large amount time deposit 고액정기
large amount transaction 고액거래
large block trading 고액거래
large capital stock 대형주
large company 대기업
large credit 고액채권
large depreciable property 대규모상각자산
large institutional investors 큰 기관투자가
large investment bank 대투자은행
large order 거액주문
large risks 거대리스크
large scale bond issue 채권을 대량으로 발행함
large shareholder 대주주
large-sized stock 대형주
Laspeyres formula 라스파이레스방식
last close price 전일종가
last cost method 최종구입원가법
last day of trading 최종거래일
last heir 최종상속인
last payment date 불입기일
last price 종가
last purchase method 최종구입원가법
last resort 라스트리조트
last resort lender 최후의 대주(貸主)
last-in first-out basis 후입선출기준
last-in first-out method 후입선출법
last fee 지연손해금
late payment charge 지연손해금
late presentation 제시지연
late shipment 선적지연
latent assets 비밀적립금
latent call option 잠재적인 콜옵션
latent demand 잠재수요
latent equity holdings 보유주포함
latent loss 비밀손실
latent return 비밀수익
latent unemployment 잠재실업
latent warrant 잠재워런트
latter half 하반기
latter half of the year 후기
lattice approach 격자법
launch 런치
launch date 발행개시일
launch spread 런치스프레드
launching 기채;모집발표
laundered money 위장자금
law 법률
Law Amending Part of the Commercial Code 상법 등의 일부를 개정한 법률

K L

law change 법률변경
Law Concerning Central Securities Depository and Book-Entry Transfer 주권 등의 보관 및 대체에 관한 법률
Law Concerning Government Bonds 국채에 관한 법률
law concerning restrictions on money lending business 대금업규제법
law concerning restrictions on the acceptance of subscription; deposit and interest rate, etc. 출자법
law concerning restrictions on the maximum interest rate 이자제한법
Law Concerning Seciruties Investment Trust and Securities Investment Companies 증권투자신탁 및 증권투자법인에 관한 법률
law for foreign securities company 외국증권업법
law of diminishing return 수익체감의 법칙
law of exception 예외의 원칙
law of increasing public expenditures 경비팽창의 원칙
law of indifference 일물일가(一物一價)의 법칙
law of large numbers 대수의 법칙
law of member firms 회원법
law of nations 국제법
law of nature 자연법
law of obligations 채권법
law of ship's flag 기국법;선적국법
law of subscription 출자법
law of substitution 대체법률
law of succession 상속법
law office 법률사무소
law on bills 어음법
Law on Securitization of Specified Assets 특정자본의 유동화에 관한 법률
law relating to tax reduction and postponement of collection for disaster victims 재해감면법
law with expiration date 시한입법
lawful 적법의
lawful age 성년
lawsuits 소송
lawyer 변호사
lawyer's fee 변호사료
lawyer's liability 변호사책임
lawyer's liability insurance 변호사배상책임보험
lay 풋내기의
lay-days 상륙기간
layoff 레이오프
LBO fund LBO 펀드
L/C beneficiary 신용장수익자
L/C confirming bank 신용장확인은행
L/C margin money 신용장개설부증금
lead 이르게 하다;이끌다
lead analyst 주임애널리스트
lead manager 주간사
lead time 리드타임
leader of long side 구입장본인
leader of short side 매출장본인
leaders 주도주
leadership personality 지도력
leading case 지도적인 판례
leading counsel 주임변호인
leading domestic demand 내수를 이끄는
leading edge 최첨단
leading index of business conditions 경기선행지수
leading indicator 경기선행지수
leading series 선행계열
leading share 선두주
leading stock 선도상품
leads and lags 리즈앤드래그즈
leak of know-how 노하우누설
leap 대폭증가
learning curve 학습곡선
lease accounting 리스회계
lease bond 임대보증증권
lease contract 임대계약
lease financing 리스금융
lease in perpetuity 영대차지권

lease liability 리스채무
lease obligation bond 리스재원채
lease of property 자산임대
lease period 리스기간
lease property 리스물건
lease receivable 리스채권
lease tenant right 차지권
lease-holder 차지인
lease-up 리스업
leaseback 리스백
leased asset 리스자산
leased land 임차지
leasehold 차지권을 부여하는 계약
leasehold estate 임차부동산
leasehold insurance 임차보험
leaseholder 차지권자
leasing business 리스업무
leasing company 리스회사
leasing contract 리스계약
least less developed countries 후발발전도상국
least-squares method 최소제곱법
leave order 지정가격주문
ledger 원장
ledger account 원장계정
ledger assets 원장자산
ledger balance 원장잔고
ledger clerk 원장계
ledger folio 원장페이지수
ledger of accounts 계좌부
ledger of customer accounts 고객계좌부
ledger transfer 원장대체
legal 적법한
legal ability person 능력자
legal action 소송
legal adviser 법률고문
legal aid services 법률상담
legal benefit 법정급부
legal capacity 행위능력
legal capital 법정자본
legal claim 법적청구권
legal community 법조계
legal contract 적법계약
legal cost 소송비용
legal counsel 법률상담
legal defeasance 법적상환
legal department 법무부
legal document 법률서류
legal durable years 법정내용연수
legal duty 법률상의 의무
legal earned surplus reserve 법정이익준비금
legal effect 법적효력
legal entity 법적실체
legal estate 부동산권
legal evidence 법률상의 증거
legal exemption from income tax 기초공제
legal fee 변호사보수
legal framework 법체제
legal fruits 법정과실
legal guardian 법정후견인
legal interest 법정이자
legal investment 투자적격대상
legal lending limit 법정대출한도화
legal liability 법정책임;법적채무
legal lien 선취특권
legal liquidation 법적정리
legal lending limit 법정대출한도액
legal liability 법정책임
legal lien 법적리엔
legal liquidation 법적정리
legal mortgage 보통법상의 모기지
legal notice 적법한 통지
legal opinion 변호사의 의견서
legal organ 정당한 권한이 있는 기관
legal person 법인
legal portion of legacy 법정상속분
legal possession 법률상의 점유
legal presumption 법률상의 추정
legal procedure 재판절차
legal proceedings 법적수단
legal rate 법정이율

legal rate of interest 법정금리
legal relations 법률관계
legal relationship in tax 조세법률관계
legal representation 법률대리인
legal representative 법정대리인
legal reserve 법정준비금
legal resistance 법적대항권
legal responsibility 법적책임
legal risk 법적리스크
legal section 법무부
legal status of issuance 발행근거법
legal subrogation 법정대위
legal tax cut 감세
legal tender 법정통화
legal tender note 강제통용력이 있는 지폐
legal term 법정기한
legal theory 법리론
legal title 보통법상의 소유권
legal valuation 법정평가
legal valuation method of inventory 법정재고평가법
legal welfare expense 법정복리비
legally secured portion 유류분
legend 법례
legislative action 법적조치
legislative department 입법부
legislature 입법부
lended stock 대주;대여주
lender bank 대출은행
lender of last resort 최종대주
lender's preference 대출자의 선호
lender's risk 대출자의 위험
lending 대부
lending a street name 명의대여
lending ability 대출능력
lending attitude 대출자세
lending criteria 대출기준
lending loss 대손금
lending of development funds 개발자금대부
lending operation 대출업무
lending or borrowing of securities 유가증권을 대차함
lending policy 대출정책
lending practice 융자관행
lending rate 대출금리
lending securities 대증권
lending stock 대주
lending terms 대출조건
lending window 대부창구
length of service 재직기한
Leontief's paradox 레온체프의 역설
less fees 수수료차감후
less-developed country 개발도상국
lessee 임차인
lesser evil 문제가 적은 제도
lessor 임대인
let 임대
letter of acceptance 낙찰결정서
letter of administration 유산관재장
letter of allotment 할당장
letter of attorney 위임장
letter of award 낙찰결정서
letter of comfort 각서
letter of confirmation of collateral 담보차입증
letter of credit 신용장
letter of credit advising bank 신용장통지은행
letter of credit beneficiary 신용장수익자
letter of credit confirming bank 신용장확인은행
letter of guarantee 보증장
letter of indemnity 손해보전계약서
letter of intent 합의확인서
letter of license 지불기일연기서면
letter of recommendation 추천장
letter of undertaking 각서
letter or credit issuing bank 신용장발행은행
letter securities 비등록사모채
letter stock 매각제한주식
letters patent 특허증
level 수준
level annual premium method 평준적립방식

level annuity 정액연금
level contribution 평준거출
level of education 교육수준
level of employment 고용수준
level of living 생활수중
level pay floating rate note 정액지불변동이부채
level payment 원리균등분할반제
level premium 평준보험료
level yield 일정이율
leverage 자금효율
leverage effect 레버리지효과
leverage factor 레버리지지수
leverage factor ratio 레버리지비율
leverage ratio 부채비율
leverage test 부채비율
leveraged buyout 레버리지드 바이아웃
leveraged holding 레버리지드 홀딩
leveraged lease 레버리지드 리스
leveraged option 레버리지드 옵션
leveraged position 레버리지드 포지션
leveraged recapitalization 레버리지드 리캐피털리제이션
leveraged stock 레버리지드 스톡
leveraged strategic acquisition 레버리지드 스트래티직 액퀴지션
levy in kind 물납세
levy of attachment 재산차압
levy of tax 과세
liabilities account 부채계정
liabilities and capital 부채 및 자본
liabilities and stockholders' equity 부채 및 자본부문
liabilities exceeding assets 채무초과
liabilities for guarantee 보증채무
liabilities for guarantee against repairs 수선보증예비금
liabilities off the book 장부외 채무
liabilities reserve 부채성 준비금
liability accounting 부채회계
liability for damage 책임소재
liability for endorsement 보증채무
liability hedge 부채헤지
liability limits 보상한도액
liability management 부채관리
liability of estimated amount 견적에 따른 채무
liability rate 부채금리
liability ratio 부채이율
liability reserve 책임준비금
liability side 부채측
liability structure 부채구조
liability swap 채무스와프
liability with interest 유이자부채
liaison office 주재원사무소;연락사무소
liberalization of capital transactions 자본거래자유화
liberalization of exchange control 환자유화
liberalization of interest rate 금리자유화
liberalization of trade 무역자유화
liberalization rate 자유화율
liberty 자유
liberty of contract 계약자유의 원칙
Libor 런던은행간 거래금리;리보
license 허가
license agreement 라이센스계약
license expense 면허료
license tax 면허세
licensed tax accountant 세무사
licensing system 면허제
lien 선취특권;리엔
lien of partners 조합원 선취득권
lien theory 선취특권이론
lienor 선취특권자
life 기간
life and annuity 생명보험 및 연금
Life and Health Insurance Guaranty Association 생명건강보험보증협회
Life and Health Insurance Guaranty Association Model Act 생명건강보험보증협회모델법
Life and Health Insurance Guaranty Fund

KL

생명건강보험보증기금
life annuity 종신연금
life annuity insurance 종신연금보험
life consultant 라이프컨설턴트
life cycle 라이프사이클
Life Income Tax Act of 1959
1959년 생명보험회사소득세법
life insurance 생명보험
life insurance company 생명보험회사
life insurance company purchase 생보구입
life insurance credit 생명보험료공제
life insurance policy 생명보험증권
life insurance premium 생명보험료
life insurance premiums deduction
생명보험료공제
life interest 일생의 권리
life table 생명표
life tenancy 영대차지인
life-long education 평생교육
life-to-call 기전상환까지의 거치기간
lifelong wages 생애임금
lifetime employment 종신고용
lifo adaptation of retail method
후입선출매가환원법
LIFO reserve 후입선출법준비금
lifting charges 취급수수료
lifting of gold embargo 금수출해금
light and fuel expenses 광열비
light oil delivery tax 경유거래세
light vehicle tax 경차세
like goods 동종상품
limit calculation 가격지정산정법
limit down 스톱저
limit high 스톱고
limit low 스톱저
limit of a loan 대부한도
limit of deductible of entertainment expense
교제비편입한도액
limit of liability 배상책임한도액
limit of overdrawn account 수표발행한도
limit of price 가격한도
limit on foreign investors' holdings of stocks
외국인지주제한
limit order 지정가격주문
limit to credit reserve for bad debts
대손준비금계정편입한도액
limit up 스톱고
limitation 제한
limitation of actions 출소기한
limitation on dividend 배당제한
limitation on interlocking 업무겸업제한
limitational factor 제한요인
limited annuity 유한연금
limited audit 한정감사
limited branching 특정지역지점설치
limited company 유한책임회사
limited convertibility 제한적인 교환성
limited distribution 한정적인 판로
limited guarantee 제한적인 보증
limited income method 소득원천세
limited legal tender 제한법화
limited liability 유한책임
limited life assets 유한내용연수자산
limited life preferred stock 기한부 우선주
limited obligation bond 특정재원채
limited offering 한정모집
limited opinion 한정의견
limited partnership 유한책임조합
limited private company 유한회사
limited recourse loan 제한상환청구권부 론
limited tax liability 제한납세의무
limited tax rate 제한세율
line department 라인부문
line item 계정과목
line of business 영업과목
line of credit 대출예약한도
linear accelerator 선형가속도계수
linear bond 리니어채
linear programming 선형계획법
linear regression 선형회귀
linear warranty 승계담보
linked bond 링크채

liquid assets 유동자산
liquid capital 유동자본
liquid deposit 유동성예금
liquid part 유동부분
liquid ratio 유동비율
liquid reserve 유동성준비금
liquid stock 유통문제
liquid-asset hypothesis 유동자산가설
liquidate 현금화하다
liquidated account 확정계정
liquidated company 청산회사
liquidated corporation 청산한 법인
liquidated damages 손해배상금
liquidated debt 확정채무
liquidating partner 청산인
liquidation 현금화;청산
liquidation accounts 청산계정
liquidation affairs 청산사무
liquidation balance sheet 청산대차대조표
liquidation company 청산회사
liquidation dividend 청산배당
liquidation event 청산사유
liquidation final return 청산확정신고
liquidation income 청산소득
liquidation income due to merger 합병에 따른 청산소득
liquidation income from dissolution 해산에 따른 청산소득
liquidation matter 청산사무
liquidation of claim 채권변제
liquidation of clearing margin 거래증거금환금
liquidation of duties 관세사정
liquidation of investments 투자매각
liquidation of liabilities 사무처리
liquidation of special bad debts 채권상각특별계정제거
liquidation of speculative accounts 투기계정을 정리함
liquidation of the assets 자산매각
liquidation office 청산사무소
liquidation preference 청산우선권
liquidation price 청산치
liquidation proceedings 청산수속
liquidation profit and loss 청산손익
liquidation tax 청산소득세
liquidation value 청산가치
liquidator 청산인
liquidator of a corporation 회사정산인
liquidity 유동성
liquidity adjusted 유동성조정필
liquidity analysis 유동성분석
liquidity creation 유동성창출
liquidity crisis 유동성위기
liquidity crunch 신용경색
liquidity differential 유동성격차
liquidity dilemma 유동성딜레마
liquidity diversification 유동성분산
liquidity effect 유동성효과
liquidity facility 신용공여한도
liquidity in hand 소지한 유동성
liquidity index 유동지수
liquidity management 유동성관리
liquidity of the banking system 은행유동성
liquidity position 유동성포지션
liquidity preference theory 유동성선호이론
liquidity premium 유동성프리미엄
liquidity ratio 유동성비율
liquidity risk 유동성리스크
liquidity scarcity 유동성부족
liquidity trap 유동성의 함정
liquidity-driven issue 유동성상장주
liquidity-driven market 유동성지향상장
liquidity-motivated transactions 유동성동기로 인한 매매
list of beneficiary shareholders 실질주주명부
list of differences between 대조표
list of members 회원명부
list of property 재산목록
list of shareholders 주주명부
list quotation 상장표
listed bond market 상장채권시장

listed bonds 상장채권
listed brand 상장상품
listed company 상장회사
listed foreign stocks 상장외국주식
listed futures 상장선물
listed investment trusts linked to Nikkei 300 Stock Price Index 닛케이삼백주가지수연동형 상장투자신탁
listed issue 상장문제
listed options 상장옵션
listed product 상장상품
listed securities 상장증권
listed stock 상장주
listed stock price index 상장주가지수
listed stocks used in the computation of indices 지수용 상장주식
listed warrants 상장신주인수권증권
listing 상장
listing agent 상장대리인
listing application 상장신청
listing by application 신청에 따른 상장
listing criteria 상장기준
listing examination 상장심사
listing examination fees 상장심사비
listing fee 상장비용
listing on the First Section 일부상장
listing on the Second Section 이부상장
listing regulations 상장규정
listing requirements 상장요건
livestock insurance 동물보험
living 생계
living cost 생계비
living expenses 생활비
living standards 생활수준
living trust 생전신탁
Lloyd's policy 로이즈증권
load charges 판매수수료
loading 부가보험료
loading charges 적재비용
loading surplus 부가이익
loan account 대부계정
loan agreement 금전대차계약
loan application 융자신청
loan association 금융조합
loan business on real property 부동산대부업
loan by the Bank of Japan 일본은행대출
loan capital 차입자본
loan claims 론채권
loan extension 차관공여
loan for carrying unsold inventory 체화융자
loan for consumption 소비론
loan for exchange 교환대차
loan from banks 은행차입
loan guarantees for defense industry 국방산업에 대한 융자보증
loan in trust 대부신탁
loan insurance 대부금보험
loan interest rate 대출이율
loan ledger 대부원장
loan limit 융자한도
loan loss 대손금
loan loss allowance 대손준비금
loan loss coverage 채권손실커버리지
loan loss provision 대손준비금
loan of subscription payment funds 불입융자대부
loan on bill 어음대부
loan on deeds 증서대부
loan on personal guarantee 보증대출
loan on real estate 부동산대부
loan on real property 부동산대부
loan on security 담보대출
loan outstanding 차입금잔고
loan participation 대부지분참가
loan payable 차입금
loan rate 대출금리
loan receivable 대부금
loan receivable in securities 대부유가증권
loan received 차관수령
loan redemption 차입금상환
loan restrictions 융자규제
loan risk 융자리스크

loan sales 론채권매매
loan secured by deposit 예금담보대부
loan secured by government bonds or corporate debentures 공사채담보대부
loan secured by real estate 부동산저당대부금
loan secured by securities 유가증권담보대부금
loan securities 대부증권
loan shark 고리대
loan society 금융조합
loan spread 론스프레드
loan stock 대금주
loan subparticipation 대출채권분매
loan swap 론스와프
loan to affiliated companies 계열융자
loan to customers account 대부금계정
loan to financial institutions 금융기관대부금
loan to subsidiary 자회사대부금
loan transaction 대차거래
loan trust 대부신탁
loan with third party's guarantee 보증부 대부
loan without interest 무이자대부
loan-deposit ratio 예금대출율
loan-to-value ratio 융자비율
loanable fund 대부자금
loanable funds theory 대출자금이론
loanable resources 대출자금
loanable value 담보
loans and bills discounted 대출금
loans and bills discounted accounts 대출금계정
loans and discounts by industry 업종별 대출통계
loans by private financial institutions 민간금융기관대출
loans by public financial institutions 공적금융기관대출
loans in margin transactions 신용거래대부금
lobbying 원외운동
lobbying contract 원외계약
local allocation tax 지방분여세
local area network 기업내 고속정보통신망
local authorities 지방자치체
local authority bond 지방채
local autonomy 지방자치
local bank 지방은행
local bond 지방채
local company 지방기업
local consumption tax 지방소비세
local content 로컬컨텐트
local content ratio 현지조달율
local cost 현지코스트
local credit 국내발행신용장;로컬크레디트
local currency 현지통화
local dealers 증권거래소의 회원
local distribution tax 지방배포세
local expenditure 지방세
local finance 지방재정
local finance bureau 재무국
local government 지방자치체
local government bond 지방채
local grant tax 지방교부세
local law 지역법
local production factory 현지생산공장
local public entity 지방자치체
local public finance 지방재정
Local Public Finance Law 지방재정법
local public goods 지방공공재
local stock exchange 지방증권거래소
local tax 지방세
Local Tax Law 지방세법
local tax payment 지방세납세
local transfer tax 지방양여세
locals 로컬즈
location 소재지
location of loss or damage 손실발생지
location quotient 특화계수
lock-in 확정
lock-in effect 록인효과
lock-up 록업
lock-up option 록업옵션
lock-up period 록업기간

lockbox 록박스
locked market 동결시장
loco price 현장인도가격
locomotive theory 기관차이론
log 기록
log linear 대수선형
logarithmic chart 대수그래프
logarithmic spiral 등각나선;로그스파이럴
lognormal distribution 대수정규분포
Lombard borrowing 롬바르드차입
Lombard credit 롬바르드대부
Lombard lending 롬바르드대출
Lombard rate 롬바르드레이트
Lombard Street 롬바르드가
London acceptance 런던인수
London clearing banks 런던어음교환소가맹은행
London Club 런던클럽
London Depositary Receipts 런던예탁증서
London Discount Market Association 런던할인시장협회
London gold market 런던금시장
London Inter-Bank Offered Rate 런던은행수취금리
London interbank bid rate 런던은행간 수취금리
London International Financial Futures Exchange 런던국제금융선물거래소
London Metal Exchange 런던금속거래소
London refinance 런던리파이낸스
London school 런던학파
long account 매매계약을 하였으나 아직 결제하지 않은 주식이나 상품
long and medium-term interest rate 장중기금리
long butterfly spread transaction 롱버터플라이스프레드거래
long calendar spread transaction 롱캘린더스프레드거래
long call 롱콜
long cash period 장기현물기간
long condor 롱콘더
long coupon 롱쿠폰
long exchange 장기환
long hedge 매입헤지
long hedging 매입헤징
long position 매입보유
long position risk 매입보유리스크
long positions 매매계약을 하였으나 아직 결제하지 않은 주식이나 상품
long put 롱풋
long service allowance 근속수당
long straddle 롱스트래들
long strip 롱스트립
long the swap 스와프를 구입하다
long treasury bond 미국재무부 장기채권
long waves 장기파동
long-arm jurisdiction 역외적용관할권
long-dated bill 장기어음
long-dated forwards 장기선도거래
long-dated issue 장기채
long-form audit report 장문식 감사보고서
long-form report 장문식 보고서
long-run 장기
long-run equilibrium 장기균형
long-run supply curve 장기공급곡선
long-run trend 장기트렌드
long-term accounts payable in foreign currency 장기외화기준채무
long-term accounts receivable in foreign currency 장기외화기준채권
long-term asset ratio to equity capital 자기자본장기자산율
long-term bill 장기어음
long-term bond 장기채
long-term borrowing 장기차입금
long-term business 장기사업
long-term buying 장기구입
long-term capital 장기자본
long-term capital balance 장기자본수지
long-term capital gains 장기양도소득
long-term capital transaction 장기자본거래

long-term comprehensive insurance 장기종합보험
long-term contract 장기청부공사
long-term credit 장기신용
long-term credit bank 장기신용은행
long-term debt 장기채무
long-term debt assumed 장기채무증가
long-term finance 장기금융
long-term forward exchange agreement 장기환예약
long-term fund 장기자금
long-term government bond 장기국채
long-term interest rate 장기금리
long-term investment 장기투자
long-term liabilities 장기채무
long-term loan 장기대부금
long-term loan payable 장기차입금
long-term loan receivable 장기대부금
long-term money market 장기금융시장
long-term national bond of England 영국장기국채
long-term postponement of credit 채무보류
long-term prime rate 장기프라임레이트
long-term solvency 장기지불능력
long-term suspended claims 장기연기채권
long-term yield 장기이율
long-term-lease 장기임대차계약
longest remaining life bonds 장기기채
look-back option 룩백옵션
look-back option transaction 룩백옵션거래
loose leaf book 루즈리프식 장부
Lorenz curve 로렌츠곡선
losers game 패자의 게임
loss 손실
loss account 손실계정
loss adjustment 손해사정
loss allocation 손실배분
loss and gain 손익
loss and gain account 손익계정
loss and gain statement 손익계산서
loss and profit brought forward 이월손익
loss arising from casualty 재해로 인한 소실
loss brought forward from the previous term 전기이월손실
loss carried forward to the following term 차기이월차손금
loss carry back 차손금을 되돌림
loss contingency 우발손실
loss cut 손해를 피해 철수하다
loss due to disaster 재해손실금
loss due to spoiled work 손해비용
loss for the current year 당기손실금
loss forwarded 이월차손금
loss from amalgamation 합병차손
loss from bad debts 대손손실
loss from capital reduction 감자차손
loss from damaged business assets 피해사업용 자산의 손실
loss from difference of price 차손금
loss from dividend income 배당소득손실
loss from fluctuation of foreign exchange rate 환차손
loss from foreign exchange rate fluctuation 환율변동에 따른 손실
loss from liquidation of properties 자산청산에 따른 손실
loss from merger 합병차손
loss from putting on reserve for deferred income tax 압축준비금편입손
loss from redemption of bond 사채상환차손
loss from revaluation of securities 유가증권평가손
loss from the revaluation of fixed assets 고정자산평가손
loss from the sale of fixed assets 고정자산매각손
loss from valuation of property 자산평가손
loss function 손실함수
loss incurred from exchange rate 환차손
loss leader 로스리더
loss making division 불채산부문
loss making operations 적자경영

K L

loss not yet realized 미실현손실
loss not yet recognized 미확인손실
loss of productivity claims 생산성상실 클레임
loss of profits insurance 이익보험
loss of property 자산손실
loss of sovereignty 국가주권상실
loss of work 작업손실
loss on assets 자산손실
loss on foreign exchange 외국환차손
loss on insurance claims 보험금차손
loss on property abandoned 자산폐기손
loss on property destroyed 자산상실비
loss on property revaluation 자산평가손
loss on retirement of fixed assets 제거손실
loss on sale 매각손
loss on sale of property 자산매각손
loss on sale of real estate 부동산매각손
loss on sale returns 반품차손비
loss on securities sold 유가증권매각손
loss payable clause 제삼자지불약관
loss per share 일주당 손실
loss provision 손실준비금
loss qualifying for necessary expenses 필요경비에 해당하는 손실
loss ratio 손해율
loss recognition 손실인식
loss recovery 손실회수율
loss reserves 책임준비금
loss resulted from valuation 평가손
loss resulting from casualty 재해손실
lost card 분실카드
lost-or-not-lost clause 소급조항
lot bond 로트채
lot consolidation 단주정리
lot money 경매수수료
lot size 거래규모
lottery 곡선
lotting out 분양
Louvre accord 루브르합의
low beta portfolio 베타수치가 낮은 포트폴리오
low capacity utilisation 낮은 설비투자율
low capital intensive industry 자본집약성이 낮은 산업
low cost 저비용
low dividend stock 저배주
low grade stocks 저위주
low growth 저성장
low growth industries 저성장산업
low income countries 저소득국
low interest loan 저금리론
low level 저수준
low par issue 저액면주식
low price 싼값
low price stock 저위주
low risk stocks 안전성이 높은 주식
low turnover 한산한 거래;소액매매
lower closing quotation 저고정가격
lower end of the market 저가격시장
lower in quotation 저가격
lower order goods 저가재
lower price 낮은 가격
lower-of-cost-or-market method 저가법
lower-of-cost-or-market value basis 저가주의
lowering of interest rate 금리인하
lowest taxable limit 과세최저한
loyalty rebate 특약리베이트
lucrative terms 유리한 조건
lump sum contract 정액청부계약
lump sum freight 총괄운임
lump sum payment 일괄지불
lump sum payment of dividends at maturity 만기일괄지불
lump sum payment regarded as retirement allowance 퇴직수당으로 처리하는 일시금
lump sum pension 일시불연금
lump sum purchase 일괄구입
Luxembourg Monetary Institute 룩셈부르크금융협회
luxurious house for rent 고급임대주택
luxury tax 사치세

M

M 0 growth M 제로신장
M 2+CD Statistics M2+CD통계
M 2's behaviour M2의 움직임
M 3 growth M3의 신장
MacFadden Act of 1927 맥패든법
machine bookkeeping 기계부기
machine-hour rate 기계시간율
machine-hour rate method 기계시간율 배부법
machinery-credit insurance 기계류 신용보험
machinery industry 기계업계
machinery insurance 기계보험
macro accounting 매크로회계
macro analysis 기계보험
macro hedge 매크로헤지
macro model 매크로모델
macro view 대세관
macroeconomic analysis 매크로경제분석
macroeconomic factor 매크로경제요인
macroeconomic indicators 최종지표
macroeconomic model 매크로경제모델
macroeconomic policy 매크로경제정책
MACRS 메이가즈(수정가속상각법)
magnitude of economic change 경제변화의 정도
magnitude of the cycle 경기순환의 진폭
mail confirmation 메일컨퍼메이션
mail credit 메일크레디트
mail credit facility 메일크레디트퍼실리티
mail days 우편일수
mail exchange bill 문서환
mail order 통신판매
mail transfer 보통발송송금;우편환
mail transfer payable 송금환
mail-order loan 메일론
mailing cost 우송료
main account 주요계정
main books 주요장부
main budget 본예산
main customer 주요거래
main income earner 주소득자
main materials 주요원재료
main office 주사무소;본사
mainstream 주류
maintenance 유지
maintenance and repairs 수선비
maintenance bond 하자보수보증증권
maintenance call 추가증거금
maintenance clause 부양약관
maintenance cost 유지비
maintenance department 보수과
maintenance expense 유지비;계약유지비
maintenance fee 관리비
maintenance funds 유지자금
maintenance lease 메인터넌스리스
maintenance margins 유지증거금
maintenance of books and records 장부서류를 정리하고 보존함
maintenance of capital 자본유지
maintenance of financial capital 화폐자본유지
maintenance of membership 조합원자격유지
maintenance of physical capital 실제자본유지

maintenance reserve 유지준비금
major 큰;주요한
major acquisition 대형매수
major banks 주요은행
major bottom 기초;토대
major commodity 주요상품
major cycles 주순환
major foreign stock price indexes 외국주요주가지수
major industrial nations 선진국
major industry 주요산업
major investments 대규모투자
major leagues 선진공업국
major market index 메이저마켓지수
major medical expense insurance 고액의료비보험
major move 메이저무브
major nations 주요국
major order 대량수주
major peak 메이저피크
major product 주제품
major raw materials 주요한 원재료
major relationship bank 주력은행
major stockholders 주요주주
major trend 주요트렌드
majority decision 다수결
majority interest 과반수지분
majority of stockholders 주요주주
majority of voting rights 의결권다수결
majority owner 과반수주주
majority-owned subsidiary 과반수소유종속회사
make-ready time 준비시간
maker's credit 연불수출
making a claim for a refund 환부청구
making a downward revision 하향수정함
making a trial balance 시산표를 작성함
making two-sided markets 양방향부과
making up for loss 손실보전
making up of a deficit 적자보전
maldistribution 편재
Maloney Act of 1938 마로니법
malpractice 부당행위
man hour rate 공수율
managed asset 관리자산
managed crawling peg 관리크롤링페그
managed currency 관리통화
managed currency system 관리통화제도
managed float 관리플로트
managed floating rate system 관리플로트제
Managed Fund Contract 매니지드펀드계약
managed futures 상품펀드
managed issues 관리상품
managed liabilities 관리채무
managed price 관리가격
managed receivable 관리자산
managed trade 관리무역
management 운용
Management & Coordination Agency 총무청
management accounting 관리회계
management agreement 경영위탁계약
management audit 경영감사
management business of investment trust 투자신탁위탁업무
management buyout 매니지먼트바이아웃
management consultant 경영컨설턴트
management consulting 기업진단
management cultures 경영본질
management decision 경영의사결정
management fee 간사수수료
management group 인수간사단
management index 경영지표
management information system 경영정보시스템
management know-how 경영노하우
management labor relation 노사관계
management of clearing margin 거래증거금관리
management of collateral 담보관리
management of juristic act 법무처리
management of property 재무처리

management of supply 공급관리
management of the default compensation reserve 위약손실보상준비금운용
management organization 경영조직
management participation 경영참가
management participation right 경영참가권
management philosophy 경영이념
management plan 경영계획
management resources 경영자원
management responsibility 경영자책임
management science 매니지먼트사이언스
management service for bill for collection 수금어음관리서비스
management strategy 경영전략
management supervisor 감독관
management team 경영진
management through figures 계수관리
manager 간사
manager-client relations 투자관리자와 고객의 관계
manager's contribution 매니저의 기여도
managerial auditing 경영감사
managerial choices 경영판단
managerial investment trust 관리형 투자신탁
managerial philosophy 경영이념
managerial resources 경영자원
managers 간사단
managing bank 간사은행
managing committee 경영위원회
managing director 상무이사
managing governor 상무이사
managing underwriter 간사증권
mandate 맨데이트;명령
mandate bid 맨데이트입찰
mandate letter 맨데이트레터
mandate on remission 환송명령
mandatory clause 필수조건
mandatory collateral substitution 강제담보변환
mandatory control 법적규제
mandatory convertible bond 강제전환사채
mandatory injunction 강제금지명령
mandatory line of credit 법정신용한도
mandatory redemption 강제상환
mandatory securities valuation reserve 법정유가증권평가준비금
mandatory sinking fund requirement 강제적인 감채기금조항
manifest 적재목록
manipulation 조작
manipulation of account 분식
manipulation of the market 가격조작
manner of amortization 상각방법
manner of depreciation 상각방법
manner similar to straight line depreciation method 정액법에 준거한 방법
manual of accounting instructions 회계집무규정
manual of accounting procedure 회계절차규정
manufacture order 제조지도서
manufactured goods 제품
manufacturer's risks 제조자리스크
manufacturing accounting 공업회계
manufacturing bases 생산거점
manufacturing bookkeeping 공업부기
manufacturing burden 제조간접비
manufacturing cost accounting 제조원가계산
manufacturing costing 제조원가계산
manufacturing department 제조부문
manufacturing expenses 제조경비
manufacturing expenses budget 제조간접비예산
manufacturing expenses ledger 제조간접비원장
manufacturing license 제조허가
manufacturing payroll 제조업고용자수
manufacturing process 제조공정
manufacturing statement 제조원가보고서
manufacturing taxation 제조과세
manufacturing technology 생산기술
mapleleaf coin 메이플리프코인

margin 위탁증거금;차금;중간이윤
margin account 증거금계정;신용거래구좌
margin buying 신용구입
margin call 추가증거금
margin collateral 신용거래위탁증거금
margin cost 증거금코스트
margin debt 증거금부채
margin deficiency 증거금부족
margin deposit 수입증거금
margin for borrowed stocks 대주담보금
margin for stocks lent 신용거래대주수입금
margin for transactions 매매증거금
margin improvement 이익금확대
margin money system 증거금제도
margin of safety 안전성 마진;
투자안전확보범위
margin on commodity futures
상품선물거래의 증거금
margin purchase 신용구매
margin rate 증거금율
margin ratio 이익률
margin required method 필요증거금법
margin rule 증거금규칙
margin system 증거금시스템
margin trading 신용거래
margin transaction 증거금거래
marginal analysis 한계분석
marginal balance 한계이익
marginal benefit 한계편익
marginal capital coefficient 한계자본계수
marginal capital expenditure 한계자본지출
marginal clauses 난외약관
marginal condition 한계조건
marginal cost 한계비용
marginal cost curve 한계비용곡선
marginal cost of production 한계생산비
marginal costing 한계원가계산
marginal credit 한계신용
marginal deduction system 한계공제제도
marginal demand 한계수요
marginal efficiency 한계효율
marginal efficiency of capital 기본한계효율
marginal efficiency of investment
투자한계효율
marginal factor 한계요소
marginal firm 한계기업
marginal income 한계이익
marginal income ratio 한계이익률
marginal income statement 한계손익계산
marginal loan-deposit ratio 한계예대율
marginal net suitability 한계순적합도
marginal principle 한계원리
marginal production 한계생산
marginal productivity 한계생산성
marginal profit 한계이익
marginal profit ratio 한계이익률
marginal propensity to consume
한계소비성향
marginal propensity to import 한계수입성향
marginal propensity to save 한계저축성향
marginal rate of return 한계수익률
marginal ratio 한계비율
marginal returns 한계수익
marginal revenue 한계수입
marginal rise 미미하게 늘어남
marginal seal 난외에 찍어두는 도장
marginal tax rate 한계세율
marginal theory 한계이론
marginal unit cost 한계단위원가
marginal utility 한계효용
marginal utility of money 화폐의 한계효용
marginal value 한계가치
marginal value curve 한계가치곡선
margins of solvency 지불여력
Marine and Fire Insurance Association of Japan 일본손해보험협회
marine and transport insurance
해상 및 운송보험
marine bill of landing 해상선하증권
marine cargo insurance 화물해상보험
marine cargo policy 화물해상보험증권
marine insurance 해상보험

marine insurance account 해상보험계정
Marine Insurance Act of 1906 영국해상보험법
marine perils 해상위험
marine surveyor 해사검사인
marine transportation 해운
marine transportation industry 해운업
mariner's lien 선원의 선취특권
maritime 해사의
maritime belt 영해
maritime bonds 해사채
maritime court 해사재판소
maritime hypothecation 해사저당
maritime law 해사법
maritime lien 해사선취특권
maritime perils 해상위험
maritime traffic 해운
mark bond 마크채
mark down 가격인하
mark to market 마크투마켓
mark-downs 중개료
mark-to-market account 시가평가계정
mark-to-market analysis 시가분석
mark-to-market basis 시가기준
mark-to-market date 시가일
mark-to-market value 시가가치
mark-up ratio 마크업률
mark-ups 중개료
marked checks 기호수표
market analysis 시장분석
market basket contract 마켓바스켓방식
market basket index 마켓바스켓지수
market behavior 시장동향
market beta 시장베타
market cap 시가총액
market capitalization 시장시가총액
market conduct 시장행동
market congestion 기채러시
market consensus 시장예측
market control 시장지배
market crash 상장의 하락
market creating effect 시장창조효과
market cycle 시장의 주기
market data 시장동향
market demand 시장수요
market demand curve 시장수요곡선
market discipline 시장원리
market discount rate 시장경제모델
market economy 시장경제
market economy model 시장경제모델
market efficiency 시장의 효율성
market equilibrium 시장균형
market equilibrium curve 시장균형곡선
market exiting 시장후퇴
market expansion effect 시장확장효과
market expectation 시장예측
market extinction 시장삭감
market failure 시장의 실패
market hours 입회시간
market impact 시장에 대한 영향
market index 시장지수
market information 시황정보
market information center 시황정보센터
market information system 시황정보시스템
market integrity 시장의 완전성
market interest rate 시중금리
market leaders 시장의 주도주
market liberalisation 시장규제완화
market maker 마켓메이커
market making condition 마켓메이킹상황
market making function 마켓메이킹기능
market manipulation 상장조종
market mechanism 시장원리
market method 시가법
market milking 시장을 조종함
market model 시장모델
market momentum 시장의 힘
market mood 시장의 경향
market of a stock exchange 증권거래소시장
market on close 종가지정주문
market opening 시장개방
market opportunity 시장기회

market order 성행주문
market out clause 마켓아웃조항
market overt 공개시장
market overview 시장개황
market penetration 시장침투
market place 시장
market player 시장참가자
market portfolio 시장포트폴리오
market practice 시장관행
market prediction 시장예측
market price 시장가격
market price basis 시가주의
market price of risk 리스크의 시장가격
market price of stock 주가
market principle 시장원리
market psychology 시장심리
market quotation 시장분위기
market rate 시장상장; 실세레이트
market rate of interest 시장이자율
market rate of return 투자수익률
market recovery 시황회복
market reform 시장개혁
market report 시황보고
market research 시장조사
market rhythm 시장의 기조
market risk 가격리스크;시장리스크
market sector 시장섹터
market sensitivity 시장감응도
market sentiment 시장센티멘트
market share 시장점유율
market stabilization 시장안정조작
market structure 시장구조
market study 시장조사
market supervision 매매감리
market survey 시장조사
market theory 시장이론
market timer 마켓타이머
market timing 마켓타이밍
market timing assessment
시장타이밍을 평가함
market transaction 거래
market valuation 시장평가
market value 시장가격
market value accounting 시가회계
market value analysis 시가분석
market value basis 시가주의
market value in case of purchase 구입시가
market value method 시가법
market value of inventory 재고자산의 시가
market value per share 주가
market value weighted index
시장가격가중평균지수
market volatility 시장변동성
market yield 시장이율
market-if-touched order 마켓이프터치드오더
market-on-close order 마켓온클로즈오더
marketability 시장성
marketable debt securities
시장성이 있는 채권
marketable order 시장성이 있는 주문
marketable securities 시장성증권
marketable securities listed on a securities exchange 증권거래소에 상장된 유가증권
marketable title 매매에 적합한 권리
marketing budget 마케팅예산
marketing channel 판매경로
marketing cost 판매비
marketing expense 마케팅비
marketing function 마케팅기능
marketing mix 마케팅믹스
marketing pull 마케팅풀
marketing push 마케팅푸시
marketing structure 유통기구
Markowitz theory 마코위츠이론
marry 매리
marrying transaction 증권매리
Marshall curve 마샬곡선
Marshall Plan 마샬플랜
Marshallian demand curve 마샬수요곡선
Marshallian K 마샬의 K
Maruyu program
(일본의)소액저축비과세제도

mass communication 매스커뮤니케이션
mass consumption society 대중소비사회
mass production 대량생산
mass production techniques 대량생산기술
mass risks 대중리스크
mass sales 대량추천판매
massive potential 거대한 잠재력
master agreement 마스터계약
master contract 기본계약
master L/C 원신용장
master plan 기본계획
master trust 마스터트러스트
match 일치시키다
match making 균형
matched book 매매일치
matched maturities 기간일치
matched order 담합매매
matching 대응; 매칭; 약정
matching costs and revenues 비용과 수익의 대응
matching of bids and offers 지정가격대응
matching ratio 조회적합률
matching swap 대응스와프
matching transaction 매칭거래
material alternation 중요한 변수
material cost 재료비
material cost budget 재료예산
material distribution sheet 재료분개장
material evidence 중요한 증거
material fact 중요사실
material for repair 수리용 재료
material impact 중대한 영향
material in process 중도재료비
material in storage 저장원재료
material inventory 재료재고고
material ledger 재료원자
material misrepresentation 중대한 부실표현
material on hand 보유자재
material price standard 재료표준가격
material price variance 재료가격차이
material purchased 재료구입고
material purchased report 원재료구입보고서
material quantity variance 재료수량차이
material received report 원재료수입보고서
material requisition 출고표
material requisition note 출고표
material specification 재료사양서
material usage variance 재료수량차이
material variance 재료비차액;실질적인 차이
materiality 중요성
materiality principle 중요성 원칙
materialized securities 증서가 발행된 증권
materials for investigation 조사자료
mathematical economics 수리경제학
mathematical reserve 수리적인 책임준비금
mathematical statistics 수리통계
matrix 매트릭스
matrix bookkeeping 행렬부기
matrix multiplier 행렬승수
matrix trading 매트릭스트레이딩
matter 기초사실
matter in deed 증서사항
matter in issue 쟁점사항
matter of record 기록사항
matters to be notified 신고사항
matters to be reported 보고사항
mature 기한이 오다
mature company 성숙기업
mature economy 성숙경제
mature phase 성숙단계
mature plans 성숙한 플랜
matured bill 만기어음
matured bond 만기채권
matured liability 만기채무
maturing bonds 만기가 된 채무
maturing liability 만기가 된 채무
maturity 만기
maturity basket 만기바스켓
maturity date 만기일
maturity distribution range 만기분포의 차이
maturity gap exposure 운용과 조달 사이의 기간 차

maturity guarantee 만기보증
maturity list 만기일표
maturity mismatch 기간의 미스매치
maturity repayment 만기반려금
maturity stripping 매츄리티스트리핑
maturity structure 만기일구성
maturity swap 매츄리티스와프
maturity value 상환가액
maturity-designated time deposit 만기일지정정기예금
maverick risk 이단자리스크
maximal collateral 근저당
maximam operating ratio 최유리조업도
maxims 법률격언
maximum and minimum tariff system 최고최저세율제
maximum capacity 최대생산능력
maximum inventory 최대재고량
maximum level 최고수준
maximum likelihood method 최대우도법
maximum limit for interest rate 이자부 최고한도
maximum limit of fluctuation 스톱치
maximum limit of overdraft 대출초과한도액
maximum limit system 최고발행액제한제도
maximum loan value 대출한도액
maximum loan estimates 최대손실추정치
maximum price 최고가격
maximum special depreciation allowance 특별상각한도액
mean absolute deviation 평균절대편차
mean deviation 평균편차
mean difference 평균차
mean price 중간값
mean reversion 평균회귀
mean reverting process 평균회귀과정
mean squared error 평균제곱오차
mean value 중간치
meaning of redemption 상환정의
means for hedging 헤지수단
means of foreign payment 대외지불수단
means test 자산조사
measure for monetary ease 금융완화조치
measure of investment 투자척도
measure of return 수익률측정
measure of risk 리스크측정
measure of value 태도측정
measurement contract 측정계약
measurement date 측정일
measurement method 측정방법
measurement principles 측정기준
measures in case of vacancy 결원이 생길 때의 조치
measuring gap 메저링갭
mechanical trading 기계화거래
mechanism 기구
mechanization method 기계화방식
mechanized accounting 기계화회계
media advertising 매체광고
media commission 매체수수료
media mix 매체믹스
media strategy 미디어전략
median 중앙치
mediate descent 간접상속
mediate powers 부수권한
mediation 중개
mediation regulations 중개규정
Medicaid 국민의료보조제도
medical benefit 의료급부
medical corporation 의료법인
medical costs 의료비
medical credit 의료비공제
medical examination 진사(생명보험을 계약할 때 피보험인의 건강상태를 조사함)
medical expenses 의료비
medical expenses deduction 의료비공제
medical industry 의료산업
medical jurisprudence 법의학
Medicare 노인의료보험제도
medium gilt 중기길트채
medium of capital transfer 자본이전수단
medium rating 신용등급

medium-sized stock 중형주
medium-term bond 중기채
medium-term coupon-bearing government bonds 중기이자부 국채
medium-term financial assets 중기금융자산
medium-term fixed rate government bond 중기이자부 국채
medium-term funding 중기자금조달
medium-term government bond fund 중기국채펀드
medium-term government securities funds 중기국채펀드
medium-term loan 중기대부
medium-term note 미디엄텀노트
medium-term outlook 중기전망
meeting of bond-holders 사채권자집회
meeting of promoters 발기인회
melon cutting 고액배당
member bank 가맹은행
member bank of the Second Association of Regional Banks 제 2 지방은행
member banks of the clearing house 어음교환소가맹은행
member banks of the Second Association of Regional Banks 제 2 지방은행
member firm 회원회사
member governor 회원이사
member of stock exchange 거래소회원
member organization 회원회사
member representative 회원대표자
member securities company 회원증권회사
member's fee 거래소회비
member's mark 회원표식
member's store 가맹점
member's voluntary winding-up 주주에 의한 임의청산
membership 가맹권
membership admission 회원가입
membership business 회원비즈니스
membership certificate 회원증서
membership corporation 회원조직법인
membership equity 회원증서
membership fee 회비
membership guarantee deposit 회원신임금
membership in the capacity of a corporation 회사명의회원
membership organization 회원제조직
memorandum account 비망계정
memorandum for offering 모집요강
memorandum of association 기본정관
memorandum of balance sheet audit 대차대조표감사의 각서
memorandum of protest 거절증서
memorandum of understanding 각서
memorandum price 비방가액
memorandum value 비망가격
memorandum-check 제시하지 않는 특약수표
memorial dividend 기념배당
menu approach 메뉴어프로치
mercantile agency 상사대리
mercantile law 상업법
mercantile paper 상업어음
mercantile partnership 상업조합
mercantile risk 상품위험
merchandise 상품
merchandise account 상품계정
merchandise book 상품매매장
merchandise bookkeeping 상업부기
merchandise cost 상품원가
merchandise in transit 미달상품
merchandise inventory 상품재고;재고상품
merchandise inventory account carried over 이월상품계정
merchandise ledger 상품원장
merchandise management 상품관리
merchandise mix 상품구성
merchandise procurement cost 상품조달원가
merchandise resources 구입처
merchandise turnover ratio 상품회전율
merchant bank 머천트뱅크
merchant banker 투자은행가
merchant fee 가맹점수수료

merchant law 상업법
merchant outlet 가맹점 점포
merchantable 시장성이 있는
merely nominal persons 단순명의인
merger 합병;혼동
merger accounting 합병회계
merger and acquisition 합병과 매수
merger and acquisition business M&A 비즈니스
merger of a domestic corporation 내국법인합병
merger of corporation 회사를 흡수합병함
merger of guaranty 보증계약을 혼동하여 소멸함
merger ratio 합병비율
merger terms 합병조건
merit goods 가치재(價値財)
merit increase 성공보수
metal products industry 금속제품업계
method 수법
method based on the calendar year 역년기준에 따른 방법
method of average price at the close of the preceding month 이월평균단가지불법
method of comparative analysis 비교분석법
method of historical cost 취득원가법
method of making a resolution 의결방법
method of resolution 결의방법
method of simple interest 단리법
methodology 방법론
metropolitan inhabitant tax 도민세
mezzanine bond 열후사채
mezzanine bracket 메자닌브라켓
mezzanine debt 메자닌채무
mezzanine finance 메자닌파이낸스
mezzanine money 전환사채
micro accounting 마이크로 회계
micro hedge 마이크로 헤지
microanalysis 마이크로 분석
microeconomic 마이크로 경제의
microeconomy 마이크로 경제
Mid-America Commodity Exchange 중미상품거래소
mid-market level 중가
mid-maturities 중기물
mid-range product 중가격품
middle range technology 중간기술
middle rate 중가
middle-sized companies 중견기업
middle-sized stock 중견주
middleman 중개대리인
Midwest Stock Exchange 미드웨스트증권거래소
mild recession 완만한 경기후퇴
military power 군사대국
mine 마인
mineral product tax 광산세
mineral properties mining right 광업권
mini investment 미니투자
mini stock 미니주식시장
mini tap 미니탭
mini . max . bond 미니맥스채
mini-refunding 미니리펀딩
minimum access 최저한수입업무
minimum annual return 최저연간이익
minimum bid 최저입찰가격
minimum capital requirements 최저자본금
minimum capital system 최저자본금제도
minimum cost rule 원가비교법
minimum denomination 최저권면단위
minimum denomination on which interest is calculated 이자 단위
minimum exempt income 최저면세소득
minimum fluctuation unit 최소변동단위
minimum freight 최저운임
minimum funding standard 최저적립기준
minimum guarantee 최저보증금
minimum inventory 최저재고
minimum lease payment 최저리스지불액
minimum lending rate 최저대출비율
minimum liability 최소부채
minimum liquidity ratio 최저유동성비율

minimum margin 최저 이폭
minimum margin requirement 최저증거금율
minimum marginal cost 최소한계비용
minimum payment 최저지불액
minimum profit 최소이윤
minimum quantity 최저주문량
minimum rate 최저요율
minimum rate of interest 최저이율
minimum sacrifice 최저의 희생
minimum stock 최저재고
minimum surplus 자본의 최저한도
minimum tax 최저과세
minimum value 최소치
minimum wage 최저임금
mining accounting 광업회계
mining and manufacturing 광공업
mining industry 광업
mining lease 광업임차권
mining partnership 광업조합
mining property 광업자산
ministerial ordinance 부령(部令)
ministerial power 사무권한
Ministry of Agriculture; Forestry and Fisheries 농림수산부
Ministry of Economy; Trade and Industry 경제통상산업부
Ministry of Education, Culture, Sports, Science and Technology 교육과학기술부
Ministry of Finance 재무부
Ministry of Finance Securities 재무부 증권
Ministry of Foreign Affairs 외무부
Ministry of Health; Labour and Welfare 후생노동성
Ministry of International trade and Industry 무역부
Ministry of Justice 법무부
Ministry of Land ; Infrastructure and Transport 국토교통부
Ministry of Public Management; home Affairs; Posts and Telecommunications 총무부
Ministry of the Environment 환경부
minor 미성년자
minor account 미성년자의 거래계좌
minor cycle 소순환
minor rally 본래 상태로 조금 되돌아감
minor tax credit 미성년자공제
minority buy-out 소수주주지분매입
minority control 소수지배
minority interest 소수주주지분
minority representation 소수대표법
minority shareholders 소수주주
minority shareholders' right 소수주주권
mint par of exchange 법정평가
mint price 주조가격
minus factor 마이너스요인
minus growth 마이너스성장
minus tick 마이너스틱
minus-ceiling 마이너스실링
minutes 의사록
minutes of meeting of the board of directors 이사회의사록
mirror swap 반대스와프
mirrored trade 반대거래
misappropriation 배임
misappropriation of funds 부당지출
misappropriation of goods 물품횡령
miscalculation 계산착오
miscellaneous accounts payable 여러 미불금
miscellaneous accounts receivable 여러 미수금
miscellaneous assets 잡자산
miscellaneous expenses 잡비
miscellaneous gains 잡익
miscellaneous income 잡소득
miscellaneous local taxes 잡종세
miscellaneous losses 잡손
miscellaneous provision 잡칙
miscellaneous receipts 잡수입
miscellaneous revenue 잡수익
misconduct 위반행위
misfeasance 불법행위
misfit return 부적합리터닝

misfit risk 부적합리스크
misfit-portfolio 부적합포트폴리오
mismatch between assets and liabilities 자산과 부채의 미스매치
mismatch risk 미스매치리스크
mismatched FRN 미스매치변동이자부채
mismatching 미스매칭
misnomer 성명오기
mispriced security 상대적으로 비싸거나 값싼 증권
mispricing 미스프라이싱
misrepresentation 부실표시
missing the market 시장상실
mission 사명
mission statement 기본규약
mistake of fact 사실착오
mistake of law 법률착오
mitigation 경감
mixed 혼성의;엇갈린
mixed account 혼합계정
mixed assets 혼합자산
mixed capitalist economy 혼성자본주의체제
mixed collateral 혼성저당
mixed contract 혼합계약
mixed economy 혼합경제
mixed farming 혼성농업
mixed gift 혼합증여
mixed insurance 혼합보험
mixed inventory 혼합재고정리
mixed policy 혼합보험
mixed property 혼합재산
mixed question of law and fact 법률과 사실이 혼재된 문제
mixed reserve 혼합준비금
mixed surplus 혼합잉여금
mixed tariff 혼성관세
mixed transaction 혼합거래
mixed trust 믹스트러스트
mixed undertaking 공사(公私)혼합기업
mixed variance 혼합차이
mobile shop 이동점포
mobilization 동원
mode 최빈치;최빈값
mode of transportation 수송방법
model 모델
model analysis 모델분석
model price 모델가격
moderation 축소
modern economics 근대경제학
modern market economy 근대경제학
modern portfolio theory 현대포트폴리오이론
modernization of smaller enterprise 중소기업의 근대화
modest economic expansion 경기가 서서히 회복됨
modest rebound 경기가 서서히 회복됨
modestly-priced 적당한 가격의
modification 수정
modified accelerated cost recovery system 수정가속상각법
modified accounts 수정재무제표
modified all-inclusive theory 수정포괄주의
modified capitalism 수정자본주의
modified duration 모디파이드듀레이션
modified endowment 수정양로보험계약
modified pass-through 모디파이드패스스루
Modigliani-Miller theory 모딜리아니-밀러의 명제
moment 모멘트
momentum oscillator 모멘텀오실레이터
monadic operation 단항연산
monetarism 통화주의
monetarist 통화주의자
monetarization of government bonds 국채화폐화
Monetary Agency of Singapore 싱가폴통화감시청
monetary aggregate 통화총량
monetary agreement 통화협정
monetary analysis 화폐분석
monetary and credit control 금융신용규제
monetary and financial policy 통화금융정책

monetary approach
화폐적인 어프로치; 모네터리어프로치
monetary assets 금융자산
monetary authority 통화당국
monetary bloc 통화블록
monetary capital 화폐자본
monetary control 통화관리
monetary crisis 통화위험
monetary easing 금융완화
monetary excess 과잉유동성
monetary expansion 금융확대
monetary financial assets 통화성 금융자산
monetary growth 금융확대
monetary growth model 화폐성장모델
monetary illusion 화폐환상
monetary indicators 금융지표
monetary instability 통화불안
monetary interest rate 화폐이자율
monetary items 금전항목
monetary liabilities 금전채무
monetary management 통화관리
monetary multiplier 화폐승수
monetary policy 금융정책
monetary reform 통화개혁
monetary regime 금융체제
monetary reserve 통화준비
monetary restraint 금융긴축
monetary restraint policy 금융긴축정책
monetary stability 통화안정
monetary standard 본위제도
monetary standard policy 본위정책
monetary stringency
돈의 융통이 막힘; 자금이 딸림
monetary survey 모니터리서베이
monetary system 화폐제도
monetary target 모네터리타겟
monetary tightening 금융긴축
monetary transfer 모네터리트랜스퍼
monetary union 통화동맹
monetary unit 통화단위
money analysis 화폐분석
money at call 단기융자
money bill 금전법안
money borrowed for short-term 단기차입금
money borrowed to purchase stocks
주식취득을 위한 차입금
money broker 금융업자
money capital 화폐자본
money center bank 대형전국은행
money changer 환전상
money claim 금전채권
money creation 신용창조
money deposited 예금
money earmarked 충당금
money exchange 환전소
money flow 자금순환
money flow analysis 머니플로분석
money flow table 머니플로표
money game 머니게임
money illusion 화폐환각
money in bank 예금
money in token of sympathy 위로금
money in trust 위탁금
money income 현금수입
money judgment 금전판결
money laundering 자금세정
money lender 금융업자
money lending business 금전대부업
money making 영리
money manager 자산운용자
money market 단기금융시장
money market account 단기금융계정
money market broker 단기업자
money market certificate
시장금리연동형 정기예금
money market conditions index
금융시장정세지표
money market data 금융시장데이터
money market dealer 단자회사
money market deposit account
단기금융시장예금계정
money market fund 단기금융상품투자신탁

money market index 단기금융시장지수
money market instrument 단기금융상품
money market intervention 금융시장에 대한 개입
money market loan 시장금리연동형 대출
money market management 금융조절
money market mutual funds 단기증권투자신탁
money market note 머니마켓노트
money market operations 단기금융시장조작
money market preferred stock 머니마켓우선주
money market rate 시중금리
money market securities 금융시장증권
money market unit trust 머니마켓유닛트러스트
money market yield 머니마켓이율
money multiplier 통화승수
money of the world 세계화폐
money order 송금환
money paid-in part 내금
money paid temporarily 일시금
money paid under mistake 비채변제
money position 머니포지션
money purchase plan 보험료기준연금제도
money rate 금리
money received 입금
money spread 머니스프레드
money stock 통화스톡
money supply 통화공급량
money supply control 머니서플라이관리
money trust 금전신탁
money veil theory 화폐베일이론
money yield 명목이율
monitoring 감시
monitoring of delivery 인도감시
monitoring post 감시포스트
monoline insurance company 전문보험회사
monometalic competition 단본위제도
monopolistic competition 독점적인 경쟁
monopoly 독점권
monopoly assessment 전매과세
monopoly capital 독점자본
monopoly price 독점가격
monopoly profit 전매이익
monopurpose credit card 단일목적카드
monorate of exchange system 단일환시장제
Monroe Doctrine 먼로주의
Monte Carlo simulation 몬테카를로시뮬레이션
month order 먼스오더
month to which the last trading day pertains 최종거래일에 속하는 월
month-end 월말
month-end average method 이월평균단가불출법
month-end delivery 월말인도
monthly accounting 월말결산
monthly allotment of depreciable period 감가상각의 월할계산
monthly average 월중평균
monthly average method 월차총평균법
monthly balance sheet 월차대차대조표
monthly chart 매달 차트
monthly closing average 종가월중평균
monthly high and low 월간고저
monthly income statement 월차손익계산서
monthly installment 월부
monthly installment sales 월부판매
monthly investment plan 월부투자계획
monthly payment 매월지불
monthly report 월보
monthly reversal 먼스리리버설
monthly statement 월차계산서
monthly statement of account 월계표
monthly trial balance 월차시산표
Moody's 무디즈
moral consideration 도덕상의 약인
moral hazard 도덕적 해이
moral obligation 자연채무
moral obligation bond 도의적인 지불보증채권

moral risks 모랄리스크
moral suasion 도의적인 설득
moral turpitude 부도덕행위
moratorium 지불정지;모라토리엄
moratorium period 지불유예기간
moratory interest 손해배상이자
more margin 증거금
more or less terms 수량과부족용인조건
moribund property 소멸해가는 재산
morning session 전장
morning trading session 전장
mortality 폐기물
mortality profit 죽은 차익
mortgage 저당권; 모기지
mortgage backed bond 모기지담보채권
mortgage backed securities 모기지증권
mortgage bank 저당은행
mortgage bond 물상담보부사채
mortgage bond coupon 모기지사채금리
mortgage business 주택론사업
mortgage clause 저당권설정약관
mortgage collateral type 모기지담보형
mortgage company 저당금융회사
mortgage credit 주택저당세액공제
Mortgage Credit Association 저당신용조합
mortgage credit bond 저당신용채
mortgage creditor 모기지권자
mortgage debenture 저당신용채
mortgage debenture in trust 담보부 사채신탁
mortgage debentures trust law 담보부 사채신탁법
mortgage debtor 저당권설정자
mortgage documents 저당증서류
mortgage elasticity 모기지의 가격탄력성
mortgage fund 모기지펀드
mortgage guaranty insurance 모기지증권보험
mortgage indebtedness 모기지채무
mortgage insurance 저당보험
mortgage interest deduction 주택론금리공제
mortgage investment trust 담보부 투자신탁
mortgage lending 부동산담보대부
mortgage loan 저당론
mortgage market 모기지증권시장
mortgage note 저당증권
mortgage of goods 동산모기지
mortgage of ship 선박저당권
mortgage participation certificates 모기지참여증권
mortgage pass-through securities 모기지패스루증권
mortgage pass-through certificate 모기지패스스루증권
mortgage payable 저당차입금
mortgage pool 모기지풀
mortgage portfolio 모기지포트폴리오
mortgage rate 저당론금리
mortgage refinancing 모기지재금융
mortgage securities 저당증권
mortgage strips 모기지스트립증권
mortgage the right 권리를 담보로 삼다
mortgageable chattels 저당이 될 수 있는 동산
mortgagee 저당권자
mortgages receivable 담보부 대부금
mortgagor 저당권설정자
most deliverable bond 인도최적채권
most favored nation clause 최혜국조항
most favored nation treatment 최혜국대우
most recent purchase method 최종구입원가법
most seriously affected countries 최대피영향국
mother fund 마더펀드
Mothers 마더즈
motion 신청;동의
motion day 신청심리일
motivation 동기부여
motivation research 동기조사
motor insurance 자동차보험
mounting 설치
movable and immovable assets account 동산부동산계정

movable band 무버블밴드
movable property in trust 동산신탁
movables 동산
movables comprehensive insurance 동산종합보험
movement of funds 자금이동
movement of price 가격변동
moving average 이동평균
moving average convergence 이동평균수속
moving average cost method 이동평균법
moving average deviations 이동평균치
moving average index 이동평균지수
moving average method 이동평균법
moving downward 하강
moving equilibrium 이동평균
moving weighted average method 이동가중평균법
multi currency loan 멀티커런시론
multi-currency clause 다통화조항
multi-currency intervention 복수통화개입
multi-factor model 복수요인모델
multi-factor house 다세대주택
multi-sectoral analysis 다부문분석
multibank holding company 복수은행지주회사
multilateral agreement 다국간 협정
multilateral clearing agreement 다각적인 청산협정
multilateral initiative 다국간 교섭
Multilateral Investment Guarantee Agency 다수국간투자보증기관
multilateral lending institutions 국제금융기관
multilateral settlement 다각결제
multilateral trade negotiations 다각적 무역교섭
multilevel marketing system 멀티상법
multinational bank 다국적은행
multinational firm 다국적기업
multiperiod model 다기간모델
multiple 정수배
multiple banking system 복수은행제도
multiple correlation 다중상관
multiple currency accounting 다통화회계
multiple equilibria 복수균형
multiple evidence 다원적인 증거
multiple line agent 생명손해보험동시판매외무원
multiple maturity deposit 복수만기예금
multiple option funding facilities 멀티풀옵션펀딩퍼실리티
multiple payment credit card 할부카드
multiple purpose bank account 종합계좌
multiple step 구분식
multiple step income statement 구분손익계산서
multiple tariff system 복합세제
multiple tax rate 복수세율
multiple-step form 다단계식
multiple step statement 복수구분계산서
multiplicity of action 소송중복
multiplied effect 파급효과
multiplier analysis 승수분석
multiplier effect 승법효과
multiplier theory 승수이론
multiply listed company 중복상장기업
multivariate analysis 다변량해석
municipal bond 지방채
municipal bond fund 지방공공단체채권펀드
municipal bond interest 지방채이자
municipal bond unit investment trust 단위형 지방채투자신탁
municipal bylaws 조례
municipal corporation 지방공공단체
municipal finance 도시재정
municipal futures 지방채선물
municipal inhabitants tax 시읍면세
municipal law 조례
municipal note 지방채
municipal ordinance 시조례
municipal securities 지방채증권
municipal securities dealer 공공채딜러

municipal tobacco tax 시읍면담배세
mutilated check 훼손된 수표
mutual account 상호계산
mutual agreement procedure 상호협의
mutual aid 공제
mutual aid association of government offices 관공서공제조합
mutual aid contract for retirement allowance 퇴직금공제계약
mutual aid money 공제금
mutual aid organization for specific retirement allowance 특정퇴직금공제단체
mutual aid premiums 공제부금
mutual aid system 공제금제도
mutual association 상호보험조합
mutual benefit association 공제조합
mutual benefit society 상호조합
mutual company 상호회사
mutual condition 상호조건
mutual covenant 상호날인계약
mutual credits 상호대차
mutual debt 상대채무
mutual fund 뮤추얼펀드
mutual fund underwriters 뮤추얼펀드인수업자
mutual installment 상호부금
mutual insurance 상호보험
mutual life insurance company 상호생명보험회사
mutual offset system 상호결제제도
mutual pension 공제연금
mutual promise 상호약속
mutual savings bank 상호저축은행
mutual vote 공선
mutual wills 상호조언
mutual-aid pension 공제연금
mutuality of obligation 채무의 상호성
mutuality of remedy 구제의 상호성
mutually exclusive event 상호독립적인 사건

N

NACT 전미기업재무담당자협회
Nagoya Stock Price Index 나고야증권주가지수
naked call 네이키드콜
naked contract 무상계약
naked option 네이키드옵션
naked position 네이키드포지션
naked warrant 네이키드워런트
name borrowing 명의차용
name list 인명부
name share 기명주
name transfer 명의변경
named bill 기명어음
named peril 특정위험
nano-second 나노초
narrative form 보고식
narrow 축소하다
narrow based stock index 업종별 주가지수
narrow market 한산시장
narrow market security 물량이 적은 주
narrow movement 소폭왕래
narrow range 소폭
narrow seas 해협
narrow spread 시세변동으로 매매차익금이 적어지다
narrowing of spread 시세변동으로 매매차익금이 적어지다
NASDAQ 나스닥
NASDAQ Composite Index 나스닥종합주가지수
NASDAQ Japan 나스닥 저팬
National Accounting Office 주계국
national accounts 국민계정
national assets 고유재산
National Association of Accountants 미국회계인회계
National Association of Cost Accountants 미국원가계산사협회
National Association of Insurance Commissioners 미국보험감독관협회
National Association of Securities Dealers 미국증권업협회
National Association of Securities Dealers Automated Quotations 장외상품시황자동정보시스템
national averages 전국평균
national balance sheet 국민대차대조표
National Bank Act of 1863 국립은행법
national bond futures market 국채선물시장
national capital 국민자본
national capital account 국민자본계정
national capital sheet 국민자본표
National Conference of Stock Exchanges 전국증권거래소협의회
national credit 국가신용
National Credit Union Administration 전국신용조합본부
national debt 국가채무
national debt service expenditure 공채비
national disposable income 국민가처분소득
national economic accounting 국민경제재산
national economic budget 국민경제예측

national economy 국민경제
national expenditure 국민지출
National Federation of Credit Guarantee Corporations 전국신용보증협회연합회
national finance 국가재정
national full line firm 종합증권회사
National Futures Association 전미선물협회
national government debts 정부채무
national health insurance tax 국민건강보험세
national income 국민소득
national income accounting 국민소득회계
national income accounts 국민소득계정
national income analysis 국민소득분석
national income distributed 분배국민소득
national income statistics 국민소득통계
national interest 국익
national markets 국내시장
national median 전국중앙치
national minimum 내셔널미니멈
national pension 국민연금
National Police Agency 경찰청
national property 국유재산
National Public Safety Commission 국가공안위원회
National Public Service Law 국가공무원법
national reserve fund 전국평균기금
National Securities Clearing Corporation 미국증권거래소결제기관
national subsidy 국고보조금
national tariff 국정세율
national tax 국세
National Tax Administration Agency 국세청
National Tax Collection Law 국세징수법
National Tax College 세무대학교
National Tax Council 국세심사회
National tax procedure law 국세통칙법
National Tax Receipt Fund 국세수납금정리자금
National Tax Tribunal 국세불복심판소
National Tax Violations Control Law 국세범칙감독법
national treasury 국고
national treatment 내국민대우
national trust 내셔널트러스트
national wealth 국부(國富)
national wealth statistics 국부통계
nationalization 국유화
natural attrition 자연감
natural boundary 자연경계
natural business year 자연영업연도
natural capital 자연자본
natural diaster 천재지변
natural disaster relief loans 천재자금
natural fruits 천연과실
natural law 자연법
natural liberty 자연적인 자유
natural logarithm 자연대수
natural person 자연인
natural premium 자연보험료
natural presumption 자연적인 추정
natural rate of interest 자연이자율
natural rate of unemployment 자연실업률
natural rights 자연권
natural support 자연적 지지
natural year 역년(曆年)
nature of business 사업종류
Naval Court 해사심판소
navigable 항행가능한
near future 머지 않아
near maturity 만기에 가까운
near money 준통화
near the money 니어더머니
near time prospect 전망
near-panic market 공황상장
near-term bond 만기에 가까운 채무
near-term outlook 단기예측
nearby contract 기근물
nearest month 가장 가까운 달
necessaries 생활필수품
necessary documentary evidence

필요한 증거서류
necessary expense 필요경비
necessary expenses in the case of closing business 사업을 폐지한 경우의 필요 경비
necessary household furniture 필수가구
necessary party 필요당사자
necessary tax procedure 필요한 세무수속
neck line 네크라인
negative account 평가계정
negative amortisation 음의 상환
negative amortization 마이너스상각
negative assets 소극자산
negative assurance 소극적인 보증
negative averments 소극적인 주장
negative capital 부채
negative carry 네거티브캐리
negative cash flow 네거티브캐시플로
negative clause 담보보류조항
negative confirmation 소극적인 확인
negative correlation 부의 상관관계
negative covenant 경쟁제한특약
negative duration 부정적인 듀레이션
negative effect 부정적인 효과
negative evidence 소극적인 증거
negative factor 마이너스요인
negative goodwill 소극적인 주
negative growth 마이너스성장
negative income tax 역소득세
negative interest 역금리
negative interest rate spread 시중은행의 할인율상회
negative leverage effect 부정적인 레버리지
negative list 신용불량자리스트
negative monetary position 금전채무상태
negative plea 소극적인 항변
negative pledge clause 담보제한조항
negative pledge pari passu clause 네거티브 플레지 패리 패스 조항
negative prescription 소멸시효
negative property 소극재산
negative spread 당연히 비싸야 할 종목이 싸고; 싸야 할 종목이 비싼 상태
negative statute 금지법
negative testimony 소극적인 증언
negative valuation accounts 소극적인 평가계정
negative yield 단기금리가 장기금리보다 비싼 상태
negative yield curve 오른쪽 아래 방향으로 향하는 이율곡선
negligence 과실
negligence clause 면책조항
negligible in amount 무시할 수 있는 가격
negotiable 양도가능
negotiable asset 양도가능한 자산
negotiable bill 유통어음
negotiable certificate of deposit 양도가능정기예금증서
negotiable instrument 유통증권
Negotiable Instruments Act 유통증권법
negotiable L /C 매입가능신용장
negotiable order of withdrawal account 양도가능환불지도예금계정; NOW 계정
negotiable order of withdrawal deposit NOW 예금
negotiable securities 유가증권
negotiable time certificates of deposits 양도가능정기예금증서
negotiated contracts 수의계약
negotiated market 상대매매시장
negotiated sale 협의발행
negotiated trade 상대거래
negotiated trading 상대거래
negotiated transaction 상대거래
negotiated underwriting 협의인수
negotiating bank 어음유통은행
negotiation charge 어음유통수수료
negotiation credit 외국환유통신용장
negotiation for budget draft 부활절충
negotiation on terms and conditions 조건교섭
neighborhood benefits 인지자의 수익

neighborhood effect 근린효과
neighboring countries 근린제국
neo-quantity theory of money 신화폐수량설
nervous market 신경질적인 시장
nervous shock 정신적인 충격
net amount after provision for loss 대손준비금공제후의 금액
net amount principle 순액주의
net asset per share 일주당 순자산
net asset value 순자산가치
net asset value per unit 유닛당 순자산가치
net asset worth per share 일주당 순자산
net assets 순자산
net assets value 순자산가액
net avails 순수취액
net balance 넷밸런스
net base 순액(純額)베이스
net block flow 넷블록플로
net book value 순장부가액
net borrowed reserves 순차입준비
net budget 예산순계
net capital stock 조자본스톡
net carryover cost 순이월비용
net cash 넷캐시
net cash flow 넷캐시플로
net cash inflows 순현금유입
net changes in each element 과목별 순변동액
net collectible amounts 순회수가능액
net commodity terms of trade 순상품교역조건
net cost 순원가
net creditor country 넷채권국
net current assets 순유동자산
net cycle time 순운전시간
net debt 순부채
net deposit 실세예금
net earned surplus forwarded 이월이익잉여금
net earnings 순이익
net equity assets 순지분자산
net export 순금융수입
net external assets 대외순자산
net foreign credit 대외순대출
net free reserves 순자유준비
net income 순익
net income for the year 당기순이익
net income ratio 순이익률
net income to sales 매상순이익률
net increase 순증가
net interest 순이자
net interest cost 순이자비용
net interest income 순수취이자
net investment 순투자
net lease 넷리스
net liabilities 순부채
net liabilities balance 순유동성수지
net long positions 매초수량
net loss 순손실
net loss carried forward 이월결손금
net monetary items 순금전항목
net monetary position 순화폐포지션
net national product 국민순생산
net national welfare 국민복지지표
net of income taxes 소득세를 공제하고
net of reserves 대손준비금공제후 수취채권
net open position 넷오픈포지션
net operating cycle 순영업순환일수
net operating earnings 경상순익액
net operating loss 순영업손실
net operating loss assumed from a transfer of corporation 피합병회사로부터 승계한 결손금
net operating profit 순영업이익
net output 순산출
net pay 급료
net plan assets 연금플랜순자산
net position 넷포지션
net premium 순수입보험료
net present value 순현재가치
net price 순가격
net price index 넷프라이스인덱스
net price trading 넷프라이스트레이딩

net proceeds 순수취액
net production value 순생산고
net profit 순이익
net profit after depreciation 상각후 순이익
net profit before corporation tax 법인세공제전 순이익
net profit before depreciation 상각전 순이익
net profit before the adjustment of tax 세금조정전 순이익
net profit for the year 당기순이익
net profit margin 매상순이익률
net profit on sales 매상순익
net profit or loss 순손익
net profit or loss account 순손익계산
net profit or loss section 순손익구분
net profit ratio 순익률
net profit to net worth 자기자본이익률
net profit to sales 매상순이익률
net purchase 매입초과;순구입고
net quick assets 순당좌자산
net realizable value 순실현가능가격
net realized capital gain 순실현캐피탈게인
net receipt 순수취금
net receivable 순채권
net return 순수익
net sales 순매상고
net saving 순저축
net settlement 차금결제
net short hedging 순매연결
net succession 순상속재산
net supply of industrial funds 산업자금공급상황
net surplus 순잉여금
net tangible asset ratio to long-term debt 장기부채순고정자산
net tangible assets 순고정자산
net taxable assets 순과세재산
net trading volume 넷거래고
net value 순가격
net working capital 순운전자본
net worth 순자산
net worth equity 순자산
net worth equity capital 자기자본
net worth method 자산부채증감법
net worth of collateral 담보여력
net worth ratio 자기자본비율
net worth tax 부유세
net worth to debts 자본부채비율
net worth to fixed capital 자본고정비율
net write-off 순대손상각
net yield 세인이율
netting 네팅
netting arrangement 네팅계약
neutral equilibrium 중립적인 균형
neutral hedge 뉴트럴헤지
neutral money principle 중립화폐정책
neutrality 중립성
neutrality of taxation 조세의 중립성
new account 신규계정
new banking law 신은행법
new bond 신발채
new capacity 신설비
New Deal 뉴딜
new debt issues 신발채를 발행함
new design 신안
new face bond 신안채
new field 신규분야
new foreign resource bonds 신규재원채
new foreign exchange law 신외국환관리법
new futures 신선물
new high 신고치
New Institute Cargo Clauses 신협회화물약관
new issue 신규발행
new issue of stocks 신주발행
new issue value of outstanding bonds 공사채현존액
new issue volume of outstanding bonds 공사채발행액
new job offers 신규구인수
new lending 신규대출
new listing 신규상장
new loan 신규대출

new low 신저치
new monetary adjustment system 신금융조절
new money 신규자금
new mortgage 신규모기지
new order 신규수주
new permits 주택착공허가건수
new premium 신규프리미엄
new share 신주
new share issuing expense 신주발행비
new share off 신주하락
new shares issued through rights-offerings 신주락에 관계되는 증가신주
new shares issued through stock-dividends 주식배당락에 관계되는 증가신주
new social indicators 국민생활지표
new stock 신주
new stock issuing expenses 신주발행비
new stock price indexes 신주가지수
new trial 재심
new type of gold standard 신형 금본위제
new welfare economics 신후생경제학
New York acceptance credit 뉴욕인수신용장
New York Futures Exchange 뉴욕선물거래소
New York inter-bank offered rate 뉴욕은행간 제안금리
New York Mercantile Exchange 뉴욕상품거래소
New York money market 뉴욕금융시장
New York Offshore Center 뉴욕오프쇼어시장
New York refinance 뉴욕리파이낸스
New York Stock Exchange 뉴욕증권거래소
New York Stock Exchange Composite Stock Index 뉴욕증권거래소주가지수
newly deficit 적자전락
newly industrialized countries 신공업국군
newly issued corporate bond 신규발행사채
newly listed company 신규상장회사
next closing of account 차기결산
next day fund 익일자금화 자금
next-in next-first method 나중에 취득한 재고자산부터 먼저 가격을 산정하는 재고자산평가법
niche 니치
nifty fifty 인기 50문제
night deposit safe 야간금고
night session 야간거래
Nikkei 225 Future 닛케이 225선물거래
Nikkei 225 Index option 닛케이 225 지수옵션
Nikkei 225 Options 닛케이 225 옵션
Nikkei 300 Futures 닛케이 300 선물거래
Nikkei 300 Investment Trust 닛케이 300 투자신탁
Nikkei 300 Options 닛케이 300 옵션
Nikkei 300 Stock Price Index 닛케이 300 주가지수
Nikkei 300 Dow-Jones Average 닛케이다우평균
no consideration 무약인항변
no dividend 무배당
no dividend company 배당이 없는 기업
no effect 무효
no fault automobile insurance 노폴트자동차보험
no load fund 노로드펀드
no loss no profit 손실도 없고 수익도 없음
no protest 거절증서가 필요 없음
no-down 노다운
no-par-value stock 무액면주식
node 절점
node method 노드방식
noise 노이즈
nominal account 명목계정
nominal amount 액면가액
nominal assets 명목자산
nominal capital 명목자산
nominal coupon 표면이율
nominal deposit 표면예금
nominal GNP 명목 GNP
nominal gross deposit 표면예금

nominal income 명목수입
nominal interest rate 표면금리
nominal liabilities 명목부채
nominal partner 명목상의 파트너
nominal profit 명목이익
nominal proxy 무권대리
nominal quotation 분위기; 시황
nominal rate 표면금리
nominal rate of discount 명목할인율
nominal rate of interest 명목이율
nominal rate of protection 명목보호율
nominal rate of return 명목수익률
nominal transaction 명목상거래
nominal value 액면가; 공칭가
nominal wage 명목임금
nominal wealth tax 명목상의 재산세
nominal yield 명목이율
nominalism 명목주의
nominate 지명하다
nominated subcontractor 지정하청업자
nominee 명의인
non-accrual 이자계상정지
non-amortizable securities 일시불유가증권
non-bank financial institution 비은행금융기관
non-basic shareholder of family corporation 비동족주의
non-borrowed reserve 여잉준비
non-business activity 비사업활동
non-business expenses 사업외경비
non-business property 비영업용 자산
non-callable bond 논콜러블본드
non-cancellable guarantee 취소불능보증
non-cash assets 비현금자산
non-cash items 비현금항목
non-claim 청구불이행
non-concealed assets 장부외자산
non-controllable cost 관리불능원가
non-cost items 비원가항목
non-cumulative dividend 비누적형 배당
non-cumulative preferred stock 비누적형 우선주식
non-current assets 비유동자산
non-current liabilities 장기채무
non-declarant 미선언자
non-delivery 인도불이행
non-depositary correspondent 논디포지터리 코레스펀던트
non-depreciable assets 비상각자산
non-depreciable property 비상각자산
non-detachable warrant 분리불능 워런트
non-determined period 규정하지 않은 기간
non-diversified investment company 비분산투자형 투자회사
non-dividend 무배당
non-draft export 외화를 주고받지 않는 수출
non-draft import 외화를 주고받지 않는 수입
non-expendable fund 사용불능자금
non-family corporation 비동족회사
non-financial accounts 비금융계정
non-financial assets 비금융자산
non-financial market 비금융시장
non-financial transaction 비금융거래
non-fleet insured 논플리트계약자
non-forfeiture act 불몰수법
non-forfeiture condition 불몰수조건
non-fulfillment 불이행
non-fulfillment of a contract 계약불이행
non-fund transactions 수지를 수반하지 않는 거래
non-genuine agreement 이면계약
non-government bond 민간채
non-homogeneity 비동질성
non-inclusion of income tax credit in deductible expenses 소득세공제액손금불산입
non-installment 비할부
non-installment card 일괄지불카드
non-interest-bearing bond 비이자부채
non-interest-sensitive item 금리비감응항목
non-investment cooperative association 비출자조합

non-joinder 불병합
non-juridical organization 법인격이 없는 단체
non-legal standards 법률이 아닌 기준
non-life insurance 손해보험
non-life insurance agent 손해보험대리점
non-life insurance company 손해보험회사
Non-Life Insurance Institute of Japan 일본손해보험사업연구소
non-liquid assets 비유동성자산
non-marine agency system 논마린대리점제도
non-market economy 비시장경제
non-market risk 비시장성 리스크
non-market risk sources 비시장성 리스크의 원천
non-marketable issue 비시장성 증권
non-marketable securities 비시장성 증권
non-member governor 회원외이사
non-member securities company 비회원회사
non-monetary indirect security 비화폐간접증권
non-monetary items 비금전항목
non-money trust 금외신탁
non-operating 영업외의
non-operating expenditure 영업외비용
non-operating expenses 영업외경비
non-operating income 영업외수입
non-operating profit 영업외이익
non-operating profit and loss 영업외손익
non-operating revenue 영업외수익
non-operating section 영업외손익구분
non-opinion report 무한정감사보고서
non-order bill 지도금지어음
non-par stock 무액면주
non-par-value stock 무액면주식
non-payments 미납
non-personal family corporation 비동족의 동족회사
non-personnel expenses 물건비
non-proportional reinsurance 비례할당하지 않는 재보험
non-rate earnings assets 비금리자산
non-rate-paying liability 비금리부채
non-rate-sensitive liability 금리비감응부채
non-reciprocal 비상호적인
non-recourse 논리코스
non-registered 등기미제
non-resident foreign currency account 비거주자외화예금계정
non-resident won deposit 비거주자 원예금
non-risk assets 비위험자산
non-risk interest rate 비위험이자율
non-settled 비계약자
non-stochastic model 비확률 모델
non-strategic division 비전략 부문
non-suit 소송각하
non-tariff barriers 비과세장벽
non-tie-up loan 비제휴론
non-voting stock 의결권이 없는 주
noncancellable 해약불가능한
noncash financing activities 수지를 동반하지 않는 재무활동
noncash investing activities 수지를 동반하지 않는 투자활동
noncommercial enterprise 비영리회사
noncommercial trader 비상업트레이더
noncompetitive tender 비경쟁입찰
nondeductible taxes 손금불산입조세과금
nonequity index futures 비주식지수선물
nonexclusive 비독점적인
nonfeasance 의무불이행
nonferrous metals industry 비철금속업계
nonfinancial transactions 비금융거래
nonfulfillment of settlement 결제불이행
nonnegotiable 유통성이 없는
nonnegotiable bill 이서금지어음
nonnegotiable endorsement 비유통증권
nonnegotiable safekeeping receipts 양도불능보호증서
nonparticipating insurance 무배당보험
nonparticipating preferred stock 비참가우선주식

nonpayment protest 부도통지
nonperformance 불이행
nonperformance of contract 계약불이행
nonperforming assets 불가동자산
nonperforming loans 불량채권
nonpermanent resident 비주거자
nonprofit corporation 비영리법인
nonprofit foundation 공익법인
nonprofit institution 비영리기관
nonprofit making business 비영리사업
nonprofit making organization 비영리조직
nonprofit-making activity 공익사업
nonprofit-making company 비영리법인
nonrecurring cost 경상외비용
nonrecurring item 감시손익항목
nonrecurring profit 감시이익
nonrecurring profit and loss 경상외손익
nonresident 비거주자
nonresident foreign currency account 비거주자외화예금계정
nonresident won account 비거주자원예금계정
nonstatistical sampling 비통계적 샘플링
nontax payment 세외부담
nontax receipts 세외수입
nontaxable corporation 비과세법인
nontaxable document 비과세문서
nontaxable exchange of properties 수용환지
nontaxable goods 면세품
nontaxable income 비과세소득
nontaxable interest from deposits for tax payment 납세준비예금이자의 비과세
nontaxable interest income 비과세이자소득
nontaxable property 비과세재산
nontaxable receiving 미납세인수
nontaxable savings 비과세저축
nontaxable securities 비과세유가증권;면세증권
nontaxable transaction 비과세거래
nontaxable-goods for special use 특수용도면세
nontraditional asset class 비전통적인 어셋클래스
nonuser 불행사
Nordic Council 북유럽협의회
Nordic Council of Ministers 북유럽각료회의
Norin Chukin Bank 일본농림중앙금고
normal and average use hours 통상사용시간
normal asset mix 노멀어셋믹스
normal auditing procedures 정규감사절차
normal balances 정상잔고
normal burden rate 정상배부율
normal cost 정상원가
normal depreciation 정상상각
normal distribution 정규분포
normal equation 정규방정식
normal goods 정상재
normal market 노멀마켓
normal operating cycle 정상적인 상업순환
normal probability distribution 정규확률분포
normal procedure 정규절차
normal profit 정상이윤
normal rate of exchange 정상환상장
normal return 정상이익
normal standard cost 정상표준원가
normal stock 정상재고고
normal target allocation 노멀타겟앨로케이션
normal tax 보통세
normal yield curve 순일드
normalized EPS 표준EPS
North America Free Trade Agreement 북미자유무역협정
North Atlantic Assembly 북대서양의회
North Atlantic Free Trade Area 북대서양자유무역지역
North Atlantic Treaty Organization 북대서양조약기구
North Brent 북해 브렌트
north-south problem 남북문제
north-south summit 남북서미트
north-south trade 남북무역
nostro 자국

Nostro account 당방계정
not otherwise provided 별도의 규정이 없는 한
notarial charges 공증료
notarial deed 공정증서
notarial document 공정증서
notary 공증인
note at sight 일람불약속어음
note auctions 중기채입찰
note discounted 할인어음
note dishonoured 부도어음
note endorsed 이서양도어음
note for payment of tonnage dues 톤세 납부서
note issuance facility 노트이슈언스퍼실리티 ; NIF
note issued by a third person 제3자가 발행한 어음
note of payment 지불통지서
note of protest 거절각서
note payable 지불약속어음
note payable register 지불어음기입장
note purchase agreement 채무매입계약
note received discounted 할인어음
note register 어음기입장
noteholders meeting 채권보증자회의
notes and accounts payable 지불채무
notes and accounts receivable 수취채권
notes and bills discounted 할인어음
notes and bills endorsed 이서어음
notes and bills payable 지불어음
notes and bills receivable 수취어음
notes endorsed for payment 이서양도어음
notes of financial statements 재무제표각주
notes payable book 지불어음기입장
notes receivable 수취어음
notes receivable register 수취어음기입장
notes to the financial statement 재무제표각주
noteworthy 주목할 만한
notice deposit 통지예금
notice of abandonment 위임통지
notice of acceptance 인수통지
notice of demand to guarantor 납부최고서
notice of determination 결정통지서
notice of lien 선취특권통지
notice of loss and damage 사고통지
notice of redemption 상환통지
notice of seizure 차압통지서
notice to inform of taking effect 효력발생통지서
notice to inform of taking effect of securities registration statement 유가증권신고효력발생통지서
notice to produce 문서제출요구서
notice to quit 해약예고
noticeably fluctuating goods 가격변동이 심한 물품
notification 최고서
notification in writing 문서통지
notification of appropriation of refund 환부금충당통지서
notification of audit 사전조사통지
notification of depreciation method 상각방법신고
notification of estimated tax prepayment 예정납세액통지
notification of incorporation 설립계
notification of opening of business 개업계
notification of payment of refund 환부금지불통지서
notification of tax agent 납세관리인신고
notification of tax payment 납세고지서
notification of the taxable year 사업 연도신고
Notification of the Ministry of Finance 재무부 통지
notification of transfer of place of tax payment 납세지이동신고
notification procedure 통고처분
notifying bank 통지은행
notional amount 상정원본
notional certificate 의제증서
notional income 관념상의 소득

M N

notwithstanding 그럼에도 불구하고
novelty 신안(新案)
NTT bond NTT 채
nuclear energy property insurance 원자력재산보험
nuisance 불법방해
null and void 무효의
nullity 무효
number of buying and selling 매매횟수
number of days' purchases in accounts payable 외상채권회전일수
number of days' sales in inventories 재고정리자산회전일수
number of days' sales in receivables 매상채권회전일수
number of floating shares 유동주식수
number of machines installed 설치대수
number of stocks issued per old stock 구주 일주당 발행된 신주수
number of offered shares 공개주식수
number of scheduled payments 반제횟수
number of settlement transactions 결제횟수
number of shareholders 주식수
number of stocks held 보유주식수
number of stocks issued 발행필 주식수
number of years elapsed 경과연수
numbered accounts 번호계좌
numeraire 평가기준
numerical integration 수치적분법
NYSE Composite 뉴욕종합지수
NYSE Composite Stock Index NYSE 종합주가지수

O

oath 선서
object cost 요소별 원가
object of pledge 질권목적
object of taxation 과세물건
object tax 목적세
objection 이의신청
objection to discipline 처분에 대한 이의
objection to disposition 처분에 대한 이의
objective 요소별의
objective function 목적함수
objective indicator 객관지표
objective probability 객관적인 확률
objective statement 요소별 계산서
objective value 객관적인 가치
obligation 채무
obligation fees 부담비
obligation of bookkeeping 기장업무
obligation of contract 계약상의 권리
obligation of signature and seal 자필압인의무
obligation to acquire the approval 승인된 의무
obligation to file return 신고의무
obligations incurred 발생채무부담
obligations to compensate 보상의무
obligations under capital leases 리스설비자산채무
obligatory insurance 강제보험
obligee 채권자
obligor 채무자
obligor risk 채무자의 위험
obliteration 말소
observation 관찰
observed depreciation 견적감가상각
observed life table 견적내용연수표
obsolete 쓸모없게 된;진부한
obsolete assets 진부화 자산
obsolete property 진부화 자산
obstruction of navigation 항행방해죄
obtainer of employment income 급여소득자
occasional income 일시소득
occupant 점유자
occupation tax 영업세
odd date 정형화이외거래기간
odd date or broken date delivery 특정기일인도
odd lot 단주
odd lot consolidation 단주정리
odd lot dealer 단주업자
odd-lot transaction 단주거래
ODR cut 공정할인율하락
ODR operation 공정할인율조작
OECD membership OECD 가맹
OECD model double taxation convention OECD 모델조세조약
of like grade and quality 품질이 같은
off balance 오프밸런스
off balance sheet transaction 오프밸런스시트거래
off balance sheet accounting 오프밸런스회계
off balanced trade 오프밸런스거래
off limit 출입금지

off market 오프마켓
off market swap 오프마켓스와프
off-board market 장외시장
off-board transactions 시장외거래
off-board transactions of listed bonds 상장채권시장외매매고
off-exchange futures transactions 장외선물거래
off-floor distribution 입회외분매
off-hours trading 입회외매매거래
off-record lending (은행원 등이) 남의 예금을 기장하지 않고 제삼자에게 일시대출하는 부정행위
off-setting account 상쇄계정
off-the-run issue 주변상품
offense 범죄
offer 제출;신청
offer by subscription 예약공모
offer curve 오퍼곡선
offer for sale 팔다
offer side 오퍼사이드
offer the deposit 예탁하다
offered price 매호치
offered rate 오퍼레이트
offering 모집
offering circular 모집안내서
offering for sale 매출
offering for subscription 공모
offering price 매출가격
offering size 입찰총액
offering to shareholder 주주할당
office audit 책상조사
office copy 관제등본
office expense account 영업비계정
office expenses 사무비
office expenses book 영업내역장
office found 국고귀속인정
office furniture 영업용집기
office grant 강제이행
office hours 영업시간
office manual 사무규정
Office of Administrative Law Judges(SEC) 행정소송심판관실(SEC)
Office of Administrative Service(SEC) 행정서비스실(SEC)
Office of Chief Accountant(SEC) 주임회계사실(SEC)
Office of Comptroller(SEC) 관리사실(SEC)
Office of Consumer Affairs and Information Service(SEC) 소비자업무정보서비스실(SEC)
Office of Economic Analysis(SEC) 경제분석실(SEC)
Office of EDGAR management(SEC) 에드가관리실(SEC)
Office of Executive Director(SEC) 사무국장실(SEC)
Office of General Counsel(SEC) 법률 고문실(SEC)
Office of Information System Management (SEC) 정보시스템관리실(SEC)
Office of Opinion and Review(SEC) 의견기초실(SEC)
Office of Personnel(SEC) 인사실(SEC)
Office of Public Affairs(SEC) 공보실(SEC)
Office of Public Utility Regulation(SEC) 공익사업규제실(SEC)
Office of Secretary 비서실(SEC)
Office of the Comptroller of the Currency 통화감독관사무소(SEC)
office or other fixed place of business 사무소 혹은 다른 일정한 사무소
office overhead 사무소제경비
office regulation 사내규정
officer de jure 법률상의 직원
officer's bonus 임원상여금
officer's compensation 임원보수
officer's salary 임원급료
officers retiring allowance 임원퇴직금
official approval 인허가
official assessment 부과과세제도
official check 은행수표

official credits 공적채권
official deposit 공금예금
Official Development Assistance 정부개발원조
official discount rate 공정률
official exchange market 공정시장
official exchange rate 공정환상장
official foreign exchange reserves 외화준비고
official information 공보
official inspection 임검
official interest rate 정책금리
official intervention 공적개입
official invoice 공용 인보이스
official mandate 정식맨데이트
official power 직권
official rate 공정레이트
official receiver 관선수익관리인
official reserve transactions balance 공적결제수지
official retain 영치
official to receive national tax 국세수납관리
offset 상쇄
offset account 상쇄계정
offset error 상쇄오진
offset item 상쇄항목
offsetting order 반대주문
offsetting position 상쇄포지션
offshoot 자회사
offshore account 오프쇼어계정
offshore assets 해외자산
offshore banking center 오프쇼어뱅킹센터
offshore banking facility 오프쇼어은행간 시장
offshore banking unit 오프쇼어뱅킹유닛
offshore borrowing 오프쇼어조달
offshore center 오프쇼어센터
offshore fund 오프쇼어펀드
offshore guarantee 오프쇼어보증
offshore lease 오프쇼어리스
offshore market 오프쇼어시장
offshore production 오프쇼어해외시장
offshore purchase 역외조달
offshore trade 삼국간 무역
oil and coal product industry 석유석탄제품업계
oil concession 석유채굴권
oil pollution liability insurance 원유오염배상책임보험
oil refinery 석유정제업
oil stock 석유주
old account 잔존계정
old age pension 노령연금
old bank act 구은행법
old bond 올드본드
old foreign exchange act 구외국환관리법
old person allowance 노령자공제
old share 구주
old-aged; survivor and disability insurance 노령유족장애자연금
oligopolistic control 과점지배
oligopolistic economy 과점경제
oligopoly 과점
oligopoly industry 과점산업
oligopoly price 과점가격
omitted dividend 무배당
omnibus account 공동계정
omnium 담보차입주식총액
on a simple interest basis 단리(單利)베이스
on balance 온밸런스
on balance volume 온밸런스볼륨
on board notation 선적이서
on call 청구 즉시
on cost 제조비
on customer's account 위탁계정으로
on demand selling rate 도착지불판매상장
on one's own account 자기계정으로
on one's proprietary account 자기계정으로
on or before 기일 또는 기일전에
on our risk 당방부담
on passage 운송중
on the books 외상장부에서

on the job accidents 업무상의 사고
on-balance-sheet transaction 온밸런스거래
on-hours trading 입회내 매매거래
on-line banking system 온라인뱅킹시스템
one bank holding company 단일은행지주회사
one contract 일계약
one day contract 일일계약
one day reversal 원데이리저벌
one day skipped 영업일이 지나서
one factor 단일요인
one factor model 단일요인모델
one hundred percent income statement 백분율손익계산서
one man company 일인회사
one name paper 단명어음
one share shareholder 일주주주
one shot customer 일회성 고객
one sided hedge 편도헤지
one stop filing 원스톱파일링
one time trading 청산매매
one way 편도
one year budget principle 예산단년도주의
one year rule 일년기준
one's own house system 지가제도(持家制度)
onerous contract 유상계약
onerous gift 부담을 조건으로 한 증여
ones own convenience 자기사정
ongoing assessment 계속평가
onshore 자국내
onshore market 온쇼어마켓
open account 미결계정
open air market 야외시장
open and current account 상호계산계정
open auction 공개경쟁
open bidding 일반경쟁입찰
open board of broker 공개거래회관
open book 오픈북
open buying 신규구입
open check 보통수표
open contract 특약이 없는 계약
open corporation 공개회사
open court 공개법정
open cover 오픈커버;포괄보험
open credit 오픈크레디트
open down 오픈다운
open economy 개방경제
open group 개방단체
open inflation 개방형 인플레이션
open insurance 포괄예정보험
open interest 미결제거래잔고
open interest in margin transactions 신용거래잔고
open interest on buyer's side 매입 측의 거래잔고
open interest on seller's side 매출 측의 거래잔고
open L/C 매취은행무지정신용장
open ledger 미결제원장
open market 공개시장
open market operations 공개시장조작
open market quotation 시중상장
open market rate 시중금리
open market selling operation 매출오퍼레이션
open money market 공개단기금융시장
open mortgage 해방담보
open mortgage clause 단순저당채권자불약관
open order 무조건주문
open outcry method 공개경쟁매매방식
open policy 포괄보험증서
open position 아직 결제하지 않은 주식이나 상품
open price 포괄보험증서
open rate method 오픈레이트방식
open repo 공개시장조작
open selling 신규매출
open tendering 일반경쟁입찰
open theft 현행절도죄
open-end 개방식의
open-end bond investment trust 공사채투자신탁
open-end fund 오픈엔드형 펀드

open-end investment trust 오픈형 투자신탁
open-end lease 오픈엔드형 리스
open-end mortgage 개방식 담보
open-end mortgage bond 개방식 담보부사채
open-end type 추가형
pen-up of money market 금융시장개방
opener 신용장발행의뢰인
opening balance 기초잔고
opening balance account 개시잔고계정
opening bank 개설은행
opening charge 신용장발행수수료
opening commission 발행수수료
opening entry 이월기장
opening inventory 기초재고고
opening price 시가
opening quotation 시가
opening rate 시가
opening rate closing rate 시가와 종가
opening session 오프닝세션
opening tone 오프닝톤
operand 연산수
operated days 조업일수
operating accounts 영업활동계정
operating activities 영업활동
operating assets 운용자산
operating budget 영업예산
operating business 영리회사
operating capital 운전자금
operating condition 영업상황
operating cost 운전비용
operating cycle 영업순환
operating cycle rule 영업순환기준
operating efficiency 경영효율
operating expenses 영업경비
operating fund 운전자금
operating income 영업수익
operating income on sales 매상영업이익률
operating income to sales 영업이익률
operating lease 오퍼레이팅리스
operating ledger 영업원장
operating leverage analysis 오퍼레이팅레버리지 분석
operating leverage effect 영업면의 증익 효과
operating loss 영업손실
operating margin 영업이익률
operating perfomance ratios 업적비율
operating profit 영업이익
operating profit and loss 영업손익
operating profit level 영업이익단계
operating profit margin 영업이익률
operating profit on sales 매상고 영업이익률
operating rate 조업도
operating ratio 가동률
operating receipt 영업수입
operating report 영업보고
operating reserve 영업준비금
operating results 영업성적
operating revenue 영업수익
operating section 영업손실구분
operating standing 영업상태
operating statement 영업활동계산서
operating surplus 영업잉여
operating target 조작목표
operating variable 조작변수
operation audit 업무감사
operation capacity 조업도
operation efficiency 작업능률
operation expenses 작업비
operation in the secondary market 유통시장조작
operation of law 법의 작용
operation ratio 조업률
operation variance 조업도차이
operational efficiency 효율성
operations for stabilizing the stock market price 주가안정조작
opinion 의견
opinion of auditors 감사의견서
opinion of independent certified public accountant 감사보고서

opinion expression 이견포명
opportunity cost 기회비용
opportunity gain 기회이익
opportunity loss 기회손실
opposite accounts 반대계정
opposite party 상대방
oppression 직권남용죄
optimal bond portfolio 최적채권포트폴리오
optimal capital structure 최적자본구성
optimal condition 최적조건
optimal growth model 최적성장모델
optimal hedge instrument 최적헤지수단
optimal operating ratio maximal operating ratio 최적조업도와 최유리조업도
optimal policy mix 최적폴리시믹스
optimal portfolio 최적포트폴리오
optimal scale 최적규모
optimal threshold return 적성상하한계수익률
optimality criterion 최적성기준
optimization 최적화
optimum allocation of resources 최적자원배분
optimum capacity 최적조업도
optimum currency 최적통화지역
optimum distribution 최적분배
optimum foreign exchange reserves 적정외화준비고
optimum inventory 최적재고량
optimum output 최적생산량
optimum rate of growth 최적성장률
optimum rate of interest 최적이자율
opting-out 옵팅아웃
Option 25 옵션 25
option adjusted spread 옵션조정후 스프레드
option adjusted yield 옵션조정후 이율
option bond 옵션부채
option buyer 옵션바이어
option clearing corporation 옵션청산회사
option combination 풋콜조합옵션
option delivery 풋콜인도
option delta 옵션델타
option expiration date 옵션만기일
option forward 옵션포워드
option gamma 옵션감마
option market 옵션시장
option money 특권료
option performance index 옵션퍼포먼스지수
option period 선택권행사가능기간
option pool 옵션풀
option position 옵션포지션
option premium 옵션프리미엄
option pricing model 옵션가격결정모델
option pricing theory 옵션가격결정이론
option seller 최적규모
option spread 옵션스프레드
option theta 옵션세타
option to double 배액감채약관
option trading based on government securities 국채증권선물옵션
option trading based on the stock price index 주가지수옵션거래
option transaction 옵션거래
option warrants 주식매수권증서
option writer 옵션매도자
optional assessment 원천선택과세
optional cancellation 임의해약
optional cargo 양륙지 선택화물
optional redemption 임의상환
optional repayment provision 선택상환조항
optional reserve 임의준비금
options based on securities 유가증권옵션
options contract value 옵션거래대금
options on stock index futures 주가지수선물옵션
options on stock price index 주가지수옵션
options trading 옵션거래
options trading on Japanese government bond futures 일본국채증권선물옵션거래
options trading on securities 유가증권옵션거래
oral testimony 구두증언
order 주문

order and disposition 명의상의 소유
order B /L 지도인식 선하증권
order backlog 수주잔
order book 주문기록부
order book official 오더북오피셜
order book trading 주문부거래
order by telephone 전화주문
order entry 주문엔트리
order for attachment of property 차압명령
order for collection 징수명령
order for relief 구제명령
order increase 수주증가
order negotiation 주문상대
order of application 적용순서
order of credit 채권순위
order of liquidity 유동성배열법
order of preference 선호순위
order stock 현품주문
order to outside manufacturer 외주
order to pay 지불명령
order volume 수주액
order-filling cost 주문불이행
order-taking hours 주문접수시간
orderly export marketing 질서 있는 수출
orderly marketing agreement 시장질서유지협정
orders in hand 수주잔고
ordinance by local government 조례
ordinance of competent minister 주무부령
ordinary agent 생명보험외무원
ordinary and necessary expenses 보통 필요한 경비
ordinary and necessary movable property for living 생활에 보통 필요한 동산
ordinary and normal recurring operations 통상운영
ordinary annual expenditure 경상세출
ordinary annual revenue 경상세입
ordinary annuity 보통연금
ordinary bank 보통은행
ordinary bill 통상어음
ordinary budget 경상예산
ordinary care 통상주의
ordinary charges 통상비용
ordinary collection 보통징수
ordinary conveyance 통상양도증서
ordinary corporation 보통법인
ordinary corporation income 보통소득
ordinary deposit 일반예금
ordinary depreciation 보통상각
ordinary dividend 보통배당
ordinary expenditure 경상비용
ordinary foreign tax credit 통상외국세액공제
ordinary general meeting 통상총회
ordinary income 경상수입
ordinary individual life insurance 보통개인보험
ordinary insurance 보통보험
ordinary interest rate 보통이자율
ordinary life insurance 보통생명보험
ordinary local grant tax 보통교부세
ordinary loss or gain 경상손익
ordinary tosses 통상손해
ordinary partnership 보통조합
ordinary payment 통상결제
ordinary private company 일반적인 사회사
ordinary profit 경상이익
ordinary profit and loss 경상손익
ordinary remittance 보통송금
ordinary risks of employment 사업상의 통상위험
ordinary share 보통주
ordinary shareholder 보통주주
ordinary shareholder's equity 보통주주지분
ordinary stock 보통주
ordinary tax 경상세
ordinary trades trading 매매입회를 통한 거래
organic composition of capital 유기적인 자본구성
organization audit 조직감사
organization committee 창립위원
organization expenses 창업비

O P

organization expenses amortize 설립상각비
Organization for Economic cooperation and Development 경제협력개발기구
Organization for European Economic Cooperation 유럽경제협력기구
Organization for Security and Cooperation in Europe 유럽안보협력기구
organization form 조직형태
organization meeting 창립총회
Organization of American States 미주기구
Organization of Arab Petroleum Exporting Countries 아랍석유수출국기구
Organization of Central American States 중미기구
organization of loan 론조성
Organization of Pacific Economic Cooperation 태평양지역경제협력기구
Organization of Petroleum Exporting Countries 석유수출국기구
organization office 창립사무소
organization planning 조직계획
organizational changes 조직개혁
organizational unit 조직단위
organizations of primary commodity producers 일차산품생산국기구
organized margin transactions 제도신용거래
organizer 창립자
original capital 원시자본
original cost 취득원가
original cost method 취득원가법
original credit 원신용장
original document 원본
original entry 원시기입
original equipment manufacturing OEM
original insurance 원보험
original insurance policy 원보험증서
original issue discount 발행시할인
original jurisdiction 제 1심관할권
original margin 기본증거금
original maturity 기초만기
original money 본원화폐
original package 원포장
original premium 기초보험료
original purchaser 당초구입자
original register 원부
original trading partner 기본상대방
originator 발기인
Osaka Securities Exchange 오사카증권거래소
Osaka Stock Price Index 오사카증권주가지수
oscillation theory 진동이론
oscillator 오실레이터
Oslo Stock Exchange Index 오슬로증권거래소지수
OTC company 장외등록기업
OTC firm 장외거래상품
OTC interest rate option 장외금리옵션
OTC margin stock 장외증거금주식
OTC option 장외옵션
OTC sales yield of public and corporate bonds 공사채장외매매이율
OTC stock quotation exchange system 주식장외시황발표제도
other accounting 타회계
other insurance clause 타보험조항
other reserve 별도적립금
our account 당방계정
our side 당방
out of date 기한경과
out of the money 아웃오브더머니
out town bill 타소불어음
out town check 타소불수표
out town delivery 타소인도
out-in transaction 외내거래
out-of-court settlement 시담해결
out-of-date check 실효수표
out-of-pocket cost 현금지불비용
out-of-pocket expense 현금지출비
out-out loan 외외론
out-out transaction 외외거래
outbuilding 부속건물

outgo 지출
outlay 지출
outlay cost 지출원가
outlay expiration 지출소비
outlay for advertisement 광고비
outlay tax 간접세
outline 아웃라인
outlook for consumer spending 소비예상
output coefficient 산출계수
output cost 제조원가
output method 생산고비례법
output reduction 조업단축
outright 아웃라이트
outright base 무조건오퍼
outright buying and selling 단순매매
outright exchange rate 아웃라이트환상장
outright forward delivery with option 옵션부 순월인도
outright forward fixed date delivery 순월확정일인도
outright forward rates fixed date 순월확정일상장
outright purchase 매절
outright sales 품절
outright transaction 아웃라인거래
outside capital 타인자본
outside day 아웃사이드데이
outside dealing 장외거래
outside director 사외이사
outside environment 외부환경
outside money inside money 외부화폐와 내부화폐
outside pressure 외압
outside product 외주제품
outsider 장소에 어울리지 않는 사람
outsourcing service expenses 업무위탁비
outstanding account 미결제계정
outstanding at year-end 연말잔고
outstanding balance of issue amount 발행잔고
outstanding balance of loan 융자잔고
outstanding balances 잔존원본
outstanding balances of credit 신용잔고
outstanding bond 발행필 채권
outstanding capital 발행필 자본
outstanding capital stock 자본금현재고
outstanding contract amount 계약잔고
outstanding debt 한도를 넘은 차용
outstanding liabilities 미불부채
outstanding loan 융자잔고
outstanding loans and discounts of all banks by terms 기한별 대출통계
outstanding premiums 미수보험료
outstanding principal 잔존원본
outstanding principal amount 잔존원본액
outstanding shares 발행필 주식
outstanding stock 발행필 주식
outstanding title 제삼자의 권원
outstanding warrants 발행필 워런트
outward freight 왕로운임
outward investment 대외투자
over and short account 과부족계정
over funding 오버펀딩
over insurance 초과보험
over month repurchase 익월물
over par 오버퍼
over subscription 오버서브스크립션
over time 시간경과에 따른
over time price of bond 시간경과에 따른 채권가격
over-absorbed cost 배부초과원가
over-and-out option 오버앤드아웃옵션
over-capacity 설비과잉
over-carrying cost 이월비
over-competition 과당경쟁
over-hedge 과대헤지
over-indebted person 고액채무자
over-indebtedness 채무과다
over-investment 과잉투자
over-issue 한도초과발행상품
over-loan 대출초과
over-month loan 익월물

over-paid 과다지불한
over-payment 과납
over-payment of corporation tax due to window dressing
분식결산에 따른 법인세과다납부
over-priced 고가
over-speculation 과당투기
over-the-counter currency option
장외통화옵션
over-the-counter managed issues
장외관리상품
over-the-counter market 장외시장
over-the-counter option 장외옵션
over-the-counter sales yield 장외매매이율
over-the-counter stock 장외주
over-the-counter transaction 장외거래
over-the-month delivery 익월인도
over-the-top warrant 오버더탑워런트
over-used hours 초과사용시간
overabsorbed burden 간접비배부초과액
overabsorption 초과배부
overall balance 종합수지
overall balance of foreign exchange
외환보유고
overall effective tax rate 종합효과세율
overall position 종합지고
overborrowing 차입초과
overbought market 과잉매입상장
overbought position 과잉매입포지션
overcapitalization 과대자본
overdraft 당좌초과인출
overdraft account 당좌대월계정
overdraft economy 초과인출경제
overdraft facilities 당자대월약정
overdraft interest 초과발행이자
overdrafts for export bills 환당좌대출
overdrawing 초과대출
overdrawn 초과대부
overdrawn account 초과대출계정
overdressing 과도한 분식
overdue account 기한경과계정
overdue bill 기한경과어음
overdue check 기한경과수표
overdue interest 연체이자
overdue interest on loan on bills
어음대부연체이자
overdue interest per diem 연체일변; 연체일보
overdue loan 기한경과대부
overdue payment 기일도래채권
overestimate 과대평가
overestimation of goods traded in
보상판매상품을 과대평가함
overestimation of inherited assets
인계자산을 과대평가함
overestimation of investment in kind
현물출자를 과대평가함
overexuberant economy 과열경제
overfunded 자금이 크게 팽창한
overhang 공급과잉
overhauling 수선
overhead 제경비
overhead allocation 제조간접비배부
overhead cost 간접비
overhead cost distribution 간접비배부
overhead distribution basis 간접비배부기준
overhead distribution sheet 부문비계산표
overhead expenses 경상비
overhead rate 간접비배부율
overhead variance 간접비차이
overheated economy 과열경제
overheating of business activity 경기과열
overhung dollar 달러과잉
overland freight 육상운송비
overlapping account 중복계정
overlapping debt 중복채무
overlay 추가증액
overnight 익일반제
overnight call 익일반제콜
overnight call rate 익일반제콜금리
overnight delivery 익일인도
overnight money 익일물
overnight rate 오버나이트레이트

overnight repo 익일물레포
overnight transaction 오버나이트거래
overpayment 과오납금;과납
overproduction 생산과잉
overreaching clause 소유권유보조항
overriding 우선시키다
overrun 초과의
overs and shorts 과부족
overseas affiliated firm 해외관계회사
overseas assets 해외자산
overseas business 해외사업
Overseas Economic Cooperation Fund 해외경제협력기금
overseas finance subsidiary 해외금융자회사
overseas flotation 해외기채분
overseas interest rate 해외금리
overseas interests 대외이권
overseas investment 대외투자
overseas investment report 해외투자보고서
overseas legal reserves 해외법정준비금
overseas liabilities 해외부채
overseas listing 해외상장
overseas major market 해외주요시장
overseas market development reserve 해외시장개척준비금
Overseas Private Investment Corporation 해외민간투자공사
overseas production capacity 해외생산능력
overseas production ratio 해외생산비율
overseas securities financing 해외증권발행
overseas technical service transaction 해외기술거래
overseas transaction 해외거래
overseas travel accident insurance 해외여행상해보험
overseas undertaking corporation 해외사업법인
overselling 초과매출
overshoot 지나친 행위
overstatement 과대표시
overstatement of taxable income 과대신고
overstock 과잉재고
oversupply 공급과다
overt 명백한;공공연한
overt act 명백한 행위
overvaluation 과대평가
overvalued 고가
overvalued futures 고가선물
overview of the business results 업적개요
owing 지불해야 할
owing to bank 은행차입
own account 자기계정
own bill 자행인수
own capital 자기자본
own named cards 자사카드
own shares 자기자본
own usance 자행유전스
owner control 소유자지배
owner of record 명의상의 주주
owner's equity 소유주지분
owner's risk 하주위험부담
owner's capital 주주자본
owner's equity to total assets 자기자본비율
ownership certificate 소유권증
ownership right 소유권
ownership structure 주주구조

P

Paasche formula 파쉐계산식
Pac-man defense 팩맨디펜스
pace of economic expansion 경제성장률
Pacific basin 환태평양
Pacific Basin 환태평양지역
Pacific Economic and Cultural Enclave 환태평양경제문화권
Pacific Insurance Conference 태평양보험회의
Pacific Stock Exchange 퍼시픽증권거래소
package automobile policy 자동차종합보험
package deal contract 패키지딜
package lease 패키지리스
package policy 패키지폴리시
packing and wrapping expenses 포장비
packing charge 포장비
packing credit 패킹크레디트
packing list 포장명세서
pact 협약
paid amount 지불금액
paid cash book 현금지불장
paid check 지불필 수표
paid interest 반제이자
paid-in advances 신주불입금
paid-in capital 불입자본
paid-in capital in excess of par 주식불입잉여금
paid-in capital increase 유상증자
paid-in outstanding shares 유채발행필 주식
paid-in surplus 불입잉여금
paid-up capital 불입자본
paid-up insurance 보험료지불필 보험
painting the tape 가격조작
panic market 공황시장
panic selling 공포투매
paper audit 서면감사
paper company 페이퍼컴퍼니
paper credit 종이홍수
paper currency 지폐
paper profit 가공이익
paperless trading 페이퍼리스트레이딩
par 주식액면
par bond 액면매매사채
par forward 파포워드
par issue 액면발행
par price 액면가격
par value 액면가격
par value of exchange rate 환평가
par value share 액면주식자본금
par value stock 액면주식
par yield 파일드
paradox of value 가치패러독스
paradoxical view 역설적인 견해
paragraph 항;단락
parallel clearing 상호결제
parallel import 평행수입
parallel issue 평행기채
parallel loan 상호대출
parallel market 패럴렐마켓
parallel money market 병행시장
parallel rate shift 금리평행이동
parallel shift 평행이동

parallel standard 평행본위제도
parallel transaction 평행거래
parameter 매개변수;파라미터
parametric method 파라메트릭방법
paramount right 우월한 권리
parent base 단독베이스
parent company 친회사
parent sales 단독베이스매상
parent store 본점
parent-basis earning outlook 단독베이스수익예측
parenthetical notes 본체주기
Pareto's constant 파레토 상수
pari passu 동순위로
pari passu clause 파리패스조항
pari-mutuel betting 경마식 도박
Paris bourse 파리거래소
Paris Club 파리클럽
parity 평가
parity account 패리티계산
parity adjustment 평가조정
parity grid 패리티그리드
parity index 패리티지수
parity line 패리티직선
parity of official exchange rate 공정평가
parity quotation 평준상장
parity rate of exchange 액면평가
parity value 패리티가치
parking 피난
parol contract 구두계약
part-owners 공유자
partial abandonment 일부위탁
partial acceptance 일부인수
partial assignment 일부양도
partial audit 부분감사
partial correlation of securities investment trust 증권투자신탁을 부분해약함
partial costing 부분원가계산
partial delivery 일부인도
partial derivative 편도함수
partial draw down 분할인출
partial elasticity 편탄력성
partial endorsement 일부이서
partial equilibrium 부분균형
partial legal tender 불완전법화
partial loss 분손
partial payment 일부지급
partial performance 일부이행
partial reserve system 일부준비제도
partial shipment 분할선적
partial tax transfer to local government 지방분여세
partial withdrawal 부분철수
partially covered option 부분적인 커버드옵션
partially finished goods 반제품
partially finished goods ledger 반제품원장
participant 참가자
participating annuity 이익배당부 연금
participating bank 참여은행
participating bond 이익참가사채
participating insurance 참가보험
participating interests 참여지분
participating preferred stock 참가우선주식
participating stock 이익배당주
participating whole life insurance 배당부 종신보험
participation 참가
participation agreement 파티서페이션계약
participation certificate 참가증권
participation fee 참가금
participation in seizure 참가차압
participation loan 참가융자
participation method 참가방식
participation stock 참가주
particular average 단독해손
particular interest 이해함수
particular lien 특정리엔
particular loss 분손
particulars 내역
particulars of account 계정명세
particulars of transaction 거래내용
parties to lawsuit 소송당사자

partition 공유물분할
partition of corporation 회사분할
partition of the estate 유산분할
partition finished product 반제품
partly paid bond 일부불입채권
partner 출자사원
partnership 파트너십
partnership agreement 파트너십계약
partnership assets 조합재산
partnership property 조합재산
parts account 부품계정
party 당사자
party insuring 보험계약자
pass dividend 무배당으로 하다
pass on 전가하다
pass-through 패스스루
pass-through rate 패스스루비율
pass-through securities 패스스루증권
passage 통과
passage of title 소유권이전
passbook 통장
passbook savings account 통장저축예금계좌
passed dividend 무배당
passenger liability insurance 승객배상책임보험
passengers traffic receipts 여객수입
passengers tax 통행세
passing off 사칭통용
passive bond 무이자사채
passive debt 무이식채무
passive investment management 소극적인 투자관리
passive loss 패시브손실
passive management 소극적인 관리
passive partner 패시브파트너
passive strategy 안전형 운용
passive trust 소극신탁
past cost 과거원가
past due bill 기한경과어음;부도어음
past due interest 연체이자
past due loan 연체론
past performance 과거의 실적
past service liability 과거근무채무
patent 특허
patent account 특허권계정
patent ambiguities or defects 명백한 의미불명료 혹은 오류
patent ambiguity 명백한 의미불명료
patent applied for 특허출원중
patent attorney 특허변리사
Patent Bureau 특허국
patent dispute 특허분쟁
patent fee 특허료
patent infringement 특허권침해
patent law 특허법
patent pending 특허출원중
patent period 특허유효기간
patent right 특허권
patented article 특허품
patentee 특허권자
path 경로
path dependent option 경로의존형 옵션
path-independency 경로독립성
pattern information processing 패턴정보처리
pattern of portfolio return 포트폴리오수익패턴
pattern recognition 패턴인식
pawn 저당물
pawn-shop 전당포
Pax Americana 팍스아메리카나
pay 임금
pay according to ability 능력급
pay according to function 직무급
pay after tax 세금공제급여
pay back method 회수기간법
pay by card 카드결제
pay down 현금지불
pay off 완제하다
pay on application 확인지불
pay roll audit 급료감사
pay-as-you-earn 원천과세
pay-as-you-go 현금지불주의

pay-as-you-go-system 부과방식
pay-freeze 임금동결
pay-in-kind bond 현물배당주
pay-off 일괄완제
pay-off diagram 페이오프다이어그램
pay-off function 이득함수
pay-off matrix 페이오프행렬
pay-roll register 임금급료지불부
pay-through bond 페이스루채권
pay-up 추가지불
payable 지불기일이 도래한
payable at sight 일람불
payable on a fixed date 확정일불
payable on demand 요구불
payable register 지불전표기입장
payable to bearer 지참인불
payable to holder 소지인불식; 소지인출급식
payable to order 지도식 또는 소지인불식
payables 매입채무
payables to sales ratio 매상채무비율
payback period 회수기간
payee 수취인
payer 지불인
paying & warrant agency agreement 지불워런트 대리인계약서
paying agent 지불대리인
paying bank 지불은행
paying in slip 입금전표
paying tax 납부
paying; collecting and refunding tax 세액납부; 징수 및 환급
paymaster 회계주임; 경리담당자
payment 결제
payment account agreement 지불준비계정계약
payment against acceptance 인수불
payment against document 서류상환지급
payment agreement 지불협정
payment and receipt of cash 현금수수
payment at regular fixed times 정시불
payment at short date 단기불
payment book 지불기입장
payment by beneficiary 수익자부담금
payment by bill 어음지불
payment by cash 현금지불
payment by installment 분할지불
payment by rough estimate 개산지불
payment by the result 성과배분
payment credit 지불신용장
payment date 지불기일
payment day 지불일
payment default 결제불이행
payment for another 대납
payment handling bank 불입취급은행
payment in advance 선급으로
payment in full 전액불입
payment in installments 분할납부
payment in kind 물납
payment in lump sum 일시불입
payment in part 일부지급
payment in subrogation 대위납부
payment in substitution 대물변제
payment into court 공탁
payment mismatches 이자지불미스매치
payment of capital contribution 출자금불입
payment of retirement allowance for termination 퇴직금중간정산지급
payment of tax 세금납부
payment of unrealized profit 계산상의 이익을 지출함
payment on account 일부지급
payment on delivery 선불
payment on interest and discount rate 이자 및 할인료
payment order 지불지도
payment periods 반제기간
payment rate 지불률
payment record 지불조서
payment regarded as dividends 간접배당
payment slip 출금전표
payment statement 지불명세
payment stop 지불정지

O P

payment supra 참가지불
payment system 결제수단
payment terms 지불조건
payment on to be made by a lump sum at maturity 기간일괄불
payment to nonresidents 비거주자의 급여소득
payment to nonresidents and foreign corporation 비거주자 및 외국법인에 대한 지불
payment to rendered services 역무제공에 대한 지불
payment-in-kind preferred stock 페이먼트인카인드 우선주
payout 배당지불
payout ratio 배당성향
payroll 급료;임금지불장
payroll book 임금대장
payroll deduction 임금공제
payroll deduction type investment trust 급여공제형 투신
payroll tax 임금세
peak load 피크로드
pearl harbor file 펄하버파일
peculiar benefits 특수수익
pecuniary considerations 금전적인 보수
pecuniary damage 금전적인 손해
pecuniary legacy 금전유증
pecuniary relation 금전상의 관계
pecuniary transaction 금전거래
peer 동료
peer companies 동업타사
peer review 피어리뷰
pegged exchange 고정환상장
pegged exchange rate system 고정환상장제도
pegged market 고정상장
pegged stock 고정주
pegging 가격안정화
penal 형사상의
penal interest 위약이자
penal provision 벌칙
penal sum 위약금액
penalty 위약금
penalty against employer and employee 양벌규정;쌍벌규정
penalty charge 지연손해금
penalty heavier than imprisonment 금고 이상의 형벌
penalty on delayed delivery 연체보상금
penalty rate 벌칙금리
penalty tax 가산세
pending 미결의
pending lawsuit 계쟁중인 소송
penetration of phones 전화보급률
penetration of tight money policy 금융긴축정책이 침투함
penetration price 침투가격
penetration rate 가입률
pennant 페넌트
penny stock 저가주
pension 연금
pension and life insurance schemes 기업연금; 기업보험
pension assets 연금자산
Pension Benefit Guarantee Corporation 연금보장공사
pension benefits 연금급부
pension business 연금업무
pension contract 연금계약
pension cost 연금코스트
pension expense 연금비용
pension financing method 재정방식
pension fund 연금기금
pension fund beneficiary 연금기금의 수익자
pension fund management 연금기금관리
pension fund spread 연금기금 스프레드
pension fund surplus 연금기금잉여
pension plan 연금계획
pension point system 연금포인트제도
pension program 연금제도
pension reserve 연금적립금
pension right 연금권

pension scheme 연금제도
pension trust 연금신탁
pensionable age 지급개시연령
penultimate 끝에서 두번째
pent road 막다른 길
people meter 피플미터
People's Finance Corporation 국민금융공사
People's Insurance Company of China 중국인민보험공사
peppercorn rent 명목상의 지대
per annum 일년당
per annum rate 연리
per capita 일인당
per capita gross national product 일인당 국민총생산
per capita income 일인당 소득
per capita incomes 일인당 GNP
per capita levy 균등할세율
per capita product 일인당 생산
per capita rate 일인당 세율
per contra account 대조계정
per contra noted discounted account 할인보증계정
per diem 일일당
per diem allowance 일당
per share data 일주당 수치
per share earning ratio 주가수익률
per-diem rate for call loan 콜금리
percent of capacity use 가동율
percentage analysis 구성비율
percentage balance sheet 백분율대차대조표
percentage depletion 비율법감모상각
percentage grant 정율보조금
percentage lease 퍼센티지리스
percentage method 백분율법
percentage of capital structure 자본구성비율
percentage of completion basis 공사진행기준
percentage of credit losses 대손율
percentage of debt collection 회수율
percentage of delinquency 연체율
percentage of each classification of assets to total assets 자산구성비율
percentage of profits available on net worth 자기자본이익률
percentage on diminishing value plan 정율상각법
percentage statements 백분율재무제표
percentage table 백분율표
perception 점유하다
peremptory 단정적인
peremptory instruction 결정적인 설시
peremptory nonsuit 결정적인 각하
perennial tax 영구세
perennial tenant right 영대소작권
perfect competition 완전경쟁
perfect hedge 완전헤지
perfect monopoly 완전독점
perfect obligation 완전채무
perfect title 완전권원
perfected security interest 대항요건을 구비한 담보권
perfection of the interest 대항력을 구비함
perfection standard cost 완전표준원가
perfectly negatively correlated returns 완전부상관수익률
perfectly positively correlated returns 완전정상관수익률
performance accounting 업적평가회계
performance appraisal 업적평가
performance attribution 퍼포먼스특성
performance audit 업무감사
performance bond 이행보증증권
performance bond insurance 이행보증보험
performance evaluation 업적평가
performance fund 퍼포먼스펀드
performance guarantee 이행보증
performance guarantee deposit 이행증거금
performance indicators 업적지표
performance margin 퍼포먼스증거금
performance measurement 퍼포먼스측정
performance model 업적모델
performance of business 사업수행

performance of obligations 채무이행
performance of obligations of guarantee 보증채무이행
performance report 업적보고서
performance-based fee system 퍼포먼스비례보수체계
performing loans 가동중인 론
peril 위험
peril point 위험점
perils clause 위험약관
perils insured against 피보험위험
perils of the sea 해상고유의 위험
period analysis 기간분석
period call market 정기콜시장
period charge 기간비용
period commencing on but excluding the date of 개시일포함
period cost 기간원가
period expense 기간비용
period for tax 납기
period of economic growth 경제성장기
period of economic stability 경제안정기
period of depreciation 상각기간
period of grace 예비기간
period of request for reconsideration 심사청구기간
periodic actual inventory 정기실지재고
periodic allocation of cost 원가기간배분
periodic audit 정기감사
periodic average method 총평균법
periodic balance sheet 기말대차대조표
periodic financial accounts 기간재무제표
periodic income 기간이익
periodic inventory 정기재고조사
periodic loss 기간손실
periodic pension cost 연금의 기간원가
periodic securities report 유가증권보고서
periodic trial balance 기말시산표
periodical accounting 기간계산
periodical accounting of profit and loss 기간손익계산
periodical deposits 정기적금
periodical return 정기수익
periodical transaction 정기거래
periodicals 정기간행물
permanent account 영구계정
permanent assets 영구자산
permanent auditor 상임감사역
permanent debt 영구공채
permanent difference 영구차이
permanent domicile 본적
permanent establishment 항구적인 시설
permanent facility 항구적인 시설
permanent financing 영구대출
permanent health insurance 종신건강보험
permanent income hypothesis 상설소득가설
permanent injunction 영구금지명령
permanent liabilities 영구부채
permanent life insurance 종신보험
permanent loan 영구임대
permanent preferred stock 영구우선주
permanent trespass 계속적인 침해
permissible error 허용오차
permutation 교환
pernor 수익자
pernor of profits 수익취득자
perpetual annuity 종신연금
perpetual bond 영구권
perpetual injunction 영구금지명령
perpetual inventory 계속재고
perpetual inventory method 계속기록법
perpetual issue 영구채
perpetual lease 영대차지권
perpetual lessee 영대차지인
perpetual subordinated debt 영구열후채
perpetual warrant 영구워런트
perpetuating testimony 증언을 증거로 보전함
persistence rate 계속률
persistent 완고한; 지속성의
person adjudged incompetent 금치산자
person for handling securities 유가증권관리책임자

person receiving employment income 급여소득자
personal accident insurance 상해보험
personal account 인명계정
personal action 인적소송
personal assets 동산
personal average tax rate 평균개인세율
personal bankruptcy 개인파산
personal bias 개인적인 편향
personal bill 개인어음
personal check 퍼스널체크
personal checking account 개인당좌계정
personal consumption expenditure 개인소비
personal contract 동산계약
personal covenant 인적 약관
personal credit 개인신용
personal deposit 개인예금
personal distress 동산차압
personal dividend income 개인배당소득
personal estate 동산
personal exclusion from taxation 인적과세제외
personal exemption 기초공제
personal expenditure 개인지출
personal family corporation 동족주주의 동족회사
personal financing 개인금융
personal guarantee 개인보증
personal hereditament 인적상속재산
personal holding company 동족회사
personal identification number 비밀번호
personal immunity 개인의 비밀보유권
personal income 개인소득
personal income from property 개인재산소득
personal income tax 개인소득세
personal insurance 개인보험
personal interest income 개인이자소득
personal judgment 인적판결
personal knowledge 직접인식
personal ledger 인명원장
personal liability 개인부채
personal liability insurance 개인배상책임보험
personal liberty 인신의 자유
personal loan 개인론
personal opinion 자기의견
personal pension 개인연금
personal pension insurance 개인연금보험
personal pension scheme 개인연금제도
personal property 개인재산
personal property floater 가재포괄보험
personal property tax 동산세
personal rental income 개인임대료소득
personal representatives 인격대표자
personal saving 개인저축
personal sector 개인부문
personal security 인적담보
personal service 역무
personal tax 동산세
personal taxation 인적과세
personal trust 개인신탁
personal trust fund 개인신탁펀드
personal valuation 개인적인 평가
personality 인적재산
personification theory 의인화 이론
personnel audit 인사감사
personnel expenses 인건비
personnel management 인사관리
personnel policy 인사방침
personnel reduction 인원소멸
persons in overseas service 국외근무자
pertinent information 관련정보
perusal 정독
peseta 페세타
pessimistic scenario 비관적인 시나리오
petition 청원
petition in bankruptcy 파산신청
petition of right 권리청원
petitioner 신청인
petrobond 원유가격연동형 사채
petrochemical complex 석유화학콤비나트

petrochemical industry 석유화학산업
petroleum act 석유업법
petroleum gas tax 석유가스세
petroleum revenue tax 석유수입세
petroleum tax 석유세
Petroleum tax law 석유세법
petty average 소규모해손
petty cash 소액현금
petty cash account 소액현금계정
petty cash book 소액현금출납장
petty cash payment 소액현금지불
petty cash system 소액현금제도
petty current deposit 소액현금예금
petty deposits 소액예금
petty expense analysis book 잡비내역장
petty expenses 잡비
petty imprest 소액전도금
petty loss and profit 잡손익
petty offense 소죄
petty-sum depreciable assets 소액감가상각자산
petty-sum depreciable property 소액상각자산
petty-sum wasting property 소액감모자산
pharmaceutical industry 의약품업계
phase of expansion 경기확대국면
phase of recession 경기후퇴국면
phased construction 단계적인 건설
phases of economic cycle 경기순환국면
Philadelphia plan 필라델피아플랜
Phillips curve 필립스곡선
philosophy of management 경영철학
physical access member 입회장에서 거래할 수 있는 회원
physical age 물리내용연수
physical capital 실체자본
physical contingency 물리적인 예비비
physical counts 실지재고
physical delivery 현실인도
physical depreciation 물리적인 감가
physical distribution 물류
physical evidence 물적증거
physical inventory 실지재고정리
physical life 물리적인 내용연수
physical security 현물증권
physical variance 추량차이
physical wear and tear 물리적인 감모
physically handicapped person allowance 장애자공제
physician's expense insurance 치료비보험
pick up 상승
pick-up of inflation rate 인플레율상승
pick-up of yield 이익개선
picker 도둑; 소매치기
pickup in demand 수요회복
piece rate plan 성과급
pilot plant 파일럿플랜트
pilot unit 시작기
PIN number PIN 번호
pit 피트
pit broker 피트브로커
pit reporter 피트리포터
place of abode 주소
place of delivery 인도장소
place of fiduciary 수탁취급장소
place of issue 발행지
place of payment 지불지
placement commission 판매수수료
placement of bond 사채판매
placement of unlisted note 사모채발행
placing memorandum 사모요령
plain deal 플레인딜
plain language 보통주
plain vanilla 플레인바닐라
plain vanilla floater 플레인바닐라변동이자부채
plain vanilla swap 플레인바닐라스와프
plaintiff 원고
plan assets 연금자산
plan beneficiaries 플랜수익자
plan documents 연금플랜규정서
plan termination insurance 연금제도종료보험

planned economy 계획경제
planned monetary system 관리통화제도
plant 공장
plant account 공장설비계정
plant and equipment 공장설비
plant capacity 생산설비
plant fund 설비자금
plant investment 설비투자
plant ledger 고정자산원장
plant outages 조업정지
plants and buildings 건물
plastic money 플라스틱머니; 신용카드
playing cards tax 트럼프세
playright 흥행권
Plaza Accord 플라자합의
pledge 담보물
pledge account 질권계좌
pledged assets 저당자산
pledged revenue 반제원자
pledged security 차입유가증권
pledgee 동산질권자
pledgee's lien 동산질권자의 유치권
pledging 플레징
pledgor 질권설정자
plenipotentiary 전권
plowing-back 이익을 재투자함
plum 특별배당
plunge 대폭하락
plunger 무모한 투기꾼
plus-tick 플러스틱
point and figure 포인트앤드피규어
point and figure chart 포인트앤드피규어차트
point and figure method 포인트앤드피규어법
point elasticity 점탄력성
point of sales 판매시점정보관리
point of sales system POS 시스템
points 주장의 요점
points reserved 보류논점
poison pill 독소조항방위
poison pills 포이즌필
Poisson distribution 포이즌분포
policy asset allocation 폴리시어셋앨로케이션
policy asset mix 폴리시어셋믹스
policy assignment 정책수단을 할당함
policy coordination 정책협조
policy depreciation 정책적인 감가상각
policy dividend 계약자배당금
policy fee 증권발행수수료
policy for promoting competition 경쟁촉진정책
policy for restricting competition 경쟁제한정책
policy loan 보험증권대부
policy mix 폴리시믹스
policy objective 최종목표
policy of insurance 보험증권
Policy Proof of Interest 수익보험증권
policy rate 정책금리
policy reserve 책임준비금
policy state 정책포지션
policy summary 계약개요
policy term 보험기간
policy years basis 보험인수연도별 계산
policy-holders' dividend 보험계약자배당금
policyholder 보험계약자
policyholder dividend 계약자배당
policyholder loan 보험가입자론
policyholder obligations 보험가입자의 채무
policyholder's surplus 보험계약자잉여금
Policyholders' Protection Act 보험계약자보호법
political accountability 정치적인 책임
political corporation 정치단체
political crisis 정치위기
political risk 정치리스크
political system stability index 정치안정지수
political turmoil 정치적인 혼란
politics of pensions 연금의 정치적인 측면
poll tax 인두세
pollution control reserve 공해방지준비금
pool agreement 풀협정
pool balance 풀잔고

pool of financial assets 금융자산풀
pool of financing 풀오브파이낸싱
pool of fund approach 자금풀법
pool of funds 자금풀
pool operation 풀조작
pooled common stock account 합동보통주계정
pooled common stock and publicly traded bond account 합동보통주 및 공모채계정
pooled first mortgage 공동제일저당권
pooled fund 풀펀드
pooled private placement bond account 합동사모채계정
pooled publicly traded bond account 합동공모채계정
pooled real property account 합동부동산계정
pooling accounting 풀링회계
pooling arrangement 재보험풀
pooling contracts 공동계산계약
pooling of interest method 지분풀링방식
pooling of interests 지분풀링
poor economy 경기침체
poor securities trading 증권거래침체
poorly capitalized 자금력이 빈약함
popular action 민중소송
popular stock 인기주
population 모집단
population density 인구밀도
population mean 모평균
population statistics 인구통계
port charges 항만료
port dues 입항세
port risks insurance 계선보험
port toll 양륙세
portable pension 이동계속연금
portfolio analysis 포트폴리오분석
portfolio approach 포트폴리오수법
portfolio balance approach 포트폴리오밸런스어프로치
portfolio bond 소지채권
portfolio bonds 보유채권
portfolio characteristic line 포트폴리오의 특성선
portfolio diversification 포트폴리오분산투자
portfolio engineers 포트폴리오엔지니어
portfolio gains 자산매각익
portfolio insurance 포트폴리오보험
portfolio investment 자산운용투자
portfolio management 포트폴리오관리
portfolio manager 포트폴리오매니저
portfolio method 전자산합동방식
portfolio mix 포트폴리오믹스
portfolio monitoring 포트폴리오모니터링
portfolio of investment trust 투신상표
portfolio optimization 포트폴리오최적화
portfolio optimizer 포트폴리오 옵티마이저
portfolio pricing methodology 포트폴리오가격결정법
portfolio restructuring 포트폴리오재편
portfolio revision 포트폴리오수정
portfolio risk model 포트폴리오리스크모델
portfolio selection 자산선택
portfolio stocks 보유주식
portfolio theory 포트폴리오이론
portfolio trade 포트폴리오거래
portfolio value 포트폴리오가치
portfolio view 포트폴리오뷰
portfolio's yield 포트폴리오이율
position 환보유고
position adjustment 포지션조정
position bookkeeping 평형부기
position delta 포지션델타
position gamma 포지션감마
position instruction 포지션지도
position risk 포지션리스크
position sheet 운용장
position theta 포지션세타
position trader 포지션트레이더
position trading 포지션매매
positional goods 지위재

positions established with index arbitrages 재정거래와 관련된 현물포지션
positions on customer's account 고객의 위탁과 관련해서 아직 결제를 하지 않은 상태
positive adjustment policies 적극적인 조정정책
positive carry 포지티브캐리
positive condition 적극조건
positive confirmation 적극적인 확인
positive correlation 정의 상관관계
positive covariance 정의 분포도
positive credit file 포지티브정보
positive curve 순일드
positive economics 실증경제학
positive figure 흑자
positive financial policy 적극재정;팽창재정
positive law 실정법
positive leverage effect 정의 레버리지효과
positive monetary position 금전채무의 초과상태
positive prescription 취득시효
positive property 적극재산
positive spread 긍정적인 격차
positive yield 순일드
positive yield curve 정의 이율곡선
possession 점유
possession in deed 현실점유
possession in law 법정점유
possession of land 토지점유
possession of property 자산소유
possessory lien 점유적인 리엔
post audit 사후감사
post close account 마감후 계정
post entry 추가기입
post for stocks to be delisted 정리포스트
post industrial society 탈공업화 사회
post Keynesian 포스트케인시안
post to the ledger 원장에 옮겨적다
post-balance sheet date 결제일후
post-balance sheet event 후발사상
post-closing entry 마감후 기입
post-closing trial balance 이월계산표
post-qualification 사후자격심사
post-tax profit 세금공제후 이익
postage 우송료
postage paid 우송료지불필
postage to be paid on delivery 우송료선불
postal agencies 우정관서
postal check 우편수표
postal deposit 우편저금
postal life insurance 간이보험
postal money order 우편환
postal savings 우편저금
Postal Savings Law 우편저금법
postal transfer account 대체계좌
postdate 사후일부
postdated bill 사후일부 어음
postdated check 사후일부 수표
posted price 공시가격
posterior analysis 사후분석
posting 옮겨 적기
posting of contract price 약정가격공표
postponement of investment 투자연기
postponement of payment 지불유예
postponement of tax collection 징수유예
postponement of tax payment 연납
postretirement benefit 퇴직후 급부
postulate of accounting period 회계연도를 공준함
postulate of auditing 감사공준
postulate of business entity 기업실체를 공준함
potential customer 잠재고객
potential demand 잠재수요
potential existence 잠재적인 존재
potential growth 잠재성장률
potential over-supply produced by new issues 증자압박
pound bloc 펀드블록
pound crisis 펀드위기
pound sterling commercial paper 영국펀드 CP

pound sterling currency futures 영국펀드 통화선물
pound sterling depositary interest futures 영국펀드 예금금리선물
pound sterling time deposit 영국펀드 정기예금
poverty line 빈곤선
poverty rate 빈곤율
power 권한
power expense 전력비
power in gross 독립지명권
power of appointment 지명권
power of attorney 위임장
power of collection 징수권
power of sale 매각권
power theory of wages 임금세력설
practicable 실무적으로 가능한
practicable consequence 실무적인 귀결
practical economy 실천경제
practicable guidance 현실적인 지침
practicable seminar 실천세미나
practice 실천
practice standards 업무기준
practitioner 실무가
pragmatic decisions 현실주의적인 결정
pragmatic judgment 실제판단
pragmatic reasons 현실적인 이유
prayer 청구취지신청
pre-acquisition profit 취득일 이전의 유보이익
pre-date 전일부
pre-deposited stock certificates 예탁전 주권
pre-maturity redemption 조기상환
pre-preparatory period 사전준비기간
preamble 서문
preaudit 사전감사
prebid agreement 프레비드계약
precarious right 불확실한 권리
precedence 우위
precedence of bids and offers 지정가격순위
precedence of customer's order 징수순위
precedent 선례
preceding 이전의
preceding article 전조
preceding fiscal year 전년도
preceding month 전월
preceding page 전페이지
preceding taxable year 전사업연도
preceding year 전년
precise value 정확한 가치
precision instruments industry 정밀기계업계
precision machinery 정밀기계
precision technology 정밀기술
precontact 선계약
predate 전일부로 하다
predecessor company 피합병회사
predetermined burden rate 예정배부율
predetermined cost 예정원가
predetermined cost system 예정원가계획
predetermined price 미리 설정한 가격
predictability 예측가능성
predicted cost 예사원가
prediction error 예측오차
prediction of investment return 투자수익을 예측함
predictors of default 채무불이행 예측지표
preemption 우선매수권
preemption entry 선취권을 등록; 신청함
preemptive right 신주우선인수권
prefectural bond 지방채
prefectural inhabitants tax 지방세
prefectural location 지방분포
prefectural tax 도시세
preference 선호;우선권
preference dividend 우선배당
prefectural for gold 금선호
preference for interest rate 금리선호
preference of financial assets 금융자산선호
preference ordering 선호순서
preferential 특혜적인
preferential bill 우선채권
preferential creditor 우선채권자
preferential duty 특혜관세

preferential payment 우선지불
preferential payment in bankruptcy 파산우선지불
preferential right 우선권
preferential tariff 특혜관세
preferred bidder 우선입찰자
preferred creditor 우선채권자
preferred creditors' right 선취특권
preferred dividend 우선배당
preferred dividend coverage ratio 우선배당부담배율
preferred equity 우선주
preferred equity securities 우선출자증권
preferred liability 우선채무
preferred ordinary share 우선적인 보통주
Preferred Providers Organization 특약의료기구
preferred stock 우선주
preferred stock capital 우선주식자본
preferred stockholder 우선주의 주주
prejudice 권리훼손;편견
preliminary 속보
preliminary advice 사전조언
preliminary audit 예비감사
preliminary balance sheet 예비대차대조표
preliminary claim 예비클레임
preliminary disclosure of settlement of accounts 결산예비발표
preliminary information 예비정보
preliminary prospectus 사업설명서
preliminary rating 예비등급
premature delivery futures system 계약금제도
premerger notification 사전병합신고
premier 우량의
premise of a going concern 계속기업을 전제로
premises 택지
premises and equipment 동산과 부동산
premises and compensation for removal 권리금과 입퇴금
premium bond 프리미엄채
premium borrower 우량발행체
premium cap 고급카드
premium condition 보험료프리미엄
premium deficiency 보험료결손
premium due 지불기일이 온 보험료
premium in addition to the original contract price 청부대금거치금
premium in arrears 미수보험료
premium income 수입보험료
premium issue 프리미엄발행
premium loan 보험료대체대부
premium on bonds payable 사채할증발행차금
premium on debt 채무증권발행차금
premium on redemption 환급프리미엄
premium over conversion value 전환가격을 넘는 금액
premium payment of a retirement annuity 퇴직연금부금
premium quotation system 프리미엄시가방식
premium reserve 보험료적립금
premium sale 경품부 판매
premium securities 프리미엄증권
premium tax 보험료세
preopening expenses 창립준비비
prepaid 선불의
prepaid asset 전불자산
prepaid card 프레페이드카드
prepaid commission 선불수수료
prepaid expense 선불비용
prepaid freight 선불운임
prepaid income 선불이익
prepaid income taxes 선불법인세
prepaid insurance 선불보험료
prepaid insurance premiums 미경과보험료
prepaid interest 선불이자
prepaid rents on buildings 선불가임
prepaid salaries and wages 선도임금
preparatory audit 사전조사
preparing the financial statements 재무제표를

작성함
prepay 선불하다
prepay risk 기한전 환급리스크
prepayment indicator 기한전 상환율지표
prepayment model 기한전 상환모델
prepayment of income tax 예정납세
prepayment of tax 조세예납
prepayment of tax on liquidation income 청산소득에 대한 법인세예납
prepayment option 선불옵션
prepayment projection 조기상환예상
prepayment rate 기한전 상환율
prepayment right 기한전 반제권
prepayment risk 조기상환리스크
preproduction cost 시작품원가
prequalification 사전자격심사
presale order 사전판매
prescribe 규정하다
prescribed format 통일양식
prescript 법령
prescription 시효
prescription extinctive 소멸시효
present cost 현재원가
present data analysis 현상분석
present goods 현재재
present market value 시가
present price 현재가격
present value 현재가치
present value accounting 현재가치회계
present value discounted at compound interest 복리현가
present value method 현가법
present value of annuity 연금현가
present value rate 현가율
present worth 현재가치
presentation 제시
presentation bill 일람불어음
presentation for acceptance 인수를 위한 제시
presentation for payment 지불제시
presentation period for payment 지불제시기간
presenting bank 제시은행
presentment of bill of exchange 환어음제시
preservation 몰수보존
preservative attachment 채권보전
preservative security 보전담보
preservative seizure 보전차압
preside over 통괄하다
president 이사장
president of TSE TSE이사장
president-ELECT 차기대통령
press club 기자클럽
press law 출판법
pressure group 압력단
pressure on price 명예가격
pressure to cut interest rates 이율하락압력
presumption 추정
presumption of a real obtainer of income 소득귀속을 추정함
presumption of fact 사실상의 추정
presumption of rights 권리추정
presumptive evidence 추정증거
presumptive heir 법정추정상속인
pretax accounting income 세금공제전 회계이익
pretax income 세금공제전 이익
pretax income to sales 매상세금공제전 이익률
pretax life earnings 생명보험부문 세금공제전 이익
pretax profit 세금공제전 이익
prevailing interest rate 시장실세이율
prevailing price 일반가격
prevailing rate 시장금리
prevailing value 재조달가치
prevailing wage 일반임금
previous close price 전일종가
previous indorsements guaranteed 선행이서진정증명
previous mouth 전월
previous term 전기
previous year 전년

price action 가격행동
price adjustment 가격조정
price agreed upon 협정가격
price analysis 가격분석
price appreciation 증가(增價)
price auction 가격입찰
price before tax 세전가격
price book-value ratio 주가순자산배율
price boost 가격상승
price cartel 가격카르텔
price cashflow ratio 캐시플로배율
price competition 가격경쟁
price concession 가격양보
price contingency 인플레예비비
price contract 가격계약
price control 가격통제
price determination 가격결정
price difference 가격폭
price differential 가격차이
price discovery 가격발견
price discrepancies 가격차이
price discrimination 가격차별
price divergence 가격차이
price dividend ratio 배당이율
price earnings multiple 주가수익률
price earnings ratio 가격수익률
price effect 가격효과
price elasticity 가격탄력성
price elasticity of supply and demand 수요가격탄력성
price factor 가격계수
price filter 프라이스필터
price fixing 가격결정
price flexibility 가격신축성
price fluctuation 가격변동
price fluctuation reserve 가격변동준비금
price freeze 가격동결
price hike 가격인상
price including tax 세입가격
price index 물가지수
price index of listed securities 상장유가증권지수
price indication method 가격표시방법
price information 가격정보
price insurance 가격보험
price leader 프라이스리더
price level 물가수준
price limit 가격폭제한
price limit on commodity futures 상품선물거래가격폭제한
price line 가격폭제한
price line of futures price 선물가격곡선
price maker 프라이스메이커
price margin 가격차익
price mechanism 가격메카니즘
price movement limit 가격폭제한
price movement of stocks 주가동향
price of corporate bond 사채가격
price of introduced stock 공개가격
price of new stocks on the day to be paid in 지불기일현재의 신주가격
price outlook 인플레예측
price pattern 가격패턴
price policy 가격정책
price policy of agricultural products 농산물가격정책
price priority 가격우선
price protection 가격보호
price quotation 시세; 시가; 가격표
price range 가격폭
price revision 가격개정
price rise 가격상승
price risk 가격리스크
price sensitivity 가격감응성
price stability 가격안정
price stabilization policy 물가안정정책
price standards 가격표준
price structure 가격구조
price support subsidy 가격유지보조금
price supporting 가격안정조작
price system 가격체계
price theory 가격이론

price trend on stocks 주식트렌드
price variance 가격차이
price variation 물가변동
price volatility 가격변동률
price weighted 평균가격가중
price weighted index 평균가격가중지수
price yield curve 가격이율곡선
price-fixing agreement 가격담합협정
price-specie-flow mechanism 물가정화유출입기구
prices minus tax 세금공제가격
pricing 금리결정;가격결정
pricing calculation 가격계산
pricing of policies 보험료설정
pricing risk 세율설정리스크
pricing strategy 가격결정전략
pricing tool 가격결정툴
prima facie 얼핏 보기에는
primary account 일차계정
primary activity 기채활동
primary advance 일차적인 부동산이동행위
primary benefit rule 제일수익자원칙
primary bond market 신발채시장
primary capital 일차자본
primary dealer 프라이머리딜러
primary demand 기본적인 수요
primary deposit 본원적인 예금
primary distributions 일차분매
primary goods 일차산품
primary industry 일차산업
primary industry product export 일차산품수출
primary liability 일차부채
primary market 기채시장
primary materials 원재료
primary money 일차화폐
primary mortgage market 신규모기지발행시장
primary objective 최대목표
primary obligor 주요채무자
primary paper 신발채
primary regulation notice 기본통달
primary reserve assets 일차준비자산
primary securities 직접증권
primary securities market 증권발행시장
primary user 주요이용자
prime bank 유력은행
prime bankers acceptance 일류은행인수어음
prime bill 우량어음
prime borrower 우량발행체
prime contract 원계약
prime corporate bonds 일류사채
prime cost 구입원가
prime cost method 직접원가배부법
prime credit 원신용장
prime factor 주요인
prime interest rate 프라임레이트
prime issuer 우량발행체
prime letter of credit 원시용장
prime name bank 초일류은행
prime name CD 프라임네임 CD
prime paper 우량어음
prime product 주제품
prime rate 우선대출금리;프라임레이트
principal 원본;본인
principal account 주요계정
principal accounts of financial institution for small-business 중소기업금융기관계정
principal amortization schedule 원본상환방법
principal amount 원금
principal and interest 원리
principal books 주요장부
principal company 주체회사
principal guaranteed 원본보증
principal member 프린시펄멤버
principal only 원본만
principal outstanding 잔존원본액
principal paying 주지불
principal paying agent 주지불대리인
principal payment 원본지불
principal place of business 영업상의 본거

principal production order 주요제조지도서
principal products 주제품
principal tax 본세
principal transaction 자기거래
principal-equal monthly payment 원본균등반제
principal-only securities PO 증권
principal of all-inclusiveness 포괄주의원칙
principal of ascertained claim 권리확정주의
principle of balanced budget 건전재정주의
principle of clarity 명료성의 원리
principal of comparability 비교성의 원칙
principle of comparative advantage 비교우위의 원리
principle of conservatism 보수주의의 원칙
principle of consistency 계속성의 원칙
principle of cost allocation 비용배분의 원칙
principle of cross liabilities 교차책임주의
principle of disclosure 공개성의 원칙
principal of double-entry bookkeeping 복식부기원칙
principle of effective demand 유효수요의 원리
principle of equilibrium 대차평균의 원리
principle of equivalence 수지상등의 원칙
principle of gross budget accounting 총액예산주의
principle of increasing risk 위험체증의 원리
principle of matching 대응의 원칙
principle of matching costs with revenues 수익비용대응의 원칙
principle of materiality 중요성의 원칙
principle of need 필요성원칙
principle of orderly system of bookkeeping 정규부기의 원칙
principle of perennial tax 영구세주의
principle of priority of national tax claim 국세채권우선의 원칙
principle of priority to first seizure 차압선착순주의
principle of realization 실현주의의 원칙
principle of single budget 예산단일주의
principle of surplus section 잉여금구분의 원칙
principle of taxation 조세원칙
principle of taxation on a substantial income earner 실질소득자과세의 원칙
principle of taxation on actual beneficiary 실질주의
principle of the freedom of contract 계약자유의 원칙
principle of truth 진실성의 원칙
principle of unified accounting 회계단일원칙
principles of consolidation 연결방침
printed matter 인쇄물
prior analysis 사전분석
prior approval 사전인가제도
prior bond 우선권부 사채
prior cost 과거근무비용
prior lien 선취유치권
prior lien bond 선취특권채; 우선담보권부 사채
prior notice 사전신고
prior pension cost 과거근무비
prior period adjustment 전기손익수정
prior preferred stock 제일우선주
prior redemption 만기전 상환
prior service cost 과거근무비용
prior taxable year 전사업연도
prior year adjustment items 과년도손익수정항목
priority 우선성
priority between national tax and local tax 국세와 지방세간의 우열
priority creditor 우선채권자
priority of attachment 우선차압권
priority of mortgage 저당우선권
priority of taxes 조세우선권
priority order of application 충당순위
private account 개인명의계좌
private accountant 사적인 회계사
private activity bond 민간사업비

private automobile policy 자가용자동차보험
private banking 프라이베이트뱅킹
private bill 개인어음
private bond 민간채
private business 민간기업
private capital 민간자본
private company 비공개기업
private consumption 민간소비
private contract 수의계약
private convertible note 사모(私募)전환사채
private corporation 민간회사
private debt 민간채무
private demand 민간수요
private enterprise 민영사업
private financial institution 민간금융기업
private holding company 동족회사
private insurance 자가보험
private international law 국제사법
private investor 민간투자가
private label card 제휴자사카드
private ledger 사용(私用)원장
private market 민간시장
private member 개인회원
private mortgage insurance 민간모기지보험
private note 사모채
private offering 사모(私募)
private offering bond 사모채
private passthrough 프라이베이트패스스루
private pension 기업연금
private placement 사모(私募)발행
private placement bond 연고채
private placement local bond 연고지방채
private placement local government bond 연고지방채
private placement municipal bond 연고지방채
private placement securities 사모(私募)증권
private placement special bond 연고특별채
private placement straight bond 사모(私募)보통사채
private placement syndicate 사모채신디케이트
private placing 사모발행
private right 사권(私權)
private risk 프라이베이트리스크
private sale 폐쇄매각
private settlement 시담
private subscription 연고모집
private subscription bond 연고채
private tender 지명입찰
private transaction 민간거래
private trust 개인신탁
private undertaking 민간사업
private use 사적인 사용
privately placed bond 비공모채
privatisation scheme 민영화계획
privatization 민영화
privilege tax 영업세
privileged allocation of issuance to stockholders 주주우선배정
privileged debts 우선지불채무
privileges and immunities 특권 및 면제
privity of contract 계약관계
prize of raffle 복권당첨금
prize offered for advertisement of the business 사업광고를 위한 상품
pro forma account sales 견적매상계정서
pro forma adjustment 견적수정
pro forma amount 참고수치
pro forma balance sheet 견적대차대조표
pro forma bill 견적환어음
pro forma draft 견적환어음
pro forma estimated cost 견적
pro forma figure 시산베이스
pro forma financial statements 견적재무제표
pro forma statement 견적재무제표
pro rata 비례배분한
pro rata payment 비례지불
pro-business 경기중시
pro-forma invoice 프로포마인보이스
pro-rata clause 프로라타조항
pro-trade biased growth 순무역편향성장

probabilistic characteristic lines 확률적 특성선
probabilistic forecasting 확률예측
probability curve 확률곡선
probability distribution 확률분석
probability model 확률모델
probability-proportional-to-size 확률비례
probable 확률이 높은
probable cause 상당한 이유
probable dividend 예상배당
probable life 예상내용연수
probable maximum loss 예상최대손해액
probable yield 예상이익
probate 검증하다
problem assets 불량자산
problem loan 불량채권
procedural audit 절차감사
procedure 소송절차
procedure for collection of tax delinquency 체납처분
procedure of the compulsory conversion into money 강제환가절차
procedures for bond futures trading 채권선물거래제도요강
procedures for the convocation 소집절차
procedures of closing the books 결산절차
procedures of tax adjustments 세무조사절차
proceedings 의사
proceeds 수취금
proceeds account agreement 지불준비계정계약
proceeds from disposals 처분수입
proceeds from external bond issuance 외채발행대금
proceeds from long-term debt 장기차입에서의 자금증가
proceeds of life insurance 생명보험금
proceeds of loan 대부수익
proceeds of sale 매상고
process analysis 공정분석
process control 공정관리; 프로세스 관리
process cost accounting 공정별 원가계산
process cost system 종합원가계산
process costing 공정별 원가계산
process for the recovery of taxes in arrears 세금체납처분
process innovation 프로세스이노베이션
process of garnishment 채권절차
process production 일관생산
process study 공정분석
processing 가공
processing cost 가공비
processing deal 위탁가공무역
processing deal trade 가공무역
processing expenses 가공비
processing expenses arising from outside manufacturer 외주가공비
processing tax 가공세
procurator 대리인
procurement cost 조달비
producer price index 생산자물가지수
producer's cartel 생산국카르텔
producer's inventory of finished goods 생산품제품잭
producer's surplus 생산자잉여
producer's value 생산자가격
producing departments cost 제조부문비
product 제품
product analysis 상품분석
product cost 제품원가
product cost accounting 제품원가계산표
product cycle theory 프로덕트사이클론
product development 상품개발
product group 제품군
product innovation era 상품혁신의 시대
product investment 상품투자
product liability 제조물책임
product liability insurance 제조물책임보험
product life-cycle 제품라이프사이클
product market 생산시장
product mix 제품믹스
product on consignment 위탁품

product portfolio management 제품포트폴리오매니지먼트
product price 제품가격
product standards 제품기준
product warranties 제품보증
production 생산고
production accord 생산협정
production account 생산계정
production base 생산거점
production budget 제조예산
production capacity 생산능력
production capital 생산자본
production card 작업표
production control 생산관리
production department 제조부문
production efficiency variance 제조능률차이
production equipment 제조설비
production expenses 제조경비
production facility 생산설비
production function 생산함수
production goods 생산재
production indexes 생산지수
production labor cost 생산노무비
production level 조업도
production loan 프로덕션론
production method 생산고비례법
production order 제조지도서
production order cost accounting 개별원가계산
production process 생산공정
production report 생산고보고서
production sharing 생산분배
production statement 제조보고서
production variance 제조차이
production volume budget 조업도차이
productive ability 생산능력
productive life 생산연수
productive wages 직접임금
productivity 생산성
productivity accounting 생산성회계
productivity analysis 생상성분석
productivity gain 생산성향상
productivity of capital 자본생산성
productivity ratio 생산성지표
products and completed operation liability insurance 생산물배상책임보험
products in progress 제작중인 물건
professional accountant 직업회계사
professional auditor 직업감사인
professional discipline 직업상의 규범
professional ethics 직업윤리
professional liability insurance 전문직업인배상책임보험
professional's market 전문적인 상장
professionals 전문가
profit 이익
profit account 이익계정
profit accrued from valuation 평가익
profit accruing from insurance 보험차익
profit accruing from refund of bonds and debentures 공사채상환익
profit after expenses 경비공제후 이익
profit after tax 세공제후 이익
profit and loss 손익
profit and loss account 손익계정
profit and loss break-even point 손익분기점
profit and loss carried forward 이월손익
profit and loss equation 손익계산서등식
profit and loss method 손익법
profit and loss on valuation of real estate 부동산평가손익계정
profit and loss report 손익보고
profit and loss statement 손익계산서
profit and loss transaction 손익거래
profit available for dividend 배당가능이익
profit before tax 세공제전 이익
profit center 프로핏센터
profit chart 이익도표
profit commission 이익반환
profit contribution 이익공헌도
profit control 이익관리
profit control chart 이익도표

profit corporation 영리법인
profit curve 이익곡선
profit debenture 수익사채
profit for the current term 당기이익금
profit forecast 수익예측
profit form amalgamation 합병차익
profit from capital reduction 감자차익
profit from consolidation 합병차익
profit from immovables transactions 부동산매매익
profit from merger 합병차익
profit from private funds offered 사재제공익
profit from redemption 상환차익
profit from sales of stocks 주식매각익
profit from the difference between new and old official prices 가격차익금
profit from trust 신탁이익
profit from valuation of assets 자산평가익
profit goal 목표이익
profit growth 이익신장
profit growth rate 이익성장률
profit increase 증익
profit inflation 이윤인플레이션
profit insurance 이익보험
profit making business 영리사업
profit management 이익관리
profit margin 이폭
profit margin of interest rate 이익금
profit not yet realized 미실현이익
profit on assets sold 재산매각익
profit on bad debt recovered 상각채권수금익
profit on redemption of discount bond 할인채상환익
profit on sale 매각익
profit on sale of real estate 부동산매각익
profit on securities sold 유가증권매각익
profit or loss brought forward from previous business term 전기손익금
profit or loss from installment sales 할부판매손익
profit or loss from retirement of fixed assets 제각손익
profit or loss from revaluation of fixed asset 고정자산평가손익
profit or loss from valuation 평가손익
profit or loss on foreign exchange 외환환산손익
profit or loss resulting from valuation of assets 자산평가손익
profit per share 일주당 이익
profit potential 잠재이익
profit prior to consolidation 연결전 이익
profit prior to incorporation 회사설립전 이익
profit profile 수익구조
profit quota 이익할당
profit rate of total liabilities and net worth 총자본수익률
profit ratio 이익률
profit ratio indices 수익관련지표
profit ratio of capital 자본이익률
profit ratio of net worth 자본이익률
profit ratio of operating capital 경영자본이익률
profit ratio of paid-up capital 불입자본수익률
profit resulting from sale of the trust estate 신탁재산을 처분해서 발생한 매각이익
profit sharing 이익배분
profit sharing bond 이익배분사채
profit sharing securities 이윤증권
profit sharing system 이익배분제도
profit sharing trust 이윤분배신탁
profit slide 이익감
profit taking 가격차이로 이익얻기
profit tax 수익세
profit transferred 대체이익
profit volume graph 한계이익도표
profit volume ratio 매상고한계이익률
profit-driven market 업적상장
profit-sharing plan 이익분배플랜
profitability 수익성

profitability and investment analysis ratio 수익성분석
profitability index 수익성지표
profitable 수익률이 높은
profitable line of business 채산라인
profiteer 부당이득자
program budgeting 프로그램예산
program trading 프로그램매각
progress payment 생산고지불
progressive audit 진행감사
progressive average inventory method 총평균법
progressive cost 체증비
progressive income tax 누진소득세
progressive ledger 연속원장
progressive nature 누진제
progressive rate 누진세율
progressive tax 누진세
progressive tax rate 누진세율
progressive taxation 누진과세
progressiveness of income tax 소득세누진도
prohibited period 금지기간
prohibition of deposit transfer 예금양도금지
prohibition of endorsement 이서금지
prohibition of management official interlocks 관리직원겸업금지
prohibition of seizure on social insurance payment 사회보험급부차압금지
prohibition of set off for national taxes 국세에 대한 상쇄금지
prohibition of transfer 양도금지
prohibitive tax 금지세
prohibitory injunction 금지명령
project finance 프로젝트파이낸스
project loan 프로젝트론
project risk 프로젝트리스크
projected balance sheet 견적대차대조표
projected benefit obligation 예측급부채무
projected demand 예측수요량
projected dividend 예상배당
projected financial statements 견적재무제표
projected holding period rate of return 기대보유기간수익률
projected income statement 견적손익계산서
prolonged 장기화한
prominent 탁월한
promisee 수약자
promisor 계약자
promissory note 약속어음
promoter 발기인
promoter's profits 창업자이익
promoter's share 발기인주
promoting mergers tax credit 합병촉진세액공제
promotion expenses 창업비
prompt payment 즉시지불
promulgation 공포
proof of loss 손해증명
propensity to consume 소비성향
propensity to import 수입성향
propensity to invest 투자성향
propensity to save 저축성향
proper card 자사카드
proper journal 보통분개장
proper law 준거법
properties put to use for business 사업목적에 사용되는 자산
property 재산
property acquired 취득자산
property acquired by subsidy 보조금으로 얻은 자산
property acquired by the specified investment in kind 특정현물출자로 취득한 자산
property and equipment 고정자산
property and liability insurance 손해보험
property basis applicable to inventories 재고자산에 적용되는 자산기준
property damage 재물손괴
property for advertisement 광고선전용 자산
property for exchange 교환용 자산
property for experimental and research 시험연구용 자산

property for residence 거주용 자산
property for substitution 대체자산
property for transfer 양도자산
property generally prohibited from seizure 일반차압금지재산
property held for a long time 장기보유자산
property in possession 담보권행사부동산
property income 재산소득
property insurance 동산보험
property ledger 재산원장
property market 부동산시장
property not qualifying for capital gain 양도소득의 근거로 분류되지 않는 자산
property not subject to seizure 차압금지재산
property portfolio 부동산포트폴리오
property prices 부동산가격
property put into business 사업용으로 사용되는 자산
property received in the exchange 교섭으로 취득한 자산
property replaced by purchase 매환자산
property reserved 준비필 재산
property right 재산권
property subject to seizure 차압대상재산
property tax 고정자산세
property tax cadaster 고정자산과세대장
property tax rate 고정자산세율
property ward 재산구
property; plant and equipment 유형고정자산
proportional allocation 비례배분
proportional calculation 비례원가계산
proportional cost 비례비
proportional expenses 비례비
proportional method 일괄비례배분방식
proportional reinsurance 비례재보험
proportional reserve method 비례준비금
proportional reserve system 비례준비제도
proportional tax 비례세
proportional taxation 비례과세법
proportional equal terms 비례평등조건
proportionally variable cost 비례적인 가변비용
proposal letter 프로포절레터
proposal method 프로포절방식
proposal budget 예산안
propound 제안하다
proprietary account 자본주계정
proprietary company 사회사
proprietary order 자기주문
proprietary right 소유권
proprietary trading 자기계정매매
proprietor 소유자
proprietor deduction 사업주공제
proprietor punishment 업무주처벌제도
proprietors special expense reserve 사업주특별경비준비금
proprietorship 개입기업;소유주지분
proprietorship account 소유주계정
prosecutor 검찰관
prosecutors office 검찰청
prospect 예측
prospective cash receipts 입금예측액
prospective dividend rate 예상배당율
prospective PER 예측 PER
prospective profit 기대이익
prospective rating 경험요율법
prospective return 예상수익률
prospective usable 사용가능기간
prospective yield 예상이익
prospective yield average 예상평균이익
prospectus 설립취지서;내용설명서
prospectus for securities registration 신고계획서
prospectus of promotion 회사설립취지서
prosperous days 호경기시대
protecting the currency 통화방위
protection 보호영장
protection and indemnity association 선주책임상호보험조합
protection and indemnity risks P&I 보험
protection of investor 투자자보호
protection of investors 투자가보호

protection of the full deposited amount 예금전액보호
protectionist economic regionalism 보호주의경제권
protectionist policies 보호주의정책
protective duty 보호관세
protection put 프로텍티브풋
protective put trading 프로텍티브풋 거래
protective tariff 보호관세
protective trust 보호신탁
protectorate 보호령
protest charges 거절증서작성수수료
protest waived 거절증서불요문언
protested check 부도수표
protester 비판적인 시청자
protocol 조약의정서;프로토콜
provable debt 입증할 수 있는 채권
prove 증명하다
proven 확인의
provided that 단
provision account 준비금계정
provision for bad debts 대손준비손
provision for employee bonus 상여준비금
provision for overseas legal reserves 해외법정준비금편입
provision for possible loan loss 대손준비금편입
provision for repairs 수선준비금편입
provision for reserve for overseas investments 해외투자손실준비금편입
provision for reserve for price fluctuation 가격변동준비금편입
provision for surplus 적립이월
provision for tax 납세준비금
provisional 임시의
provisional attachment 가차압
provisional budget 잠정예산
provisional disposition 가처분
provisional execution 가집행
provisional insurance 예정보험
provisional liquidator 잠정청산인
provisional order 가명령
provisional policy 예정보험
provisional rating 임시가격설정
provisional registration 가등기
provisional residence 가주소
provisional return 예정신고
provisional seizure 가차압
provisional settlement of account 가결산
provisional sum 프로비저널섬;PS단가
provisional tariff 잠정세율
provisional tax payment system based on the previous year's tax amount 예정납세제도
provisions of mutatis mutandis application 준용규정
proviso 조건;단서
provisory 단서의
provisory clause 단서조항
provocation 도발
proximate cause 주원인
proximate damage 직접손해
proxy 대리
proxy contest 위임장경합
proxy currency 대용통화
proxy fight 위임장쟁탈전
proxy solicitation 위임장근유
proxy statement 주주총회소집통지
proxy vote 위임장투표
prudence 주의
prudent man rule 신중인원칙
prudent person rule 수탁자책임
pseudo-random numbers 유사난수
psychological effect 심리효과
psychological line 사이콜로지컬라인
psychological theory of exchange 환심리설
public account law 회계법
public accountant 공인회계사
public acknowledgment 인지
public and corporate bond 공사채
public and corporate bond investment trust 공사채투자신탁
public announcement 공고

public assistance 생활보호
public auction 공매
public bidding 공개입찰
public body 공공단체
public bond 공채
public bond dealing 공채매매
public bond investment trust 공사채투자신탁
public bonds 모채
public company 공개기업
public compensation bond 교부공채
public corporation 공사;공단
public corporation bond 공사채
public corporation bonds 공단공고채
public debt securities 공공채
public disclosure 공시
public dues 공과
public economics 공공경제학
public enterprise 공적기업
public expenditure 공공지출
public facilities tax 공동시설세
public finance 국가재정
public finance corporation 공고
Public Finance Law 재정법
public finance institution 공적금융기관
public float 공개주
public fund 공모펀드
public goods 공공재
public governor 공익대표이사
public hearing 공청회
public impost 공과
public information 공개정보
public interest 공익
public interest corporation 공익법인
public investment 공공투자
public law 공법
public market 대중상장
public measurer 공인검량인
public money 공적자금
public monopoly 전매
public notary 공증인
public notification 공시최고
public notification of auction 공매광고
public notification of returns 신고서공시
public offering 공모
public offering auction system 공모입찰방식
public offering business 공모업무
public offering of municipal bond 지방채공모
public offering of stock 주식공모
public offering of straight bond 보통사채공모
public offering of government bonds 국채시중소화
public order 공공질서
public pension 공적연금
public placement 공모
public policy 공익
public procurement 정부조달
public responsibility 공공책임
public sale 공개매각
public sector 공공센터
public sectors deficit 재정적자
public securities market 공모증권시장
public service 공공사업
public spending 공공지출
public subscription 공모
public summons 공시최고
public telecommunication business 공공통신사업
public tender 공개입찰
public trust 공익신탁
public use 공공용
public utility 공공사업
public utility accounting 공익사업회계
public utility bond 공익사업채
public utility charges 공공요금
public works outlays 공공사업지출
public-sectors accounting 공공부문회계
publicly held company 공개회사
publicly held stock 공개주
publicly offered share 매출주
publicly subscribed share 공모주

publicly traded company 상장회사
publishing right 출판권
puffer 경매인의 한통속
pull strategy 풀전략
pulling-back 후퇴
pulp and paper industry 펄프제지업계
pump-priming effect 마중물효과;실마리효과
punishment on penalty tax 추징처분
punitive damages 징벌적인 손해배상
punitive tariff 제재관세
purchase 구매
purchase acquisition 흡수합병
purchase agent 매입대리인
purchase agreement 매수계약서
purchase allowance 구입가할인
purchase amount 구입고
purchase and assumption 예금승계방식
purchase and sale statement 매입계산서
purchase book 구입장
purchase commission 구입수수료
purchase commitments 구입약정
purchase contract 선물매수계약
purchase discount 구입할인
purchase face amount 매수액면금액
purchase fund 매입자금
purchase group 매입그룹
purchase investigation 매수를 임의조사함
purchase ledger 구입처원장
purchase method 매수법
purchase money 구입대금
purchase money mortgage 토지대금모기지
purchase of goods and services by government 정부가 재화와 서비스를 구입함
purchase of new issues of public and corporate bonds 공사채소화
purchase on credit 외상구입
purchase payment fund 외상적립기금
purchase price 구입대금
purchase rebate with special payment terms 특약지불조건부 구입할부
purchase return 구입반품
purchase tax 구입세
purchase-money obligation 매입대금채무
purchased parts 매입부품
purchaser 매주
purchases and sales 매매
purchases budget 구입예산
purchases rebate 구입환불
purchases year 구입년
purchasing cost 구입원가
purchasing expenses 구입비용
purchasing manager 구매부장
purchasing power 구매력
purchasing power gain or loss 구매력변동손익
purchasing power of money 화폐의 구매력
purchasing power 구매력평가
purchasing power parity theory 구매력평가설
purchasing power risk 구매력리스크
purchasing price 구입단가
pure cap 퓨어캡
pure deferred life annuity 순수거치종신연금
pure discount bond 순할인채
pure endowment insurance 생존보험
pure risk 순수위험
pure swap 순수스와프
purpose loan 목적융자
purview 본문
push pull 푸시풀
put and call 풋앤드콜
put bond 상환청구권부 채권
put diagram 풋다이어그램
put holder 풋보유자
put option 풋옵션
put ratio back spread trading 풋레이쇼백스프레딩
put swaption 풋스왑션
put warrant 풋워런트
put-call ratio 풋콜레이쇼
put-value line 풋가격선
putative 추정의

puttable bond 푸터블채권
puttable swap 푸터블스와프
puttable swaption 푸터블스왑션
puttable warrant 푸터블워런트
putting-out system 전대제도
pyramid management method
피라미드형 관리방식
pyramiding process 피라미딩과정

Q

quadratic function 이차함수
quadratic programing 이차계획서
qualification 한정사항;적격성;면채사항
qualification for trade 거래자격
qualified 적격인
qualified acceptance 조건인수
qualified acceptance heritage 한정상속
qualified acceptance of bill 단순하지 않은 인수
qualified audit certificate 한정감사보고서
qualified auditor's report 한정의견감사보고서
qualified bond 적격채권
qualified business unit 퀄리파이드비즈니스유니트
qualified certificate 한정의견증명서
qualified endorsement 한정이서
qualified inheritance 한정상속
qualified institutional investor 적격기관투자가
qualified investment 적격투자액
qualified opinion 한정의견
qualified pension contract 적격퇴직연금계약
qualified pension funds 적격퇴직연금적립금
qualified pension plan 적격퇴직연금
qualified pension system 적격퇴직연금제도
qualified property 제한적인 재산권
qualified report 한정보고서
qualified securities 적격증권
qualified spouse for deduction 공제대상배우자
qualifying reserve 한정준비금
qualifying stock option 종업원자사주구입권
qualitative analysis 정성분석
qualitative credit control 질적인 금융통제
qualitative economic policy 질적인 경제정책
qualitative information 정성정보
qualitative parameters 질적인 요인
qualitative substantiality test 질적실질성의 원칙
quality class 고품질클래스
quality control 품질관리
quality of earnings 이익의 질
quality standards 품질기준
quality stock 우량주
quantitative analysis 정량분석
quantitative asset allocation 정량적인 어셋앨로케이션
quantitative credit control 양적인 신용규제
quantitative economic policy 양적인 경제정책
quantitative monetary indicator 양적인 금융지표
quantitative substantiality test 수량실질성의 원칙
quantitative tool 수량화 수단
quantity adjustment 수량조정
quantity discount 수량할인
quantity of output 산출량
quantity of production 생산량
quantity sold 판매수량
quantity standard 수량표준

quantity theory of money 화폐개량설
quantity variance 추정량차이
quarter 4반기
quarter-days 4계지불지급일
quarter-on-quarter 전기대비
quarterly auction 4반기입찰
quarterly earnings 4반기이익
quarterly real growth rate 4반기 베이스의 실질성장률
quarterly refunding 4반기 리펀딩
quarterly reports 4반기보고서
quash 각하하다
quasi contract 준계약
quasi currency 준통화
quasi easement 준지역권
quasi equity 준주식
quasi estoppel 준금반언(準禁反言)
quasi final return 준확정신고
quasi incompetent person 준금치산자
quasi judicial power 준사법권력
quasi loan for consumption 준소비대차
quasi member 준회원
quasi money 준화폐
quasi public corporation 제 3섹터
quasi-debt obligations 준채무
quasi-fiduciary relationship 확신인관계
quasi-government agency 준정부기관
quasi-incompetent person 피보좌인
quasi-loan 준차입
quasi-reorganization 준갱생
queuing 대기행렬
quick assets 당좌자산
quick assets ratio 당좌비율
quick assets to year's cash expenses 연간지출당좌비율
quick deposit 당좌예금
quick liabilities 단기부채
quick ratio 당좌비율
QUICK-terminal 퀵단말
quiet market 보합상장
quitting of business 사업폐지
quorum 법정수
quorum for a general meeting 총회정족수
quota 할당량
quota share treaty reinsurance 비례특약재보험
quotation 시황
quotation exchange center 시세정보교환센터
quotation of over-the-counter issue 장외시세
quotation on overseas markets 해외상장
quote 호가
quote reporter 쿼트리포터
quoted company 상장회사
quoted driven 호가주도형
quoting high 시세를 높게 부르다

R

raider 적대적인 매수를 고려하는 주식취득자
raiding the market 시장을 어지럽힘
railroad bonds 철도채
raising of funds 자금조달
raising of interest rate 금리인상
rally 시세가 회복되다
rally in the bond market 채권상장상승
random number 난수
random price changes 불규칙한 가격변동
random sample 무작위추출법
random walk theory 랜덤워크이론
range 변동폭
range forward contract 레인지포워드거래
range trading 시세가 오르락내리락함
range-bound market 박스권의 움직임
ranking of advances 상승순위
ranking of declines 하락순위
rapid expansion 급증
rare stock 희귀주
rasure 소거
ratable distribution 비례배당
ratable value 과세견적가격
ratchet effect 래칫효과
rate adjustment 금리조정
rate cap 금리캡
rate cut 요율인하
rate floor agreement 금리플로어계약
rate hike 요율인상
rate in foreign currency 외화통화유통
rate in home currency 자국통화유통
rate in overseas market 해외상장
rate issue 부과
rate of awareness 지명도
rate of change 변화율
rate of charge 징수율
rate of depreciation of total assets 총자산상각률
rate of earnings on total capital 총자본순이익률
rate of efficiency of depreciation 감가상각효과
rate of estimated expenses 개산경비율
rate of increase 상승률
rate of listed bond 공사채를 상장한 상장
rate of operating 가동률
rate of output 조업도
rate of premium 보험료율
rate of return on invested capital 투자이익률
rate of return on investment 투자이익률
rate of returned goods unsold 반품률
rate of returns 수익률
rate of stock-turn 상품회전율
rate of taxation 세율
rate of technical progress 기술진보율
rate of temporary duty 잠정세율
rate of variable expenses 변동비율
rate of wage increase 임금상승률
rate outlook 금리예측
rate papers 납세고지서
rate sensitive assets 금리감응자산
rate sensitive liability 금리감응부채
rate spread 이익금

ratepayer 조세부담자
ratification 비준
rating 부과;평가;등급
rating agency 평가기관
rating change 등급변경
rating downgrade 등급하락
rating of bond 채권의 등급을 매김
rating organization tariffs 산정회 요율
rating outlook 등급예측
rating system 등급제도
ratio 비;비율
ratio analysis 비율분석
ratio call spread transaction 레이쇼콜스프레드거래
ratio method 비율분석법
ratio of bond issue to total expenditure 공채의존도
ratio of cash to thirty-day debts 현금대비일개월부채비율
ratio of cost of sales 매상원가율
ratio of current assets to total deposits 유동자산비율
ratio of current expenses to current income 경상수지율
ratio of current liabilities to net worth 유동부채비율
ratio of depreciation 감가상각률
ratio of direct and indirect taxes 직간접비율
ratio of dividends to shareholders' equity 주주자본배당률
ratio of earnings to dividends 이익금대비배당률
ratio of expenses to revenues 수익비율
ratio of fixed assets to long term capital 고정자산장기자본비율
ratio of fixed liabilities to net worth 고정부채비율
ratio of general expenses to current income 일반경비율
ratio of gross profit to inventory investment 교차비율
ratio of gross profit to net sales 매상총이익률
ratio of individual stock ownership 개인지주비율
ratio of inventory to net working capital 고정자산순운전자본비율
ratio of leasehold to land value 차지권비율
ratio of merchandise to receivables 상품재고대비수취계정비율
ratio of necessary expenses to gross revenue 경비율
ratio of net profit on sales 매상이익률
ratio of net profit to capital 자본이익률
ratio of net profit to gross revenues 순이익대비총수익비율
ratio of net worth to total capital 자기자본비율
ratio of net worth to total debt 자기자본대비부채비율
ratio of operating profit to revenue 영업이익률
ratio of ordinary profits to total capital 총자본경상이익률
ratio of personnel expenses 인건비율
ratio of profit to capital 자본이익률
ratio of profit to net sales 매상고이익률
ratio of profit to net worth 자기자본이익률
ratio of receivable to inventories 인수계정대비재고자산비율
ratio of replacement of assets 자산갱신율
ratio of shareholding 지주비율
ratio of special depreciation deduction 특별상각률
ratio of total liabilities to net worth 부채비율
ratio of wage-hikes 임금인상률
rational structure 합리적인 구조
rationale 근거
rationalization of production 생산합리화
rationalize 합리화를 계획하다
rationalized 합리적인
rationing 배급제도

raw and processed materials 원재료
raw material 재료
raw material inventory 원재료재고
re-auction 재공매
re-correction 재갱정
re-cross-examination 재반대심문
re-entry 부동산점유회복
re-exchange 역환어음
re-export 재수출
re-leasing 재리스
reacquired share 자기주식
reaction curve 반응곡선
reactionary fall 반락
readjusting entry 재수정기입
readjustment of taxation system 세제정리
ready money 소지현금
ready reckoner 계산조견표
real account 실재계정
real action 대물소송
real assets 실물자산
real balance effect 실질화폐잔고효과
real capital 실물자본
real chattels 물적동산
real compensation 실질임금
real contract 대물계약
real cost 실질원가
real credit 대물신용
real deposits 실질예금
real disposable income 실질가처분소득
real distress 부동산차압
real earnings 실질소득
real economy 실체경제
real entity theory of corporation 법인실재설
real estate 부동산
real estate acquisition tax 부동산취득세
real estate broker 부동산브로커
real estate held for sale 판매용 토지
real estate in trust 부동산신탁
real estate income 부동산소득
real estate industry 부동산업
real estate investment trust 부동산투자신탁
real estate loan receivable 부동산저당장기대부금
real estate mortgage 부동산모기지
real estate security 부동산담보
real estate stock 부동산주
real estate tax 고정자산세
real estate yield 부동산주의 투자이율
real evidence 물적증거
real GNP growth rate 실질 GNP 성장률
real gross investment 실질투자자
real growth 실질성장
real growth rate 실질성장률
real guarantee 물상보증
real income 실질소득
real income earner 실질소득자
real interest rate 실질금리
real investment 실물투자
real investment return 실질투자수익률
real money 실질화폐
real multiplier 실질승수
real net investment 실질순투자
real obtainer of dividend income 배당소득으로 귀속됨
real obtainer of interest income 이자소득으로 귀속됨
real property 부동산
real property acquisition tax 부동산취득세
real rate 실질이율
real rate of exchange 실세환상장
real rate of return 실질이율
real right 물권
real security 물적담보
real term 실질단위
real time 리얼타임
real time communication 실시간통신
real time gross settlement 즉시그로스결제
real time processing 리얼타임처리
real transfer 실질적인 트랜스퍼
real unit labor cost 실질단위노동코스트
real value 실질가치
real water 순수한 물; 진수

real yield 실질이율
real-bills doctrine 상업어음주의
real-time price 현재가치
realignment 재조정
realignment negotiation 재조정교섭
realizable value 실현가능가액
realization basis 실현주의
realization of gains 수익실현
realization of profit and losses 손익실현
realization of tax liability 납세의무성립
realization principle 실현주의
realization sales 환금판매
realized appreciation 실현증가액
realized depreciation 실현감가상각
realized gain 실현이익
realized gross profit on installment sales 할부매상익
realized income 실현이익
realized loss 실현손익
realized profit 실현이익
realized return 실현수익
realized revenue 실현수익
realized value 실현가치
realized volatility 실현가격변동률
realized yield 실효이율
realty business 부동산업
reappraisal 재평가;재검토
rearrangement of budget item 예산항목이체
reason for dishonor 부도사유
reasonable 합리적인
reasonable and probable cause 합리적이고 상당한 원인
reasonable depreciation 상당한 상각
reasonable doubt 합리적인 의문
reassessment 재평가
reassessment of income tax 소득세갱정결정
reassessment of taxes 과세갱정결정
reassessment of section 재지정
reassessment of markets 상장시장변경
rebalance 재평가
rebalancing 조변환
rebalancing strategies 리밸런싱전략
rebate 리베이트;환불
rebate on sales 매상반려
rebound 반등
rebound in spending 소비회복
rebut 반항하다
rebutting evidence 반증
recapitalization 자본형성;자본수정
recapitalization of legal reserve 결정준비금자본편입
recapture 탈환; 회복
recapture of depreciation 감가상각액회복
receipt and payment bookkeeping 수지부기
receipt and payment of treasury accounts with the public 재정자금대비민간수지
receipt in full 전액영수서
receipt of business 영업양수
receipt of orders 수주
receipt slip 입금전표
receipts and disbursements break-even point 수지분기점
receipts and payments 수지지출
receipts of dividends 배당수입
receipts of money 입금
receivable and payable contract 채권채무계약
receivable from affiliate 관계회사외상금
receivable from portfolio 채권포트폴리오
receivables 채권
receivables from customers 입체금
receivables not qualifying for the bad debts reserve 대손준비금으로 편입할 수 없는 자금
receivables pool 채권풀
receivables turnover 매상채권회전률
received margin 수입증거금
receiver 파산관재인
receiver in bankruptcy 파산관재인
receivership 채권자구제수속
receiving 수납계정
receiving bank 피발송은행

receiving order 재산관리명령
receiving quotation 수취계정기준상장
receiving report 수납보고서
recent standards 최근수준
reception stamp 수납인
recess 휴회
recession 경기후퇴;불황
recession period 경기후퇴기
recession risk 경기후퇴리스크
recessionary economic 경기혼미
recipient country 수입국
reciprocal account 대응계정
reciprocal consignment 상호위탁판매
reciprocal contract 쌍무계약
reciprocal credit 상호신용장
reciprocal demand curve 상호수요곡선
reciprocal distribution method 상호배부법
reciprocal duty 호혜관세
reciprocal transfer of property 상호자산교환
reciprocity 교환재보험;상호주의
recital 증서의 설명부분
recklessness 부주의
reckoning of useful life 내용연수계산
reclaimed land 매립지
reclaimed materials 재생원재료
reclassification 재분류
recognised stock exchange 공인증서거래소
recognition log 인지래그
recognition method 인지법
recognition of gain and loss 손익인식
recognition of losses 손실인식
recognition of sales 매상고를 인식함
recognized clearing house 공인청산기관
recommendation 권고
recommendation to a member
회원에 대한 권고
recommended accounting practices
회계실무권고서
recommended stock 추천주
reconciliation 조정
reconciliation account 조정계정
reconciliation item 조정항목
reconciliation of deficit 부족금처리
reconciliation of surplus 잉여금조정서
reconciling type 잔고조정식
reconstruction expense 개축비
reconstruction works 개축공사
reconversion 재전환
record date 기준일
record high 사상최고
record keeping 기록보존
record low 사상최저
record of seizure 차압조서
record on removal 이송신청기록
record price 고가
recorded cost 장부원가
recoup 손해를 회복하다
recoupment 공제권
recourse 구상권
recourse agreement 리코스계약
recourse loan 리코스론
recourse obligations 소급의무
recourse right 파급권
recover high 고가로 회복함
recoverable 회수가능한
recovery cost 회수가능원가
recovery expectations 경기회복기대
recovery expenditure 회수가능지출
recovery from deficit 흑자전환
recovery of bad debt 대손금회수
recovery of credits 채권회수
recovery of doubtful accounts 대손금회수
recovery of loss 결손회수
recovery of the bad debts 대손금회수
recovery period 원가회수기간
recovery value 회수가능가치
recruiting expense 모집비
recruitment 사원채용
rectangular distribution 직각분포
recurring audit 연속감사
recurring gain or loss 경상손익
recurring profit 경상이익

recurring profit and loss 경상손익
recycling 환류
red B/L 적선하증권
red clause credit 레드클로즈신용장; 전대신용장
red-balance 적자잔액
red-herring prospectus 레드헤링계획서
red-ink entry 적자기입
redeem before maturity 조기상환하다
redeemable bond 상환채권
redeemable preferred stock 상환우선주식
redeemable stock 상환주식
redemption 상환
redemption and coupon payments 원리지불
redemption at fixed date 정시상환
redemption at market value 시가상환
redemption at maturity 만기상환
redemption before maturity 중도환금
redemption by drawing 추첨상환
redemption by lottery 추첨상환
redemption by purchase 매입상각
redemption by the number of drawing 추첨상환
redemption by yearly installment 연부상환
redemption date 상환기일
redemption fee 해약수수료
redemption from tax sale 공매에서 되찾음
redemption fund 상환기금
redemption gain 상환차익
redemption of external loan 외채상환
redemption of government securities 정부증권상환
redemption of pledge 저당을 되찾음
redemption of principal 원본상환
redemption of stock by distribution of net profit 이익처분에 따른 주식상각
redemption premium 상환프리미엄
redemption price 상환가격
redemption profit 상환익
redemption risk 상환리스크
redemption system 감채제도
redemption through secondary market purchase 매입상환
redemption value 상환가격
redemption yield 상환이율
rediscount 재할인
rediscount policy 재할인정책
rediscount rate 재할인금리
redistributed cost 재배부원가
redistribution 재분배
redistribution of income 소득재분배
redress 구제
reduced asset price 감자산가격
reduced borrowing costs 조달코스트삭감
reduced capital adequacy requirements 자기자본기준완화
reduced dividend 감배
reduced liquidity 유동성결핍
reduced losses 적자축소
reduced profit 이익감액
reduced tax rate 경감세율
reduced tax rate on dividend paid 배당경과
reduced tax rate on specified medical corporation 특정의료법인의 특별세율
reducing balance method 체감잔고법
reducing unemployment rate 실업률감소
reduction and exemption of taxes 감면
reduction entry 압축기장
reduction in price 가격인하
reduction of business 사업규모축소
reduction of capital stocks 자본감소
reduction of capital without compensation 무상감자
reduction of expenditures 경비절감
reduction of incidence 부담경감
reduction of operation 조업단축
reduction of taxes 감세
reduction or exemption of tax 조세감면
reduction surplus 감자잉여금
reductions in long-term debt 장기차입반제액
redundancy 과잉; 여분
referable name 확인해야 할 곳

referee in bankruptcy 파산심리인
referee in case of need 예비지불인
reference 조합
reference bank 조회처은행
reference document 참조서류
reference index 지표가 되는 지수
reference period 참고기간
reference range 참고상장권
reference rate 기준금리
reference statistics 참고통계
reference yield 참고이율
reference zone 참고상장권
referral fees 소개수수료
referred to as 칭하다
refinance of redemption 차환발행
refinancing 자금재조달
refinancing bond 차환채
refinancing issue 차환발행
refinancing system 리파이낸스방식
refix date 갱신일
reflation 통화재팽창
reflation policy 경기부양책
reform of financial system 금융제도개혁
reform of international monetary system 국제통화제도개혁
reform of the administrative structure 행정개혁
reform of the deposit insurance system 예금보험기구개혁
refresher 추가사례금
refund bond 전불금반환보증증권
refund by carrying a loss back to a prior year 반복에 따른 환급
refund by final return 확정신고에 따른 환부
refund claim 환부신청서
refund deferred life annuity 상환거치종신연금
refund of clearing margin 거래증거금 환급
refund of fees 수수료반환
refund of overpayment 과오납금환부
refund of principal 원본상환
refund of taxes 세금환부
refund retroactive to the past taxable years 과년도를 소급한 환급
refund tax 환부세
refunded corporation tax 환부법인세
refunding 자금재조달
refunding bonds 차환채
refunding of equity 지분환급
refunding securities 차환증권
refundment 반려금
refundment guarantee 전불금반환보증
refundment of stockholders' equity 주주지분상환
refusal to deal 거래거부
refusal to receive 불수리
regional bank 지방은행
regional bank card 지방은행카드
Regional Bank Association of Japan 일본전국지방은행협회
regional cartel 지역카르텔
regional development 지역개발
regional economics 지역경제학
regional economy 지역경제
regional exchange 지방거래소
regional government bond 지방채
regional office 지방사무소
regional policy 지역정책
regional portfolio 특정지역 포트폴리오
regionalism 지역주의
regionals 지방업자
register 등기부
register of cancellation of attachment 차압지소등기
register of government bonds 국채등록부
register of settlement of mortgage 저당권설정등기
registered 등기필
registered bond 기명사채;등록채
registered design 의장권
registered financial institution 등록금융이관
registered form 기명식

registered gilts 등록길트채
registered government bonds 등록국채
registered issues 등록명
registered letters 등기우편
registered number 등기번호
registered office 본사사무소
registered owner 등록명의인
registered public accountant 경리사
registered representative 증권외무원
registered securities 기명식 증권
registered share 등록주
registered society 등록조합
registered stock 기명주식
registered trade-mark 등록상표
registered trader 등록트레이더
registrar of companies 회사등기소
registration 신고
registration act for corporate bond 사채등록법
registration agency 등록기관
registration and license tax 등록면허세
Registration and License Tax Law 등록면허세법
registration certificate 권리증
registration fee 등기료
registration formalities 등기수속
registration of a new design 신안등록
registration of alteration 변경등기
registration of copyright 판권등록
registration of design 의장등록
registration of establishment 설립등기
registration of incorporation 회사설립등기
registration of signet for financial futures transaction 금융선물거래소용 인감계
registration of the right of pledge 질권등기
registration of transfer 이전등기
registration statement 유가증권계출서
registration statement of tender offer 공개매부신고서
registration statement of withdrawal of tender offer 공개매부철회신고서
registration tax 등록세
regression 회귀
regression analysis 회귀분석
regression analysis method 회귀분석법
regression coefficient 회귀계수
regression equation 회귀방정식
regression model 회귀모델
regressive expectations 회귀기대
regressive tax 역진세
regressive taxation 역진과세
regular audit 정시감사
regular delivery 통상인도
regular dividend 보통배당
regular fee 통상비용
regular general meeting 정기총회
regular general meeting of shareholders 정기주주총회
regular interest 정규권
regular meeting of the Board of Governors 정례이사회
regular member 정회원
regular member handling off-floor distribution 입회외분매취급정회원
regular members of the Tokyo Stock Exchange 도쿄증권거래소정회원
regular panel 소집배심원명부
regular settlement 익영업일인도
regular wage 기본급
regular way of delivery 통상인도
regular way transaction 보통거래
regularity 규칙성
regulated company 규제대상기업
regulated interest rate 규제금리
regulated investment company 규제투자회사
regulated market 규제시장
regulated prices 규제가격
regulation 규정
regulation of debt collection 회수규제
regulation of lending 융자규제
regulation of stock price 주가규제
Regulation T excess T 규칙초과증거금

regulations according to the labor agreement 노동계약에 따른 규정
regulations of financial statements 재무제표규칙
Regulations of Procedures of Hearings by the Ministry of Finance 재무부청문절차규칙
regulations on foreign banks 외국은행규제
regulations on large-lot loans 고액융자규제
regulatory action 행정조치
regulatory agency 규제당국
regulatory attention 규제당국의 주목
regulatory capital adequacy 자기자본비율규제
regulatory field 규제분야
regulatory measures 규제조치
rehabilitation 갱생
rehearing 재심리
rehypothecation 재담보설정
reimbursed expenses 입체경비
reimbursement 변상
reimbursement authorization 보상지불수권서
reimbursement method 생산고지불제
reimbursement obligation 보상채무
reimbursing bank 상환은행
reinstate 복권하다
reinsurance 재보험
reinsurance accounting 재보험회계
reinsurance agreement 재보험계약
reinsurance broker 재보험브로커
reinsurance clause 재보험조항
reinsurance commission 재보험수수료
reinsurance leverage 재보험레버리지
reinsurance premium 재보험료
reinsurance recovery 재보험금
reinsurance transaction 재보험거래
reinsurance treaty 재보험특약
reinvested earnings 이익잉여금
reinvestigation organization 이의심리청
reinvestment 재투자
reinvestment rate 재투자이율
reinvestment risk 재투자리스크
REIT 부동산투자신탁
rejected check 지불거절수표
rejection 기각
rejection certificate 거절증서
rejection rate 기각률
related cost 관련원가
related issue 관련상품
related laws 관계법령
related obligations 관련채무
related party 관련당사자
relational database 관련데이터베이스
relationship bank 거래은행
relationship lending 관련대부
relationship management system 거래처종합관리
relative 상대
relative advantage 비교우위
relative credit risk 상대적인 신용리스크
relative error 상대오차
relative excepted risk 상대적인 면책위험
relative income 상대소득
relative index 상대력지수
relative measures 상대적인 측도
relative performance 상대적인 퍼포먼스
relative price 상대가격
relative revenue 상대수익
relative share 분배율
relative strength 상대적인 강약도
relative strength index 상대력지수
relative value 상대가치
relaxation 완화
relaxation of credit 금융완화
relaxation of regulations 규제완화
relaxation of tight money policy 금융완화정책
release from debts 채무면제
release of lien 리엔방기
release of security 담보해제
release of seizure 차압해제
relegation 추방

relevancy 관련성
relevant authorities 관계당국
relevant benefit 적격급부
relevant cost 관련원가
relevant market 관련시장
relevant range 적합범위
relevant risk 관련리스크
reliability 신뢰성
relief loan 구제금융
relief merger 구제합병
religious corporation 종교법인
relinquishing of business 사업폐지
reload 리로드
relocation 이전
remainder 잔존
remainder price 잔존가격
remainder type 차액식
remaining carry 잔존캐리
remaining economic age 경제적인 잔존내용연수
remaining period 잔존기간
remaining period of the lease 임대계약의 잔존기간
remaining useful life 잔존내용연수
remargin 추가수익
remeasurement 재측정
remedy 구제방법
remedy for violation of private right 권리구제제도
reminder price 비망가격
remittance abroad 외국송금
remittance advice 송금통지서
remittance bill 송금환
remittance check 송금수표
remittee 환수취인
remitting bank 발송은행
removal expenses 제거비용
removed assets 철거자산
remuneration 보수
remuneration for personal services 인적역무의 대가
remuneration of officers 임원보수
render 언도하다
rendering of service 역무제공
renegotiated loans 금리감면채권
renegotitation 재교섭
renewal 갱신
renewal after the maturity 기한 후 자동지속
renewal charge 갱신료
renewal commission 갱신수수료
renewal expenses 대체비용
renewal fee 갱신료
renewal of bills and notes 어음갱신
renewal or change of the lease 차지계약갱신 및 변경
renewal premium 계속보험료
renounce 거절하다
rent arrears 연체지대(地代)
rent charge 지대(地代)부담
rent expense 리스료
rent income 임대료수입
rent on real estate 부동산임대료
rent payable 지불임대료
rent reasonably fixed 정당한 지대(地代)
rent receivable 미수임대료
rent roll 지대표(地代表)
rent service 지대봉사
rent-free 임대료 없이
rental agents' commissions 임차수수료
rental allowance 가임수당
rental expense 렌탈비용
rental income 가임(家賃)소득
rental market value 가임(家賃)상장
rental of real property 부동산대부
rental revenue 리스료
rental service 임대업
rental starts 임대주택의 착공호수
rental value 임대가격
rented house 차가
rented house right 차가권
renter 임차인

QR

rentier class 불로소득자층
rents and royalties 임대료 및 사용료 수입
rents received 부동산수입
reorganization bond 정리사채
reorganization of corporation 회사갱생
reorganization of industry 농업재편성
reorganization proceedings 갱생수속
reorganization scheme 재건계획
repackage bond 리패키지채
repair 수선
repair equalization reserve 수선평균적립금
repair-shop 수선공장
repairing budget 수선비예산
repairing cost 수선비
repairing expenses 수선비
repairing risks insurance 선박수선보험
repairs and maintenance 수선유지비
reparations 배상금
repayment at one time 일괄반제
repayment date 반제기일
repayment instalment 분할반제
repayment money 환부금
repayment moratorium 채무반제연기
repayment mortgage 원리반제형모기지
repayment of interest and principal 원리지불
repayment of liabilities 채무반제
repayment rate 반제율
repeated calculation 반복계산
repeating audit 반복감사
repercussion effect 파급효과
replaced property 대치자산
replacement 교체
replacement assets 교체자산
replacement by purchase 대치
replacement cost 교체원가
replacement cost accounting 교체원가회사
replacement deposit 차환예탁금
replacement investment 갱신투자
replacement method 50%상각법
replacement of business property 사업용 자산을 대치함
replacement of collateral 대체담보
replacement of loan 차관반제
replacement of stock certificates 주권교체
replacement price 교체가격
replacement property by purchase 대체를 통한 자산교환
replacement risk 재취득리스크
replacement unit 교체단위
replacement value 교체가치
replacement value insurance 신가보험
replenishment 보충
repo market 현선시장
repo rate 기준금리
report date 결산일
report form 보고식
report form balance sheet 보고식 대차대조표
report on examination 검사보고서
report on the issuer's own stock repurchase 자기주주매부상황보고서
report system 보고제도
reported asset value 공표베이스자산가치
reported equity 재무보고서상의 주주자본
reported period 당기
reported profit 공표이익
reported term 당기의
reporting audit standards 감사보고기준
reporting companies 결산회사
reporting currency 보고통화
reporting requirement 보고의무
repos 현선매매
repossession 철수;반환
representation 표명
representation work 표시작업
representative democracy 대표민주제
representative director 대표이사
representative liquidator 대표청산인
representative money 대표화폐
representative of corporation 법인의 대표자
representative office 주재원사무소
representative suit 대표소송
representatives or administrators

대표자 및 관리인
representing issue 대표상품
repricing date 금리변경시점
repricing interval 금리변경기간
reproduction 재생산
reproduction cost 재생산원가
reproduction on a diminishing scale 축소재생산
repudiation 거절;방기
repurchase 되사기
repurchase agreement 환매조건부 거래
repurchase obligation 환매의무
repurchase price 환매가;재취득가격
repurchase rate 재취득비율
repurchase right 환매청구권
repurchases of bond 채무해약
reputation 평판
reputed owner 명의상의 소유자
request 청구
request for correction 갱정청구
request for reconsideration 심사청구
request for reinvestigation 이의제기
request for share distribution 교부요구
request for wage increase 임상요구
request payment by securities 증권위탁납부
requested return 의뢰반송
required amount 소요액
required capital coefficient 필요자본계수
required margin 증거금소요액
required reserve 법정준비
required reserve ratio 법정준비율
required return 예정투자수익률
requirements 요건
requirements for issuing bonds 적채기준
requirements for setting up against 대항요건
requisite 필요요건
requisition 의뢰서
resale 재판;전매
resale price 재판가격
resale price maintenance 재판가격유지
resale price method 재판매가격기준법
rescheduling 리스케줄링;채무반제계획변경
rescission 해약
rescue bond 레스큐채
rescue package 지원책
research and development 연구개발
research and development cost 연구개발비
research and development expenditures 연구개발비
research cost 연구비
research expenditure 조사비
reservation 유보사항
reservation of ownership 소유권보류
reserve 적립금
reserve account 준비금계정
reserve accounting 적립금회계
reserve adequacy 준비금의 타당성
reserve against decline in price 가격변동준비금
reserve assets 준비자산
reserve bank 준비은행
reserve capital 준비자본
reserve cash 현금준비
reserve currency 준비통화
reserve deposit requirement system 준비예금제도
reserve for accidents 재해준비금
reserve for additions 증설적립금
reserve for after-care of products 제품보증준비금
reserve for amortization 상각준비금
reserve for bad debts 대손준비금
reserve for bad loan 대손준비금
reserve for bond dealing losses 채권거래손실준비금
reserve for bonus payment 상여준비금
reserve for compensation for completed works 완성공사보상준비금
reserve for construction 신축적립금
reserve for corporation tax 법인세준비금
reserve for dead loan 대손준비금
reserve for deferred income tax 압축준비금

QR

reserve for depreciation 감가상각준비금
reserve for depreciation of real estate 부동산감가상각준비금
reserve for development of overseas market 해외시장개척준비금
reserve for discount 할인준비금
reserve for employees retirement allowance 종업원퇴직급여준비금
reserve for encumbrance 지출부담준비금
reserve for equalization of dividend 배당평균준비금
reserve for expansion 설비확장적립금
reserve for foreign exchange fluctuation 외국환변동준비금
reserve for improvement of structure of small-and medium-sized enterprise 중소기업구조개선준비금
reserve for intercompany profit 대체이익준비금
reserve for inventory fluctuation 가격변동준비금
reserve for liability 부채준비금
reserve for liability for commodity transactions 상품거래책임준비금
reserve for liability for security transactions 증권거래책임준비금
reserve for loss from fluctuation of foreign exchange rate 환변동손실준비금
reserve for loss securities transactions 증권거래손실준비금
reserve for loss on goods unsold 반품조정준비금
reserve for losses 결손전보적립금
reserve for losses from securities transactions 증권거래책임준비금
reserve for outstanding claims 지불준비금
reserve for overhead 간접비준비금
reserve for overseas investment loss 해외투자손실준비금
reserve for pension fund 퇴직급여적립금
reserve for pensions 연금준비금
reserve for prevention of pollution 공해방지준비금
reserve for price fluctuation 가격변동준비금
reserve for renewals and replacements 개축적립금
reserve for repairs 수선준비금
reserve for retirement and severdance allowance 은퇴급여준비금
reserve for retirement annuity 퇴직연금적립금
reserve for retirement of preferred stock 우선주상환준비금
reserve for self-insurance 자가보험준비금
reserve for sinking fund 감채기금적립금
reserve for special depreciation 특별상각준비금
reserve for special purpose 특정준비금
reserve for specific purpose 목적적립금
reserve for stock dealing losses 주식거래손실준비금
reserve for tax payment 납세준비금
reserve fund 적립금
reserve position 준비포지션
reserve rate 지불준비율
reserve ratio 지불준비율
reserve requirement policy 지불준비율정책
reserve requirements 예금준비
reserve requirements of depositary institutions 예금수입기관의 요소준비
reserve requirements system 지불준비제도
reserve system 준비제도
reserve tranche 리저브트란시
reserved common stock 유보주식
reserved profit 유보이익
reserved surplus 준비잉여금
reserves for credit losses 대손준비금
reset bond 리셋채
reset date 금리갱신일
reset frequency 갱신빈도
resident 거주자
resident alien 거주외국인

resident auditor 주재감사인
resident doctor 연수의
resident foreign corporation 거주외국법인
resident foreign currency deposits 거주자외화예금
resident tax 주민세
residential investment 주택투자
residential property 거주용 재산
residential property market 주택용 부동산시장
residual analysis 잔여분석
residual assets 잔여재산
residual benefit 잔여이익
residual claim 잔여청구권
residual class 잔여클래스
residual cost 잔여원가
residual equity 잔여지분
residual income 잔여이익
residual interest 잔여지분
residual net income 잔여순이익
residual profits 잔여이익
residual property 잔여재산
residual ratio 잔존율
residual return 잔차수익률
residual risk 잔여리스크
residual share 잔여배분
residual standard deviation 잔여표준편차
residual value 잔존가격
residuary estate 잔여재산
residuary outlay 잔여지출
residue 잔여부분
resiliency 신속한 조정
resistance level 관문
resistance line 저항선
resolution 결의
Resolution Trust Corporation 정리신탁공사
resource allocation 자원배분
resources 자원
resources on business 경영자원
respective 각각의
respite 변제연기
response of market 시장반응
responsibility 책임
responsibility accounting 책임회계
responsibility costing 책임원가계산
responsible and recognized dealer 주요딜러
rest 휴식하다;잔여
restated 수정후
restatement of balance sheet 대차대조표를 재표시함
restitution 원상회복;손해배상금
restoration 복원
restoration of suspended membership 회원복권
restraining order 금지명령
restraint 제지; 억제
restraint measures 억제정책
restraint of trade 영업제한
restraint on alienation 양도금지
restraint on anticipation 미수이익처분금지
restrict sales 한정매출
restricted account 제한부 계정
restricted asset 구속자산
restricted credit 매취은행지정신용장
restricted period 제한기간
restricted receipts 특정수입고
restricted share 제한주식
restricted stock 제한주
restricted surplus 제한부 잉여금
restriction of order acceptance 수탁제한
restriction of price range 가격폭제한
restriction of transfer 양도제한
restriction on the growth of bank loans 대출증가액규칙
restriction on transfer of shares 주식양도제한
restriction on transferability 양도제한
restrictive covenant 한정조항;부작위약관
restrictive financial covenant 재무제한조항
restrictive monetary policy 금융긴축정책
restrictive provision 제한조항
restructuring charge 구조조정비용

restructuring period 구조조정기간
restructuring plan 구조조정계획
restructuring related stock 리스트럭처링 관련주
results of the current term 당기실적
resulting trust 추정신탁;복귀신탁
results announcement 결산발표
results of business 영업실적
results of operations 영업성적
results of ordinary operations 경상손익
results of the tax examination 세무조사결과
resumption of dividend 복배
resumption of suspended trading 거래재개
resumption of trading 거래재개
resurgence 재연
retail 소매
retail accounting 소매업회계
retail and consumer spending sector stock 소비지출관련주
retail bank 소매은행
retail banking 리테일뱅킹
retail business 소매업
retail cost 소매원가
retail credit card 유통계 카드
retail excise 소매세
retail industry 소매업계
retail institutions 소매금융기관
retail inventory method 재고조사법
retail investor 최종투자가
retail market 소매시장
retail method 매가환원법
retail price 소매가격
retail price inflation 소매물가인플레이션
retail sales 소매매상고
retail selling price 소매매가
retail store inventories 소매재고
retail trade industry 소매업
retained cash flow 소지캐시플로
retained earnings 유보이익
retained earnings appropriated for bond 감채적립금
retained earnings at the beginning of a period 전기이월이익금
retained earnings ratio 사내유보율
retained earnings statement 이익잉여금계산서
retained income 유보이익
retained profit 내부유보
retained surplus 이익준비금
retaining fee 변호사고문료
retaining lien 변호사리엔
retaliatory duties 보복관세
retention money 유보금
retention of earnings 이익유보
retention quotient 순보험료비율
retirement 소각
retirement accounting 제거회계
retirement allowance 퇴직급여
retirement allowance in a lump sum 퇴직금을 일괄지급함
retirement allowance regulations 퇴직급여규정
retirement annuity 퇴직연금
retirement annuity business 퇴직연금업무
retirement annuity reserve 퇴직연금적립금
retirement by purchase 매입상각
retirement cost 제거비
retirement income 퇴직소득
retirement income policy 퇴직소득부 보험
retirement lump sum grants 퇴직일시금
retirement method 폐기법
retirement of bond 사채소각
retirement of company's own stocks 자기주식소각
retirement of redeemed preferred stock 상환우선주를 상환함
retirement of shares 주식상각
retirement pay 퇴직금
retirement pension 퇴직연금
retirement plan 퇴직금제도
retirement price 제거가액
retirement related benefits 퇴직관련급부

retirement unit 제거단위
retractable maturity 단기가능만기
retroactive 소급해서
retroactive adjustments 소급수정
retroactive discount 소급할인율
retroactive levy 소급징수
retroactive restatement 소급수정보고서
retroactively to a date in the past 과거로 소급해서
retrogressive accounting 소구계산
retrospective law 소급법
retrospective policy 소급보험
return after due date 기한후 신고
return and payment 신고 및 납부
return blank 신고용지
return commission 환급수수료
return form for insurance premium deduction 보험료공제신고서
return form for retirement income 퇴직소득신고서
return freight 반환운임
return inward 반품
return line 리턴라인
return maximizer 리턴극대자
return of capital 자본회수
return of investment 자본이익률
return on assets 총자산수익률
return on common stockholders' equity 주주자본이익률
return on equity 주주자본이익률
return on equity capital 주주자본이익률
return on fixed assets 고정자본에 대한 수익률
return on investment 투자수익;투자수익률
return on long-term liabilities plus equity capital 자기자본이익률
return on net worth 주주자본이익률
return on physical capital 물적자본이익률
return on sales 매상고이익률
return on the capital investment 설비투자이익률
return on total assets 총자산이익률
return outward 반품
return premium for cancellation 해약반려금
return to equilibrium 평형으로 회귀함
return to shareholder 주주에게로 회귀함
return without voting 무투표당선
returned goods unsold 반품
returned materials report 원재료반환표
returning of premium 프리미엄환원
revaluation 절상;재평가;평가절상
revaluation excess 재평가차액
revaluation of assets 자산평가환
revaluation of stocks 주식평가환
revaluation profit 재평가익
revaluation surplus 재평가잉여금
revaluation surplus reserve 재평가적립금
revealed preference 현시선호
revenue 매상(비제조업)
revenue account 수입계정
revenue agency 세입대리점
revenue and expenditure budget 세입세출예산
revenue anticipation note 세입예측증권
revenue bond 특정재원채
revenue curve 수익곡선
revenue deficit 세입결함
revenue distribution 수익분포
revenue expenditure 수익지출
revenue from account-opening fees 계좌개설금수입
revenue from fund operations 기본재산운용수입
revenue from government enterprise 관영수입
revenue from leases 리스수익
revenue from operations 영업수익
revenue from public bond 공채수입
revenue maximization hypothesis 매상고최대화가설
revenue officer 수세관
revenue pressures 감수압력
revenue projection 수익예측

revenue realization 수익실현
revenue recognizing standard 수익인식기준
revenue reserve amount 수익적립금액
revenue reserves 이익적립금
revenue sources 세입원
revenue stamp 수입인지
revenue tax 소득세
reversal 상장의 반전
reversal auction 역입찰
reversal cost method 역산법
reversal day 반전일
reversal entry 반대분개
reversal of judgment 판결파기
reversal of reserve for overseas investments 해외투자손실준비금환수
reversal of reserve for price fluctuation 가격변동준비금환수
reversal of surplus 적립금반환
reversal of taxation 과세처분취소
reversal pattern 반전패턴
reversal assets effect 역자산효과
reverse direction 역방향
reversal dual currency bond 리버스듀얼커런시채
reversal floater 연변동이부채
reversal floating rate note 역변동이부채
reverse for extraordinary casualties 이상위험준비금
reverse hedge 역헤지
reverse income tax 역소득세
reverse offset 역상태
reverse operation 역산
reverse remittance 역송금
reverse repo 리버스레포
reverse split of stocks 주식병합
reverse swap 역스와프
reverse takeover 반대매매
reverse telegraphic transfer 전신거래환
reverse trade 반대매매
reverse yield gap 역일드갭
reverse zero coupon swap 리버스제로쿠폰스와프
reversed and remanded 파기반송
reversed swap 역스와프
reversing entry 반대기입
reversion 복귀재산권
revert to the following day 다음날로 늦추다
revert to the previous day 전일로 앞당기다
review 심사
review of financial statements 재무제표리뷰
revised average stock price 수정평균주가
revised budget 수정예산
revised return 수정신고
revised statutes 수정법률
revision 정정
revision of office regulation 내규개정
revival of judgment 판결부활
revival of monetary policy 금융정책부활
revival of will 유언부활
revived quotation 급등한 가격
revocable L/C 취소가능신용장
revocation 철회
revocation of approval to filing blue return 청색신고승인취소
revocation of probate 검인철회
revocation of will 유언철회
revocation suit 취소소송
revoke 취소하다
revolving card 리볼빙카드
revolving collateral 근담보
revolving credit 회전신용장; 리볼빙 크레디트
revolving fund 회전자금
revolving guarantee 근보증
revolving letter of credit 회전신용장
revolving line of credit 한계대부선
revolving loan 리볼빙론
revolving trade 회전무역
revolving underwriting facility 리볼빙 언더라이팅 퍼실리티
reward 보수
reword 바꾸어 쓰다
rewriting 고쳐 씀; 다시 씀

Ricardo effect 리카도효과
rider 부가조항
right and interest 이권
right in rem 물권
right not to pay before due date 기한이익
right of access 억세스권
right of access to courts 재판청구권
right of auditing 감사권
right of avoidance 부인권
right of beneficiary 수익권
right of cancellation 해약권
right of claim 청구권
right of collective bargaining 단체교섭권
right of credit availability 크레디트이용권
right of demanding compensation 구상권
right of design 의장권
right of eminent domain 토지수용권
right of first refusal 최우선인수권
right of inheritance 상속권
right of lease 임차권
right of petition 청원권
right of pledge 질권
right of priority 선취권
right of recourse 상환청구권
right of redemption 권리반환권
right of recision 계약해제권
right of resumption 회복권
right of taxation 과세권
right of telephone 전화가입권
right of trademark 상표권
right of use 사용권
right to begin 개시권
right to counsel 변호사의 도움을 받을 권리
right to obtain foreign money 외화할당권
right to revoke fraudulent act
사해행위취소권
rights and liabilities of members 사원권
rights and obligations 권리와 의무
rights existing on real property
부동산상의 권리
rights for profit-sharing 공익권
rights issue 주주할당발행증자
rights of repurchase 환매권
rights off 권리하락
rights offering 주주할당
rights on 권리부
rights to claim the refund 반환청구권
rigidity of price 가격경직성
ring 링
rise in price 가격상승
rise in yield 이율상승
rise interest rate 금리상승
rise on stock price 주가상승
rise-and-fall market 왕래상장
rising of the court 폐정
rising phase 상승상장
rising quotation 상승상장
risk appetite 리스크선호
risk arbitrage 리스크를 수반한 재정거래
risk assessment 리스크평가
risk asset ratio 위험자산비율
risk assets 위험자산
risk averse 리스크회피형의
risk averse attitude 리스크회피적인 태도
risk aversion 위험회피
risk averter 리스크회피자
risk based capital standards
리스크베이스의 자기자본기준
risk capital 위험자본리스크
risk characteristics 리스크특성
risk control 리스크관리
risk country control 리스크컨트리컨트롤
risk covered 담보위험
risk differentials 리스크격차
risk disclosure statement 리스크개시서
risk evaluation 리스크평가
risk exposure 위험노출
risk factor 리스크팩터
risk free 신용리스크가 없는
risk hedge 위험회피; 리스크헤지
risk information 리스크정보
risk lover 위험선호자

risk management 리스크매니지먼트
risk neutral 리스크중립자
risk neutral attitude 리스크뉴트럴자세
risk parameter 리스크요인
risk penalty 리스크페널티
risk preference 리스크선호도
risk premium 리스크프리미엄
risk profile 리스크특성
risk reduction measure 리스크경감수단
risk reduction strategy 리스크경감전략
risk sector 리스크섹터
risk seeking attitude 리스크선호태도
risk selection 리스크선택
risk sensitive index 리스크감응도지표
risk sharing 리스크분포
risk structure 리스크구조
risk structure of discount rate 할인율의 리스크구조
risk taking 리스크부담
risk tolerance 리스크허용도
risk weight 리스크웨이트
risk-adjusted analysis 리스크조정분석
risk-adjusted approach 리스크조정법
risk-adjusted capital 리스크조정필 자본
risk-based capital 리스크기반자본금
risk-controlled 리스크제어
risk-free assets 무리스크자산
risk-free interest rate 무리스크금리
risk-free securities 무리스크증권
risk-neutral valuation 무리스크뉴트럴
risk-return group 리스크수익그룹
risk-return relationship 리스크와 수익의 관계
risk-return trade-off 리스크와 수익의 트레이드오프
riskless arbitrage 무리스크재정
riskless assets 안전자산
riskless transaction 리스크가 없는 거래
risky 리스크가 큰
risky assets 위험자산
risky assets mix 위험자산믹스
risky securities 리스크증권
robot teller 로봇텔러
robust earnings 업적호조
robust home sales 주택판매호조
rocket scientist 하이테크상품개발자
ROI 투자수익률
roll down 롤다운
roll forward 롤포워드
roll over 만기서환
rollback 롤백
roller coaster swap 롤러코스터스와프
rolling readjustment 파동조정
rolling yield 롤링일드
rolling-forward procedure 선송법
rollover loan 롤오버론
roly poly CD 롤리폴리 CD
Roosa bond 로자본드
Roosa effect 로자효과
Roosa plan 로자구상
root of title 권원의 기초
rotational system 윤번제
rough balance system 개산대차대조표
rough cost 개산원가
rough cost book 개산원가표
rough number 어림값
round lot 최저거래단위
round number 어림수
round trip transaction 왕복거래
round up 올림
round-the-clock market 24시간거래시장
roundabout production 우회생산
roundabout trade 우회무역
rounding off in calculation 끝수계산
rounding reversal pattern 라운딩리버설패턴
routed order 루티드오더
routine tasks 단순작업
royalties received for use of patents 수입특허권사용료
royalty 로얄티
royalty as to know-how 노하우사용료
royalty interest 소유권이권
royalty of patent right 특허권사용료

royalty of the copyright 저작권사용료
royalty on a book 인세
royalty to be paid every fixed time 정시불사용료
RP market 레포시장
rubber product industry 고무제품업계
ruin the reputation 신용을 실추시키다
rule 규칙
rule absolute 절대명령
rule against accumulations 영구적립금지규칙
rule against perpetuities 영구권금지원칙
rule day 명령일
rule of law 법의 지배
rule of reason 합리원칙
rule to show cause 이유개시
rules of auction 경쟁매매원칙
Rules of Fair Practice 공정관습규칙
rules of thumb 경험칙
ruling 결정
ruling out 제외
run upon a bank 단골은행
run-down 상장표요약
runaway gap 런어웨이갭
running account 당좌계정
running cost 운전비
running inventory 상시재고
running inventory method 계속재고법
running of the market 시황상황
running price 시가
running royalty 계속사용료
running stock 정상재고
rush order 주문이 쇄도함

S&P 100 spot option S & P 100선물옵션
S&P 500 Stock Price Index
S&P 500종 주가지수
S&P futures S & P 선물
sacrifice sale 투매; 헐값으로 팔기
saddle point 안상점
safe custody 보호예금
safe deposit 보호예금
safe deposit box insurance 대금고보험
safe harbor 세이프하버
safe harbor accord 세이프하버협정
safe harbor lease 세이프하버리스
safe keeping 보관
safe-pledge 보석보증인
safeguard provision 세이프가드조항
safety factor 안전율
safety margin 안전계수
safety nets 예금자보호시스템
safety reserves 안전준비금
safety stock 안전재고
safety valve 안전밸브
sag 처짐; 늘어짐
salaries 급료
salaries and wages 임금
salary from secondary source
이차재원으로 급여를 지급함
salary scale 급여지수
sale and purchase on credit 외상매매
sale and return 해제조건부 매매
sale bond 판매보증증권
sale by agent 대리판매
sale by brand 브랜드매매
sale by bulk 일괄매매
sale by description 표시를 통한 매매
sale by grade or type 규격매매
sale by specification 사양서매매
sale by subscription 예약판매
sale for cash 현금판매
sale in gross 일괄매출
sale leaseback transaction 세일리스백거래
sale on account 외상매출
sale on an underwriting basis 인수매출
sale on commission 위탁판매
sale on customer's account
고객의 수탁에 기반을 두고 팔아치움
sale on standard 표준품매매
sale or return 반환권부 매매
sale price 거래가격
sale to arrive 미착품판매
sale-leaseback 세일리스백
sales 매상
sales account 매상계정
sales accounting 판매회계
sales allowance 매출에누리
sales amount 판매금액
sales analysis 매상분석
sales and general administrative expense
판매관리비
sales and purchases on commission
수수료매매
sales at unreasonably high price
굉장히 높은 가격으로 판매함

sales basis 매상기준
sales book 매상장
sales commission 판매수수료
sales contract 매매계약
sales contracts commitments 선물인도계약
sales cost 매상원가
sales cost ratio 매상원가율
sales credit 외상거래채권
sales discount 판매할인
sales earnings 영업수입
sales finance 판매금융
sales finance company 판매금융회사
sales for this term 당기매상고
sales force 판매력
sales forecasting 매상고예측
sales growth rate 매상성장률
sales invoice 매상송장
sales journal 매상분개장
sales ledger 매상원장
sales method 판매방법
sales mix 세일즈믹스
sales network 판로
sales of bond 채권설정
sales of corporate bonds by purchasers 사채소화상황
sales of investment trusts 투자신탁설정
sales office 영업소
sales on approval 시용판매
sales on consignment 수탁판매
sales price 매출가격
sales proceeds 매상액
sales profit ratio 매상이익률
sales promotion 판매촉진
sales promotion expense 판매촉진비
sales rebate 매상할인
sales rebate with special payment terms 특별지출조건부 매상할인
sales record 판매장부표
sales returns 매상되돌림
sales revenues 매상수익
sales slip 매상전표
sales subsidiary 판매자회사
sales tax 매상세
sales to accounts receivable 외상채권율
sales to cash 현예금회전율
sales to fixed assets 고정자산매상률
sales to inventories 재고정리자산매상률
sales to receivables 외상채권회전율
sales to total assets 총자산매상률
sales to working capital 운전자본매상률
sales type lease 판매형 리스
sales under agreement to repurchase 환매를 조건으로 매각함
sales volume 생산고
sales volume budget 매상고예산
sales year 매각연도
Sallie Mae 미국장학자금금고; 샐리메이
Sallie Mae debenture 샐리메이채
salvage 해난구조
salvage charges 구조료
salvage loss 구조물매득금차인정산
salvage prices 잔존가격
salvage value 처분가치
same day effective order 당일유효주문
same day settlement 동일결제
sample 상품견본
sample mean 표본평균
sample shipment 견본적송품
sample expense 견본비
sampling distribution 표본분포
sampling error 표본추출오차
sampling survey 표본조사
sampling unit 표본단위
samurai bond 사무라이채
samurai commercial paper 사무라이 CP
sanction 제한조치
sandwich spread 샌드위치스프레드
sans recourse 상환청구에 응하지 않은
satellite market 위성시장
satisfaction of mortgage 모기지개방증서
satisfactory 만족할 만한
satisfying principle 만족기준

Saturday Night Special 새터데이나이트스페셜
saucer 소스
Saudi Arabian Monetary Agency 사우디아라비아통화청
saving account 저축계정
saving clause 유보사항
saving function 저축함수
savings at call 통지예금
savings bank 저축은행
savings bond 저축채권
savings debenture 저축채권
savings deducted at source 공제저금
savings deposit 저축예금
savings in preparation for tax payment 납세적금
savings note 저축채권
savings rate 저축률
savings ratio 저축률
savings share 저축주
savings-and-loan association 저축대부조합
savings-for-tax association 납세저축조합
savings-investment theory of income determination 저축투자소득결정론
savings-investment theory of interest-rate determination 저축투자이자율결정론
SBF 120 SBF 120종 주가지수
scale analysis 척도분석
scale economies 규모의 경제
scale merit 규모의 이익
scale of central and local public finance 재정규모
scale order 등급주문
scale trading 평가하기 어려운 매매
scalper 당장의 이윤을 노려 사고파는 사람
scalping 당장의 이윤을 노려 사고 팜
scandal 스캔들
scarce currency clause 희소통화조항
scarce resources 희소자원
scarce stock 적은 주
scarcity of stock 주식부족
scatter chart 산포도표
scenario analysis 시나리오분석
schedule 각종명세
schedule form 보고식
schedule of bonds payable 사채명세표
schedule of capital 자본금명세표
schedule of depreciation 감가상각비명세표
schedule of securities 유가증권명세표
schedule of tangible fixed assets 유형고정자산명세표
schedule of the cost of goods manufactured 제조원가명세표
schedule of the marginal efficiency of capital 자본한계효율표
schedule of transactions 거래명세
schedule payment 스케줄페이먼트
scheduled cost 표시원가
scheduled payment 약정반제
scheduled repayment 정시상환
scheduler income taxation 분류소득
schedules of financial statements 재무제표부속명세표
schema of reproduction 재생산표식
scheme of arrangement 채무정리계획
scheme of operation 사업방법서
Schuldschein Darlehen 채무증서대부
scissors-form difference in price 낫모양가격표
scope of assessment 과세범위
scope of audit 감사범위
scope of authority 권한범위
scope of business 사업범위
scope of exemption of property tax 고정자산세비과세범위
scope of income subject to withholding income tax 원천징수의 대상이 되는 소득
scope of opinion 의견구분
scope of securities 유가증권의 범위
scorched earth defense 초토작전
scrap 찌꺼기; 토막
scrap equipment 폐잔설비

scrap value 잔존가액
scrapped property 제거자산
scrapping of equipment tax credit 특정설비폐기세액공제
scrapping of property 자산제거
screening 심사
screening of application for loan 대출심사
scrip 단주주권
scrip certificate 임시주권
scrip dividend 증서배당
script 원문서
scrutiny 심사
SDR denominated bond SDR 기준채
sea brief 중립선증명서
sea law 해사법규
sea letter 중립국선증명서
sea peril 해상위험
seal 검인
seal impression 인감
season sale 계절매출
seasonal adjustment 계절조정
seasonal average 계절평균
seasonal duties 계절관세
seasonal factor 계절요인
seasonal fluctuation adjustment 계절변동조정
seasonal fund 계절자금
seasonal goods 계절상품
seasonal index 계절지수
seasonal merchandise 계절상품
seasonal moves 계절요인
seasonal selling pressure 계절적인 매출압력
seasonal unemployment 계절적인 요인으로 인한 실업
seasonal variation 계절변동
seasonally adjusted 계절변동조정필
seasoned bond 만기에 가까운 채권
seasoned issue 이미 발행한 상품
seasoned loan 경과기간이 긴 론
seat 회원권
seaworthy 항해에 견디는
SEC accounting SEC 회계
SEC Accounting Releases SEC 회계연속통보
SEC Docket SEC 다킷
SEC schedules SEC 부속명세서
SEC standards SEC 기준
secession from a corporation 입퇴료
second deliverance 재인도
second generation on-line system 이차 온라인
second half of the year 하반기
second mortgage 이차저당
second mortgage bond 이차저당부 사채
second surplus treaty 이차초과액특약
second tier 2위군;후발주자
second-distress 이차차압
second-lien mortgage loan 이순위모기지론
secondary activities 부수업무
secondary bond dealing 유통시장에서의 채권딜링
secondary boycott 이차보이콧
secondary capital 보완적인 자기자본
secondary claim 후순위청구권
secondary conveyance 이차부동산이전행위
secondary distribution 이차분매
secondary evidence 이차적인 증거
secondary industry 이차산업
secondary liability 이차부채
secondary liquidities 이차유통자본
secondary market 유통시장
secondary market for Japanese government bonds 일본국채유통시장
secondary market liquidity 유통시장의 유동성
secondary offering 매출
secondary rally 이차부채
secondary securities 이차증권
secondary tax liability 이차납세의무
secondary trend 이차트렌드
secrecy agreement 수비의무계약
secret account 비밀계정
secret commission 비밀수수료

secret language 암호
secret liability 비밀부채
secret partnership 익명조합
secret reserve 비밀적립금
secret service expenses 기밀비
secret trust 비밀신탁
secretariat 총무처;사무국
Secretary of State 국무장관
section of revenue 수세과
sectional calculation 부문계산
sectional income statement 구분손익계산서
sectional journal 분할분개장
sectional ownership 구분소유권
sectional surface rights 구분지상권
sector 섹터
sector balance sheet 부문별 대차대조표
sector-stock price index 업종별 주가지수
sectoral approach 섹터방식
secular decline 장기저하
secular pressure 구조적인 압력
secular reason 구조요인
secured account 보증계정
secured advance 담보부 대부
secured bond 저당권부 사채
secured call loan 유담보론
secured claim 갱생담보권
secured credit 담보 부대출
secured debenture 담보부 부채
secured debt 담보부 대출
secured liabilities 담보부 부채
secured loan 담보대출
secured loan on securities 증권담보론
secured note 담보부 약속어음
secured party 담보권자
secured securities 담보부 증권
secured transactions 담보부 거래
securing completion of transaction 거래의 안전을 도모함
securities 유가증권
securities account 유가증권계정
securities acquired by the specified investment in kind 특정현물출자증권
Securities Act of 1983 1983년 증권법
securities administration 증권행정
securities administration trust 유가증권관리신탁
securities analysis 증권분석
Securities and Exchange Commission 미국증권거래위원회
Securities and Exchange Law 증권거래법
Securities and Exchange Surveillance Commission 증권거래감사위원회
Securities and Investments Board 증권투자위원회
securities borrowed 차입유가증권
securities broker 증권브로커
securities business 증권업
securities business tax law 증권거래세법
securities called by lot 추선상환증권
securities capital 증권자본
securities clearing 증권클리어링
securities companies by size of capital 자본금계층별 증권회사
securities company 증권회사
securities dealer 증권딜러
securities deposited as collateral 담보차입유가증권
securities deposited from others 보관유가증권
securities eligible for settlement 결제물건
securities exchange 증권거래소
securities exchange commission 증권거래심의회
Securities Exchange Surveillance Commission 증권거래감사위원회
securities finance company 증권금융회사
securities financing 증권금융
securities firm 증권회사
securities for fiduciary issue 보증준비
securities for sale 매각가능증권
securities futures 증권선물거래
securities handling clerk 유가증권취급자

securities held for investment trust 투자신탁유가증권
securities holdings 보유증권
securities house dealer 증권회사딜러
securities in foreign currency 외화증권
securities in lieu of cash 대용유가증권
securities in portfolio 소지증권
securities in trust 유가증권신탁
securities industry 증권업계
Securities Industry Association 전미증권업자협회
securities inventory 증권회사가 판매를 위해 보유한 채권
securities investment 증권투자
securities investment advisory service 증권투자상담
securities investment by financial institution 금융기관이 보유한 유가증권
securities investment trust 증권투자신탁
securities investment trust sales company 투자신탁판매회사
Securities Investor Protection Act of 1970 증권투자가보험법
securities investor protection corporation 증권투자가보호회사
securities issuance 증권발행
securities issued by government related agency 정부계 기관증권
securities ledger 유가증권원장
securities lent 대부유가증권
securities loan 증권금융
securities loaned 대부유가증권
securities management 증권관리
securities market 증권시장
securities market line 증권시장선
Securities Market Reform Act 증권시장개혁법안
Securities Market Stabilization Act 증권시장안정화법안
securities of affiliated company 관계회사유가증권
securities on property 물적증권
securities on the shelf 일괄등록필 증권
securities outstanding 발행필 증권
securities owned 상품유가증권
securities ownership by investment trusts 투자신탁의 유가증권보험
securities purchase 유가증권매입
securities received as collaterals 보관유가증권
securities received for guarantee 세금유가증권
securities register 유가증권기입장
securities registration statement 유가증권신고서
securities regulations 증권규칙
securities report 유가증권보고서
securities report for listing application 상장신고를 위한 유가증권보고서
securities reserve 유가증권준비
Securities Supervisory Board 증권감독원
securities trading 증권거래
securities transaction tax 유가증권거래세
securities transaction tax law 유가증권거래세법
securities transfer tax 유가증권거래세
securities underwriting business law 유가증권인수업법
securities with irregularities 사고증권
securities yield 증권이율
securitisation law 증권화법
securitisation market 증권화시장
securitization 증권화
securitization by pooling 풀링에 따른 증권화
securitization of bad loans 불량채권의 증권화
securitization of real estate 부동산의 증권화
securitized assets 증권화 자산
security account 보증계정
security analyst 증권분석전문가
security credit 증권금융
security credit by banks 은행을 통한 증권금융

security credit by brokers and dealers 브로커와 딜러를 통한 증권금융
security deposits 담보예금
security financing 주식자금조달
security financing by listed companies 상장회사자금조달액
security for costs 소송비용담보
security for obligation 채권담보
security for tax payment 납세담보
security income and expense 유가증권손익
security interest 담보권
security of tax payment 납세보증
security right 담보권
security risk curve 증권리스크
security suretyship 보증인
security yield curve 증권이율곡선
security-specific risk 증권고유리스크
securtised asset 증권화된 자산
seed money 초기투입자금
segment accounting 세그먼트회계
segment reporting 사업구분별 손익보고
segmental breakdown 부문별 내역
segmental information 세그먼트정보
segmental sales 부문별 매상
segmental sales breakdown 부문별 매상내역
segmentation 세분화;세그멘테이션
segmentation theory 시장분단이론
segregated account 분리계정
segregated accounts 분별관리
segregation of clearing margin 거래증거금을 구분함
segregation of margin 증거금분리
seized 점유한
seized goods 차압물건
seizor 차압인
seizure 차압
selected issue 선정문제
selection of a necessary appraisal method 필요한 평가방법을 선정함
selection of depreciation method 상각방법을 선정함
selection of risk 위험선택
selection of valuation method 평가방법을 선정함
selective bid 지명경쟁입찰
selective buying 물색매매
selective credit regulation 선택적인 신용규제
selective financing 선별융자
selective function 선택적인 기능
selective lending 선별융자
selective selling 특약판매
selective tendering 지명경쟁입찰
self-accounting system 독립회계제
self-addressed check 자기앞수표
self-assessed income tax 신고소득세
self-assessment 자기신고
self-assessment of taxation 신고납세
self-assessment system 자기신고납부제도
self-balancing 독자평균
self-balancing type 증감대조식
self-consumption 자가소비
self-defense 정당방위
self-disserving evidence 자신에게 불리한 증거
self-employed 자영의
self-employed pension 자영업자연금
self-employed retirement annuity 자영업자퇴직연금
self-employment income 자가영업소득
self-enforcement 자력집행권
self-finance 자기금융
self-finance ratio 자기금융비율
self-insurance 자가보험
self-insurance fund 자가보험기금
self-insurance plan 자가보험제도
self-insurance reserve 자가보험준비금
self-issue cards 자사카드
self-liquidity 자기유동성
self-management 자영
self-produced fixed assets 자기생산에 관련된 고정자산
self-produced inventories 자기제조에 관련된 재고자산

self-regarding evidence 자신에 대한 증거
self-registration 일괄등록제도
self-regulations 자주규제
self-regulatory organization 자주규제기관
self-restraint 자주규제
self-restraint agency 자주규제기관
self-restraint interest 자주규제금리
self-return 자기신고
self-serving declaration 자기에게 이익이 되는 공술
self-support accounting 독립채산
self-support subsistence 독립생계
self-supporting accounting system 독립채산제
self-sustained personal accident insurance 자손사고보험
sell back 되팔다
sell down 셀다운(간사단 이외에 판매함)
sell low 싸게 팔다
sell on the spot 즉매하다
sell side 셀사이드
sell signal 매신호
sell-and-lease agreement 대차계약
seller 파는 쪽
seller's monopoly 판매자독점
seller's option 매주선택
seller's option trading 셀러즈옵션거래
seller's option transaction 특약일거래
seller's price 부르는 값
sellers over 전매장
sellers' market 파는 자의 시장
selling agreement 판매계약
selling and administrative expenses 판매관리비
selling charges 판매비용
selling climax 셀링클라이막스
selling commission 매상수수료
selling concession 판매수수료
selling contract 판매예약
selling cycle 판매순환
selling exchange 판매환
selling expense 판매비
selling expense variance 판매비차이
selling group 판매단
selling group agreement 판매단계약서
selling off 투매
selling offer 판매오파
selling on a consignment basis 위탁판매
selling on a rising scale 매상
selling on balance 평균매출
selling on rally 되팔기
selling on spurt 급등매출
selling on temporary 되팔기
selling operation under repurchase agreement 환매조건부 매출오퍼레이션
selling operations 판매오퍼
selling opportunity 매장
selling order 매주문
selling out 처분매출
selling overhead 판매간접비
selling pressure 매압력
selling price 파는 값
selling price inventory 매가재고조사법
selling price per unit 상품 하나당 매매가격
selling rate 매상장
selling regular member 매부정회원
selling right 파는 권리
selling sample 매출견본
selling short 공매
selling short against the box 가격하락위험을 피하기 위해 현물을 보유하였으면서도 신용거래로 판매하는 행위
selling side 매출사이드
selling support 매출인기
selling; general and administrative expenses 일반관리비; 판매일반관리비
semi-annual audit 중간감사
semi-annual audit report 중간감사보고서
semi-annual closing of accounts 중간결산
semi-annual compounding calculation 반년마다 복리로 계산함
semi-annual coupon 반년불쿠폰

semi-annual report 반기(半期)보고서
semi-finished goods 반제품
semi-fixed cost 준고정비
semi-inflation 준인플레이션
semi-installment 반기지불
semi-variable charge 준변동비
semi-variable cost 준변동원가
semi-variable expenses 준변동비항목
sender 적송인
senior accountant 상급회계사
senior bond 상위사채
senior co-manager 상급부간사
senior creditor 선순위채권자
senior debt 우선채무
senior executive 경영자
senior issue 상위증권
senior lender 선순위대수
senior loan 우선대부
senior managing director 전무이사
senior managing governor 전무이사
senior mortgage 선순위양도저당
senior mortgage bond 선순위담보부사채
senior securities 우선증권
senior subordinated note 상위열후사채
senior trader 시니어트레이더
senior tranche 상위트란시
senior unsecured debt 무담보상위채무
seniority order wage system 연공서열임금제도
seniority system 연공제
sensitive market 민감한 시장
sensitivity 감응성
sensitivity adjustment 감응도 조정
sensitivity analysis 감응도 분석
sensitivity coefficient 감응도 계수
sentiment 감정;정서
sentiment index 센티멘트지표
separable cost 분리가능원가
separate account 별도계정
separate and restricted account 별단계정
separate bill 별계정
separate estate 부인의 고유재산
separate financial statements 단독재무제표
separate investment account 분리계정
separate maintenance 별거수당
separate property 특유재산
separate return 개별신고서
separate taxation from other income 분리과세
separate trading of registered interest and principal of securities 스트립채
separate withholding tax 분리과세
separated taxation on dividend income 배당분리과세
separation between capital and administration 자본경영분리
sequence of deduction 공제순서
sequence of tax credits 세액공제순서
sequential cost system 공정별 종합원가계획
serial bond 연속상환채권
serial correlation 계열상관
serial issue 연속발행
serial securities 연속상환증권
serial zero-coupon bond 연속제로쿠폰채
series 시리즈
service account 무역외 수지
service balance 무역외 수지
service by public notification 공시송달
service contribution 역무출자
service cost 용역원가
service department 보조부문
service departmental charge 보조부문비
service division 보조부문
service industry 서비스업
service life 내용연수
service office 영업소
service trade 서비스무역
service transaction 서비스거래
service unit 용역단위
service-yield basis 생산고비례법
servicer 서비서
services output method 용역생산고법

servicing burden 채무반제부담
servicing fee 서비싱수수료
servicing fee income 서비싱수수료수입
servitude 지역권
servitude for use of water 용수지역권
servitude holder 지역권자
session 회기
session period 입회시간
set bill 복수어음
set of accounts 회계장표
set off 상쇄
set up against 대항하다
setback 감소
setting 설정
setting up overdraft 대월설정
settle 청산하다
settle accounts 결산하다
settled account 청산계정
settled additional tax due amount 갱정결정으로 확정한 추가세액
settlement 결제
settlement account 결제계정
settlement at Japan Securities Clearing Corporation 일본증권결제상황
settlement date 결제일
settlement day 인도일
settlement discount 결제할인
settlement facility 결제기구
settlement for the first half of the year 중간결산
settlement index 청산지수
settlement method 결제방식
settlement of accounts 수지결산
settlement of accounts for the latter half 하기결산
settlement index 청산지수
settlement method 결제방식
settlement of accounts 결산
settlement of accounts for the latter half 하기결산
settlement of balance 평균결제
settlement of claim 채권변제
settlement of debt 정산
settlement of easement 지역권설정
settlement of mortgage 저당권설정
settlement of subsidy 보조금반제
settlement of superficies 지상권설정
settlement of tax amount 세액확정
settlement of unsettled transactions 미결제거래정리
settlement out of court 시담
settlement period 변제기한
settlement price 결산가격
settlement risk 인도리스크
settlement statements 결산서류
settlement time 결제시한
settlement trade 거류지무역
settlement value 결제대금
settlement variation 세틀먼트바리에이션
settlement volume 인도결제수량;결제건수
settlements rate 결제비율
settlor 신탁설정자
setup time 조직편제시간
sever 분리하다
several contract 분할계약
several covenant 가분조항
several liability 개별책임
several ownership 분할소유권
severally 단독으로
severally but not jointly 비연대보증
severally liable 개별책임의
severance 분리
severance benefit 퇴직수당
severance of actions 소송을 분리함
shadow account 섀도우어카운트
shadow cabinet 재야내각
shadow price 잠재가격
shaking-out 투매
share account 주식계정
share allotment certificate 주식할당증서
share allotment letter 주식할당통지
share broker 주식브로커

share capital 주식자본
share consolidation 주식합병
share deposits 출자예금
share draft account 주식어음계정
share drafts 쉐어드래프트
share earnings 일주당 이익
share exchange 주식교환
share handling 주식취급
share holding ratio 주식보유율
share in expense of public service 공공시설부담액
share ledger 주식대장
share of no par value 무액면주식
share of one kind 단일주식
share of the residual property 잔여재산여분
share price 주가
share price level 주가수준
share price performance 주가동향
share repurchase 자사주구매
share split-down 주식합병
share split-up 주식분할
share with par value 액면주식
share-handling service agent 주식사무대행기관
share-issuing expense 신주발행비
shared equities 공유지분
shareholder 주주
shareholder activism 주주행동주의
shareholder litigation 주주가 소송함
shareholder's account 주주계정
shareholder's interest 주주지분
shareholder's right 주주권
shareholder's rights 주주권리
shareholders of record 등록주주
shareholders-oriented management 주주중시경영
shareholders' equity 주주자본
shareholders' ledger 주주원장
shareholders' list 주주명부
shareholders' meeting 주주총회
shareholders' representative suit 주주대표소송
shareholders' resolution 주주결의
shareholdings 지분주
shares bought on margin 신용구매
shares held by investment trusts 투신편입주식
shares held in a long position 상장된 주식
shares lent by members 자기자본
shares outstanding 발행필 주식
shares registered in the name of depository 보관대체기관명의주식
shares sold short 신용판매
sharing costs 경비분담
sharp advance market 급등상장
sharp decline 격감
sharp decline market 급락상장
sharp drop 폭락
sharp fall 급락
sharp increase 급등
sharp loss 급반락
sharp rally 반등
sharp rise 급등
sharp setback 급반락
sharp upward revision 대폭상향수정
shelf offering 일괄모집
shelf registration 발행등록
shelf registration statement 발행신고서
shell branch 겉보기가격
shell corporation 페이퍼컴퍼니
Sherman Anti-trust Act 셔먼 반트러스트법;독점금지법
shift in interest rate 금리변동
shift to won 원시프트
shiftability theory 전가성이론
shifting of business center 영업본거이동
shifting of tax burden 조세를 전가함
shinkin bank 신용금고
ship mortgage 선박모기지
ship order 출하지도서
ship's bill 선장용 선하증권
ship's husband 선박관리인

ship's paper 선박비부서류
shipment 적송품
shipments index 출하지수
shipped quality terms 선적품질조건
shipper 적송인
shipper's usance 수출신용
shipping 해운
shipping articles 선원고용계약서
shipping charge 운송비
shipping commissioners 해사고용감독관
shipping document 선적서류
shipping expense 발송비
shipping market 해운시장
shipping marks 하인(荷印)
shipping receipts 해운수입
shipping tax 선박세
ships and vessels 선박
shogun bond 쇼군채
shogun convertible bond 쇼군 CB
shop 공장
shop act 상점법
shop cost 공장원가
shop inspection 공장검사
shopbook rule 상품부기의 법칙
shopkeepers' books 소매상인의 장부
shopping around 쇼핑어라운드
short 쇼트
short account 쇼트어카운트
short book 쇼트북
short butterfly 쇼트버터플라이
short call 쇼트콜
short coupon 쇼트쿠폰
short covering 환매결제
short covering at a loss
값을 어림짐작하여 매기다
short delivery 부족
short drawing 쇼트드로잉
short fall 단기투자이익
short form 간이형
short form audit report 단문식 감사보고서
short forward position 선물매출포지션
short hedge 매출헤지
short interest 차입주잔주; 차주잔고
short lined rally 일시적인 반등
short market 단기상장
short period 단기
short period cost 단기비용
short position 쇼트포지션
short position risk 쇼트포지션리스크
short positions
팔기로 예정하고 아직 결제하지 않은 상품
short put 쇼트풋
short rate 단기금리
short run equilibrium 단기균형
short run supply curve 단기공급곡선
short sale against the box
시세를 예상하여 매각함
short sale ratio 공매비율
short securities transaction 공매
short selling 공매
short squeeze 쇼트스퀴즈
short straddle 쇼트스트래들
short strangle 쇼트스트랭글
short strap 쇼트스트랩
short strip 쇼트스트립
short supply 공급부족
short swap 단기스와프
short swing profits 단기매매익
short term asset 단기자본
short the swap 스와프를 단기로 하다
short title 약칭
short-dated bond 단기채
short-term 단기
short-term bond 단기채
short-term borrowing 단기차입
short-term capital 단기자본
short-term capital balance 단기자본수지
short-term capital gain 단기양도소득
short-term capital transaction 단기자본거래
short-term credit market 단기금융시장
short-term debt 단기차입금
short-term debt rating 단기등급

short-term economic survey of all businesses 전국기업단기경제관측
short-term economic survey of principal enterprises 주요기업단기경제관측
short-term facility rate 단기자금레이트
short-term finance 단기금융
short-term fund 단기자금
short-term government bond 단기국채
short-term government securities 정부단기증권
short-term investment 단기투자
short-term interest rate 단기금리
short-term investment 단기투자
short-term investment account 단기투자계정
short-term liabilities 단기부채
short-term liquidity factor 단기유동성요인
short-term loan 단기대부
short-term loan payable 단기차입금
short-term loan receivable 단기대부
short-term loans 단기대부금
short-term margin 단기차입보증금
short-term money house 단자업자
short-term money market 단기금융시장
short-term note 단기채권
short-term oriented 단기지향
short-term outlook 단기예측
short-term prime rate 프라임레이트
short-tenn returns 단기투자수익
short-term securities borrowed 단기차입유가증권
short-term solvency 단기지불능력
short-term transaction 단기거래
short-term yield 단기이율
shortage 부족액
shortage in deliverable securities 상품부족
shortage of funds 자금부족
shortage of special depreciation 특별상각부족액
shortening of a prearranged period of a construction work 예정공기간축
shortening of useful life 내용연수단축
shortfall 부족
shrinkage variance 감모차이
shut for dividend 명의변경저지
sickness benefit 질병급부
sight bill 일람불환어음
sight credit 사이트크레디트
sight draft 일람불어음
sight L/C 일람불신용장
sight note 일람불약속어음
sight of a bill 어음사이트
sight rate 일람불환상장
sight selling rate 일람불상장
sight-seeing tax 관광세
sign manual 자서
sign of fragility 취약성
signature and seal 기명날인
signed and sealed 서명날인
signed check 기명식 수표
signed transfer 기명양도
significant amount 중요한 금액
significant subsidiaries 중요한 자회사
signs 징조
silence 침묵
silent base 익명참가베이스
silent participation 익명참가
silent partner 익명참가자
silver exchange 은환
silver standard 은본위제
similar goods 유사품
similar investment media 유사한 투자매체
simple accounting 단식부기
simple aggregate 단순총화
simple arbitrage 단순재정
simple arithmetic average index 단순산술평균지수
simple assault 단순폭행
simple average 단순해손;단순평균
simple average cost method 단순평균법
simple average stock price 단순평균주가
simple average yield 단순평균이율
simple confession 단순자백

simple contract 약식계약
simple cost accounting 단순종합원가계산
simple guarantor 단순보증인
simple hypothesis 단순가설
simple index 단순지수
simple interest 단리
simple journal 단순분개장
simple jump model 단순점프모델
simple listing 간이상장
simple margin 단리마진
simple mean value 단순평균치
simple moving average 단순이동평균
simple multiplier 단순승수
simple obligation 단순채무
simple prediction 단순예측
simple reserve method 단순준비법
simple tariff system 단일세율제
simple trust 단순신탁
simple yield 직접이율
simplified bookkeeping system 간이부기
simplified employee pension 간이종업원퇴직연금
simplified method of depreciation 간편상각
simplified tax system 간이과세제도
simulated 허위의
simulation 시뮬레이션
simultaneous tax audit 동시조사
Singapore inter-bank offered rate 싱가폴은행간 기준금리
Singapore International Monetary Exchange 싱가폴국제금융거래소
single account system 단회계제도
single balance sheet 단일대차대조표
single banking license 단일은행면허
single bill 채무부담날인채무증서
single bond 채무부담날인채무증서
single currency 단일통화
single customer separate account 단일고객분리계정
single employer defined benefit pension plan 단일사업주형 급부기준연금제도
single entry 단식기입
single entry bookkeeping 단식부기
Single European Act 단일유럽의정서
single exchange rate 단일환레이트
single expression 단식
single index model 단일지표모델
single market 시장통합
single maturity deposit 단일만기예금
single name 단명
single name paper 단명어음
single option 싱글옵션
single order term 일정기한지불
single pay life insurance 일시불생명보험
single payment 일괄지불
single payment annuity 일시지불
single payment loan 일회불대부
single premium 일시불보험료
single premium deferred annuities 일시불거치연금
single premium endowment insurance 일부지불양로보험
single proprietorship 개인사업주
single purpose 전용의
single step 무구분식
single step form 무단계식
single step income statement 단일구분손익계산서
single tariff 단일세율
single tax 단일세
single transaction 단일거래
single-step statement 단일구분계산서
sinking 침몰
sinking fund 감채기금
sinking fund account 감채기금계정
sinking fund method 상각기금법
sinking fund obligation 감채기금채무
sinking fund payments 감채기금편입
sinking fund preferred stock 감채기금우선주
sinking fund requirements 감채기금적립액
sinking fund reserve 감채기금적립금
sister company 자매회사

sit in camera 비공개개정
site 소재지
site audit 현장감사
site survey 실지조사
six column journal 6자리 분개장
six month closing of accounts 중간기 결산
60-year redemption rule 60년 상환룰
size effect 규모효과
skeleton form account T자형 계정
skip-day settlement 3일후 결제
skyrocketing 급상승
skyrocketing price 급상승가격
slack 완만한
slacken 느슨한; 줄인
slackness of money market 금융완만
slaughter sale 투매
sleeping account 휴면구좌
sleeping member 휴면회원
sliding cheap 슬라이딩칩
sliding tariff 슬라이드관세
slight negligence 경과실
slight tightening 가벼운 긴장
slight ups and downs 소부동
slightly firmer 작은 가게
slimmer profit margins 이익률저하
slip 전표
slip bookkeeping 전표식 부기
slip system 전표제도
slip system of accounting 전표식회계법
slope risk 경사리스크
slow 늦다
slowdown 둔화
slower growth 저성장
slowing demand 수요감소
slowing economy 경기둔화
sluggish 완만한
slumpflation 슬럼프플레이션
small 스몰(100만 달러 단위의 거래)
small and medium-sized enterprises 중소기업
small capital stock 소형주
small enterprise mutual aid plan 소규모기업공제
small gain 소폭이익
small investor 소액투자가
small loan 소액금융
small lot order 소액주문
small lot trade 소액매매
small lot trading 소액거래
small margin 소폭
small revaluation 소폭절상
small savers certificate 소액예금증권
small scale enterprises 소규모사업자
small sized business proprietor 소규모기업가
small spread 스몰스프레드
small sum and important property 소액중요자산
small sum deferred assets 소액거치자산
small sum deposit 소액예금
small sum properties 소액자산
small sums of deposits and savings 소액예저금
small sums of dividend income 소액배당소득
small sums of pension paid to old-age persons 소액노령연금
small trend 소규모트렌드
small- and medium-sized enterprise modernization activities 중소기업근대화시책
small-sized stock 소형주
smart money 현명한 투자가
Smithsonian Agreement 스미소니언합의
Smithsonian rate 스미소니언레이트
Smithsonian system 스미소니언체제
smooth absorption 원만한 소화
smooth consumption 순조로운 소비
smooth trading operation 원만한 유통
smoothing method 평활법
smoothing of income 이익이 평활화됨
smoothing operation 안정화개입
smoothing out operation 스무딩아웃오퍼레이션
smuggling 밀수

snake in the tunnel 터널 속의 뱀
soar 급등
soaring market 고등시장
social accounting 사회회계
social and entertainment expenses provided in lump sum 적정교환비
social assistance 공적부조
social assumption 사회적인 가정
social audit 사회감사
social capital 사회자본
social club 사교클럽
social consciousness 사회의식
social contract 사회계약
social contribution burden 사회보장부담
social cost 사회비용
social expenses 교제비
social indicator 사회지표
social indifference curve 사회적인 무차별곡선
social insurance 사회보험
social insurance premiums 사회보험료
social insurance premiums deduction 사회보험료공제
social insurance tax 사회보험세
social marginal cost 사회적인 한계비용
social responsibility of enterprise 기업의 사회적 책임
social security 사회보장
Social Security Act 연방사회보장법
social security benefits 사회보장급부
social security number 사회보장번호
social security recipient 사회보장급부자
social security system 사회보장제도
Social Security tax rate 사회후생함수
society 조합
Society for Worldwide International Financial Telecommunications 스위프트; SWIFT
soft currency 연화;교환불능통화
soft currency country 연화국
soft dollar 소프트달러
soft landing 소프트랜딩
soft loan 소프트론
soft market 연조(軟調)시장
sola bill 솔라빌(1통만의 수출어음)
solatium 위문금
sold bill 할인어음
sold book 상품매상장
sold-out market 물량이 적은 상장
sole agency 일수판매
sole agent 일수판매대리점
sole proprietor 개인사업주
sole proprietorship 개인기업
sole right 독점권
solicitation 권유
soliciting 모집
soliciting agent 모집기관
solid demand 견실한 수요
solidity ratio 고정비율
solvency 지불능력
solvency margin 솔벤시마진
solvency ratio 유동성 비율
solvent 지불능력이 있는
sophisticated arrangements 복잡한 거래
sophisticated market 고도의 시장
sound banking 건전한 은행업무
sound buy idea 건전한 구매테마
sound capitalisation 자기자본충실
soundness 건전성
source 출처
source and application of funds 자금의 원천과 용도
source and disposition statement 원천 및 용도계산서
source of funds 자금원
source of income 소득원천
source of revenue 재원
source of taxation 세원
sources in increase in outstanding shares 상장회사의 발행필 주식 증감상황
sovereign 주권자
sovereign act 통치행위

sovereign analyst 소브린분석가
sovereign balance sheet 국가의 밸런스시트
sovereign bank 소브린은행
sovereign ceiling 소브린실링
sovereign immunity 외국주권면제
sovereign issuer 소브린발행체
sovereign loan 소브린론
sovereign name 소브린상품
sovereign power 주권
sovereign rating 소브린비율
sovereign risk 주권리스크
sovereign state 주권국
sovereignty 주권
space arbitrage 스페이스재정
span of control 관리한계
spare plant capacity 유휴설비
special account 특별회계
special account for distribution of local allocation and shared taxes 교부세 및 양도세 배부특별회의
special account for inward portfolio investment 증권특별계정
Special Account Law of the Government Debt Consolidation Fund 국채정리기금특별회계법
special account of gains on insurance claim 보험차익특별계정
Special Accounts 특별회계
special admission fee 특별가입금
special advances rate 특별대출금리
special assessment 특별과징금
special audit 특별감사
special automobile policy 자가용자동차종합보험
special bad debts reserve 채권상각특별계정
special bank account firm 특별은행계정업자
special benefit theory of taxation 특별편익설
special bid 특별대량구매
special bills for installment sales credit 할부판매전용어음
special bond 특별채
special bracket group 스페셜브래킷그룹
special charges 특별비용
special clause 특별약관
special clearance 특별청산
special collecting agent 특별징수의무자
special collection 특별징수
special collection of inhabitants tax 주민세특별징수
special committee 특별위원회
special committee for public and corporate bond 공사채전문위원회
special conditions of the contract 특별조건서
special contingency reserve 우발손실준비금
special corporation 특수회사
special corporation surtax 법인특별세
special cost studies 특수원가조사
special credit 스페셜크레디트
special credit for acquisition of dwelling house 주택취득특별공제
special credit of corporation tax 법인세액특별공제
special crossed check 특정횡선수표
special damage 실손해
special day delivery transaction 특약일결제거래
special deduction 특별공제
special deduction for blue return 청색신고특별공제
special deduction for capital gains 양도소득특별공제
special deduction for occasional income 임시소득특별공제
Special Deficit-Financing Bond Law 특례공채법
Special Deficit-Financing Bonds 특례공채
Special Deficit for the Default Compensation Fund 위약손실보상기금특별위탁금
special deposit scheme 특별예금제도
special deposits 별단예금
special depreciation 특별상각

special depreciation method 특별한 상각방법
special depreciation reserve 특별상각준비금
special dividend 특별배당
Special Drawing Rights 특별인출권
Special Dues 특별부담금
special economic benefit 특별한 경제적 이익
special endorsement 기명식 이서
special examiner 특별국세조사관
special exchange 특별교환
special exemption for spouse 배우자특별공제
special expenses 특별비
special general meeting 임시총회
special incentive measures 촉진세제
special income tax 특별소득세
special interest party 특별이해관계자
special interests 이익집단
special intermediary institution 특별매개기관
special item 특별항목
special journal 특수분개장
special L/C 매입은행지정신용장
special landholding tax 특별토지보유세
special law 특별법
special ledger 특무원장
special lien 스페셜리엔
special loan account interest rate 특별대부계정금리
special local consumption tax 특별지방소비세
special local grant tax 특별지방교부세
special loss 특손
special margin requirement 특별증거금요건
special margin transaction 특별신용거래
Special Maruyu program (일본)특별소액저축비과세제도
special meeting of the Board of Governors 임시이사회
special member 특별회원
special membership fee 특별회의
special methods of computing depreciation 특별한 감가상각방법
special outlay 별도지출
special participant 특별참가자
special participant deposit 특별참가자 예탁금
special participant in equity options trading 주권옵션거래특별참가자
special participant in futures trading based on government bonds 국채증권선물거래특별참가자
special participant in stock price index futures trading 주가지수선물거래특별참가자
special participant participation fee 특별참가자참가금
special participants in futures trading and the like 선물거래 등의 특별참가자
special payment 특별결제
special product firm 전문상품취급업자
special production order 특정제조지도서
special profit and loss 특별손익
special purpose company 특별목적회사
special purpose financial statement 특정목적재무제표
special purpose financial statements 개별목적재무제표
special purpose tax 목적세
special purpose trust 특별목적트러스트
special quotation 특별청산지수
special rate 특별요율
special repair expenses 특별수선비
special reserve 특별적립금
special resolution 특별결의
special revenue officer 특별국세징수관
special risks 특별위험
special rule 특례
Special Rule for Brokerage Agreement Standards 수탁계약준칙특례
special rule of the business regulations 업무규정특례
special rule relating to margin 증거금특례
special surplus fund 특별적립잉여금
special tax bond 특별목적세채권

special tax preferences 우대세제
special tax reduction bond 특별감세국채
special tax treatment for property replacement 매환특례
special taxation measures 조세특별조치
Special Taxation Measures Law 조세특별조치법
special tonnage due 특별톤세
special trades trading 과오정정입회외 거래
special trading accounts 특정거래계정
special trading income or loss 특정거래손익
special treatment 특례
special valuation method 특별한 평가법
special ward 특별구
special ward inhabitants tax 특별구민세
special won 특별원
specialist 스페셜리스트
specialist block purchases 특별대행구매
specialist book 스페셜리스트북
specialist insurer 개인보험자
specialization 전문화;특화
specialized foreign exchange bank 외국환전문은행
specialized fund 특정전문투자신탁
specialty goods 전문품
specie money 정화
specie points 금의 현송점
specie reserve 정화준비(正貨準備)
specific bonds 특수채
specific charge 특정담보
specific consumption tax 개별소비세
specific cost 개별원가
specific duty 종량세
specific performance 특정이행
specific productive factors 특수생산요소이론
specific property tax 개별재산세
specific reinsurance 개별재보험
specific risk 고유리스크
specific storage 종량보관료
specific tariff 종량세율
specific tax 종량세
specific-order cost system 개별원가계산제도
specification 명세서;시방서
specification cost 시방서원가
specified assets 특정자산
specified benefit 확정급부
specified current account 특정당좌예금
specified day transaction 특정거래
specified disease insurance 특정질병보장보험
specified donation 특정기부금
specified interest 특정이자
specified investment in kind 특정현물출자
specified medical corporation 특정의료법인
specified money in trust 특정금전신탁
specified pool trade 풀특정거래
specified portion 지정상속분
specified stock 특정주
specimen of stock certificate 주권견본
specimen of certificates of the security 유가증권견본
specter 스펙터
spectral analysis 스펙터 분석
speculating for difference 차금거래
speculation 투기
speculation for difference 가격차액으로 이익을 얻음
speculation for margin 차금거래
speculation in stocks 주식투기
speculation transaction 투기거래
speculative buyers 투기꾼
speculative buying 투기구매; 매점매석
speculative dealing 투기전
speculative demand 가수요
speculative enthusiasm 투기열
speculative fund 트기자금
speculative gain 투기이윤
speculative grade 투기적인 등급
speculative grade bond 투기적인 채권
speculative import 가수입
speculative market 투기시장
speculative money 투기자금
speculative motive 투기동기

speculative name 구입상품
speculative risk 투기리스크
speculative stock 투기주
speculative transaction 투기거래
speculator buying 투기구입
speculators 투기자
speed resistance line 스피드레지스턴스라인
speedy trial 신속한 재판
spending 지출
spending cut 예산삭감
spending increase 지출증대
spending program 재정지출계획
spending spree 산포
spending variance 예산차이
spendthrift trust 낭비자신탁
spike 감당할 수가 없는
spillover effect 유출효과
spin-off 스핀오프
split 스풀릿
split ledger account 분할원장계정
split order 대량주문을 소량집행함
split rating 다른 비율
split sale 분할판매
split taxation 이분이승법
split-funding 분할각출
split-ups of stocks 주식분할
splining a cause of action 청구원인분할
spoilage expenses 손상품비
spoiled goods 손상품
sponsor selectivity 스폰서의 선택력
sponsor tolerance to risk 스폰서의 리스크 허용도
sponsor's role 스폰서의 역할
sponsored research 위탁연구
sponsoring member 간사회의
sponsoring securities firm 간사증권회사
spontaneous combustion 자연발화
sporadic buying 도발적인 구매
sports gambling 스포츠도박
spot 직물
spot dealing 직물거래
spot delivery 현물인도
spot exchange 현물환
spot exchange rate 현물상장; 직물환상장
spot forward 스폿포워드
spot fund 스폿펀드
spot market 현물시장
spot next 스폿넥스트
spot operation 직물거래
spot period 스폿기간
spot position 직물위치
spot price 현물가격
spot quotation 현물상장
spot rate 현물상장
spot sale 즉매
spot share 현주
spot trading 직물거래
spot transaction 직물거래
spot value 현물가격
spot yield 스폿금리
spot-forward spread 직물선물스프레드
spouse tax credit 배우자공제
spread 스프레드
spread account 스프레드계정
spread banking 스프레드뱅킹
spread between spot rate and futures rate 직물상장과 선물상장의 가격차
spread curves 스프레드곡선
spread income 스프레드수입
spread loan 스프레드론
spread lock agreement 스프레드록계약
spread toss reinsurance 초과손해재보험
spread position 스프레드포지션
spread risk 스프레드리스크
spread sheet 스프레드시트
spread trading 스프레드트레이딩
spread trading between contract months 한정개월간 스프레드거래
spread transaction 스프레드거래
spurt 급증
square 스퀘어
square matrix 정방행렬

square position 스퀘어포지션
squeeze 압박
stability 안정성
stability analysis 안정성분석
stability condition 안정조건
stability of the foreign exchange market 환수급안정성
stabilization operation 안정조작
stabilization policy 안정화 정책
stabilizing 안정촉진적인
stabilizing transaction 안정조작
stable dividend 안정배당
stable dollar assumption 화폐가치일정공준
stable economic growth 안정경제성장
stable money principle 안정화폐론
stable stock 안정주
stable stockholder 안정주주
stable stockholder operation 주주안정공작
stagflation 스태그플레이션
staggering maturity 만기분산
stagnant industry 정체산업
stagnant market 저속상장
stable B/L 시기경과선하증권
stale check 연체수표
stamp 인지
stamp duty 인지세
stamp duty law 수입인지세법
stamp revenue 인지수입
stamp tax 인지세
stand alone investment 단순한 투자대상
stand in debt 채무가 있는
stand-by agreement 스탠드바이약정
stand-by credit 스탠드바이신용장
stand-by underwriting 잔액인수발행
Standard & Poor's 스탠다드앤드푸어스
Standard & Poor's 400 Industrial 스탠다드앤드푸어스 400종 공업주가지수
Standard & Poor's 500 스탠다드앤드푸어스 500종
Standard & Poor's 500 index 스탠다드앤드푸어스 500종 주가지수
Standard & Poor's Composite Index 스탠다드앤드푸어스종합지수
Standard & Poor's Stock Price Index 스탠다드앤드푸어스주가지수
standard amount of clearing margin 거래증거금 기준액
standard basket 표준바스켓방식
standard burden rate 표준배부율
standard clause 표준약관
standard commission 표준수수료
standard correlation 표준상관계수
standard cost 표준원가
standard cost accounting 표준원가계산
standard cross default provision 표준크로스디폴트조항
standard currency basket system 표준바스켓방식
standard date 표준일
standard deduction 개산공제
standard depletion expenses 표준손료
standard deviation of volatility 변동율표준오차
standard documentation 표준서식
standard error 표준오차
standard error of beta 베터표준오차
standard error of estimate 추정치표준오차
standard industrial classification 표준산업분류
standard interest rate 표준금리
standard issue 표준상품
standard labor cost 표준노무비
standard machine time 표준기계시간
standard manufacturing expense 표준제조간접비
standard material cost 표준재료비
standard money 본위화폐
standard of price 도량표준
standard of price for margin calculation 증거금기준액
standard profit 표준이익
standard quantity of materials consumed

재료표준소비량
standard rate 기준요금
standard rate of charge 징수표준율
standard silver dollar 표준은달러
standard stocks 표준주
standard system 본위제도
standard tax rate 표준세율
Standard Valuation Law 표준책임준비금평가법
standard values 표준치
standard values for clearing margin rate calculation 거래증거금율산정기준치
standard wage 기준임금
standard-cost system 표준원가계산제도
standard-run quantity 표준생산량
standardization 표준화
standardized bonds 표준물
standardized financial statements 표준재무제표
standardized volatility 표준화 볼라틸리티
standards 기준
standards of audit procedures 감사절차기준
standby agreement 잔액인수;스탠드바이인수
standby arrangement 차입예약
standby credit 스탠드바이크레디트;스탠드바이신용장
standby facilities 스탠드바이퍼실리티
standing auditor 상임감사역
standing body 상설기관
standing charge 항상비용
standing committee 상설위원회
standing cost 항상단가
standing expenses 고정비
standing governor 상임이사
standing order 계속주문
standing production order 계속제도명령서
standing proxy 상임대리인
standstill 스탠드스틸
standstill provision 스탠드스틸조항
star system 스타시스템
starting-load cost 당초부담원가
state and local government debt 공채
state bank 주법은행
state bankruptcy 국가파산
state bond 주채
state branching 주내지점설치
state capital 국가자본
state capitalism 국가자본주의
state enterprises 국영사업
state franchise tax 주법인세
state government bond 주정부채권
state government bond and debenture 주정부채권
state government securities 주정부증권
state guaranteed debt 정부보증채
state income tax 주소득세
state insurance department 주보험국
state law 주법
state monopoly payment 전매납부금
state of observance 준수상황
state of the union message 일반교서
State Redress Law 국가배상법
state-chartered association 주면허조직
state-owned company 국유기업
stated capital 확정자본금
stated interest rate 약정이율
stated liabilities 표시부채
stated value 장부기재가격
stated value no-par stock 기재식 무액면주식
statement 계산서
statement classified by account title 계정과목내역명세서
statement form 보고식
statement of account 결산보고
Statement of Accounting Standard 회계기준서
statement of assets 재산목록
statement of assets and liabilities 자산과 부채계산서
statement of capital surplus 자본여잉금계산서
statement of cash flow 자금수지표

statement of cash receipts and disbursement 자금조표
statement of changes in financial position 재정상태변동표
statement of changes in stockholders' equity 자본계정보고서
statement of declaration 선언서
statement of disagreement 보복신청
statement of earned surplus 이익잉여금계산금
statement of estimated application of fund 견적자금운용표
statement of facts 합의사실기재서
statement of financial condition 재정상태계산서;대차대조표
statement of financial position 대차대조표
statement of income and expense 수지일람표
statement of income and retained earnings 잉여금결합계산서
statement of intent 고지서
statement of items 내역서
statement of liquidations 청산서
statement of loss 손익계산서(순손실의 경우)
statement of net assets 순자산계산서
statement of notification of the specified issuance of securities 유가증권통지서
statement of operation earnings 경상이익계산서
statement of position on the tender offer 공개구매의견표명보고서
statement of principles 기본방침
statement of production cost 제조원가보고서
statement of realization and liquidation 처분청산계산서
statement of receipts and disbursement 수지계산서
statement of retained earnings 이익여잉금계산서
statement of settlement of accounts 수지결산서
statement of source and application of funds 자금운용표
statement of source and uses of funds 자금운용표
statement of stockholders' equity 주주지분계산서
statement of stockholders' net worth 주주지분계산서
statement of surplus 잉여금계산서
statement of withdrawal 취소신고서
statement of withdrawal of shelf registration 발행등록취소신고서
statement on auditing procedures 감사절차서
Statements on Auditing Standards 감사기준서
static analysis 정태분석
static equilibrium 정적균형
static model 정학모델
static multiplier 정학승수
static ratio 정태비율
static risk 정태리스크
static statistics 정태통계
stating part 주요부분
stationary state 정상상태
statistical analysis 통계분석
statistical decision theory 통계가정이론
statistical error 통계오차
statistical measure 통계척도
statistical model 통계모델
statistical procedure 통계처리
statistical terminology 통계용어
statistical theory 통계이론
statistics 통계학
Statistics Bureau of the Management and Coordination Agency 총무청 통계과
statistics of foreign currency reserves 외화준비통계
statistics on international balance of payment 국제수지통계
statistics on money supply 머니서플라이분석
statistics on money supply analysis

머니서플라이분석통계
statistics on national income 국민소득통계
status law 제정법
status of limitation 시효
status of limitation on collection 징수권소멸시효
status of limitation on refund claim 환부청구권시효
statutory 법령에 의한
statutory accounting principle 법정회계원칙
statutory assignment 제정법상의 양도
statutory audit 법정감사
statutory debt limit 법정발행한도액
statutory depletion method 법정감모상각법
statutory depreciation 법정상각
statutory depreciation method 법정상각방법
statutory due date of tax payment 법정납기한
statutory due date of tax return 법정신고기한
statutory merger 강제합병
statutory rate of interest 법정이율
statutory reserve 법정준비금
statutory tariff 법정세율
statutory useful life 법정내용연수
statutory valuation method 법정평가방법
statutory valuation method of securities 유가증권법정평가법
stay of proceedings 소송중지
steady 견고
steady market 견고한 시황
steady rise 착실한 신장
steady sales 순조로운 매상
step ladder payment method 스텝상환
step-down bond 스텝다운채
step-up bond 스텝업채
step-up coupon 스텝업쿠폰
step-up swap 스텝업스와프
stepped cost 단계원가
stepped coupon bond 단계이부채
sterling balance 펀드잔고
sterling currency futures 펀드통화선물
sterling exchange standard 본드환본위제
sterling floaters 펀드기준변동이부채
sterling swap rate 펀드스와프레이트
stiffen 경화시키다;완고하게 하다
stimulative fiscal policy 경기자극형 재정정책
stimulus package 자극책
stipulated damages 약정손해배상액
stipulated price 협정가격
stipulated security 약정담보권
stipulation 조항
stochastic 확률적인
stochastic calculus 확률해석
stochastic model 확률모델
stochastic process 확률프로세스
stochastic sequence 확률계열
stochastic simulation 확률시뮬레이션
stock abbreviation 주식약어
stock account 자본계정
stock acquired by borrowed money 차입금으로 취득한 주식
stock acquired by capital increase 증자로 취득한 주식
stock acquired by merger 합병으로 취득한 주식
stock acquired by the investment in kind 현물출자취득주
stock acquisition 주식매수; 주식구입에 의한 매수; 주식취득
stock adjustment 스톡조정
stock allotted to third persons 제3자 할당주
stock arbitrage 주식제정거래
stock at par 액면주
stock authorized 수권자본
stock bonus plan 스톡보너스플랜
stock book 재고품대장; 주식대장
stock broker 주식중매인
stock buy-back 주식환매
stock certificate 주권
stock certificate to bearer 무기명주권
stock clearing corporation 대체결제회사

stock collateral loan 주식담보금융
stock compensation plan 주식보상제도
stock consolidation 주식병합
stock controlling other business 기업지배주식
stock cum rights 증자권리부 주식
stock dealing 주식거래
stock dividend 주식배당
stock equity 주주지분
stock equity value 주식지분가치
stock exchange 주식거래소
Stock Exchange Automated Quotation 런던증권거래소시황정보시스템
stock exchange clearing house 주식청산소
stock exchange daily official list 주식거래소공보
stock exchange holiday 주식거래소휴일
stock exchange loan 주식거래소대부
stock exchange panic 주식공황
stock exchange seat 주식거래소회원권
stock exchange share 당소주(當所株)
stock exchange transaction 거래소거래
stock flow 스톡플로
stock for guarantee 보증주
stock for inflation hedging 인플레헤지주
stock for margin trading 신용거래주
stock for which listing application is made 상장신고에 관계된 주식
stock funding 주식자금조달
stock futures 주시선물
stock futures transaction 주식선물거래
stock holding ratio of foreigners 외국인지주비율
stock in hand 현재품
stock ill the inventory 재고품
stock in trade 재고품
stock inflation 스톡인플레이션
stock investment 주식투자
stock investment in subsidiary 자회사주식투자
stock investment trust 주식투자신탁
stock issue at market price 시가발행주식
stock issuing expenses 주식발행비용
stock ledger 주식대장
stock lending 증권임차
stock level 소지재고수준
stock listing agreement 상장계약자
stock loan market 대주시장
stock market 주식시장
stock market crash 주식공황
stock market fluctuation 주식시장의 변동
stock mind 스톡마인드
stock mini-investment 주식미니투자
stock name 주식명
stock name transfer expense 명의변경비
stock of affiliated company 관계회사주식
stock on hand 소지주
stock option 주식매입선택권; 스톡옵션
stock option plan 주식구입선택권
stock option type warrant 스톡옵션형 워런트
stock portfolio 주식편입상황
stock power 주권양도위임장
stock premium 주식발행차금
stock price 주가
stock price analysis 주가분석
stock price average 평균주가
stock price average by size of stocks 규모별 주식평균
stock price index 주가지수
stock price index arbitrage transaction 주가지수재정거래
stock price index by size of stocks 규모별 주가지수
stock price index call option 주가지수콜옵션
stock price index futures 주가지수선물
stock price index futures by industry 업종별 주가지수선물거래
stock price index futures contract 주가지수선물계약
stock price index futures trading 주가지수선물거래
stock price index on the market value

시가총액방식주가지수
stock price index put option 주가지수풋옵션
stock price manipulation 주가조작
stock purchase option 주식매입옵션
stock purchase plan 주식구입계획
stock purchase right 신주인수권
stock purchase warrant 신주인수권
stock quotations 주가정보
stock rating 주식비율
stock receipt 주권양도증
stock recommended for purchase
권장주; 추천주
stock redemption 주식상환
stock register 주식원장
stock repurchase plan 주식환매계획
stock right 증자신주매수권
stock risk estimation 주식리스크추정
stock speculation 주식투기
stock split-up 주식분해
stock subscription 주식응모
stock swap 주식스와프
stock symbol 주식심볼
stock taking 실제재고
stock trading transaction loss reserve
주식매매손실준비금
stock trust 주식투신
stock turnover 재고회전율
stock turnover tax 유가증권거래세
stock used in the average 평균주가채용주
stock valuation 주식평가
stock valuation based on dividend
배당환원주식평가
stock valuation summary 주식평가개요
stock warrants 스톡워런트
stock with par value 액면주식
stock without par value 무액면주식
stock yield 주식이율
stock-to-sales ratio 재고율
stockholder 주주
stockholder's equity 주주지분
stockholder's right 주주권
stockholder's equity 주주자본
stockholder's equity per share
일주당 주주자본
stockholder's meeting 주주총회
stockholding limit for foreign investors
외국인지주제한
stockpile financing 체화금융
stolen bill 도난어음
stolen check 도난수표
stop limit order 가격폭주문
stop loss buy order 역지정가격구매주문
stop loss coverage 초과손해보험
stop loss order 손절주문
stop loss reinsurance 초과손해재보험
stop order 공탁금 지불금지명령;지정가격주문
stop payment order 지불정지통지
stop-and-go policy 스톱앤드고정책
stop-high 스톱고
stop-limit order 역지정가격주문
stop-loss order 스톱로스주문
stop-loss trading 스톱로스트레이딩
stop-out price of T-bond T-본드입찰최저가
stop-payment order 지불정지통지
stoppage of business 영업정지
storage accounts receivable 미수보관료
storage charges 보관비
storage costs 저장경비
storage management 저장품관리
storage of inventories 재고자산보관
store business interruption insurance
점포휴업보험
store of value 가치보장수단
stored goods 저장품
storekeepers' comprehensive insurance
점포종합보험
stores ledger 원재료원장
stores purchase book 재료구입장
straddle 스트래들
straddle position transaction
스트래들포지션거래
straddle trading 스트래들거래

straight average cost method 단순평균법
straight B/L 기명식 선하증권
straight bankruptcy 단순파산
straight bond 보통사채
straight cash vehicles 현물상품
straight climb 수직상승
straight corporate bond 보통사채
straight credit 매입불능신용장
straight currency swap 스트레이트커런시스와프
straight debt 보통차입채무
straight equity 보통주
straight fall 시세가 폭락함
straight government bond 보통국채
straight life annuity 종신연금
straight line amortization 정액상각법
straight line method 직선법
straight-line depreciation 정액감가상각법
Straits Times Industrial Index 스트레이트타임즈공업주가지수
strangle 스트랭글
strangle position transaction 스트랭글포지션거래
strap 스트랩
strategic alliance 전략적인 제휴
strategic decision 전략적인 의사결정
strategic field 전략분야
strategic industries 전략산업
strategic partner 전략적인 파트너
strategic risk 전략리스크
strategy 전략
stratified 층별의
straw bail 공보증인
straw man 거짓증자
street 금융가
street broker 장외중매인
Street economist 시장분석가
street name 명의
street price 입회후 상장
strengthen 해결하다
strengthening 정리;해결
strengthening of managerial function 관리기능강화
strict construction 엄격해석
strict foreclosure 대물변제담보물을 취득함
strike price 권리행사가격
strike rate 행사금리
stringent policy 긴축정책
strip 스트립
strip bond 스트립채
strip curve 스트립커브
strip guarantee 스트립보증
strip player 스트립플레이어
strip spread 스트립스프레드
strip yield 스트립일드
stripped cap 스트립캡
stripped interest rate cap 스트립금리캡
stripped issue 스트립상품
stripped zero-coupon 스트립제로쿠폰
strips 스트립채
strong and weak 강약
strong feeling 강한 느낌
strong form 스트롱폼
strong growth 강한 성장
strong incentive 호재료
strong market 강세시황
strong sentiment 강한 느낌
strong tone 시세가 오를 듯한 기세
strong won 원고
structural 구조적인
structural adjustment 구조조정
structural adjustment facility 구조조정융자
structural analysis 구조분석
structural change 구조변화
structural choice 구조선택
structural equation 구조방정식
structural impediments initiative talks 구조협의
structural inflation 구조적인 인플레이션
structural liquidity 구조적인 유동성
structural outline 구도
structural reform 구조개혁

structural risk 구조리스크
structural unemployment 구조적인 실업
structure 구축물
structure of interest rates 금리구조
structure of the government bond futures market 국채선물시장구조
structured arbitrage 구조재정거래
structured equity product 주식구조상품
structured finance 구조화 금융
structured finance market 구조화 금융시장
structured securities 구조화 증권
structured trade 구조화 거래
structured transaction 구조화 거래
student comprehensive insurance 학생종합보험
sub-LIBOR LIBOR 이하
sub-par bond 언더파채권
sub-prime 서브프라임
sub-underwriter 하인수업자
subcontract 하청
subcontract factory 하청공장
subcontractor 하청업자
subduct 제거하다
subdued economic growth 경기혼미
subject 과목
subject market 서브젝트마켓
subject of futures trading 선물거래대상
subject-matter of insurance 보험의 목적
subjective judgment 주관적인 판단
subjective probability 주관적인 확률
sublease 부동산전대차
subordinate ledger 보조원장
subordinate tranche 열후트란시
subordinated 예속의
subordinated bond 하위사채
subordinated capital 여후자본
subordinated claims 열후청구권
subordinated clause 열후조항
subordinated creditor 하위채권자
subordinated debenture 하위사채
subordinated debt 하위채권
subordinated debt market 열후채시장
subordinated deposit 열후예탁금
subordinated discount bond 열후할인채
subordinated funding 열후자금조달
subordinated interest 열후지분
subordinated loan 열후론
subordinated payment-in-kind bond 하위페이먼트인카인드채
subordinated securities 열후증권
subordinated stock 하위주
subordinated unsecured debenture 하위성 무담보사채
subordination 후순위
subrogated performance 대위변제
subrogated right 대위채무
subrogation 대위
subrogation arising out of salvage 잔존물대위
subrogation payment 대위납부
subrogation receipt 대위영수서
subrogation right of obligee 채권자대위권
subscribed capital stock 미불입자본
subscriber's yield 응모자이율
subscription 응모
subscription agent 모집대리인
subscription agreement 모집계약
subscription blank 주식신청서
subscription book closed 주식모집마감
subscription book open 주식모집개시
subscription by Bank of Japan 일본은행응모
subscription by the Trust Fund Bureau 자금운용부 인수
subscription certificate 출자증권
subscription for shares 주식응모
subscription for stock 주식인수
subscription money 신청금
subscription of bonds by non-government funds 시중소화국채
subscription period 판매기간
subscription price 응모가격
subscription rights 신주인수권

subscription warrant 신주인수권증서
subscription/contribution government bond 출자/거출국채
subscription's receivable account 주식인수계정
subsequent events 후발사상
subsequent measurements 사후측정
subsequent review 후발사상리뷰
subsequent taxable year 다음사업연도
subsidiary 자회사
subsidiary accounts 보조원장계정
subsidiary book 보조장부
subsidiary coin 보조화폐
subsidiary department 보조부문
subsidiary journal 보조기입장
subsidiary ledger 보조원장
subsidiary material cost 보조재료비
subsidiary money 보조화폐
subsidies from the government or local public entities 국가나 지방공공단체의 보조금
subsidized export 보조금을 받는 수출
subsidy 보조금
subsidy charged to the special account 특별계정에 산입된 보조금
subsidy government bond 교부국채
substance 본질
substance over form 실질우선
substandard loan 회수에 문제가 있는 대부
substantial evidence 실질적인 증거
substantial performance 실질이행
substantial shareholding report 대량보유보고서
substantive 실질적인
substantive evidence 실질증거
substantive law 실체법
substantive test 실질성 검사
substitute 대용물
substitute assets 대체자산
substitute certificate for government bond 국채대용증서
substitute fixed assets 대체고정자산
substitute member representative 임시회원대표
substitute property 대체자산
substitute representative 대표자대리인
substitute securities 대용유가증권
substituted expenses 대체비용
substitution 대체
substitution account of IMF IMF 대체계정
substitution effect 대체효과
substitution of land lot 환지처분
substitution swap 대체스와프
subtraction 공제
subzero growth 마이너스성장
succession 승계
succession of book value in the case of merger 합병시의 장부가격으로 인수함
succession of endorsement 이서연속
succession of liabilities 채무인계
succession of national tax liability 국세채무승계
succession of property 유산상속
succession of right of taxation 과세권승계
succession of tax liability 납세의무계승
succession of tax obligation 납부의무계승
successive inheritance 상차상속
successor 후계자
successor of the deceased 사망자의 상속인
suction to cash 현금에 부착함
sue and labor charges 손해방지비용
sue and labor clause 손해방지조항
sue out 신청하여 취득하다
sufficiency 충족
sufficient solvency to settle the credit in full 채권을 지불할 수 있을 만한 능력
suggested resale price 권장재판매가격
suitor 소송인
sum insured 보험금액
sum insured left 잔존보험금액
sum payable at death 사망보험금
sum total 합계

sum-of-the-years-digits method 산술급수법
summary 종합계정; 요약
summary account 집계계정
summary budget 총괄예산
summary journal 종합분개장
summary measure 집약척도
summary of earnings 영업성적
summary of statistics 총괄표
summary posting 합계전기
summary procedure 감독절차
summary proceedings 약식소송절차
summary sheet 집계표
summary statement of business 사업개황설명서
summer time 서머타임
summing-up 증거요약
summons 호출장
sums insured method 보험금액비례주의
sundries 잡비
sundry account 잡계정
sundry expenses 제잡비
sundry goods 잡화
sundry income 잡수입
sundry receipts 잡수입
sundry supplies 소모품
sunk cost 회수불능원가
super 301 Article 슈퍼 301조
super floater swap 플로터스와프
super gold tranche 슈퍼골드트란시
super long-run 초장기
super majority provision 슈퍼메이저터리조항
super NOW account 슈퍼나우계정
super prime rate 슈퍼프라임레이트
super-long government bonds 초장기국채
Superannuation Plan 재직사망보험부 퇴직금적립제도
superannuation reserve 퇴직금적립금
supercargo 화물관리인
superior courts 상급법원
superior obligation 재단채권
supernational organisations 국제기관
supersede 대체하다
supertax 부가세
supervision 감리
supervision and order 감리명령
supervisor 슈퍼바이저
supplemental 보충의
supplemental policies 보완보험
supplementary budget 보정예산
supplementary cost 간접원가;보충비용
supplementary document 추보서류
Supplementary Documents to the Shelf Registration Statement 발행등록추보서류
supplementary financial measure 보충융자
supplementary income statement information 손익계산서의 보충자료
supplementary insurance 보조보험
supplementary proceedings 보충절차
supplementary prospectus 보충계획서
supplementary provision 부칙
supplementary rate 보충률
supplementary special deposits scheme 추가특별예금제도
supplementary statement 부속명세서
supplier's credit 연불신용
supplies account 소모품계정
supplies expenses 소모품비
supply 지급
supply and demand 수급
supply arrangements 공급계약
supply capacity 공급능력
supply curve 공급곡선
supply function 공급함수
supply of credit 신용공급
supply of investible funds 자금공급
supply price 공급가격
supply source 공급원
supply-side economics 서플라이사이드경제학
support level 지지선
support line 하치지시선
support operation 급격한 시세변동을 막음
support price 유지가격

support tranche 서포트트란시
support trust 부조신탁
supporter 부양자
supporting documents 부속서류
supporting order 매매유지주문
suppression of deposition 공술녹취서금지
supranational agencies 국제기관
supreme advisor 최고고문
Supreme Court 최고법원
supreme law of the land 국가의 최고법규
surcharge 가중세;과징금
surety 보증인
surety bond 보증증권
surety money 보증채무
surety obligation 구상권
suretyship 보증
surface right 지상권
surgical expense insurance 수술비보험
surplus 잉여금
surplus account 잉여금계정
surplus adjustment 잉여금수정
surplus analysis 잉여금분석
surplus appropriated for redemption fund 채무상환적립금
surplus appropriation statement 잉여금처분계산서
surplus at liquidation 청산잉여금
surplus at the beginning of the period 전기이월이익잉여금
surplus at the opening of the period 기초잉여금잔고
surplus available for dividend 배당가능이익
surplus brought forward from the previous term 전기이월이익금
surplus capacity 생산여력
surplus charge 잉여금부과
surplus country 흑자국
surplus equipment 유휴설비
surplus finance 흑자재정
surplus from capital reduction 감자잉여금
surplus from consolidation 연결잉여금
surplus from merged company 합병차익
surplus from revaluation 재평가잉여금
surplus funds 잉여금
surplus insurance 잉여인슈런스
surplus profit 잉여익금
surplus profit carried forward to the following term 차기이월이익금
surplus reserves 잉여적립금
surplus reserves transferred to income 적립금 반려
surplus section 잉여금구분
surplus transaction 잉여금거래
surplus treaty reinsurance 초과액특약재보험
surplus value 잉여가치
surprises in earnings 예상외의 이익변동
surrender 권리방기
surrender of bill 어음인도
surrender ratio 해약률
surrender value 해약반려금
surtax 과징금
surtax on land tax 지조부가세
surtax on national tax 국세부가세
surveillance 감시
survey data 조사데이터
survey fee 감정료
survey of households 가계조사
survey report 감정보고서
surveying 측량
surveyor 사정인
survival bond 서바이벌본드
survival function 서바이벌함수
surviving company 존속회사
surviving entity 존속실체
survivor 's annuity 유족연금
survivorship 생존자에 대한 권리의 귀속
sushi bond 스시본드
suspended trading 매매정지
suspense account 미결계정
suspense payment 가불금
suspense payment account 가불금계정
suspense receipts 가수금

suspense receipts account 가수금계정
suspension 정지
suspension from bank account 은행거래정지
suspension of banking transaction 은행거래정지처분
suspension of business 사업중지
suspension of business activity 영업활동정지
suspension of convertibility 교환성정지
suspension of execution 집행정지
suspension of payment 지불정지
suspension of prescription 정지시효
suspension of qualification for trade 거래자격정지
suspension of right 권리정지
suspension of seizure 차압유예
suspension of statute of limitations 시효정지
suspension of trading 거래정지
suspension of transactions 입회정지
suspension of work claims 중단클레임
suspicion 혐의
sustain 유지하다
sustainable development 지속가능한 개발
sustainable equilibrium exchange rate 유지가능한 균형상장
sustainable growth rate 지속성장률
sustained economic expansion 지속적인 경제성장
sustenance 생계
swap 스와프
swap agreement 스와프협정
swap arrangement 스와프협정
swap bid rate 스와프비드레이트
swap bond 스와프채
swap broker 스와프브로커
swap cost 스와프코스트
swap coupon 스와프쿠폰
swap deal 스와프거래
swap margin 스와프마진
swap of bond 채권스와프
swap offer rate 스와프오퍼레이트
swap portfolio 스와프포트폴리오
swap price 스와프가격
swap profit 스와프이익
swap rate 스와프레이트
swap rate basement 스와프레이트의 최저권
swap spread 스와프스프레드
swap spread curve 스와프스프레드커브
swap strike 스와프스트라이크
swap trading 스와프거래
swap transaction 스와프거래
swaps clearing system 스와프결제시스템
swaption 스왑션
sweep account 스윕어카운트
sweetener 조미료
SWIFT 국제은행간 데이터통신시스템
swing 스윙
swing facilities 스윙퍼실리티
swing line 신용공여화
swing loan 스윙론
Swiss franc note 스위스프랑기준채
switch 환승
switch finance 스위치금융
switch from won to dollars 원달러시프트
switch reversal 역입체
switch-back option 스위치백옵션
Sydney Futures Exchange 시드니선물거래소
symbol system of accounts 계정기호법
symbolic delivery 상징적인 인도
symmetrical distribution 대칭분포
symmetrical triangle 대칭트라이앵글
symmetrical triangle pattern 대칭트라이앵글
syndicate 인수단
syndicate composition 신디케이트구성
syndicate manager 신디케이트간사
syndicate of banks 은행단
syndicate underwriting 신디케이트인수
syndicated credit 신디케이트론
syndicated loan 협조융자;신디케이트론
syndicated term loan 중장기협조융자
syndication 신디케이트단
synergy 상승
synergy effect 상승효과

synopsis sheet 개요시트
synthesis 합성
synthesis tax rate 종합세율
synthetic asset 합성어셋
synthetic assets 합성자산
synthetic bond 신세틱채권
synthetic cash arbitrage transaction 합성현물재정거래
synthetic cash instrument 신세틱캐시
synthetic currency 합성통화
synthetic floating rate 합성변동금리
synthetic index fund 합성지수펀드
synthetic instrument 복합상품
synthetic long 신세틱론
synthetic portfolio 합성포트폴리오
synthetic position 합성포지션
synthetic put 신세틱풋
synthetic securitization 신세틱 세큐리티제이션
synthetic short 신세틱쇼트
synthetic swap 합성스와프
system approach 시스템어프로치
system audit 시스템
system bid and offer 시스템호가
system engineering 시스템공학
system for purchase of foreign exchange bills 외국환어음매수제도
system for sale of bills drawn by the Bank of Japan 일본은행매출어음제도
system issue 시스템문제
system of accounts 회계조직
system of fixed rate of exchange 고정상장제
system of interest rates 이자율체계
System of National Account 국민경제계산체계
system of note issue 발권제도
system of taxation 조세체계
system repos 시스템레포
system risk 시스템리스크
systematic risk 시스티매틱리스크

T

T form account T자형 계정
T+3 4영업일 인도
T+7 8영업일 인도
T-account method T형 계정
T-Bond Futures T-Bond 선물거래
T-bond futures option T-Bond 선물옵션
T-note 재무부 중기증권
table 계산표
table of price factors 환산계수테이블
table of random numbers 난수표
table of the present value 현재가격표
tabular cash book 다행식 현금출납장
tabular ledger 표식원장
tabular standard 계산본위
tabulating machine 회계기
tacit 묵시의
tacit contract 묵계
tactical asset allocation 전술적인 자산배분
tail 테일
tail hedge 테일헤지
tailgating 상승
tailor made 특주의
tailored swap transactions 특수구조스와프
take out 차액수입
take-home pay 세금공제급여
take-or-pay contract 산출물인수 혹은 지불계약
takedown 인출
takeout loan 테이크아웃론
takeover 매입
takeover bid 주식공개매입
takeover boom 매수붐
taking a bath 투기전에서 손해를 봄
taking a flier 투기행위
talk down 구두개입(하락)
talk up 구두개입(상승)
tally 조합
tally man 검수인
tandem currencies 탠덤통화
tangible assets 유형자산
tangible depreciable property 유형상각자산
tangible fixed assets 유형고정자산
tangible property 유형고정자산
tangible value 유형자산가치
tap bills 탭빌
tap issue 탭발행
tap stock 탭채
tapping of resources 자원개발
target assets value 대상자산가액
target company 대상회사
target cost 목표원가
target income 목표이익
target issue 타겟발행
target level 유도목표
target payout ratio 목표배당성향
target portfolio 목표포트폴리오
target price 목표가격
target profit 목표이익
target range 목표변동폭
target return 타겟리턴
target risk 거대위험
target securities 대상상품

target stock 대상주식
target yield 목표이율
target zone 타겟존; 목표상장권
target zone of exchage rate 목표환상장
tariff 관세
tariff autonomy 관세자주권
tariff barrier 관세장벽
tariff by agreement 협정요율
tariff commission 세율위원회
tariff cuts 관세인하
tariff escalation 경사관세
tariff in jeopardy 긴급관세
tariff negotiations 관세교섭
tariff quota 관세할당
tariff quota system 관세할당제도
tariff rate 관세율
tariff union 관세동맹
tariff wall 관세장벽
tariff war 관세전쟁
task 사업
tax 조세
tax absorption 조세흡수
tax absorption credit 원천과세부담방식
tax accountant 조세계정
tax accountant examination 세리사시험
tax accountant fee 세리사보수
tax accounting 세무회계
tax adjustments 세무조사
Tax Administration Bureau 국세청
tax administration system 세무행정조직
tax advantages 세제상의 우대조치
tax advisor 세무고문
tax agency 세무대리
tax agent 납세관리인
tax agent of property tax
고정자산세납세관리인
tax allocation 세금의 기관배분
tax allowance 공제
tax amount 과세액
tax amount settled 조정세액
tax and public charge 공조공과
tax and public dues 공조공과
tax and revenue anticipation 세수세입예측
tax and stamp revenues 조세 및 인지수입
tax anticipation bill 조세준비증권
tax anticipation note 세수예상어음
tax anticipation warrant 세수예상워런트
tax arbitrage 세금재정
tax assessment 조세사정
tax audit 세무감사
tax authorities 세무당국
tax avoidance 조세회피
tax base 과세기준
tax base of enterprise tax on corporation
법인사업세과세표준
tax bearer 담세자
tax bearing capacity 담세력
tax benefit for exchange of property
자산교환세법상의 특전
tax benefit rule 세효과규칙
tax benefits 세제상의 우대조치
tax bill 과세통지서
tax bracket 세율등급
tax burden 조세부담
tax burden ratio 조세부담율
tax charge 법인세부담
tax claims 조세채권
tax clause 세금조항
tax collected 조세수탁금
tax collection 징세
tax collection by stamp 증지징수
tax collection system 징세기구
tax collector 수세관
Tax Commission 세제조사회
tax computation basis 세액계산기준
tax concessions for nonresident
비거주자에 대한 감면
tax consultation 세무상담
tax convention 조세조약
tax court 세무법원
tax credit 세액공제
tax credit for dividend 배당공제

tax credit for minor 미성년자공제
tax criminal 조세범
tax cut by law 감세
tax cutback 택스컷백
tax deducted at the source 원천과세
tax deductible items 과세공제비목
tax deduction 세공제
tax deduction of interest payment 지불이자과세공제
tax deed 공매증서
tax delinquency 세금체납
tax dispute 세무쟁소
tax documents 세무서류
tax dodger 탈세자
tax dodging 탈세
tax due 납세액
tax effect 세효과
tax effect accounting 세효과회계
tax evader 탈세자
tax evasion 탈세
tax examination 세무조사
tax exempt 비과세
tax exempt bond 면세채
tax exempt organization 비과세기관
tax exemption 면세
tax exemption for agricultural income 농업소득면세
tax exemption for dependents 부양공제
tax exemption for specific use 특정용도면제
tax exemption limit 면세점
tax for default 가산세
tax for transfer of securities 유가증권이전세
tax forms 납세신고용지
tax free 비과세
tax free article 비과세품
tax free corporation 비과세법인
tax free income 면세소득
tax free investment 면세투자
tax free purchase 비과세구입
tax free reserve 비과세준비금
tax free small-sum public bond investment system 소액공채별 한도비과세제도
tax gathering season 세수기
tax haven 세금피난처
tax holiday 면세기간
tax home 과세상의 주소
tax in arrears 연체세
tax in jeopardy 긴급과세
tax in kind 물납세
tax incentive 세리상의 우대조치
tax incidence 조세귀착
tax income 세수
tax increase 증세
tax items 세목(稅目)
tax jurisdiction 세관할지
tax jurisprudence 세법학
tax law 세법
tax lease 택스리스
tax leverage lease 택스레버리지리스
tax liabilities 조세채무
tax liability 납세의무
tax liability of foreign corporation 외국법인의 납세의무
tax lien 조세선취특권
tax loss carry-back 결손금 되풀이
tax loss carry-forward 결손금이월
tax manager 납세관리인
tax obligation 납세의무
tax office 세무서
tax on admission 입장세
tax on bank note system 태환권발행세
tax on business 기업과세
tax on construction 건축세
tax on consumption 소비에 대한 세금
tax on deposit 예금이자세
tax on dividend 이익배당세
tax on enterprise 기업과세
tax on excess issue 제한외발행세
tax on goods and possessions 물세
tax on income 소득에 대한 세금
tax on property 자산세
tax on redemption profit 상환차익과세

S T

tax on the aquisition of immovable property 부동산취득세
tax on the write-up 자산재평가세
tax on transaction 거래에 대한 세금
tax on undistributed profits 유보소득에 대한 세
tax on unutilized land 미이용지세
tax oriented transaction 절세거래
tax papers 납세고지서
tax paradise 조세피난처
tax payable 미불세금
tax payable account 미불세금계정
tax payment 납세
tax payment and subrogation by third party 제삼자납부 및 대위
Tax Payment Association 납세협회
tax payment by securities 증권납부
tax payment by self-assessment 신고납세
tax payment by stamp 인지납부
tax payment by transfer account 대체납세
tax payment in kind 현물납부
tax payment in money 금전상납
tax payment place 납세지
tax payment slip 납부서
tax period appearing on tax bill 세납통지서 상의 세납기간
tax policy 조세정책
tax practitioner 세리사
tax procedures 세무상의 수속
tax proxy 세무대리
tax rate 세율
tax rate applied to upper part of income 상적세율
tax rate higher than standard 초과세율
tax rate of gift tax 증여세율
tax rebate 환불세
tax receivable 미수세
tax reduction 감세
tax regulations 세법
tax relief 조세부담경감
tax relief bonds 감세채권
tax requisition 과세요건
tax reserve 세금준비금
tax resort 세금휴양소
tax return 세무신고서
tax return form 납세신고서
tax revenue 세수
tax roll 과세대장
tax rule 세법규
tax sale 환가처분
tax saving 절세
tax saving association 납세저축조합
tax seal 세인
tax shelter 세금회피수단
tax sparing 간주세액공제
tax sparing credit system 간주외국세액공제
tax state 조세국가
tax structure 조세구조
tax suit 세무소송
tax surcharge 부가세
tax swap 택스스와프
tax table 세액표
tax take 세금으로 빼앗기는 금액
tax threshold 과세최저한
tax transaction 조세거래
tax treatment 세무처리
tax treaty 조세조약
tax tribunal examiner 국세심사관
tax unpaid 납세미제
tax value 과세가격
tax-exempt paper 면세채
tax-exempt securities 면세증권
taxable 과세할 수 있는
taxable amount 과세가격
taxable bond 과세채
taxable capacity 세부담능력
taxable depreciation 유세상각
taxable document 과세문서
taxable estate 과세유산
taxable goods 과세품
taxable income 과세소득
taxable income earned by nonresident

비거주자의 과세소득
taxable income entitled to reduced tax rate 경감세율적용소득금액
taxable item 과세대상
taxable minimum of property tax 고정자산세면세점
taxable period 과세기간
taxable poolings 과세풀링
taxable property 과세재산
taxable purchases 과세구입
taxable sales 과세매상
taxable undistributed profits 과세대상유보금액
taxable unit 과세단위
taxable valuation 과세평가액
taxable value of gift tax 증여세과세가격
taxable year 사업연도
taxable year of foreign corporation 외국법인사업연도
taxable year of merger 합병사업연도
taxation 과세
taxation according to legal portion of legacy 법정상속분과세
taxation allowance for life insurance premium 생명보험료공제
taxation allowance for non-life insurance premium 손해보험료공제
taxation at the source 원천과세
taxation at time of receipt from bonded area 인수과세
taxation by applying upper bracket 상적과세
taxation by estimate 추계과세
taxation division 수세과
taxation of income basis 소득할과세
taxation office 세무서
taxation on aggregate income 종합과세
taxation on capital gain 캐피탈게인과세
taxation on corporation tax basis 법인세할과세
taxation on deemed corporation 간주법인과세
taxation on dividend 배당에 대한 과세
taxation on enterprise 기업과세
taxation on entertainment and social expense 교제비과세
taxation on government monopoly 전매과세
taxation on interest or capital gains separately withheld from other income 원천분리과세
taxation on per capita basis 균등할과세
taxation on retirement annuity 퇴직연금과세
taxation on retirement pension 퇴직연금과세
taxation on shipment 이출과세
taxation on small business 소기업과세
taxation system 세제
taxation upon the general-public 대중과세
taxation upon total income 종합과세
taxes and rates 국세 및 지방세
taxes assessed by taxpayers 신고세
taxflation 택스플레이션
taxing authority 세무당국
taxing power 징세권
taxpayer 납세자
taxpayer dealing with foreign countries 외국과 거래하는 납세자
taxpayer filing a blue return 청색신고자
taxpayer identification number 납세자번호
taxpayer identification number system 납세자번호제도
taxpayer with limited tax liability 제한납세의무자
taxpayer's association 납세조합
taxpayer's option 납세자의 선택
taxpayer's suit 납세자소송
TB operation TB 오퍼
TB rate TB 금리
Teachers' Insurance Annuity Association of America 전미교직원보험퇴직연금조합
technical analysis 기술적인 분석
technical assistance 기술지원
technical change 사선으로 교차된 줄무늬
technical cooperation 기술제휴

ST

technical forecast 기술적인 예측
technical graph 기술분석용 그래프
technical index 기술지표
technical indicator 기술분석지표
technical innovation 기술혁신
technical position 시장내부요인
technical progress 기술진보
technical rally 기술적인 반등
technical reaction 기술적인 반응
technical rebound 자율반등
technical standard 기술수준
technical terms 전문용어
technical theory 기술이론
technical trading 테크니컬트레이딩
technically insolvent corporation 기술적으로 지불불능한 기업
technological advance 기술진보
technological changes 기술진보
technological forecasting 기술예측
technological support 기술지원
technology export 기술수출
technology fund 하이테크주펀드
technology gap 기술격차
technology shares 하이테크주
technology transfer 기술이전
technology transfer agreement 기술이전계약
TED spread TED 스프레드
TED spread trading TED 스프레드거래
telecommunication business 전기통신사업
telecommunication carriers 전기통신사업자
telecommunication market 전기통신시장
telegraphic transfer 전신환
telegraphic transfer bought 매환
telegraphic transfer buying rate 전신매상장
telegraphic transfer payable 송금환
telegraphic transfer rate TT 레이트
telegraphic transfer receivable 수금환
telegraphic transfer selling rate 전신매상장
telephone banking 텔레폰뱅킹
telephone booth 전화부스
telephone loan 텔레폰론
telephone market 텔레폰마켓
telephone rates 전화요금
telephone subscription right 전화가입권
teller 텔러
temporal diversification 기간분산
temporal method 템포럴법
temporary 임시의
temporary account 임시계정
temporary advance 일시입체
temporary bond 템퍼러리본드
temporary boom 일시적인 호황
temporary borrowing 일시차입금
temporary change 임시변동
temporary halt 일시중단
temporary holding 일시보류
temporary holding of trading session 매매입회일시보류
temporary income 임시소득
temporary injunction 임시금지명령
temporary investment 일시투자
temporary loan 일시대부금
temporary loan before bond flotation 기채연결융자
temporary loan on property 일시적인 자산대부
Temporary Money Rates Adjustment Law 임시금리조정법
temporary payment 가불금
temporary rally 일시적인 반등
temporary receipts 가수금
temporary receipts account 가수금계정
temporary repairs 가수선
temporary residence 거소
temporary seal 가봉
temporary suspension 임시정지
Temporary Tariff Measures Law 관세잠정조치법
temporary tariff rate 잠정세율
temporary tax accountant 임시세리사
temporary use 일시사용
10 line treaty 10라인 특약

10 year government bond futures 장기국채선물거래
ten years comparative financial summary 10년간 비교재무제표
10-K report 10-K 레포트
10-Q report 10-Q 사반기보고서
10-year coupon-bearing government bonds 10년 이부채권
tenancy 부동산권
tenancy at will 임의부동산대차권
tenancy in common 전구성원이 공유함
tenant 차지인
tenant right 차지권; 대차권
tender 입찰인수; 견적사양서
tender bill 텐더빌
tender bond 입찰보증서
tender offer 주식공개매부
tender offer report 공개매부보고서
tender operation 입찰오퍼
tender option 텐더옵션
tender panel 텐더패널
tender period 입찰기간
tender price 텐더가격
tenement 보유재산
tension 긴장
tentative agreement 잠정합의
tentative auction date 잠정입찰일
tentative balance sheet 가대차대조표
tentative budget 잠정예산
tentative validity 공정력
tenure of office 임기
tenure of the office 재임
term bonds 단일만기채
term call 만기물
term deposits 정기예금
term fed 텀페드
term fed fund rate 텀페드펀드레이트
term federal fund 텀페더럴펀드
term financing 중장기파이낸스
term financing rate 기간차입금리
term for evaluation 평가시기
term for which the bonus payment is computed 상여지급액 계산기간
term insurance 정기보험
term life insurance 정기생명보험
term loan 텀론
term of engaging in the business 사업에 종사하는 기간
term of execution 집행기간
term of insurance 보험기간
term of office 재직기한
term of payment 지불기한
term of validity 유효기한
term receivable 텀채권
term repo 정기선물
term risk 기간리스크
term RP 정기선물
term sheet 조건개요서
term structure 기간구조
term structure of interest rates 금리기간구조
term structure of yield 이율기간구조
term swap 텀스와프
term-end 기말
term-end account 기말계정
term-end settlement of accounts 기말결산
terminal funding 연금원가적립방식
terminal funding method 연금현물충족방식
terminal market 정기시장
terminal pay allowance 퇴직수당
terminal value 최종가치
termination 기간만료
termination benefit 퇴직급부
termination claim 만기청구액
termination date 터미네이션데이트
termination events 해약사유
termination of a term 기간만료
termination provisions 해약조항
terms and conditions 조건
terms of delivery 인도조건
terms of trade 교역조건
terrier 토지대장
territorial waters 영해

tertiary industry 3차산업
test marketing 시험판매
test of controls 내부통제테스트
test of hypothesis 가설검정
test statistic 검정통계량
testamentary trust 유언신탁
testify 증언하다
testimony 증언
testing 시험
testing audit 시험조사
testing expenses 시작비
textile and apparel industry 섬유의류업계
their account 선방계정
thematic apperception test 회화통각검사; TAT
theoretical 이론적
theoretical capacity 이론상의 생산능력
theoretical future price 이론선물가격
theoretical price 이론가격
theoretical rate of exchange 이론적인 환상장
theoretical rates 이론금리
theoretical valuation 이론가격
theoretical value 이론가치
theory of accounts 계정이론
theory of approximation 근사치이론
theory of asset preference 자산선호이론
theory of asset valuation 자산평가론
theory of comparative advantage 비교우위설
theory of comparative cost 비교생산비설
theory of credit creation 신용창조론
theory of foreign exchange 외환학설
theory of games 게임이론
theory of imputation 귀속이론
theory of interest 이자이론
theory of international indebtedness 국제대차설
theory of liabilities taxation 조세채무관계설
theory of optimum tariff 최적관세이론
theory of portfolio selection 자산선택이론
theory of probability 확률론
theory of tax accounting 세무회계론
thereupon 즉시
thief 절도범
thin 한산
thin capitalization 과소자본
thin margin 소규모차액이익금
thing in action 무체동산
things real 부동산
third country bill 삼국어음
third generation 삼차
third generation on-line system 3차 온라인 시스템
third market 장외거래시장
third party 제삼자
third party credit 할부구입알선업
third party liability cover 제3자배상특약보험
third party liability insurance 제3자배상책임보험
third party sales credit 할부구입알선
third sect 제3구역
Third World 제3세계
third world countries 제3세계 각국
third-party credit support 제3자 신용보상
third-party risk 제삼자리스크
threat 협박
three digit PER 3자리수 주가수익률
360 day basis 360일 베이시스
three line converting method 3선 전환법
three-month moving average 3개월 이동평균
threshold 한계
threshold of divergence 괴리한도
thrift and savings plans 저축제도
thrift bank 저축금융기관
thrift industry 저축금융업계
thrift institution 저축금융기관
through B /L 통과선하증권
through the decision 결정으로
through transportation 일관수송
through-put contract 스루풋조항
throughout accounting 일관회계
throughout the target issues 대상문제전체의

throughput contract 생산고보증계약
throw-back rule 스로우백원칙
thumb-rule 경험칙
tick 틱
tick size 호가단위
tick-test rule 틱테스트룰
ticker 주식상장표시판
ticket 전표
ticket of leave 가석방허가증
ticket sale finance 티켓판매금융
tie-in sale 포함판매
tie-up loan 제휴론
tied aid 조건부 구조
tied loan 조건부 융자
tied-agent 전속중개자
tier 계층
Tier 1 capital guideline 기본항목기준
Tier 2 capital 자기자본보완항목
tight 단단히
tight budget 긴축재정
tight credit 신용압박
tight fiscal package 긴축재정안
tight fiscal policy 재정긴축정책
tight money policy 금융긴축정책
tightened inspection 엄격한 검사
tightened liquidity 자금조달악화
tightening 협박;긴축
tightening monetary policy 긴축정책
tightening of liquidity 유동성압박
tighter monetary policy 긴축금융정책
tightness of money 자금이 딸림
timber delivery tax 목재거래세
timber income 산림소득
time adjusted 시간조정필
time bargains 정기거래
time bias 타임바이어스
time bill 기한부 어음
time card 타임카드
time cost 시간원가
time decay 타임디케이
time deposit 정기예금
time deposit account 정기예금계정
time deposit certificate 정기예금증서
time deposits available within one year 일년 이내의 정기예금
time difference theory 시차설
time draft 일람후 정기불환어음
time effect 시간효과
time expired 기한무효
time factor 시간적인 요소
time filter 타임필터
time for tax payment 납기한
time horizon 거래기간
time lag 타임래그
time limit 기한
time limit of the subscription for new stock 신주신청기한
time limitation 기간제한
time loan 정기대부
time of inclusion in expenses of enterprise tax 사업세손금산입시기
time of payment 지불시기
time of presentation 제시기간
time of receipts 수입시기
time of recognizing gain 수익계상시기
time of recognizing loss 손실계상시기
time option 타임옵션
time policy 기간보험
time precedence 시간우선
time preference 시간선호
time priority 시간우선의 원칙
time sales 할부판매
time saving 정기예금
time series analysis 시계열분석
time series behavior 시계열변동
time series behavior of earnings 이익의 시계열변동
time series data 시계열데이터
time span 타임스팬
time spread 시간스프레드
time to expiration 잔여기간
time to maturity 잔존기간

time transaction 정기거래
time value 시간가치
time value of option 옵션의 시간가치
time variance 시간차이
time weighted return 시간가중수익률
timely disclosure 적시정보개시
Timely Disclosure Network 적시개시정보전달시스템
times interest earned 이자부담배율
times interest earned ratio 이자부담배율
times per year 연간회전횟수
timing differences 기간차이
timing mismatch 시기가 어긋남
timing option 타이밍옵션
timing swap 타이밍스와프
tip 정보누설
title deeds 권원
title document 권리증서
title insurance 부동산권이서
title insurance company 권원보험;소유권보증
title paramount 계정과목
title report 권원보고서
tobacco consumption tax 담배소비세
Tobin's q 토빈의 **q**
tokkin 토킨펀드
tolerable deviation rate 허용면세율
tolerable rate 허용률
tolerance 허용차;공차
tolerance level 허용수준
tolerance limit 허용한도
toll 통행료
toll charges 통행세
toll gate 도로요금소
toll traverse 사유지통행료
tombstone ad 묘석광고
tomorrow-next 익일차입; 삼일후 반제
tone 시황
tonnage due 톤세
tontines 톤틴연금
tool 수법
tools of analysis 분석방법
top 상위
top bidder 최고가입찰자
top line 매상고
top straddle 톱스트래들
top tax rate 최고세율
top vertical combination 톱버티컬컴비네이션
top-down forecasting 톱다운형 예측
top-down investment 톱다운형 투자
top-reversal day 톱리버설데이
TOPIX index option TOPIX 지수옵션
TOPIX futures TOPIX 선물옵션
TOPIX New Index Series TOPIX 뉴스인덱스시리즈
TOPIX option TOPIX 옵션
TOPIX trends TOPIX 추이
topless 주가가 천정부지로 치솟음
Toronto Futures Exchange 토론토선물거래소
Toronto Industrial Index 토론토공업주지수
Toronto Stock Exchange 토론토증권거래소
Torrens System 토런스시스템
total 합계
total amount of insurance in force 보유계약
total asset turnover ratio 총자산회전율
total assets 총자산
total book value of assets 총자산장부가액
total buying contract 총매입계약
total capital 자본금합계
total capital profit ratio 총자본수익률
total capitalization 총장기자금
total cost 전부원가
total cost curve 총비용곡선
total cost of transaction 거래총비용
total costing 전부원가계산
total delta 총델타치
total deposit 총예금
total earnings 총수익
total gamma 총감마수치
total kappa 총캐퍼수치
total liabilities and net worth 총자본
total loss 전손
total loss only 전손만의 담보

total market capitalizatioin 주식시가총액
total market delta 총시장델타치
total market value 총시장가액
total maximum liability 책임한도액
total money supply 총통화공급고
total net income 총소득금액
total net worth 자기자본합계
total of shares outstanding 총발행필 주식수
total payment of installments 할부가격
total production 총생산
total rate of return 총수익률
total receipts 총수입
total receivables 미수수취계정합계
total reserve system 전액정화준비제도
total reserves 총준비
total return 종합이율
total return swap 토탈리턴스와프
total roh 총로치
total sales 총매상고
total selling contract 총매출계약
total starts 착공호수전체
total stocks issued 총발행필 주식수
total sum 총계
total taxable income 과세총소득금액
total taxation 종합과세
total theta 총세타수치
total turnover 총생산고
totally-held subsidiary 100퍼센트 자회사
touching the bottom 최저시세로 떨어짐
tourist income 관광수입
tourist tax 여행자세
town 마을
town planning scheme 도시계획
traceable cost 추적가능원가
track record 과거기록
tracking error 연동오차
tracking stock 자회사수익연동주식
trade 영업
trade acceptance 수출인수어음
trade acceptances payable 인수어음
trade account 영업계정
trade account payable 외상매입금
trade account receivable 외상매출금
trade against the trend 인기가 높을 때 팔고 낮을 때 삼
trade agreement 무역협정
trade assets 영업자산
trade associations 증권거래업자협회
trade balance 무역수지
trade by agreement 협정무역
trade claim 무역클레임
trade contractor 직별업자
trade control 무역통제
trade creation effect 무역창출효과
trade credit 무역금융
trade creditor 구입처
trade debtor 외상판매처
trade deficit 무역적자
trade description 상품설명
trade discount 업자할인
trade expansion act 통상확대법
trade expenses 영업비
trade figure 무역수지실적
trade friction 무역마찰
trade liability 영업채무
trade mark 상표
trade matrix analysis 무역연관분석
trade name 상호
Trade Negotiations Committee 무역교섭위원회
trade off 트레이트오프
trade on commission 위탁무역
trade on one's own account 스스로 붙임
trade payables 지불채무
trade position 무역수지
trade receivable 매상채권
trade receivables 수취채권
trade rights 영업권
trade secret 영업상의 비밀
trade secrets 기업비밀
trade settlement 결제
trade sharing 적취비율

trade statistics 무역통계
trade surplus amount 무역수지흑자폭
trade suspension 거래정지; 매매정지
trade tax 영업세
trade term 거래조건
trade terms 정형무역조건
trade ticket 트레이드티켓
trade union 노동조합
trade-in 신품을 고가로 인수함
trade-in articles 고가로 인수한 신품
trade-mark infringement 상표권침해
trade-mark registration law 상표등록법
trade-related investment measures 무역관련투자조치
traded option 거래옵션
traded securities 유통증권
trader 트레이더
trading account 매매계정
trading account assets 상품계정자산
trading area 상세권
trading collateral 거래담보금
trading conditions 거래조건
trading day 거래일
trading days 입회일수
trading firm finance 상사금융
trading floor 거래소
trading hour 입회시
trading hours 매매입회시
trading income of loss 매매손익
trading know-how 거래노하우
trading limits 가격폭제한
trading market 유통시장
trading mechanism 매매구조
trading on equity 자기자본대용
trading on the over-the-counter market 장외거래
trading outside the floor 입회외 거래
trading partner 무역상대국
trading pool 트레이딩풀
trading post 거래포스트
trading profit 증권매매익
trading profit and loss account 매매손익계정
trading qualification 거래자격
trading range 거래범위
trading regulations 거래규칙
trading securities 트레이딩목적유가증권
trading stamp 트레이딩스탬프
trading system 거래시스템
trading tax 거래세
trading to correct errors 과오정정거래
trading unit 거래단위
trading unit system 거래단위제도
trading value 매매대금
trading volume 생산고
trading volume of over-the-counter bonds 공공채장외매매고
traditional market 전통시장
traffic personal accident insurance 교통사고상해보험
trailing PER 실적기준 PER
traitor 신뢰를 배신한 자
tramper 부정기선
tranche 분할발행
tranche issue 트란시방식
trandint haet 거래중단
transaction 거래
transaction account 결제계정
transaction approach 개별거래마다 리스크를 평가함
transaction collation 매매조회
transaction cost 거래코스트
transaction fee 거래수수료
transaction in assets 자산거래
transaction motive 거래동기
transaction of near delivery 기근물거래
transaction on a dealer basis 자기매매
transaction on exchange 거래소거래
transaction shift 거래소시프트
transaction tax 거래세
transaction with delayed settlement 착지거래
transaction with rights receipts 권리증서매매
transaction effected by member for the

accounts of others 수탁거래
transaction for customers' accounts 수탁거래
transaction for members' account 자기거래
transaction in securities 유가증권매매
transcript 등본
transfer account 대체계정
transfer agent 명의변경대리인
transfer at low price 저액양도
transfer books closed 주권명의변경정지
transfer books open 주권명의변경정지해제
transfer contract 양도계약
transfer entry 환기입
transfer expenditure 이전경비
transfer expenses 양도비용
transfer fee 양도수수료
transfer income 이전소득
transfer ledger 환원장
transfer mechanism 트랜스퍼메카니즘
transfer number 환번호
transfer of a share-certificate 주권명의변경
transfer of assets 자산양도
transfer of business 영업양도
transfer of current account 당좌계정부체
transfer of endorsed note 이서양도
transfer of fixed assets given in pledge 담보부 고정자산양도
transfer of fund 자금이동
transfer of land tax 지대위양
transfer of name 명의변경
transfer of operations 영업양도
transfer of ownership 소유권이전
transfer of positions 매매계약을 한 채 아직 결제하지 않은 상품을 이전함
transfer of property 자산양도
transfer of property due to the delivery of substitute property 환지처분에 따른 양도
transfer of real property 부동산양도
transfer of rights 이권양도
transfer of securities 유가증권양도
transfer of the business 영업양도
transfer of the place of tax payment 납세지이동
transfer of the whole business 전영업양도
transfer of transferable credit 신용장양도
transfer of unsettled transactions 미결제약정인계
transfer payment 이전지출
transfer price 양도가격
transfer pricing 이전가격조작
transfer pricing taxation system 이전가격세제
transfer problem 트랜스퍼문제
transfer profit 환이익
transfer property 양도자산
transfer risk 결제리스크
transfer savings account 환저금계좌
transfer service delegatee 명의변경사무수탁자
transfer slip 환전표
transfer tax 양도세
transfer transactions 환거래
transferable account 환가능계정
transferable credit 양도가능신용장
transferable deposits 통화제예금
transferable loan 양도가능대출
transferable loan certificate 양도가능대부증서
transferable loan facility 양도가능대부
transferable RUF 양도가능러프
transferable securities 양도성 증권
transferee 양수인
transferee corporation 합병법인
transferee of membership equity 회원지분양수인
transferor 양도인
transferor corporation 피합병회사
transferred debt 이관채권
transferred positions 매매계약을 한 채 아직 결제하지 않은 상품이 이관됨
transferring charge 대체수수료
transfers between geographic areas

지역간 대체
transformation of tax transit 세금소전
transgression 침해
transire 화물운송면장
transit account 미달계정
transit clause 운송약관
transit trade 통과무역
transition matrix 천이확률행렬
transition period 과도기
transition stage 과도기
transition years 과도기연수
transitional measure 경과조치
transitory income 변동소득
transitory phenomena 일시적인 현상
translation adjustments 환환산조정
translation gains and losses 환환산차액
translation method at historical rates 취득시 환산표
translation method at the current exchange rate 기말시 환산법
translation of foreign currency statements 외화표시부분을 환산함
translation of foreign currency transactions 외화기준거래환산
transmission mechanism 파급경로
transmitting bank 단골은행
transnational corporation 초국적기업
transparent 투명성이 있는
transport insurance 운송보험
transportation 운송
transportation bond 교통채
transportation business 운송업
transportation charges 운송료
transportation claim 운송클레임
transportation company 운송업자
transportation cost 수송비
transportation equipment 운송설비
transportation equipment futures 운송용기기품선물
transportation equipment industry 운송용기기품업계
transportation in bond 보세운송
transportation insurance 운송보험
transshipment 짐을 옮겨실음
transshipment bill of lading 적환선하증권
travel advances 전불여비
traveling audit 순회감사
traveling benefits 여비수당
traveling expenses 여비교통비
traveling expenses for business 출장여비
traveller's letter of credit 여행신용장
travelling salesman 순회판매인
traverse 부인하다
treasurer 재무부장
treasury auction 국채입찰
treasury bill 재무부증권;단기증권
Treasury Bill issued 재무부발행증권
Treasury bill market 재무부단기증권시장
treasury bills 할인단기국채
treasury bond 재무부장기증권
treasury bonds 재무부증권
Treasury Bonds Investment Series 재무부투자채권
Treasury Certificate of Indebtedness 재무부채무증서
Treasury Eurodollar spread TED 스프레드
treasury financing 국채입찰
treasury financing bills 재무부증권
treasury fund remittance 국고금송금
treasury investments and loans 재정투융자
treasury note 재무부중기증권
treasury notes 국고채권
treasury product 재무상품
treasury savings notes 재무부중기저축채권
treasury securities market 재무부증권시장
treasury stock 자기주
Treasury strip 국채스트립채
treasury surplus 국고여유금
treasury tax and loan account 조세공채계정
treasury tax and loan note accounts 재무부조세국채증권계정
Treasury yield 재무부증권이율

treating 교섭하다
treaty 조약
treaty of commerce 통상조약
treaty reinsurance 특약재보험
treaty shopping 트리티쇼핑
treaty wording 재보험특약서
trebletariff 삼중관세율
tree structure 트리구조
trend 추세
trend analysis 추세분석
trend channel 트렌드채널
trend follower 트렌드플라워
trend line 트렌드라인
trend of earnings 수익경향
trend pattern 경향선
trend series 경향지수
trend towards luxury spending 고급품소비지향
trial 시산
trial balance of balances 잔고시산표
trial balance of totals 합계시산표
trial balance of totals and balances 합계잔고시산표
trial balance sheet 시산표
trial employment period 시용기간
trial jury 공판배심
trial manufacture 시작
trial period 시용기간
trial product 시작품
trial running expenses 시운전비
trial running of manufacturing equipment 생산설비를 시운전함
triangle reversal patterns 트라이앵글 리버설 패턴
triangular trade 삼각무역
tribunal 심판기관
trickle down 통화침투설의
trigger event 해약이유
trigger price 트리거가격
Trilateral Commission 삼극위원회
trilemma 삼도논법
tripartite agreement 삼국간 협정
triple bottom 삼중바닥
triple crossover method 트리플크로스오버법
triple merit 삼중익
triple settlement 4일후 인도
triple top 트리플톱
troubled-loan cleanup 불량채권처리
trough 경기의 저점
truck system 현물급여
true and fair 진실하며 공정함
true and fair view 진실하며 공정한 의견
true reserve 진정한 준비금
trust account 신탁계정
trust accounting 신탁업회계
trust accounts of all banks 전국은행신탁계정
trust agreement 신탁계약
trust assets 신탁재산
trust bank 신탁은행
trust business 신탁업
trust by act of law 법정신탁
trust company 신탁회사
trust contract 신탁약관
trust deed 신탁증서
trust deposit 신탁예금
trust estate 신탁재산
trust fee 신탁보수
trust for value 유상신탁
trust fund 신탁기금
Trust Fund Bureau 자금운용부
Trust Fund Bureau Special Account 자금운용부 특별회계
trust fund plan 신탁형연금
trust income 신탁수입
trust indenture 신탁증서
trust instrument 신탁증서
trust joint 합동
Trust Law 신탁법
trust money 위탁금
trust obligation participating securities 톱스; TOPS
trust principal 신탁원본

trust property 신탁재산
trust receipt 수입담보화물보관증
trust securities 신탁증권
trust theory 신탁설
trust under agreement 계약신탁
trustee 수탁자
trustee bank 수탁은행
trustee company 수탁회사
trustee for bond issuance 사채발행수탁자
trustee in bankruptcy 파산관재인
trustor 신탁설정자
truth in lending 진성대부법
truth in securities act 증권법의 진실
TSE 도쿄증시
TSE Stock Price Average 도쿄증시평균
turn around 반전
turn to red figures 적자전락
turndown 급락
turning point 전환점
turning upward 저점이탈
turnkey 턴키
turnkey contract 턴키계약
turnover increase rate 매상증가율
turnover of commodity 상품회전수
turnover of funds 자금회전율
turnover of gross and net working capital 총운전자본 및 순운전자본회전율
turnover of payables 매입채무회전율
turnover of receivables 인수계정회전율
turnover of total capital 총자본회전율
turnover of total operating assets 경영자본회전율
turnover period 회전기간
turnover rate 회전율
turnover rate of capital 자본회전율
turnover ratio 회전율
turnover ratio of total liabilities 타인자본회전율
turnover ratio of total liabilities and net worth 총자본회전율
turnover tax 거래고세
turnovers of net worth 자기자본회전율
24 hours trading 24시간 거래
24 Ore Figure 이탈리아 24오레종합주가지수
20% depreciation method 1/5상각법
20 year government bond futures 초장기국채선물
20 year Japanese government bond 일본초장기국채증권선물
twin deficits 쌍둥이적자
twin-card 트윈카드
twisting (왜곡된 권유로 인한) 부당생명보험계약
2 dollar broker 2달러브로커
two tier market 이중구조시장
two tier offer 이단계오퍼
two way account 상호계정
two way market 투웨이마켓
two way price 쌍방시세
type of holding 보유형태
type of licenses 면허종류

U

U.S.dollar short-term interest futures
달러단기금리선물
U.S.Government General Accounting Office
미국일반회계국
U.S.savings bond 미국저축채
U.S.term 미국방식
ultimate fact 주요사실
ultimate lender 주요 대주(貸主)
ultimatum 최후통첩
ultra vires activities 월권행위
umbrella export credit facility
포괄수출신용방식
umbrella liability policy
기업포괄배상책임보험; 포괄책임보험
umbrella master agreement 포괄표준계약서
umpire 심판인
unabsorbed burden 간접비 배부부족액
unadjusted trial balance 미수정잔고시산표
unalienable 양도할 수 없는
unallocated funding instrument
비할당적립방식
unamortized balance 미상각잔고
unamortized bond discount 미상각사채할인
unamortized cost 미상각원가
unamortized debt discount and expenses
사채발행차금
unamortized discount 미상각발행차금
unamortized discount on debenture accounts
채권이연계정
unamortized interest during construction
미상각건설이자
unamortized obligation 미상각채무
unamortized premium on bonds
사채발행차익
unanimous 전원일치로
unappropriated deficit 미처리결손금
unappropriated earned surplus
미처분이익잉여금
unappropriated earned surplus for current term 당기미처분이익잉여금
unappropriated income 미처분이익
unappropriated retained earnings
미처분잉여금
unappropriated surplus at the end of year
기말이월이익금
unappropriated surplus for the current taxable
당기처분이익잉여금
unassigned surplus 미분배잉여적립금
unaudited 비감사
unauthorized card 무권카드
unauthorized member 무효회원
unauthorized use 부정사용
unavoidable accident 불가피한 사고
unavoidable circumstances 부득이한 사정
unavoidable cost 회피불가능원가
unavoidable dangers 불가피한 위험
unavoidable risk by diversified investment
분산투자로 배제할 수 없는 위험
unbalanced 미결산의
unbalanced account 미결산계정
unbalanced book 미결산장부
unbalanced budget 적자예산

unbalanced open 미결산
uncertain 불확실한
uncertain factor 불투명요인
uncertainty 불투명
unchange 수준유지
unchanged 불변의
unchanged to slightly higher 강세수준유지
unchanged to slightly lower 약세수준유지
unclaimed 소유자불명의
unclaimed check 미청구수표
unclaimed dividends 미청구배당금
unclaimed stock 실권주
unclaimed wages 미불임금
unclassified expenses 잡비
unclear energy insurance 원자력보험
unclear energy liability insurance 원자력손해배상책임보험
uncollateralized call 무담보콜
uncollected balance 미수금
uncollected commission 미수수수료
uncollected funds 미수자금
uncollected income 미수수익
uncollected interest 미수이자
uncollected premium 미수보험료
uncollected rent 미수지대
uncollected revenue 미수수익
uncollectible loan 언콜렉터블론
uncommitted facilities 무인수방식
uncommitted tranche 비약정트란시
uncompleted works 미완성공사
unconditional 무조건의
unconditional contract 단순계약
unconditional debt 무조건채무
unconditional drawing right 무조건인출권
unconditional estimate 무조건추정
unconditional grant 무조건보조금
unconditional liquidity 무조건유동성
unconditional operation 무조건오퍼레이션
unconditional reserve 별도적립금
unconfirmed credit 불확인신용장
unconscionable bargain 비양심적인 계약
unconsolidated affiliates 연결대상외 관련회사
unconsolidated subsidiaries 비연결자회사
unconstitutional 위헌의
uncontrollable cost 관리불능비
uncontrollable expenses 관리불능비
uncorrelated return 무상관수익률
uncovered interest arbitrage 언커버드금리재정
uncovered option 언커버드옵션
uncovered position 언커버드포지션
uncrossed check 보통수표
undated bill 무일부어음
undated issue 영구채
undefended 무방비의
undepreciated balance 미상각잔고
undepreciated wasting property 미상각감모자산
under absorbed 배부부족
under development 개발중
under dressing 언더드레싱
under insurance 일부보험
under lease 전대차
under liquidity 과소유동성
under par 액면할
under protest 지불거절
under repair 수선중
under reserve 유보조건
under separate cover 별봉(別封)으로
under-depreciation 과소상각
undercapitalization 과소자본
underdepreciation carried forward 상각부족액이월
underemployment 과소고용
underemployment equilibrium 과소고용균형
underemployment multiplier 불완전고용승수
underestimation 과소평가
underground economy 지하경제
underground money 지하자금
underhedging 과소헤지
underinvestment 과소투자
underlying 원자산의

underlying accounting date 기초적인 회계데이터
underlying assets 원자산
underlying cause 근본원인
underlying collateral 담보물건
underlying index 대상지표
underlying inflation rate 기초인플레이션율
underlying market 현물시장
underlying retention 보유손해액
underlying securities 원증권;대상증권
underlying share 현물주
underlying size 거래단위
underlying stock 대상주식
underlying swap 대상스와프
underlying value 직물가격
underpayment 과소납부
underperforming loans 불량채권
underperforming mortgages 불량모기지
understanding 이해
undertaker 사업자
undertaking 약속
undertone 전반적인 시황
undervaluation 과소평가
undervalued 값이 쌈
undervalued asset 값싼 자산
underwriter 인수업자
underwriters' allocation 인수업자의 할당액
underwriting 인수업무
underwriting account balance 영업계정수지잔고
underwriting agreement 인수계약서
underwriting business 인수업무
underwriting by the Bank of Korea 한은(韓銀)인수
underwriting by the Trust Fund Bureau 자금운용부 인수
underwriting commission 인수수수료
underwriting company 인수회사
underwriting contract 증권인수업자수수료
underwriting fee 인수수수료
underwriting firm 인수회사
underwriting group 인수단
underwriting of government securities 국채인수
underwriting of new issue securities 신증권인수
undisbursed loans 미실행대출
undischargeable claim 파면책채권
undisclosed reserve 비밀적립금
undisposed 미처분
undisposed deficit 미처분결손
undistributed earnings 미분배이익
undistributed profits 유보금액
undivided bequest 미분할유산
undivided interest 불가분권
undivided profit 미처분이익
undue influence 부당위압
undue risks 과대한 리스크
unearned 미수
unearned discount 미경과할인료
unearned income 불로소득
unearned interest 미경과이자
unearned premium 미경과보험료
unearned revenue 전수익금
unemployment 실업
unemployment benefit 실업급부
unemployment compensation 실업보험
unemployment insurance 실업보험
unemployment rate 실업율
unencumbered assets 담보권을 설정할 수 없는 자산
unexpected property loss 임시자산손실
unexpired 미경과
unexpired cost 미소비원가
unexpired expenses 미경과비용
unexpired insurance premium 미경과보험료
unexpired interest 미경과이자
unfair advantage 부정이익
unfair call 부당이행청구
unfair competition 부정경쟁
unfair dismissal 부당해고
unfair labor practice 부당노동행위

unfair method of competition 불공정한 경쟁방법
unfair trade 부당한 거래
unfair trade practice 부당영업행위
unfavorable balance 지불초과
unfavorable factor 악재료
unfavorable leverage effect 부정적인 증익효과
unfilled orders 현품주문
unfixed interest bearing 불확정이자부
unforeseen event 예견되지 않은 사고
unforeseen liabilities 예측하지 못한 채무
unfunded accrued pension cost 미불연금비용
unfunded debt 단기채무
unguaranteed residual value 무보증잔존자격
unhedge 언헤지
unhedged bond 언헤지본드
unified brand 통일상표
unified operation 통일적인 운용
uniform 일률적
uniform accounting regulations 통일경리기준
uniform accounting standards 통일회계기준
uniform accounting system 통일회계제도
Uniform Commercial Code 통일상사법전
uniform cost accounting 통일원가계산
uniform cost accounting system 통일원가계산제도
Uniform Life Insurance Act 통일보험법
Uniform Practice Code 전미증권업협회통일관습규칙
uniform practice code 통일관습규칙
Uniform Securities Act 통일증권법
unilateral contract 편무계약
unilateral record 일방적인 기록
unilateral transaction 일방적인 거래
unincorporated company 법인격이 없는 회사
unincorporated joint venture 비회사형 합변사업
uninscribed stock 무기명주식
uninsured peril 비담보위험
union label 조합증표
union mortgage clause 표준저당권자 지불약관
unique selling proposition 유니크셀링프로포지션
unissued capital stock 미발행자본
unissued certificate 예비주권
unissued stock 미발행주식
unit 단위
unit banking system 단일은행제도
unit cost 단위원가
unit credit method 단위연금적립증가방식
unit depreciation 개별상각
unit grant 단위보조금
unit investment trust company 투자회사
Unit Linked Life Insurance 유닛링크보험
unit method 개별감가상각법
unit of account 계산단위
unit of account bond 유닛오브어카운트채
unit of investment securities 투자법인에 출자하는 단위
unit of production method 생산고비례법
unit of taxation 과세단위
unit of trading 매매단위
unit posting 개별전기
unit price 단가
unit pricing 단가적산법
unit sales 매상수령
unit shares 단위주
unit trust 유닛트러스트
unit type 단위형
unit type investment trust 단위형 투신
unit-price contract 단가계약
unitary exchange rate system 단일환율제도
unitary tax 합산과세
unitary taxation 합산과세
United Nations Capital Development Fund 국제연합자본개발기금
United Nations Conference on Trade and Development 국제연합무역개발회의
United Nations Economic Development

Administration 국제연합경제개발국
United States trustee 연방관재관
unity of possession 점유합동
unity of title 권원합동
universal agent 총대리인
universal banking 유니버설뱅킹
universal currency 세계통화
universal legacy 포괄유증
universal legatee 포괄수유자
universal life insurance 유니버설보험
universal pension 일률급부연금
unjust disbursement 부당지출
unjust enrichment 부당이득
unjustified 부당한
unknown clause 부지약관
unlawful 불법인
unlawful act 불법행위
unlawful assembly 불법집회
unlawfulness 불법
unless otherwise specified 다른 결정이 없는 한
unlimited company 무한책임회사
unlimited facility 무제한퍼실리티
unlimited legal tender 무제한법화
unlimited liability 무한책임
unlimited liability company 무한책임회사
unlimited partnership 합명회사
unliquidated claim 불확정채권
unlisted assets 부외자산
unlisted company 비상장회사
unlisted liability 부외채무
unlisted loan 부외차금
unlisted note 비상장채
unlisted securities 장외증권
unlisted stock 비상장주
unloading 물건이나 주식을 팔아서 큰 이득을 보고 물러남
unmatched book 언매치드북
unofficial capital flight 비공식자본이 유출됨
unpaid 미불
unpaid balance of national tax 국세미불액
unpaid capital 미불입자본
unpaid claims 미불보험금
unpaid dividend 미불배당금
unpaid donation 미불기부금
unpaid draft 부도어음
unpaid returns 미불반려금
unpaid tax 미불세금
unperfomed part of obligation 채무미이행분
unproductive capital 미가동자본
unprofitable company 실적이 좋지 않은 회사
unqualified financial statements 미감사재무제표
unqualified opinion 무한정의견
unqualified opinion report 무조건감사보고서
unqualified report 무제한적정의견
unrated entity 무등급법인
unrealised loss 미실현손
unrealised profit 미실현익
unrealised profits and losses 포함손익
unrealizable assets 환가불능자산
unrealized gains in securities 증권포함익
unrealized gross profit on installment sales 할부매상미실현익
unrealized income 미실현이익
unrealized profit 미실현수익
unrealized profit and loss 계산상의 손익액
unrealized profits 미실현이익
unrealized revenue 미실현수익
unreasonable taxation 부당과세
unreasonably 현저하게
unrecognized net gain /loss 미인식순손익
unrecovered cost 미회수원가
unregistered 미등기
unregistered debenture 미등록사채
unregistered stock 무등록주
unrelated business income 비관련사업이익
unsalable stock 매잔재고
unsealed deposit 개봉예금
unseaworthy 내항력이 없는
unsecured 무담보의
unsecured account 무담보계정

unsecured bond 무담보사채
unsecured call loan 무담보콜
unsecured credit 무담보신용
unsecured creditor 일반채권자
unsecured debt 무담보채
unsecured liability 무담보부채
unsecured loan 무담보융자
unsecured obligations 무담보채무
unsecured trading 무담보거래
unsettled 미결제의
unsettled account 미결제계정
unsettled transactions 미결제거래; 미결제약정
unsettled transactions on proprietary account 자기계산에 따른 미결제약정
unsigned vote 무기명투표
unsold 팔다남은
unsolicited rating 무의뢰평가
unsubordinated 비열후
unsubordinated debenture 비열후담보부사채
unsystematic risk 비(非)시스티매틱리스크
untied loan 언타이드론
untrue 사실에 반한
untruncated multiplier 비단절승수
unused buildings 유휴건물
unused land 유휴토지
unusual casualty reserve 이상위험준비금
unusual gains or losses 임시손익
unusual item 이상항목
unusual loss 이상손실
unusual movement 이상한 움직임
unusual profit or loss item 이상손익항목
unusual risks reserve 이상위험준비금
unvalued policy 미평가보험
unwritten law 비제정법
up and put option 업앤드풋옵션
up front 일괄전불
up gap 업갭
up-down ratio 등락레이쇼
up-front payment 계약일시금
up-front premium 선불프리미엄
up-pressure 상승력
up-tick 상향
update 갱신하다
upper limit of a loan 대부한도액
ups and downs 성쇠
upset price 최저경매가격
upstairs market 계상시장
upswing on business results 실적상승
uptrend 업트렌드
upturn 호전
upturn in gearing 부채비율상승
upward pressure 상승압력
upward revision 상향수정
upward trend 상승기조
upwards 기조를 올림
Urban Development Corporation 도시기반정비공단
urban remodeling enterprise 도시개량사업
urbanization 도시화
Uruguay Round 우루과이라운드
usable period of used property 중고자산사용가능기간
usable years 사용기간
usage 관습
usance 유전스
usance bill 기한부 환어음
usance bill rate 기한부 어음상장
usance buying rate 기한부 어음매상장
usance granted by foreign banks 외국은행유전스
usance L/C 기한부 신용장
usance rate 유전스레이트
use and file 사용후 신고제
use of funds 자금용도
use value 사용가치
used hours 사용시간
used property 중고자산
useful information 유용한 정보
useful life 내용연수
useful life table 내용연수표
user 소비자
user cost 사용자원가

usher 안내인
usual covenants 통상약관
usurer 고리대부
usury 고리
usury law 이자제한법
utilities bond 전력채
utilities stock 전력가스주
utility company 공익기업
utility consumption 유틸리티소비
utility function 효용함수
utility indicator 효용지표
utility model 실용신안
utility model patent 실용신안권
utility rate 공공요금
utility service 용역제공
utility theory 효용이론
utility value 사용가치
utilization rate 설비가동률
utilization variance 조업도차이
utilized cost 이용원가
utmost good faith 최대선의

V

vacancy 결원
vacant building 빈 건물
vacant land tax 공간지세
vacant lot 공지
vacation 비워 줌; 내줌
vacation pay 휴가수당
vacation with pay 유급휴가
valid 유효한
validate 정당하다고 인정하다
validation 타당성확인
validity 정당성
valuable consideration 유가약인(有價約因)
valuable papers 유가증권
valuation 평가액
valuation account 평가계정
valuation actuary 보험계리인
valuation at cost 원가법
valuation at selling price 시가법
valuation basis 평가기준
valuation by lower of cost or market method 저가법에 따른 평가
valuation by multiplier 배율평가
valuation by road rating 노선가격방식에 따른 평가
valuation characteristics 평가특성
valuation clause 보험평가액조항
valuation date 평가일
valuation form 적하가격신고서
valuation item 평가과목
valuation loss 평가손
valuation modeling 평가모델
valuation of assets 자산평가
valuation of bond 공사채평가
valuation of call option 콜옵션평가
valuation of common stock 보통주평가
valuation of copyright 저작권평가
valuation of farmland 순농지평가
valuation of fixed assets 고정자산평가
valuation of goods 자재평가
valuation of goodwill 영업권평가
valuation of house 가옥평가
valuation of inventory 재고자산평가
valuation of leasehold 차지권평가
valuation of listed stock 상장주식평가
valuation of loan 대부금채무평가
valuation of occupancy right 점용권평가
valuation of patent right 특허권평가
valuation of preemptive right 신주인수권평가
valuation of property 재산평가
valuation of residential site 택지평가
valuation of right of lease 임차권평가
valuation of securities 유가증권평가
valuation of stock without quotation 거래시세가 없는 주식평가
valuation of work in process 시제품평가
valuation on perfect competitive market 완전경쟁시장에서의 평가
valuation principle 평가원칙
valuation profit 평가익
valuation reserve 평가성 준비금
valuation standards of fixed assets 고정자산

평가기준
value 가액
value accounting 가치회계
value added 부가가치
value added analysis 부가가치분석
value added network 부가가치통신망
value added tax 부가가치세
value agreement endorsement on dwelling risks 가격협정보험
value approach 밸류어프로치
value at-risk 밸류앳리스크
value date 기산일(起算日)
value declared 신고가격
value diagram 밸류다이어그램
value engineering 가치공학
value exchange system 가치교환시스템
value in use 사용가치
value investor 가치 목적의 투자가
value line 정보서비스
value line average 밸류라인평가
value line composite index 밸류라인종합지수
value line index 밸류라인인덱스
value line option 밸류라인옵션
value line ranking 밸류라인랭킹
Value Line Stock Index 밸류라인주가지수
value next month 익월인도
value of assessment 과세가격
value of lease 임대가격
value of the transaction 거래가격
value productivity 가치생산성
value received 대가수령
value today 당일인도
value tomorrow 익일인도
value variance 가액차이
value-added product 고부가가치제품
valued policy 평가필 보험
vanilla structure 단순한 방식
vanilla swaps 바닐라스와프
variability 불안정성
variability factor 변동지수
variable 변수
variable annuity 변액연금
variable budget 변동예산
variable capital 가변자본
variable cash reserve requirements 가변형 현금준비제도
variable charge 변동비
variable constant 가변상수
variable cost and expenses 변동비
variable cost ratio 변동원가율
variable costing 변동소득계산
variable expenses 변동비
variable insurance 변액보험
variable interest rate 변동이율
variable investment tax 가변투자세
variable overhead 변동관리비
variable profit 변동이익
variable rate mortgage loan 변동금리형 부동산론
variable repo 금리입찰방식레포
variable universal life insurance 변액유니버설보험
variable zone 변동가격권
variable-rate debt 변동금리채무
variable-rate interest 변동금리
variable-rate loan 변동금리론
variables sampling 변수샘플링
variance 차이
variance account 원가차액계정
variable accounting 변동분석회계
variance analysis 분산분석
variance of the estimate 평가차액
variance ratio 분산비
variation from budget 예산차이
variation margin 변동증거금
variance margin call 변동증거금지불
various kinds of income 각종소득
various kinds of tax benefits 세법상의 특전
vega 베가
vega-neutral 베가뉴트럴
velocity of circulation 유통속도
velocity of circulation of money 화폐유통속도

vendee 구입자
vendor 판매자
venture 사업
venture business 벤처비즈니스
venture capital 벤처캐피탈
venue 행위지
verbal 구두의
verdict 평결
verification 검증
verification by telephone 전화확인
verification of a seal impression 인감조회
verification purpose 조회목적
versus ~와 대비하여
vertical analysis 수직분석
vertical integration 수직통합
vertical M&A 수직적인 M&A
vertical merger 수직합병
vertical specialization 수직적인 국제분업
vertical spread 버티컬스프레드
vertical spread transaction 버티컬스프레드거래
vertical territorial customer restrictions 수직적인 고객제한
vertical trade 수직적인 무역
vessel unknown 적재한 선박의 이름을 알지 못함
vest 권리를 주다
vested benefit obligation 확정급부채무
vested in interest 발생확정시키다
vested in possession 현재 소유한
vested interest 확정권리
vested remainder 확정잔여권
vested rights 기득권
vesting 수급권부여
Veterans Administration 재향군인관리국
veto 거부
viable 성장할 수 있는
vice chairman 부의장
vice president 부총재
vicinity of the upper limit 천정권
vicious cycle 악순환
vicious member merchant 악질가맹점
view of lowering interest rate 금리가 낮으리라 예상함
vigorous change 강력한 변화
vintage of capital 평균자본연령
violation of a contract 계약위반
violation of just and equitable principles 신의칙위반
violent fluctuation 시세난조
virtually unchanged 큰 변화가 없는
virtuous cycle 호순환
visual curve-fitting method 작도법
visual inspection 실제조사
vital statistics 인구동태통계
void 무효의
void agreement 무효합의
void contract 무효계약
void transaction 효력이 없는 법률행위
volatile market 변동시장
volatility 볼라틸리티
volatility ratio 변동율
volatility spread 볼라틸리티스프레드
volatility value 볼라틸리티가치
volume accumulation 누적생산고
volume accumulator 볼륨어큐뮬레이터(누적지표의 한 종류)
volume cost 양산원가
volume efficiency 양산효과
volume indicator 조업도지수
volume of business 거래고
volume of inventories 재고량
volume of issuance 발행규모
volume of over-the-counter transaction 장외매매고
volume ratio 볼륨레이쇼
volume variance 조업도 차이
voluntary 임의의; 약인 없이
voluntary accumulation plan 임의형 계속투자플랜
voluntary additions 임의편입액
voluntary adjustment 자기부인

voluntary arbitration 임의중재
voluntary association 자발적인 조직
voluntary audit 임의감사
voluntary bankruptcy 자기파산
voluntary conveyance 무상양도
voluntary depreciation 임의상각
voluntary depreciation method 임의상각법
voluntary dissolution 임의해산
voluntary export restraint 수출자주규제
voluntary insurance 임의보험
voluntary liquidation 임의정리
voluntary method of computing depreciation 임의상각법
voluntary partnership 임의조합
voluntary place of tax payment 임의납세지
voluntary reserve 임의준비금
voluntary restraint program 자주규제계획
voluntary restriction of export 수출자주규제
voluntary saving 자발적인 저축
voluntary settlement 무상승계적인 부동산처분
voluntary tax payment 자주납부
voluntary unemployment 자발적인 실업
voluntary winding up 임의해산
volunteer 무상취득자
Vostro account 상대편계정
voting 투표
voting bond 의결권부 사채
voting company 결의권회사
voting right 의결권
voting right of stockholder 주주의결권
voting stock 의결권주식
voting trust 의결권신탁
voting trust certificate 의결권신탁증서
voucher 전표
voucher for disbursement 불출증표
voucher payable register 지불전표기입장
voucher system 지출전표제도
vouching 전표대조
voyage policy 항해보험
vulnerability 취약성
vulnerable 취약한

W

wage assignment 급료공제
wage ceiling 임금상한설정
wage contract 임금협정
wage in kind 현물급여
wage income 임금소득
wage increase 임금인상
wage level 임금수준
wage negotiation 노사교섭
wage rate 임률
wage structure 임금체계
wage system 임금체계
wage unit 임금단위
wage variance 임금차이
wage-bracket table 간이세류표
wage-earner 임금생활자
wage-freeze 임금동결
wage-hike drive 임금투쟁
wage-price control 임금물가통제
wage-price guideline 임금물가 가이드라인
wage-push inflation 임금인플레이션
wager policy 도박보험
wages ledger 임금원장
wages on job evaluation 직능급
wages payable 미불임금
wait and see 시황관망
wait for reaction 반응을 기다림
waiting for further development 전개를 기다림
waiting period 대기기간
waiver 권리방기
waiver clause 권리방기조항
waiver of obligation 채무면제
waiver of premium 보험료불입면제
wall flower 인기가 떨어진 물건
Wall Street 월가
Wall Street Journal 월스트리트저널
war bereaved 전몰자 유족
war clause 전쟁약관
war perils 전쟁위험
warehouse charges 차고료
warehouse expenses 보관료
warehouse fee 창고료
warehouse receipt 예금증권
warehouse rent 보관료
warehousing and carrying charge 보관비
warehousing and harbor transportation service industry 창고운송관련업
warning against fraud 부정행위에 대한 경고
warrant 위임장; 워런트
warrant agent 워런트대리인
warrant agreement 워런트계약서
warrant bond 워런트채
warrant in bankruptcy 파산자 재산차압명령
warrant market 워런트시장
warrant of attachment 차압명장
warrant outstanding 발행필 워런트
warrant parity 워런트패러티
warrant value 워런트밸류
warranted rate of growth 적정성장률
warranty 보증

warranty obligation 보증채무
Warsaw Treaty Organization 바르샤바조약기구
wash order 와시오더
wash sale 가장매매
waste 폐기물
watch and wait 관망
watch committee 공안위원회
watch list 요주의명부
water-bailiff 수로주변감시관
watered assets 수증자산
watered capital 의제자본;수할자본
watered stock 수증주식
wave function 파동함수
Wave Theory 웨이브이론
way 통행권
way for subscription 모집방법
weak form 위크폼
weak tone 약한 시세
weaker economy 경기후퇴기
weaker U .S . dollar 달러약세
weakness 연조(軟調)
wealth tax 부유세
wear and tear 손모
weather insurance 날씨보험
wedge 웨지
wedge formation 웨지포메이션
Wednesday-factor 수요일요인
week order 위크오더
weekend effect 주말효과
weekly accounting 주차결산
weekly chart 매주의 차트
weekly payment 일주간지불
weekly reversal 위클리리저벌
weight of evidence 증거의 무게
weighted 가중
weighted arithmetic average 가중산술평균
weighted average 가중평균
weighted average cost method 가중평균원가법
weighted average method 가중평균법
weighted average number of common share outstanding 가중평균보통주수
weighted average of market capitalization 시가총액가중평균치
weighted basis trade 가중평균베이스무역
weighted index 가중지수
weighted mean 가중평균
weighted mean method 가중평균법
weighted rebalancing 가중재편성
weighted stock price average 가중평균주가
weighting ratio 편입률
welcome enterprise 기업유치
welfare economics 후생경제학
welfare expense 복리후생비
welfare facilities 복리후생시설
welfare pension 후생연금
welfare pension insurance 후생연금보험
what if 가정에 기반을 둠
when-issued basis 발행일기준
when-issued transaction 발행일거래
where got and where gone statement 투자원천운용표
white knight 백마 탄 왕자;매수위기의 기업을 구하기 위해 개입하는 제 3의 기업
white paper on economic cooperation 경제협력백서
white return 백색신고
whole life insurance 종신보험
wholesale 도매량
wholesale accounting 도매회계
wholesale bank 홀세일뱅크
wholesale banking 도매은행업무
wholesale business 도매업
wholesale dealer 도매상
wholesale establishment 도매사업
wholesale group insurance 단체급계약
wholesale price 도매가격
wholesale price index 도매물가지수
wholesale trade 도매업
wholesale trade industry 도매업계
wholesaler 도매업자

wholly owned subsidiary 완전소유자회사
wide fluctuation of market 난조시장
widening gap 확대되는 격차
wider band 변동폭이 있는 고정제
wider margin 확대상장변동
widow-and-orphan stock 안정배당주
widow's pension 미망인연금
width of currency movements 환변동폭
wild card option 와일드카드옵션
wild card period 와일드카드기간
willful 고의의
willfully evading the tax 고의적인 탈세
willfully false 고의적인 허위
Williams Act 윌리엄즈법
willingness to pay 반제의지
windfall loss 예상 밖의 손실
windfall loss or gain 우발적인 손익
windfall profit 뜻밖의; 행운의
winding up 해산
winding-up Act 해산법
winding-up by the court 강제청산
winding-up of pending affairs 잔무정리
winding-up order 청산명령
window 창구
window dressing 분식(粉飾)
window dressing deposit 분식예금
window dressing financial statement 분식제무제표
window dressing settlement 분식결산
window guidance 창구지도
windstorm and flood insurance 풍수해보험
wire houses 개인고객을 상대하는 증권회사
wire transfer 전신송금
with a proviso 조건부
with average 분손담보
with discount 액면이하
with premium 액면이상
with recourse credit 상환의무를 면제하지 않는 신용장
with the exception of 제외하고는
withdraw 물러나다
withdrawl 철수
withdrawl from membership 회원탈퇴
withdrawl of certificate 증서교부
withdrawl of deposited margin 증거금인출
withdrawl of membership 탈퇴
withdrawl of receipt 수리철회
withdrawl of stock certificates 주권교부
withdrawal plan 인출플랜
withdrawing member 탈퇴회원
withholding agent 원천징수의무자
withholding and payment 원천징수와 납부
withholding at the source 원천징수
withholding exemption certificate 원천징수표
withholding income tax 원천징수소득세
withholding of customs appraisement 관세평가금지
withholding of employment income 급여소득에 대한 원천징수
withholding record of employment income 급여소득원천징수표
withholding tax 원천과세
withholding tax credit 원천세액공제
withholding tax on income 원천소득세
withholding tax option 원천선택
withholding tax system 원천징수제도
within limits on value of call option 콜옵션가치범위
within the due date of filing the return 신고서제출기한내
without credit at sight buying rate 신용장이 없는 일람불어음매입상장
without prejudice 권리를 손상하지 않고
without prejudice to preliminary 기득권을 범하지 않고
without recourse 상환의무를 지지 않는
without recourse credit 상환의무면제신용장
words of limitation 내용표시문언
work 작업
work in process ledger 제작 중인 물건의 원장
work in progress 제작 중인 물건

work order 제조지도서
work rules 취업규제
work sheet 정산표
workable competition 유효경쟁
worker's property accumulation savings 재형저축
workers union 종업원조합
workers' s accident comprehensive insurance 노동재해종합보험
working account 활동계정
working assets 운용자산
working balance 운용잔고
working budget 실행예산
working capital 운전자금
working capital analysis 운전자본분석
working capital control 운전자금관리
working capital position 운전자본상태
working capital ratio 유동비율
working condition 작업조건
working cost 영업비
working days 작업일수
working fund 운전자금
Working Group of Financial Markets 금융시장협의회
working hours 작업시간
working interest 임차권이권
working inventory 운전재고자산
working place 사업장
working rules of audit procedures in reporting 감사보고준칙
working trial balance 감사시산표
working trial balance sheet 시산표
working year 영업연도
working-capital ratio 운전자본비율
working-hours method 운전시간법
workmen's compensation 노동재해보험
workmen's compensation acts 노동자재해보상법
workmen's compensation insurance 노동자재해보상보험
workmen's compensation law 노동자배상법
worksheet method 정산표방식
workshop 작업장
World Bank 세계은행
World Bank bond 세계은행채
World Bank group 세계은행그룹
world class investor 세계규모의 투자가
world crisis 세계공황
world enterprise 세계기업
world index 월드인덱스
World Intellectual Property Organization 세계지적소유권기관
world market 세계시장
world market portfolio 포트폴리오
world market price 국제시장가격
world marketing 세계마케팅
world money 세계화폐
worth and fixed assets ratio 자본고정자산비율
worth to current debt ratio 자본유동부채비율
worth to debts ratio 자본부채비율
worth to fixed debt ratio 자본고정부채비율
worth to fixed ratio 자본고정비율
wrapping-up 종료
write off bad debts 대손을 상각하다
write up 과대평가하다
write-down 평가감
write-off 상각
write-off from special bad debts reserve 채권상각특별계정소멸
write-up 평가증
writer 매출자
writing 주식신용거래나 상품선물거래에서 성립된 판매주문
written agreement 서면계약
written application 서면신청
written assignment 양도증서
written bid and offer 기재한 호가
written contract 서면계약
written decision 재결서
written down value 평가감후 가격
written examination 필기시험

written inquiry 서면문의
written law 성문법
written option 판매옵션
written premium 계상보험료
written proxy 대리권을 증명하는 서류
wrong doing 부정행위
wrongful dismissal 부당해고

Y

Yankee bond 양키본드
Yankee bond market 미국달러채시장
year end stock 기말재고
year in brief 당년도의 개황
year to which listing day pertains 상장일의 연도
year-end 연말
year-end adjustment 연말조정
year-end demand for fund 연말자금수요
year-end dividend 기말배당
year-end market 연말상장
year-end settlement 연말조정
year-to-year changes 경년변동율
year-to-year percentage change 전년대비변화율
yearly earnings 연간총익
yearly installment 연부(年賦)
yearly taxation 연세주의(年稅主義)
years elapsed after foundation 설립후 경과연수
yield auction 이율입찰
yield based on weighted average 가중평균이익
yield book 이익표
yield by simple interest 단리이익
yield curve 일드커브
yield curve differential 이율격차
yield curve flattening 이율곡선평준화
yield curve inversion 역일드
yield curve risk 이율곡선리스크
yield curve swap 일드커브스와프
yield differential 이익격차
yield enhancement 이익향상
yield factor 이익요인
yield for average life 평균잔존연한이익
yield for holding period 소유기간이익
yield improvement switch 이익개선스위치
yield of bond transaction 채권매매이율
yield on already issued bond 기발채이익
yield on bond 채권이익
yield on investment 운용이익
yield on public and corporate bond 공사채응모자이익
yield rate 이율비
yield rate variance 이율비차이
yield spread 이익격차
yield standard 이익수준
yield structure 이익구조
yield swap 일드스와프
yield to call 임의상환이익
yield to maturity 만기이익
yield to subscriber 응모자이익
yield-to-call 조상상환이익
yield-to-put 매입청구이익
yields of public and corporate bonds 공사채이율
yo-yo stock 요요주식
yours 유어즈(팔았을 때)

Z

zai-tech 재테크
zaibatsu 재벌
zero-beta portfolio 제로베타포트폴리오
zero-cost collar 제로코스트칼라
zero-cost option 제로코스트옵션
zero-cost option trading 제로코스트옵션거래
zero-coupon bond 제로쿠폰채
zero-coupon curve 제로쿠폰커브
zero-coupon issue 제로쿠폰채
zero-coupon T-note 제로쿠폰 T노트
zero-plus tick 제로펄스틱
zero-sum game 제로섬게임
Zillmer quota 질멜비율
Zillmerized reserve 질멜식 책임준비금

[KOREAN-ENGLISH]

한영편

ㄱ

가감하다 added or deducted
가격감응성 price sensitivity
가격개정 price revision
가격결정 price determination; price fixing
가격결정전략 pricing strategy
가격결정툴 pricing tool
가격경쟁 price competition
가격경쟁력 cost competitiveness
가격경직성 rigidity of price
가격계산 pricing calculation
가격계수 price factor
가격계약 price contract
가격구조 price structure
가격담합협정 price-fixing agreement
가격대비성능비 cost performance
가격동결 price freeze
가격리스크 price risk
가격리스크;시장리스크 market risk
가격메카니즘 price mechanism
가격발견 price discovery
가격변동 movement of price; price fluctuation
가격변동률 price volatility
가격변동수정 adjustment for price fluctuations
가격변동이 심한 물품 noticeably fluctuating goods
가격변동준비금 price fluctuation reserve; reserve against decline in price; reserve for inventory fluctuation; reserve for price fluctuation
가격변동준비금편입 provision for reserve for price fluctuation
가격변동준비금환수 reversal of reserve for price fluctuation
가격변동폭제한 fluctuation limit
가격보험 price insurance
가격보호 price protection
가격분석 price analysis
가격상승 price boost; price rise; rise in price
가격상승국면에서 at an increase in price
가격수익률 price earnings ratio
가격수준변동회계 accounting for price-level change
가격신축성 price flexibility
가격안정 price stability
가격안정조작 price supporting
가격안정화 pegging
가격양보 price concession
가격우선 price priority
가격유지보조금 price support subsidy
가격이 상승한 토지 accommodation lands
가격이론 price theory
가격이율곡선 price yield curve
가격인상 price hike
가격인하 mark down; reduction in price
가격인하불안 downsizing
가격인하여지 downside risk
가격입찰 price auction
가격정보 price information
가격정책 price policy

가격조작 manipulation of the market; painting the tape
가격조정 price adjustment
가격지정산정법 limit calculation
가격차별 price discrimination
가격차액으로 이익을 얻음 speculation for difference
가격차이 price differential; price discrepancies; price divergence; price variance
가격차이로 이익얻기 profit taking
가격차익 price margin
가격차익금 profit from the difference between new and old official prices
가격체계 price system
가격카르텔 price cartel
가격탄력성 price elasticity
가격통제 price control
가격패턴 price pattern
가격폭 price difference; price range
가격폭제한 daily price limit; price limit; price line; price movement limit; restriction of price range; trading limits
가격폭주문 stop limit order
가격표시방법 price indication method
가격표준 price standards
가격하락 falling in price
가격하락위험을 피하기 위해 현물을 보유하였으면서도 신용거래로 판매하는 행위 selling short against the box
가격하향국면에서 at a decrease in price
가격한도 limit of price
가격행동 price action
가격협정보험 value agreement endorsement on dwelling risks
가격효과 price effect
가결산 provisional settlement of account
가결산일 assumed settling day
가계 household
가계부 family bookkeeping
가계부문 household sector
가계비 household expenses; housekeeping expenses
가계소비지출 household consumption expenditure
가계약 interim contract
가계조사 survey of households
가계조사(家計調查) family income and expenditure survey
가계채무 household debt
가공 processing
가공거래 fictitious transaction
가공계좌 fictitious account
가공매상전표 fictitious sales slip
가공명의예금 fictitious name deposit
가공무역 improvement trade; processing deal trade
가공비 cost of processing; processing cost; processing expenses
가공세 processing tax
가공이익 fictitious profit; paper profit
가능성조항 availability clause
가대차대조표 tentative balance sheet
가동률 operating ratio; rate of operating
가동시간 hours worked
가동율 percent of capacity use
가동이익 income earned
가동중인 론 performing loans
가등기 provisional registration
가망이 없는 상실 irretrievable deprivation
가맹권 membership
가맹은행 member bank
가맹점 member's store
가맹점수수료 merchant fee
가맹점점포 merchant outlet
가맹점획득회원 acquiring member
가명령 provisional order
가법감산 additive substruction
가벼운 긴장 slight tightening
가변상수 variable constant
가변자본 variable capital
가변투자세 variable investment tax

가변형 현금준비제도 variable cash reserve requirements
가봉 temporary seal
가분조항 several covenant
가분채권 divisible claim
가분채무 divisible obligation
가불 borrowing in advance
가불금 suspense payment; temporary payment
가불금계정 suspense payment account
가사관련비 expenses incurred for maintaining household
가산 homestead right
가산세 additional tax; penalty tax; tax for default
가석방허가증 ticket of leave
가설검정 test of hypothesis
가설상의 상정 hypothetical assumption
가속감가상각 accelerated depreciation
가속도계수 acceleration coefficient
가속도원리 acceleration principle
가속상각 accelerated amortization
가속상각법 accelerated cost recovery system; accelerated depreciation methods
가수금 suspense receipts; temporary receipts
가수금계정 suspense receipts account; temporary receipts account
가수선 temporary repairs
가수선비 cost of temporary repair
가수요 fictitious demand
가수요 speculative demand
가수입 speculative import
가액 value
가액차이 value variance
가영수증 interim receipt
가옥평가 valuation of house
가이드라인 guideline
가이드라인 내생연수 guideline service life
가임(家賃)상장 rental market value
가임(家賃)소득 rental income
가임료 house rent income
가임수당 rental allowance
가입 acquisition of membership
가입금 admission fee
가입률 penetration rate
가입연령 age at entry
가입연령방식 entry age cost method
가입코스트 entry cost
가장 가까운 달 nearest month
가장 아래 first bottom
가장매매 wash sale
가장행위 disguised act
가재도구 household goods
가재포괄보험 personal property floater
가전제품 consumer electronics
가정 assumptions; hypothesis
가정에 기반을 둠 what if
가정이익 but-for income
가족보험 family policy
가족상해보험 family personal accident policy
가족수당 dependent allowance; family allowance
가주소 provisional residence
가중 weighted
가중사요 aggravation
가중산술평균 weighted arithmetic average
가중세;과징금 surcharge
가중재편성 weighted rebalancing
가중지수 weighted index
가중평균 weighted average; weighted mean
가중평균법 weighted average method; weighted mean method
가중평균베이스무역 weighted basis trade
가중평균보통주수 weighted average number of common share outstanding
가중평균원가법 weighted average cost method
가중평균이익 yield based on weighted average
가중평균주가 weighted stock price average
가증서; 보험인수증 cover note
가집행 provisional execution
가차압 ancillary attachment
가차압 provisional attachment; provisional seizure

가처분 provisional disposition
가처분소득 disposable income
가처분이익 available profit; disposable profit
가치 목적의 투자가 value investor
가치공학 value engineering
가치교환시스템 value exchange system
가치를 높이다 enhance
가치보장수단 store of value
가치생산성 value productivity
가치재(價値財) merit goods
가치패러독스 paradox of value
가치회계 value accounting
가트;관세와 무역에 관한 일반협정 General Agreement on Tariffs and Trade
각각의 respective
각국통화단위 denominated in each currency
각사업연도의 소득액 amount of income for each taxable year
각서 letter of comfort; letter of undertaking; memorandum of understanding
각종명세 schedule
각종소득 classified income; various kinds of income
각주 footnote
각하하다 ignore; quash
간사 manager
간사단 managers
간사수수료 management fee
간사은행 managing bank
간사증권 managing underwriter
간사증권회사 sponsoring securities firm
간사회의 sponsoring member
간섭 interference
간이과세제도 simplified tax system
간이보험 industrial insurance; postal life insurance
간이부기 simplified bookkeeping system
간이상장 simple listing
간이세류표 wage-bracket table
간이종업원퇴직연금 simplified employee pension
간이형 short form
간접공제 indirect credit
간접금융 indirect financing
간접노무비 indirect labor cost
간접매매 indirect sales
간접무역 indirect trade
간접발행 indirect issue
간접배당 payment regarded as dividends
간접법 indirect method
간접보증 indirect guarantee
간접부문비 indirect department cost
간접부수비용 indirect incidental expenses
간접부채 indirect liability
간접비 business commencement expenses
간접비 indirect cost; indirect expenses; overhead cost
간접비 배부부족액 unabsorbed burden
간접비(원재료와 노무비 이외) burden on cost
간접비배부 overhead cost distribution
간접비배부기준 overhead distribution basis
간접비배부율 distribution rate of overhead cost; overhead rate
간접비배부초과액 overabsorbed burden
간접비분배 distribution of overhead cost
간접비준비금 reserve for overhead
간접비차이 overhead variance
간접비할부 application of overhead
간접비할부표 application rate of overhead cost
간접사업세 indirect business tax
간접상각 indirect method of depreciation
간접상속 mediate descent
간접생산 indirect production
간접세 indirect tax; outlay tax
간접세협력단체 cooperative association on indirect taxes
간접손해 consequential damage
간접송달 constructive service
간접수요;파생수요 derived demand
간접예금 indirect deposit

간접외국세액공제 indirect foreign tax credit
간접원가; 보충비용 supplementary cost
간접이익 indirect yield
간접임금 indirect wage
간접재료비 indirect material cost
간접재정 indirect exchange arbitrage
간접증거 indirect evidence
간접증권 indirect securities
간접투자 indirect investment
간접표시 indirect presentation
간주교부금 deemed bounty
간주기부금 deemed donations
간주배당 consent dividend
간주배당 constructive dividends
간주배당 deemed dividend
간주법인 deemed corporation
간주법인과세 taxation on deemed corporation
간주사업연도 deemed accounting period
간주상속재산 deemed inherited property
간주세액공제 tax sparing
간주소유 constructive ownership
간주심사청구 deemed request for reconsideration
간주양도 deemed transfer
간주외국세액공제 tax sparing credit system
간주이자 fictitious coupon
간판뿐인 가게 brass-plate office
간편상각 simplified method of depreciation
갈고리모양의 hooked
갈고리손 hook damage
감가상각 depreciation
감가상각가능한 depreciable
감가상각고 amount to be written off as depreciation
감가상각기금 depreciation fund
감가상각기초액 depreciation base
감가상각누계액 cumulative amount of depreciation
감가상각누적액 accumulated depreciation
감가상각단위 depreciation unit
감가상각률 ratio of depreciation; depreciation rate
감가상각발생액 accrued depreciation
감가상각법 depreciation method
감가상각부담 depreciation burden
감가상각비 depreciation expense
감가상각비누계 aggregate of depreciation deduction
감가상각비명세표 schedule of depreciation
감가상각액회복 recapture of depreciation
감가상각연수 depreciation period
감가상각예비금 allowance for depreciation
감가상각의 월할계산 monthly allotment of depreciable period
감가상각자산 depreciable assets
감가상각자산취득가액 acquisition cost of depreciable assets
감가상각준비금 depreciation reserve; reserve for depreciation
감가상각준비금비율 depreciation reserve ratio
감가상각타당성 depreciation adequacy
감가상각특례 exception to depreciation deduction
감가상각필 fully depreciated
감가상각회계 depreciation accounting
감가상각효과 rate of efficiency of depreciation
감가상각후 가액 depreciated value
감가상각후 원가 depreciated cost
감가상각후 원시원가 depreciated original cost
감가수당금 depletion allowance
감가율에 따른 상각 depreciation by depreciation rate
감가적립금 debenture redemption reserve
감가정율법 fixed percentage method; fixed percentage on declining balance method
감당할 수가 없는 spike
감독관 management supervisor
감독절차 summary procedure
감리 supervision
감리명령 supervision and order
감리위원회 board of supervisors

감마 gamma
감마분포 gamma distribution
감마익스포저 gamma exposure
감면 reduction and exemption of taxes
감면세액공제 deduction for tax reduction
감모가능한 depletive
감모상각 depletion; depletion assets
감모상각원가법 cost method of depletion
감모차이 shrinkage variance
감배 dividend cut; dividend decrease; reduced dividend
감사 audit
감사공준 postulate of auditing
감사권 right of auditing
감사기준 auditing standards; general audit standards
감사기준서 Statements on Auditing Standards
감사기준심의회 Auditing Standards Board
감사범위 scope of audit
감사법인 auditing corporation
감사보고기준 reporting audit standards
감사보고서 accountant report; audit report; auditor's report; opinion of independent certified public accountant
감사보고준칙 working rules of audit procedures in reporting
감사보수 audit fee
감사상각원가 depreciable cost
감사시기 audit time
감사시산표 working trial balance
감사실시기준 field-work audit standards
감사역 comptroller
감사역;감사 auditor
감사연도 audit year
감사의견 audit opinion
(비공식) 감사의견서; 각서 comfort letter
감사의견서 opinion of auditors
감사이론 auditing theory
감사인의 독립성 auditors' independence
감사인의 의견 auditor's opinion
감사인의 책임 auditors' liability
감사절차 audit procedure; auditing procedure
감사절차기준 standards of audit procedures
감사절차서 statement on auditing procedures
감사절차위원회 committee on auditing procedure
감사조사서 audit file
감사증거 audit evidence
감사증명 audit certification
감사증명서 audit certificate
감사타이밍 audit timing
감사표명 audit representation
감사필 금액 audited amount
감사필 연차재무보고서 annual audited financial statement
감사필 재무제표 certificated financial statement
감세 legal tax cut; reduction of taxes; tax cut by law; tax reduction
감세국채 government bond for tax reduction
감세채권 tax relief bonds
감소 setback
감속경향 decelerating trend
감수 decreased receipts
감수압력 revenue pressures
감시 monitoring; surveillance
감시손익항목 nonrecurring item
감시이익 nonrecurring profit
감시포스트 monitoring post
감액 abatement
감액청구 abatement claim
감응도 계수 sensitivity coefficient
감응도 분석 sensitivity analysis
감응도 조정 sensitivity adjustment
감응성 sensitivity
감익 decreased earnings
감자 capital decrease; capital reduction
감자산가격 reduced asset price
감자잉여금 reduction surplus; surplus from capital reduction
감자차손 loss from capital reduction
감자차익 gains from capital stock reduction;

gains from stock retirement; profit from capital reduction
감자회사 company with reduced capital
감정;정서 sentiment
감정료 survey fee
감정보고서 survey report
감정인 assessor
감채기금 sinking fund
감채기금계정 sinking fund account
감채기금우선주 sinking fund preferred stock
감채기금적립금 reserve for sinking fund; sinking fund reserve
감채기금적립액 sinking fund requirements
감채기금채무 sinking fund obligation
감채기금편입 sinking fund payments
감채적립금 retained earnings appropriated for bond
감채제도 redemption system
감추다 harbor
값싼 자산 undervalued asset
값을 깎아 내려가는 경매 Dutch auction
값을 끌어올림 bidding up
값을 어림짐작하여 매기다 short covering at a loss
값이 쌈 undervalued
값이 오른 이익 capital appreciation
강력한 변화 vigorous change
강보합 firmer; gaining
강세 bullish tone
강세 리버설패턴 bullish reversal patterns
강세 콘솔리데이션패턴 bullish consolidation pattern
강세; 약세 bull and bear
강세근성 bull clique
강세매입 bull buying
강세수준유지 unchanged to slightly higher
강세스프레드거래 bull spread transaction
강세시장 bull market
강세시황 strong market
강약 strong and weak
강약세 bull bear bond
강약지수 bull and bear index
강제감사 compulsory audit
강제경매 compulsory sale by auction; forced auction
강제교환 forced exchange; involuntary conversion
강제금지명령 mandatory injunction
강제담보변환 mandatory collateral substitution
강제매각 forced sale
강제매매 juridical sale
강제보험 compulsory insurance; obligatory insurance
강제상환 mandatory redemption
강제소송참가 cross claim
강제이행 office grant
강제자산양도 compulsory transfer of property
강제저축 forced saving
강제적인 coercive; compulsory
강제적인 감책기금조항 mandatory sinking fund requirement
강제적인 양도 involuntary transfer
강제전환 forced conversion
강제전환사채 mandatory convertible bond
강제지불불능 involuntary insolvency
강제집행 compulsory execution; forcible execution
강제채무증서 bill obligatory
강제처분 forcible disposition
강제처분가치 forced-sale value
강제철수 compulsory withdrawal
강제청산 compulsory liquidation; compulsory winding-up; forced liquidation
강제청산 winding-up by the court
강제통용력이 있는 지폐 legal tender note
강제파산 involuntary bankruptcy
강제하다 enforce
강제합병 statutory merger
강제해약 compulsory cancellation
강제화의 compulsory composition
강제환가 compulsory conversion into money

강제환가절차 procedure of the compulsory conversion into money
강한 느낌 strong feeling; strong sentiment
강한 성장 strong growth
강한 재료 bullish factor
강한 저항선 bullish resistance line
강한 지지선 bullish support line
강한 채널 bullish channel
강행규정 forcible provisions
강행할 수 있는 enforceable
강화하다 beef up
개념 concept
개량 improvement
개량비 betterment expense; improvement cost; improvement expense
개량특허 improvement patent
개발격차 development gap
개발규제 development regulation
개발도상국 developing countries; less-developed country
개발부담금 charge for development
개발비 development cost; development expenses
개발수입 develop and import scheme
개발업자 developer
개발자금 development fund
개발자금대부 lending of development funds
개발자본 development capital
개발중 under development
개방경제 open economy
개방단체 open group
개방식 담보 open-end mortgage
개방식 담보부사채 open-end mortgage bond
개방식의 open-end
개방하다 affranchise
개방형 인플레이션 open inflation
개별감가상각법 unit method
개별거래마다 리스크를 평가함 transaction approach
개별경쟁매매 individual auction
개별공제 itemized deduction
개별과세 individual taxation
개별기업 고유의 company-specific
개별기준 individual basis
개별내용연수 individual useful life
개별매매방식 individual dealing system
개별목적재무제표 special purpose financial statements
개별법 identified cost method
개별상각 individual depreciation; item depreciation; unit depreciation
개별상품 individual issue
개별생산 individual production
개별소비세 specific consumption tax
개별신고서 separate return
개별원가 job cost; specific cost
개별원가계산 job cost system; job order costing
개별원가계산 production order cost accounting
개별원가계산법 job order cost system
개별원가계산제도 specific-order cost system
개별재보험 specific reinsurance
개별재산세 specific property tax
개별전기 unit posting
개별중재 ad hoc arbitration
개별책임 several liability
개별책임의 severally liable
개봉예금 unsealed deposit
개산가격 approximate price; approximate value
개산경비공제 deduction of estimated expenses
개산경비율 rate of estimated expenses
개산공제 standard deduction
개산대차대조표 rough balance system
개산액 approximate amount
개산요구 estimate of budget requests
개산원가 approximate cost; estimated cost; rough cost
개산원가표 rough cost book
개산지불 payment by rough estimate
개선 amelioration; betterment
개설은행 opening bank

개시 disclosure; inception
개시권 right to begin
개시범위 extension of disclosure
개시원칙 disclosure philosophy
개시일 commencement date
개시일포함 period commencing on but excluding the date of
개시잔고계정 opening balance account
개업계 notification of opening of business
개업비 expenses incurred for opening of business
개업비 initial cost of business
개요 executive summary
개요시트 synopsis sheet
개인가처분소득 disposable personal income
개인건강보험 individual health insurance
개인고객을 상대하는 증권회사 wire houses
개인공제 individual exclusion
개인금융 personal financing
개인금융자산 financial assets of individuals
개인기업 sole proprietorship
개인당좌계정 personal checking account
개인론 personal loan
개인명의계좌 private account
개인배당소득 personal dividend income
개인배상책임보험 personal liability insurance
개인변액연금 individual variable annuity
개인보증 personal guarantee
개인보험 personal insurance
개인보험자 specialist insurer
개인부문 personal sector
개인부채 personal liability
개인사업주 single proprietorship; sole proprietor
개인생명보험 individual life insurance
개인소득 personal income
개인소득세 individual income tax; personal income tax
개인소비 personal consumption expenditure
개인신용 personal credit
개인신용정보 consumer's credit file
개인신탁 personal trust; private trust
개인신탁펀드 personal trust fund
개인어음 personal bill; private bill
개인연금 individual annuity; personal pension
개인연금보험 personal pension insurance
개인연금제도 personal pension scheme
개인예금 personal deposit
개인의 비밀보유권 personal immunity
개인이자소득 personal interest income
개인임대료소득 personal rental income
개인재산 personal property
개인재산소득 personal income from property
개인저축 personal saving
개인적인 편향 personal bias
개인적인 평가 personal valuation
개인주민세 individual inhabitant tax
개인주주 individual stockholder
개인지주비율 ratio of individual stock ownership
개인지출 personal expenditure
개인퇴직연금제도 individual retirement account
개인퇴직적립계정 Individual Retirement Account
개인투자가의 투자방침 investment policy of personal investor
개인파산 personal bankruptcy
개인회원 private member
개입 intervention
개입구입 intervention purchase
개입금리 intervention rate
개입기업;소유주지분 proprietorship
개입수준 intervention level
개입점 intervention point
개입조작 intervention operation
개입통화 intervention currency
개정대금업법 amended usury lax
개축공사 reconstruction works
개축비 reconstruction expense
개축적립금 reserve for renewals and replacements

ㄱ

객관적인 가치 objective value
객관적인 확률 objective probability
객관지표 objective indicator
갭 GNP gap GNP
갭(일반적으로 사용되는 회계원칙) GAAP
갭기간 gapping horizon
갭법 gap management technology
갭분석 gap analysis
갱생 rehabilitation
갱생담보권 secured claim
갱생수속 reorganization proceedings
갱생절차개시 commencement of reorganization proceedings
갱생회사 corporation in need of reorganization
갱신 renewal
갱신료 renewal charge; renewal fee
갱신빈도 reset frequency
갱신수수료 renewal commission
갱신일 refix date
갱신차금 difference by renewal
갱신투자 replacement investment
갱신하다 update
갱정;조정 correction
갱정결정으로 확정한 추가세액 settled additional tax due amount
갱정청구 claim for correction; request for correction
거대리스크 large risks
거대위험 target risk
거대한 잠재력 massive potential
거래 market transaction; transaction
거래가격 sale price; value of the transaction
거래거부 refusal to deal
거래계정 dealing account
거래고 volume of business
거래고세 turnover tax
거래관계를 청산하다 close one's position
거래규모 lot size
거래규칙 trading regulations
거래기간 time horizon
거래내용 particulars of transaction
거래노하우 trading know-how
거래단위 trading unit; underlying size
거래단위제도 trading unit system
거래담보금 trading collateral
거래동기 transaction motive
거래를 중개함 intermediation of trading
거래명세 schedule of transactions
거래범위 trading range
거래비용 dealing cost
거래세 trading tax; transaction tax
거래소 bourse; trading floor
거래소; 경마장에서 부당이익을 얻는 사람 bucketeer
거래소거래 exchange trade; stock exchange transaction; transaction on exchange
거래소거래세 bourse transaction tax
거래소매입 exchange acquisition
거래소법 exchange act; exchange law
거래소별세 exchange tax
거래소분배 exchange distribution
거래소세 bourse tax
거래소시장 exchange market
거래소시프트 transaction shift
거래소중매인 commission broker
거래소회비 member's fee
거래소회원 exchange member; member of stock exchange
거래수수료 transaction fee
거래시세가 없는 주식평가 valuation of stock without quotation
거래시스템 trading system
거래약정서 agency arrangement; customer's agreement and consent
거래에 대한 세금 tax on transaction
거래옵션 traded option
거래은행 relationship bank
거래의 신의칙 just and equitable principle of transactions
거래의 안전을 도모함 securing completion of transaction
거래의 종류 kinds of transaction

거래일 trading day
거래자격 qualification for trade; trading qualification
거래자격을 부여함 granting of trading qualification
거래자격정지 suspension of qualification for trade
거래재개 resumption of suspended trading; resumption of trading
거래정지 suspension of trading
거래정지;매매정지 trade suspension
거래정지처분 disposition by suspension of business
거래조건 business terms; trade term; trading conditions
거래종류별 by types of trading
거래중단 trandint haet
거래증거금 clearing margin
거래증거금 기준액 standard amount of clearing margin
거래증거금율산정기준치 tandard values for clearing margin rate calculations
거래증거금 환급 refund of clearing margin
거래증거금관리 management of clearing margin
거래증거금액산정기준일 base date for clearing margin calculation
거래증거금을 구분함 segregation of clearing margin
거래증거금환급 liquidation of clearing margin
거래처 clients
거래처수입보증금 customer's deposits
거래처원장 customer's ledger
거래처종합관리 relationship management system
거래총비용 total cost of transaction
거래코스트 transaction cost
거래포스트 trading post
거래확인 confirmation of transaction
거류지무역 settlement trade
거미집순환 cobweb cycle
거부 veto
거소 temporary residence
거액의 투자 considerable investment
거액주문 large order
거울삼아 in the light of
거절 disclaimer; discontinuity
거절;방기 repudiation
거절각서 note of protest
거절증서 memorandum of protest; rejection certificate
거절증서가 필요없음 no protest
거절증서불요문언 protest waived
거절증서작성수수료 protest charges
거절하다 renounce
거주 abode
거주외국법인 resident foreign corporation
거주외국인 resident alien
거주용 자산 property for residence
거주용 재산 residential property
거주자 resident
거주자외화예금 resident foreign currency deposits
거주자유러엔채 Euroyen bond for resident
거짓증자 straw man
거출금;분담금 contribution
거출잉여금 contributed surplus
거출자본 contributed capital
거출제도 contribution plan
거출형의 contribution defined
거치기간 grace period
거치저금 deferred savings
거치종신연금 deferred life annuity
거치형 연금 deferred annuity
건강보험 health insurance
건강보험료 health insurance premium
건강유지기구 Health Maintenance Organization
건물 plants and buildings
건물 등이 들어서지 않은 택지 land lot without construction
건물감가상각 depreciation of building
건물을 생산적인 사용변경함 conversion of

building for productive use
건설가계정 construction in process account
건설공사 construction work
건설공사보험 contractors' all risks insurance
건설공사수입 construction work revenue
건설국채 construction bond
건설비계정 construction account
건설업 construction industry
건설이자 interest incurred during construction
건설조성금 construction subsidy; government subsidy for capital expenditure
건설중인 건물 building under construction
건설지출 construction expenditure
건전성 soundness
건전성유지계약 keep-well agreement
건전재정주의 principle of balanced budget
건전한 구매테마 sound buy idea
건전한 은행업무 sound banking
건조중량 dry weight
건축계정 building account
건축대부조합 building and loan association
건축대차권 building lease
건축비 building expenses
건축세 building tax; tax on construction
건축조합 building societies
검사 inspection
검사보고서 report on examination
검사위원회 committee of inspection
검사증명서 inspection certificate
검수인 tally man
검인 seal
검인철회 revocation of probate
검정통계량 test statistic
검증 verification
검증하다 probate
검찰관 prosecutor
검찰청 prosecutors office
겉보기가격 shell branch
게산조견표 calculator
게임이론 game theory; theory of games
게임플랜 game plan
겐사키시장 gensaki
격감 sharp decline
격려 encouragement
격려금 bounty
격자법 lattice approach
격차균등화 equalizing divergences
격화 intensification
견고 steady
견고한 시황 steady market
견본비 sample expense
견본적송품 sample shipment
견식 knowledge and discernment
견실한 경영 conservative management
견실한 수요 healthy demand; solid demand
견적 pro forma estimated cost
견적감가상각 observed depreciation
견적공사원가 estimated cost of construction work
견적금액변경 changes in estimates
견적내용연수 expected life; estimated useful life
견적내용연수표 observed life table
견적대차대조표 budgeted balance sheet; estimated balance sheet; pro forma balance sheet; projected balance sheet
견적매각가격 estimated exit value
견적매상계정서 pro forma account sales
견적비용 estimated expenses
견적세액 estimated tax
견적손익계산서 estimated profit and loss statement; projected income statement
견적수정 pro forma adjustment
견적에 따른 채무 liability of estimated amount
견적원가 estimate cost
견적원가계산 estimated cost accounting
견적원가계산제도 estimated cost accounting system
견적원가제도 estimating-cost system
견적이익 estimated profit
견적자금운용표 statement of estimated application of fund

견적재무제표 pro forma financial statements; pro forma statement; projected financial statements
견적채무 estimated liabilities
견적환어음 pro forma bill; pro forma draft
결과책임 absolute liability
결론 conclusion
결론의 근거 basis for conclusions
결산 closing of accounts; closing the book; settlement of accounts
결산가격 settlement price
결산기 book closing period; fiscal year closed
결산발표 results announcement
결산보고 statement of account
결산분개 closing entries
결산서류 settlement statements
결산예비발표 preliminary disclosure of settlement of accounts
결산일 closing date; report date
결산일레이트 current rate
결산절차 account closing procedure; procedures of closing the books
결산정리 closing adjustment
결산조정 adjustment in settling accounts
결산하다 settle accounts
결산회사 reporting companies
결손 deficiency
결손계정 deficiency account
결손금 되풀이 tax loss carry-back
결손금계산서 deficit statement
결손금계정 deficit account
결손금액 deficit amount
결손금이월 carry over of deficit; tax loss carry-forward
결손금처리계산서 deficit disposition statement; deficit reconciliation statement
결손금환금공제 carry back of losses
결손금환급 carry back of deficit
결손액 amount of loss
결손전보적립금 reserve for losses
결손회수 recovery of loss
결원 vacancy
결원이 생길 때의 조치 measures in case of vacancy
결의 resolution
결의권회사 voting company
결의방법 method of resolution
결재하여 허가함 homologation
결점 demerit; flaw
결정 decision; ruling
결정계수 coefficient of determination
결정권 casting vote
결정으로 through the decision
결정적인 각하 peremptory nonsuit
결정적인 설시 peremptory instruction
결정적인 추정 conclusive presumption
결정준비금자본편입 recapitalization of legal reserve
결정통지서 notice of determination
결제 delivery versus payment settlement DVP; payment; settlement; trade settlement
결제계정 settlement account; transaction account
결제기구 settlement facility
결제대금 settlement value
결제를 위해 수수하는 금전 cash to be payed or received for settlement
결제리스크 transfer risk
결제물건 securities eligible for settlement
결제방식 settlement method; settlement method
결제불이행 default on clearing obligation; failure to settle; nonfulfillment of settlement; payment default
결제불이행에 대한 반제 compensation for the failure to settle
결제비율 settlements rate
결제사무 clearing business
결제사무를 위임함 entrustment clearing business
결제성 예금 checkable deposit
결제수단 payment system

결제수지 balance of clearing
결제시 clearing time
결제시한 settlement time
결제에 필요한 수수료 fee for settlement
결제이행 fulfillment settlement
결제일 delivery date; settlement date
결제일후 post-balance sheet date
결제할인 settlement discount
결제횟수 number of settlement transactions
결함품;하자품 defective goods
결합대차대조표 combined balance sheet
결합비용 joint cost
결합상각법 combined depreciation
결합손익계산서 combined profit and loss statement
결합재무제표 combined financial statement
겸무임원 director having duties in an employee's capacity
겸임중역 interlocking directors
경감 extenuation; mitigation
경감세율 reduced tax rate
경감세율적용소득금액 taxable income entitled to reduced tax rate
경계 bounds; fear
경계선 boundary
경계하는 자세 cautious stance
경과계정 deferred and accrued accounts
경과기간이 긴 론 seasoned loan
경과보험료 earned premium
경과시간 lapsed time
경과실 slight negligence
경과실수 actual number of days elapsed
경과연수 elapsed years; number of years elapsed
경과연수; 연령조사 aging
경과이자 accrual rate
경과이자; 미불이자 accrued interest
경과일수 lapsed days
경과조치 interim measure; interim measures; transitional measure
경과항목 accrued item
경기 business climate; business conditions; economic environment
경기가 서서히 회복됨 modest economic expansion; modest rebound
경기과열 overheating of business activity
경기냉각 faltering economies
경기동향조사 business survey
경기동향지표 diffusion index
경기둔화 slowing economy
경기변동 business fluctuation; economic fluctuation
경기부양책 reflation policy
경기선행지수 composite index of leading indicators
경기선행지수 leading index of business conditions; leading indicator
경기순환 business cycle; economic cycle
경기순환국면 phases of economic cycle
경기순환의 진폭 magnitude of the cycle
경기순환주 business cyclical stock
경기순환형 기업 business cyclical company
경기예측 business forecast
경기의 고점 cyclical peak
경기의 저점 cyclical trough; trough
경기자극책 economic stimulus package; business stimulating measure
경기자극형 재정정책 stimulative fiscal policy
경기조정 business adjustment
경기중시 pro-business
경기증대 boost
경기지수 business barometer
경기지표 business indicator
경기침체 poor economy
경기통계 fundamental statistics
경기혼미 recessionary economic; subdued economic growth
경기확대국면 phase of expansion
경기확대기간 expansion period
경기회복 cyclical upturn; economic recovery
경기회복기대 recovery expectations
경기후퇴 economic recession; economic

slump
경기후퇴; 불황 recession
경기후퇴국면 phase of recession
경기후퇴기 recession period; weaker economy
경기후퇴리스크 recession risk
경년변동율 year-to-year changes
경로 path
경로독립성 path-independency
경로의존형 옵션 path dependent option
경로의존형 파생상품 history-dependent derivative
경리과 accounting department
경리규정 accounting regulations
경리사 registered public accountant
경리사무 accountant business
경리의 하이라이트 financial highlights
경마식 도박 pari-mutuel betting
경매 auction sale
경매수수료 lot money
경매시장 auction market
경매인 auctioneer
경매인의 한통속 puffer
경매조건 conditions of sale
경비계정잔고 expense account balance
경비공제후 이익 profit after expenses
경비보고 expense report
경비보상금 compensation for expense and loss
경비분담 sharing costs
경비소멸 curtailment of expenditure; expense reduction
경비예산 estimated appropriation; expense budget
경비원장 expense ledger
경비율 expense ratio; ratio of necessary expenses to gross revenue
경비절감 financial retrenchment; reduction of expenditures
경비차액 factory expenses variance
경비팽창의 원칙 law of increasing public expenditures
경비할당 expenses quota
경사관세 tariff escalation
경사리스크 slope risk
경상거래 current transaction
경상계정수지 balance of current account
경상계획 business plan
경상달러 current dollar
경상분석 business analysis
경상비 overhead expenses
경상비 이상의 above the line
경상비용 current expenses; ordinary expenditure
경상세 ordinary tax
경상세입 ordinary annual revenue
경상세출 ordinary annual expenditure
경상손익 ordinary profit and loss; results of ordinary operations; income before extraordinary items; ordinary loss or gain; recurring gain or loss; recurring profit and loss
경상수입 ordinary income
경상수지 current account balance; current balance
경상수지율 ratio of current expenses to current income
경상수지흑자 favorable balance on current account
경상순익액 net operating earnings
경상예산 current budget; ordinary budget
경상외비용 nonrecurring cost
경상외손익 nonrecurring profit and loss
경상이익 current profit; ordinary profit; recurring profit
경상이익계산서 statement of operation earnings
경상이익수지 current transfers
경상이전 current transfer
경상적자 current account deficit
경상지불 current payment
경상지출 current expenditure

ㄱ
ㄴ

경상통계 business statistics
경상판단의 원칙 business judgment principle
경영감사 management audit; managerial auditing
경영계획 management plan
경영노하우 management know-how
경영본질 management cultures
경영분석 analysis of the affairs of a business
경영위원회 managing committee
경영위탁계약 management agreement
경영의사결정 management decision
경영이념 management philosophy; managerial philosophy
경영자 senior executive
경영자보험 key executive insurance
경영자본이익률 profit ratio of operating capital
경영자본회전율 turnover of total operating assets
경영자연금 executive pension
경영자원 management resources; managerial resources; resources on business
경영자책임 management responsibility
경영전략 management strategy
경영정보시스템 management information system
경영조직 management organization
경영지배권 controlling interest
경영지표 management index
경영진 management team
경영참가 management participation
경영참가권 management participation right
경영철학 philosophy of management
경영컨설턴트 management consultant
경영판단 managerial choices
경영하다 carry on
경영효율 operating efficiency
경유거래세 light oil delivery tax
경쟁가격 competitive price
경쟁관할권 concurrent jurisdiction
경쟁력 competitive edge; competitiveness
경쟁매매 competitive auction
경쟁매매원칙 rules of auction
경쟁매장 auction
경쟁압력 competition pressure
경쟁입찰 bid by advertising; competitive bid; competitive tender
경쟁적인 평가절하 competitive depreciation
경쟁제한정책 policy for restricting competition
경쟁제한특약 negative covenant
경쟁촉진정책 policy for promoting competition
경쟁판매 competitive sale
경쟁품취급금지계약 exclusive dealing
경제개발검토위원회 Economic and Development Review Committee
경제개혁 economic reform
경제경과 economic path
경제계 economic circles
경제계획 economic plan
경제공황 economic crisis
경제교류 economic exchange
경제구조조정 economic structural adjustment
경제권 economic bloc
경제규모 economic size
경제기초조건 중시파 fundamentalist
경제기초조건;펀드멘털즈 fundamentals
경제기초조건을 바탕으로 움직이는 상장 fundamental market
경제기획청 Economic Planning Agency
경제논리 economic event
경제단체연합회 Federal of Economic Organizations
경제대국 economic big power; economic power; economic superpower
경제동맹 economic union
경제리스크 economic risk
경제마찰 economic friction
경제모델 economic model
경제백서 economic white paper
경제변화의 정도 magnitude of economic change
경제봉쇄 economic blockade
경제분석 economic analysis

경제분석실(SEC) Office of Economic Analysis (SEC)
경제사상 economic event
경제사정 conditions of the national economy
경제상황 economic conditions
경제생활 economic life
경제성 공학 economic engineering
경제성장 economic growth
경제성장기 period of economic growth
경제성장률 economic growth rate; pace of economic expansion
경제성장모델 economic growth model
경제성장정책 economic growth policy
경제센터 economic center
경제순환 circular flow of economic system
경제실체 economic entity
경제안전보장 economic security
경제안정기 period of economic stability
경제연보 annual economic review
경제예측 economic forecast; economic outlook; economic prediction
경제외교 economic diplomacy
경제원가 economic cost
경제원조 economic aid
경제윤리 economic ethics
경제의 실체 economic reality
경제의 연속성 economic continuity
경제의 이중구조 dual structure of the economy
경제의 흐름 economic tide
경제재 economic goods
경제적 이익 economic earnings
경제적 이익의 베타수치 economic earnings beta
경제적 후생 economic welfare
경제적인 성숙 economic maturity
경제적인 잔존내용연수 remaining economic age
경제적인 진부화 economic obsolescence
경제적인 편익 economic benefits
경제전망 economic prospect
경제전쟁 economic war
경제정보 business information
경제정보서비스 business information service
경제정책 economic policy
경제제재 economic sanction
경제조직 economic organization
경제지수 economic index
경제지표 economic barometer; economic figure; economic indexes; economic indicator
경제지표효과 economic number effect
경제진보 economic progress
경제질병 economic malaise
경제질서 economic order
경제철학 economic philosophy
경제체제 economic regime; economic system
경제통계 economic statistics
경제통상산업부 Ministry of Economy; Trade and Industry
경제통합 economic integration
경제표 economic table
경제학 economics
경제학자 economist
경제해석 economic interpretation
경제협력 economic assistance
경제협력 economic cooperation
경제협력개발기구 Organization for Economic cooperation and Development
경제협력백서 white paper on economic cooperation
경제활동 economic activity
경제활동자극책 economic activity stimulating measure
경제회계 economic accounting
경차세 light vehicle tax
경찰청 National Police Agency
경품부 판매 premium sale
경합기업 competitor
경합하다 compete; consolidate
경향선 trend pattern
경향지수 index number trend series; trend series

경험상의 판단 experienced judgment
경험요율법 prospective rating
경험적 어프로치 empirical approach
경험칙 rules of thumb; thumb-rule
경화 hard currency
경화시키다;완고하게 하다 stiffen
계량경제모델 econometric model
계량모델예측 forecast by the econometric model
계량분석 econometric analysis
계몽활동 enlighteening activities
계산가격 computed price
계산기초 basis of the calculation
계산다툼 footing
계산단위 unit of account
계산본위 tabular standard
계산상의 손익액 unrealized profit and loss
계산상의 이익을 지출함 payment of unrealized profit
계산서 statement
계산서류 financial documents
계산절차 computation procedure
계산조견표 ready reckoner
계산차이 errors in calculation
계산착오 miscalculation
계산표 table
계산하다 calculate
계상보험료 accrued premium; written premium
계상시장 upstairs market
계상이익 declared profit
계상하다 appropriate
계선보험 port risks insurance
계속개시 continuous disclosure
계속기간 duration
계속기록법 perpetual inventory method
계속기업을 전제로 premise of a going concern
계속률 persistence rate
계속보험료 renewal premium
계속비 continued expenses
계속사업부문이익 earnings from continuing operations
계속사용료 running royalty
계속성의 원칙 principle of consistency
계속시장;연속거래 continuous market
계속재고 perpetual inventory
계속재고법 running inventory method
계속적인 신용공여 evergreen credit
계속적인 침해 permanent trespass
계속제도명령서 standing production order
계속주문 standing order
계속평가 ongoing assessment
계수 coefficient
계수관리 management through figures
계약 contract
계약 engagement
계약;약정 agreement
계약각서 articles of agreement
계약개요 policy summary
계약곡선 contract curve
계약관계 privity of contract
계약규모 contract size
계약금 contract money; God's penny
계약금액; 거래금액 contract value
계약금제도 premature delivery futures system
계약기간 contract term
계약내용을 실행함;인출 closing
계약능력 capacity to contract
계약당사자 contract party
계약률 contract ratio
계약보증 contract bond
계약불이행 non-fulfillment of a contract; nonperformance of contract
계약상의 권리 obligation of contract
계약상의 권리를 침해함 impairment of contract
계약서 contractual documents
계약서류작성은행 documentation bank
계약서에 씌어있지 않더라도 by default
계약선수금 advance received on contract
계약성립 done

계약수수료 contract charge
계약시장 contract market
계약신탁 trust under agreement
계약운임제 contract rate system
계약위반 violation of a contract; breach of contract
계약의 목적을 달성하지 못함 frustration
계약이행 fulfillment of a contract
계약일시금 up-front payment
계약자 promisor
계약자배당 policyholder dividend
계약자배당금 policy dividend
계약자유의 원칙 liberty of contract; principle of the freedom of contract
계약잔고 contract balance; outstanding contract amount
계약전도금 advance made on contract; contract deposit paid
계약전수금 contract deposit received
계약조건 contract terms
계약증거금 earnest money
계약채무 commitments
계약체결 conclusion of a contract
계약초과금액 excess receipt over contract price
계약포지션 contract position
계약해제 annulment of a contract
계약해제권 right of recision
계약형 contract type
계약형 계속투자플랜 contract type accumulative investment plan
계약형 투자신탁 contract type investment trust
계열금융기관 affiliated financial institute
계열상관 serial correlation
계열융자 loan to affiliated companies
계열화 affiliation
계쟁중인 소송 pending lawsuit
계절관세 seasonal duties
계절매출 season sale
계절변동 seasonal variation
계절변동조정 seasonal fluctuation adjustment
계절변동조정필 adjusted to seasonal variations; seasonally adjusted
계절상품 seasonal goods; seasonal merchandise
계절요인 seasonal factor; seasonal moves
계절자금 seasonal fund
계절적인 매출압력 seasonal selling pressure
계절적인 요인으로 인한 실업 seasonal unemployment
계절조정 seasonal adjustment
계절지수 seasonal index
계절평균 seasonal average
계정;계좌;고객 account
계정과목 account headings; account title; line item; title paramount
계정과목내역명세서 statement classified by account title
계정과목번호표시법 account number plan
계정과목일람표 account chart; classification of accounts
계정과목코드 account code
계정과목표 card of accounts; chart of accounts
계정구 check-out counter
계정기호법 symbol system of accounts
계정명세 particulars of account
계정분석 account analysis
계정서 account statement
계정시스템 account system
계정식 account form; balanced form
계정식손익계산서 account form income statement; account from profit and loss statement
계정이론 theory of accounts
계정잔고 account balance
계정장부 book of account
계정항목 item of account
계좌개설금수입 revenue from account-opening fees
계좌관리기관 book-keeping institution

계좌대체 account transfer
계좌번호 account number
계좌부 ledger of accounts
계좌에서 대리납부함 direct debit
계좌이체 automatic fund transfer
계좌폐지 discontinuance of accounts
계좌해약 account termination
계층 tier
계획경제 planned economy
고가 high price; higher in quotation; higher quotation; over-priced; overvalued; record price
고가로 인수한 신품 trade-in articles
고가로 회복함 recover high
고가상품 big ticket goods
고가선물 overvalued futures
고가주 high-priced stock
고객 customer
고객계정 customer's account
고객계정을 확보한 브로커 carrying broker
고객계좌부 ledger of customer accounts
고객관계 customer relations
고객기반 customer base
고객단가 customer transaction
고객동원력 customers mobilizing power
고객보고 customer repos
고객의 수탁에 기반을 두고 팔아치움 sale on customer's account
고객의 위탁과 관련해서 아직 결제를 하지 않은 상태 positions on customer's account
고객전수금 advance by customers
고객주문 customer's order
고객효과 clientele effect
고금리 high interest rate
고금리시대 era of high interest rate
고금리정책 dear money policy; high interest rate policy
고급임대주택 luxurious house for rent
고급카드 premium cap
고급품소비지향 trend towards luxury spending
고도의 시장 sophisticated market
고도장애 disability
고도정보통신시스템 information network system
고등시장 soaring market
고리 usury
고리대 feneration; loan shark
고리대부 usurer
고리부 사채 high-interest-bearing debenture
고무제품업계 rubber product industry
고문 advisor
고발 accusation
고보합 holding high
고부가가치제품 value-added product
고수준 healthy trend
고수준의 경기 high level of business activity
고액거래 large amount transaction; large block trading
고액납세자 high income brackets; high taxpayers
고액배당 melon cutting
고액예금금리 large amount deposit interest
고액융자규제 regulations on large-lot loans
고액의료비보험 major medical expense insurance
고액정기 large amount time deposit
고액채권 large credit
고액채무자 over-indebted person
고열경제 heated up economy
고용 employment
고용계약 employment contract
고용기회 job availability; job opportunities
고용기회균등 equal employment opportunities
고용데이터 employment data
고용보험 employment insurance
고용수준 level of employment
고용승수 employment multiplier
고용신장 employment growth
고용예측 employment prospectus
고용조정 employment adjustment
고용지수 employment index

고용통계 employment statistics; labor market data
고유리스크 specific risk
고유재산 national assets
고율적용제도 higher interest rates application system
고의의 intentional; willful
고의적인 탈세 willfully evading the tax
고의적인 허위 willfully false
고이율채 high yield bond
고이율쿠폰 generous coupon
고장어음 foul bill
고저법 high-low method
고정가격 fixed price
고정가격계약 fixed price contract
고정관념 abiding sense
고정금리 fixed rate
고정금리기준모기지 graduated payment mortgage
고정금리부채 fixed rate liability
고정금리스와프 fixed rate swap
고정금리자산 fixed rate assets
고정금리지불인 fixed rate payer
고정금리캐시플로 fixed cash flow
고정급 fixed salary; fixed wages
고정단위형 투자신탁 fixed unit investment trust
고정대부금 fixed loan
고정부채 fixed liabilities
고정부채비율 ratio of fixed liabilities to net worth
고정비 constant cost; constant expenses; fixed costs and expenses; fixed expenses; fixed overhead; standing expenses
고정비율 fixed asset to net worth ratio; fixed ratio; solidity ratio
고정비회수계획 capacity cost plan
고정상장 pegged market
고정상장제 system of fixed rate of exchange
고정성 배열법 capital arrangement; fixed arrangement
고정세율 fixed general tariff
고정수입 fixed income
고정수입이 있는 개인 individual with regular income
고정쉐어 fixed share
고정예산 fixed budget
고정웨이트지수 fixed weight index
고정유동비율제도 fixed liquidity reserve requirements
고정이율증권 fixed return securities
고정이자부 채권 fixed rate bond
고정자본 fixed capital
고정자본에 대한 수익률 return on fixed assets
고정자본투자 fixed capital investment
고정자산 fixed assets; property and equipment
고정자산과세대장 property tax cadaster
고정자산납세기한 due date of property tax payment
고정자산대장 fixed asset ledger; fixed asset register
고정자산매각손 loss from the sale of fixed assets
고정자산매각손익 gains or losses from sales of fixed asset
고정자산매각익 gains from sale of fixed assets
고정자산매상률 sales to fixed assets
고정자산명세표 fixed asset schedule
고정자산비율 fixed asset ratio
고정자산세 fixed asset tax; property tax; real estate tax
고정자산세납세관리인 tax agent of property tax
고정자산세면세점 taxable minimum of property tax
고정자산세비과세범위 scope of exemption of property tax
고정자산세율 property tax rate
고정자산순운전자본비율 ratio of inventory to net working capital

고정자산원장 plant ledger
고정자산자기자본율 equity capital ratio to fixed assets
고정자산장기자본비율 ratio of fixed assets to long term capital
고정자산증감명세표 lapsing schedule of fixed assets
고정자산처분 disposal of fixed assets
고정자산평가 valuation of fixed assets
고정자산평가기준 valuation standards of fixed assets
고정자산평가손 loss from the revaluation of fixed assets
고정자산평가손익 profit or loss from revaluation of fixed asset
고정자산평가심의회 Fixed Asset Valuation Council
고정자산평가익 gains from revaluation off fixed assets
고정자산회전율 fixed asset turnover ratio
고정주 pegged stock
고정차입금 fixed debt
고정채시장;채권시장 fixed income market
고정평가제 fixed parity system
고정환상장 pegged exchange
고정환상장제도 pegged exchange rate system
고정환율 fixed exchange rate
고정환율제도 fixed exchange rate system
고지서 statement of intent
고지서취급 insurance without medical examination
고지의무 duty of disclosure
고지효과 announcement effect
고차재(高次財) higher order goods
고쳐 쓴;다시 쓴 rewriting
고충처리위원회 grievance committee
고충처리절차 complaint procedures
고품질클래스 quality class
곡선 curve; lottery
곤궁화 정책 impoverishing theory
곤란함 embarrassing
골드러시 gold rush
골드센터 gold center
골드트란시 gold tranche
골드트란시 IMF gold tranche IMF
골든크로스 golden cross
골든패러슈트 golden parachute
골든핸드커프스 golden hand cuffs
골퍼보험 golfers' insurance
공간지세 vacant land tax
공개가격 price of introduced stock
공개거래회관 open board of broker
공개경쟁 open auction
공개경쟁매매방식 open outcry method
공개구매의견표명보고서 statement of position on the tender offer
공개기업 public company
공개단기금융시장 open money market
공개매각 public sale
공개매부보고서 tender offer report; registration statement of tender offer
공개매부철회신고서 registration statement of withdrawal of tender offer
공개법정 open court
공개성의 원칙 principle of disclosure
공개시장 market overt; open market
공개시장조작 open market operations; open repo
공개입찰 public bidding; public tender
공개정보 public information
공개주 introduced stock; public float; publicly held stock
공개주식수 number of offered shares
공개초안 exposure draft
공개회사 open corporation; publicly held company
공격자 aggressor
공격적인 정도 aggressiveness
공격적인 증권 aggressive securities
공격적인 투자 aggressive investment
공고 government financial corporation; public announcement; public finance corporation

공공경제학 public economics
공공단체 public body
공공부문회계 public-sectors accounting
공공사업 public utility; public service
공공사업비 expenditure for public works
공공사업지출 public works outlays
공공센터 public sector
공공시설건설부담액 allotted amount in constructing public facility
공공시설부담액 share in expense of public service
공공요금 public utility charges; utility rate
공공용 public use
공공재 public goods
공공지출 public expenditure; public spending
공공질서 public order
공공채 public debt securities
공공채딜러 municipal securities dealer
공공채발행 issue of public bonds
공공채장외매매고 trading volume of over-the-counter bonds
공공책임 public responsibility
공공통신사업 public telecommunication business
공공투자 public investment
공과 public dues; public impost
공권부여 enfranchisement
공권을 박탈하다 disfranchise
공금예금 official deposit
공급가격 supply price
공급계약 supply arrangements
공급곡선 supply curve
공급과다 oversupply
공급과잉 overhang
공급관리 management of supply
공급능력 supply capacity
공급부족 short supply
공급원 supply source
공급탄성치 elasticity of supply
공급함수 supply function
공기연장 extension of time for completion
공단공고채 public corporation bonds
공동감사 joint audit
공동개발 joint development
공동계산계약 pooling contracts
공동계정 common account; omnibus account
공동관계 joint relationship
공동구매 joint purchase
공동발행인 co-maker
공동법정상속인 co-heir
공동변동상장 joint currency float; joint floating exchange rate
공동변동장 joint-floating market system
공동보증 joint guarantee
공동보증인 cosureties
공동보험 co-insurance
공동시설세 public facilities tax
공동시장 common market
공동신고 joint return
공동융자 co-finance; joint financing
공동의 joint
공동인수 club deal
공동제일저당권 pooled first mortgage
공동주간사 co-lead-manager
공동채권매입기구 Cooperative Credit Purchase Corporation
공동책임 joint liability
공동체 community
공동파트너 joint partners
공동판매 combination sale; cooperative marketing; joint marketing; joint sales
공동플로팅 EC joint floating system EC
공동해손 general average
공동해손맹약서 average bond
공동해손분담액 general average contribution
공동해손비용 general average expenditure
공동해손희생손해 general average sacrifice
공리 axiom
공매 public auction; selling short; short securities transaction; short selling
공매광고 public notification of auction
공매보증금 deposit for public auction

공매비율 short sale ratio
공매에서 되찾음 redemption from tax sale
공매증서 tax deed
공매처분 disposition by public sale
공모 offering for subscription; public offering; public placement; public subscription
공모업무 public offering business
공모입찰 bidding for public offering
공모입찰방식 public offering auction system
공모주 publicly subscribed share
공모증권시장 public securities market
공모채 bond for public offering
공모펀드 public fund
공무 civil service
공법 public law
공보 official information
공보실(SEC) Office of Public Affairs(SEC)
공보증인 straw bail
공분산 covariance
공분산분석 covariance analysis
공사(公私)혼합기업 mixed undertaking
공사;공단 public corporation
공사공단채 authority bond
공사관리 care of works
공사미수금 construction work account receivable
공사부담금 contribution in aid of construction
공사비 cost of construction
공사수입 construction revenue
공사전도금 deposit paid on construction work
공사진행기준 percentage of completion basis
공사채 public corporation bond; government bonds and corporate debentures; public and corporate bond
공사채담보금융 bond collateral loans
공사채담보대부 loan secured by government bonds or corporate debentures
공사채를 상장한 상장 rate of listed bond
공사채발행액 new issue volume of outstanding bonds
공사채상환익 profit accruing from refund of bonds and debentures
공사채소화 purchase of new issues of public and corporate bonds
공사채응모자이익 yield on public and corporate bond
공사채이율 yields of public and corporate bonds
공사채인수협회 Bond Underwriters Association
공사채장외매매이율 OTC sales yield of public and corporate bonds
공사채전문위원회 special committee for public and corporate bond
공사채투신 bond trust
공사채투자신탁 public bond investment trust; bond investment trust; open-end bond investment trust; public and corporate bond investment trust
공사채평가 valuation of bond
공사채현선매매 bonds transaction with repurchase agreement
공사채현존액 new issue value of outstanding bonds
공선 mutual vote
공수율 man hour rate
공술녹취서금지 suppression of deposition
공시 announcement; public disclosure
공시가격 posted price
공시기능 disclosing function
공시송달 service by public notification
공시자본 declared capital
공시제도 disclosure system
공시최고 public notification; public summons
공식 formula
공안위원회 watch committee
공업국 industrialized countries
공업부기 industrial bookkeeping; factory bookkeeping; manufacturing bookkeeping
공업생산 industrial production
공업소유권 industrial property; industrial

right
공업어음 industrial bill
공업재단 industrial foundation
공업주 industrial stock
공업주가지수 Industrial Ordinary Shares Index
공업회계 industrial accounting; manufacturing accounting
공용 인보이스 official invoice
공용징수 expropriation
공유 co-ownership; joint ownership
공유물분할 partition
공유자 co-owner; part-owners
공유자산 common property
공유지분 shared equities
공유지선행취득 accelerated land purchase
공익 public interest; public policy
공익권 rights for profit-sharing
공익기업 utility company
공익대표이사 public governor
공익법인 public interest corporation; corporation in public interest; corporation of public utility; juridical person for public interest; nonprofit foundation
공익사업 nonprofit-making activity
공익사업규제실(SEC) Office of Public Utility Regulation(SEC)
공익사업채 public utility bond
공익사업회계 public utility accounting
공익사업회사예금 deposit with public utility corporation
공익신탁 charitable trust; public trust
공인검량인 public measurer
공인기관 authorized agency
공인은행 authorized bank
공인의 chartered
공인증권분석전문가 chartered financial analyst
공인증서거래소 recognised stock exchange
공인청산기관 recognized clearing house
공인회계사 certified public accountant; chartered public accountant; public accountant
공인회계사가 작성한 감사보고서 audit report of certified public accountant
공인회계사법 Certified Public Accountant Law
공장 factory; plant; shop
공장간접비 factory burden
공장검사 shop inspection
공장계정 factory account
공장비품 factory fitting; factory furnitures and fixtures
공장설비 plant and equipment
공장설비계정 plant account
공장용 소모품 factory supplies
공장용 집기 factory furniture
공장원가 factory cost; ground price; shop cost
공장원계정 factory ledger account
공장원장 factory ledger
공장인도 ex works
공장회계 factory accounting
공적개입 official intervention
공적결제수지 official reserve transactions balance
공적금융기관 public finance institution
공적금융기관대출 loans by public financial institutions
공적기업 public enterprise
공적부조 social assistance
공적불법방해 common nuisance
공적연금 public pension
공적연금공제 deduction for public pension
공적자금 public money
공적자금주입 injection of public pund
공적채권 official credits
공정가격 fair price
공정가치 fair value
공정거래국 fair trade bureau
공정거래위원회 Fair Trade Commission
공정과 형평 fair and equitable
공정관리;프로세스관리 process control
공정관습규칙 Rules of Fair Practice

ㄱ
ㄴ

공정금리인하 key rate cut
공정레이트 official rate
공정력 tentative validity
공정률 official discount rate
공정별 원가계산 process cost accounting; process costing
공정별 종합원가계산 departmental process cost system
공정별 종합원가계획 sequential cost system
공정분석 process analysis; process study
공정시장 official exchange market
공정시장가격;시가 fair market value
공정증서 notarial deed; notarial document
공정평가 parity of official exchange rate
공정한 가격형성 fair price formation
공정한 경쟁 equal footing
공정한 이익 equity margin
공정할인 Bank of Japan discount rate
공정할인율인하 discount rate cut
공정할인율조작 discount rate policy; ODR operation
공정할인율하락 ODR cut
공정환상장 official exchange rate
공제 deduction; mutual aid; subtraction; tax allowance
공제권 recoupment
공제금 mutual aid money
공제금제도 mutual aid system
공제단체 benefit association
공제대상배우자 qualified spouse for deduction
공제부금 mutual aid premiums
공제순서 sequence of deduction
공제액 amount deducted; exempted amount
공제연금 mutual pension; mutual-aid pension
공제저금 deposit through deduction from monthly pay; savings deducted at source
공제조건부 보험 deductible
공제조합 aid societies; benefit society; fraternal society; mutual benefit association
공제조항 deductible clause
공제해야 하는 채무 deductible liabilities
공제후의 상황 after-session undertone
공조공과 tax and public charge; tax and public dues
공증료 notarial charges
공증인 notary; public notary
공지 vacant lot
공채 government debt; public bond; state and local government debt
공채관리정책 debt management policy
공채매매 public bond dealing
공채발행 flotation of government bond
공채비 expenditure for public bond; national debt service expenditure
공채수입 revenue from public bond
공채의존도 ratio of bond issue to total expenditure
공채이자 interest on government bond
공채정리 consolidation of public loans
공청회 public hearing
공칭자본금 capital stock registered
공탁 payment into court
공탁금 지불금지명령;지정가격주문 stop order
공탁물 deposited article
공탁법 deposit law
공탁소 deposit office
공탁자 depositor
공통계정 joint account
공통관세 common tariff
공통기반 common background
공통기사;틀에 박힌 문구 boilerplate
공통농업정책 common agriculture policy
공통담보 common collateral
공통대수 common logarithm
공통법신탁 common law trust
공통요인리스크 common factor risk
공통원가 common cost
공통재 common goods
공판배심 trial jury
공평성 fairness
공평하게 fairy and impartially

공평하고 질서 있는 시장 fair and orderly market
공평한 fair
공평한 납세 equalization of tax payment
공평한 징수 equalization of tax collection
공포 promulgation
공포투매 panic selling
공표 dissemination
공표베이스자산가치 reported asset value
공표이익 reported profit
공표자본금 disclosed capital stock
공표하다 disseminate
공하(空荷)운임 dead freight
공해(公海) high seas
공해방지준비금 pollution control reserve; reserve for prevention of pollution
공헌이익 contribution margin
공헌이익식 contribution margin form
공황 crisis
공황상장 near-panic market
공황시장 panic market
과거근로채무의 상각액 amortization of prior service cost
과거근무비 prior pension cost
과거근무비용 prior cost; prior service cost
과거근무채무 past service liability
과거기록 track record
과거로 소급해서 retroactively to a date in the past
과거실적 historical earning
과거원가 past cost
과거의 수요 backward needs
과거의 수치폭 historical trading range
과거의 실적 past performance
과거최고치 historical peak
과납 over-payment
과년도를 소급한 환급 refund retroactive to the past taxable years
과년도손익수정항목 prior year adjustment items
과다지불한 over-paid
과당경쟁 excessive competition
과당경쟁 over-competition
과당투기 over-speculation
과대신고 exaggerated final return; overstatement of taxable income
과대자본 overcapitalization
과대평가 overestimate; overvaluation
과대평가하다 write up
과대표시 overstatement
과대한 리스크 undue risks
과대헤지 over-hedge
과도기 transition period; transition stage
과도기연수 transition years
과도한 분식 overdressing
과목 subject
과목별 순변동액 net changes in each element
과반수소유종속회사 majority-owned subsidiary
과반수주주 majority owner
과반수지분 majority interest
과부족 excess and deficiency; overs and shorts
과부족계정 over and short account
과세 importation of tax; levy of tax; taxation
과세가격 dutiable value; tax value; taxable amount; value of assessment
과세갱정결정 reassessment of taxes
과세견적가격 ratable value
과세고지일 date of tax to be levied
과세공제비목 tax deductible items
과세구입 taxable purchases
과세권 right of taxation
과세권승계 succession of right of taxation
과세금 assessed tax
과세기간 taxable period
과세기준 tax base
과세단위 taxable unit
과세단위 unit of taxation
과세대상 taxable item
과세대상유보금액 taxable undistributed profits
과세대장 tax roll

과세매상 taxable sales
과세매상고 amount of taxable purchase
과세면제소득 franked income
과세문서 taxable document
과세물건 object of taxation
과세범위 scope of assessment
과세상의 주소 tax home
과세소득 assessable income; taxable income
과세액 tax amount
과세액평가 appraisal of dutiable value
과세연기 deferment of taxation
과세요건 tax requisition
과세원부 assessment roll
과세유산 taxable estate
과세의 공평 impairment of value
과세재산 taxable property
과세채 taxable bond
과세처분취소 reversal of taxation
과세총소득금액 total taxable income
과세최저한 lowest taxable limit; tax threshold
과세통지서 tax bill
과세평가심사위원회 Board of Review
과세평가액 taxable valuation
과세표준 base of taxation
과세풀링 taxable poolings
과세품 article subject to taxation; taxable goods
과세할 수 있는 taxable
과소고용 underemployment
과소고용균형 underemployment equilibrium
과소납부 underpayment
과소상각 under-depreciation
과소신고가산금 additional charge for deficient return
과소신고가산세 additional tax for deficient returns
과소유동성 under liquidity
과소자본 inadequate capital; thin capitalization; undercapitalization
과소투자 underinvestment
과소평가 underestimation; undervaluation
과소헤지 underhedging
과실 culpa; fault; gross error; negligence
과열경제 overexuberant economy; overheated economy
과열장세 feverish market
과오납금;과납 overpayment
과오납금환부 refund of overpayment
과오정정거래 trading to correct errors
과오정정입회외 거래 special trades trading
과잉;여분 redundancy
과잉거래 excessive trading
과잉구매고 amount overbought
과잉달러 dollar overhung
과잉매입상장 overbought market
과잉매입포지션 overbought position
과잉매출고 amount oversold
과잉설비;과잉능력 excess capacity
과잉소비 excessive consumption
과잉유동성 excess liquidity; excessive liquidity; monetary excess
과잉융자 excessive lending
과잉재고 inventory excess; overstock
과잉저축 excessive savings
과잉투자 over-investment
과점 oligopoly
과점가격 oligopoly price
과점경제 oligopolistic economy
과점산업 oligopoly industry
과점지배 oligopolistic control
과징금 surtax
과태료 fine
관계당국 relevant authorities
관계법령 related laws
관계자 affiliate
관계회사 affiliated company
관계회사사채 bond of affiliated company
관계회사외상금 receivable from affiliate
관계회사외상매출금 account receivable due from affiliated company
관계회사유가증권 securities of affiliated company

관계회사주식 stock of affiliated company
관계회사채권 indebtedness of affiliates
관계회사출자금 contributions to affiliated company
관계회사출자금 investment in affiliates
관공서공제조합 mutual aid association of government offices
관광세 sight-seeing tax
관광수입 tourist income
관념상의 소득 notional income
관련당사자 related party
관련대부 relationship lending
관련데이터베이스 relational database
관련리스크 relevant risk
관련산업 correlative industry
관련상품 related issue
관련성 relevancy
관련성이 없는 irrelevant
관련시장 relevant market
관련원가 related cost; relevant cost
관련정보 pertinent information
관련채무 related obligations
관련회사 associate company
관료 bureaucracy
관리가격 administered price; managed price
관리가격인플레이션 administered-price inflation
관리가능원가 controllable expenses
관리감사 administrative audit
관리기구 control mechanism
관리기능강화 strengthening of managerial function
관리무역 managed trade
관리불능비 uncontrollable cost; uncontrollable expenses
관리불능원가 non-controllable cost
관리비 general administration expenses; maintenance fee
관리사실(SEC) Office of Comptroller(SEC)
관리상품 managed issues
관리시장 governed market
관리자산 managed asset; managed receivable
관리직원겸업금지 prohibition of management official interlocks
관리채무 managed liabilities
관리책임 care and custody
관리크롤링페그 managed crawling peg
관리통화 controlled currency; managed currency
관리통화제도 managed currency system; planned monetary system
관리플로트 managed float
관리플로트제 managed floating rate system
관리한계 control limit; span of control
관리형 투자신탁 managerial investment trust
관리회계 administration accounting; management accounting
관망 watch and wait
관문 resistance level
관선수익관리인 official receiver
관성효과 inertia effect
관세 customs; customs duty; tariff
관세교섭 tariff negotiations
관세동맹 customs union; tariff union
관세면제품 article on the free list
관세법 customs law
관세사정 liquidation of duties
관세사중손실 dead weight loss of customs duty
관세율 tariff rate
관세율표 customs tariff table
관세인하 tariff cuts
관세자주권 customs autonomy; tariff autonomy
관세잠정조치법 Temporary Tariff Measures Law
관세장벽 tariff barrier; tariff wall
관세전쟁 tariff war
관세정율법 customs tariff law
관세평가금지 withholding of customs appraisement
관세할당 tariff quota
관세할당제도 tariff quota system

관세환부제도 customs duty refund system
관세환불 drawback
관습 consuetude; usage
관습가설 habit persistence hypothesis
관습법 common law
관습상의 보유권 customary tenure estates
관영수입 revenue from government enterprise
관재명령 administration order
관재인 administrator
관제등본 office copy
관찰 observation
관청부기 government bookkeeping
관청회계 governmental and municipal accounting
관할 jurisdiction
관할이전 change of venue
관할차이 jurisdictional defect
관행 customary practice
광고 advertisement
광고규제 advertising regulation
광고기획자 account executive
광고료 advertising rate
광고매체 advertising media
광고비 advertising expenses; outlay for advertisement
광고선전비 advertising and general publicity expenses
광고선전용 자산 property for advertisement
광고세 advertisement tax; advertising tax
광고쪽지;등귀 flier
광공업 mining and manufacturing
광공업생산지수 industrial production index
광범위한 시장지표 broad market index
광산세 mineral product tax
광업 mining industry
광업권 mineral properties mining right
광업임차권 mining lease
광업자산 mining property
광업조합 mining partnership
광업회계 mining accounting
광열비 light and fuel expenses
광의유동성 broadly-defined liquidity
괴리 divergence
괴리율 disparate ratio
괴리지표 divergence indicator
괴리한도 divergence threshold; threshold of divergence
굉장히 낮은 가격 considerable low price
굉장히 높은 가격으로 판매함 sales at unreasonably high price
교묘한 elaborate
교부공채 compensation bond; government compensation bond; public compensation bond
교부국채 delivery bond; subsidy government bond
교부세 및 양도세 배부특별회의 special account for distribution of local allocation and shared taxes
교부수수료 fees for withdrawals of stock certificates
교부요구 request for share distribution
교부청구 demand for withdrawal
교섭력 bargaining power
교섭으로 취득한 자산 property received in the exchange
교섭하다 treating
교양비 expenses for education and culture
교역조건 barter terms of trade; terms of trade
교역조건지수 index of terms of trade
교육과학기술부 Ministry of Education; Culture; Sports; Science and Technology
교육론 education loan
교육비 education expense
교육산업 education industry
교육수준 level of education
교제비 entertainment and social expenses; social expenses
교제비공제 deduction of entertainment expenses
교제비과세 taxation on entertainment and social expense

교제비편입한도액 limit of deductible of entertainment expense
교차비율 ratio of gross profit to inventory investment
교차신청 cross offer
교차책임주의 cross liabilities basis; principle of cross liabilities
교차탄력성 cross elasticity
교차통화금리스와프 cross-currency interest rate swap
교체 alternation; replacement
교체가격 replacement price
교체가치 replacement value
교체단위 replacement unit
교체원가 replacement cost
교체원가회사 replacement cost accounting
교체자산 replacement assets
교통사고상해보험 traffic personal accident insurance
교통채 transportation bond
교화경제 exchange economy
교환 permutation
교환가격 exchange value
교환가능전환우선주 convertible exchangeable preferred stock
교환공문 exchange of notes
교환대차 loan for exchange
교환방정식 equation of exchange
교환비손금불산입 exclusion from expenses of entertainment and social expenses
교환비율 convertible ratio
교환성정지 suspension of convertibility
교환용 자산 property for exchange
교환잔고표 clearing-house balance
교환재보험;상호주의 reciprocity
교환차금 difference from exchange of property
교환차익 gains from exchange of properties
교환처분 involuntary exchange
구도 structural outline
구두개입(상승) talk up
구두개입(하락) talk down
구두계약 parol contract
구두의 verbal
구두증언 oral testimony
구매 purchase
구매대전도금 advance for purchase
구매력 buying power; purchasing power
구매력리스크 purchasing power risk
구매력변동손익 purchasing power gain or loss
구매력침식 erosion in purchasing power
구매력평가 purchasing power
구매력평가설 purchasing power parity theory
구매부장 purchasing manager
구매신청 buying offer
구매오퍼레이션 buying operation
구매자차관 buyer's guide
구매장 buying opportunity
구매헤지 buying hedge
구분; 부문 division
구분소유권 sectional ownership
구분손익계산서 multiple step income statement; sectional income statement
구분식 multiple step
구분식 시산표 classified trial balance
구분지상권 sectional surface rights
구상 claim for compensation
구상권 guarantor's right of indemnity; indemnity right; recourse; right of demanding compensation; surety obligation
구상기간 claim period
구상무역 compensating trade or transactions; compensation trade
구상액 amount of claim
구상은행 claiming bank
구성;시담 composition
구성부분 building block
구성비 composition ratio
구성비율 component percentages; distribution ratio; percentage analysis
구성비율분석 component analysis
구성요건 composition requirements

구속력이 있는 binding
구속자산 restricted asset
구속잔고 compensating balance
구속조항 binding clause
구역외의 extramural
구외국환관리법 old foreign exchange act
구은행법 old bank act
구입가격 buying price; cost price
구입가할인 purchase allowance
구입고 purchase amount
구입년 purchases year
구입단가 purchasing price
구입대금 purchase money; purchase price
구입대리점 buying agent
구입대장 bought ledger
구입반품 purchase return
구입비용 purchasing expenses
구입상품 speculative name
구입선불대금 advance on account of sellers
구입세 purchase tax
구입수수료 purchase commission
구입시가 market value in case of purchase
구입액 amount of goods purchased
구입약정 purchase commitments
구입에너지 buying energy
구입예산 purchases budget
구입운임 freight inward; freight-in
구입원가 buying cost; cost of goods purchased; cost of purchase; first cost; prime cost; purchasing cost
구입의사 intention to purchase
구입자 vendee
구입장 purchase book
구입장본인 leader of long side
구입전불대금 deposit paid to trade creditors
구입조건 buying terms
구입주문 buying order
구입지원 buying support
구입처 merchandise resources; trade creditor
구입처원장 creditors ledger; purchase ledger
구입총액 gross purchase
구입측 buying side
구입한 물품을 수출함 export of goods purchased
구입할인 purchase discount
구입환불 purchases rebate
구제 redress
구제계획 bailout plan
구제금융 relief loan
구제명령 order for relief
구제방법 remedy
구제상장 bailout market
구제의 상호성 mutuality of remedy
구제조치 bailout
구제조항 bailout clause
구제하다 bail out
구제합병 relief merger
구제합병방식 assisted acquisition
구조개혁 structural reform
구조료 salvage charges
구조리스크 structural risk
구조물매득금차인정산 salvage loss
구조방정식 structural equation
구조변화 structural change
구조분석 structural analysis
구조선택 structural choice
구조요인 secular reason
구조재정거래 structured arbitrage
구조적인 structural
구조적인 실업 structural unemployment
구조적인 압력 secular pressure
구조적인 유동성 structural liquidity
구조적인 인플레이션 structural inflation
구조조정 structural adjustment
구조조정계획 restructuring plan
구조조정기간 restructuring period
구조조정비용 restructuring charge
구조조정융자 structural adjustment facility
구조협의 structural impediments initiative talks
구조화 거래 structured trade; structured transaction
구조화 금융 structured finance

구조화 금융시장 structured finance market
구조화 증권 structured securities
구주 old share
구주 일주당 발행된 신주수 number of stocks issued per old stock
구축물 structure
구축하다 construct
국 (局) bureau
국가공무원법 National Public Service Law
국가공안위원회 National Public Safety Commission
국가나 지방공공단체의 보조금 subsidies from the government or local public entities
국가배상법 State Redress Law
국가신용 national credit
국가신용도 country risk
국가예산누적적자 cumulative fiscal deficit
국가의 밸런스시트 sovereign balance sheet
국가의 최고법규 supreme law of the land
국가의 행위 act of state
국가자본 state capital
국가자본주의 state capitalism
국가재정 national finance; public finance
국가주권상실 loss of sovereignty
국가채무 national debt
국가파산 state bankruptcy
국경세 frontier tax
국경세조정 border tax adjustment
국경없는 정보 cross border information
국경인도 delivered at frontier; frontier delivery
국경인도가격 delivered at frontier price
국고 national treasury
국고 대 민간수지 government fund transactions with the public
국고귀속인정 office found
국고금송금 treasury fund remittance
국고보조금 national subsidy
국고수지 government fund transactions
국고여유금 treasury surplus
국고재무대리인 fiscal agent for treasury fund
국고채권 treasury notes
국내가격 domestic price
국내국채 government bonds in domestic currency
국내균형 domestic equilibrium
국내기관투자가 domestic institutional investor
국내론방식 domestic loan system
국내무역 internal trade
국내발행신용장;로컬크레디트 local credit
국내사업 domestic operations
국내소득 domestic income
국내시장 domestic market; national markets
국내신용 domestic credit
국내어음 inland bill
국내요인 domestic factor
국내원천 domestic source
국내원천소득 domestic source income; income accrued from domestic sources; income from Korean sources
국내자본 domestic capital
국내주 domestic stock
국내지출 domestic expenditure
국내총생산 gross domestic product
국내총자본형성 gross domestic capital formation
국내투자 domestic investment
국립은행법 National Bank Act of 1863
국무장관 Secretary of State
국민가처분소득 national disposable income
국민건강보험세 national health insurance tax
국민경제 national economy
국민경제계산체계 System of National Account
국민경제예측 national economic budget
국민경제재산 national economic accounting
국민계정 national accounts
국민금융공사 People's Finance Corporation
국민대차대조표 national balance sheet
국민복지지표 net national welfare
국민생활지표 new social indicators
국민소득 national income
국민소득계정 national income accounts

국민소득분석 national income analysis
국민소득순환 circulation of national income
국민소득통계 national income statistics; statistics on national income
국민소득회계 national income accounting
국민순생산 net national product
국민연금 national pension
국민연금예탁금 deposits of funds of national annuities
국민의료보조제도 Medicaid
국민자본 national capital
국민자본계정 national capital account
국민자본표 national capital sheet
국민지출 national expenditure
국민총공급 gross national supply
국민총생산 gross national product
국민총수요 gross national demand
국민총자산 gross national wealth
국민총지출 gross national expenditure
국방산업에 대한 융자보증 loan guarantees for defense industry
국별한도 country limit
국부(國富) national wealth
국부통계 national wealth statistics
국세 national tax
국세 및 지방세 taxes and rates
국세미불액 unpaid balance of national tax
국세범칙감독법 National Tax Violations Control Law
국세부가세 surtax on national tax
국세불복심판소 National Tax Tribunal
국세수납관리 official to receive national tax
국세수납금정리자금 National Tax Receipt Fund
국세심사관 tax tribunal examiner
국세심사회 National Tax Council
국세에 대한 상쇄금지 prohibition of set off for national taxes
국세와 지방세간의 우열 priority between national tax and local tax
국세징수법 National Tax Collection Law
국세채권우선의 원칙 principle of priority of national tax claim
국세채무승계 succession of national tax liability
국세청 National Tax Administration Agency; Tax Administration Bureau
국세통칙법 National tax procedure law
국세환부가산액 additional amount to a refund of national tax
국영사업 state enterprises
국외근무자 persons in overseas service
국외상장 cross border listing
국유기계설비교환 exchange of machinery and equipment owned by the government
국유기업 state-owned company
국유재산 national property
국유화 nationalization
국익 national interest
국정세율 national tariff
국제감사실무위원회 International Auditing Practices Committee
국제개발부흥은행협정 Agreement of the International Bank for Reconstruction and Development
국제개발협회 International Development Association
국제거래통화 international transaction currency
국제결제 international settlement
국제결제기관 International Securities Clearing Corporation
국제결제은행 Bank for International Settlements
국제결제통화 international settlement currency
국제경쟁력 international competitiveness
국제경제학 international economics
국제경제협력은행 International Bank for Economic Cooperation
국제경제협력회의 Conference on International Economic Cooperation
국제공모 international offerings
국제공법 international public law

국제공헌 international contribution
국제관리통화제도 international managed currency system
국제관습법 international custom
국제균형 international equilibrium
국제금융 international finance
국제금융거래소 International Monetary Exchanges
국제금융공사 International Finance Corporation
국제금융기관 international financial institution; multilateral lending institutions
국제금융시장 global credit market; international financial market; international money market
국제금융제도 international financial system
국제기관 supernational organisations; supranational agencies
국제기관채권 bond of international agency; international agency bond
국제기업회계 international accounting
국제기준 International standards
국제노동기관 International Labor Organization
국제농업개발기금 International Fund for Agricultural Development
국제단기금융시장 international short-term money market
국제단기부동자금;핫머니 hot money
국제단기자본거래 international short-term capital transaction
국제단위 international unit
국제대차 balance of international indebtedness; international indebtedness
국제대차설 theory of international indebtedness
국제론포트폴리오 international loan portfolio
국제리스 international lease
국제마케팅 international marketing
국제무역 international trade
국제무역위원회 International Trade Commission
국제민간항공기관 International Civil Aviation Organization
국제법 international law; law of nations
국제보호 international custody
국제부흥개발은행 International Bank for Reconstruction and Development
국제부흥개발은행특별조치 IBRD special law
국제분산투자 international diversified investment; international portfolio diversification
국제분업 international division of roles
국제브로킹 international broking
국제비교 international comparables; international comparison
국제사법 private international law
국제사업 international business
국제상공회의소 International Chamber of Commerce
국제상업중재 international commercial arbitration
국제상품 international merchandise
국제상품협정 international commodity agreement
국제소비자기구 International Organization of Consumer's Unions
국제수지 balance of international payments; international balance of accounts; international balance of payment
국제수지조정과정 adjustment process of balance of payments
국제수지탄력성 elasticity of the balance of payments
국제수지통계 balance of payments statistics; statistics on international balance of payment
국제수지흑자 favorable balance of payments
국제수출신용보험기구 International Union of Credit and Investment Insurers
국제스와프딜러 International Swap Dealers Association
국제시장 cross border market; international market

국제시장가격 international market price; world market price
국제시장조사 international marketing research
국제신디케이트 international syndicate
국제업무 international operation
국제연합경제개발국 United Nations Economic Development Administration
국제연합무역개발회의 United Nations Conference on Trade and Development
국제연합자본개발기금 United Nations Capital Development Fund
국제예탁증서 international depositary receipts
국제위기 international crisis
국제유동성 international liquidity
국제은행간 데이터통신시스템 SWIFT
국제은행법 International Banking
국제은행업무 international banking; international banking facility; international banking operation
국제은행업무계정(IBF계정) international banking facilities account
국제이중과세 international double taxation
국제이코노미스트 international economist
국제인수단 international consortium; international underwriting group
국제자금 international fund
국제자금이동 international movements of funds
국제자본 international capital
국제자본이동 international capital market; international capital movement
국제자산운용 international asset management
국제자원은행 International Resources Bank
국제장기자본이동 international long-term capital movement
국제적인 금융관리 international money management
국제적인 석유주 international oil plays
국제전기통신연합 International Telecommunication Union
국제조세법 international tax law
국제조약 international conventions
국제주권 international stock
국제주식시장 international equity market
국제증권 international securities
국제증권거래소연합 International Federation of Stock Exchanges
국제증권거래위원회기구 International Organization of Securities Commissions
국제증권투자 international portfolio investment
국제채권 international bond
국제채권트레이딩 international bond trading
국제채무딜러협회 Association of International Bond Dealer
국제청산동맹 International Clearing Union
국제카르텔 international cartel
국제통화 international currency
국제통화기금 International Monetary Fund
국제통화기금협정 Agreement of the International Monetary Fund
국제통화불안 international monetary turmoil
국제통화시장 International Monetary Market
국제통화제도 international currency system; international monetary system
국제통화제도개혁 reform of international monetary system
국제투자 international investment
국제투자신탁 international investment trust
국제투자은행 international bank for investment; international investment bank
국제트란시 international tranche
국제표준화기구 International Standardization Organization
국제항공운송협회 IATA; International Air Transport Association
국제해사기관 International Maritime Organization
국제해상보험연합 International Union of Marine Insurance
국제화 internationalization
국제환 international exchange
국제회계기준 IAS; international accounting

standards
국제회계기준위원회 IASC; International Accounting Standards Committee
국제회계전문가협회 Association of International Accountants
국제 CMS international cash management service
국채 government bond
국채관리정책 government bond management policy
국채대리점 government bond agency
국채대용증서 substitute certificate for government bond
국채대체결제제도 government bond book-entry system
국채등록부 register of government bonds
국채모집인수단·컨소시엄 consortium
국채발행 government bond issuance
국채비 debt service payment
국채사무취급비 administrative fees
국채상환 government bond redemption
국채선물거래 government bond futures
국채선물시장 national bond futures market
국채선물시장구조 structure of the government bond futures market
국채스트립채 Treasury strip
국채시중소화 public offering of government bonds
국채에 관한 법률 Law Concerning Government Bonds
국채에 대한 사무 government bond administration
국채이율 government bond yield
국채이자 interest on government securities
국채인수 underwriting of government securities
국채입찰 auction of government bond; treasury auction; treasury financing
국채입찰제도 government bond auction system
국채정리기금 Government Debt Consolidation Fund
국채정리기금특별회계법 Special Account Law of the Government Debt Consolidation Fund
국채제도 government bond system
국채증권선물거래 futures trading based on government securities
국채증권선물거래특별참가자 special participant in futures trading based on government bonds
국채증권선물옵션 option trading based on government securities
국채화폐화 monetarization of government bonds
국토교통부 Ministry of Land; Infrastructure and Transport
국회제정법 act of parliament
군사대국 military power
군중;대중;동아리 crowd
굳히다;경화하다 harden
굴신제한제도 elastic limit system
굴절수요곡선 kinked demand curve
권고 recommendation
권리구제제도 remedy for violation of private right
권리금 foregift; keymoney
권리금과 입퇴금 premises and compensation for removal
권리남용 abuse of rights
권리담보조항 covenant of seisin
권리락 ex-rights
권리락;신주락으로(의) ex-new
권리를 담보로 삼다 mortgage the right
권리를 부여하다 entitle
권리를 손상하지 않고 without prejudice
권리를 주다 vest
권리반환권 right of redemption
권리방기 abandonment of right; surrender; waiver
권리방기조항 waiver clause
권리부 rights on

권리상실소장 bill for foreclosure
권리서 abstract of title
권리서기탁 deposit of title-deeds
권리소멸조항 defeasance
권리수록 acquisition of right
권리양도 assignment of rights
권리와 의무 rights and obligations
권리장전 bill of rights
권리정지 suspension of right
권리증 registration certificate
권리증권 document of title
권리증서 deed of title; title document
권리증서매매 transaction with rights receipts
권리청원 petition of right
권리추정 presumption of rights
권리취득 accession
권리침해 infringement
권리하락 rights off
권리행사 exercise of right
권리행사가 인정된 거래량 exercise limit
권리행사가격 exercised value; strike price
권리행사기간 exercise period
권리행사를 지시함 instruction of exercise
권리행사수량 exercise volume
권리행사일 exercise day; expiration day of the exercise
권리행사통지 exercise notice
권리행사할당 assignment of exercise
권리확보 entitlement
권리확정주의 principal of ascertained claim
권리훼손;편견 prejudice
권면;디노미네이션 denomination
권원 title deeds
권원(權原)구입 buying title
권원보고서 title report
권원보험;소유권보증 title insurance company
권원의 기초 root of title
권원합동 unity of title
권유 solicitation
권유장을 내어 판매함 follow-up selling
권유텔렉스 invitation telex
권장재판매가격 suggested resale price
권장주;추천주 stock recommended for purchase
권한 authority; power
권한내에서 intra vires
권한담보조항 covenant for title
권한범위 ambit; scope of authority
권한부여 delegation
권한위임 delegation of authority
권한을 부여하다 authorize
권한이 있는 당국 competent authority
귀납적 통계 inductive statistics
귀속 imputation
귀속가격 imputed price
귀속가치 imputed value
귀속소득 imputed income
귀속시키다 impute
귀속원가;부가원가 imputed cost
귀속이론 theory of imputation
귀속이익 attributable profit
귀속이자 imputed interest
귀속주의 attributable income principle
귀속지분 attributable interest
귀책과실 imputed negligence
규격매매 sale by grade or type
규모별 주가지수 stock price index by size of stocks
규모별 주식평균 stock price average by size of stocks
규모의 경제 economy of scale; scale economies
규모의 이익 scale merit
규모확대 addition of scale
규모효과 size effect
규정 code; regulation
규정집 book of regulations
규정하다 prescribe
규정하지 않은 기간 non-determined period
규제가격 regulated prices
규제금리 regulated interest rate
규제금리부채 administered rate liabilities

규제당국 regulatory agency
규제당국의 주목 regulatory attention
규제대상기업 regulated company
규제분야 regulatory field
규제시장 regulated market
규제완화 deregulation; relaxation of regulations
규제조치 regulatory measures
규제투자회사 regulated investment company
규칙 rule
규칙성 regularity
규칙에 대한 위임 delegation of authority to rules
균등가중평균 equal-weighted average
균등평준연차배당 equivalent level annual dividend
균등할과세 taxation on per capita basis
균등할세율 per capita levy
균분 equally divided
균일요금 flat price
균일요율;균일레이트 flat rate
균일의;배당락의 flat
균일환예약 flat exchange contract
균형 match making
균형가격 equilibrium price
균형분석 equilibrium analysis
균형세력 balanced growth
균형예산 balanced budget
균형예산정리 balanced budget theorem
균형이자율 equilibrium rate of interest
균형재정 balanced finance
균형점 equilibrium point
균형환상장 equilibrium rate of exchange
그 자체 in return
그람러드만법 Gramm-Rudman-Hollings Law
그랜빌의 법칙 Granville theory
그랜트엘리먼트 grant element
그럼에도 불구하고 notwithstanding
그레샴의 법칙 Gresham's law
그레이터풀이론 greater fool theory
그로스거래고 gross trading volume
그로스상환 gross redemption
그로스섹션 Growth Section
그로스업방식 gross up method
그로스펀드 growth fund
그로스펀드포지션 gross fund position
그룹과세 consolidated tax return system
그룹세액공제 group relief
그리드 grid
그린메일 green mail
그린카드제도 green card system
근거 rationale
근거있는 조항 grounding clause
근담보 revolving collateral
근대경제학 modern economics; modern market economy
근로소득공제 earned income allowance
근로소득세 earned income tax
근로학생공제 allowance for working student; exemption for working student
근린궁지화정책 beggar-my-neighbor policy
근린제국 neighboring countries
근린효과 neighborhood effect
근보증 revolving guarantee
근본원인 underlying cause
근사치이론 theory of approximation
근속수당 long service allowance
근인주의 cause proximate
근저당 maximal collateral; fixed collateral
근저당권 fixed mortgage
근접의 adjoining
글래스스티걸법 Glass-Steagall Act
글로벌경제 global economy
글로벌노트퍼실리티 global note facilities
글로벌마케팅 global marketing
글로벌무기명예탁증서 global bearer certificate
글로벌본드 global bond
글로벌예탁증권 global depository certificate
글로벌장기채권 global long-term bond
글로벌증권 global certificate
글로벌커스터디 global custody
글로벌트레이딩 global trading

글로벌포트폴리오 global portfolio
금고 이상의 형벌 penalty heavier than imprisonment
금괴 bullion
금구입워런트 gold purchase warrant
금기준치결정 gold fixing
금달러준비 gold and dollar reserve
금담보 gold collateral
금리 Fed fund rate FF; interest rate; money rate; TB rate TB
금리가 낮으리라 예상함 view of lowering interest rate
금리감면채권 renegotiated loans
금리감응도 interest rate sensitivity
금리감응부채 rate sensitive liability
금리감응자산 rate sensitive assets
금리감응항목 interest rate sensitive items
금리감응형 상품 interest-sensitive products
금리감응형 종신보험 Interest Sensitive Whole Life
금리갱신일 reset date
금리결정;가격결정 pricing
금리구조 structure of interest rates
금리기간구조 term structure of interest rates
금리동향 interest rate movement
금리리스크 exposure to interest rate; interest exposure; interest rate risk
금리마인드 interest rate minded
금리마진 interest rate spread
금리만 interest only
금리민감주 interest rate sensitive stock
금리방향 direction of interest rate
금리변경기간 repricing interval
금리변경시점 repricing date
금리변동 interest rate fluctuation; shift in interest rate
금리변동리스크 interest volatility risk
금리부담율 interest coverage ratio
금리부문 interest component
금리비감응부채 non-rate-sensitive liability
금리비감응항목 non-interest-sensitive item
금리상승 rise interest rate
금리선도거래 forward rate agreement
금리선물 interest futures; interest rate futures
금리선물계약 interest rate futures contracts
금리선물옵션거래 interest rate futures option trading
금리선호 preference for interest rate
금리세금공제전 이익 earnings before interest and taxes
금리수준 interest rate level
금리스와프 interest rate swap; interest swap
금리스와프채 interest swap bond
금리스트리프채 interest strips
금리예측 rate outlook
금리옵션 interest rate option
금리옵션거래 interest option transaction
금리유도목표 Fed fund target FF
금리인상 interest rate raise; raising of interest rate
금리인하 lowering of interest rate
금리입찰방식레포 variable repo
금리자유화 liberalization of interest rate
금리재정 interest arbitrage; interest rate arbitrage
금리재정거래 interest rate arbitrage transaction
금리정책 interest rate policy
금리조작 interest rate control
금리조정 interest rate adjustment; rate adjustment
금리차 interest rate differential; interest spread
금리차익 interest surplus
금리칼라 interest rate collar
금리캡 rate cap
금리캡거래 interest cap trading
금리평가 interest parity
금리평행이동 parallel rate shift
금리평형세 interest equalization tax
금리플로어 interest rate floor
금리플로어계약 rate floor agreement
금리하락 falling interest rate

금반언(禁反言) estoppel
금보유고 gold holdings
금본위제 gold standard
금본위제도붕괴 fall of gold standard
금불태화정책 gold sterilization policy
금선물 gold futurues
금선물계약 gold bullion futures contract
금선물옵션 gold futures option
금선호 prefectural for gold
금속제품업계 metal products industry
금수입점 gold import point
금수출점 gold export point
금수출해금 lifting of gold embargo
금액 amount
금액가중수익율 dollar-weighted return
금약관 gold clause
금외신탁 non-money trust
금워런트 gold warrant
금융가 street
금융거래 financial transaction
금융계정 balance of monetary movements; cash account; financial accounts
금융공황 financial crisis; financial panic
금융규제 financial regulation
금융기관 banking facilities; financial institution
금융기관대부금 loan to financial institutions
금융기관예금 deposit at financial institutions
금융기관의 알선 good offices of banking facilities
금융기관이 보유한 유가증권 securities investment by financial institution
금융긴박 financial strain and stress
금융긴축 credit squeeze; credit tightening; monetary restraint; monetary tightening
금융긴축정책 monetary restraint policy; restrictive monetary policy
금융긴축정책 tight money policy
금융긴축정책이 침투함 penetration of tight money policy
금융난 financial difficulty
금융단기증권 financing bills
금융담보 financial exposure
금융리스 financial lease
금융면의 결단 financial decision
금융모델 financial model
금융보증보험 financial guaranty insurance
금융부담 financing burden
금융부채 financial liability
금융불황 financial recession
금융붕괴 financial collapse
금융비용 finance charge; financial expenses; financing charge
금융비용커버리지 fixed charge coverage
금융상품 financial instrument; financial product
금융서비스 financial facilities; financial service
금융서비스법 Financial Services Act
금융선도계약 financial forward contract
금융선물 financial futures
금융선물거래 financial futures transaction
금융선물거래계좌개설신청서 application for financial futures transaction account
금융선물거래계좌설정약정서 agreement for the account for financial futures transaction
금융선물거래설명서 explanatory leaflet for financial futures transaction
금융선물거래소 financial futures exchange
금융선물거래소용 인감계 registration of signet for financial futures transaction
금융선물거래에 관한 확인서 confirmation for financial futures transaction
금융선물계약 financial futures contract
금융선물상품 financial futures instrument
금융선물시장 financial futures market
금융선물옵션 financial futures option
금융섹터 financial sector
금융수단 financing vehicle
금융수익 financial income; financial margin; financial profit
금융시장 financial market

금융시장개방 open-up of money market
금융시장글로벌화 financial market globalization
금융시장데이터 money market data
금융시장분석 financial market analysis
금융시장에 대한 개입 money market intervention
금융시장에 억세스함 access to capital market
금융시장자유화 financial market liberalization
금융시장정세지표 money market conditions index
금융시장증권 money market securities
금융시장협의회 Working Group of Financial Markets
금융신용규제 monetary and credit control
금융어음 finance accounting
금융업 financial operations
금융업계 financial community; financing business industry
금융업자 money broker; money lender
금융연구소 financial research center
금융옵션 financial option contract
금융옵션시장 financial option market
금융완만 slackness of money market
금융완화 easing of credit; monetary easing; relaxation of credit
금융완화정책 easy monetary policy; relaxation of tight money policy
금융완화조치 measure for monetary ease
금융원조 financial aid
금융자본 finance capital; financial capital
금융자본시장자유화 deregulation of financial and capital market
금융자산 financial assets; monetary assets
금융자산가치 financial asset value
금융자산부채잔고표 financial assets and liabilities account
금융자산선호 preference of financial assets
금융자산풀 pool of financial assets
금융자유화 deregulation of finance; financial liberalization
금융자유화대책자금 Financial Liberalization Fund
금융자유화정책 financial liberalization policy
금융자회사 captive finance company
금융정책 financial policy; monetary policy
금융정책부활 revival of monetary policy
금융제도 financial system
금융제도개혁 reform of financial system
금융제도조사회 Financial system Research Council
금융조달방침 financing policy
금융조절 money market management
금융조합 loan association; loan society
금융주 financial sector stocks
금융중개기관 financial intermediaries or brokers; intermediating financial institution
금융중심지 financial center
금융지주회사 financial holding company
금융지표 financial indexes; monetary indicators
금융채 bank debenture
금융채권 financial claim
금융채무 financial obligation
금융체제 monetary regime
금융크로스 crossing for the purpose of financing
금융통계 financial statistics
금융파생상품시장 derivatives market
금융항목 financial item
금융혁명 financial revolution
금융혁신 financial innovation
금융협정 financial agreement
금융확대 monetary expansion; monetary growth
금융환경 financial environment
금융활동 financial activities
금융회사 finance company; financing corporation
금은복본위제도 gold and silver bimetallism
금의 현송점 specie points

금전거래 pecuniary transaction
금전대부업 money lending business
금전대차계약 loan agreement
금전법안 money bill
금전상납 tax payment in money
금전상의 관계 pecuniary relation
금전신탁 money trust
금전신탁이익 income from trust deposits
금전유증 pecuniary legacy
금전의 인환권 exchange check for money
금전적인 보수 pecuniary considerations
금전적인 손해 pecuniary damage
금전채권 money claim
금전채무 monetary liabilities
금전채무상태 negative monetary position
금전채무의 초과상태 positive monetary position
금전채무인증서 due bill
금전취급자 cash forward handling clerk
금전판결 money judgment
금전항목 monetary items
금전환증권 gold convertible securities
금준비 gold reserve
금준비법 Gold Reserve Act
금지 ban
금지금본위제 gold bullion standard
금지기간 prohibited period
금지명령 injunction; prohibitory injunction; restraining order
금지법 negative statute
금지세 prohibitive tax
금지절차 injunction proceedings
금채권 gold bond
금치산 incompetency
금치산자 incompetency person; person adjudged incompetent
금태환 conversion to gold
금투자계좌 gold accounts
금평가 gold par value
금평가 gold parity
금풀 gold pool
금현송점(金現送點) gold points
금화본위제 gold coin standard
금환 gold exchange
금환본위제 gold exchange standard
금환준비 gold exchange reserve
급격한 시세변동을 막음 support operation
급등 high rise; sharp increase; sharp rise; soar
급등매출 selling on spurt
급등상장 sharp advance market
급등한 가격 revived quotation
급락 sharp fall; turndown
급락상장 sharp decline market
급료 net pay; salaries
급료;임금지불장 payroll
급료감사 pay roll audit
급료공제 wage assignment
급료선불 advance of salary
급반락 sharp loss; sharp setback
급부 benefit
급부수령권 accrued benefit
급상승 skyrocketing
급상승가격 skyrocketing price
급성장 fast growth
급여공제형 투신 payroll deduction type investment trust
급여기준 basis on the amount of salary
급여로 간주하는 연금 annuity regarded as salaries and wages
급여소득 employment income
급여소득공제 employment income deduction; deduction for employment income; employment income exemption
급여소득에 대한 원천징수 withholding of employment income
급여소득원천징수표 withholding record of employment income
급여소득자 employment income earner; obtainer of employment income; person receiving employment income
급여지수 salary scale
급증 considerable rise; rapid expansion; spurt

급파하다;급파 dispatch
긍정적인 격차 positive spread
긍정적인 약인 affirmative covenants
긍정적인 증익효과 favorable leverage effect
기각 rejection
기각률 rejection rate
기간 life
기간경과 elapse of the time
기간계산 periodical accounting
기간구조 term structure
기간내의 세금배분 intraperiod tax allocation
기간내의 소득과세배분 intraperiod income tax
기간리스크 term risk
기간만료 termination; termination of a term
기간보험 time policy
기간분산 temporal diversification
기간분석 period analysis
기간비용 period charge; period expense
기간산업 key industry
기간세 fundamental tax
기간손실 periodic loss
기간손익계산 periodical accounting of profit and loss
기간안분이율 interpolated rate
기간원가 period cost
기간의 미스매치 maturity mismatch
기간이익 periodic income
기간일괄불 payment on to be made by a lump sum at maturity
기간일치 matched maturities
기간재무제표 periodic financial accounts
기간제한 time limitation
기간지표 current coupon
기간차이 timing differences
기간차입금리 term financing rate
기간평균 average over period
기간효과 extension effect
기계류 신용보험 machinery-credit insurance
기계보험 machinery insurance; macro analysis
기계부기 machine bookkeeping
기계시간율 machine-hour rate
기계시간율배부법 machine-hour rate method
기계업계 machinery industry
기계운전시작업 in-cycle work
기계화거래 mechanical trading
기계화방식 mechanization method
기계화회계 mechanized accounting
기관 institution
기관구매 equity purchases by institutions
기관구입 buying by institutional investors
기관매입 institutional buying
기관매출 institutional selling
기관중재 institutional arbitration
기관차이론 locomotive theory
기관투자가 institutional investors
기관투자가간 시장 fourth market
기관투자가지수옵션 institutional investors' index option
기구 mechanism
기국법;선적국법 law of ship's flag
기근물 nearby contract
기근물거래 transaction of near delivery
기금단위계정 fund unit account
기금이자 interest on guaranty capital
기념배당 commemorative dividend; memorial dividend
기능 function
기능별 계산서 functional statement
기능별 원가 functional cost
기능별 조직 functional organization
기능별 회계 functional accounting
기능분석 functional analysis
기능적인 가격설정 functional pricing
기능적인 감가 functional depreciation
기능통화법 functional currency method
기대가설 expectation hypothesis
기대갭 expectation gap
기대만기이율 expected yield-to-maturity
기대보유기간수익률 expected holding-period rate of return; projected holding period rate

of return
기대상속인 expectant heir
기대수익 expected earnings
기대연간조업도 expected annual volume
기대이론 expectation theory
기대이윤 expected profit
기대이율 expected yield
기대이익 prospective profit
기대이익성장률 expected earnings growth rate
기대자금효과 expected wealth effect
기대치 expected value
기득권 acquired right; vested rights
기득권을 범하지 않고 without prejudice to preliminary
기득권조항 grandfather provision
기록 log
기록미제출 failing of record
기록보존 record keeping
기록사항 matter of record
기록에 의한 by record
기말 end of the period; term-end
기말감사 completed audit; final audit
기말결산 term-end settlement of accounts
기말계정 term-end account
기말대차대조표 periodic balance sheet
기말배당 year-end dividend
기말시 환산법 translation method at the current exchange rate
기말시산표 periodic trial balance
기말에 제작중인 물건 goods in process at the end of period
기말이월이익금 unappropriated surplus at the end of year
기말잔고 balance at the end of the term; closing balance; ending balance
기말잔고;최종잔고 final balance
기말잔고계정 closing balance a/c
기말재고 year end stock
기말재고고 closing inventories
기말재고자산 inventory at the end of period
기말정리 adjustment at term-end
기명날인 signature and seal
기명사채;등록채 registered bond
기명식 registered form
기명식 선하증권 straight B/L
기명식 수표 signed check
기명식 이서 special endorsement
기명식 증권 registered securities
기명양도 signed transfer
기명어음 named bill
기명주 inscribed stock; name share
기명주권 inscribed stock certificate
기명주식 registered stock
기명증권 inscribed securities
기명채권 inscribed bond
기밀비 secret service expenses
기밀성 confidentiality
기발채이익 yield on already issued bond
기본가격 basic value
기본계약 master contract
기본계획 master plan
기본권리 fundamental rights
기본규약 mission statement
기본규제 fundamental rules
기본급 base pay; basic salary; regular wage
기본기간 basic period
기본방침 statement of principles
기본상대방 original trading partner
기본약정 agreement of articles
기본예산 baseline budget
기본원칙 basic principle
기본재산운용수입 revenue from fund operations
기본적인 수요 primary demand
기본정관 charter; memorandum of association
기본준비금을 적립함 accumulation of basis reserve
기본증거금 initial margin; original margin
기본통달 primary regulation notice
기본한계효율 marginal efficiency of capital
기본항목기준 Tier **1** capital guideline

기부금공제 contribution deduction; deduction for donation
기부금손금산입한도액 deduction limit applicable to donation
기부금의 손금산입한도액 deductible amount for donation
기분회계 equity accounting
기산일 initial date in reckoning; value date
기소부분 accusatory part
기소자 accuser
기술격차 technology gap
기술데이터 descriptive data
기술도입 introduction of technology
기술분석용 그래프 technical graph
기술분석지표 technical indicator
기술수준 technical standard
기술수출 technology export
기술예측 technological forecasting
기술이론 technical theory
기술이전 technology transfer
기술이전계약 technology transfer agreement
기술적으로 지불불능한 기업 technically insolvent corporation
기술적인 반등 technical rally
기술적인 반응 technical reaction
기술적인 분석 technical analysis
기술적인 예측 technical forecast
기술제휴 technical cooperation
기술지원 technical assistance; technological support
기술지표 technical index
기술진보 technical progress; technological advance; technological changes
기술진보율 rate of technical progress
기술혁신 technical innovation
기어링비율 gearing ratio
기어링효과 gearing effect
기어전동장치;기어링 gearing
기업 business concern; enterprise
기업가 entrepreneur
기업가정신 entrepreneurship
기업가치 business worth; enterprise value
기업간 분석 interfirm analysis
기업간 신용 credit among corporations
기업거래 business transaction
기업결합 business combinations
기업결합회계 accounting for business combinations
기업경영 corporate management
기업과세 tax on business; tax on enterprise; taxation on enterprise
기업규모 corporate size
기업금융 business finance; corporate banking; corporation finance
기업내 고속정보통신망 local area network
기업내 분석 intrafirm analysis
기업담보권 enterprise mortgage
기업도산 corporate bankruptcy
기업매수자 corporate raider
기업문화 corporate culture
기업보증 corporate guarantee
기업보험 corporate insurance
기업부담 employer's contribution
기업부문 corporation sector
기업부채비율 company leverage
기업비밀 trade secrets
기업사상 business event
기업수익성 corporate profitability
기업실체 business entity
기업실체를 공준함 postulate of business entity
기업안정 corporate settlement
기업연금 business annuity; private pension
기업연금; 기업보험 pension and life insurance schemes
기업연금보험 corporate pension insurance
기업원가 enterprise cost
기업유치 welcome enterprise
기업의 비공개화 going private
기업의 사회적 책임 social responsibility of enterprise
기업의 신규합병 consolidation of corporations
기업이미지 corporate image

기업이미지통합전략; corporate identity CI
기업이익 corporate profit
기업이익의 공변동 co-movement of corporate earnings
기업이익조정 adjustment of business income
기업재고 business inventory
기업재무국(SEC) Division of Corporate Finance(SEC)
기업재무담당자 corporate treasurer
기업전략 corporate strategy
기업전체의 리스크를 평가함 enterprise approach
기업조합 joint enterprise cooperative
기업지배주식 stock controlling other business
기업지분 corporation's equity
기업진단 management consulting
기업집단재무제표 group financial statements
기업집중 concentration of enterprise
기업채무 corporate debt
기업통합 corporate governance
기업투자 business investment
기업포괄배상책임보험;포괄책임보험 umbrella liability policy
기업프로필 corporate profile
기업형 corporation type
기업형 투자신탁 corporation type investment trust
기업형태 forms of enterprise
기업활동 business activities
기업활력 corporate vitality
기업회계 business accounting; corporate accounting; enterprise accounting
기업회계심의회 Business Accounting Council
기업회계원칙 accounting principles for business enterprise; business accounting principle; corporate accounting principles; financial accounting standards for business enterprise
기여과실 contributory negligence
기여분 contributory shares of estate
기여침해 contributory infringement
기일 appointed day; date
기일 또는 기일전에 on or before
기일도래원본 credit past due date
기일도래채권 overdue payment
기입 entry
기입하다 enter
기자클럽 press club
기장기 book-keeping machine
기장업무 obligation of bookkeeping
기장장소 booking center
기재식 무액면주식 stated value no-par stock
기재한 호가 written bid and offer
기전상환가격 call price
기전상환까지의 거치기간 life-to-call
기전에 계상한 대손준비금을 기말에 전부 잔액을 환산해서 새로 대손준비금을 적립하는 방법 adding back the credited reserve amount in full to the income in the following period
기조를 올림 upwards
기존자산 existing assets
기존채무 existing debt
기존특혜 existing preferential duties
기준 BIS standards BIS
기준 SEC standards SEC
기준 standards
기준가격 base price
기준금리 reference rate; repo rate
기준기간 base period
기준레이트 base rate
기준상장 basic rate
기준시간총액 base market value
기준에 따라 운용하다 apply correspondingly to
기준연도 base year
기준외국환상장 basic rate of foreign exchange
기준요금 standard rate
기준일 base date; date of record; record date
기준임금 standard wage
기준재고법 base-stock method
기준조업도 denominator level
기준채 SDR denominated bond SDR

기준통화 base currency
기준표준원가 base standard cost
기준할인레이트 basic discount rate
기준환상장 basic exchange rate
기중감사 interim audit
기중상환청구권부 전환사채 convertible bond with redemption request right
기증자 donator
기채 bond flotation; flotation of loan; issue of bond
기채;모집발표 launching
기채러시 market congestion
기채비용 floatation cost
기채시장 bond flotation market; bond issuing market; primary market
기채연결융자 temporary loan before bond flotation
기채활동 primary activity
기초 basis; beginning of the period; initial
기초;토대 major bottom
기초가치 fundamental value
기초공제 basic allowance; basic deduction; basic exemption; legal exemption from income tax; personal exemption
기초공준 basic convention
기초금융상품어프로치 fundamental financial approach
기초만기 original maturity
기초법규 basic regulations
기초보험료 original premium
기초불균형 fundamental disequilibrium
기초비용견적 base cost estimate
기초사실 matter
기초상정 basic assumption
기초세율 basic tax rate
기초수익 base earnings
기초수지 basic balance of payments
기초연구 basic research
기초연도 basic year
기초원가 basic cost
기초율 experience assumptions
기초인플레이션율 underlying inflation rate
기초잉여금잔고 surplus at the opening of the period
기초자본 initial capital
기초잔고 balance at the beginning of the period; beginning balance; initial balance; opening balance
기초재고고 opening inventory
기초재고자산 initial inventories; inventory at the beginning of the period
기초재무제표 basic financial statements
기초적립금 basic reserve
기초적인 회계데이터 underlying accounting date
기초정리 fundamental theorem
기초제작중인 물건 initial goods in process
기초제작품계정 initial work in process account
기초통계 basic statistics
기초퇴직연금기금 basic retirement funds
기축통화 key currency
기탁신용장 escrow letter of credit
기탁자금 escrow fund
기탁회사 deposit company
기하모델 geometric model
기하평균 geometric average
기한 time limit
기한경과 out of date
기한경과계정 overdue account
기한경과대부 overdue loan
기한경과수표 overdue check
기한경과어음 overdue bill
기한경과어음;부도어음 past due bill
기한만료 expiry
기한무효 time expired
기한별 대출통계 outstanding loans and discounts of all banks by terms
기한부 신용장 usance L/C
기한부 어음 time bill
기한부 어음매상장 credit buying rate
기한부 어음매상장 usance buying rate
기한부 어음상장 usance bill rate

기한부 우선주 limited life preferred stock
기한부 환어음 usance bill
기한의 이익을 상실한 채무 debts accelerated
기한이 끝난 카드 expired card
기한이 오다 become due; mature
기한이익 right not to pay before due date
기한이익상실 acceleration
기한이익상실조건 acceleration clause
기한이익의 상실사유 event of default
기한전 반제권 prepayment right
기한전 반제요구 acceleration demand
기한전 상환 early amortization
기한전 상환모델 prepayment model
기한전 상환율 prepayment rate
기한전 상환율지표 prepayment indicator
기한전 해약 cancellation before the maturity; early termination
기한전 환급리스크 prepay risk
기한전의 계약위반 anticipatory breach of contract
기한후 신고 return after due date
기한후 이자 interest after the maturity
기한후 자동지속 renewal after the maturity
기항지체류조항 "clause touch and stay"
기호수표 marked checks
기회비용 opportunity cost
기회소집 convocation of general meetings
기회손실 conditional loss; opportunity loss
기회이익 opportunity gain
긴급과세 tax in jeopardy
긴급관세 emergency duty; emergency tariff; tariff in jeopardy
긴급상각 emergency amortization
긴급수입 emergency import
긴급융자 emergency loan
긴급입법 emergency legislation
긴장 tension
긴축금융정책 tighter monetary policy
긴축예산 austere budget
긴축재정 austere fiscal policy; tight budget
긴축재정안 tight fiscal package
긴축정책 stringent policy; tightening monetary policy
길더채 guild bond
길드채입찰 gilt auction
길트에지채 gilt-edged bond
길트에지채;금연증권 gilt-edged securities
길트채이율 gilt yield
깁슨의 역설 Gibson paradox
깃발 flag
꼭 필요한 만큼만 구입함 hand-to-mouth buying
끝수계산 rounding off in calculation
끝에서 두 번째 penultimate

ㄱ ㄴ

ㄴ

나고야증권주가지수 Nagoya Stock Price Index
나노초 nano-second
나스닥 NASDAQ
나스닥저팬 NASDAQ Japan
나스닥종합주가지수 NASDAQ Composite Index
NOW 예금 negotiable order of withdrawal deposit
NYSE 종합주가지수 NYSE Composite Stock Index
나중에 취득한 재고자산부터 먼저 가격을 산정하는 재고자산평가법 next-in next-first method
낙담 disappointing
낙성계약 consensual contract; contract entered into by mutual consensus
낙찰결정서 letter of acceptance; letter of award
낚시보험 anglers' insurance
난수 random number
난수표 table of random numbers
난외약관 marginal clauses
난외에 찍어두는 도장 marginal seal
난조시장 wide fluctuation of market
날씨보험 weather insurance
날인의 인장을 조회함 collation of seals
날인증서 deed
날인증서계약을 위반함 breach of covenant
남북무역 north-south trade
남북문제 north-south problem
남북서미트 north-south summit
(은행원 등이) 남의 예금을 기장하지 않고 제삼자에게 일시대출하는 부정행위 off-record lending
납기 period for tax
납기연장 extension of due date
납기한 due date for tax payment; time for tax payment
납부 paying tax
납부독촉 demand for tax payment
납부서 tax payment slip
납부위탁 consignment of tax payment
납부의무계승 succession of tax obligation
납부최고서 notice of demand to guarantor
납세 tax payment
납세고지서 notification of tax payment; rate papers; tax papers
납세관리인 administrator of tax payment; tax agent; tax manager
납세관리인신고 notification of tax agent
납세담보 security for tax payment
납세미제 tax unpaid
납세보증 security of tax payment
납세부담 burden of paying tax
납세신고서 tax return form
납세신고용지 tax forms
납세액 tax due
납세예비금 accrued taxes on income
납세위탁 consignment ledger; consignment of

tax liability
납세의무 tax liability; tax obligation
납세의무가 있는 법인 corporation liable to taxation; corporation subject to taxation
납세의무계승 succession of tax liability
납세의무부담 burden of tax liability
납세의무성립 realization of tax liability
납세의무자분류 classification of a taxpayer
납세의무확정 establishment of tax liability
납세자 taxpayer
납세자번호 taxpayer identification number
납세자번호제도 taxpayer identification number system
납세자소송 taxpayer's suit
납세자의 선택 taxpayer's option
납세저축조합 savings-for-tax association; tax saving association
납세적금 savings in preparation for tax payment
납세조합 taxpayer's association
납세준비금 accrued income taxes; deposit for tax payment; provision for tax; reserve for tax payment
납세준비예금 deposit for tax
납세준비예금이자의 비과세 nontaxable interest from deposits for tax payment
납세준비증권 anticipation tax bill
납세증명서 certificate of tax payment
납세지 tax payment place
납세지변경 change of the place of tax payment
납세지이동 transfer of the place of tax payment
납세지이동신고 notification of transfer of place of tax payment
납세지지정 designation of place for tax payment
납세필 duty-paid
납세필 증서 certificate of compliance
납세협회 Tax Payment Association
납회 final session of a month
낫모양가격표 scissors-form difference in price
낭비자신탁 spendthrift trust
낮은 가격 lower price
낮은 설비투자율 low capacity utilisation
낳다 bear
내각부 Cabinet Office
내구소비재 consumers' durables; durable consumer goods
내구재수주 durable goods order
내국민대우 national treatment
내국법인 domestic corporation
내국법인합병 merger of a domestic corporation
내국세 internal tax
내국세입국 Bureau of Internal Revenue
내국주식 domestic share
내국채 internal bond
내국환 inland exchange
내국환어음 inland bill of exchange
내규개정 revision of office regulation
내금 money paid-in part
내림차순 descending order
내부감사 internal audit
내부감사기준 internal audit standard
내부감사보고서 internal audit report
내부감사인 internal auditor
내부감사제도 internal audit system
내부거래 internal transaction
내부견제 internal check
내부견제제도 internal check system
내부경영분석 internal business analysis
내부구조 internal structure
내부규정 internal regulations
내부금융 internal financing
내부노동시장 internal labor market
내부대체 intracompany transfer
내부대체가격 intracompany transfer price
내부대체이익 interdepartmental profit
내부대체차액 inter-company transfer variance
내부보고 internal reporting
내부보고제도 internal reporting system
내부보고회계 accounting for internal reporting
내부부채 internal liability
내부분석 internal analysis
내부수익률 internal rate of return

내부신용보완 internal credit enhancement
내부유보 retained profit
내부유보금 internal reserve
내부이익 internal profit
내부이자율 internal rate of interest rate
내부자거래와 증권사기에 대한 규제법 Insider Trading and Securities Fraud **1988** Enforcement Act of
내부자금 internal fund
내부자료 internal document
내부자본 internal capital
내부정보 inside information
내부정합성 internal consistency
내부증거 internal evidence
내부캐시플로 internal cash flow
내부통제 internal control
내부통제테스트 test of controls
내부화주문 internalized order
내부회계통제 internal accounting control
내생변수 endogenous variable
내생변화 endogenous change
내셔널미니멈 national minimum
내셔널트러스트 national trust
내수 domestic demand
내수관련주 domestic demand related stock
내수를 이끄는 leading domestic demand
내수산업 domestic demand oriented industry
내수진흥 domestic demand stimulation
내수확대 domestic demand expansion; increasing domestic demand
내역 break-down; particulars
내역계정서 itemized bill
내역서 detailed statement; statement of items
내외금리차 international interest-spread
내용연수 durable years; service life; useful life
내용연수계산 computation of useful years; reckoning of useful life
내용연수단축 shortening of useful life
내용연수표 useful life table
내용증명우편 content-certified mail
내용표시문언 words of limitation
내입금 initial down payment; initial installment; initial payment
내재적인 콜가격 implicit call price
내재화 internalization
내지근무 home service
내채 internal debt
내포금리 implicit interest
내항력이 없는 unseaworthy
내항화물해상보험 coastwise cargo insurance
내화건축물을 증가상각함 additional depreciation on fire-proof buildings
냉각기간 cooling time
넓이 breadth
네거티브캐리 negative carry
네거티브캐시플로 negative cash flow
네거티브플레지패리패스조항 negative pledge pari passu clause
네덜란드의 **ANP-CBS** 종합주가지수 ANP /CBS General Index
네이키드옵션 naked option
네이키드워런트 naked warrant
네이키드콜 naked call
네이키드포지션 naked position
네크라인 neck line
네팅 netting
네팅계약 netting arrangement
넷거래고 net trading volume
넷리스 net lease
넷밸런스 net balance
넷블록플로 net block flow
넷오픈포지션 net open position
넷채권국 net creditor country
넷캐시 net cash
넷캐시플로 net cash flow
넷포지션 net position
넷프라이스인덱스 net price index
넷프라이스트레이딩 net price trading
노다운 no-down
노다지;대성공 bonanza
노동경제학 labor economics

노동계수 labor coefficient
노동계약에 따른 규정 regulations according to the labor agreement
노동금고 labor credit associations
노동력 labor force
노동법 industrial law; labor laws
노동법규 labor regulations
노동분배율 labor share
노동분쟁 labor trouble
노동비차이 labor variance
노동생산 industrial output
노동소득 labor income
노동시장 labor market
노동입법 labor legislation
노동자나 소매상의 저축; 융자를 담당하는 금융기관 industrial bank
노동자배상법 workmen's compensation law
노동자이동 labor turnover
노동자재해보상법 workmen's compensation acts
노동자재해보상보험 workmen's compensation insurance
노동재해 industrial injury
노동재해보험 workmen's compensation
노동재해종합보험 workers' s accident comprehensive insurance
노동쟁의 industrial dispute; labor dispute
노동조합 labor union; trade union
노동집약적 산업 labor-intensive industry
노동협약 labor agreement
노드방식 node method
노령연금 old age pension
노령유족장애자연금 old-aged; survivor and disability insurance
노령자 aged person
노령자공제 allowance for old person; deduction for old-age person; exemption for aged person; old person allowance
노로드펀드 no load fund
노멀마켓 normal market
노멀어셋믹스 normal asset mix
노멀타겟앨로케이션 normal target allocation
노무감사 labor audit
노사관계 labor relation
노사관계 management labor relation
노사교섭 wage negotiation
노선가격방식에 따른 평가 valuation by road rating
노이즈 noise
노인부양친족 aged dependent
노인의료보험제도 Medicare
노임 labor cost
노트이슈언스퍼실리티; NIF note issuance facility
노폴트자동차보험 no fault automobile insurance
노하우누설 leak of know-how
노하우사용료 royalty as to know-how
녹다운제품 knock-down product
논디포지터리코레스펀던트 non-depositary correspondent
논리코스 non-recourse
논마린대리점제도 non-marine agency system
논콜러블본드 non-callable bond
논플리트계약자 non-fleet insured
농림수산부 Ministry of Agriculture; Forestry and Fisheries
농림수산업 fishery; agriculture and forestry industry
농림어업금융기관 financial institution for agriculture forestry and fisheries
농산물가격정책 price policy of agricultural products
농산물관세 agricultural tariff
농업경영비 agricultural expenditure
농업경제학 agricultural economics
농업금융 agricultural credit
농업보조금 farm subsidy
농업보험 agricultural insurance
농업부기 agricultural bookkeeping
농업생산법인 agricultural production corporation

농업선취특권 agricultural lien
농업소득 agricultural income
농업소득면세 tax exemption for agricultural income
농업은행 agricultural bank
농업재편성 reorganization of industry
농업조합 agricultural society
농업회계 farm accounting
높은 가능성 high possibility
높은 유동성 high liquidity
뇌물;뇌물을 줌 bribery
뇌물수수; 부패 corruption
누가법 cumulative method
누적 accumulation; buildup; cumulative loss
누적과세 cumulative taxation
누적급부채무 accumulated benefit obligation
누적배당 accumulated dividend; cumulative dividend
누적배당우선주식 accumulated preferred stock
누적배당형 주식 accumulative stock
누적변동성 historical volatility
누적비율 accumulative rate
누적생산고 volume accumulation
누적세 cascade tax
누적시스템 accumulation system
누적액 accumulated amount
누적우선주 cumulative preferred stock
누적유닛 accumulation unit
누적유증 cumulative legacy
누적이익 accumulated income
누적이자 accumulated interest
누적적인 accumulative
누적적자 accumulated deficit; cumulative deficit
누적제한 cumulative limitation
누적증가예산 incremental budget
누적채무 accumulated debt
누적채무 debt accumulation
누적투자 accumulated investment; cumulative investment
누적투자기간 accumulative investment period
누적투자유닛 accumulative investment unit
누적투자플랜 accumulative investment plan
누적투표 cumulative voting
누적판결 accumulative judgment
누적한도액 cumulative maximum amount
누적한도액기준 cumulative limit
누적형 거래고세 cascade type turnover tax
누적흑자 cumulative surplus
누진과세 graduated taxation; progressive taxation
누진세 progressive tax
누진세율 progressive rate; progressive tax rate
누진소득세 progressive income tax
누진제 progressive nature
뉴딜 New Deal
뉴스인덱스시리즈 **TOPIX** New Index Series TOPIX
뉴욕금융시장 New York money market
뉴욕리파이낸스 New York refinance
뉴욕상품거래소 New York Mercantile Exchange
뉴욕선물거래소 New York Futures Exchange
뉴욕어음교환소의 은행간 자금이체지급제도; Clearing House Inter-Bank Payment System CHIPS
뉴욕연방준비은행 Federal Reserve Bank of New York
뉴욕오프쇼어시장 New York Offshore Center
뉴욕은행 Bank of New York
뉴욕은행간 제안금리 New York inter-bank offered rate
뉴욕인수신용장 New York acceptance credit
뉴욕종합지수 NYSE Composite
뉴욕증권거래소 Big Board; New York Stock Exchange
뉴욕증권거래소주가지수 New York Stock Exchange Composite Stock Index
뉴트럴헤지 neutral hedge
느슨한;줄인 slacken

능력 ability
능력급 pay according to ability
능력이 있는 당사자 competent parties
능력이 있음 competency
능력자 legal ability person
능률감사 efficiency audit
능률차이 efficiency variance
늦다 slow
니어더머니 near the money
니치 niche
닛케이 225 선물거래 Nikkei 225 Future
닛케이 225 지수옵션 Nikkei 225 Index option
닛케이 300 옵션 Nikkei 300 Options
닛케이 300 주가지수 Nikkei 300 Stock Price Index
닛케이 300 투자신탁 Nikkei 300 Investment Trust
닛케이 225 옵션 Nikkei 225 Options
닛케이 300 선물거래 Nikkei 300 Futures
닛케이다우평균 Nikkei 300 Dow-Jones Average
닛케이 300 주가지수연동형 상장투자신탁 listed investment trusts linked to Nikkei 300 Stock Price Index

ㄷ

다각결제 multilateral settlement
다각적 무역교섭 multilateral trade negotiations
다각적인 청산협정 multilateral clearing agreement
다각화의 경제성 economies of scope
다각화전략 diversification strategy
다국간 교섭 multilateral initiative
다국간 협정 multilateral agreement
다국적기업 multinational firm
다국적은행 multinational bank
다기간모델 multiperiod model
다단계식 multiple-step form
다른 결정이 없는 한 unless otherwise specified
다른 계좌 different account
다른 비율 split rating
다목적재무재표 all-purpose financial statement
다변량해석 multivariate analysis
다부문분석 multi-sectoral analysis
다세대주택 multi-factor house
다소 높은 유도 aggressively held up
다수결 majority decision
다수국간투자보증기관 Multilateral Investment Guarantee Agency
다양한 diverse
다우 **20**종 채권지수 Dow Jones 20 Bond Index
다우공공주 **15**종 평균 Dow Jones 15 Public Utility Average
다우공업주 Dow Jones Industrial
다우공업주 **30**종 평균 Dow Jones 30 Industrial Average
다우식 상품지수 Dow-Jones Commodity Index
다우운송주 **20**종 평균 Dow Jones 20 Transportation Average
다우이론 Dow Theory
다우평균 Dow Jones Average; Dow Jones Industrial Average
다운앤드아웃콜옵션 down and out call option
다원적인 증거 multiple evidence
다음날로 늦추다 revert to the following day
다음사업연도 subsequent taxable year
다이나믹승수 dynamic multiplier
다이나믹전략 dynamic strategies
다이나믹크레디트스와프 dynamic credit swap
다이나믹포트폴리오 dynamic portfolio
다이나믹프로그램 dynamic programming
다이나믹헤지 dynamic hedge scheme
다이랙트뱅킹 direct banking
다이렉트어음 direct paper
다이묘본드 daimyo bond
다이아몬드포메이션 diamond formation
다중상관 multiple correlation
다중채무 card-holic
다지라인 Dodge Line
다킷 **SEC** Docket SEC
다통화조항 multi-currency clause

다통화회계 multiple currency accounting
다행식 시산서 artificial statement
다행식 현금출납장 tabular cash book
단 provided that
단가 unit price
단가계약 unit-price contract
단가적산법 unit pricing
단계원가 stepped cost
단계이부채 stepped coupon bond
단계적인 건설 phased construction
단계적인 평가변동방식 crawling peg system
단골은행 run upon a bank; transmitting bank
단기 short period; short-term
단기가능만가 retractable maturity
단기거래 short-term transaction
단기공급곡선 short run supply curve
단기국채 government bill; short-term government bond
단기균형 short run equilibrium
단기금리 short rate; short-term interest rate
단기금리가 장기금리보다 비싼 상태 negative yield
단기금융 short-term finance
단기금융계정 money market account
단기금융상품 money market instrument
단기금융상품투자신탁 money market fund
단기금융시장 money market; short-term credit market; short-term money market
단기금융시장예금계정 money market deposit account
단기금융시장조작 money market operations
단기금융시장지수 money market index
단기대부 short-term loan; short-term loan receivable
단기대부금 short-term loans
단기등급 short-term debt rating
단기로 매매하는 in-and-out trading
단기매매익 short swing profits
단기부채 quick liabilities; short-term liabilities
단기불 payment at short date
단기비용 short period cost
단기상장 short market
단기스와프 short swap
단기양도소득 short-term capital gain
단기업자 money market broker
단기예측 near-term outlook; short-term outlook
단기유동성요인 short-term liquidity factor
단기융자 money at call
단기이율 short-term yield
단기자금 short-term fund
단기자금레이트 short-term facility rate
단기자금조달비용 cost of short-term funds
단기자본 short term asset; short-term capital
단기자본거래 short-term capital transaction
단기자본수지 short-term capital balance
단기증권투자신탁 money market mutual funds
단기지불능력 short-term solvency
단기지향 short-term oriented
단기차입 borrowing short; short-term borrowing
단기차입금 bank loans; money borrowed for short-term; short-term debt; short-term loan payable
단기차입금(장기차입의 1년 내 반제분) current period of long-term debt
단기차입보증금 short-term margin
단기차입유가증권 short-term securities borrowed
단기채 short-dated bond; short-term bond
단기채권 short-term note
단기채무 unfunded debt
단기투자 current investment; short-term investment; short-term investment
단기투자가 day-to-day trader
단기투자계정 short-term investment account
단기투자수익 short-tenn returns; short fall
단기파동; 키친사이클 Kitchen cycles
단단히 tight
단독베이스 parent base
단독베이스매상 parent sales

단독베이스수익예측 parent-basis earning outlook
단독보유 entire tenancy
단독으로 severally
단독재무제표 separate financial statements
단독해손 particular average
단리 simple interest
단리(單利)베이스 on a simple interest basis
단리마진 simple margin
단리법 method of simple interest
단리이익 yield by simple interest
단명 single name
단명어음 one name paper; single name paper
단문식 감사보고서 short form audit report
단본위제도 monometalic competition
단서의 provisory
단서조항 provisory clause
단수 fractional figure
단수금융 fractional sum
단수이자 fractional interest
단순가설 simple hypothesis
단순계약 unconditional contract
단순매매 outright buying and selling
단순명의인 merely nominal persons
단순보증인 simple guarantor
단순부동산권 fee simple
단순분개장 simple journal
단순산술평균지수 simple arithmetic average index
단순승수 simple multiplier
단순신탁 simple trust
단순예측 simple prediction
단순이동평균 simple moving average
단순자백 simple confession
단순작업 routine tasks
단순재정 simple arbitrage
단순저당채권자불약관 open mortgage clause
단순점프모델 simple jump model
단순종합원가계산 simple cost accounting
단순준비법 simple reserve method
단순지수 simple index
단순채무 simple obligation
단순총화 simple aggregate
단순파산 straight bankruptcy
단순평균법 simple average cost method; straight average cost method
단순평균이율 arithmetic dividend yield average; simple average yield
단순평균주가 arithmetic stock price average; simple average stock price
단순평균치 simple mean value
단순폭행 simple assault
단순하지 않은 인수 qualified acceptance of bill
단순한 방식 vanilla structure
단순한 투자대상 stand alone investment
단순해손;단순평균 simple average
단식 single expression
단식기입 single entry
단식부기 bookkeeping by single entry; simple accounting; single entry bookkeeping
단위 unit
단위미만주 fractional share
단위미만주식 fractional shares
단위보조금 unit grant
단위연금적립증가방식 unit credit method
단위원가 unit cost
단위주 even lot; unit shares
단위형 unit type
단위형 지방채투자신탁 municipal bond unit investment trust
단위형 채권투자신탁 bond unit trust
단위형 투신 unit type investment trust
단일거래 single transaction
단일고객분리계정 individual separate account; single customer separate account
단일구분계산서 single-step statement
단일구분손익계산서 single step income statement
단일대차대조표 single balance sheet
단일만기예금 single maturity deposit
단일만기채 term bonds

단일목적카드 monopurpose credit card
단일사업주형 급부기준연금제도 single employer defined benefit pension plan
단일세 single tax
단일세율 single tariff
단일세율제 simple tariff system
단일요인 one factor
단일요인모델 one factor model
단일유럽의정서 Single European Act
단일은행면허 single banking license
단일은행제도 unit banking system
단일은행지주회사 one bank holding company
단일주식 share of one kind
단일지표모델 single index model
단일통화 single currency
단일환레이트 single exchange rate
단일환시장제 monorate of exchange system
단일환율제도 unitary exchange rate system
단자시장 call loan market; call money and discount market; call money market
단자업자 short-term money house
단자협회 Association of Call Loan and Discount Companies
단자회사 call loan dealer; money market dealer
단정적인 peremptory
단주 fractional lot; odd lot
단주거래 odd-lot transaction
단주분을 포함하지 않음 based on round lots
단주업자 odd lot dealer
단주정리 lot consolidation; odd lot consolidation
단주주권 scrip
단주주문 fractional order
단지보험 apartment dwellers' comprehensive insurance
단체거치연금계약 group deferred annuity contract
단체건강보험 group health insurance
단체교섭 collection bargaining
단체교섭권 right of collective bargaining
단체급계약 wholesale group insurance
단체모기지보상생명보험 group mortgage insurance
단체보험 group insurance
단체상해보험 group accident insurance; group life insurance
단체신용생명보험 group credit life insurance
단체신용생명보험조합 group credit insurance association
단체양로보험 group endowment insurance
단체연금 group pension
단체연금보험 group annuity insurance
단체예탁관리계약 group deposit administration contract
단체장기보험계약 group permanent insurance contract
단체정기보험 group term insurance
단체협약 collection bargaining agreement
단축 cutback
단항연산 monadic operation
단회계제도 single account system
달러가중수익률 dollar-weighted rate of return
달러계정 dollar account
달러계좌개설서류 documents for opening a U. S. dollar account
달러고기조 firm tone of the U. S. dollar
달러과잉 overhung dollar
달러기준 denominated in U. S. dollar
달러기준으로 in dollar terms
달러기준의 dollar denominated
달러기준전환사채 dollar convertible bond
달러기준채무 ebt in U. S. dollar
달러단기금리선물 U S dollar short-term interest futures
달러매출개입 intervention by selling dollars
달러방위 defense of the dollar
달러불황 dollar shortage
달러블록 dollar bloc
달러선호 dollar preference
달러시프트 dollar shift
달러약세 weaker U S dollar

ㄷ ㄹ

달러위기 dollar crisis
달러저 depreciation of dollar
달러지폐 buck
달러콜옵션 dollar call option
달러평가 dollar parity
달러평균 dollar averaging
달러평균법 dollar average method
달러풀 dollar pool
달러풋옵션 dollar put option
달러화약세 forward discount of U.S. dollar
달러환율 exchange rate per dollar
달성가능한 attainable
달성하다 attain
담;울타리 enclosure
담배소비세 tobacco consumption tax
담보 collateral; loanable value
담보 부대출 secured credit
담보가치 collateral value
담보계정 assigned accounts
담보관리 management of collateral
담보권 security interest; security right
담보권 행사 exercise of security right
담보권을 설정할 수 없는 자산 unencumbered assets unexpected
담보권자 secured party
담보권행사 foreclosure
담보권행사부동산 property in possession
담보권행사에 따른 매각 foreclosure sales
담보권행사자금 foreclosed assets
담보대부 collateral loan
담보대출 loan on security; secured loan
담보를 통한 은행차입 bank loans secured by mortgage
담보목록 inventory of security
담보물 pledge
담보물건 guaranty; underlying collateral
담보물건을 가격보다 낮게 평가할 때의 비율 assessment rate of collateral
담보범위 coverage
담보보류조항 negative clause
담보부 거래 secured transactions
담보부 고정자산양도 transfer of fixed assets given in pledge
담보부 대부 secured advance
담보부 대부금 mortgages receivable
담보부 대출 secured debt
담보부 부채 secured debenture; secured liabilities
담보부 사채신탁 mortgage debenture in trust
담보부 사채신탁법 mortgage debentures trust law
담보부 수입 collateral import
담보부 신탁채권 collateral trust bond
담보부 약속어음 collateral note; secured note
담보부 예금 collateral deposit
담보부 인수 acceptance on security
담보부 증권 secured securities
담보부 투자신탁 mortgage investment trust
담보여력 net worth of collateral
담보예금 deposit as collateral; security deposits
담보위험 risk covered
담보자산 hypothecated assets
담보제공액 assigned amount
담보제한조항 negative pledge clause
담보주 collateral shares
담보차입동의서 hypothecation agreement
담보차입유가증권 securities deposited as collateral
담보차입자산 assets subject to lien
담보차입주식총액 omnium
담보차입증 letter of confirmation of collateral
담보해제 release of security
담세능력설 ability theory of taxation
담세력 tax bearing capacity
담세자 tax bearer
담수에 젖음 fresh water damage
담합거래 accommodation trades
담합경매 knock out
담합매매 matched order
당국 authorities
당기 current period; current taxable year;

current term; current year; reported period
당기결산 current term settlement
당기만기부분 current maturity
당기매상고 sales for this term
당기미처분이익잉여금 unappropriated earned surplus for current term
당기세액 current taxes
당기손실금 deficit for the current term; loss for the current year
당기순손실 current term net loss
당기순손익 current term net profit or loss
당기순이익 current term net profit; net income for the year; net profit for the year
당기순익 current term net income
당기실적 results of the current term
당기업적주의 current operating performance theory
당기업적주의에 따른 손익계산서 current operating performance income statement
당기영업이익 current operating profit
당기의 reported term
당기이익 bottom line; current income
당기이익금 profit for the current term
당기지출원가 current-outlay cost
당기처분이익잉여금 unappropriated surplus for the current taxable
당년도의 개황 year in brief
당면의 유동성 immediate liquidity
당방 our side
당방계정 our account; Nostro account
당방부담 on our risk
당사자 party
당소주(當所株) stock exchange share
당연히 비싸야 할 종목이 싸고, 싸야 할 종목이 비싼 상태 negative spread
당월에 한해 유효한 주문 good this month order
당일만 유효한 주문 day order
당일변동상황 intraday deviations
당일유효주문 same day effective order
당일인도 value today
당일중의 변동율 intraday fluctuation rate
당일중의 변동폭 intraday fluctuation margin
당자대월약정 overdraft facilities
당장 immediate future
당장의 이윤을 노려 사고 팜 scalping
당장의 이윤을 노려 사고파는 사람 scalper
당좌계정 account current; book account; checking account; current account; running account
당좌계정부체 transfer of current account
당좌대부 demand loan
당좌대월계정 overdraft account
당좌대월약정서 agreement for overdraft
당좌대출 cash credit
당좌비율 acid ratio; quick assets ratio; quick ratio
당좌수표 current account cheek
당좌예금 cash at bank; checking deposits; current deposit; deposit in current account; quick deposit
당좌자금 current fund
당좌자산 quick assets
당좌초과인출 overdraft
당초구입자 original purchaser
당초부담원가 starting-load cost
당초측정 initial measurements
대가;약인 consideration
대가구입 counterpurchase
대가수령 value received
대각스프레드 diagonal spread
대고객환상장 exchange quotation
대공황 great depression
대규모상각자산 large depreciable property
대규모투자 major investments
대금고보험 safe deposit box insurance
대금교환인도 cash on delivery
대금업규제법 law concerning restrictions on money lending business
대금주 loan stock
대금평균 average value
대기기간 waiting period

대기업 large company
대기행렬 queuing
대납 payment for another
대납회 final session of a year
대내간접투자 indirect inward investment
대내증권투자 foreign investment in Korean securities; foreign investment in Korean stocks
대내직접투자 inward direct investment
대내투자 inward investment
대달러환상장 exchange rate against dollar
대당거래 cross transaction
대등한 입장에서 at arm's length
대등합병 amalgamation on an equal basis
대량거래 block transaction
대량구입 bulk purchase
대량매매거래 block sales
대량보유보고서 substantial shareholding report
대량생산 mass production
대량생산기술 mass production techniques
대량수주 major order
대량주문을 소량집행함 split order
대량추천판매 mass sales
대륙법 continental law
대륙식 원장마감수속 continental form of closing the ledger
대리 deputy; proxy
대리교환 clearing for nonmember
대리권을 증명하는 서류 written proxy
대리대부 agency loan
대리수수료 agent commission
대리인 attorney in fact; procurator
대리인;중개인 agent
대리인부기 agency bookkeeping
대리인을 통해서 by proxy
대리인자금 agency fund
대리점 agency
대리점경비 agency cost
대리점계약 agency contract
대리점계약서 agency agreement
대리점계정 agency account; agent account
대리점대출 agency account receivable; current credit accounts with agencies
대리점수수료 agency commission; agency fee
대리점원장 agency ledger
대리판매 sale by agent
대립하는 이해 competent interest
대면 confrontation
대물계약 real contract
대물관할권 jurisdiction of the res
대물담보 impersonal security
대물배상보험 automobile property damage liability insurance
대물변제 accord and satisfaction; payment in substitution
대물변제담보물을 취득함 strict foreclosure
대물소송 real action
대물신용 real credit
대발회 first session of a year
대변잔고 credit balance
대변전표 credit note
대부 lending
대부계정 advance account; loan account
대부금 loan receivable
대부금;상승;입체금 advance
대부금계정 loan to customers account
대부금리 credit rate
대부금보험 loan insurance
대부금액 amount advanced
대부금이자 interest on loans
대부금이자반려 interest on loans rebated
대부금채무평가 valuation of loan
대부금회수 collection of loans
대부미수이자 accrued interest on loan
대부수익 proceeds of loan
대부신탁 loan in trust
대부신탁 loan trust
대부신탁예상배당률 expected return ratio of loan trust
대부예약 forward commitment

대부원장 loan ledger
대부유가증권 loan receivable in securities; securities lent; securities loaned
대부자금 loanable fund
대부증권 loan securities
대부지분참가 loan participation
대부창구 lending window
대부한도 limit of a loan
대부한도액 upper limit of a loan
대상(大商) dramatic surge
대상;큰장사 broad market
대상문제전체의 throughout the target issues
대상상품 target securities
대상스와프 underlying swap
대상자산가액 target assets value
대상주식 target stock; underlying stock
대상지표 underlying index
대상회사 target company
대세관 macro view
대손 bad loan; credit losses
대손계정 bad debt account; bad account
대손금 bad debt loss; dead loan; lending loss; loan loss
대손금;불량채권 bad debt
대손금상각 (대손상각) bad debt written-off
대손금회수 recovery of bad debt; recovery of doubtful accounts; recovery of the bad debts
대손상각 charge off
대손손실 loss from bad debts
대손예비금 allowance for bad debt; allowance for uncollectable accounts
대손율 percentage of credit losses
대손을 상각하다 write off bad debts
대손준비금 allowance for bad loan; allowance for doubtful accounts; bad debt provision; loan loss allowance; loan loss provision; reserve for bad debts; reserve for bad loan; reserve for dead loan; reserves for credit losses
대손준비금계정편입한도액 limit to credit reserve for bad debts
대손준비금공제후 수취채권 net of reserves
대손준비금공제후의 금액 net amount after provision for loss
대손준비금으로 편입할 수 없는 자금 receivables not qualifying for the bad debts reserve
대손준비금편입 provision for possible loan loss
대손준비손 provision for bad debts
대수그래프 logarithmic chart
대수선형 log linear
대수의 법칙 law of large numbers
대수정규분포 lognormal distribution
대외관계 international affairs
대외균형 external equilibrium
대외수지 external account
대외순대출 net foreign credit
대외순자산 net external assets
대외이권 overseas interests
대외준비고 international reserves
대외지불수단 foreign means of payment
대외지불수단 means of foreign payment
대외지불을 위한 환 exchange for means of foreign payment
대외차입 international borrowing
대외채권 foreign debt
대외채권채무 foreign claims and debt
대외채무 international debts
대외채무반제 foreign debt servicing
대외채무이자지불 interest payments on foreign debt
대외투자 outward investment; overseas investment
대용물 substitute
대용유가증권 securities in lieu of cash; substitute securities
대용증권 collateral security
대용증권담보율 collateral value of substitute security
대용통화 proxy currency

대용할 수 있는 fungible
대월설정 setting up overdraft
대위 subrogation
대위납부 payment in subrogation; subrogation payment
대위변제 subrogated performance
대위영수서 subrogation receipt
대위채무 subrogated right
대위통지서 advice of subrogation
대응;매칭;약정 matching
대응계정 reciprocal account
대응스와프 matching swap
대응의 원칙 principle of matching
대응조정 correlative adjustment
대인배상보험 automobile bodily injury liability insurance
대조계정 contra account; per contra account
대조표 list of differences between
대조한 등본 examined copy
대주 lending stock
대주;대여주 lended stock
대주담보금 margin for borrowed stocks
대주시장 stock loan market
대주주 big shareholder; large shareholder
대중과세 taxation upon the general-public
대중리스크 mass risks
대중상장 public market
대중소비사회 mass consumption society
대중투자가 investing public
대증권 lending securities
대차거래 debt-credit transaction; loan transaction
대차계약 sell-and-lease agreement
대차계정 debtor and creditor accounts
대차대조표 balance sheet; financial position statement; statement of financial position
대차대조표감사의 각서 memorandum of balance sheet audit
대차대조표등식 balance sheet formula
대차대조표를 재표시함 restatement of balance sheet
대차대조표분석 balance sheet analysis
대차대조표일후의 발생사항 event subsequent to balance sheet date
대차대조표항목 balance sheet items
대차란 debtor side
대차은행 debtor bank
대차평균의 원리 principle of equilibrium
대체 book-entry transfer; substitution
대체가능성 fungibility; fungible goods
대체결제수수료 fee for book-entry transfer
대체결제제도 book-entry clearing system
대체결제회사 stock clearing corporation
대체계정 transfer account
대체계좌 postal transfer account
대체고정자산 substitute fixed assets
대체기입 cross entry
대체납세 tax payment by transfer account
대체담보 replacement of collateral
대체를 통한 자산교환 replacement property by purchase
대체미니멈세 alternative minimum tax
대체법률 law of substitution
대체보관기관 custody and transfer institution
대체보관기관에 예탁함 deposit with depository
대체비용 alternative costs; renewal expenses; substituted expenses
대체수수료 book-entry transfer fee; transferring charge
대체스와프 substitution swap
대체안 alternatives
대체영수증 journal voucher
대체원장 journal ledger
대체유동성 alteration liquidity; alternative liquidity
대체이익 profit transferred
대체이익준비금 reserve for intercompany profit
대체자금 alternative fund
대체자산 property for substitution; substitute assets; substitute property

대체전표 cross slip; journal slip
대체제품 alternate product
대체증권 fungible securities
대체탄력성 elasticity of substitution
대체하다 supersede
대체회계원칙 alternative accounting principles
대체효과 substitution effect
대출계정 creditor account
대출금 loans and bills discounted
대출금계정 loans and bills discounted accounts
대출금리 interest rate on loans; lending rate; loan rate
대출금이자 interest on loans and discount
대출기준 lending criteria
대출능력 lending ability
대출란 creditor side
대출리스크 debt exposure
대출메모 credit memorandum
대출수수료 fee on loans
대출심사 examination of loan application; screening of application for loan
대출액 amount financed
대출약정평균금리 average contractual interest rate on bank loan
대출업무 lending operation
대출예약한도 line of credit
대출은행 creditor bank; lender bank
대출이율 loan interest rate
대출자금 loanable resources
대출자금이론 loanable funds theory
대출자세 lending attitude
대출자의 선호 lender's preference
대출자의 우선권분석 analysis of lender's preference
대출자의 위험 lender's risk
대출정책 lending policy
대출조건 lending terms
대출조건명시 disclosure of terms and conditions of loans
대출준비금 borrowed reserves
대출증가액규칙 restriction on the growth of bank loans
대출채권 finance receivable
대출채권분매 loan subparticipation
대출초과 over-loan
대출초과한도액 maximum limit of overdraft
대출한도액 maximum loan value
대출한도액 적용제도 credit ceiling application system
대출한도액;신용한도 credit line
대치 replacement by purchase
대치자산 replaced property
대칭변수 antithetic variable
대칭분포 symmetrical distribution
대칭트라이앵글 symmetrical triangle; symmetrical triangle pattern
대투자은행 large investment bank
대폭발 Big Bang
대폭상향수정 sharp upward revision
대폭증가 leap
대폭하락 plunge
대폭할인 deep discount
대표민주제 representative democracy
대표상품 representing issue
대표소송 representative suit
대표이사 executive directors; representative director
대표자 및 관리인 representatives or administrators
대표자대리인 substitute representative
대표청산인 representative liquidator
대표화폐 representative money
대항력 countervailing power
대항력을 구비함 perfection of the interest
대항요건 requirements for setting up against
대항요건을 구비한 담보권 perfected security interest
대항하다 set up against
대행은행 agent bank
대행카드 credit cards issued by the agent
대형매수 large acquisition; major acquisition

대형발행 jumbo issue
대형전국은행 money center bank
대형주 large capital stock; arge-sized stock
더미계정 dummy account
더미회사 dummy company
더블레버리지 double leverage
더블업 double-up
더블옵션 double option
더블크로스오버 double crossover
더블톱 double top
더빈-왓슨비 Durbin-Watson ratio
더치길더채 Dutch guilder bond
더치방식 Dutch system
더티플로트;관리변동환율제도 dirty float
덤벨포트폴리오 dumbbell portfolio
덤핑 dumping
덤핑제소 dumping petition
데디케이트포트폴리오 dedicated portfolio
데모그라픽분석 demographic analysis
데모그라픽스코어링 demographic scoring
데몬스트레이션효과 demonstration effect
데이터가공업무 data processing business
데이터뱅크 data bank
데이터베이스 data base
데이터수집 data capture
데이터통신 data communications
데이트레이더 day trader
데트에퀴티스와프 debt equity swap
데트워런트 fixed income warrant
데트워런트채 bond with debt warrant; debt warrant
데트크로스 debt cross
델타 delta
델타수치 delta value
델타헤지 delta hedge
도난보험 burglary insurance
도난수표 stolen check
도난어음 stolen bill
도덕상의 약인 moral consideration
도덕적 해이 moral hazard
도둑;소매치기 picker
도떼기(고물, 벼룩)시장 flea market
도량표준 standard of price
도로요금소 toll gate
도매가격 wholesale price
도매량 wholesale
도매물가지수 wholesale price index
도매사업 wholesale establishment
도매상 wholesale dealer
도매업 wholesale business; wholesale trade
도매업계 wholesale trade industry
도매업자 wholesaler
도매은행업무 wholesale banking
도매회계 wholesale accounting
도미노효과 domino effect
도민세 metropolitan inhabitant tax
도박 gambling
도박보험 wager policy
도발 provocation
도발적인 구매 sporadic buying
도수분포 frequency distribution
도시 City
도시개량사업 urban remodeling enterprise
도시계획 town planning scheme
도시계획세 city planning tax
도시기반정비공단 Urban Development Corporation
도시세 prefectural tax
도시은행 city bank
도시재정 municipal finance
도시화 urbanization
도움 aid and comfort
도의적인 설득 moral suasion
도의적인 지불보증채권 moral obligation bond
도이머이정책(베트남의 개혁정책) Doi Moi
도입예금 deposit to be relent to a third party
도착원가 laid-down cost
도착지불판매상장 on demand selling rate
도착후 일람불어음 arrival draft
도쿄증권거래소정회원 regular members of the Tokyo Stock Exchange

도쿄증시 TSE
도쿄증시평균 TSE Stock Price Average
도피자금 flight money
도함수 derived function
도형 diagram
독단적인 arbitrary
독립감사 independent audit
독립계약 independent contract
독립기업간 가격 arm's length price
독립기업원칙 arm's length principle
독립생계 self-support subsistence
독립세 independent tax
독립지명권 power in gross
독립채산 self-support accounting
독립채산제 business accountability; self-supporting accounting system
독립책임액비례주의 independent intermediary
독립투자 autonomous investment
독립판매조직 independent marketing organization
독립회계사 independent accountant
독립회계제 self-accounting system
독소조항방위 poison pill
독일 FAZ 지수 Frankfurter Allgemeine Zeitung Index
독일마르크 Deutch mark
독일무기명증서 German bearer certificate
독일연방은행 Bundesbank
독자평균 self-balancing
독점가격 monopoly price
독점권 exclusive privilege; exclusive right; monopoly; sole right
독점금지법 anti-monopoly law
독점대리점 exclusive agent
독점도 degree of monopoly
독점자본 monopoly capital
독점적인 경쟁 monopolistic competition
독점판매권 exclusive distributorship
독점판매대리점 exclusive selling agent
독점판매업자 exclusive distributor
독촉료 charge for call
독촉장 collection letter
돈의 융통이 막힘; 자금이 딸림 monetary stringency
동결계정 frozen account
동결시장 locked market
동결자산 frozen assets
동기 cause inducement
동기부여 motivation
동기조사 motivation research
동남아시아국가연합 Association of South-East Asian Nations
동료 peer
동류증권그룹 homogeneous security group
동맹 alliance
동맹; 연맹 Bund
동맹회사 allied company
동물보험 animal insurance
동물보험 livestock insurance
동비용곡선 equal cost curve
동산 chattel; movables; personal assets; personal estate
동산계약 personal contract
동산과 부동산 premises and equipment
동산대부 chattel loan
동산모기지 mortgage of goods
동산보험 property insurance
동산부동산계정 movable and immovable assets account
동산세 personal property tax
동산세 personal tax
동산신탁 movable property in trust
동산유증 bequest
동산저당 chattel mortgage
동산저당증권 chattel paper
동산종합보험 movables comprehensive insurance
동산질권자 pledgee
동산질권자의 유치권 pledgee's lien
동산차압 personal distress
동산회복소송 claim and delivery

동순위로 pari passu
동순위선취특권 concurrent liens
동시거래정지 circuit breaker
동시조사 simultaneous tax audit
동아시아보험회의 East Asian Insurance Congress
동아프리카공동체 East African Community
동업조합 craft union
동업조합 guild
동업타사 peer companies
동원 mobilization
동의 consent
동의하지 않음 disagreement
동일결제 same day settlement
동일성 identity
동일한 identical with
동일한 성장률 flat growth
동족관계회사 affiliated family corporations
동족조합 family partnership
동족주주의 동족회사 personal family corporation
동족회사 closed corporation; family company; personal holding company; private holding company
동종상품 like goods
동종의 in kind
동질성 homogeneity
동질시장 homogeneous market
동태분석 dynamic analysis
동태적인 위험 dynamic risks
동태통계 dynamic statistics
동학적인 산업연관분석 dynamic input-output analysis
동향 behavior
동화 assimilation
되사기 repurchase
되사다 buy back
되팔기 selling on rally; selling on temporary
되팔다 sell back
두뇌유출 brain drain
두자리수성장기조 double-digit recurring profit growth
둔조(鈍調)시장 heavy market
둔화 deceleration; slowdown
뒤떨어지다 lag
듀레이션가중이익 duration-weighted yield
듀레이션갭 duration gap
듀레이션매칭 duration-matching
듀레이션법 duration method
듀얼전환사채 dual convertible bonds
듀얼커런시채 dual currency bonds
듀얼클로즈드엔드형 펀드 dual closed-end fund
듀얼펀드 dual fund; dual-purpose bond
듀엣채 duet bond
드래곤채 dragon bond
드러난 본문 bare body
드롭록채 drop-lock bond
드롭아웃옵션 dropout option
등가 equivalence
등가계수 equivalent coefficient
등가교환 equivalent exchangee; exchange of equivalents
등가이율 equivalent yield
등각나선;로그스파이럴 logarithmic spiral
등귀 appreciation
등금액 포트폴리오 equal weighted portfolio
등급 degree
등급변경 rating change
등급별 원가계산 group cost system
등급예측 rating outlook
등급제도 rating system
등급주문 scale order
등급하락 rating downgrade
등기료 registration fee
등기미제 non-registered
등기번호 registered number
등기변경예고 caution
등기부 register
등기수속 registration formalities
등기우편 registered letters
등기필 registered

등락레이쇼 increase and decrease ratio; up-down ratio
등락선 advance-decline line
등락순위 biggest single day advances and declines
등록 enrollment
등록국채 registered government bonds
등록금융이관 registered financial institution
등록기관 registration agency
등록길트채 registered gilts
등록말소 cancellation of register
등록면제거래소 exempt stock exchange
등록면허세 registration and license tax
등록면허세법 Registration and License Tax Law
등록명 registered issues
등록명의인 registered owner
등록상표 registered trade-mark
등록세 registration tax
등록조합 registered society
등록주 registered share
등록주주 shareholders of record
등록트레이더 registered trader
등본 duplicate tenor; transcript
등분산 constant variance
디노미네이션 denomination reduction
디노미네이션관련주 denomination related stocks
디맨드풀인플레;초과수요인플레 demand pull inflation
디스인플레이션 disinflation
디퍼드스와프 deferred swap
디포지터리코러스폰던트; 예치환거래은행 depository correspondent
디폴트리스크가 없음 default free
디폴트손실 default loss
디폴트채권 default receivable
디프디스카운트채 deep discount bond
디프록주의 deep rock doctrine
디프인더머니 deep in the money
디플레갭 deflationary gap
디플레기간 deflationary period
디플레기대 deflation expectation
디플레압력 deflationary pressure
디플레이션 deflation
디플레이션갭 deflation gap
디플레이터 **GDP** deflator GDP
디플레이터 **GNP** deflator GNP
디플레이터;가격수정인자 deflator
디플레정책 deflation policy
디플레효과 deflationary effect
딜러 dealer
딜러론 dealer loan
딜러수수료 dealer's fee; dealer commission
딜러시장 dealer market
딜러어음 dealer paper
딜러옵션 dealer's option
딜러참가 dealer participation
딜러포지션 dealer's position
딜레마 dilemma
딜링거래시스템 computer assisted execution system
딜링리스크 dealing risk
뜻밖의; 행운의 windfall profit
뜻에 반하여 against the will

ㄹ

라스트리조트 last resort
라스파이레스방식 Laspeyres formula
라운딩리버설패턴 rounding reversal pattern
라이센스계약 license agreement
라이프사이클 life cycle
라이프컨설턴트 life consultant
라인부문 line department
래그분석 lag analysis
래그효과 lag effect
래칫효과 ratchet effect
래터곡선 Latter curve
랜덤워크이론 random walk theory
런던국제금융선물거래소 London International Financial Futures Exchange
런던금속거래소 London Metal Exchange
런던금시장 London gold market
런던리파이낸스 London refinance
런던보험업자협회 Institute of London Underwriters
런던어음교환소가맹은행 London clearing banks
런던예탁증서 London Depositary Receipts
런던은행간 거래금리;리보 Libor
런던은행간 수취금리 London interbank bid rate
런던은행수취금리 London Inter-Bank Offered Rate
런던인수 London acceptance
런던증권거래소시황정보시스템 Stock Exchange Automated Quotation
런던클럽 London Club
런던학파 London school
런던할인시장협회 London Discount Market Association
런어웨이갭 runaway gap
런치 launch
런치스프레드 launch spread
레드클로즈신용장;전대신용장 red clause credit
레드헤링계획서 red-herring prospectus
레버리지드리스 leveraged lease
레버리지드리캐피털리제이션 leveraged recapitalization
레버리지드바이아웃 leveraged buyout
레버리지드스톡 leveraged stock
레버리지드스트래티직액쿼지션 leveraged strategic acquisition
레버리지드옵션 leveraged option
레버리지드포지션 leveraged position
레버리지드홀딩 leveraged holding
레버리지비율 leverage factor ratio
레버리지지수 leverage factor
레버리지효과 leverage effect
레스큐채 rescue bond
레온체프의 역설 Leontief's paradox
레이쇼 book to bill ratio BB
레이쇼콜스프레드거래 ratio call spread transaction
레이오프 layoff
레이트 **BA** rate BA

레이트 **telegraphic transfer** rate TT
레인지포워드거래 range forward contract
레포시장 RP market
레포트 **10-K** report 10-K
렌지포워드거래 flexible forward contract
렌탈비용 rental expense
로렌츠곡선 Lorenz curve
로봇텔러 robot teller
로스리더 loss leader
로얄티 royalty
로이즈증권 Lloyd's policy
로자구상 Roosa plan
로자본드 Roosa bond
로자효과 Roosa effect
로컬즈 locals
로컬컨텐트 local content
로트채 lot bond
록박스 lockbox
록업 lock-up
록업기간 lock-up period
록업옵션 lock-up option
록인효과 lock-in effect
론갱신 balance renewal
론스와프 loan swap
론스프레드 loan spread
론조성 organization of loan
론채권 loan claims
론채권매매 loan sales
롤다운 roll down
롤러코스터스와프 roller coaster swap
롤리폴리 **CD** roly poly CD
롤링일드 rolling yield
롤백 rollback
롤오버론 rollover loan
롤포워드 roll forward
롬바르드가 Lombard Street
롬바르드대부 Lombard credit
롬바르드대출 Lombard lending
롬바르드레이트 Lombard rate
롬바르드차입 Lombard borrowing
롱버터플라이스프레드거래 long butterfly spread transaction
롱스트래들 long straddle
롱스트립 long strip
롱캘린더스프레드거래 long calendar spread transaction
롱콘더 long condor
롱콜 long call
롱쿠폰 long coupon
롱풋 long put
루브르합의 Louvre accord
루즈리프식 장부 loose leaf book
루티드오더 routed order
룩백옵션 look-back option
룩백옵션거래 look-back option transaction
룩셈부르크금융협회 Luxembourg Monetary Institute
리니어채 linear bond
리드타임 lead time
리로드 reload
리밸런싱전략 rebalancing strategies
리버스듀얼커런시채 reversal dual currency bond
리버스레포 reverse repo
리버스제로쿠폰스와프 reverse zero coupon swap
리베이트;환불 rebate
리볼빙론 revolving loan
리볼빙언더라이팅퍼실리티 revolving underwriting facility
리볼빙카드 revolving card
리셋채 reset bond
리스계약 leasing contract
리스금융 lease financing
리스기간 lease period
리스료 rent expense; rental revenue
리스물건 lease property
리스백 leaseback
리스설비자산채무 obligations under capital leases
리스수익 revenue from leases
리스업 lease-up

리스업무 leasing business
리스자산 leased asset
리스재원채 lease obligation bond
리스채권 lease receivable
리스채무 lease liability
리스케줄링;채무반제계획변경 rescheduling
리스크가 없는 거래 riskless transaction
리스크가 큰 risky
리스크감응도지표 risk sensitive index
리스크개시서 risk disclosure statement
리스크격차 risk differentials
리스크경감수단 risk reduction measure
리스크경감전략 risk reduction strategy
리스크관리 risk control
리스크구조 risk structure
리스크기반자본금 risk-based capital
리스크뉴트럴자세 risk neutral attitude
리스크를 수반한 재정거래 risk arbitrage
리스크매니지먼트 risk management
리스크베이스의 자기자본기준 risk based capital standards
리스크부담 exposure to risk; risk taking
리스크분산 diversification of risks
리스크분포 risk sharing
리스크선택 risk selection
리스크선호 risk appetite
리스크선호도 risk preference
리스크선호태도 risk seeking attitude
리스크섹터 risk sector
리스크수익그룹 risk-return group
리스크어태치 attachment of the risk
리스크와 수익의 관계 risk-return relationship
리스크와 수익의 트레이드오프 risk-return trade-off
리스크요인 risk parameter
리스크웨이트 risk weight
리스크의 시장가격 market price of risk
리스크정보 risk information
리스크제어 risk-controlled
리스크조정법 risk-adjusted approach
리스크조정분석 risk-adjusted analysis
리스크조정필 자본 risk-adjusted capital
리스크중립자 risk neutral
리스크증권 risky securities
리스크측정 measure of risk
리스크컨트리컨트롤 risk country control
리스크특성 risk characteristics; risk profile
리스크팩터 risk factor
리스크페널티 risk penalty
리스크평가 risk assessment; risk evaluation
리스크프로파일 exposure profile
리스크프리미엄 risk premium
리스크허용도 risk tolerance
리스크회피자 risk averter
리스크회피적인 태도 risk averse attitude
리스크회피형의 risk averse
리스트럭처링 관련주 restructuring related stock
리스회계 lease accounting
리스회사 leasing company
리얼타임 real time
리얼타임처리 real time processing
리엔방기 release of lien
리엔보유자 holder of lien
리저브트란시 reserve tranche
리즈앤드래그즈 leads and lags
리카도효과 Ricardo effect
리코스계약 recourse agreement
리코스론 recourse loan
리턴극대자 return maximizer
리턴라인 return line
리테일뱅킹 retail banking
리파이낸스방식 refinancing system
리패키지채 repackage bond
링 ring
링크채 linked bond

ㅁ

마감시산표 closing trial balance
마감일 cutoff date
마감장의 고가 higher quotation at the close
마감필 계정 closed account
마감후 계정 post close account
마감후 기입 post-closing entry
마구 팔기 bear the market
마더즈 Mothers
마더펀드 mother fund
마로니법 Maloney Act of 1938
마샬곡선 Marshall curve
마샬수요곡선 Marshallian demand curve
마샬의 **K** Marshallian K
마샬플랜 Marshall Plan
마스터계약 master agreement
마스터트러스트 master trust
마을 town
마이너스상각 negative amortization
마이너스성장 minus growth; negative growth; subzero growth
마이너스실링 minus-ceiling
마이너스요인 adverse element; minus factor; negative factor
마이너스틱 minus tick
마이크로경제 microeconomy; microeconomic
마이크로분석 microanalysis
마이크로헤지 micro hedge
마이크로회계 micro accounting
마인 mine
마중물효과;실마리효과 pump-priming effect
마찰로 인한 실업 frictional unemployment
마케팅기능 marketing function
마케팅믹스 marketing mix
마케팅비 marketing expense
마케팅예산 marketing budget
마케팅푸시 marketing push
마케팅풀 marketing pull
마켓메이커 market maker
마켓메이킹기능 market making function
마켓메이킹상황 market making condition
마켓바스켓방식 market basket contract
마켓바스켓지수 market basket index
마켓아웃조항 market out clause
마켓온클로즈오더 market-on-close order
마켓이프터치드오더 market-if-touched order
마켓타이머 market timer
마켓타이밍 market timing
마코위츠이론 Markowitz theory
마크업률 mark-up ratio
마크채 mark bond
마크투마켓 mark to market
막다른 길 pent road
막대그래프 bar chart
만기 final maturity; maturity
만기가 된 채무 maturing bonds; maturing liability
만기까지 보유함 hold-to-maturity
만기물 term call
만기바스켓 maturity basket
만기반려금 maturity repayment

만기보증 maturity guarantee
만기분산 staggering maturity
만기분포의 차이 maturity distribution range
만기상환 redemption at maturity
만기서환 roll over
만기어음 matured bill
만기에 가까운 near maturity
만기에 가까운 채권 seasoned bond
만기에 가까운 채무 near-term bond
만기이익 yield to maturity
만기일 date of maturity; due date; expiration date; maturity date
만기일괄상환 bullet maturity
만기일괄상환상품 bullet issue
만기일괄상환채 bullet bond
만기일괄지불 lump sum payment of dividends at maturity
만기일구성 maturity structure
만기일지정정기예금 maturity-designated time deposit
만기일표 maturity list
만기전 상환 prior redemption
만기전 인수 anticipated acceptance
만기전이서 before due endorsement
만기지불고 amount due
만기채권 matured bond
만기채무 matured liability
만기청구액 termination claim
만기후 이서 after maturity endorsement
만능대차대조표 all-purpose balance sheet
만리장성;큰 방해물 Chinese wall
만성적인 chronic
만성적인 디플레이션 chronic deflation
만성적인 인플레이션 deep-rooted inflation; chronic inflation
만성적인 태업 chronic absenteeism
만족기준 satisfying principle
만족할 만한 satisfactory
말소 obliteration
매가 labeled price
매가재고조사법 selling price inventory
매가환원법 retail method
매각가능증권 securities for sale
매각권 power of sale
매각손 loss on sale
매각연도 sales year
매각익 profit on sale
매각제한주식 letter stock
매개변수;파라미터 parameter
매니저의 기여도 manager's contribution
매니지드펀드계약 Managed Fund Contract
매니지먼트바이아웃 management buyout
매니지먼트사이언스 management science
매달 차트 monthly chart
매력주 glamor stock
매리 marry
매립지 reclaimed land
매매 bargain; buying and selling; purchases and sales
매매;흡수합병 absorption
매매감리 market supervision
매매계약 sales contract
매매계약선수금 advanced collection on sale contracts
매매계약양도 assignment of sales contract
매매계약을 하였으나 아직 결제하지 않은 주식이나 상품 long account; long positions
매매계약을 한 채 아직 결제하지 않은 상품을 이전함 transfer of positions
매매계약을 한 채 아직 결제하지 않은 상품이 이관됨 transferred positions
매매계약체결 contract formation
매매계정 trading account
매매구조 trading mechanism
매매단위 unit of trading
매매대금 trading value
매매를 위한 시설 facilities for buying and selling
매매보고서 bought and sold note
매매손익 trading income of loss
매매손익계정 trading profit and loss account
매매수요 floating supply

매매에 적합한 권리 marketable title
매매유지주문 supporting order
매매일임계정 discretionary account
매매일임계정거래 discretionary account transaction
매매일치 matched book
매매입회구분 division of trading sessions
매매입회를 통한 거래 ordinary trades trading
매매입회시 trading hours
매매입회일시보류 temporary holding of trading session
매매정지 suspended trading
매매조회 transaction collation
매매증거금 margin for transactions
매매차익금 down spread
매매채권 absorbed bond
매매확인서 contract slip
매매횟수 number of buying and selling
매번 반기마다 half-yearly
매부위탁입체금 advance on indent
매부정회원 selling regular member
매상 sales; selling on a rising scale
매상(비제조업) revenue
매상계산기준 basis for recording sales
매상계산서 account of sales
매상계정 sales account
매상고 amount of sales; proceeds of sale; top line
매상고를 인식함 recognition of sales
매상고영업이익률 operating profit on sales
매상고예산 sales volume budget
매상고예측 sales forecasting
매상고이익률 ratio of profit to net sales; return on sales
매상고최대화가설 revenue maximization hypothesis
매상고한계이익률 profit volume ratio
매상기준 sales basis
매상되돌림 sales returns
매상반려 rebate on sales
매상분개장 sales journal
매상분석 sales analysis
매상성장률 sales growth rate
매상세 sales tax
매상세금공제전 이익률 pretax income to sales
매상송장 sales invoice
매상수령 unit sales
매상수수료 selling commission
매상수익 sales revenues
매상순이익률 net income to sales; net profit margin; net profit to sales
매상순익 net profit on sales
매상액 sales proceeds
매상영업이익률 operating income on sales
매상원가 cost of goods sold; sales cost
매상원가율 ratio of cost of sales
매상원가율 sales cost ratio
매상원장 sales ledger
매상이익률 ratio of net profit on sales; sales profit ratio
매상장 sales book; selling rate
매상전표 sales slip
매상증가 gains in sales; increase of sales
매상증가율 turnover increase rate
매상채권 trade receivable
매상채권회수기간 average collection period
매상채권회전률 receivables turnover
매상채권회전일수 number of days' sales in receivables
매상채무비율 payables to sales ratio
매상총손실 gross loss on sales
매상총이익 gross margin; gross profit on sales
매상총이익률 gross profit margin; ratio of gross profit to net sales
매상할인 sales rebate
매수 buying over
매수계약서 purchase agreement
매수를 임의조사함 purchase investigation
매수법 purchase method
매수부담 buyer's risk

매수붐 takeover boom
매수시장 buyer's market
매수시황 bid quotation
매수액면금액 purchase face amount
매수율 bid rate
매수자금리 interest rate payable by buyer; interest rate receivable by seller
매수잔고 buying balance
매수전략 acquisition strategy
매수추천 buy recommendation
매수하다 buy out
매수회사 acquisition accounting
매스커뮤니케이션 mass communication
매신호 buy signal; sell signal
매압력 selling pressure
매월지불 monthly payment
매입 takeover
매입;처분매입 buying
매입가능신용장 negotiable L/C
매입계산서 purchase and sale statement
매입그룹 purchase group
매입대금채무 purchase-money obligation
매입대리인 purchase agent
매입대상채권 instruments for buying operation
매입률 buying rate
매입보유 long position
매입보유리스크 long position risk
매입부품 purchased parts
매입불능신용장 straight credit
매입상각 redemption by purchase; retirement by purchase
매입상환 redemption through secondary market purchase
매입수수료 buying commission; commission for purchase
매입외국환 foreign exchange bills bought
매입은행무지정신용장 general letter of credit
매입은행지정신용장 special L/C
매입을 촉진하여 급격한 시세 변동을 막음 holding the market
매입인수 bought deal; firm commitment underwriting
매입자금 funds for purchase; purchase fund
매입채무 payables
매입채무회전율 turnover of payables
매입청구이익 yield-to-put
매입초과;순구입고 net purchase
매입측의 거래잔고 open interest on buyer's side
매입헤지 long hedge
매입헤징 long hedging
매잔재고 unsalable stock
매장 chance to sell; selling opportunity
매절 outright purchase
매점 buying up; cornering
매주 purchaser
매주문 selling order
매주선택 seller's option
매주의 차트 weekly chart
매주지불보증대리인 del credere agent
매체광고 media advertising
매체믹스 media mix
매체수수료 media commission
매초수량 net long positions
매출 offering for sale; secondary offering
매출가격 issue price; offering price; sales price
매출견본 selling sample
매출발행 best efforts issue
매출사이드 selling side
매출어음 bill drawn for sale
매출에누리 sales allowance
매출오퍼레이션 open market selling operation
매출우세 bears over
매출인기 selling support
매출자 writer
매출장본인 leader of short side
매출주 publicly offered share
매출측의 거래잔고 open interest on seller's side

매출헤지 short hedge
매취은행무지정신용장 open L/C
매취은행지정신용장 restricted credit
매츄리티스와프 maturity swap
매츄리티스트리핑 maturity stripping
매칭거래 matching transaction
매크로경제모델 macroeconomic model
매크로경제분석 macroeconomic analysis
매크로경제요인 macroeconomic factor
매크로경제정책 macroeconomic policy
매크로모델 macro model
매크로헤지 macro hedge
매크로회계 macro accounting
매트릭스 matrix
매트릭스트레이딩 matrix trading
매호치 asked price; offered price
매환 exchange bought; exchange sold; telegraphic transfer bought
매환자산 property replaced by purchase
매환특례 special tax treatment for property replacement
맥패든법 MacFadden Act of 1927
맨데이트;명령 mandate
맨데이트레터 mandate letter
맨데이트입찰 mandate bid
머니게임 money game
머니마켓노트 money market note
머니마켓우선주 money market preferred stock
머니마켓유닛트러스트 money market unit trust
머니마켓이율 money market yield
머니서플라이관리 money supply control
머니서플라이분석 statistics on money supply
머니서플라이분석통계 statistics on money supply analysis
머니스프레드 money spread
머니포지션 money position
머니플로분석 money flow analysis
머니플로표 money flow table
머지않아 near future
머천트뱅크 merchant bank
먼로주의 Monroe Doctrine
먼스리리버설 monthly reversal
먼스오더 month order
멀티상법 multilevel marketing system
멀티커런시론 multi currency loan
멀티풀옵션펀딩퍼실리티 multiple option funding facilities
메뉴어프로치 menu approach
메이가즈(수정가속상각법) MACRS
메이저마켓지수 major market index
메이저무브 major move
메이저피크 major peak
메이플리프코인 mapleleaf coin
메인터넌스리스 maintenance lease
메일론 mail-order loan
메일컨퍼메이션 mail confirmation
메일크레디트 mail credit
메일크레디트퍼실리티 mail credit facility
메자닌브라켓 mezzanine bracket
메자닌채무 mezzanine debt
메자닌파이낸스 mezzanine finance
메저링갭 measuring gap
면세 duty exemption; exemption from taxation; tax exemption
면세기간 tax holiday
면세소득 tax free income
면세수입품 duty free imports
면세의 duty free; exempt from taxation
면세점 exemption point; tax exemption limit
면세증권 tax-exempt securities
면세채 tax exempt bond; tax-exempt paper
면세투자 tax free investment
면세특권 extraterritoriality on tax laws
면세품 free article; free goods; nontaxable goods
면소되다 acquit
면역화 immunization
면제 immunity
면제사회사(私會社) exempt private company
면직;각하 dismissal
면책 exoneration; indemnity

면책법 act of indemnity
면책약관 exemption agreement
면책위험 excepted perils
면책율조항 franchise clause
면책조항 escape clause; exemption clause; hedge clause; negligence clause
면책조항삭제 deletion of exclusion
면허료 fees and permits; license expense
면허세 by types of licenses; license tax
면허제 licensing system
면허종류 type of licenses
명도지체 delay of evacuation
명령일 rule day
명령하다 enjoin
명료성의 원리 principle of clarity
명목계정 nominal account
명목보호율 nominal rate of protection
명목부채 nominal liabilities
명목상거래 nominal transaction
명목상의 재산세 nominal wealth tax
명목상의 지대 peppercorn rent
명목상의 파트너 nominal partner
명목수익률 nominal rate of return
명목수입 nominal income
명목이율 money yield; nominal rate of interest; nominal yield
명목이익 nominal profit
명목임금 nominal wage
명목자산 nominal assets; nominal capital
명목주의 nominalism
명목할인율 nominal rate of discount
명목 **GNP** nominal GNP
명백성 certainty
명백한 위험 apparent danger
명백한 의미불명료 patent ambiguity
명백한 의미불명료 혹은 오류 patent ambiguities or defects
명백한 행위 overt act
명백한;공공연한 overt
명백한;외견의 apparent
명세서;시방서 specification
명시계약 express contract
명시담보 express warranty
명시모델 explicit model
명시신탁 express trust
명시적 비용 explicit cost
명시하지 않은 비용 implicit cost
명예가격 pressure on price
명예회장 chairman emeritus
명의 street name
명의대여 lending a street name
명의변경 name transfer
명의변경 transfer of name
명의변경대리인 transfer agent
명의변경비 stock name transfer expense
명의변경사무수탁자 transfer service delegatee
명의변경수수료 fees for stock name transfers
명의변경저지 shut for dividend
명의변경청구 demand for name registration
명의상의 소유 order and disposition
명의상의 소유자 reputed owner
명의상의 주주 owner of record
명의인 nominee
명의주 dummy stock
명의주배당 dividend on dummy stock
명의차용 name borrowing
모기지개방증서 satisfaction of mortgage
모기지권자 mortgage creditor
모기지담보채권 mortgage backed bond
모기지담보형 mortgage collateral type
모기지사채금리 mortgage bond coupon
모기지스트립증권 mortgage strips
모기지의 가격탄력성 mortgage elasticity
모기지재금융 mortgage refinancing
모기지증권 mortgage backed securities
모기지증권보험 mortgage guaranty insurance
모기지증권시장 mortgage market
모기지참여증권 mortgage participation certificates
모기지채무 mortgage indebtedness
모기지패스스루증권 mortgage pass-through securities; mortgage pass-through

certificate
모기지펀드 mortgage fund
모기지포트폴리오 mortgage portfolio
모기지풀 mortgage pool
모네터리타겟 monetary target
모네터리트랜스퍼 monetary transfer
모니터리서베이 monetary survey
모델 model
모델가격 model price
모델분석 model analysis
모든 소비자 all buyers
모든 종류를 포함하는;일괄의 across the board
모디파이드듀레이션 modified duration
모디파이드패스스루 modified pass-through
모랄리스크 moral risks
모멘텀오실레이터 momentum oscillator
모멘트 moment
모방하다 emulate
모범기업 exemplar company
모집 offering; soliciting
모집계약 subscription agreement
모집기관 soliciting agent
모집단 population
모집대리인 subscription agent
모집방법 way for subscription
모집비 recruiting expense
모집안내서 offering circular
모집요강 memorandum for offering
모채 public bonds
모평균 population mean
모험 adventure
모호;불명료함 ambiguity
목재거래세 timber delivery tax
목적세 earmarked tax; object tax; special purpose tax
목적융자 purpose loan
목적적립금 reserve for specific purpose
목적함수 objective function
목전 in the near term
목표가격 target price
목표배당성향 target payout ratio
목표변동폭 target range
목표원가 target cost
목표이율 target yield
목표이익 desired profit; profit goal; target income; target profit
목표포트폴리오 target portfolio
목표환상장 target zone of exchage rate
몬테카를로시뮬레이션 Monte Carlo simulation
몰수 confiscation; forfeiture
몰수보존 preservation
몹시 차가와지다 at low ebb
묘미가 있는 attractive
묘석광고 tombstone ad
무간섭주의 laissez-faire
무관계한 impertinent
무구분식 single step
무권대리 nominal proxy
무권카드 unauthorized card
무기명사채 bearer debenture
무기명식수표 bearer check
무기명예탁증권 Bearer Depositary Receipts
무기명주 bearer stock
무기명주권 stock certificate to bearer
무기명주식 uninscribed stock; bearer share
무기명증권 bearer securities
무기명채권 bearer bond
무기명투표 unsigned vote
무기한보증 continuing guaranty
무기한차압 distress infinite
무단계식 single step form
무담보 freedom from encumbrance
무담보거래 unsecured trading
무담보계정 unsecured account
무담보부채 unsecured liability; unsecured bond
무담보상위채무 senior unsecured debt
무담보신용 unsecured credit
무담보신용장 documentary clean credit
무담보융자 unsecured loan

무담보의 unsecured
무담보채 unsecured debt
무담보채무 unsecured obligations
무담보콜 uncollateralized call; unsecured call loan
무등급법인 unrated entity
무등록주 unregistered stock
무디즈 Moody's
무리스크금리 risk-free interest rate
무리스크뉴트럴 risk-neutral valuation
무리스크자산 risk-free assets
무리스크재정 riskless arbitrage
무리스크증권 risk-free securities
무모한 투기꾼 plunger
무방비의 undefended
무배당 no dividend; non-dividend; omitted dividend; passed dividend
무배당보험 nonparticipating insurance
무배당으로 하다 pass dividend
무배당지속 continued no dividend
무배전락기업 companies previously paying dividend
무버블밴드 movable band
무보증잔존자격 unguaranteed residual value
무상 gratis
무상감자 reduction of capital without compensation
무상계약 gratuitous contract; naked contract
무상관수익률 uncorrelated return
무상기탁 gratuitous bailment
무상론 grant loan
무상승계적인 부동산처분 voluntary settlement
무상양도 voluntary conveyance
무상주 free share
무상주식 bonus issues
무상취득자 volunteer
무상환사채 debenture stock
무세 free of taxation
무세품표 free list
무시할 수 있는 가격 negligible in amount
무신고 failure to file a return
무신고가산세 additional tax due to failure to file a return
무액면주 non-par stock
무액면주식 no-par-value stock; non-par-value stock; share of no par value; stock without par value
무약인항변 no consideration
무역관련투자조치 trade-related investment measures
무역교섭위원회 Trade Negotiations Committee
무역금융 foreign trade finance
무역금융 trade credit
무역마찰 trade friction
무역부 Ministry of International trade and Industry
무역산업부 Department of Trade and Industry
무역상대국 trading partner
무역수지 balance of trade; trade balance; trade position
무역수지실적 trade figure
무역수지흑자 favorable balance of trade
무역수지흑자폭 trade surplus amount
무역신용 foreign trade credit
무역연관분석 trade matrix analysis
무역외 invisible trade
무역외수지 service account; service balance; balance of invisible trade; invisible account; invisible trade balance
무역자유화 liberalization of trade
무역적자 foreign trade deficit; trade deficit
무역정책 foreign trade policy
무역지수 index of trade
무역창출효과 trade creation effect
무역클레임 trade claim
무역통계 foreign trade statistics; trade statistics
무역통제 trade control
무역협정 trade agreement
무의뢰평가 unsolicited rating
무이식채무 passive debt

무이자대부 loan without interest
무이자사채 passive bond
무인수방식 uncommitted facilities
무일부어음 undated bill
무작위추출법 random sample
무제한법화 unlimited legal tender
무제한적정의견 unqualified report
무제한퍼실리티 unlimited facility
무조건감사보고서 unqualified opinion report
무조건매매 absolute sales
무조건보조금 unconditional grant
무조건오퍼 outright base
무조건오퍼레이션 unconditional operation
무조건유동성 unconditional liquidity
무조건의 unconditional
무조건인도 absolute delivery
무조건인출권 unconditional drawing right
무조건주문 open order
무조건채무 unconditional debt
무조건추정 unconditional estimate
무차별곡선 indifference curve
무채발행 free issue
무체권 intangible right
무체동산 chose in action; thing in action
무체재산 incorporeal property
무투표당선 return without voting
무한정감사보고서 non-opinion report
무한정의견 unqualified opinion
무한책임 unlimited liability
무한책임사원 general partner
무한책임파트너십 general partnership
무한책임회사 unlimited liability company; unlimited company
무해한 오진 harmless error
무형감가상각자산 intangible depreciable assets
무형고정자산 intangible fixed assets; intangibles
무형상각자산 intangible depreciable property
무형자본 immaterial capital; intangible capital
무형자산 intangible assets; invisible assets
무형자산감가상각 amortization of intangibles
무형재산 immaterial property; intangible property
무형효과 intangible effects
무효 no effect; nullity
무효계약 void contract
무효라 할 수 없는 indefeasible
무효로 할 수 있는 defeasible
무효의 null and void; void
무효카드 invalid card
무효판결 decree of nullity
무효합의 void agreement
무효화 annulment
무효회원 unauthorized member
무휴동산 incorporeal chattel
묵계 tacit contract
묵시담보 implied warranty
묵시신탁 implied trust
묵시의 tacit
묵시허용 implied license
묵인 acquiescence; connivance
문서열람 inspection of documents
문서위조 forgery
문서의 본문 body of an instrument
문서제출요구서 notice to produce
문서통지 notification in writing
문서환 mail exchange bill
문제가 적은 제도 lesser evil
물가 commodity price
물가변동 price variation
물가수준 price level
물가안정정책 price stabilization policy
물가정화유출입기구 price-specie-flow mechanism
물가지수 price index
물건비 non-personnel expenses
물건이나 주식을 팔아서 큰 이득을 보고 물러남 unloading
물권 real right; right in rem
물납 payment in kind
물납세 levy in kind; tax in kind

물량이 적은 상장 sold-out market
물량이 적은 주 narrow market security
물러나다 withdraw
물류 physical distribution
물리내용연수 physical age
물리적인 감가 physical depreciation
물리적인 감모 physical wear and tear
물리적인 내용연수 physical life
물리적인 예비비 physical contingency
물물교환 barter
물상담보부사채 mortgage bond
물상보증 real guarantee
물색매매 selective buying
물세 impersonal tax
물세 tax on goods and possessions
물적계정 impersonal account
물적공제 impersonal deduction
물적과세제외 impersonal exclusion from taxation
물적담보 collateral on property; real security
물적동산 real chattels
물적자본이익률 return on physical capital
물적증거 physical evidence; real evidence
물적증권 securities on property
물품납부 delivery of articles
물품세 commodity excise; commodity tax; excise duty
물품세법 commodity tax law
물품화폐 commodity money
물품횡령 misappropriation of goods
뮤츄얼펀드 mutual fund
뮤츄얼펀드인수업자 mutual fund underwriters
미가동자본 unproductive capital
미감사재무제표 unqualified financial statements
미결계정 open account; suspense account
미결산 unbalanced open
미결산계정 unbalanced account
미결산보험금 insurance claims unsettled
미결산의 unbalanced
미결산장부 unbalanced book
미결의 pending
미결제거래;미결제약정 unsettled transactions
미결제거래를 조정함 arrangement of unsettled transaction; completion of unsettled transaction
미결제거래잔고 open interest
미결제거래정리 settlement of unsettled transactions
미결제계정 outstanding account; unsettled account
미결제약정인계 transfer of unsettled transactions
미결제원장 open ledger
미결제의 unsettled
미경과 unexpired
미경과보험료 prepaid insurance premiums; unearned premium; unexpired insurance premium
미경과비용 expenses paid in advance; unexpired expenses
미경과이자 unearned interest; unexpired interest
미경과할인료 unearned discount
미국경영자협회 American Management Association
미국공인증권분석가협회 Institute of Chartered Financial Analyst
미국공인회계사협회 American Institute of Certified Public Accountants
미국국무부 Department of State
미국내국세입법 Internal Revenue Code
미국내국세입청 Internal Revenue Service
미국내부감사인협회 Institute of Internal Auditors
미국달러채시장 Yankee bond market
미국대학교직원퇴직변액연금기금 College Retirement Equities Fund
미국방식 U. S. term
미국법률협회 American Law Institute
미국법조협회 American Bar Association

미국보험감독관협회 National Association of Insurance Commissioners
미국상무부 Department of Commerce
미국상품선물거래위원회 Commodity Futures Trading Commission
미국선물업자협회 Futures Industry Association
미국수출입은행 Export-Import Bank of USA
미국예탁주식 American depositary share
미국예탁증권 American Depositary Receipts
미국원가계산사협회 National Association of Cost Accountants
미국은행협회 American Bankers Association
미국인정생명보험사회 American . Society of C. L. U.
미국일반회계국 U S Government General Accounting Office
미국장학자금금고;샐리메이 Sallie Mae
미국재무부 장기채권 long treasury bond
미국저축채 U. S. savings bond
미국정부주택저당금고증권 GNMA debenture
미국증권거래소 American Stock Exchange
미국증권거래소결제기관 National Securities Clearing Corporation
미국증권거래위원회 Securities and Exchange Commission
미국증권업협회 National Association of Securities Dealers
미국형 American type
미국형 옵션 American option
미국회계사협회 American Institute of Accountants
미국회계인회계 National Association of Accountants
미국회계학회 American Accounting Association
미기입장부 blank book
미납 non-payments
미납세인수 nontaxable receiving
미니리펀딩 mini-refunding
미니맥스채 mini. max. bond
미니주식시장 mini stock
미니탭 mini tap
미니투자 mini investment
미달거래 dealing in transit
미달계정 account in transit; transit account
미달러지폐 greenback
미달상품 merchandise in transit
미달의 in transit
미달항목 item in transit
미달현금 cash in transit
미드웨스트증권거래소 Midwest Stock Exchange
미등기 unregistered
미등록사채 unregistered debenture
미디어전략 media strategy
미디엄텀노트 medium-term note
미래리스크 future risk
미래원가 future cost
미래원가계산 accounting for future cost
미루어 판단함 implication
미리 설정한 가격 predetermined price
미망인공제 allowance for widow
미망인연금 widow's pension
미미하게 늘어남 marginal rise
미발행자본 unissued capital stock
미발행주식 unissued stock
미분계수 differential coefficient
미분방정식 differential equation
미분배이익 undistributed earnings
미분배잉여적립금 unassigned surplus
미분할유산 undivided bequest
미분할유산의 상속세 inheritance tax on undivided bequest
미불 unpaid
미불계정 accrued account
미불공임 accrued wages
미불금 amount in arrears; debt service
미불급여 accrued payroll; employee compensation
미불기부금 accrued donation; unpaid

donation
미불반려금 unpaid returns
미불배당금 dividend payable; unpaid dividend
미불배당액 accrued dividend
미불법인세 income taxes payable
미불보험금 unpaid claims
미불부채 outstanding liabilities
미불비용 accrued charge; accrued expenses; accrued expenses payable
미불세금 tax payable; unpaid tax
미불세금계정 tax payable account
미불수수료 accrued commission
미불수수료 commission payable
미불연금비용 unfunded accrued pension cost
미불이자 interest payable
미불임금 unclaimed wages; wages payable
미불임차금 accrued rent
미불입액 capital stock unpaid
미불입자본 subscribed capital stock
미불입자본 unpaid capital
미불채무 accrued liability
미상각감모자산 undepreciated wasting property
미상각건설이자 unamortized interest during construction
미상각발행차금 unamortized discount
미상각사채할인 unamortized bond discount
미상각원가 unamortized cost
미상각잔고 unamortized balance; undepreciated balance
미상각채무 unamortized obligation
미상환채권 bond outstanding
미선언자 non-declarant
미성년자 minor
미성년자공제 minor tax credit; tax credit for minor
미성년자의 거래계좌 minor account
미소비원가 unexpired cost
미수 unearned
미수금 accounts due; uncollected balance
미수금경과기간 accounts-receivable aging
미수급료 accrued salaries
미수배당 dividend receivable
미수보관료 storage accounts receivable
미수보증금 claim for guarantee
미수보험금 insurance claim
미수보험료 deferred premium; due and deferred premiums; outstanding premiums; premium in arrears; uncollected premium
미수세 tax receivable
미수수수료 commission receivable; uncollected commission
미수수익 uncollected revenue; uncollected income
미수수취계정합계 total receivables
미수은행예금이자 interest receivable on bank deposits
미수이익 accrued income; accrued revenue
미수이익처분금지 restraint on anticipation
미수이자 uncollected interest
미수임대료 rent receivable
미수자금 uncollected funds
미수정잔고시산표 unadjusted trial balance
미수지계정 accruals
미수지대 uncollected rent
미스매치리스크 mismatch risk
미스매치변동이자부채 mismatched FRN
미스매칭 mismatching
미스프라이싱 mispricing
미승적격자산 admitted assets
미실행대출 undisbursed loans
미실현손 unrealised loss
미실현손실 loss not yet realized
미실현수익 unrealized profit; unrealized revenue
미실현이익 profit not yet realized; unrealized income; unrealized profits
미실현익 unrealised profit
미완료거래 incomplete transaction
미완성공사 uncompleted works
미이용지세 tax on unutilized land

미인식순손익 unrecognized net gain / loss
미주개발은행 Inter-American Development Bank
미주기구 Organization of American States
미착품 goods in transit
미착품판매 sale to arrive
미처리결손금 unappropriated deficit
미처분 undisposed
미처분결손 undisposed deficit
미처분이익 unappropriated income; undivided profit
미처분이익잉여금 unappropriated earned surplus
미처분잉여금 unappropriated retained earnings
미청구배당금 unclaimed dividends
미청구수표 unclaimed check
미평가보험 unvalued policy
미확인손실 loss not yet recognized
미확정의 계약 (미확정계약) executory contract
미활동계정 inactive account
미회수원가 unrecovered cost
믹스트러스트 mixed trust
민간거래 private transaction
민간금융기관대출 loans by private financial institutions
민간금융기업 private financial institution
민간기업 private business
민간모기지보험 private mortgage insurance
민간사업 civilian enterprise; private undertaking
민간사업비 private activity bond
민간소비 private consumption
민간수요 private demand
민간시장 private market
민간은행대출 commercial bank credit
민간자본 private capital
민간채 non-government bond; private bond
민간채무 private debt
민간투자가 private investor
민간트란시 commercial tranche
민간회사 private corporation
민감한 시장 sensitive market
민법 civil code; civil law
민사상의 구제조치 civil remedy
민사소송 civil suit; common law action
민사의 civil
민사의 (민사소송) civil action
민사집행 civil execution
민수 civilian demand
민영사업 private enterprise
민영화 privatization
민영화계획 privatisation scheme
민주화 democratization
민중소송 popular action
밀러의 명제 - 모딜리아니 Modigliani-Miller theory
밀수 smuggling

ㅂ

바꾸어 쓰다 reword
바닐라스와프 vanilla swaps
바닥 bottom
바닥값 bottom price
바닥시세 floor price
바람직한 자금흐름을 만들어내는 능력 ability to generate favorable cash flows
바람직한 현금의 흐름 favorable cash flows
바르샤바조약기구 Warsaw Treaty Organization
바벨전략 barbell strategy
바스켓 basket
바스켓거래 basket trading; basket transaction
바스켓대당거래 basket cost trading
바스켓방식 basket system
바스켓워런트 basket warrant
바이사이드 buy side
바이앤드라이트전략 buy and write strategy
바이어스 bias
바이어즈크레디트 buyer's credit
바젤위원회 Basel Committee
바젤합의 Basel agreement
바코드 bar code
바터무역 barter trade
바트(타이의 화폐단위) baht
박스권의 움직임 range-bound market
박스스프레드 box spread
박스젠킨스모형 Box-Jenkins method
반기(半期)보고서 semi-annual report
반기보고서 half-yearly report
반기지불 semi-installment
반년마다 복리로 계산함 semi-annual compounding calculation
반년불쿠폰 semi-annual coupon
반대거래 mirrored trade
반대계정 opposite accounts
반대기입 reversing entry
반대매매 closing transaction; reverse takeover; reverse trade
반대분개 reversal entry
반대소송 cross action
반대스와프 mirror swap
반대오퍼 counteroffer
반대의견 dissenting opinion; contrary opinion
반대주문 offsetting order
반대증서 counterdeed
반대청구 cross-demand
반대하다 dissent
반등 false rally; rebound; sharp rally
반락 reactionary fall
반려금 refundment
반복감사 repeating audit
반복계산 repeated calculation
반복에 따른 환급 refund by carrying a loss back to a prior year
반사회세력 anti-social power
반소(反訴) demand in reconvention
반순환적인 contra-cyclical; countercyclical
반순환정책 countercyclical policy
반응곡선 reaction curve

반응을 기다림 wait for reaction
반전 turn around
반전일 reversal day
반전패턴 reversal pattern
반제기간 payment periods
반제기일 repayment date
반제수출 collateral export
반제원자 pledged revenue
반제율 repayment rate
반제의지 willingness to pay
반제이자 paid interest
반제품 half-finished goods; partially finished goods; partition finished product; semi-finished goods
반제품원장 partially finished goods ledger
반제횟수 number of scheduled payments
반증 rebutting evidence
반품 goods returned to vendor; return inward; return outward; returned goods unsold
반품률 rate of returned goods unsold
반품조정준비금 reserve for loss on goods unsold
반품차손비 loss on sale returns
반하는 in violation of
반항하다 rebut
반향원리 echo principle
반향효과 echo effect
반환권부 매매 sale or return
반환운임 return freight
반환청구권 rights to claim the refund
반환청구하다 claim the refund
발견위험의 원칙 doctrine of discovered peril
발권은행 bank of issue
발권제도 system of note issue
발기인 incorporator; originator; promoter
발기인주 promoter's share
발기인회 meeting of promoters
발매가격 exit price
발매가액 exit value
발생 accrual
발생기간 accrual period
발생시레이트 historical rate
발생주의 accrual basis; accrual method
발생주의회계 accrual accounting; accrual basis accounting
발생채무부담 obligations incurred
발생확정시키다 vested in interest
발송비 delivery expenses; shipping expense
발송송금환 bill sent
발송운임 freight and cartage outward
발송은행 remitting bank
발송지 destination
발송지지입인도(관세입) delivered duty paid
발송지지입인도(관세제외) delivered duty unpaid
발송통지서 advice note
발주자면책조항 disclaimer clause
발췌계산서 abstract of accounts
발행 drawing
발행가격 issue value
발행개시일 launch date
발행고 amount issued
발행권 drawing right
발행규모 volume of issuance
발행근거법 legal status of issuance
발행등록 shelf registration
발행등록추보서류 Supplementary Documents to the Shelf Registration Statement
발행등록취소신고서 statement of withdrawal of shelf registration
발행목적 issuance purpose
발행상사 issuing house
발행세 issue tax
발행수수료 opening commission
발행시장 issue market
발행시할인 original issue discount
발행신고서 shelf registration statement
발행액 issuance volume
발행어음 drawn bill
발행예정채권 bond in a pipeline
발행은행 drawing bank; issuing bank
발행이율 issuing yields

발행인 drawer
발행일 issue date
발행일거래 when-issued transaction
발행일거래취소 cancellation of when-issued transaction
발행일기준 when-issued basis
발행자비용 issuer's cost
발행잔고 **CD** outstanding CD
발행잔고 outstanding balance of issue amount
발행전 유통시장 gray market
발행조건 conditions of issuance; issue terms
발행지 place of issue
발행채채권불이행 issuer defaults
발행필 워런트 outstanding warrants; warrant outstanding
발행필 자본 outstanding capital
발행필 자본금 capital stock issued
발행필 주식 issued share; issued shares; issued stocks; outstanding shares; outstanding stock; shares outstanding
발행필 주식수 number of stocks issued
발행필 주식자본금 issued capital stock
발행필 증권 securities outstanding
발행필 채권 bond issued
발행필 채권 outstanding bond
발행필 총주식수 all issued stocks
발행하다 draw
발행회사 issuer; issuing corporation
발회 first session of a month
발효일 effective date
방계혈족 collateral consanguinity
방관자 bystander
방기 abandonment
방기가치 abandonment value
방문판매업자 call-sales merchant
방법론 methodology
방위매입 defensive purchase
방위비 defense expenditure
방위주 defensive stock
방위증권 defensive securities
방위채 defense bond
방위청 Defense Agency
방위투자 defensive investment
방출;면책 discharge
방해클레임 disruption claims
방향성 directional movement
방향성지수 directional index
방화벽 fire wall
방화어음 bill in domestic currency
배가 뒤집힌;전복된 capsized
배경 backdrop
배경사항 background information
배급제도 rationing
배달증명우편 delivery-certified mail
배당 dividend
배당 dividend distribution
배당가능이익 profit available for dividend; surplus available for dividend
배당가능잉여금 divisible surplus
배당결정 determination of dividend
배당경과 reduced tax rate on dividend paid
배당계정 dividend account
배당공제 credit for dividend; deduction for dividends; dividend credit; dividend exclusion; tax credit for dividend
배당금을 지불할 법인 agent handling payment of the dividends
배당금이동회사 companies changing the amount of dividend
배당금재투자 dividend reinvestment plan
배당금지불 delivery of dividends
배당금총액 amount of dividends paid
배당능력 ability to pay dividend
배당락 dividend off; ex-dividend
배당락일 ex-dividend date
배당률 dividend growth rate; dividend rate
배당부 cum dividend; dividend on
배당부 종신보험 participating whole life insurance
배당분리과세 separated taxation on dividend income
배당사채 income bond

배당성향 dividend payout ratio; payout ratio
배당소득 dividend income
배당소득손실 loss from dividend income
배당소득으로 귀속됨 real obtainer of dividend income
배당손금법 dividend-paid deduction method
배당수입 receipts of dividends
배당액으로 간주하는 금액 amount regarded as dividend
배당에 대한 과세 taxation on dividend
배당에 배려가 결핍됨 failure to consider dividend policy
배당예정 dividend schedule
배당우선주식 dividend preferred stock
배당원천선택과세 alternative withholding tax on dividends
배당이 없는 기업 no dividend company
배당이율 price dividend ratio
배당이익 dividend yield
배당이익이 없는데도 배당함 bogus dividend
배당적립금 dividend reserve
배당제한 limitation on dividend
배당주 dividend stock
배당지불 dividend payment; payout
배당지불은행 dividend payment bank
배당평균적립금 dividend equalization reserve
배당평균준비금 dividend equalization fund; reserve for equalization of dividend
배당포함 cum-dividend
배당포함주가지수 dividend-included stock price indices
배당플로 dividend flow
배당할인 dividend discount
배당할인율 dividend discount rate
배당환원가액 capitalized value of stock
배당환원모델 dividend discount model
배당환원방식 dividend discount method
배당환원주식평가 stock valuation based on dividend
배당회사 dividend paying company
배부계정 absorption account
배부기준 apportionment base
배부를 마친 제조간접비 absorbed burden
배부부족 under absorbed
배부세 apportioned tax; distribution tax
배부율 absorption rate
배부초과원가 over-absorbed cost
배분 admeasurement; allocation
배분모델 allocation model
배분비율 allocation ratio
배분지관리인 allotment warden
배분판결 decree of distribution
배상금 claims; reparations
배상책임한도액 limit of liability
배액감채약관 option to double
배액정율법 double declining balance method
배우자공제 deduction for spouse; exemption for spouse; spouse tax credit
배우자특별공제 special exemption for spouse
배율평가 valuation by multiplier
배임 misappropriation
배제가능리스크 avoidable risk
배치거래시스템 batch trading system
백마 탄 왕자;매수위기의 기업을 구하기 위해 개입하는 제 3의 기업 white knight
백분율대차대조표 common-size balance sheet; percentage balance sheet
백분율법 percentage method
백분율손익계산서 common-size income statements; one hundred percent income statement
백분율재무제표 common-size financial statements; percentage statements
백분율표 percentage table
백색신고 white return
백업라인 back-up line
백업퍼실리티 back-up facility
백오피스;배후부문;비영업부문 back office
백지로 in blank
백지식이서 endorsement in blank; indorsement in blank
백지양도 assignment in blank

백지어음 blank bill
백지위임 carte blanche
백지이서 blank endorsement
백지인수 blank acceptance
백지주식 blank stock
백투백거래 back to back transaction
백투백론 back to back loan
백화점매상고 department store sales
밴드앤드크롤 band and crawl
밴드왜건효과 band wagon effect
밴콜 ban call
밸런스시트어프로치 balance sheet approach
밸런스펀드 balanced fund
밸런스펀드포트폴리오 balanced fund portfolio
밸런스형 매니저 balanced manager
밸류다이어그램 value diagram
밸류라인랭킹 value line ranking
밸류라인옵션 value line option
밸류라인인덱스 value line index
밸류라인종합지수 value line composite index
밸류라인주가지수 Value Line Stock Index
밸류라인평가 value line average
밸류앳리스크 value at-risk
밸류어프로치 value approach
뱅크라인 bank line
뱅크럽시리모트 bankruptcy remote
뱅크베이시스 bank basis
뱅크와이어 bankwire
뱅크유전스 bank usance
버블경제 bubble economy
버터플라이스프레드 butterfly spread
버터플라이스프레드거래 butterfly spread trading
버텀리버설데이 bottom reversal day
버텀업형 bottom-up process
버텀업형 예측 bottom-up forecasting
버티컬스프레드 vertical spread
버티컬스프레드거래 vertical spread transaction
번호 **PIN** number PIN
번호계좌 numbered accounts
벌금 amercement
벌금을 부과하다 amerce
벌룬모기지 ballon mortgage
벌룬상환 ballon maturity
벌칙 penal provision
벌칙금리 penalty rate
벌크카고 bulk cargo
범용카드 all purpose card; general purpose card
범죄 offense
법규재량 controlled discretion
법령 prescript
법령에 의한 statutory
법례 legend
법률 law
법률격언 maxims
법률고문 counselor; legal adviser
법률고문실**(SEC)** Office of General Counsel (SEC)
법률과 사실이 혼재된 문제 mixed question of law and fact
법률관계 legal relations
법률대리인 legal representation
법률변경 law change
법률사무소 law office
법률상 de jure
법률상담 legal aid services; legal counsel
법률상담료 fee for legal advice
법률상의 의무 legal duty
법률상의 점유 legal possession
법률상의 증거 legal evidence
법률상의 직원 officer de jure
법률상의 추정 legal presumption
법률서류 legal document
법률시행국**(SEC)** Division of Enforcement (SEC)
법률에 저촉됨 conflict of laws
법률에서 요구하는 형식 form required by law
법률위반 breach of law

법률위임 authorization by law
법률이 아닌 기준 non-legal standards
법률적인 소멸에 따른 대손 bad debt caused by the legal effect
법률적인 추정 artificial presumptions
법률착오 mistake of law
법률학 jurisprudence
법률행위 judicial act; juristic act
법리론 legal theory
법무부 legal department; legal section; Ministry of Justice
법무처리 management of juristic act
법외이익 exorbitant profit
법원 forum
법의 작용 operation of law
법의 재량 discretion of law
법의 지배 rule of law
법의 행위 act of law
법의학 medical jurisprudence
법인 artificial person; corporation; Juridical person; legal person
법인격 juridical personality
법인격이 없는 단체 non-juridical organization
법인격이 없는 회사 unincorporated company
법인고객 corporate customer
법인권 corporate right
법인기업 corporate business
법인단체 corporate body
법인등록부 corporate registration
법인매입 institution buying
법인사업세 enterprise tax on corporation
법인사업세과세표준 tax base of enterprise tax on corporation
법인설립 establishment of corporation; incorporation of enterprise
법인세 corporate income tax; corporate tax; corporation tax
법인세공제 corporation tax credit; credit against corporation tax
법인세공제전 순이익 net profit before corporation tax
법인세법 corporation tax law
법인세부담 tax charge
법인세액손금불산입 exclusion from expenses of corporation tax
법인세액특별공제 special credit of corporation tax
법인세율 corporation tax rate
법인세준비금 reserve for corporation tax
법인세할과세 taxation on corporation tax basis
법인세할주민세 corporation levy
법인세확정신고서제출 filing of final return on corporation tax
법인소득 corporate income
법인소득세비용 corporate income taxes expenses
법인소득세율 corporate income tax rate
법인신탁 corporate trust
법인실재설 real entity theory of corporation
법인예금 corporate deposit
법인의 대표자 representative of corporation
법인이득세 corporation profit tax
법인이론 entity theory
법인이익금 gross income of corporation
법인인감 corporate seal
법인저축 corporate savings
법인주민세 corporate inhabitant tax
법인주주 corporate shareholder; institutional stockholder
법인카드 corporate card
법인투자가 corporate investor
법인특별세 special corporation surtax
법인해산 dissolution of corporation
법인화 incorporation
법인회원 corporation member
법적규제 mandatory control
법적대항권 legal resistance
법적리스크 legal risk
법적리엔 legal lien
법적상환 legal defeasance
법적수단 legal proceedings

법적실체 legal entity
법적정리 legal liquidation; legal liquidation
법적조치 legislative action
법적책임 legal responsibility
법적청구권 legal claim
법적효력 legal effect
법정감모상각법 statutory depletion method
법정감사 statutory audit
법정과실 legal fruits
법정금리 legal rate of interest
법정급부 legal benefit
법정기한 legal term
법정납기한 statutory due date of tax payment
법정내용연수 legal durable years; statutory useful life
법정대리인 legal representative
법정대위 legal subrogation
법정대출한도액 legal lending limit
법정대출한도화 legal lending limit
법정발행한도액 statutory debt limit
법정복리비 legal welfare expense
법정상각 statutory depreciation
법정상각방법 statutory depreciation method
법정상속동산 heir-looms
법정상속분 legal portion of legacy
법정상속분과세 taxation according to legal portion of legacy
법정상속인 heir apparent
법정세율 statutory tariff
법정수 quorum
법정신고기한 statutory due date of tax return
법정신용한도 mandatory line of credit
법정신탁 trust by act of law; constructive trust
법정외 보통세 general tax not stipulated in Local Tax Law
법정유가증권평가준비금 mandatory securities valuation reserve
법정이율 legal rate; statutory rate of interest
법정이익준비금 legal earned surplus reserve
법정이자 legal interest
법정자본 legal capital
법정재고평가법 legal valuation method of inventory
법정점유 possession in law
법정준비 required reserve
법정준비금 legal reserve; statutory reserve
법정준비율 required reserve ratio
법정책임 legal liability
법정책임;법적채무 legal liability
법정추정상속인 presumptive heir
법정통화 legal tender
법정평가 judicial valuation; legal valuation; mint par of exchange
법정평가방법 statutory valuation method
법정회계원칙 statutory accounting principle
법정후견인 legal guardian
법조계 legal community
법체제 legal framework
베가 vega
베가뉴트럴 vega-neutral
베어본드 bear bond
베어불본드 bear bull bond
베어스프레드거래 bear spread trading
베어인덱스채 bear index bond
베어콜스프레드 bear call spread
베어허그(강한 포옹) bear hug
베이비펀드 baby fund
베이스머니 base money
베이시스갭 basis gap
베이시스거래 basis trading; basis transaction
베이시스리스크 basis risk
베이시스마켓 basis market
베이시스스와프 basis swap
베이시스포인트 basis point; bp
베타 beta
베타계수 beta coefficient
베타서비스 beta service
베타수치 beta value
베타수치가 낮은 포트폴리오 low beta portfolio
베타수치에 기반을 둔 정보원 information

sources on beta value
베타예측방정식 beta value prediction equation
베터표준오차 standard error of beta
벤처비즈니스 venture business
벤처캐피탈 venture capital
벤치마크포트폴리오 benchmark portfolio
벨로우더라인 below the line
벨로우마켓 below market
변경;변조 alteration
변경등기 registration of alteration
변경요청 alteration demand
변경일 change date
변경클레임 change claims
변경할 수 있는 ambulatory
변동가격권 variable zone
변동계수 coefficient of variation
변동관리비 variable overhead
변동금리 floating rate; variable-rate interest
변동금리 CD floating rate certificate of deposit
변동금리대출 floating rate lending
변동금리론 variable-rate loan
변동금리모기지 adjustable mortgage; adjustable rate mortgage
변동금리지불인 floating-rate payer
변동금리지표 floating rate index
변동금리채무 variable-rate debt
변동금리형 부동산론 variable rate mortgage loan
변동분석 fluctuation analysis
변동분석회계 variable accounting
변동비 variable cost and expenses; variable charge; variable expenses
변동비율 rate of variable expenses
변동상장 floating system
변동상한금리부 계정 floating interest rate account with ceiling
변동소득 fluctuating income; transitory income
변동소득 및 임시소득 fluctuating and extraordinary income
변동소득계산 variable costing
변동소득평균과세 averaging taxation on fluctuating income
변동시장 volatile market
변동예산 variable budget
변동원가율 variable cost ratio
변동율 volatility ratio
변동율표준오차 standard deviation of volatility
변동이율 floating interest rate; variable interest rate
변동이율우선주 adjustable rate preferred stock
변동이익 variable profit
변동이자부 모기지 floating rate mortgage
변동이자부 채권 floating rate note; floater; floating rate bond
변동이자부 채권시장 floating rate market
변동조항 fluctuation clause
변동증거금 variation margin
변동증거금지불 variance margin call
변동지수 variability factor
변동폭 band; range
변동폭이 있는 고정제 wider band
변동하다 fluctuate
변동환율 floating exchange rate
변동환율제 flexible exchange rate; floating exchange rate system
변명;면책사유 excuse
변상 indemnification; reimbursement
변수 variable
변수샘플링 variables sampling
변액보험 interest sensitive policy
변액보험 variable insurance
변액연금 variable annuity
변액유니버설보험 flexible-premium variable life insurance; variable universal life insurance
변익분석 benefit analysis
변익비용분석 benefit cost analysis

변제기한 settlement period
변제연기 respite
변조카드 forged cards
변존임차권 concurrent lease
변칙결산회사 companies having changed their fiscal terms
변호사 advocate; attorney; lawyer
변호사고문료 retaining fee
변호사료 lawyer's fee
변호사리엔 attorney's lien; retaining lien
변호사배상책임보험 lawyer's liability insurance
변호사보수 legal fee
변호사의 도움을 받을 권리 right to counsel
변호사의 의견서 legal opinion
변호사책임 lawyer's liability
변화 change
변화율 rate of change
변환계수 conversion factor
별거수당 separate maintenance
별계정 separate bill
별단계정 separate and restricted account
별단예금 special deposits
별도계정 separate account
별도의 규정이 없는 한 not otherwise provided
별도적립금 other reserve; unconditional reserve
별도지출 special outlay
별로 마음이 내키지 않음 dull
별명 alias
별봉(別封)으로 under separate cover
병위채 exchange bill payable
병존원인 concurrent cause
병합 annexation
병행시장 parallel money market
보강증거 corroborating evidence
보강하다 corroborate
보건 health service
보건급부 health benefit
보고사항 matters to be reported
보고서 account record
보고식 schedule form; narrative form; report form; statement form
보고식 대차대조표 report form balance sheet
보고의무 reporting requirement
보고제도 report system
보고통화 reporting currency
보관 custody; safe keeping
보관계정 custodial account
보관계좌 custody account
보관대체기관명의주식 shares registered in the name of depository
보관대체제도 central custody and book-entry transfer services
보관료 charge for custody; custody fee; warehouse expenses; warehouse rent
보관비 inventory carrying cost; storage charges
보관비 warehousing and carrying charge
보관상자 box
보관수수료 fees for custody
보관유가증권 securities received as collaterals; customers' securities; securities deposited from others
보관은행 custodian bank
보관품 article in custody
보급률 diffusion rate
보드거래 board trading
보드브로커 board broker
보류논점 points reserved
보복관세 retaliatory duties
보복신청 statement of disagreement
보상계약 contract of indemnity
보상금 indemnity allowance
보상액;보험금 claim paid or payable
보상예금 compensatory deposit
보상융자 compensatory financing facility
보상의 약속을 하다 indemnify
보상의무 obligations to compensate
보상지불수권서 reimbursement authorization
보상채무 reimbursement obligation
보상판매상품을 과대평가함 overestimation

of goods traded in
보상하다 carry out compensation
보상한도액 liability limits
보석계약서 bail-piece
보석금상실 forfeiture of bail
보석보증인 safe-pledge
보세 in bond
보세운송 transportation in bond
보세지역 bonded area
보수 compensation; remuneration; reward
보수과 maintenance department
보수적인 견해 conservative view
보수적인 회계 conservative accounting
보수주의 conservatism
보수주의의 원칙 principle of conservatism
보스턴증권거래소 Boston Stock Exchange
보완론 complementary loan
보완보험 supplemental policies
보완재 complementary goods
보완적인 자기자본 secondary capital
보완펀드 completeness fund
보유계약 total amount of insurance in force
보유기간상대가치 holding period value-relative
보유기간수익률 holding period return
보유손익 holding gain or loss
보유손해액 underlying retention
보유자재 material on hand
보유재산 tenement
보유주식 portfolio stocks
보유주식수 number of stocks held
보유주포함 latent equity holdings
보유증권 securities holdings
보유채권 bond held; portfolio bonds
보유품 goods carried over
보유형태 type of holding
보이지 않는 비용 hidden cost
보이지 않는 손 invisible hand
보일러룸 boiler room
보전담보 preservative security
보전차압 preservative seizure
보정여잉 compensatory surplus
보정예산 additional budget; supplementary budget
보정예산정책 compensatory budget policy
보정재정정책 compensatory fiscal policy
보정항목 compensatory item
보정효과 compensatory effect
보조 accessory
보조공채 aid bond
보조규제 auxiliary rules
보조금 subsidy
보조금교부 delivery of subsidies
보조금반제 settlement of subsidy
보조금반환면제 exemption from return of subsidy
보조금으로 얻은 자산 property acquired by subsidy
보조금으로 취득함 acquisition by subsides
보조금을 받는 수출 subsidized export
보조금전망채 grant anticipation note
보조기입장 subsidiary journal
보조보험 supplementary insurance
보조부 auxiliary book
보조부문 service department; service division; subsidiary department
보조부문비 service departmental charge
보조원장 auxiliary ledger; subordinate ledger; subsidiary ledger
보조원장계정 subsidiary accounts
보조의 ancillary
보조장부 auxiliary journal; subsidiary book
보조재료비 subsidiary material cost
보조화폐 subsidiary coin; subsidiary money
보증 guarantee; suretyship; warranty
보증계약 contract of guarantee
보증계약을 혼동하여 소멸함 merger of guaranty
보증계정 secured account; security account
보증금 caution money; deposit received; guarantee deposits; guarantee money
보증대출 loan on personal guarantee

보증론 guarantee loan
보증료 guarantee charge
보증발행 fiduciary issue
보증보험 guarantee insurance
보증부 대부 loan with third party's guarantee
보증부 워런트 guaranteed warrant
보증부 위임 commission del credere
보증사채 assumed bond; guaranteed bond
보증액 guaranteed amount
보증업무 guarantee business
보증위탁계약 indemnity agreement
보증은행 guarantor bank
보증인 guarantor; security suretyship; surety
보증잔고 guarantees outstanding
보증장 letter of guarantee
보증주 guaranteed stock; stock for guarantee
보증준비 securities for fiduciary issue
보증증권 guaranteed securities; surety bond
보증증권주식 bond form
보증차입유가증권 deposit of securities on contracts
보증채무 liabilities for guarantee; liability for endorsement; surety money; warranty obligation
보증채무담보 customers' liabilities on guaranties
보증채무의 cautionary
보증채무이행 performance of obligations of guarantee
보증투자계약 guaranteed investment contract
보충 replenishment
보충계획서 supplementary prospectus
보충률 supplementary rate
보충융자 supplementary financial measure
보충의 supplemental
보충절차 supplementary proceedings
보통 필요한 경비 ordinary and necessary expenses
보통개인보험 ordinary individual life insurance
보통거래 regular way transaction
보통교부세 ordinary local grant tax
보통국채 straight government bond
보통발송송금;우편환 mail transfer
보통배당 common dividend; ordinary dividend; regular dividend
보통법상의 모기지 legal mortgage
보통법상의 소유권 legal title
보통법인 ordinary corporation
보통법주식회사 common law corporation
보통보험 ordinary insurance
보통보험약관 general insurance clause
보통분개장 general journal; proper journal
보통사채 straight bond; straight corporate bond
보통사채공모 public offering of straight bond
보통상각 ordinary depreciation
보통생명보험 ordinary life insurance
보통세 general tax; normal tax
보통소득 ordinary corporation income
보통송금 ordinary remittance
보통수표 open check; uncrossed check
보통연금 ordinary annuity
보통은행 ordinary bank
보통이자율 ordinary interest rate
보통조합 ordinary partnership
보통주 ordinary share; ordinary stock; plain language; straight equity
보통주배당금 dividend on common stock
보통주보유에 관한 통계 common stock ownership statistics
보통주식 common stock
보통주식일주당 순이익 earnings per share of common stock
보통주의 장부가격 common stock book value
보통주주 ordinary shareholder
보통주주지분 ordinary shareholder's equity
보통주평가 valuation of common stock
보통징수 ordinary collection
보통차입채무 straight debt
보합상장 quiet market
보험 assurance; insurance; protection and indemnity risks P&I

보험가액 insurable value; insurance value
보험가입자론 policyholder loan
보험가입자의 채무 policyholder obligations
보험감독법 insurance law
보험계리인 actuary; valuation actuary
보험계약 insurance contract
보험계약신청서 insurance proposal form
보험계약에 실패함 lapse
보험계약자 party insuring; policyholder
보험계약자배당 dividend to policyholders
보험계약자배당금 policy-holders' dividend
보험계약자보호법 Policyholders' Protection Act
보험계약자잉여금 policyholder's surplus
보험관리 insurance management
보험규제책임자 chief insurance regulators
보험금공제 deduction for insurance proceeds
보험금액 amount covered; amount insured; insurance amount; insured amount; sum insured
보험금액비례주의 sums insured method
보험금지불 claim payment
보험금지불업무 claim processing
보험금차손 loss on insurance claims
보험금청구서 debit note for premium
보험기간 policy term; term of insurance
보험기간조항 duration of risk clause
보험대리점 insurance agent
보험대상이 되는 리스크 insurable risk
보험대체기관 central securities depository
보험레버리지 insurance leverage
보험료 insurance expense; insurance premium
보험료결손 premium deficiency
보험료공제 insurance premium deduction
보험료공제신고서 return form for insurance premium deduction
보험료기준연금제도 money purchase plan
보험료대체대부 premium loan
보험료불입면제 waiver of premium
보험료설정 pricing of policies
보험료세 premium tax
보험료율 rate of premium
보험료적립금 premium reserve
보험료지불필 보험 paid-up insurance
보험료프리미엄 premium condition
보험법 general insurance law
보험브로커 insurance broker
보험브로커등록평의회 Insurance Brokers Registration Council
보험브로커법 insurance brokers act
보험비용 claim cost; cost of insurance
보험사고 event insured against
보험상품취급업자 insurance product firm
보험세 insurance tax
보험수급실업 insured unemployment
보험수리상의 기대치 actuarial expectation
보험수리에 따른 자산가치 actuarial asset value
보험수리이율 actuarial yield
보험심의회 insurance council
보험약관 insurance clause
보험업 insurance business
보험업계 insurance industry; insurance sector
보험업법 insurance business law
보험원리 insurance principle
보험의 목적 subject-matter of insurance
보험인수연도별 계산 policy years basis
보험인수증 certificate of insurance
보험자 insurer
보험재무분석가협회 Association of Insurance and Financial Analysts
보험종류변경청구권 conversion privilege
보험증권 insurance policy; policy of insurance
보험증권대부 policy loan
보험증권의 구속력에 대한 조항 clause as to the binding effect of policy
보험지주회사 insurance holding company
보험차익 gains on insurance claim; profit accruing from insurance
보험차익특별계정 special account of gains on insurance claim

보험평가액조항 valuation clause
보험풀 insurance pool
보험형 연금 insurance scheme; insured pension plan
보험회계 insurance accounting
보험회사 insurance company
보호관세 protective duty; protective tariff
보호령 protectorate
보호신탁 protective trust
보호영장 protection
보호예금 safe custody; safe deposit
보호주의경제권 protectionist economic regionalism
보호주의정책 protectionist policies
복관세 dual tariff
복권당첨금 prize of raffle
복권하다 reinstate
복귀재산권 reversion
복리 compound interest
복리계산 calculation of compounded interest
복리방식 compound interest method
복리연율 compound annual rate
복리이율 compound interest yield
복리할인 compound discount
복리현가 present value discounted at compound interest
복리후생비 welfare expense
복리후생시설 welfare facilities
복명(複名)어음 double name paper
복배 improvement from no dividend; resumption of dividend
복본위제 bimetallism
복수구분계산서 multiple step statement
복수균형 multiple equilibria
복수기업이 주식을 소유함 cross-holding
복수만기예금 multiple maturity deposit
복수보험자 composite insurer
복수세율 multiple tax rate
복수어음 set bill
복수요인모델 multi-factor model
복수은행제도 multiple banking system
복수은행지주회사 multibank holding company
복수통화개입 multi-currency intervention
복식기장법 bookkeeping by double entry
복식부기 double accounting; double entry book keeping
복식부기원칙 principal of double-entry bookkeeping
복원 restoration
복잡한 complex
복잡한 거래 sophisticated arrangements
복제펀드 clone fund
복지시설부담액 contribution to welfare facilities
복합거래 compound transaction
복합기입 compound entry
복합상품 synthetic instrument
복합세제 multiple tariff system
복합승수 compound multiplier
복합옵션 compound option
복합운송서류 combined transport documents
복합자본 hybrid capital
복합증권 hybrid securities
본격적인 유통시장 full-fledged secondary market
본결산 full year business result
본국 home country
본드트레이더 bond trader
본드환본위제 sterling exchange standard
본래 상태로 조금 되돌아감 minor rally
본래의 가격을 밑돌다가 매각된 증권 bargain counter
본문 body; purview
본사계정 head office account
본사사무소 registered office
본선인도 free on board
본선지입인도 delivered ex ship
본세 principal tax
본소(本訴) formal lawsuits
본예산 main budget
본원예금 intrinsic deposit

본원적인 가치 intrinsic value
본원적인 예금 primary deposit
본원화폐 original money
본위정책 monetary standard policy
본위제도 monetary standard; standard system
본위화폐 standard money
본적 permanent domicile
본점 head office; parent store
본점계정 home office account
본지점계정 inter-office account
본지점레이트 inter-office rate
본질 substance
본체주기 parenthetical notes
본클레임 final claim
볼라틸리티 volatility
볼라틸리티가치 volatility value
볼라틸리티스프레드 volatility spread
볼록한 모양 convexity
볼륨레이쇼 volume ratio
볼륨어큐뮬레이터(누적지표의 한 종류) volume accumulator
봉쇄 blockade
봉쇄경제 closed economy
부(副)의 duplicate
부가가치 added value; value added
부가가치계산서 added value statement
부가가치분석 value added analysis
부가가치세 value added tax
부가가치통신망 value added network
부가계정 adjunct account
부가급부 fringe benefits
부가보험료 loading
부가세 supertax; tax surcharge
부가수정 adjustment of the carrying amount
부가위험 extraneous risk
부가이익 loading surplus
부가조항 rider
부간사 co-manager
부과 rate issue
부과;평가;등급 rating
부과결정 assessment and decision
부과과세제도 official assessment
부과기일 base date for assessment
부과방식 current disbursement approach; pay-as-you-go-system
부과식 보험 assessment plan
부과액 amount imposed
부과징수 assessment and collection
부급보증 benefit security
부기 bookkeeping
부기계 book keeper
부담 burden
부담경감 reduction of incidence
부담금 burden charge
부담비 obligation fees
부담을 조건으로 한 증여 onerous gift
부담이익배율 earning coverage ratios
부담할 수 있는 affordable
부당과세 unreasonable taxation
부당노동행위 unfair labor practice
(왜곡된 권유로 인한) 부당생명보험계약 twisting
부당영업행위 unfair trade practice
부당위압 undue influence
부당이득 excessive profit; unjust enrichment
부당이득자 profiteer
부당이행청구 unfair call
부당지출 misappropriation of funds; unjust disbursement
부당한 unjustified
부당한 거래 unfair trade
부당해고 unfair dismissal; wrongful dismissal
부당행위 malpractice
부대비용 charge extra; extra charges; incidental expenses
부대설비 fixtures
부대세 additions to tax
부대소송 incidental appeal; incidental suit
부대조건 collateral condition; condition collateral; incidental condition
부대증서 collateral bond
부도덕행위 moral turpitude

부도반각 bounce
부도사유 reason for dishonor
부도수표 dishonored check; protested check
부도어음 bill of dishonor; dishonored bill; note dishonoured; unpaid draft
부도통지 dishonor notice; nonpayment protest
부동비 idle cost
부동산 fixed property; immovable property; immovables; real estate; real property; things real
부동산;토지 landed estate
부동산가격 property prices
부동산감가상각준비금 reserve for depreciation of real estate
부동산계약 estate contract
부동산계정 immovables account
부동산공동보유 cotenancy
부동산권 legal estate; tenancy
부동산권이서 title insurance
부동산담보 real estate security
부동산담보대부 mortgage lending
부동산대부 loan on real estate; loan on real property; rental of real property
부동산대부업 business of renting property
부동산대부업 loan business on real property
부동산등기부등본 certified copy of real estate register
부동산매각손 loss on sale of real estate
부동산매각익 profit on sale of real estate
부동산매매익 profit from immovables transactions
부동산모기지 real estate mortgage
부동산브로커 real estate broker
부동산상의 권리 rights existing on real property
부동산소득 real estate income
부동산수입 income from real estate; rents received
부동산시장 property market
부동산신탁 real estate in trust
부동산양도 transfer of real property
부동산업 real estate industry; realty business
부동산업자 estate agent
부동산의 증권화 securitization of real estate
부동산임대료 rent on real estate
부동산저당대부금 loan secured by real estate
부동산저당장기대부금 real estate loan receivable
부동산전대차 sublease
부동산점유회복 re-entry
부동산주 real estate stock
부동산주의 투자이율 real estate yield
부동산차압 real distress
부동산취득세 real estate acquisition tax; real property acquisition tax; tax on the aquisition of immovable property
부동산취득세비과세 exemption of real estate acquisition tax
부동산투자신탁 real estate investment trust; REIT
부동산평가손익계정 profit and loss on valuation of real estate
부동산포트폴리오 property portfolio
부두사용료 dockage
부두지입인도 delivered ex quay
부득이한 사정 unavoidable circumstances
부령(部令) ministerial ordinance
부르는 값 seller's price
부메랑효과 boomerang effect
부문간 계정 interdepartment account
부문간 대체 interunit transfer
부문간의 interdepartmental
부문간의 대체가격을 결정함 interunit pricing
부문간접비 departmental overhead
부문간접비차이 department variance on overhead
부문감사 department audit
부문개별비 direct department cost
부문계산 sectional calculation
부문매상 divisional sales
부문별 내역 segmental breakdown

부문별 대차대조표 sector balance sheet
부문별 매상 segmental sales
부문별 매상내역 segmental sales breakdown; divisional sales breakdown
부문별 손익 divisional breakdown of profit and loss
부문별 원가계산 cost accounting by department; departmental cost accounting; departmental costing
부문별 이익 departmental profit
부문부담비 departmental burden
부문비 departmental charge; departmental expenses
부문비계산표 overhead distribution sheet
부문비예산 departmental expenses budget
부문원가 departmental cost
부분감사 partial audit
부분균형 partial equilibrium
부분원가계산 partial costing
부분적인 커버드옵션 partially covered option
부분철수 partial withdrawal
부산물 accessory product
부상사망보상금 compensation for injuries and deaths
부서하다 countersign
부속건물 outbuilding
부속명세서 **SEC** schedules SEC
부속명세서 supplementary statement
부속서류 annex; annexed letter; supporting documents
부속설비 annexed structure
부속지역권 easement appurtenant
부수권한 mediate powers
부수업무 secondary activities
부수적인 incidental
부수적인 수입 incidental gains
부스 booth
부실표시 misrepresentation
부양가족 dependent family member
부양공제 allowance for dependent; child tax credit; deduction for dependents; tax exemption for dependents
부양약관 maintenance clause
부양자 supporter
부외자산 unlisted assets
부외차금 unlisted loan
부외채무 unlisted liability
부유세 net worth tax; wealth tax
부의 상관관계 negative correlation
부의장 vice chairman
부이사장 executive vice president
부인 denial
부인권 right of avoidance
부인의 고유재산 separate estate
부인하다 traverse
부재 absence
부재소유권 absentee ownership
부재소유자 absentee owner
부재자 absentee
부적절한 disqualified
부적절한 내용 disqualified substance; inappropriate substance
부적절한 합병 inappropriate merger
부적합리스크 misfit risk
부적합리터닝 misfit return
부적합포트폴리오 misfit-portfolio
부정경쟁 unfair competition
부정기선 tramper
부정사용 unauthorized use
부정수표 defective check
부정신고 false declaration
부정이득 fraudulent gains
부정이익 unfair advantage
부정적인 듀레이션 negative duration
부정적인 레버리지 negative leverage effect
부정적인 증익효과 unfavorable leverage effect
부정적인 효과 negative effect
부정카드 fraudulent card
부정한 수단 foul means
부정행위 fraudulent act; irregular practices; wrong doing

부정행위에 대한 경고 warning against fraud
부조기금 employees relief fund
부조료과세 benefit taxation
부조신탁 support trust
부족 dearth; short delivery; shortfall
부족금처리 reconciliation of deficit
부족액 shortag; balance due
부족액보증 deficiency guarantee
부주의 recklessness
부주의한 사무처리 careless business system
부지약관 unknown clause
부차적인 결과 by-product
부채 negative capital
부채 및 자본 liabilities and capital
부채 및 자본부문 liabilities and stockholders' equity
부채계정 liabilities account
부채관리 liability management
부채구조 liability structure
부채금리 liability rate
부채기간 debt maturity
부채비율 debt equity rate; debt ratio; leverage ratio; leverage test; ratio of total liabilities to net worth
부채비율상승 upturn in gearing
부채상각준비금 amortization fund
부채성 준비금 liabilities reserve
부채이율 liability ratio
부채이자 interest on borrowed fund
부채이자공제 deduction of interest on borrowed fund
부채자산비율 debt asset ratio
부채조항 debt covenant
부채준비금 reserve for liability
부채측 liability side
부채헤지 liability hedge
부채회계 liability accounting
부총재 vice president
부칙 supplementary provision
부품계정 parts account
부활절충 negotiation for budget draft
북대서양의회 North Atlantic Assembly
북대서양자유무역지역 North Atlantic Free Trade Area
북대서양조약기구 North Atlantic Treaty Organization
북미자유무역협정 North America Free Trade Agreement
북빌딩 book building
북빌딩방식 book building method
북유럽각료회의 Nordic Council of Ministers
북유럽협의회 Nordic Council
북해 브렌트 North Brent
분개 journalizing
분개계정;명세계정 itemized account
분개기입 covering entry; journal entry
분개장 journal; journal book
분담부담보 free from particular average
분류된 주식 classified stock
분류소득 scheduler income taxation
분류소득세 classified income tax
분리 severance
분리가능워런트 detachable warrant
분리가능원가 separable cost
분리계정 segregated account; separate investment account
분리과세 separate taxation from other income; separate withholding tax
분리불능 워런트 non-detachable warrant
분리저가법 cost or market whichever is lower basis
분리하다 sever
분리형의 detachable
분매요령 details of distribution
분매집행일 distribution date
분배 distribution
분배국민소득 national income distributed
분배율 relative share
분별관리 segregated accounts
분별연령 age of discretion
분산분석 analysis of variance; variance analysis

분산비 variance ratio
분산주식투자포트폴리오 diversified portfolio on stock investment
분산투자 diversified investment
분산투자로 배제할 수 없는 위험 unavoidable risk by diversified investment
분산투자의 유효성 effectiveness of diversified investment
분산하다 diversify
분산형 보통주펀드 diversified type common stock fund
분산형 투자회사 diversified type investment company
분산형 포트폴리오 diversified type portfolio
분산화 diversification
분산화 투자 diversification investment
분석 analysis
분석가 analyst
분석데이터 analytical data
분석방법 tools of analysis
분석보고서 analytical reports
분석증명서 certificate of analysis
분석회계 analytical accounting
분손 partial loss; particular loss
분손담보 with average
분손담보조항 average clause
분식 manipulation of account; window dressing
분식결산 window dressing settlement
분식결산에 따른 법인세과다납부 over-payment of corporation tax due to window dressing
분식예금 window dressing deposit
분식제무제표 window dressing financial statement
분실카드 lost card
분양 lotting out
분양권 land for sale in lots
분위기;시황 nominal quotation
분쟁 dispute
분쟁해결 dispute settlement
분포 distribution of PBR PBR
분할 apportion
분할(계약의) apportionment
분할각출 split-funding
분할계약 several contract
분할기준 basis to prorate local tax
분할납부 payment in installments
분할반제 repayment instalment
분할반제형 대부 amortization loan
분할반제형 텀론 amortizing term loan
분할발행 tranche
분할분개장 sectional journal
분할불 easy payment
분할불구입 hire purchase
분할상속제 division of succession
분할상환기간 amortisation period
분할선적 partial shipment
분할소유권 several ownership
분할원장계정 split ledger account
분할인출 partial draw down
분할지불 installment payment; installment settlement; payment by installment
분할판매 split sale
분할하다 allot
불가동자산 nonperforming assets
불가분권 undivided interest
불가분채권 indivisible credit
불가피한 사고 inevitable accident; unavoidable accident
불가피한 위험 unavoidable dangers
불가항력 act of God; force majeure
불가효력조항 force majeure clause
불경기 depression of business
불경제;경제적이지 못함 diseconomy
불공정한 경쟁방법 unfair method of competition
불규칙한 가격변동 random price changes
불균등지불 irregular installment payment
불균형 asymmetry; disequilibrium; imbalance
불균형성장 disequilibrium growth
불납부가산세 additional tax on nonpayment

불능한 계약 impossible contract
불량대출 doubtful loan
불량모기지 underperforming mortgages
불량자산 problem assets
불량재고 dead stock
불량채권 doubtful account; nonperforming loans; problem loan; underperforming loans
불량채권상각 bad debt written-off
불량채권율 bad debt ratio
불량채권의 증권화 securitization of bad loans
불량채권처리 troubled-loan cleanup
불량회원 bad member
불로소득 unearned income
불로소득자층 rentier class
불릿스와프 bullet swap
불몰수법 non-forfeiture act
불몰수조건 non-forfeiture condition
불법 illegality; unlawfulness
불법방해 nuisance
불법의 illegal
불법인 unlawful
불법점유 dispossession
불법집회 unlawful assembly
불법취로 illegal employment
불법행위 misfeasance; unlawful act
불변리스크 constant risk tolerance
불변의 unchanged
불변자본 constant capital
불병합 non-joinder
불복신청 administrative protest
불복심사 administrative review
불상환채 irredeemable bond
불성실 bad faith
불수리 refusal to receive
불신행위 disguised conduct
불안정성 variability
불안정한 동요 erratic fluctuation
불완전경쟁 imperfect competition
불완전경쟁시장 imperfect competition market
불완전고용승수 underemployment multiplier
불완전법화 partial legal tender
불완전신탁 imperfect trust
불완전의무 imperfect obligation
불완전인도 bad delivery
불완전한 defective
불완전한 헤지 imperfect hedge
불완전확률변수 defective random variables
불이행 failure; non-fulfillment; nonperformance
불이행자 defaulter
불이행포지션 fail position
불일치 disparity
불입기일 last payment date
불입부 cum call
불입융자대부 loan of subscription payment funds
불입일 due date of payment
불입잉여금 paid-in surplus
불입자본 capital paid in; paid-in capital; paid-up capital
불입자본금 capital stock paid in
불입자본수익률 profit ratio of paid-up capital
불입지정 designation for transfer
불입출자금 contribution to equity capital
불입취급은행 payment handling bank
불채산부문 loss making division
불출증표 voucher for disbursement
불투명 uncertainty
불투명요인 uncertain factor
불특정타인을 위한 보험 insurance for account to whom it may concern
불할납세 installment payment of tax
불합리 absurdity
불행사 nonuser
불확실한 uncertain
불확실한 권리 precarious right
불확인신용장 unconfirmed credit
불확정이자 contingent interest
불확정이자부 unfixed interest bearing
불확정재산권 contingent estate
불확정채권 unliquidated claim
불환은행권 inconvertible bank note
불환지폐 inconvertible paper money

불황 depression
불황카르텔 depression cartel
붕괴 breakdown
붕락 crash
브래디구상 Brady plan
브랜드경쟁 battle of the brands
브랜드매매 sale by brand
브랜드상품 brand item
브레이크스루;돌파구 breakthrough
브레이크이븐레포레이트 break-even repo rate
브레턴우즈 Bretton Woods
브레턴우즈협정 Bretton Woods Agreement
브로드머니 broad money
브로커론 broker's loan
브로커론금리 broker's loan interest
브로커업무 broker's business; brokerage
브로커와 딜러를 통한 증권금융 security credit by brokers and dealers
브로커의 콜론 broker's call loan
브리지론;연결융자 bridge loan
브리지환 bridging exchange
블랙리스트 blacklist
블랙먼데이 Black Monday
블랙박스옥션 black box auction
블랙숄즈모델 Black-Scholes model
블랙숄즈방식 Black-Scholes method
블랙숄즈의 옵션평가식 Black-Scholes formula on option valuation
블록거래 block trading
블록경제 bloc economy
블록트레이더 block trader
블록포지셔너 block positioner
블록플로 block flow
블루칼라 blue collar
비(非)시스티매틱리스크 unsystematic risk
비; 비율 ratio
비감사 unaudited
비거주자 nonresident
비거주자 및 외국법인에 대한 지불 payment to nonresidents and foreign corporation
비거주자 원예금 non-resident won deposit
비거주자가 발행한 원기준채권 bond in won issued by nonresidents
비거주자에 대한 감면 tax concessions for nonresident
비거주자외화예금계정 non-resident foreign currency account
비거주자외화예금계정 nonresident foreign currency account
비거주자원예금계정 nonresident won account
비거주자의 과세소득 taxable income earned by nonresident
비거주자의 급여소득 payment to nonresidents
비경쟁입찰 noncompetitive tender
비계속사업 discontinued business
비계약자 non-settled
비공개개정 sit in camera
비공개기업 private company
비공개회사 closely-held company
비공모채 privately placed bond
비공식부문 informal sector
비공식자본이 유출됨 unofficial capital flight
비공식조직 informal organization
비과세 exclusion from taxation; free of tax; tax exempt; tax free
비과세거래 nontaxable transaction
비과세구입 tax free purchase
비과세기관 tax exempt organization
비과세문서 nontaxable document
비과세법인 corporation free from taxation; exempt corporation; nontaxable corporation; tax free corporation
비과세소득 exempt income; nontaxable income
비과세양도소득 capital gain free of taxation
비과세유가증권;면세증권 nontaxable securities
비과세이자소득 nontaxable interest income
비과세장벽 non-tariff barriers

비과세재산 exempt property; nontaxable property
비과세저축 nontaxable savings
비과세준비금 tax free reserve
비과세증여 exempt gift
비과세품 tax free article
비관련사업이익 unrelated business income
비관적인 시나리오 pessimistic scenario
비교 comparison
비교가능성 comparability
비교계산서 comparative statement
비교대차대조표 comparative balance sheet
비교분석 comparative analysis
비교분석법 method of comparative analysis
비교생산비설 theory of comparative cost
비교성의 원칙 principal of comparability
비교손익계산서 comparative income statement; comparative profit and loss statement
비교수지계산서 comparative statement of cash flows
비교우위 comparative advantage; relative advantage
비교우위설 theory of comparative advantage
비교우위의 원리 principle of comparative advantage
비교우위이론 comparative advantage theory
비교원가 comparative cost
비교원가조사 comparative cost studies
비교재무제표 comparative financial statement
비교통계학 comparative statistics
비교표 comparison table
비금리부채 non-rate-paying liability
비금리자산 non-rate earnings assets
비금융거래 non-financial transaction; nonfinancial transactions
비금융계정 non-financial accounts
비금융시장 non-financial market
비금융자산 non-financial assets
비금전항목 non-monetary items
비누적형 배당 non-cumulative dividend
비누적형 우선주식 non-cumulative preferred stock
비단절승수 untruncated multiplier
비담보위험 uninsured peril
비대칭바스켓방식 adjustable basket technique
비독점적인 nonexclusive
비동족의 동족회사 non-personal family corporation
비동족주의 non-basic shareholder of family corporation
비동족회사 non-family corporation
비동질성 non-homogeneity
비등록사모채 letter securities
비례과세법 proportional taxation
비례배당 ratable distribution
비례배분 proportional allocation
비례배분한 pro rata
비례비 proportional cost; proportional expenses
비례세 proportional tax
비례원가계산 proportional calculation
비례재보험 proportional reinsurance
비례적인 가변비용 proportionally variable cost
비례준비금 proportional reserve method
비례준비제도 proportional reserve system
비례지불 pro rata payment
비례특약재보험 quota share treaty reinsurance
비례평등조건 proportional equal terms
비례할당하지 않는 재보험 non-proportional reinsurance
비망가격 memorandum value; reminder price
비망계정 memorandum account
비목 expense item
비밀계정 secret account
비밀리에 이익을 처분함 hidden profit distributions
비밀번호 personal identification number
비밀부채 secret liability

비밀손실 latent loss
비밀수수료 secret commission
비밀수익 latent return
비밀신탁 secret trust
비밀유지계약 confidentiality agreement
비밀유지의무 confidentiality of information
비밀자산 hidden assets
비밀적립금 latent assets; secret reserve; undisclosed reserve
비밀적립자산주 hidden assets stock
비방가액 memorandum price
비분산투자형 투자회사 non-diversified investment company
비사업활동 non-business activity
비상각자산 non-depreciable assets; non-depreciable property
비상업트레이더 noncommercial trader
비상장주 unlisted stock
비상장채 unlisted note
비상장회사 unlisted company
비상조치 emergency measure; extraordinary measures
비상해손(海損) extraordinary average
비상호적인 non-reciprocal
비서실(SEC) Office of Secretary
비선형 추세선 curving trend line
비시장경제 non-market economy
비시장성 리스크 non-market risk
비시장성 리스크의 원천 non-market risk sources
비시장성 증권 non-marketable issue; non-marketable securities
비실명예금 deposit in a fictitious name
비싸게 사다 buy high
비싼 값으로 구입 buying at top price
비약정트란시 uncommitted tranche
비양심적인 계약 unconscionable bargain
비연결자회사 unconsolidated subsidiaries
비연대보증 severally but not jointly
비열후 unsubordinated
비열후담보부사채 unsubordinated debenture
비영리기관 nonprofit institution
비영리법인 nonprofit corporation; nonprofit-making company
비영리사업 nonprofit making business
비영리조직 nonprofit making organization
비영리회사 noncommercial enterprise
비영업용 상각자산 depreciable property for nonbusiness
비영업용 자산 non-business property
비용; 조업도; 이익 분석 cost-volume-profit analysis
비용견적 cost estimate
비용곡선 cost curve
비용과 수익의 대응 matching costs and revenues
비용대비효과분석 cost effectiveness analysis
비용데이터 cost data
비용동향 cost behavior
비용배부 expense distribution
비용배분의 원칙 principle of cost allocation
비용보증계약 guaranteed cost contract
비용분담 cost sharing
비용분류 cost classification
비용소멸 cost cutting
비용수익대응의 원칙 cost matching income principle
비용포함 free of charge
비용함수 cost function
비용효과 cost utility
비용효율이 좋은 cost effective
비워 줌; 내줌 vacation
비원가항목 non-cost items
비위험이자율 non-risk interest rate
비위험자산 non-risk assets
비유동성 illiquidity
비유동성자산 non-liquid assets
비유동자산 non-current assets
비유동적 illiquid
비유통증권 nonnegotiable endorsement
비율법감모상각 percentage depletion
비율분석 ratio analysis

비율분석법 ratio method
비은행금융기관 non-bank financial institution
비이자부채 non-interest-bearing bond
비인기채권 inactive bond
비자발적인 실업 involuntary unemployment
비자연적인 손익 involuntary loss or gain
비적격채 ineligible bill
비전략부문 non-strategic division
비전통적인 어셋클래스 nontraditional asset class
비제정법 unwritten law
비제휴론 non-tie-up loan
비주거자 nonpermanent resident
비주식지수선물 nonequity index futures
비준 ratification
비중개 disintermediation
비참가우선주식 nonparticipating preferred stock
비채무자예금 deposit of nondebtor
비채변제 money paid under mistake
비철금속업계 nonferrous metals industry
비출자조합 non-investment cooperative association
비통계적 샘플링 nonstatistical sampling
비판 criticism
비판기능 critical function
비판적인 시청자 protester
비할당적립방식 unallocated funding instrument
비할부 non-installment
비현금자산 non-cash assets
비현금항목 non-cash items
비화폐간접증권 non-monetary indirect security
비확률모델 non-stochastic model
비회사형 합변사업 unincorporated joint venture
비회원회사 non-member securities company
비효율적인 inefficient
빈 건물 vacant building
빈곤선 poverty line
빈곤율 poverty rate
빌세일 bill sale
빌트인플렉서빌러티 built-in flexibility
빌패스 bill pass
빙산이론 iceberg theory

ㅅ

사건목록 cause list
사건부 cause-books
사고 1건당 보상한도액 combined single limit
사고보험 accident insurance
사고증권 securities with irregularities
사고통지 notice of loss and damage
사교클럽 social club
사권(私權) private right
사기 actionable fraud
사기 cheat
사기양도 fraudulent conveyance; fraudulent transfer
사기채권자 fraudulent creditor
사기파산 fraudulent bankruptcy
사기표시 fraudulent misrepresentation
사기행위 fraudulent action; fraudulent conduct
사내규정 internal rule; office regulation
사내대체이익 internal transfer profit
사내보 house organ
사내유보율 retained earnings ratio
사는 쪽 bargainee; buyer
사단법인 aggregate corporation; corporate juridical person
사례금 honorarium
사망기록 bill of mortality
사망률 death rate
사망보험 insurance against death; insurance payable at death
사망보험금 sum payable at death
사망자의 상속인 successor of the deceased
사명 mission
사모(私募) private offering
사모(私募)발행 private placement
사모(私募)보통사채 private placement straight bond
사모(私募)전환사채 private convertible note
사모(私募)증권 private placement securities
사모발행 private placing
사모요령 placing memorandum
사모채 private note; private offering bond
사모채발행 placement of unlisted note
사모채신디케이트 private placement syndicate
사무간사회사 book runner
사무결합 consolidation of operation
사무관리 administration
사무국장실(SEC) Office of Executive Director(SEC)
사무권한 ministerial power
사무규정 office manual
사무라이채 samurai bond
사무라이 CP samurai commercial paper
사무법인 business company
사무비 office expenses
사무소 혹은 다른 일정한 사무소 office or other fixed place of business
사무소제경비 office overhead
사무집행 business excution
사무처리 liquidation of liabilities

사반기보고서 10-Q report 10-Q
사법부 Department of Justice
사법적인 판단을 내리다 adjudge
사법절차 judicial proceedings
사사분기 final quarter
사상최고 record high
사상최저 record low
사상최저치 all time now
사선으로 교차된 줄무늬 technical change
사실기재서 case stated
사실상 de facto
사실상 교환가능한 통화 currency convertible in fact
사실상의 존속회사 de facto existing company
사실상의 추정 presumption of fact
사실에 반한 untrue
사실조사 fact finding
사실착오 mistake of fact
사양서매매 sale by specification
사업 business; task; venture
사업개황설명서 summary statement of business
사업광고를 위한 상품 prize offered for advertisement of the business
사업구분별 손익보고 segment reporting
사업규모 business regulations
사업규모축소 reduction of business
사업금융 business loan; corporate finance
사업금융회사 business finance company
사업기회 business opportunity
사업단위 business unit
사업대부 industrial loan
사업목적에 사용되는 자산 properties put to use for business
사업방법서 scheme of operation
사업범위 scope of business
사업법 business law
사업법인 firm; industrial corporation
사업보고서 annual business report
사업보험 business insurance
사업부문간 매상 intersegment sales
사업상의 비밀 business secret
사업상의 통상위험 ordinary risks of employment
사업설명서 preliminary prospectus
사업세 business tax; enterprise tax
사업세손금산입시기 time of inclusion in expenses of enterprise tax
사업소 business establishment; business place
사업소득 business income
사업소득계산 computation of business income
사업소비 establishment expenses
사업소세 business office tax
사업소소득의 귀속 attribute of income of business office
사업수행 performance of business
사업습관 business practice
사업신탁 business trust
사업아이디어를 발견하는 사람 business finder
사업에 종사하는 기간 term of engaging in the business
사업에 주는 영향 impact on business
사업에서 생기는 소득 income derived from business
사업연도 accounting period; business year; taxable year
사업연도개시일 beginning day of the taxable year
사업연도결정 determination of taxable year
사업연도변경 change of taxable year
사업연도신고 notification of the taxable year
사업연도지정 designation of accounting period
사업외경비 non-business expenses
사업용 자산을 대치함 replacement of business property
사업용으로 사용되는 자산 property put into business
사업을 폐지한 경우의 필요경비 necessary expenses in the case of closing business
사업자 undertaker
사업자금 business fund
사업장 working place

사업전망 business expectation
사업전환 change in business
사업종류 nature of business
사업주 business proprietor
사업주공제 proprietor deduction
사업주특별경비준비금 proprietors special expense reserve
사업중지 suspension of business
사업채 industrial bond; industrial debenture
사업폐쇄 closing business
사업폐지 quitting of business; relinquishing of business
사업협동조합 cooperative business association
사업확장 business expansion
사업환경리스크지수 business environment risk index
사업활동 active conduct of business
사업회사 business corporation
사외발행보통주식 common stock outstanding
사외이사 outside director
사외이용자 external user
사용(私用)원장 private ledger
사용가능기간 estimated usable period; prospective usable
사용가치 use value; utility value; value in use
사용권 right of use
사용기간 usable years
사용불능자금 non-expendable fund
사용시간 used hours
사용시간비례법 hours-of-service method
사용용도불명금 expenditure unaccounted for
사용자 employer
사용자배상책임보험 employer's liability insurance
사용자원가 user cost
사용후 신고제 use and file
사우디아라비아통화청 Saudi Arabian Monetary Agency
사원권 rights and liabilities of members
사원예금 employee deposits
사원채용 recruitment
사원총대회 general meeting of substitutional members
사유지통행료 toll traverse
사이콜로지컬라인 psychological line
사이트크레디트 sight credit
사장회사배당상황 dividends of listed companies
사재제공익 profit from private funds offered
사적인 사용 private use
사적인 회계사 private accountant
사전가격확인제도 advance pricing agreement
사전감사 preaudit
사전병합신고 premerger notification
사전보전차압 advance preservative seizure
사전분석 ex-ante analysis; prior analysis
사전상환 advanced redemption
사전신고 prior notice
사전인가제도 prior approval
사전자격심사 prequalification
사전적립방식 advance funding method
사전조달 advance refunding
사전조사 preparatory audit
사전조사통지 notification of audit
사전조언 preliminary advice
사전준비기간 pre-preparatory period
사전징수 advance collection
사전차압 advance seizure
사전청구 advance demand
사전테스트 ex-ante test
사전판매 presale order
사정가액 assessed value
사정기관 assessing organ
사정소득액 assessed income
사정액 assessed amount
사정인 surveyor
사채 corporate bond; corporate debenture; corporate securities
사채가격 price of corporate bond
사채감채기금 bond sinking fund
사채권 bond certificate; debenture bond
사채권신탁 debenture trust

사채권양도 debenture assignment
사채권자 bond holder
사채권자집회 meeting of bond-holders
사채등록법 registration act for corporate bond
사채명세표 schedule of bonds payable
사채미발행고 bond unissued
사채발행비 bond issuing expense; debenture issuing expenses
사채발행비용 debt expense
사채발행수탁자 trustee for bond issuance
사채발행차금 debt discount and expenses; discount or premium on bond; unamortized debt discount and expenses
사채발행차금상각 amortization of bond premium
사채발행차익 unamortized premium on bonds
사채배당 bond dividend
사채상환 debenture redemption
사채상환차금 gains on bond retirement
사채상환차손 loss from redemption of bond
사채소각 retirement of bond
사채소화상황 sales of corporate bonds by purchasers
사채원부 bond register
사채이자 debenture interest; interest on bond
사채이자에 부과되는 소득세 income tax on bond interest
사채이자지불금 cash deposited for bond interest
사채최고발행한도 bond authorized
사채취득 acquisition of debenture
사채투자 investment in bonds
사채판매 placement of bond
사채평가 bond valuation
사채프리미엄발행 bond issued at a premium
사채할증발행차금 premium on bonds payable
사치세 luxury tax
사칭통용 passing off
사해행위취소권 right to revoke fraudulent act
사회감사 social audit
사회계약 social contract
사회보장 social security
사회보장급부 social security benefits
사회보장급부자 social security recipient
사회보장번호 social security number
사회보장부담 social contribution burden
사회보장제도 social security system
사회보험 social insurance
사회보험급부차압금지 prohibition of seizure on social insurance payment
사회보험료 social insurance premiums
사회보험료공제 social insurance premiums deduction
사회보험분담금 contribution for social insurance
사회보험세 social insurance tax
사회비용 social cost
사회사 proprietary company
사회의식 social consciousness
사회자본 social capital
사회적인 가정 social assumption
사회적인 무차별곡선 social indifference curve
사회적인 한계비용 social marginal cost
사회지표 social indicator
사회총자본 aggregate social capital
사회회계 social accounting
사회후생함수 Social Security tax rate
사후(事後)의 ex post facto
사후감사 post audit
사후베타수치 ex-post beta
사후분석 ex-post analysis; posterior analysis
사후수치 ex-post alpha value
사후일부 postdate
사후일부 수표 postdated check
사후일부 어음 postdated bill
사후자격심사 post-qualification
사후저축 ex-post saving
사후차이 ex-post variance
사후최적분석 ex-post optimum analysis
사후취득재산 after-acquired property
사후취득조항 after-acquired clause

사후측정 subsequent measurements
사후투자 ex-post investment
사후특성선 ex-post characteristic line
사후평가 ex-post assessment
산림소득 forestry income; timber income
산림소득특별공제 forestry income deduction
산성시험비율 acid test ratio
산술급수법 sum-of-the-years-digits method
산술평균 arithmetic mean
산술평균;단순평균 arithmetic average
산업 industry
산업간의 inter-industry
산업관련법 inter-industry-relation table
산업구조 industrial composition; industrial structure
산업구조고도화 growth of industrial structure
산업구조정책 industrial structure policy
산업별 국민순생산 industrial origin of net national product
산업분류 industrial classification
산업사고준비금 industrial-accident reserve
산업연관분석 inter industry analysis
산업의 베타수치 industry beta value
산업자금 industrial fund
산업자금공급상황 net supply of industrial funds
산업자본 industrial capital
산업정보 industry information
산업정책 industrial policy
산업집중 industry concentration
산업투자특별회계 Industry Investment Special Account
산업특정재원채 industrial revenue bond
산업합리화 industrial rationalization
산업협력방식 industrial cooperation method
산업효과 industry effect
산정 calculation; computation
산정가격 appraised price
산정기간 computation period
산정레이트 accounting rate
산정회 요율 rating organization tariffs
산출계수 output coefficient
산출량 quantity of output
산출물인수 혹은 지불계약 take-or-pay contract
산출세액 calculated tax amount
산포 spending spree
산포도표 scatter chart
삼각무역 triangular trade
삼국간 무역 intermediary trade; offshore trade
삼국간 협정 tripartite agreement
삼국어음 third country bill
삼극위원회 Trilateral Commission
삼도논법 trilemma
삼림화재보험 forest fire insurance
삼선전환법 three line converting method
삼일후 인도 double settlement
삼중관세율 trebletariff
삼중바닥 triple bottom
삼중익 triple merit
삼차 third generation
삼차산업 tertiary industry
삼차온라인시스템 third generation on-line system
상각 depreciation and amortization; write-off
상각가능한도액 final depreciable limit
상각계정 depreciation account
상각기간 period of depreciation
상각기금법 sinking fund method
상각률 amortization rate; depreciation ratio
상각방법 manner of amortization; manner of depreciation
상각방법변경 change of depreciation method
상각방법신고 notification of depreciation method
상각방법을 선정함 selection of depreciation method
상각범위 allowed depreciation
상각법 accelerated method
상각부족액이월 underdepreciation carried forward

상각비배부 appointment of depreciation
상각비용 amortization cost
상각사유 amortization event
상각액 depreciable amount
상각원가 amortized cost
상각자산 depreciable property; depreciation assets
상각전 순이익 net profit before depreciation
상각전의 이연자산 deferred charge before amortization
상각준비금 reserve for amortization
상각채권수금익 profit on bad debt recovered
상각캡 amortising cap; amortizing cap
상각필 대손금회수 collection of bad debts deducted
상각필 채권회수 bad debt recovery
상각하다 amortize
상각한도액 allowable limit for depreciation amount; allowed amortizable limit; allowed depreciation limit; depreciable limit
상각효과 amortization effect
상각후 순이익 net profit after depreciation
상각후 원가 depleted cost
상공론 commercial and industrial loan
상공업금융회사 commerce and industry finance company
상공회의소 Association Cambiste Internationale; chamber of commerce and industry
상관계수 correlation coefficient
상관관계 correlation
상관도 correlation diagram
상관분석 correlation analysis
상관비율 correlation ratio
상관습법 customs of merchant
상관표 correlation table
상근 full time
상급법원 superior courts
상급부간사 senior co-manager
상급회계사 senior accountant
상급회계학 advanced accounting
상당액 amount equivalent to
상당한 adequate
상당한 상각 reasonable depreciation
상당한 이유 probable cause
상대 relative
상대가격 relative price
상대가치 relative value
상대거래 negotiated trade; negotiated trading; negotiated transaction
상대계좌 corresponding account
상대기입 contra entry
상대력지수 relative index; relative strength index
상대론 bilateral loan
상대매매시장 negotiated market
상대방 opposite party; counterpart
상대방당사자 adversary party
상대소득 relative income
상대수익 relative revenue
상대예금 corresponding deposit
상대오차 relative error
상대적으로 비싸거나 값싼 증권 mispriced security
상대적인 강약도 relative strength
상대적인 면책위험 relative excepted risk
상대적인 신용리스크 relative credit risk
상대적인 측도 relative measures
상대적인 퍼포먼스 relative performance
상대채무 cross debt; mutual debt
상대편계정 Vostro account
상륙기간 lay-days
상무부 Commerce Department
상무이사 managing director; managing governor
상법 Commercial Code; commercial law
상법 등의 일부를 개정한 법률 Law Amending Part of the Commercial Code
상법특례 exception to the Commercial Code
상사금융 trading firm finance
상사대리 mercantile agency
상사중재 commercial arbitration

상설기관 standing body
상설소득가설 permanent income hypothesis
상설위원회 standing committee
상세 detail
상세권 trading area
상속권 right of inheritance
상속법 law of succession
상속세 death duty; estate duty; estate tax; inheritance tax
상속세공제 gift tax credit
상속세면제 exemption of inheritance tax
상속세물납 inheritance tax paid in kind
상속세법 Inheritance Tax Law
상속인 heir
상속재산 hereditaments; inherited property
상쇄 offset; set off
상쇄계정 offset account; off-setting account
상쇄관세 compensation duties; countervailing duty
상쇄액 amount of the offset
상쇄오진 offset error
상쇄오차 compensating error
상쇄이자 compensating interest
상쇄포지션 offsetting position
상쇄항목 offset item
상습관 commercial customs
상승 ascending; increase in PER; pick up; synergy; tailgating
상승각 climbing angle
상승기조 upward trend
상승력 climbing power; up-pressure
상승률 rate of increase
상승상장 rising phase; rising quotation
상승순위 ranking of advances
상승압력 upward pressure
상승커브 ascending curve
상승트라이앵글 ascending patterns triangle
상승하는 경향인 in up trend
상승효과 synergy effect
상시재고 running inventory
상업개발채권 industrial development bond
상업금융 commercial finance
상업대부 commercial lending
상업대출 commercial loan
상업등기 commercial registration
상업등기부등본 certified copy of commercial registration
상업법 mercantile law; merchant law
상업부기 commercial bookkeeping; merchandise bookkeeping
상업부동산론 commercial real estate loan
상업송장 commercial invoice
상업신용 commercial credit
상업신용보험 commercial credit insurance
상업신용장 commercial L/C
상업어음 commercial bill; commercial paper; mercantile paper
상업어음발행잔고 commercial paper outstanding
상업어음주의 real-bills doctrine
상업용 모기지 commercial mortgage
상업용 모기지담보증권 commercial mortgage backed securities
상업용 모기지풀 commercial mortgage pool
상업용 부동산 commercial real estate
상업은행가 commercial banker
상업재판소 commercial court
상업조합 mercantile partnership
상업조합중앙금고 Central Co-operative Bank for Commerce and Industry
상업통계 census bureau; commercial statistics
상업트레이더 commercial trader
상업할인 commercial discount
상업회계 commercial accounting
상업회의소 chamber of commerce
상여 employee bonus
상여수당금 accrued bonuses
상여전 소득 income before employee bonus
상여준비금 bonus payment reserve; provision for employee bonus; reserve for bonus payment
상여준비금편입한도액 allowed limit

chargeable to the bonus payment reserve
상여지급액 계산기간 term for which the bonus payment is computed
상위 top
상위사채 senior bond
상위열후사채 senior subordinated note
상위증권 senior issue
상위트란시 senior tranche
상임감사역 permanent auditor; standing auditor
상임대리인 standing proxy
상임이사 standing governor
상장 listing
상장계약위반 contravention of listing agreement
상장계약자 stock listing agreement
상장관 forecast for market tendency
상장규정 listing regulations
상장기준 criteria for listing; listing criteria
상장대리인 listing agent
상장된 주식 shares held in a long position
상장문제 listed issue
상장보통채권의 종류별 발행액 amount issued by types of straight bonds
상장보통채권의 종류별 상장총액 amount listed by types of straight bonds
상장비용 listing fee
상장상승 higher quotations
상장상품 exchange-traded issue; listed brand; listed product
상장선물 listed futures
상장시장변경 reassessment of markets
상장신고를 위한 유가증권보고서 securities report for listing application
상장신고에 관계된 주식 stock for which listing application is made
상장신주인수권증권 listed warrants
상장신청 listing application
상장신청서 application for listing; application to list
상장심사 examination for listing; listing examination
상장심사비 listing examination fees
상장옵션 listed options
상장외국주식 listed foreign stocks
상장요건 listing requirements
상장유가증권지수 price index of listed securities
상장의 대전환일 key reversal day
상장의 반전 reversal
상장의 하락 market crash
상장일의 연도 year to which listing day pertains
상장조종 market manipulation
상장주 listed stock
상장주가지수 listed stock price index
상장주식평가 valuation of listed stock
상장주식평균이율 average yield of listed stocks
상장증권 listed securities
상장채권 listed bonds
상장채권시장 listed bond market
상장채권시장외매매고 off-board transactions of listed bonds
상장폐지 delisting
상장폐지기준 criteria for delisting
상장표 list quotation
상장표요약 run-down
상장회사 listed company; publicly traded company; quoted company
상장회사의 발행필 주식 증감상황 sources in increase in outstanding shares
상장회사자금조달액 security financing by listed companies
상장후 비용 fees after listing
상적과세 taxation by applying upper bracket
상적세율 tax rate applied to upper part of income
상점법 shop act
상정원본 notional amount
상징적인 인도 symbolic delivery
상차상속 successive inheritance
상표 trade mark

상표권 right of trademark
상표권침해 trade-mark infringement
상표등록법 trade-mark registration law
상품 commodity; instrument; merchandise
상품 또는 제품 goods and products
상품 하나당 매매가격 selling price per unit
상품가격지수 commodity price index
상품간 격차 difference among issues
상품간 스프레드 intracontract spread
상품개발 product development
상품거래 commodity transaction
상품거래계좌 commodity account
상품거래고문 commodity trading adviser
상품거래법 commodity exchange act
상품거래소 commodity exchange
상품거래소위원회 commodities exchange commission
상품거래책임준비금 commodity exchange responsibility reserve; commodity transaction responsibility reserve; reserve for liability for commodity transactions
상품견본 sample
상품계정 goods account; merchandise account
상품계정자산 trading account assets
상품고객계약 commodity customers agreement
상품관리 merchandise management
상품구성 assortment of goods; merchandise mix
상품구입장 invoice-book inward
상품담보 collateral commodity
상품담보채권 commodity backed bond
상품매매장 merchandise book
상품매상장 sold book
상품발송장 invoice-book outward
상품부기의 법칙 shopbook rule
상품부족 shortage in deliverable securities
상품분석 product analysis
상품선물 commodity futures
상품선물거래가격 commodity futures price
상품선물거래가격폭제한 price limit on commodity futures
상품선물거래의 증거금 margin on commodity futures
상품선물거래청산소 clearinghouse for commodity futures
상품선물거래헤징 hedging on commodity futures
상품선물지수 commodity futures index
상품설명 trade description
상품성 commoditization
상품수요 commodity demand
상품시장 commodity market
상품옵션 commodity option
상품원가 merchandise cost
상품원장 merchandise ledger
상품위험 mercantile risk
상품유가증권 securities owned
상품재고;재고상품 merchandise inventory
상품재고대비수취계정비율 ratio of merchandise to receivables
상품조달원가 merchandise procurement cost
상품지수 commodity index
상품통계 commodity statistics
상품투자 product investment
상품투자신탁 commodities investment trust
상품펀드 managed futures
상품펀드풀운영자 commodity pool operator
상품혁신의 시대 product innovation era
상품화 commercialization
상품회전수 turnover of commodity
상품회전율 merchandise turnover ratio; rate of stock-turn
상한 ceding
상한금리 cap interest rate; ceiling rate
상해 및 건강보험 accident and health insurance
상해보험 personal accident insurance
상행위 commercial transaction
상향 up-tick
상향수정 upward revision

상호 corporate name; trade name
상호결제 parallel clearing
상호결제제도 mutual offset system
상호계산 mutual account
상호계산계정 open and current account
상호계정 two way account
상호날인계약 mutual covenant
상호대차 mutual credits
상호대출 parallel loan
상호독립적인 사건 mutually exclusive event
상호무역협정 bilateral trade agreement
상호배부법 reciprocal distribution method
상호보험 mutual insurance
상호보험조합 mutual association
상호부금 mutual installment
상호부조단체 beneficial association
상호생명보험회사 mutual life insurance company
상호수요곡선 reciprocal demand curve
상호신용장 reciprocal credit
상호약속 mutual promise
상호위탁판매 reciprocal consignment
상호입회하다 intercommon
상호자산교환 reciprocal transfer of property
상호저축은행 mutual savings bank
상호조건 mutual condition
상호조언 mutual wills
상호조합 mutual benefit society
상호협의 mutual agreement procedure
상호회사 mutual company
상환 redemption
상환가격 redemption price; redemption value
상환가능주식 callable preferred stock
상환가액 maturity value
상환거치종신연금 refund deferred life annuity
상환구조 amortisation structure
상환기간까지 보유함 held to maturity
상환기금 redemption fund
상환기일 redemption date
상환리스크 redemption risk
상환면제 discharge of repayment; forgiveness of repayment
상환연장 extension of the maturity
상환우선주를 상환함 retirement of redeemed preferred stock
상환우선주식 redeemable preferred stock
상환은행 reimbursing bank
상환의무를 면제하지 않는 신용장 with recourse credit
상환의무를 지지 않는 without recourse
상환의무면제신용장 without recourse credit
상환이율 redemption yield
상환익 redemption profit
상환재원 fiscal resources for redemption
상환재원편입 appropriation of fiscal resources for redemption
상환정의 meaning of redemption
상환주식 callable stock; redeemable stock
상환주식;상각가능주식 callable shares
상환준비예금 compulsory deposit as a condition for loans
상환차익 profit from redemption; redemption gain
상환차익과세 tax on redemption profit
상환채권 redeemable bond
상환청구 claim for reimbursement
상환청구권 claim of redemption; right of recourse
상환청구권부 채권 put bond
상환청구에 응하지 않은 sans recourse
상환통지 notice of redemption
상환프리미엄 redemption premium
새도우어카운트 shadow account
새터데이나이트스페셜 Saturday Night Special
샌드위치스프레드 sandwich spread
샐리메이채 Sallie Mae debenture
생계 living; sustenance
생계비 living cost
생계잔고 balance in hand
생계현금 cash on hand
생계현금보유고 cash in hand

생명건강보험보증기금 Life and Health Insurance Guaranty Fund
생명건강보험보증협회 Life and Health Insurance Guaranty Association
생명건강보험보증협회모델법 Life and Health Insurance Guaranty Association Model Act
생명보험 life insurance
생명보험 및 양로보험계약의 소득 income from life insurances and endowment contract
생명보험 및 연금 life and annuity
생명보험금 proceeds of life insurance
생명보험료 life insurance premium
생명보험료공제 life insurance premiums deduction; deduction for life insurance premiums; life insurance credit; taxation allowance for life insurance premium
생명보험부문 세금공제전 이익 pretax life earnings
생명보험외무원 ordinary agent
생명보험증권 life insurance policy
생명보험회사 life insurance company
생명손해보험동시판매외무원 multiple line agent
생명표 life table
생보구입 life insurance company purchase
생산거점 manufacturing bases; production base
생산계정 production account
생산고 crop; production; sales volume; trading volume
생산고보고서 production report
생산고보증계약 throughput contract
생산고비례법 output method; production method; service-yield basis; unit of production method
생산고원가 cost of work performed
생산고지불 progress payment
생산고지불제 reimbursement method
생산공정 production process
생산공학 industrial engineering
생산과잉 overproduction
생산관리 production control
생산국카르텔 producer's cartel
생산기술 manufacturing technology
생산노무비 production labor cost
생산능력 production capacity; productive ability
생산량 quantity of production
생산물배상책임보험 products and completed operation liability insurance
생산분배 production sharing
생산설비 plant capacity; production facility
생산설비를 시운전함 trial running of manufacturing equipment
생산성 productivity
생산성상실클레임 loss of productivity claims
생산성지수 index of productivity
생산성지표 productivity ratio
생산성향상 productivity gain
생산성회계 productivity accounting
생산시장 product market
생산실적 actual production
생산여력 surplus capacity
생산연수 productive life
생산요소 factors of production
생산자가격 producer's value
생산자물가지수 producer price index
생산자본 production capital
생산자잉여 producer's surplus
생산자제품재고지수 index of producers' inventory of finished goods
생산자출하지수 index of producers' shipments
생산재 production goods
생산전량구입 bulk buying
생산지수 index number of production; production indexes
생산품제품책 producer's inventory of finished goods
생산함수 production function
생산합리화 rationalization of production
생산협정 production accord

생상성분석 productivity analysis
생애임금 lifelong wages
생전신탁 living trust
생존보험 pure endowment insurance
생존자에 대한 권리의 귀속 survivorship
생활보호 public assistance
생활보호법 Daily Life Security Law
생활비 living expenses
생활비지수 cost-of-living index
생활수준 living standards
생활수중 level of living
생활에 보통 필요한 동산 ordinary and necessary movable property for living
생활필수품 necessaries
서류 document
서류상환지급 payment against document
서머타임 summer time
서면감사 paper audit
서면계약 written agreement; written contract
서면문의 written inquiry
서면신청 written application
서명날인 signed and sealed
서명하다 affix
서문 preamble
서바이벌본드 survival bond
서바이벌함수 survival function
서브젝트마켓 subject market
서브프라임 sub-prime
서비서 servicer
서비스거래 service transaction
서비스무역 service trade
서비스업 service industry
서비싱수수료 servicing fee
서비싱수수료수입 servicing fee income
서서히 절하 gradual devaluation
서약관리인 commissioners for oaths
서커스스와프 circus swap
서포트트란시 support tranche
서플라이사이드경제학 supply-side economics
석유가스세 petroleum gas tax
석유석탄제품업계 oil and coal product industry
석유세 petroleum tax
석유세법 Petroleum tax law
석유수입세 petroleum revenue tax
석유수출국기구 Organization of Petroleum Exporting Countries
석유업법 petroleum act
석유정제업 oil refinery
석유주 oil stock
석유채굴권 oil concession
석유화학산업 petrochemical industry
석유화학콤비나트 petrochemical complex
선가(船價)상각 depreciation of ship costs
선계약 precontact
선구주 forerunner stock
선권원(先權原) elder title
선금 advance payment
선금으로 payment in advance
선도 forward delivery
선도가격 forward price
선도거래 forward agreement; forward transaction
선도결제 forward settlement
선도계약 forward contract
선도금리 forward rate
선도상품 leading stock
선도예금 forward deposit
선도임금 prepaid salaries and wages
선도환 forward exchange
선두주 leading share
선량약인 good consideration
선례 precedent
선매 advance sale
선물 **S&P** futures S&P; futures
선물가격 futures price
선물가격곡선 price line of futures price
선물거래 futures trading; futures transaction
선물거래 등의 특별참가자 special participants in futures trading and the like
선물거래대상 subject of futures trading
선물거래차금 difference resulting from

offsetting futures contracts
선물계약 futures contract
선물디스카운트 forward discount
선물딜러 futures dealer
선물레이트 futures rate
선물마진 forward margin; futures margin
선물매수계약 purchase contract
선물매출포지션 short forward position
선물상장 futures quotation
선물상품 futures instrument; futures product
선물시장 forward market; futures market
선물업계 futures industry
선물옵션 futures option
선물옵션 **TOPIX** futures TOPIX
선물옵션거래계좌 futures and option trading account
선물옵션시장 futures option market
선물위탁거래업무 futures brockerage business
선물인도계약 sales contracts commitments
선물중개업자 futures commission merchant
선물평가 futures valuation
선물포지션 futures position
선물환거래 forward exchange transaction; forward operation
선물환매상장 forward bid rate; forward offer rate
선물환상장 forward exchange rate; forward quotation
선물환스프레드 forward rate spread
선물환시장 forward exchange market
선물환예약 exchange forward contract
선물환예약레이트 forward foreign exchange rate
선물환프리미엄 forward premium
선박 ships and vessels
선박건조보험 builders' risks insurance
선박관리인 ship's husband
선박모기지 ship mortgage
선박보험 hull insurance
선박비부서류 ship's paper
선박세 shipping tax
선박수선보험 repairing risks insurance
선박여객운송비 haulage
선박저당권 mortgage of ship
선방계정 their account
선별융자 selective financing; selective lending
선불 payment on delivery
선불가임 prepaid rents on buildings
선불금반환보증증권 advance payment bond
선불급여 advance salary
선불로 cash in advance
선불법인세 prepaid income taxes
선불보험료 prepaid insurance
선불비용 prepaid expense
선불수수료 prepaid commission
선불옵션 prepayment option
선불운임 advance freight; prepaid freight
선불의 prepaid
선불이익 prepaid income
선불이자 interest advance; interest prepaid; prepaid interest
선불임금 advance wages
선불프리미엄 up-front premium
선불하다 prepay
선비(船費)보험 disbursements insurance
선서 oath
선서공술서 affidavit
선-선레이트 forward-forward rate
선송법 rolling-forward procedure
선수금 advance received
선수수익 advance received profit
선순위담보부사채 senior mortgage bond
선순위대수 senior lender
선순위양도저당 senior mortgage
선순위채권자 senior creditor
선스타트스와프 forward swap
선언서 statement of declaration
선원고용계약서 shipping articles
선원의 선취특권 mariner's lien
선의계약 bona fide contracts

ㅅㅇ

선의소지자 bona fide holder
선의의 매주 innocent purchaser
선의의 부실표시 innocent misrepresentation
선의의 소지인 holder in good faith
선의의 제삼자 holder in due course
선의채권자 bona fide creditor
선일부의 dating forward
선입선출법 first-in first-out method
선장용 선하증권 ship's bill
선저침수 bilge
선적서류 shipping document
선적이서 on board notation
선적지불 cash on shipment
선적지연 late shipment
선적품질조건 shipped quality terms
선적항 home port
선정문제 selected issue
선주책임상호보험조합 protection and indemnity association
선진공업국 major leagues
선진국 advanced countries; developed countries; major industrial nations
선진국수뇌회의 Economic Summit
선취권 right of priority
선취권을 등록; 신청함 preemption entry
선취유치권 prior lien
선취특권 legal lien; preferred creditors' right
선취특권;리엔 lien
선취특권이론 lien theory
선취특권자 lienor
선취특권채;우선담보권부 사채 prior lien bond
선취특권통지 notice of lien
선측인도 free alongside ship
선택계약 alternative contract
선택권부 환예약 exchange contract with option
선택권행사가능기간 option period
선택상환조항 optional repayment provision
선택세 alternative duties
선택적인 구제 alternative remedy
선택적인 기능 selective function
선택적인 신용규제 selective credit regulation
선택주문 alternative order
선택채무 alternative obligation
선택형 가격결정 alternative pricing
선하증권 bill of lading
선행 good behavior
선행계열 leading series
선행이서진정증명 previous indorsements guaranteed
선형가속도계수 linear accelerator
선형계획법 linear programming
선형회귀 linear regression
선호;우선권 preference
선호순서 preference ordering
선호순위 order of preference
설립계 notification of incorporation
설립등기 registration of establishment
설립법 act of incorporation
설립상각비 organization expenses amortize
설립절차 formalities of incorporation
설립취지서;내용설명서 prospectus
설립후 경과연수 years elapsed after foundation
설명 clarification
설명기능 descriptive function
설명부 재무제표 descriptive financial statement
설명을 위한 통계 descriptive statistics
설명할 책임 accountability
설명회 briefing
설비 appliance; equipment; facilities
설비가동률 capacity utilization rate; capital utilization; utilization rate
설비과잉 over-capacity
설비신규구입액 additions to plant and equipment
설비신탁 equipment trust
설비자금 equipment fund
설비자금 plant fund
설비적정가격 equipment fair value

설비투자 capital investment; equipment investment; investment in plant and machinery; plant investment
설비투자 캐시플로비율 cash flow ratio to capital expenditures
설비투자계획 capital budgeting
설비투자액 amount of capital investment
설비투자의욕 capital investment intention
설비투자이익률 return on the capital investment
설비투자증가 additional capex
설비확장적립금 reserve for expansion
설정 setting
설치 installation; mounting
설치공사 installation work
설치대수 number of machines installed
섬유의류업계 textile and apparel industry
성공보수 incentive fee; merit increase
성과 fruit
성과급 piece rate plan
성과배분 payment by the result
성년 full age; lawful age
성명사기 false personation
성명오기 misnomer
성문법 written law
성쇠 ups and downs
성숙경제 mature economy
성숙기업 mature company
성숙단계 mature phase
성숙한 플랜 mature plans
성실 good faith
성실하게 in good faith
성실한 bona fide
성장경제 growing economy
성장곡선 growth curve
성장률 **GNP** growth rate GNP
성장률 growth rate
성장률변화 change in growth rate
성장성 growth potential
성장신장 growth of investment
성장이론 growth theory
성장전략 growth strategy
성장주 growth stock
성장통화 growing currency
성장할 수 있는 viable
성질이 상실됨 alteration of species
성행주문 market order
세계공황 world crisis
세계규모의 투자가 world class investor
세계기업 world enterprise
세계마케팅 world marketing
세계시장 world market
세계은행 World Bank
세계은행그룹 World Bank group
세계은행채 World Bank bond
세계적인 시장 global market
세계지적소유권기관 World Intellectual Property Organization
세계통화 universal currency
세계화 globalization
세계화폐 money of the world; world money
세공제 tax deduction
세공제전 이익 profit before tax
세공제후 이익 profit after tax
세관 customs house
세관할지 tax jurisdiction
세그먼트정보 segmental information
세그먼트회계 segment accounting
세금공제가격 prices minus tax
세금공제급여 pay after tax; take-home pay
세금공제전 이익 earnings before tax; income before income taxes; pretax income; pretax profit
세금공제전 회계이익 pretax accounting income
세금공제후 after tax
세금공제후 실수령액 after-tax gain
세금공제후 이익 after tax yield; after-tax income; after-tax yield; post-tax profit
세금공제후 이익률 after tax profit rate
세금납부 payment of tax
세금배분회계 accounting for tax allocation

세금배포회계 accounting for income tax allocation
세금분류 classification of tax
세금소전 transformation of tax transit
세금유가증권 securities received for guarantee
세금으로 빼앗기는 금액 tax take
세금의 기관배분 tax allocation
세금이 붙는 상품 dutiable goods
세금재정 tax arbitrage
세금조정전 순이익 net profit before the adjustment of tax
세금조항 tax clause
세금준비금 tax reserve
세금체납 tax delinquency
세금체납처분 process for the recovery of taxes in arrears
세금포함 before tax
세금피난처 tax haven
세금환급 amortization of taxes
세금환급청구 claim of the fund of taxes
세금환부 refund of taxes
세금회피수단 tax shelter
세금휴양소 tax resort
세납통지서상의 세납기간 tax period appearing on tax bill
세대간 이타주의 intergenerational altruism
세대간 회계 generational accounting
세대간의 intergenerational
세대과세 household taxation
세델 cedel
세리사 tax practitioner
세리사보수 tax accountant fee
세리사시험 tax accountant examination
세리사연합회 Federal of Tax Accountants
세리상의 우대조치 tax incentive
세목(稅目) tax items
세목계정식 detailed account form
세무감사 tax audit
세무고문 tax advisor
세무당국 tax authorities; taxing authority
세무대리 tax agency
세무대리 tax proxy
세무대학교 National Tax College
세무법원 tax court
세무사 certified tax accountant; licensed tax accountant
세무사법 Certified Tax Accountant Law
세무사회 certified tax accountant association
세무상담 tax consultation
세무상의 수속 tax procedures
세무상의 특례 exceptional tax treatment
세무서 tax office; taxation office
세무서류 tax documents
세무소송 tax suit
세무신고서 tax return
세무자문위원회 advisory tax board
세무쟁소 tax dispute
세무조사 tax adjustments; tax examination
세무조사결과 results of the tax examination
세무조사절차 procedures of tax adjustments
세무조정 adjustment for taxable income
세무처리 tax treatment
세무행정조직 tax administration system
세무회계 tax accounting
세무회계론 theory of tax accounting
세법 tax law; tax regulations
세법규 tax rule
세법상의 특전 various kinds of tax benefits
세법을 무시함 disregard of tax rule
세법학 tax jurisprudence
세부담능력 taxable capacity
세부담의 평준화 equalization of tax burden
세분화;세그멘테이션 segmentation
세분화하여 매입하다 buy on scale
세수 tax income; tax revenue
세수기 tax gathering season
세수세입예측 tax and revenue anticipation
세수예상어음 tax anticipation note
세수예상워런트 tax anticipation warrant
세수자연증가 automatic increase in tax revenue
세액 amount of tax
세액계산 computation of tax amount

세액계산기준 tax computation basis
세액계산기준변경 change of tax computation basis
세액공제 credit against tax; tax credit
세액공제순서 sequence of tax credits
세액납부; 징수 및 환급 paying collecting and refunding tax
세액직접공제 direct tax credit
세액표 tax table
세액확정 settlement of tax amount
세외부담 nontax payment
세외수입 nontax receipts
세원 source of taxation
세율 rate of taxation; tax rate
세율등급 tax bracket
세율설정리스크 pricing risk
세율위원회 tariff commission
세이프가드조항 safeguard provision
세이프하버 safe harbor
세이프하버리스 safe harbor lease
세이프하버협정 safe harbor accord
세인 tax seal
세인이율 net yield
세일리스백 sale-leaseback
세일리스백거래 sale leaseback transaction
세일즈믹스 sales mix
세입 annual revenue
세입가격 price including tax
세입결함 revenue deficit
세입대리점 revenue agency
세입세출예산 revenue and expenditure budget
세입예측증권 revenue anticipation note
세입원 revenue sources
세자리수 주가수익률 three digit PER
세전가격 price before tax
세제 taxation system
세제상의 우대조치 tax advantages; tax benefits
세제정리 readjustment of taxation system
세제조사회 Tax Commission
세출 annual expenditure
세틀먼트바리에이션 settlement variation
세포함 including tax
세환급증명서 customs debenture
세효과 tax effect
세효과규칙 tax benefit rule
세효과회계 accounting for income taxes; tax effect accounting
섹터 sector
섹터방식 sectoral approach
센티멘트지표 sentiment index
셀다운(간사단 이외에 판매함) sell down
셀러즈옵션거래 seller's option trading
셀룰러어프로치 cellular approach
셀링클라이막스 selling climax
셀사이드 sell side
셔먼반트러스트법;독점금지법 Sherman Anti-trust Act
소각 retirement
소개 introduction
소개수수료 referral fees
소거 elimination; rasure
소거분개 eliminating entry
소구계산 retrogressive accounting
소규모기업가 small sized business proprietor
소규모기업공제 small enterprise mutual aid plan
소규모기업공제 외상금공제 deduction for small enterprise mutual aid premiums
소규모사업자 small scale enterprises
소규모차액이익금 thin margin
소규모트렌드 small trend
소규모해손 petty average
소극신탁 passive trust
소극자산 negative assets
소극재산 negative property
소극적인 관리 passive management
소극적인 보증 negative assurance
소극적인 주 negative goodwill
소극적인 주장 negative averments
소극적인 증거 negative evidence
소극적인 증언 negative testimony

소극적인 투자관리 passive investment management
소극적인 평가계정 negative valuation accounts
소극적인 항변 negative plea
소극적인 확인 negative confirmation
소급법 retrospective law
소급보험 retrospective policy
소급수정 retroactive adjustments
소급수정보고서 retroactive restatement
소급의무 recourse obligations
소급의무면제이서 endorsement without recourse
소급조항 lost-or-not-lost clause
소급징수 retroactive levy
소급할인율 retroactive discount
소급해서 retroactive
소기업과세 taxation on small business
소득공제 deductions from income; exemption and deduction from income
소득과세를 기간상호배분함 interperiod income tax allocation
소득과세배분 income tax allocations
소득교역조건 income terms of trade
소득귀속 attribute of income
소득귀속을 추정함 presumption of a real obtainer of income
소득금액합산 aggregation of income amount
소득기준 earned income
소득베이시스 income basis
소득보상보험 disability insurance; income compensation insurance; income indemnity insurance
소득분석 income analysis
소득분포 income distribution
소득세 income tax; revenue tax
소득세감액 decrease of income tax
소득세감액승인 approval of decrease of income tax
소득세갱정결정 reassessment of income tax
소득세공제 income tax credit
소득세공제액손금불산입 non-inclusion of income tax credit in deductible expenses
소득세기본통달 fundamental directives of income tax
소득세누진도 progressiveness of income tax
소득세를 공제 net of income taxes
소득세를 과세함 importation of income tax
소득세법 income tax law
소득세속산표 income tax rapid calculation table
소득세신고 income tax return
소득세신고서 income tax return form
소득세액공제 credit for income tax
소득세연납 deferred payment of income tax
소득세율 income tax rate
소득세율표 income tax rates table
소득세의 연납에 수반되는 이자세 interest tax on authorized deferred payment of income tax
소득세탈세 evasion of income tax
소득소비곡선 income consumption curve
소득수준 income level
소득신고 declaration of income; income return
소득신고용지 income return blank
소득액을 신고하다 file income tax return
소득에 대한 세금 tax on income
소득예금 income deposit
소득요인 income factor
소득원천 source of income
소득원천세 limited income method
소득인플레이션 income inflation
소득재분배 redistribution of income
소득재분배효과 income redistribution effect
소득접근법 income approach
소득정책 income policy
소득조작 income manipulation
소득창출효과 income generating effect
소득층 income bracket
소득탄력성 income elasticity
소득할과세 taxation of income basis
소득효과 income effect

소매 retail
소매가격 retail price
소매금융기관 retail institutions
소매매가 retail selling price
소매매상고 retail sales
소매물가인플레이션 retail price inflation
소매부문 advanced processing
소매상인의 장부 shopkeepers' books
소매세 retail excise
소매시장 retail market
소매업 retail business; retail trade industry
소매업계 retail industry
소매업회계 retail accounting
소매원가 retail cost
소매은행 retail bank
소매재고 retail store inventories
소멸 extinction
소멸시효 extinctive prescription; negative prescription; prescription extinctive
소멸원가 expired cost
소멸하다 cease to exist
소멸해가는 재산 moribund property
소모 exhaustion
소모품 sundry supplies; consumables
소모품계정 supplies account
소모품비 supplies expenses
소부동 slight ups and downs
소브린론 sovereign loan
소브린발행체 sovereign issuer
소브린분석가 sovereign analyst
소브린비율 sovereign rating
소브린상품 sovereign name
소브린실링 sovereign ceiling
소브린은행 sovereign bank
소비고 amount of consumption
소비단위 consumption unit
소비동향 consumption trend
소비래그 consumption lag
소비론 loan for consumption
소비생활협동조합 consumer's cooperative society
소비성향 propensity to consume
소비세 consumption tax
소비세법 Consumption Tax Law
소비세신고 consumption entry
소비수요 consumption demand
소비수준 consumption level
소비승수 consumption multiplier
소비신장 consumption growth
소비양여세 consumption transfer tax
소비에 대한 세금 tax on consumption
소비예상 outlook for consumer spending
소비자 user
소비자관련주 consumer sector stock
소비자금리 consumer credit rate
소비자금융 consumer loan
소비자금융회사 consumer credit company; consumer finance company
소비자단체 consumer's union; consumer advocate
소비자단체 consumer group
소비자리스 consumer leasing
소비자물가지수 consumer price index
소비자신뢰 consumer confidence
소비자신용 consumer credit
소비자신용보호법 Consumer Credit Protection Act
소비자신용정보 consumer credit report
소비자업무정보서비스실(SEC) Office of Consumer Affairs and Information Service(SEC)
소비자지출 consumer expenditure; consumer spending
소비자행동 consumer's behavior
소비재 consumer goods
소비지출관련주 retail and consumer spending sector stock
소비할당 consumption quota
소비함수 consumption function
소비회복 rebound in spending
소손해면책 excess
소송 institution of law suits, lawsuits; legal

action
소송각하 non-suit
소송당사자 parties to lawsuit
소송대상이 될 만한 과실 actionable negligence
소송방기 abandonment of action
소송방식 form of action
소송비용 legal cost
소송비용담보 security for costs
소송원인 cause of action
소송원인발생 accrual of cause of action
소송을 분리함 severance of actions
소송인 suitor
소송절차 procedure
소송중복 multiplicity of action
소송중지 stay of proceedings
소수대표법 minority representation
소수점이하 버림 disregard of decimal places
소수주주 minority shareholders
소수주주권 minority shareholders' right
소수주주지분 minority interest
소수주주지분매입 minority buy-out
소수지배 minority control
소순환 minor cycle
소스 saucer
소액감가상각자산 petty-sum depreciable assets
소액감모자산 petty-sum wasting property
소액거래 small lot trading
소액거치자산 small sum deferred assets
소액공채별 한도비과세제도 tax free small-sum public bond investment system
소액금융 small loan
소액노령연금 small sums of pension paid to old-age persons
소액매매 small lot trade
소액배당소득 small sums of dividend income
소액상각자산 petty-sum depreciable property
소액예금 petty deposits; small sum deposit
소액예금증권 small savers certificate
소액예저금 small sums of deposits and savings
소액자산 small sum properties
소액전도금 petty imprest
소액전불준비금 imprest cash fund
소액주문 small lot order
소액중요자산 small sum and important property
소액채권 baby bond
소액투자가 small investor
소액현금 petty cash
소액현금계정 petty cash account
소액현금예금 petty current deposit
소액현금제도 petty cash system
소액현금지불 petty cash payment
소액현금출납장 petty cash book
소요액 required amount
소유권 ownership right; proprietary right
소유권보류 reservation of ownership
소유권유보조항 overreaching clause
소유권이권 royalty interest
소유권이전 passage of title; transfer of ownership
소유권증 ownership certificate
소유권침해 infringement of ownership
소유기간 investment horizon
소유기간이율 horizon return
소유기간이익 yield for holding period
소유부동산 estate in possession
소유자 proprietor
소유자불명의 unclaimed
소유자지배 owner control
소유재고품 goods on hands
소유제품 finished goods on hand
소유주계정 proprietorship account
소유주지분 owner's equity
소재산업 basic industry
소재지 site; location
소죄 petty offense
소지인 holder
소지인불식;소지인출급식 payable to holder
소지재고수준 stock level

소지주 stock on hand
소지증권 securities in portfolio
소지채권 portfolio bond
소지캐시플로 retained cash flow
소지한 유동성 liquidity in hand
소지현금 ready money
소집 convocation
소집배심원명부 regular panel
소집절차 procedures for the convocation
소폭 narrow range; small margin
소폭상승 edge up
소폭왕래 narrow movement
소폭이익 small gain
소폭절상 small revaluation
소프트달러 soft dollar
소프트랜딩 soft landing
소프트론 soft loan
소형주 small capital stock; small-sized stock
소화하다;요약하다;침지하다 digest
속보 preliminary
속산표 caculating table
속성 attribute
속행 further directions
손금 charge against revenues; deductible expenses
손금불산입 exclusion from expenses
손금불산입교제비 entertainment expenses not qualifying for deduction
손금불산입조세과금 nondeductible taxes
손금산입 inclusion in expenses
손금산입상여 bonus payment entered into expenses
손금산입외국세 foreign tax deductible as expenses
손금산입한도액 amount allowable
손금산입할 수 있는 준비금 deductible reserve
손모 wear and tear
손상품 spoiled goods
손상품비 spoilage expenses
손실 loss
손실계상시기 time of recognizing loss
손실계정 loss account
손실도 없고 수익도 없음 no loss no profit
손실발생지 location of loss or damage
손실배분 loss allocation
손실보상증서 back bond
손실보전 making up for loss
손실신고서 final return in the case of loss
손실인식 loss recognition; recognition of losses
손실제외 exclusion of loss
손실준비금 loss provision
손실함수 loss function
손실환급 carry back of loss
손실회수율 loss recovery
손익 gain or loss; income and expenses; income summary; loss and gain; profit and loss
손익거래 profit and loss transaction
손익계산서 earning statement; income statement; loss and gain statement; profit and loss statement
손익계산서(순손실의 경우) statement of loss
손익계산서감사 income statement audit
손익계산서계정 income statement account
손익계산서등식 profit and loss equation
손익계산서분석 analysis of income statement
손익계산서비율 income statement ratio
손익계산서어프로치 income statement approach
손익계산서원칙 income statement principles
손익계산서의 보충자료 supplementary income statement information
손익계산서항목 items on income statement
손익계정 general profit and loss account; income account; loss and gain account; profit and loss account
손익법 profit and loss method
손익보고 profit and loss report
손익분기가격 break-even price
손익분기도표 break-even chart

손익분기분석 break-even analysis
손익분기시기 break-even time
손익분기이율 break-even yield
손익분기점 break-even point; profit and loss break-even point
손익분기점분석 break-even point analysis
손익분기채권가격 break-even bond price
손익분기환상장 exchange rate at break-even point
손익실현 realization of profit and losses
손익인식 recognition of gain and loss
손익통산 aggregation of profit and loss
손절주문 stop loss order
손해 damage
손해담보계약 guaranty insurance
손해를 끼치다 inflict a loss
손해를 피해 철수하다 loss cut
손해를 회복하다 recoup
손해방지비용 sue and labor charges
손해방지의무 duty to sue and labor
손해방지조항 sue and labor clause
손해배상 compensation for damage
손해배상금 liquidated damages
손해배상액 damaged payment
손해배상이자 moratory interest
손해배상청구 claim for damage
손해변제 compensation of the damage
손해보전계약서 letter of indemnity
손해보험 damage insurance; non-life insurance; property and liability insurance
손해보험공제 deduction for damage insurance; fire and other casualty insurance premiums deduction
손해보험대리점 non-life insurance agent
손해보험료공제 taxation allowance for non-life insurance premium
손해보험회사 non-life insurance company
손해분담 apportionment of loss
손해비용 loss due to spoiled work
손해사정 loss adjustment
손해액 amount of damage
손해율 loss ratio
손해전종목보험 general insurance
손해증명 proof of loss
손해통지조항 claim notice clause
솔라빌(1통 만의 수출어음) sola bill
솔벤시마진 solvency margin
송금수표 remittance check
송금통지서 remittance advice
송금환 mail transfer payable; money order; remittance bill; telegraphic transfer payable
송금환수표 demand draft
송달부 chit book
송장;청구서 invoice
쇠퇴산업 declining industry
쇼군 CB shogun convertible bond
쇼군채 shogun bond
쇼트 short
쇼트드로잉 short drawing
쇼트버터플라이 short butterfly
쇼트북 short book
쇼트스퀴즈 short squeeze
쇼트스트래들 short straddle
쇼트스트랩 short strap
쇼트스트랭글 short strangle
쇼트스트립 short strip
쇼트어카운트 short account
쇼트콜 short call
쇼트쿠폰 short coupon
쇼트포지션 short position
쇼트포지션리스크 short position risk
쇼트풋 short put
쇼핑어라운드 shopping around
수검성변동 convergent fluctuation
수권사채 authorized bond
수권자본 authorized capital; stock authorized
수권주식 authorized shares
수금불능예상액 estimated uncollectable amount
수금수수료 charge for collection
수금어음관리서비스 management service for bill for collection

수금채무 debt for collection
수금환 exchange for collection; telegraphic transfer receivable
수금환;역환 bill receivable
수급 demand and supply; supply and demand
수급갭 gap between supply and demand
수급권부여 vesting
수급밸런스 demand-and-supply balance
수급자격 benefit eligibility
수납계정 receiving
수납기관 agency to receive tax
수납보고서 receiving report
수납인 reception stamp
수동적인 수탁자 bare trustee
수락 assent
수량과부족용인조건 more or less terms
수량실질성의 원칙 quantitative substantiality test
수량조정 quantity adjustment
수량표 bill of quantities
수량표준 quantity standard
수량할인 quantity discount
수량화 수단 quantitative tool
수렴 convergence
수렴하다 converge
수령증 accountable receipt
수로주변감시관 water-bailiff
수리경제학 mathematical economics
수리손익 actuarial gains or losses
수리용 재료 material for repair
수리적인 책임준비금 mathematical reserve
수리철회 withdrawl of receipt
수리통계 mathematical statistics
수리하다; 받아들이다 accept
수법 approach; method; tool
수비의무계약 secrecy agreement
수선 overhauling; repair
수선공장 repair-shop
수선보증예비금 liabilities for guarantee against repairs
수선비 maintenance and repairs; repairing cost
수선비 repairing expenses
수선비예산 repairing budget
수선수당금 allowance for repairs
수선유지비 repairs and maintenance
수선준비금 reserve for repairs
수선준비금편입 provision for repairs
수선중 under repair
수선평균적립금 repair equalization reserve
수세과 section of revenue; taxation division
수세관 revenue officer; tax collector
수송방법 mode of transportation
수송비 transportation cost
수수료 concession; fee and commission
수수료 각자지불 each way
수수료;비용 charge
수수료계정 commission account
수수료공제전 before fees
수수료매매 commission sale; sales and purchases on commission
수수료명세서 commission schedule
수수료반환 refund of fees
수수료사업 fee business
수수료수입 commission income; fee income; income from fees
수수료요율 commission rate
수수료차감후 less fees
수수료할인업자 discounters
수수료환급전 before refund of fees
수술비보험 surgical expense insurance
수신업무 deposit taking business
수신인 addressee
수약자 promisee
수요가격탄력성 price elasticity of supply and demand
수요감소 slowing demand
수요곡선 demand curve
수요부족 demand deficiency
수요분석 demand analysis
수요압력 demand pressure
수요예측 demand forecasting

수요일요인 Wednesday-factor
수요지수 demand index
수요탄력성 demand elasticity
수요탄성치 elasticity of demand
수요함수 demand function
수요회복 pickup in demand
수용보상금 compensation for expropriation
수용환지 nontaxable exchange of properties
수의계약 negotiated contracts; private contract
수익 earnings
수익경향 trend of earnings
수익계상시기 time of recognizing gain
수익곡선 revenue curve
수익관련지표 profit ratio indices
수익구조 profit profile
수익권 beneficiary interest; beneficiary right; right of beneficiary
수익기업 beneficiary company
수익력 earning capacity; earning power
수익력 커버리지 earning coverage
수익률 earning rate; rate of returns
수익률교차 differential of return
수익률의 상관관계 correlation of return
수익률이 높은 profitable
수익률측정 measure of return
수익리스크 earnings risk
수익면에서 in terms of revenue
수익모델 earnings model
수익보상금 compensation for revenue
수익보험증권 Policy Proof of Interest
수익분포 revenue distribution
수익비용대응의 원칙 principle of matching costs with revenues
수익비율 ratio of expenses to revenues
수익사채 profit debenture
수익성 profitability
수익성분석 profitability and investment analysis ratio
수익성지표 profitability index
수익세 earning tax; profit tax
수익실현 realization of gains
수익실현 revenue realization
수익안정성 earnings stability
수익예측 earnings outlook; profit forecast; revenue projection
수익예측컨센서스 consensus on earnings estimate
수익유보율 earnings retention rate
수익을 얻기 위한 경제활동 business activities bring profit
수익을 원본에 편입하는 형태의 투자신탁 accumulation trust
수익인식기준 revenue recognizing standard
수익자 beneficiary; pernor
수익자부담금 payment by beneficiary
수익자부담원칙 beneficiary principle
수익자산 earning assets
수익잔고계정 balance of revenue account
수익적립금액 revenue reserve amount
수익증가 augmentation of earnings
수익증권 beneficiary certificate; beneficiary interest certificate; beneficiary securities
수익지출 revenue expenditure
수익체감의 법칙 law of diminishing return
수익취득자 pernor of profits
수익회복 earnings recovery
수입결제어음제도 import settlement bill system
수입계정 revenue account
수입과징금 import surcharge
수입국 import country; recipient country
수입규제 import restriction
수입금액 amount received
수입금융 import financing
수입금지품 contraband; contraband of import
수입담보화물보관증 trust receipt
수입대체 import substitute
수입량 import volume
수입무역관리 import control
수입물가지수 import price index
수입보증금 guarantee money received; import guarantee money
수입보증료 guarantee fee received

수입보험료 premium income
수입비율 import ratio
수입성향 propensity to import
수입세 import duty; import tax; impost
수입세표 import duties tariff
수입수수료 commission received
수입승인증 import license
수입시기 time of receipts
수입신고 declaration of import
수입신용 import credit
수입어음 import bill
수입어음결제상장 acceptance rate
수입유전스 import usance
수입의존도 degree of dependence upon imports
수입이자 및 배당금 interest and dividends received
수입인지 revenue stamp
수입인지세법 stamp duty law
수입인플레 inflation led by import
수입인플레이션 import inflation
수입자금대부제도 import financing system
수입증가 augmentation
수입증거금 margin deposit; received margin
수입카르텔 import cartel
수입통관 import clearance
수입특허권사용료 royalties received for use of patents
수입할당 import quota
수입함수 import function
수입허가 import permit
수입현금 cash received
수정 modification
수정;변경 amendment
수정가속상각법 modified accelerated cost recovery system
수정기입 adjusting entry
수정발행신고서 amended shelf registration statement
수정법률 revised statutes
수정베타수치 adjusted beta value
수정분개 adjusting journal entry
수정사항결정 determination of the necessary adjustments
수정순미니멈세 adjusted net minimum tax
수정신고 amended return; revised return
수정양로보험계약 modified endowment
수정예산 amended budget; revised budget
수정원가주의 adjusted cost basis
수정자본주의 modified capitalism
수정재무제표 modified accounts
수정주주자본 adjusted equity
수정총소득 adjusted gross income
수정취득원가 adjusted historical cost
수정평균주가 revised average stock price
수정포괄주의 modified all-inclusive theory
수정하다 amend
수정회귀분석 adjusted regression analysis
수정후 restated
수정후 순이익 adjusted net profit
수주 receipt of orders
수주액 order volume
수주잔액 order backlog
수주잔고 orders in hand
수주증가 order increase
수준 level
수준유지 unchange
수중에 있는 채권 bond in portfolio
수증자산 watered assets
수증주식 watered stock
수지결산 settlement of accounts
수지결산서 statement of settlement of accounts
수지계산서 statement of receipts and disbursement
수지계정 balance of accounts
수지를 동반하지 않는 재무활동 noncash financing activities
수지를 동반하지 않는 투자활동 noncash investing activities
수지를 수반하지 않는 거래 non-fund transactions

수지방정식 income and expenditure equation
수지부기 receipt and payment bookkeeping
수지분기점 cash break-even point; receipts and disbursements break- even point
수지분석 cash flow analysis
수지상등의 원칙 principle of equivalence
수지예측 cash forecasts
수지일람표 statement of income and expense
수지지출 receipts and payments
수직분석 vertical analysis
수직상승 straight climb
수직적 컴비네이션 bottom vertical combination
수직적인 **M&A** vertical M&A
수직적인 고객제한 vertical territorial customer restrictions
수직적인 국제분업 vertical specialization
수직적인 무역 vertical trade
수직통합 vertical integration
수직합병 vertical merger
수집 capture
수집물포괄보험 collection floater
수축 contraction
수출경쟁 export competition
수출관련주 export stocks
수출구성 export mix
수출금융 export financing
수출금지 embargo
수출금지품 contraband of export
수출대금 export proceeds
수출드라이브 export drive
수출면세 export exemption
수출물가지수 export price index
수출변동보상융자제도 cooperative financing facility
수출보조금 export subsidy
수출부조 disappointing export
수출산업 export industry
수출세 export duties; export tax
수출승인 approval of export license
수출승인증 export license
수출신고 export declaration
수출신용 export credit; shipper's usance
수출신용보증 export credit guarantee
수출신용장 export letter of credit
수출신장 export growth
수출어음 export bill
수출업자신용 export supplier credit
수출유전스 export usance
수출의 수익성 export profitability
수출의존 export dependence
수출의존도 degree of dependence upon exports
수출이익 export earnings
수출인수어음 trade acceptance
수출입론 export import loan
수출입물가지수 export and import price index
수출입은행 EXIM bank; export-import bank
수출자주규제 voluntary export restraint; voluntary restriction of export
수출장려금 export bounty
수출전대계정 export advanced account
수출전대금융 export advance loan
수출전도금 export advance
수출카르텔 export cartel
수출함수 export function
수출허가 export permission
수취가임 house rent received
수취계정;외상매출금;미수금계정 account receivable
수취계정기준상장 receiving quotation
수취고 amount of proceeds
수취금 amount receivable; proceeds
수취배당금 dividend earned; dividend received
수취배당금익금불산입 dividend excluded from income
수취배당손금불산입 exclusion of dividends from gross revenue
수취수수료 commission earned
수취어음 draft receivable; notes receivable; notes and bills receivable; acceptance receivable

수취어음기입장 notes receivable register
수취이자 interest earned; interest receivable; interest received
수취인 payee
수취채권 notes and accounts receivable; trade receivables
수취할인료 discount earned
수치적분법 numerical integration
수탁 acceptance of order; bailment
수탁거래 transaction effected by member for the accounts of others; transaction for customers' accounts
수탁거래증거금 clearing margin for customer's account
수탁계약준칙 Brokerage Agreement Standards
수탁계약준칙특례 Special Rule for Brokerage Agreement Standards
수탁매매 broking
수탁매부전도금 advance received on indents
수탁은행 trustee bank
수탁자 bailor; assignee; fiduciary; trustee
수탁자배상책임보험 bailee's liability insurance
수탁자산 capital committed
수탁자책임 fiduciary responsibility; prudent person rule
수탁제한 restriction of order acceptance
수탁증거금 brokerage margin; customer's margin
수탁취급장소 place of fiduciary
수탁판매 sales on consignment
수탁판매입체금 advance on consignment-in
수탁품 goods on consignment-in; consigned goods
수탁회사 trustee company
수평무역 horizontal trade
수평분단 horizontal split
수평분석 horizontal analysis
수평분업 horizontal specialization
수평스프레드 horizontal spread
수평승수 horizontal multiplier
수평적 horizontal
수평적인 감사 horizontal audit
수평적인 국제분업 horizontal international specialization
수평적인 **M&A** horizontal M&A
수평합병 horizontal merger
수평형 통합 horizontal integration
수표기입장 check register
수표발행지 check drawer
수표발행한도 limit of overdrawn account
수표법 check act
수표장 check book
수표장원부 checkbook stub
수표제도 checking system
수표지불인 check drawee
수표지정인 check holder
수하인 consignee
수확기준 crop basis
순가격 net price; net value
순고정자산 net tangible assets
순과세재산 net taxable assets
순교역조건지수 index of net terms of trade
순금융수입 net export
순금전항목 net monetary items
순농지평가 valuation of farmland
순당좌자산 net quick assets
순대손상각 net write-off
순매상고 net sales
순매상고총계 aggregate net sales
순매연결 net short hedging
순무역편향성장 pro-trade biased growth
순보험료비율 retention quotient
순부채 net debt; net liabilities
순분검정소 assay office
순산출 net output
순상속재산 net succession
순상품교역조건 net commodity terms of trade
순생산고 net production value
순손실 net loss

순손실이월 carry forward of net operating loss; carry over of net loss
순손실환급 carry back of net loss
순손익 net profit or loss
순손익계산 net profit or loss account
순손익구분 net profit or loss section
순수거치총신연금 pure deferred life annuity
순수스와프 pure swap
순수위험 pure risk
순수익 net return
순수입보험료 net premium
순수채권 ex-warrant bond
순수취금 net receipt
순수취액 net avails; net proceeds
순수취이자 net interest income
순수한 물;진수 real water
순실현가능가격 net realizable value
순실현캐피탈게인 net realized capital gain
순액(純額)베이스 net base
순액주의 net amount principle
순영업손실 net operating loss
순영업순환일수 net operating cycle
순영업이익 net operating profit
순운전시간 net cycle time
순운전자본 net working capital
순원가 net cost
순월확정일상장 outright forward rates fixed date
순월확정일인도 outright forward fixed date delivery
순유동성수지 net liabilities balance
순유동자산 net current assets
순이월비용 net carryover cost
순이익 net earnings; net profit
순이익대비총수익비율 ratio of net profit to gross revenues
순이익률 net income ratio
순이익에 대한 지분 equity in earnings
순이자 net interest
순이자비용 net interest cost
순익 absolute profit; net income
순익률 net profit ratio
순익처분 appropriation of net income; disposition of net income
순일드 normal yield curve; positive curve; positive yield
순일수 clear days
순잉여금 actual surplus; net surplus
순자산 net assets; net worth; net worth equity
순자산가액 net assets value
순자산가치 net asset value
순자산계산서 statement of net assets
순자산인수액 acceptance price of net assets
순자유준비 net free reserves
순장부가액 net book value
순저축 net saving
순조 favorable
순조로운 매상 steady sales
순조로운 매상신장 healthy revenue growth
순조로운 소비 smooth consumption
순조로운 회복 brisk recovery
순증가 net increase
순지분자산 net equity assets
순차입준비 net borrowed reserves
순채권 net receivable
순투자 net investment
순풍개입 intervention following market
순할인채 pure discount bond
순현금유입 net cash inflows
순현재가치 net present value
순화폐포지션 net monetary position
순환변동 cyclical fluctuation
순환불황 cyclical depression
순환성장 cyclical growth
순환주 cyclical stock; cyclicals
순회감사 traveling audit
순회수가능액 net collectible amounts
순회재판소 circuit court
순회판매인 travelling salesman
숫자상으로 in number
쉐어드래프트 share drafts
쉽게 회복되지 않는 상태 insurmountable

difficulty
슈퍼 301조 301 super Article
슈퍼골드트란시 super gold tranche
슈퍼나우계정 super NOW account
슈퍼메이저터리조항 super majority provision
슈퍼바이저 supervisor
슈퍼프라임레이트 super prime rate
스로우백원칙 throw-back rule
스루풋조항 through-put contract
스몰(100만달러 단위의 거래) small
스몰스프레드 small spread
스무딩아웃오퍼레이션 smoothing out operation
스미소니언레이트 Smithsonian rate
스미소니언체제 Smithsonian system
스미소니언합의 Smithsonian Agreement
스스로 붙임 trade on one's own account
스시본드 sushi bond
스와프 swap
스와프가격 swap price
스와프거래 swap deal; swap trading; swap transaction
스와프결제시스템 swaps clearing system
스와프레이트 swap rate
스와프레이트의 최저권 swap rate basement
스와프를 구입하다 long the swap
스와프를 단기로 하다 short the swap
스와프마진 swap margin
스와프브로커 swap broker
스와프비드레이트 swap bid rate
스와프스트라이크 swap strike
스와프스프레드 swap spread
스와프스프레드커브 swap spread curve
스와프오퍼레이트 swap offer rate
스와프이익 swap profit
스와프채 swap bond
스와프코스트 swap cost
스와프쿠폰 swap coupon
스와프포트폴리오 swap portfolio
스와프협정 swap agreement; swap arrangement
스왑션 swaption
스웨덴 종합지수 Jacobson & Ponsbach General Index
스위스프랑기준채 Swiss franc note
스위치금융 switch finance
스위치백옵션 switch-back option
스위프트; SWIFT Society for Worldwide International Financial Telecommunications
스윕어카운트 sweep account
스윙 swing
스윙론 swing loan
스윙퍼실리티 swing facilities
스캔들 scandal
스케줄페이먼트 schedule payment
스퀘어 square
스퀘어포지션 square position
스타시스템 star system
스태그플레이션 stagflation
스탠다드앤드푸어스 Standard & Poor's
스탠다드앤드푸어스 400종 공업주가지수 Standard & Poor's 400 Industrial
스탠다드앤드푸어스 500종 Standard & Poor's 500
스탠다드앤드푸어스 500종 주가지수 Standard & Poor's 500 index
스탠다드앤드푸어스종합지수 Standard & Poor's Composite Index
스탠다드앤드푸어스주가지수 Standard & Poor's Stock Price Index
스탠드바이 IMF stand-by IMF
스탠드바이신용장 stand-by credit
스탠드바이약정 stand-by agreement
스탠드바이크레디트;스탠드바이신용장 standby credit
스탠드바이퍼실리티 standby facilities
스탠드스틸 standstill
스탠드스틸조항 standstill provision
스텝다운채 step-down bond
스텝상환 step ladder payment method
스텝업스와프 step-up swap
스텝업채 step-up bond

스텝업쿠폰 step-up coupon
스톡마인드 stock mind
스톡보너스플랜 stock bonus plan
스톡옵션행사 exercise of stock option
스톡옵션형 워런트 stock option type warrant
스톡워런트 stock warrants
스톡인플레이션 stock inflation
스톡조정 stock adjustment
스톡플로 stock flow
스톱고 limit high; limit up; stop-high
스톱로스주문 stop-loss order
스톱로스트레이딩 stop-loss trading
스톱앤드고정책 stop-and-go policy
스톱저 limit down; limit low
스톱치 maximum limit of fluctuation
스트래들 straddle
스트래들거래 straddle trading
스트래들포지션거래 straddle position transaction
스트랩 strap
스트랭글 strangle
스트랭글포지션거래 strangle position transaction
스트레이트커런시스와프 straight currency swap
스트레이트타임즈공업주가지수 Straits Times Industrial Index
스트롱폼 strong form
스트립 strip
스트립금리캡 stripped interest rate cap
스트립보증 strip guarantee
스트립상품 stripped issue
스트립스프레드 strip spread
스트립일드 strip yield
스트립제로쿠폰 stripped zero-coupon
스트립채 separate trading of registered interest and principal of securities
스트립채 strip bond; strips
스트립캡 stripped cap
스트립커브 strip curve
스트립플레이어 strip player
스페셜리스트 specialist
스페셜리스트북 specialist book
스페셜리엔 special lien
스페셜브래킷그룹 special bracket group
스페셜크레디트 special credit
스페이스재정 space arbitrage
스페인은행안내장 Bank of Spain Circular
스펙터 specter
스펙터분석 spectral analysis
스포츠도박 sports gambling
스폰서의 리스크허용도 sponsor tolerance to risk
스폰서의 선택력 sponsor selectivity
스폰서의 역할 sponsor's role
스폿금리 spot yield
스폿기간 spot period
스폿넥스트 spot next
스폿펀드 spot fund
스폿포워드 spot forward
스풀릿 split
스프레드 spread
스프레드 TED spread TED
스프레드거래 spread transaction
스프레드거래 TED spread trading TED
스프레드계정 spread account
스프레드곡선 spread curves
스프레드록계약 spread lock agreement
스프레드론 spread loan
스프레드리스크 spread risk
스프레드뱅킹 spread banking
스프레드수입 spread income
스프레드시트 spread sheet
스프레드트레이딩 spread trading
스프레드포지션 spread position
스피드레지스턴스라인 speed resistance line
스핀오프 spin-off
슬라이드관세 sliding tariff
슬라이딩칩 sliding cheap
슬럼프플레이션 slumpflation
승객배상책임보험 passenger liability insurance
승계 succession

승계담보 linear warranty
승법효과 multiplier effect
승수분석 multiplier analysis
승수이론 multiplier theory
승인 acknowledgment; approval; authorization; cognizance
승인되지 않은 자산 inadmitted assets
승인된 의무 obligation to acquire the approval
승인등본 attested copy
승인딜러 authorized dealer
승인신청 application for approval
시가 current price; opening price; opening quotation; opening rate; present market value; running price
시가가치 mark-to-market value
시가개산액 approximate market price
시가기준 mark-to-market basis
시가발행 issue at market price
시가발행주식 stock issue at market price
시가발행증자 capital increase by new shares at market price
시가방식 current cost method
시가법 market method; market value method; valuation at selling price
시가분석 market value analysis; mark-to-market analysis
시가상승 appreciated market price
시가상환 redemption at market value
시가와 종가 opening rate closing rate
시가일 mark-to-market date
시가전환 conversion at market price
시가주의 market price basis; market value basis
시가주의 명목가치회계 current cost / nominal dollar accounting
시가주의 안정가치회계 current cost / constant dollar accounting
시가주의회계 fair value accounting
시가총액 aggregate market value; market cap
시가총액 가중인덱스 capitalization weighted indices
시가총액가중평균치 weighted average of market capitalization
시가총액방식주가지수 stock price index on the market value
시가평가계정 mark-to-market account
시가평가액 assessed market value
시가회계 current value accounting; market value accounting
시간가중수익률 time weighted return
시간가치 time value
시간가치감가 depreciation of time value
시간경과에 따른 over time
시간경과에 따른 채권가격 over time price of bond
시간선호 time preference
시간스프레드 time spread
시간우선 time precedence
시간우선의 원칙 time priority
시간원가 time cost
시간적인 요소 time factor
시간조정필 time adjusted
시간차이 time variance
시간효과 time effect
시계열데이터 time series data
시계열변동 time series behavior
시계열분석 time series analysis
시기가 어긋남 timing mismatch
시기경과선하증권 stable B/L
시나리오분석 scenario analysis
시니어트레이더 senior trader
시담 private settlement; settlement out of court
시담해결 out-of-court settlement
시드니선물거래소 Sydney Futures Exchange
CD 시장 CD market
시리즈 series
시뮬레이션 simulation
시민단체 civil group
시방서원가 specification cost
시산 trial
시산베이스 pro forma figure
시산표 trial balance sheet; working trial

balance sheet
시산표를 작성함 making a trial balance
시세;시가;가격표 price quotation
시세가 낮을 때 물러남 closing lower
시세가 내리는 상태 downward movement
시세가 내릴 것을 예상하고 증권을 매각함 going short
시세가 내릴 때 매입하다 buy on reaction
시세가 높을 때 물러남 closing high
시세가 오르락내리락함 range trading
시세가 오를 것을 예상하고 증권을 매입함 going long
시세가 오를 듯한 기세 strong tone; firmer tone
시세가 조금씩 오르는 경향 creep back upwards
시세가 폭락함 straight fall
시세가 회복되다 rally
시세가격 indicated price; indicative price
시세난조 violent fluctuation
시세를 높게 부르다 quoting high
시세를 예상하여 매각함 short sale against the box
시세변동으로 매매차익금이 적어지다 narrow spread; narrowing of spread
시세에 파동을 일으키다 bull the market
시세정보교환센터 quotation exchange center
시세표시 indicated bid-asked quotation
시세하락을 예견하고 팔았는데 반대로 시세가 상승하여 손해를 감수하고 환매한 탓에 일시적으로 시세가 상승함 bear squeeze market
시세하락을 예상하고 매각함 hedge selling
시송품 goods on approval
시스템 system audit
시스템공학 system engineering
시스템레포 system repos
시스템리스크 system risk
시스템문제 system issue
시스템어프로치 system approach
시스템호가 system bid and offer
시스티매틱리스크 systematic risk
시용기간 trial employment period; trial period
시용판매 approval sales; sales on approval
시용판매미수금 account due from sales on approval
시운전비 trial running expenses
시읍면담배세 municipal tobacco tax
시읍면세 municipal inhabitants tax
시작 trial manufacture
시작기 pilot unit
시작비 experimental manufacturing cost; testing expenses
시작품 trial product
시작품원가 preproduction cost
시작하자마자 Just after the opening
시장 market place
시장가격 market price; market value
시장가격가중평균지수 market value weighted index
시장가치가중 capitalization weighted
시장간 inter-market
시장간 거래시스템 inter-market trading system
시장간 경쟁 competition among markets
시장간 스프레드 inter-market spread; intermarket spread
시장감응도 market sensitivity
시장개방 market opening
시장개혁 market reform
시장개황 market overview
시장경제 market economy
시장경제모델 market discount rate; market economy model
시장관행 market practice
시장구조 market structure
시장규제국(SEC) Division of Market Regulation(SEC)
시장규제완화 market liberalisation
시장균형 market equilibrium
시장균형곡선 market equilibrium curve
시장금리 prevailing rate

시장금리연동형 대출 money market loan
시장금리연동형 정기예금 money market certificate
시장기구를 평가함 evaluation of market mechanism
시장기회 market opportunity
시장내 intramarket
시장내부요인 technical position
시장동향 at the market; market behavior; market data
시장모델 market model
시장반응 response of market
시장방해 forestalling the market
시장베타 market beta
시장변동성 market volatility
시장분단이론 segmentation theory
시장분석 market analysis
시장분석가 Street economist
시장분위기 market quotation
시장삭감 market extinction
시장상실 missing the market
시장상장;실세레이트 market rate
시장성 marketability
시장성이 있는 merchantable
시장성이 있는 주문 marketable order
시장성이 있는 채권 marketable debt securities
시장성증권 marketable securities
시장섹터 market sector
시장센티멘트 market sentiment
시장수요 market demand
시장수요곡선 market demand curve
시장시가총액 market capitalization
시장실세이율 prevailing interest rate
시장심리 market psychology
시장안정조작 market stabilization
시장에 대한 영향 market impact
시장에 맞추어 above market
시장연동형 우대금리 floating prime rate
시장예측 market consensus; market expectation; market prediction
시장외거래 off-board transactions
시장원리 market discipline; market mechanism
시장원리 market principle
시장을 어지럽히다 bear raiding; raiding the market
시장을 조종함 market milking
시장의 경향 market mood
시장의 기조 market rhythm
시장의 대부분을 점유하다 dominate the market
시장의 두터움 depth of market
시장의 실패 market failure
시장의 완전성 market integrity
시장의 주기 market cycle
시장의 주도주 market leaders
시장의 효율성 market efficiency
시장의 힘 market momentum
시장이론 market theory
시장이율 market yield
시장이자율 market rate of interest
시장점유율 market share
시장조사 market research; market study; market survey
시장지배 market control
시장지수 market index
시장질서유지협정 orderly marketing agreement
시장참가자 market player
시장창조효과 market creating effect
시장침투 market penetration
시장타이밍을 평가함 market timing assessment
시장타이밍평가 assessment of market timing
시장통합 single market
시장평가 market valuation
시장포트폴리오 market portfolio
시장행동 market conduct
시장확장효과 market expansion effect
시장후퇴 market exiting
시제품평가 valuation of work in process
시조례 municipal ordinance

시중금리 market interest rate; money market rate; open market rate
시중대출 commercial bank discount and loan
시중상장 free market price; open market quotation
시중소화국채 subscription of bonds by non-government funds
시중은행;상업은행 commercial bank
시중은행의 할인율상회 back spread; negative interest rate spread
시중은행의 할인율상회시장 inverted market; backwardation market
시차설 time difference theory
시카고상공회의소 Chicago Mercantile Exchange
시카고상품거래소 Chicago Board of Trade
시카고옵션거래소 Chicago Board Options Exchange
시카고학파 Chicago school
CP 시장 CP market
시한입법 law with expiration date
시행 enforcement
시행규칙 enforcement regulations
시행세칙 detailed enforcement regulations
시행일 date of enforcement; enforcement day
시험 testing
시험연구비 experimental and research expense
시험연구비세액공제 experimental and research expense tax credit
시험연구비특별공제 credit for experimental and research expense
시험연구용 자산 property for experimental and research
시험조사 testing audit
시험판매 test marketing
시황 quotation; tone
시황가격 bid and ask quotation
시황관망 wait and see
시황보고 market report
시황보도시스템 Market Information System
시황상황 running of the market
시황정보 market information
시황정보센터 market information center
시황정보시스템 market information system
시황회복 market recovery
시효 prescription; status of limitation
시효정지 suspension of statute of limitations
시효취득 adverse possession
식량관리특별회계 Food Management Special Account
식량증권 food bill; Food Securities
식료품업계 foods industry
신가보험 replacement value insurance
신경질적인 시장 nervous market
신고 declaration; registration
신고 및 납부 return and payment
신고가격 value declared
신고계획서 prospectus for securities registration
신고기한 due date of filing return; due date of the tax return
신고납세 assessment of taxes; self-assessment of taxation; tax payment by self-assessment
신고납세액 income tax self-assessed
신고마감일 deadline for filing
신고사항 matters to be notified
신고서공시 public notification of returns
신고서를 공동제출함 joint submission of return
신고서제출기한내 within the due date of filing the return
신고세 taxes assessed by taxpayers
신고소득세 assessment of income tax; self-assessed income tax
신고시간연장승인 approval of extension of time to file
신고용지 declaration form; return blank
신고의무 obligation to file return
신고의무가 있는 법인 corporation subject to filing return
신고조정 adjustment in filing a final tax return

신고치 all-time high; new high
신고후 사용제 file and use
신공업국군 newly industrialized countries
신규계정 new account
신규구인수 new job offers
신규구입 open buying
신규대출 new lending; new loan
신규매출 open selling
신규모기지 new mortgage
신규모기지발행시장 primary mortgage market
신규발행 new issue
신규발행사채 newly issued corporate bond
신규발행채권을 발행함 issuance of new debt
신규발행후 시장 after market
신규분야 new field
신규상장 initial listing; new listing
신규상장수수료 fees for original listing
신규상장신청서 applicant for intial listing; applicant for original listing
신규상장회사 newly listed company
신규수주 new order
신규자금 new money
신규자본 fresh capital
신규재원채 new foreign resource bonds
신규주식공모 initial public offering
신규참가사업 green field business
신규프리미엄 new premium
신금융조절 new monetary adjustment system
신기원을 열다 blazing a trail
신디케이트간사 syndicate manager
신디케이트구성 syndicate composition
신디케이트단 syndication
신디케이트론 syndicated credit
신디케이트인수 syndicate underwriting
신디케이트참가자격 eligibility for syndicate membership
신뢰 confidence
신뢰계수 confidence coefficient
신뢰관계 confidential relation
신뢰구간 confidence interval
신뢰도 confidence level
신뢰를 배신한 자 traitor
신뢰성 reliability
신뢰조건 confidence building
신발채 new bond; primary paper
신발채를 발행함 new debt issues
신발채시장 primary bond market
신분증명서 identification card
신생산방식을 독점함 exclusive use of a new production
신선물 new futures
신설비 new capacity
신세틱론 synthetic long
신세틱세큐리티제이션 synthetic securitization
신세틱쇼트 synthetic short
신세틱채권 synthetic bond
신세틱캐시 synthetic cash instrument
신세틱풋 synthetic put
신속한 재판 speedy trial
신속한 조정 resiliency
신시내티증권거래소 Cincinnati Stock Exchange
신시장개척 expansion of a new market
신안(新案) new design; novelty
신안등록 registration of a new design
신안채 new face bond
신외국환관리법 new foreign exchange law
신용 및 보증보험 credit and suretyship insurance
신용감사 credit audit
신용감시시스템 credit watch system
신용거래 margin trading
신용거래계정 accounts of margin transaction
신용거래대부금 loans in margin transactions
신용거래대주수입금 margin for stocks lent
신용거래대출 customer's loan
신용거래에서 매출잔고가 매수잔고를 웃도는 상황 buyer's over
신용거래위탁증거금 margin collateral
신용거래융자잔고 adjusted debit balance
신용거래잔고 open interest in margin

ㅅ ㅇ

transactions
신용거래주 stock for margin trading
신용격차 credit spread
신용경색 liquidity crunch
신용공급 supply of credit
신용공여 credit accommodation; extension of credit; granting credit
신용공여한도 committed line of credit; liquidity facility
신용공여화 swing line
신용공황 credit crisis
신용구매 shares bought on margin; margin purchase
신용구매의 평균단위 average margin buying price
신용구입 margin buying
신용금고 shinkin bank
신용기회균등 equal credit opportunity
신용대출 credit loan
신용도 credibility; credit quality; creditworthiness
신용등급 medium rating
신용등급부여 credit rating
신용력 credit capability; credit strength; credit worthiness
신용력이 있는 creditworthy
신용리스크 credit exposure
신용리스크가 없는 risk free
신용보강 credit support
신용보완 credit enhancement
신용보증 credit guarantee
신용보증회사 credit guarantee company; financial guarantor
신용보험 credit insurance; fidelity bond
신용분석 analysis of credit
신용불량자리스트 negative list
신용불안 credit concern
신용비율 credit ratio
신용상태 credit standing condition; credit standing
신용생명보험 credit life insurance
신용압박 tight credit
신용어음 credit bill
신용완화 credit ease
신용외상거래처 credit customer
신용위험 commercial risk
신용을 실추시키다 ruin the reputation
신용잔고 outstanding balances of credit
신용장 letter of credit
신용장 없는 어음매입률 buying rate without credit
신용장개설보증금 L/C margin money
신용장발행수수료 opening charge
신용장발행은행 letter or credit issuing bank
신용장발행의뢰인 accredited party; opener
신용장보증부 할인어음 documented discount note
신용장부 일람불어음매입률 at sight buying rate with credit
신용장상의 매주 accredited buyer
신용장수익자 L/C beneficiary; letter of credit beneficiary
신용장양도 transfer of transferable credit
신용장이 없는 일람불어음매입상장 without credit at sight buying rate
신용장통지은행 letter of credit advising bank
신용장확인수수료 confirming charge
신용장확인은행 L/C confirming bank; letter of credit confirming bank
신용저하 credit decline
신용정보 credit records
신용정보센터 credit bureau
신용정책 credit policy
신용제도 credit system
신용제한 credit crunch; credit rationing
신용조건 credit terms
신용조사 credit investigation
신용조사기관 inquiry agency
신용조합 credit union; cooperative bank; credit association
신용조합단말 credit authorization terminal
신용조합환 credit union exchange

신용조회 credit inquiry; credit reference
신용증거금 credit margin
신용증권 bill of credit; credit instruments
신용창조 credit creation; money creation
신용창조론 theory of credit creation
신용카드 credit card
신용카드업무 credit card business
신용카드회사 credit card company
신용파생상품 credit derivatives
신용판단 credit decision
신용판매 shares sold short
신용평가 credit assessment
신용하지 않다 discredit
신용한도 credit ceiling; credit limit
신용한도제도 credit line system
신용할 수 있는 credible
신용화폐 credit money
신용환산계수 credit conversion factor
신원신용보험 fidelity guarantee insurance
신은행법 new banking law
신의성실의 원칙 just and equitable principle
신의신용채무 full-faith-and-credit debt
신의위반 breach of trust
신의칙위반 violation of just and equitable principles
신자원개발 exploitation of new resources
신저치 new low
신종보험;손해보증보험 casualty and surety insurance
신주 new share; new stock
신주가지수 new stock price indexes
신주락에 관계되는 증가신주 new shares issued through rights-offerings
신주발행 capitalization issue; new issue of stocks
신주발행비 new share issuing expense; new stock issuing expenses; share-issuing expense
신주부 cum new
신주분배; 할당 ex-allotment
신주불입금 paid-in advances
신주신청기한 time limit of the subscription for new stock
신주우선인수권 preemptive right
신주인수권 stock purchase warrant; common stock preemptive right; stock purchase right; subscription rights
신주인수권 행사 exercise of preemptive rights
신주인수권보 사채권 bonds with warrants to new shares
신주인수권부 cum right
신주인수권부 사채 bond with subscription warrant; bond with warrant attached
신주인수권부 사채권 bonds-cum-warrants
신주인수권증서 certificate of preemptive rights; certification of subscription rights; subscription warrant
신주인수권평가 valuation of preemptive right
신주일주당 지불가액 amount paid per new share
신주하락 new share off
신중인원칙 prudent man rule
신증권인수 underwriting of new issue securities
신청 instance
신청;동의 motion
신청금 application money; subscription money
신청심리일 motion day
신청에 따른 상장 listing by application
신청인 applicant; petitioner
신청일기준 application date base
신청증거금 advance on subscription
신청하여 취득하다 sue out
신청회원 applicant member
신축세율 flexible tariff
신축적립금 reserve for construction
신탁계약 fiduciary contract; trust agreement
신탁계정 trust account
신탁권한 fiduciary power
신탁기금 fiduciary fund; trust fund
신탁법 Trust Law
신탁보수 trust fee
신탁설 trust theory

신탁설정자 settlor; trustor
신탁수입 trust income
신탁약관 trust contract
신탁업 trust business
신탁업무 fiduciary business
신탁업회계 trust accounting
신탁예금 deposit in trust; trust deposit
신탁원본 trust principal
신탁은행 trust bank
신탁의무 fiduciary duty
신탁이익 profit from trust
신탁재산 fiduciary estate; trust assets; trust estate; trust property
신탁재산을 처분해서 발생한 매각이익 profit resulting from sale of the trust estate
신탁증권 trust securities
신탁증서 deed of trust; trust deed; trust indenture; trust instrument
신탁형연금 trust fund plan
신탁회계 fiduciary accounting
신탁회사 trust company
신파산법 Bankruptcy Reform Act of 1978
신품을 고가로 인수함 trade-in
신협회화물약관 New Institute Cargo Clauses
신형 금본위제 new type of gold standard
신화폐수량설 neo-quantity theory of money
신후생경제학 new welfare economics
신흥경제지역 emerging market
신흥기업 emerging corporation
신흥도시 boom town
신흥마켓 emerging markets
실가 actual value
실가법 actual value method
실가자산 actual assets
실권주 forfeited share
실권주 unclaimed stock
실린더 cylinder
실링방식 ceiling system
실무가 practitioner
실무수습생 articled clerk
실무적으로 가능한 practicable
실무적인 귀결 practicable consequence
실물자본 real capital
실물자산 real assets
실물투자 real investment
실비 actual expenses
실비정산계약 cost plus contract
실세레이트 effective rate
실세예금 deposit minus checks and bills on hand
실세예금 deposit on a net basis; net deposit
실세환상장 current exchange rate; real rate of exchange
실손전보 first-loss insurance
실손해 special damage
실수요 actual demand; consumer demand
실수원칙 actual demand rule
실시 implementation
실시간통신 real time communication
실시권 enforcement right
실시단계 implementation stage
실업 unemployment
실업급부 unemployment benefit
실업률감소 reducing unemployment rate
실업보험 unemployment compensation; unemployment insurance
실업보험지출 expenditure on unemployment benefit
실업율 unemployment rate
실용신안 industrial new design; utility model
실용신안권 utility model patent
실재계정 real account
실적기준 **PER** trailing PER
실적분석 historical analysis
실적상승 upswing on business results
실적예상 forecast of performance results
실적을 예상한 하향수정 downward revision on business results
실적이 좋지 않은 회사 unprofitable company
실정법 positive law
실제가격 actual price
실제가격변동율 effective volatility

실제거래행위 actual trading behavior
실제구입가액 actual purchase price
실제내용연수 actual useful life
실제로 카드를 사용하는 고객 active cardholder
실제배부율 actual burden rate
실제보다 전날일자로 하다 back dating
실제시장이율폭 current market yield spread
실제양도가액 actual transfer price
실제원가 actual cost
실제원가계산 actual cost method; actual costing
실제원가계산제도 actual cost accounting system
실제자본유지 maintenance of physical capital
실제재고 stock taking
실제전부원가계산 actual absorption costing
실제조사 visual inspection
실제조업도 actual volume
실제주의회계 actual basis accounting
실제지수 actual index price
실제취득원가주의 actual acquisition cost basis
실제판단 pragmatic judgment
실종된 채무자 absconding debtor
실증경제학 positive economics
실증분석 empirical analysis
실증연구 empirical study
실지감사 field audit
실지재고 actual inventory; physical counts
실지재고정리 physical inventory
실지조사 site survey
실질 GNP 성장률 real GNP growth rate
실질가처분소득 real disposable income
실질가치 real value
실질금리 real interest rate
실질단위 real term
실질단위노동코스트 real unit labor cost
실질베이스로 in real terms
실질성 검사 substantive test
실질성장 real growth
실질성장률 real growth rate
실질소득 effective income; real earnings; real income
실질소득자 real income earner
실질소득자과세의 원칙 principle of taxation on a substantial income earner
실질소유자 beneficial owner
실질순투자 real net investment
실질승수 real multiplier
실질연리 actual annual percentage rate
실질예금 real deposits
실질우선 substance over form
실질우선출자사원 beneficiary holders of preferred equity securities
실질원가 real cost
실질이율 real rate; real rate of return; real yield
실질이행 substantial performance
실질임금 real compensation
실질적인 substantive
실질적인 증거 substantial evidence
실질적인 트랜스퍼 real transfer
실질주의 principle of taxation on actual beneficiary
실질주주 beneficiary shareholder
실질주주명부 list of beneficiary shareholders
실질증거 substantive evidence
실질투자수익률 real investment return
실질투자자 real gross investment; beneficial investors
실질화폐 real money
실질화폐잔고효과 real balance effect
실책 blunder
실천 practice
실천경제 practical economy
실천세미나 practicable seminar
실체 entity
실체경제 real economy
실체법 substantive law
실체자본 physical capital
실체회계 entity accounting
실행가능한 feasible

실행기관 execution organ
실행예산 working budget
실현가격변동률 realized volatility
실현가능가액 realizable value
실현가치 realized value
실현감가상각 realized depreciation
실현손익 realized loss
실현수익 realized return; realized revenue
실현이익 realized gain; realized income; realized profit
실현주의 realization basis; realization principle
실현주의의 원칙 principle of realization
실현증가액 realized appreciation
실효가격 effective price
실효계약 lapsed contract
실효금리 actual interest rate; effective interest rate; effective rate of interest
실효보호율 effective rate of protection
실효성 efficacy
실효세공제후 after effective tax
실효세율 effective tariff; effective tax rate
실효수표 out-of-date check
실효스프레드 efficient spread
실효이율 effective yield; realized yield
실효적 지배 efficient allocation
실효주 lapsed share
실효환상장 effective exchange rate
심각한 문제 criteria issue
심리효과 psychological effect
심문 hearing
심사 examination; review; screening; scrutiny
심사기준 criteria for examination
심사료 examination fee
심사재결 examination and decision
심사청구 claim for examination
심사청구 request for reconsideration
심사청구기간 period of request for reconsideration
심판기관 tribunal
심판인 umpire
싱가폴국제금융거래소 Singapore International Monetary Exchange
싱가폴금거래소 Gold Exchange of Singapore
싱가폴예탁증서 Depository Receipts of Singapore
싱가폴은행간 기준금리 Singapore inter-bank offered rate
싱가폴통화감시청 Monetary Agency of Singapore
싱글옵션 single option
싸게 매입한 주를 시세가 올랐을 때 매각함 getting ashore
싸게 사다 buy on close
싸게 팔다 sell low
싸구려 물건 job lot
싼값 low price
쌍둥이 적자 twin deficits
쌍무계약 bilateral contract
쌍무계약 reciprocal contract
쌍무무역 bilateral trade
쌍방시세 two way price
쌍방향성 interaction
쓸모없게 된; 진부한 obsolete

ㅇ

아동수당 children allowance
아랍석유수출국기구 Organization of Arab Petroleum Exporting Countries
아랍연맹 Arab League
아메리카증권거래소 Amex Commodity Exchange
아메리카증권거래소 주가지수 AMEX Index
아메리카트러스트스코어 Americus Trust Scores
아부자금 coupon fund
아시아개발기금 Asian Development Fund
아시아개발은행 Asian Development Bank
아시아결제동맹(이란, 파키스탄, 스리랑카, 인도, 네팔, 방글라데시 6개국의 지역청산 지불기구) Asian Clearing Union; ACU
아시아달러 Asian dollar
아시아달러시장 Asian dollar market
아시아달러채 Asian dollar bond
아시아준비은행 Asian Reserve Bank
아시아지불동맹 Asian Payment Union
아시아태평양경제사회위원회 Economic and Social Commission for Asia and the Pacific
아시아태평양경제협력회의 Asia Pacific Economic Cooperation
아시아통화단위 Asian Currency Unit; Asian Monetary Unit
아웃라이트 outright
아웃라이트환상장 outright exchange rate
아웃라인 outline
아웃라인거래 outright transaction
아웃사이드데이 outside day
아웃오브더머니 out of the money
IMF 대체계정 substitution account of IMF
IMF 이사회 Board of Directors IMF
IMF 평가 par value IMF
IMF 차관 loan IMF
IMF 협정 agreement of IMF
IS 곡선; **LM** 곡선 I-S curve · L-M curve
아일랜드리버설패턴 island reversal pattern
아직 결제하지 않은 주식이나 상품 open position
아프리카개발은행 African Development Bank
아시아-아프리카공동시장 Afro-Asian Common Market
악성인플레이션 galloping inflation
악세 irrational tax
악세수준유지 unchanged to slightly lower
악순환 vicious cycle
악영향 adverse effects
악용 evil practice
악의의 제삼자 holder in bad faith
악재료 bad news
악재료 unfavorable factor
악질가맹점 vicious member merchant
악화 degradation; deterioration; downturn
안내인 usher
안데스공동시장 Andean Common Market
안상점 saddle point
안전계수 safety margin

안전밸브 safety valve
안전보증신청 article of the peace
안전성 마진; 투자안전확보범위 margin of safety
안전성이 높은 주식 low risk stocks
안전율 safety factor
안전자산 riskless assets
안전재고 safety stock
안전준비금 safety reserves
안전형 운용 passive strategy
안정가치로 수정한 순이익 constant dollar net income
안정가치로 수정한 재무제표 common dollar statements
안정가치회계 constant-dollar accounting
안정경제성장 stable economic growth
안정구매력 constant purchasing power
안정구매력회계 constant power purchasing accounting
안정배당 consecutive dividend; stable dividend
안정배당주 widow-and-orphan stock
안정성 stability
안정성분석 stability analysis
안정조건 stability condition
안정조작 stabilization operation; stabilizing transaction
안정주 stable stock
안정주주 stable stockholder
안정촉진적인 stabilizing
안정화 정책 stabilization policy
안정화개입 smoothing operation
안정화폐론 stable money principle
안티덤핑코드 anti-dumping code
알선인 arranger
알파벳펀드 alphabet fund
알파수치 alpha value
암딜링 black market dealing
암묵적인 implied
암묵적인 디플레이터 implicit deflator
암묵적인 전제 implicit assumption
암호 secret language
압력단 pressure group
압력단체 interest group
압류하다 attach
압박 squeeze
압축기록 advanced depreciation
압축기장 reduction entry
압축손 advanced depreciation deduction
압축준비금 reserve for deferred income tax
압축준비금편입손 loss from putting on reserve for deferred income tax
압축한도액 advanced depreciation limit
앞서감; 프런트러닝 front running
애드온금리 add-on rate
애드온방식 add on system
애로인플레이션 bottle-neck inflation
애버리지타입 선물환예약 averaged type forward contract
애콰이어 acquirer
애프터로스 after loss
액면가; 공칭가 nominal value
액면가격 par price; par value
액면가액 face value; nominal amount
액면금액 face amount
액면대로 at par
액면매매사채 par bond
액면발행 issue at face value; par issue; issued at par
액면변경 change in par value
액면이상 at a premium; with premium
액면이하 at a discount; with discount
액면이하;평가이하 below par
액면이하상품 below par issue
액면전환 conversion at par
액면전환사채 debenture convertible at par
액면주 stock at par
액면주식 par value stock; share with par value; stock with par value
액면주식자본금 par value share
액면초과금 capital in excess of par value
액면초과지불자본 capital paid in excess of

par value
액면통액 aggregate face amount
액면평가 parity rate of exchange
액면하락 drop below par
액면할 under par
액멸발행;퍼발행 issue at par
액션프로그램 actio program
액추어리즈 종합지수 FT-SE Actuaries AllShare FT-SE
액추얼포지션 actual position
액티브리스크 active risk
액티브리스크 회피도 active risk aversion
액티브리턴 active return
액티브파트너 active partner
액티브포트폴리오 active portfolio
액티비티분석 activity analysis
앨리게이터스프레드 allocator spread
M 제로신장 M 0 growth
M&A 비즈니스 merger and acquisition business
M2+CD 통계 M2+CD Statistics
M2의 움직임 M2's behaviour
M3의 신장 M3 growth
앳더머니 at the money
앳리스크 at risk
앳마켓 at-market
야간거래 night session
야간교환 exchange at night
야간금고 night deposit safe
야외시장 open air market
약세 콘솔리데이션패턴 bearish consolidation patterns
약세시세 bearish tone
약세시장 bearish market; bearish mood; bearish sentiment
약세의;내림시세의 bearish
약세저항선 bearish resistance line
약세지지선 bearish support line
약속 commitment; undertaking
약속어음 promissory note
약식계약 simple contract
약식소송절차 summary proceedings
약식승인 informal acceptance
약인 covenants
약인멸실 failure of consideration
약인조항 consideration clause
약정가격공표 posting of contract price
약정가격을 공표함 dissemination of transaction price
약정금리 agreed interest; agreed-upon interest rate; contracted interest rate
약정단계 agreed-upon price
약정담보권 stipulated security
약정만기이익 agreed yield to maturity
약정반제 scheduled payment
약정반제부 스와프 amortizing swap
약정손해배상액 stipulated damages
약정수수료 commitment fee
약정이율 contracted rate; stated interest rate
약정지수 contract index
약정통지 contract notice
약칭 short title
약한 시세 weak tone
약한 채널 bearish channel
양국간 협정 bilateral agreement
양도 alienation; assignment; cession
양도 및 이전 assignment and transfer
양도가격 transfer price
양도가능 negotiable
양도가능대부 transferable loan facility
양도가능대부증서 transferable loan certificate
양도가능대출 transferable loan
양도가능러프 transferable RUF
양도가능신용장 transferable credit
양도가능정기예금증서 negotiable certificate of deposit; negotiable time certificates of deposits
양도가능한 자산 negotiable asset
양도가능환불지도예금계정; NOW계정 negotiable order of withdrawal account
양도계약 transfer contract

양도금지 prohibition of transfer
양도금지 restraint on alienation
양도담보증서 bill of sale
양도무효조항 alienation clause
양도불능보호증서 nonnegotiable safekeeping receipts
양도비용 expenses incurred for the transfer; transfer expenses
양도상태 condition of the transfer of the property
양도성 증권 transferable securities
양도세 transfer tax
양도소득의 근거로 분류되지 않는 자산 property not qualifying for capital gain
양도소득특별공제 special deduction for capital gains
양도수수료 assignment charge; assignment fee; transfer fee
양도이서 endorsement to transfer
양도인 alienator; transferor
양도자 assignor
양도자산 property for transfer; transfer property
양도자신취득비용 cost of transferred properties
양도저당병합 consolidation of mortgages
양도제한 restriction of transfer; restriction on transferability
양도조건 assignment clause
양도증서 common assurance; deed of conveyance; written assignment
양도하다 assign
양도할 수 없는 unalienable
양도할 수 없는 권리 inalienable rights
양로모기지 endowment mortgage
양로보험 endowment insurance
양륙세 port toll
양륙지 선택화물 optional cargo
양방향부과 making two-sided markets
양벌규정;쌍벌규정 penalty against employer and employee
양산원가 volume cost
양산효과 volume efficiency
양수인 alienee; transferee
양여자 grantor
양육비 expenses of bringing up children
양일포함 both days included
양적인 경제정책 quantitative economic policy
양적인 금융지표 quantitative monetary indicator
양적인 신용규제 quantitative credit control
양키본드 Yankee bond
양허계약 concession contract
어드바이저리보드 advisory board
어드저스터블보험 Adjustable Life Insurance
어드저스터블페그 adjustable peg
어레즈주가모델 Ahlers model
어리어스와프 arrears swap
어린이종합보험 juvenile comprehensive insurance
어림값 rough number
어림수 round number
어베이러빌러티리스크 availability risk
어센딩톱스 ascending tops
어셋백커머셜페이퍼 asset-backed commercial paper
어셋베이스스와프 asset base swap
어셋스와프 asset swap
어셋스와프거래 asset swap transaction
어셋어프로치 asset approach
어셋파이낸스 asset finance
어셋패스스루증권 asset-pass-through certificate
어소시에이트멤버 associate member
어용조합 company union
어음갱신 renewal of bills and notes
어음계정장부 bill book
어음교환 bill clearing; check and bill clearing; clearance of bills
어음교환결산표 clearinghouse proof
어음교환결제 bank clearing
어음교환계정 clearing account

어음교환고 amount of clearing
어음교환소 clearinghouse
어음교환소가맹은행 clearing bank; member banks of the clearing house
어음교환제도 clearing system
어음교환차액 clearing balance
어음금액 amount of bill
어음기입장 note register
어음대부 advance on a promissory note; loan on bill
어음대부담보 collateral on loans on bills
어음대부연체이자 overdue interest on loan on bills
어음대부이자 interest on loans on bills
어음만기 due date of bills
어음매매레이트 bill buying and selling rate; bill rate
어음매매시장평균잔고 bills market average outstanding
어음매입수권서 authority to purchase
어음매입제도 bill buying system
어음발행 drawing of bill
어음발행인 drawer of bill
어음법 law on bills
어음보험 assurance of bill
어음브로커 bill broker
어음사이트 sight of a bill
어음소지자 bill bearer
어음수금수수료 charge for collection of bill
어음수신인 drawee
어음유통수수료 negotiation charge
어음유통은행 negotiating bank
어음인도 surrender of bill
어음인수 acceptance of bill; acceptance outstanding
어음인수은행 accepting bank
어음인수회사 accepting house
어음지불 payment by bill
어음할인 bill discount; discount on bill
어음할인료 discount on note
어음할인율 effective rate of discount
어음할인중개인 discount broker
어지러운 시황 boom and bust
어카운트레포트서비스 account report service
어카운트이어베이시스 account year basis
어크리에이션본드 accretion bond
어포인트상법 appointment sales
어프리시에이션스와프 appreciation swap
어피니티카드 affinity card
억세스권 right of access
억세스카드 access card
억제정책 restraint measures
억제조치 control measure
억제효과 damping effect
억지력 deterrent
언더드레싱 under dressing
언더파채권 sub-par bond
언도하다 render
언매치드북 unmatched book
언커버드금리제정 uncovered interest arbitrage
언커버드옵션 uncovered option
언커버드포지션 uncovered position
언콜렉터블론 uncollectible loan
언타이드론 untied loan
언헤지 unhedge
언헤지본드 unhedged bond
얼핏 보기에는 prima facie
엄격한 검사 tightened inspection
엄격해석 strict construction
업갭 up gap
업계 business circle; industry segments
업계관행 industry practice
업계기준 industry standard
업계스페셜리스트 industry specialist
업계재편 industry realignment
업계평균 industry average
업무 affairs
업무감사 business audit; operation audit; performance audit
업무겸업제한 limitation on interlocking
업무규정특례 special rule of the business regulations

업무기준 practice standards
업무상의 사고 on the job accidents
업무상의 수익을 보상함 compensation for profit from business
업무위탁비 outsourcing service expenses
업무주처벌제도 proprietor punishment
업앤드풋옵션 up and put option
업자간 상장 dealers' market; dealing market
업자에 의한 투기상장 broker's market
업자의 투자상장 broker's market
업자할인 trade discount
업적 achievement; earnings performance
업적개요 overview of the business results
업적모델 performance model
업적보고서 performance report
업적부진의 ailing
업적비율 operating performance ratios
업적상장 profit-driven market
업적지표 performance indicators
업적평가 performance appraisal; performance evaluation
업적평가회계 performance accounting
업적호조 robust earnings
업종 category of business
업종별 by types of industry
업종별 대출통계 loans and discounts by industry
업종별 이율 average yield by types of industry
업종별 주가지수 narrow based stock index; sector-stock price index
업종별 주가지수선물거래 stock price index futures by industry
업종별 편입률 industry weighting ratio
업트렌드 uptrend
에너지리스크 energy risk
에너지비축 energy stockpiling
에너지세 energy tax
에너지주 energy sector stock
에너지탄성 energy conservation
에누리 fictitious price
에드가 EDGAR
EDGAR 시스템 electronic data gathering analysis and retrieval system
에드가관리실(**SEC**) Office of EDGAR management(SEC)
에산감사 budget audit
에상매상고 estimated sales
에스컬레이터조항 escalator clause
에스크로계약 escrow agreement
에스크로계정 escrow account
에스크로신용장 escrow credit
에스크로신탁계약 escrow and trust agreement
에이전시마켓 agency market
에이전시이론 agency theory
AAA 등급 AAA class
에지액트법인 Edge-Act company
에퀴티보험 equities insurance
에퀴티재판소 court of equity
에퀴티파이낸스 equity finance
FT 100종 지수 FT Stock Exchange 100 Index
엑스워런트 ex-warrant
엑조틱본드 exotic bond
엑조틱옵션 exotic option
엑조틱커런시 exotic currency
엑조틱파생상품 exotic derivatives
리사법 Employee Retirement Income Security Act
엘리어트파동이론 Elliot Wave Theory
엘리트카드 elite card
엥겔지수 Engel coefficient
여객수입 passengers traffic receipts
여러 미불금 miscellaneous accounts payable
여러 미수금 miscellaneous accounts receivable
여분공사클레임 extra work claims
여비교통비 traveling expenses
여비수당 traveling benefits
여섯자리분개장 six column journal
여신공여량 credit availability
여신관리 credit control; credit exposure management
여신리스크 credit risk

여신리스크분석 credit risk analysis
여신리스크웨이트 credit risk weight
여신분석 credit analysis
여신승인 credit approval
여신업무 credit business
여신잔고 existing exposure
여잉스프레드 excess spread
여잉준비 non-borrowed reserve
여잉현금 idle cash
여행신용장 traveller's letter of credit
여행자세 tourist tax
여후자본 subordinated capital
역금리 negative interest
역년(曆年) calendar year; natural year
역년기준에 따른 방법 method based on the calendar year
역담보 countersecurity
역무 personal service
역무계약 contract for service
역무제공 rendering of service
역무제공에 대한 지불 payment to rendered services
역무출자 service contribution
역발상에 능한 주식투자가 contrarian
역방향 reverse direction
역변동이부채 reversal floating rate note
역산 reverse operation
역산법 reversal cost method
역상태 reverse offset
역선택 adverse selection
역설적인 견해 paradoxical view
역소득세 negative income tax; reverse income tax
역송금 reverse remittance
역스와프 reverse swap; reversed swap
역외적용 extraterritorial application
역외적용관할권 long-arm jurisdiction
역외조달 offshore purchase
역월도제 delivery system by calendar month
역월인도 calendar month delivery
역월제선물상장 calendar month delivery rate
역이율 inverted yield curve
역이율 현상 inverted yield curve phenomena
역이익 inverse yield
역일드 yield curve inversion
역일드갭 reverse yield gap
역일변 backwardation rate
역입찰 reversal auction
역입체 switch reversal
역자산효과 reversal assets effect
역지정가격구매주문 stop loss buy order
역지정가격주문 stop-limit order
역진과세 regressive taxation
역진세 regressive tax
역특혜 converse preference
역풍개입 intervention against market
역플로터채 inverse floater
역행렬표 inverse matrix table
역헤지 reverse hedge
역환어음 re-exchange
역흡수합병 downstairs merger
연 1회 후불 annual payment
연 2회 결산회사 corporation settling accounts twice a year
연가법 annual value method
연간생산능력 annual capacity
연간소득 annual earnings
연간수입 annual income
연간이익처분액 annual profit disposition amount
연간정액지불 equal annual payment method
연간지출당좌비율 quick assets to year's cash expenses
연간총익 yearly earnings
연간할부 annual installment
연간회전횟수 times per year
연결 consolidation
연결경상이익 consolidated current profit; consolidated recurring profit
연결계정 consolidated account
연결납세신고 consolidated return
연결대상외 관련회사 unconsolidated affiliates

ㅅㅇ

연결대차대조표 consolidated balance sheet
연결된 선의 consolidated goodwill
연결매상 consolidated sales
연결방침 consolidation policy; principles of consolidation
연결베이스 consolidated base
연결부채비율표 group gearing
연결사채 consolidated bond
연결손익계산서 consolidated profit and loss statement; consolidation statement of income statement
연결손익계산표 consolidated income statement
연결순손실 consolidated net loss
연결운전자금 consolidated working capital
연결원장 consolidation ledger
연결의 consolidated
연결이익 consolidated income
연결일 consolidation date
연결잉여금 consolidated retained earnings; consolidated surplus; surplus from consolidation
연결자본 consolidated capital
연결자산 consolidated assets
연결자회사 consolidated subsidiary
연결재무제표 consolidated financial statements
연결재무통계 consolidated financial statistics
연결전 이익 profit prior to consolidation
연결집단 consolidation group
연결초과액 consolidation excess
연결캐시플로시산서 consolidated statement of cash flow
연고모집 private subscription
연고지방채 private placement local bond; private placement local government bond; private placement municipal bond
연고채 private placement bond; private subscription bond
연고특별채 private placement special bond
연공서열임금제도 seniority order wage system
연공제 seniority system
연구개발 research and development
연구개발비 research and development cost; research and development expenditures
연구보조금 fellowship grant
연구비 research cost
연금 pension
연금가입연수 insurance year
연금계약 pension contract
연금계획 pension plan
연금구입기금 annuity purchase fund
연금구입요율 annuity purchase rates
연금권 pension right
연금급부 pension benefits
연금급부누적액 accumulated investment plan benefits
연금급부액산정방식 benefit formula
연금기금 pension fund
연금기금 스프레드 pension fund spread
연금기금관리 pension fund management
연금기금의 수익자 pension fund beneficiary
연금기금의 역할 fund's mission
연금기금잉여 pension fund surplus
연금기금적립계약 funding instrument
연금기금적립기관 funding agency
연금법 annuity method
연금보장공사 Pension Benefit Guarantee Corporation
연금보험 annuity insurance
연금부 보험 endowment annuity; income endowment; insurance with annuity
연금비용 benefit plan expense; pension expense
연금수리비용계산방식 actuarial cost method
연금신탁 pension trust
연금업무 pension business
연금원가적립방식 terminal funding
연금유닛 annuity unit
연금의 기간원가 periodic pension cost
연금의 정치적인 측면 politics of pensions
연금이율법 actuarial method

연금잉여의 금리감응도 interest sensitivity of the pension surplus
연금자산 pension assets; plan assets
연금자산실제운용수익 actual return on plan assets
연금적립금 pension reserve
연금제도 pension program; pension scheme
연금제도상의 연금회계 accounting for the cost of pension plans
연금제도종료보험 plan termination insurance
연금준비금 reserve for pensions
연금코스트 pension cost
연금특약 annuity rider
연금포인트제도 pension point system
연금플랜규정서 plan documents
연금플랜순자산 net plan assets
연금현가 present value of annuity
연금현물충족방식 terminal funding method
연금회계 accounting for pension plan
연기 adjournment
연기; 거치 deferment
연기어음 extended bill
연납 authorized deferred payment; deferment of payment; postponement of tax payment
연납과 관련된 이자세 interest tax on delayed payment
연납세 deferred tax
연납세계정 deferred tax account
연대 joint and several
연대납부책임 joint and several obligation of tax payment
연대납세의무 joint and several obligation of tax liability
연대보증 joint and several guarantee; joint and several guarantor
연대보증인 joint surety
연대보증채무 joint-and-several liability
연대순으로 chronological
연대증서 joint and several bond
연대채무 joint and several obligation
연대책임 joint and several liability
연도간 세배분 inter-period tax allocation
연도감사 annual audit
연도마감 annual closing
연도초 beginning of the fiscal year
연동오차 tracking error
연동하여 in line with
연등 consecutive advances
연락 consecutive declines
연료계정 fuel account
연료비 fuel cost
연리 interest per annum; per annum rate
연리형 론 annuity loan
연말 end of the fiscal year; year-end
연말상장 year-end market
연말자금수요 year-end demand for fund
연말잔고 outstanding at year-end
연말조정 year-end adjustment; year-end settlement
연방거래위원회 Federal Trade Commission
연방공개시장위원회 Federal Open Market Commission
연방공개시장조작 Federal Reserve open market operation
연방관재관 United States trustee
연방금융은행 federal financing bank
연방기관 federal agency
연방기관증권 federal agency securities
연방농업금융저당금고 Farmer MAC
연방법원 federal court
연방사회보장법 Social Security Act
연방소득세 federal income tax
연방신용조합법 Federal Credit Union Act of 1934
연방예금보험 federal deposit insurance
연방예금보험공사 Federal Deposit Insurance Corporation
연방은행위원회 Federal Banking Commission
연방자금 federal fund
연방자금금리 federal fund rate
연방자금시장 federal fund market
연방자문위원회 Federal Advisory Committee

연방저당금고 Federal National Mortgage Association
연방저축대부보험회사 Federal Savings and Loan Insurance Corporation
연방전신이체 Fed wire
연방정부론보증 federal loan guarantee
연방정부지출 Federal spending
연방주택국 Federal Housing Administration
연방주택금융저당금고 Federal Home Loan Mortgage Corporation
연방주택대부은행 Federal Home Loan Bank
연방주택대부은행이사회 Federal Home Loan Bank Board
연방주택대부은행제도 Federal Home Loan Bank System
연방준비개혁법 Federal Reserve Reform Act
연방준비법 Federal Reserve Act
연방준비은행 Federal Reserve Bank
연방준비제도 Federal Reserve System
연방준비제도이사회 Board of Governors of the Federal Reserve System
연방준비제도이사회 Fed; Federal Reserve Board
연방준비증서 Federal Reserve Notes
연방준비지구 Federal Reserve District
연방중개신용은행 federal intermediate credit banks
연방토지은행 Federal Land Bank
연방통신위원회 Federal Communication Commission
연방파산법 Federal Bankruptcy Act
연변동이부채 reversal floater
연복리수익률 compound annual return
연부(年賦) yearly installment
연부과세 annual fees
연부상환 redemption by yearly installment
연불기준 deferred payment basis
연불수출 maker's credit
연불신용 supplier's credit
연불조건부 청부 contract works condition of deferred payment attached
연불조건부 판매 deferred payment sales
연불쿠폰 annual coupon
연산수 operand
연산품 joint product
연생보험 joint life insurance
연서(連署) countersignature
연세주의(年稅主義) yearly taxation
연속감사 recurring audit
연속매매 continuous trading
연속발행 serial issue
연속배당 continuous dividend
연속변수 continuous variable
연속복리 continuous compound interest rate
연속복리계산 continuous compounding calculation
연속사반기 consecutive quarters
연속상환증권 serial securities
연속상환채 installment bond
연속상환채권 serial bond
연속시간 continuous time
연속원장 progressive ledger
연속제로쿠폰채 serial zero-coupon bond
연속증배 consecutive dividend increase
연속확률분포 continuous probability distribution
연속회기 continuous session
연수의 resident doctor
연수익률 annual rate of returns
연역법 deductive method
연율의 퍼센테이지 annual percentage rate
연율환산 annualised basis
연이율 annual interest rate; annualised yield
연장가능만기 extendible maturity
연장가능형 스와프 extensible swap
연장보험 extended insurance
연장클레임 extension of time claims
연조(軟調) weakness
연조(軟調) 시장 soft market
연차결산 annual accounting
연차보고서 annual report
연차재무제표 annual financial statements

연차총회 annual meeting
연체 arrearages
연체가산금 additional arrearage charge
연체금 back money; delinquency amount
연체론 past due loan
연체배당금 dividend in arrears
연체보상금 penalty on delayed delivery
연체세 deferred income taxes; delinquency tax; tax in arrears
연체세면제 discharge of delinquent tax
연체수표 stale check
연체율 percentage of delinquency
연체이자 daily interest for arrearage; default interest; deferred interest; delayed interest
연체이자 interest for delinquency; interest in arrears; overdue interest; past due interest
연체일변;연체일보 overdue interest per diem
연체일수 days in arrears
연체지대(地代) rent arrears
연체채권 arrears
연합규약 articles of confederation
연합협약 joint agreement
연화;교환불능통화 soft currency
연화국 soft currency country
연환산 annual basis
연회비 annual dues
연회원 annual member
열거하다 enumerate
열등자산 inferior assets
열망 aspiration
열화자산 deteriorated assets
열후론 subordinated loan
열후사채 mezzanine bond
열후예탁금 subordinated deposit
열후자금조달 subordinated funding
열후조항 subordinated clause
열후증권 junior securities; subordinated securities
열후지분 subordinated interest
열후채 capital debenture
열후채권 junior debt
열후채시장 subordinated debt market
열후청구권 junior claim; subordinated claims
열후트란시 subordinate tranche
열후할인채 subordinated discount bond
염가구입권 bargain purchase option
염가예상 anticipation of falling market
영구계정 permanent account
영구공채 permanent debt
영구권 perpetual bond
영구권금지원칙 rule against perpetuities
영구금지명령 permanent injunction; perpetual injunction
영구대출 permanent financing
영구부채 permanent liabilities
영구세 perennial tax
영구세주의 principle of perennial tax
영구열후채 perpetual subordinated debt
영구우선주 permanent preferred stock
영구워런트 perpetual warrant
영구임대 permanent loan
영구자산 permanent assets
영구적립금지규칙 rule against accumulations
영구차이 permanent difference
영구채 perpetual issue; undated issue
영국국내세입청 Inland Revenue
영국무역진흥회 British Export Trade Research Organization
영국법 English law
영국식 경매 English auction
영국은행협회 British Banker's Association
영국장기국채 long-term national bond of England
영국재무부 Exchequer
영국재무부장관 Chancellor of the Exchequer
영국재무부증권 exchequer bills
영국특허회계사협회 Institution of Chartered Accountants in English and Wales
영국펀드 예금금리선물 pound sterling depositary interest futures
영국펀드 정기예금 pound sterling time deposit
영국펀드 통화선물 pound sterling currency

futures
영국펀드 CP pound sterling commercial paper
영국해상보험법 Marine Insurance Act of 1906
영국회계협회 British Accounting Association

영대소작권 perennial tenant right
영대차지권 lease in perpetuity; perpetual lease
영대차지인 life tenancy; perpetual lessee
영리 money making
영리를 목적으로 한 지속적인 행위 continuous transaction of entered into for profit
영리법인 profit corporation
영리사업 commercial business; commercial enterprise; profit making business
영리회사 commercial company
영리회사 operating business
영사송장 consular invoice
영업 trade
영업경비 operating expenses
영업계정 trade account
영업계정수지잔고 underwriting account balance
영업과목 description of business; line of business
영업권 goodwill; trade rights
영업권상각 amortization of goodwill
영업권소유자 concessionaire
영업권양도 assignment of business
영업권평가 valuation of goodwill
영업내역장 office expenses book
영업면의 증익효과 operating leverage effect
영업면의 증익효과도 degree of operating leverage
영업보고 business report; operating report
영업보고서 account of business
영업본거이동 shifting of business center
영업비 business expenses; commercial expenses; trade expenses; working cost
영업비계정 office expense account
영업비상각자산 depreciable used in business
영업상의 본거 principal place of business
영업상의 비밀 trade secret
영업상태 operating standing
영업상황 actual state of business; operating condition
영업성적 business results; operating results; results of operations; summary of earnings
영업세 franchise tax; occupation tax; privilege tax; trade tax
영업소 sales office; service office
영업손실 operating loss
영업손실구분 operating section
영업손익 operating profit and loss
영업수익 operating income; operating revenue; revenue from operations
영업수입 funds from operations; operating receipt; sales earnings
영업순환 operating cycle
영업순환기준 operating cycle rule
영업시간 business hours; office hours
영업실적 results of business
영업안내 catalog
영업양도 transfer of business; transfer of operations; transfer of the business
영업양수 receipt of business
영업에 대한 간섭 interference with trade
영업연도 working year
영업예산 operating budget
영업외경비 non-operating expenses
영업외비용 non-operating expenditure
영업외손익 non-operating profit and loss
영업외손익구분 non-operating section
영업외수익 non-operating revenue
영업외수입 non-operating income
영업외의 non-operating
영업외이익 non-operating profit
영업용집기 office furniture
영업원장 operating ledger

영업이익 business profit; gain from operation; operating profit
영업이익단계 operating profit level
영업이익률 operating income to sales; operating margin; operating profit margin; ratio of operating profit to revenue
영업이익세 business profit tax
영업일 business day
영업일이 지나서 one day skipped
영업잉여 operating surplus
영업자산 trade assets
영업정지 interruption of business; stoppage of business
영업제한 restraint of trade
영업종목 items of business
영업준비금 operating reserve
영업채무 trade liability
영업행위 doing business
영업활동 operating activities
영업활동계산서 operating statement
영업활동계정 operating accounts
영업활동으로 인한 캐시플로 cash flow from operating activities
영업활동정지 suspension of business activity
영업회의 business meeting
영치 official retain
영해 maritime belt; territorial waters
영향을 주다 affect
예견되지 않은 사고 unforeseen event
예금 deposit with other bank; money deposited; money in bank
예금감소 depreciation of deposit by inflation
예금금리 deposit interest rate; interest on deposit
예금기입장 deposit diary
예금담보대부 loan secured by deposit
예금대부 deposit loan
예금대체방식 deposit transfer
예금대출율 loan-deposit ratio
예금보증금 customers' deposits
예금보험구제 deposit insurance bailout
예금보험기구개혁 reform of the deposit insurance system
예금보험제도 deposit insurance system
예금수부금 earnest money received
예금수수료 deposit fee
예금수입금융기관 depository institution
예금수입기관의 요소준비 reserve requirements of depositary institutions
예금수표 bank cashier's check
예금쉐어 deposit share
예금승계방식 purchase and assumption
예금시장 deposit market
예금양도금지 prohibition of deposit transfer
예금원장 deposit ledger
예금율 deposit-to-loan ratio
예금이율 deposit rate
예금이자세 tax on deposit
예금자보호 depositor protection
예금자보호시스템 safety nets
예금전액보호 protection of the full deposited amount
예금전쟁 deposit war
예금전표 deposit slip
예금정산불방식 deposit payoff
예금준비 reserve requirements
예금증권 warehouse receipt
예금증서 deposit certificate
예금지불준비율 cash reserve ratio
예금창구 deposit window
예금채무 deposit liability
예금통화 deposit currency; deposit money; deposit of public money
예금현금 cash in banks and hand
예대율 bank loans-deposit ratio
예보증금 deposit on contract; deposit received for guarantee; deposit received on sale
예비감사 preliminary audit
예비금설정법 allowance method
예비기간 period of grace
예비대차대조표 preliminary balance sheet

예비등급 preliminary rating
예비정보 preliminary information
예비주권 unissued certificate
예비지불인 referee in case of need
예비클레임 preliminary claim
예사원가 predicted cost
예산 budget
예산계정 budgetary account
예산단년도주의 one year budget principle
예산단일주의 principle of single budget
예산배부와 집행 allocation and execution of budget
예산배분 budget allotment
예산삭감 spending cut
예산순계 net budget
예산안 proposal budget
예산원가 budgeted cost
예산원칙 budget principle
예산위원회 Budget Committee
예산절차 budgetary procedure
예산제도 budget system
예산지출 budget outlay; budgetary expenditure
예산차이 budget variance; spending variance; variation from budget
예산차이분석 analysis of budget variance; analysis of variance from budget
예산초과 cost overrun
예산총칙 general provisions of budget; general provisions of the budget
예산통제 budgetary control
예산편성 budgetary process; compilation of the budget
예산편입 direct budget transfer
예산합의 budget agreement
예산항목이체 rearrangement of budget item
예상 밖의 손실 windfall loss
예상내용연수 probable life
예상매상고 estimate of sales; forecast of sales
예상배당 probable dividend; projected dividend
예상배당율 prospective dividend rate
예상변동률 expected volatility
예상보유기간수익률 estimated holding period return
예상손실 expected loss
예상수익 anticipated profit
예상수익률 prospective return
예상외의 이익변동 surprises in earnings
예상원가 anticipated cost
예상이익 probable yield; prospective yield
예상채무 accrued liabilities
예상최대손해액 probable maximum loss
예상평균이익 prospective yield average
예속의 subordinated
예약공모 offer by subscription
예약판매 sale by subscription
예외사항 exceptional item
예외세율 exceptional rates of tax
예외없이 모두 all and singular
예외의 원칙 law of exception; exception principle
예저금 deposit and saving
예정, 예산 따위를 앞당겨 씀 front loaded
예정공기간축 shortening of a prearranged period of a construction work
예정납세 estimated tax prepayment; prepayment of income tax
예정납세액독촉 claim of prepayment of income tax
예정납세액체납처분 disposition of failure to pay income tax in advance
예정납세액통지 notification of estimated tax prepayment
예정납세제도 income tax prepayment system; provisional tax payment system based on the previous year's tax amount
예정배부율 predetermined burden rate
예정보험 provisional insurance
예정보험 provisional policy
예정사망률 expected mortality rate
예정수입 expected income

예정신고 provisional return
예정원가 predetermined cost
예정원가계획 predetermined cost system
예정이율 assumed rate of interest
예정투자수익률 required return
예측 prospect
예측 **PER** prospective PER
예측가능성 predictability
예측급부채무 projected benefit obligation
예측모델 forecasting model
예측수요량 projected demand
예측오차 prediction error
예측하지 못한 채무 unforeseen liabilities
예탁 deposit
예탁계정 deposit account
예탁관리기금 deposit administration fund
예탁금 deposited money
예탁금에 편입함 appropriation for the deposit
예탁기한 depository period
예탁신탁회사 depository trust company
예탁유가증권 deposited securities
예탁은행 depository bank
예탁자산 depository assets
예탁전 주권 pre-deposited stock certificates
예탁주권 deposited stock certificate
예탁주식 depository shares
예탁증서 depository receipts
예탁하다 offer the deposit
오기 clerical error
오더북오피셜 order book official
오락 entertainment
오류표시 false demonstration
오른쪽 아래 방향으로 향하는 이율곡선 negative yield curve
오름차순 ascending order
오버나이트거래 overnight transaction
오버나이트레이트 overnight rate
오버더탑워런트 over-the-top warrant
오버서브스크립션 over subscription
오버앤드아웃옵션 over-and-out option
오버퍼 over par
오버펀딩 over funding
오사카증권거래소 Osaka Securities Exchange
오사카증권주가지수 Osaka Stock Price Index
오스트레일리아 종합주가지수 All Ordinaries Index
오스트레일리아달러 Aussie dollar
오스트레일리아달러채 Aussie bond
오스트레일리아회계연구재단 Australian Accounting Research Foundation
오슬로증권거래소지수 Oslo Stock Exchange Index
오실레이터 oscillator
OECD 가맹 OECD membership
OECD 모델조세조약 OECD model double taxation convention
OEM original equipment manufacturing
오전장에서 물러남 closing of the morning session
오전장의 최초 가격으로 매입하다 buy on opening
오진을 정정함 correction of errors
오차탈루 errors and omissions
오퍼 **TB** operation TB
오퍼곡선 offer curve
오퍼레이트 offered rate
오퍼레이팅레버리지 분석 operating leverage analysis
오퍼레이팅리스 operating lease
오퍼사이드 offer side
오프닝세션 opening session
오프닝톤 opening tone
오프마켓 off market
오프마켓스와프 off market swap
오프밸런스 off balance
오프밸런스거래 off balanced trade
오프밸런스시트거래 off balance sheet transaction
오프밸런스회계 off balance sheet accounting
오프쇼어계정 offshore account
오프쇼어리스 offshore lease

오프쇼어뱅킹센터 offshore banking center
오프쇼어뱅킹유닛 offshore banking unit
오프쇼어보증 offshore guarantee
오프쇼어센터 offshore center
오프쇼어시장 offshore market
오프쇼어은행간 시장 offshore banking facility
오프쇼어조달 offshore borrowing
오프쇼어펀드 offshore fund
오프쇼어해외시장 offshore production
오픈다운 open down
오픈레이트방식 open rate method
오픈북 open book
오픈엔드형 리스 open-end lease
오픈엔드형 펀드 open-end fund
오픈커버; 포괄보험 open cover
오픈크레디트 open credit
오픈형 투자신탁 open-end investment trust
옥션시스템 auction system
온라인뱅킹시스템 on-line banking system
온밸런스 on balance
온밸런스거래 on-balance-sheet transaction
온밸런스볼륨 on balance volume
온쇼어마켓 onshore market
올드본드 old bond
올리스크담보약관 all risks clause
올림 round up
올오어논 all or none(AON)
올인코스트 all in cost
옮겨 적기 posting
옵션 **TOPIX** option TOPIX
옵션가격결정모델 option pricing model
옵션가격결정이론 option pricing theory
옵션감마 option gamma
옵션거래 option transaction; options trading
옵션거래대금 options contract value
옵션계약의 이서 endorsement for option contract
옵션델타 option delta
옵션만기일 option expiration date
옵션매도자 option writer
옵션바이어 option buyer
옵션부 순월인도 outright forward delivery with option
옵션부 전환사채 convertible bonds with option
옵션부채 option bond
옵션세타 option theta
옵션소멸 expiration of option
옵션스프레드 option spread
옵션시장 option market
옵션의 시간가치 time value of option
옵션인도 delivery with option
옵션조정후 스프레드 option adjusted spread
옵션조정후 이율 option adjusted yield
옵션청산회사 option clearing corporation
옵션퍼포먼스지수 option performance index
옵션포워드 option forward
옵션포지션 option position
옵션풀 option pool
옵션프리미엄 option premium
옵션헤징 hedging on option
옵팅아웃 opting-out
와시오더 wash order
와일드카드기간 wild card period
와일드카드옵션 wild card option
완고한; 지속성의 persistent
완공보너스 completion bonus
완만한 slack; sluggish
완만한 경기후퇴 mild recession
완만한 약세인(물가) easy
완성공사고 construction of completion
완성공사보상준비금 reserve for compensation for completed works
완성공사원가 cost of completed work
완성기준 completed contract method
완성매매계약 executed contract of sale
완성보증 completion guarantee
완성품 finished goods; finished products
완전감사 complete audit
완전개시 full disclosure
완전경쟁 perfect competition
완전경쟁시장에서의 평가 valuation on

perfect competitive market
완전고용 full employment
완전고용재정여잉 full employment surplus
완전고용정책 full employment policy
완전권원 perfect title
완전균형 full equilibrium
완전독점 perfect monopoly
완전법정통화 full legal tender
완전변제 direct payment
완전부상관수익률 perfectly negatively correlated returns
완전상각 full amortization
완전소유자회사 wholly owned subsidiary
완전수급자격일 full eligibility date
완전연결 full consolidation
완전연금 full pension
완전이용산출량 full capacity output
완전정상관수익률 perfectly positively correlated returns
완전조업 full capacity
완전증명 full proof
완전채무 perfect obligation
완전특화 complete specialization
완전표준원가 perfection standard cost
완전한 커버드옵션 fully covered option
완전합의조항 entire agreement clause
완전헤지 perfect hedge
완전화폐 full bodied money
완제하다 pay off
완충재고 buffer stock
완충재고융자 buffer stock financing facility
완화 easing; relaxation
왕래상장 rise-and-fall market
왕로운임 outward freight
왕복거래 round trip transaction
왜곡 distor
외교 diplomacy
외교관과세특권 fiscal privileges of diplomat
외국거래 foreign transactions
외국과 거래하는 기업 corporation carrying on foreign trade
외국과 거래하는 납세자 taxpayer dealing with foreign countries
외국국채증권 foreign government bonds
외국기관 foreign institution
외국기업 foreign company
외국대리점계정 foreign agents accounts
외국무역승수 foreign trade multiplier
외국무역통계 export and import statistics
외국법인 alien corporation; foreign corporation; foreign juridical person
외국법인사업연도 taxable year of foreign corporation
외국법인세 foreign corporation tax
외국법인세액공제 foreign corporation tax credit
외국법인의 납세의무 tax liability of foreign corporation
외국보험회사 alien insurer
외국비상장주 foreign stocks unlisted
외국세액 foreign tax
외국세액공제 credit for foreign taxes
외국세액공제방식 foreign tax credit method
외국세액공제제도 foreign tax credit system
외국세액공제한도액 creditable amount of foreign taxes
외국세액면제방식 foreign tax exemption method
외국세액손금산입 deduction for foreign taxes
외국세액을 이월공제함 carry over of foreign tax
외국세액의 공제한도액을 이월함 carry over of foreign tax credit limit
외국세액직접공제 direct foreign tax credit
외국소득면제방식 exemption method
외국소득세 foreign income tax
외국송금 remittance abroad
외국송금환 foreign money order
외국시장 foreign market
외국신용보험협회 Foreign Credit Insurance Association
외국어음 foreign bill

외국-외국 채권 bond issued and purchase by offshore parties
외국원천소득 income accrued from foreign sources
외국은행규제 regulations on foreign banks
외국은행유전스 usance granted by foreign banks
외국의 원조 international aid
외국의 판결 foreign judgment
외국인 alien
외국인구매 foreign buying
외국인재산 alien property
외국인지주비율 foreign stock holding ratio; stock holding ratio of foreigners
외국인지주제한 limit on foreign investors' holdings of stocks; stockholding limit for foreign investors
외국인투자 foreigner's investment; investment by foreign investors
외국인투자가 foreign investors
외국자회사 foreign subsidiary corporation
외국주권면제 sovereign immunity
외국주식시장 Foreign Section; foreign stock market
외국주요주가지수 major foreign stock price indexes
외국증권 foreign securities
외국증권거래소 foreign securities exchange
외국증권업법 law for foreign securities company
외국증권회사 foreign securities company
외국지점발송계정 foreign branch-our account
외국지점예금 due from foreign banks(our a/c)
외국지점피발송계정 foreign branch-their account
외국채권 foreign bond
외국채증권 foreign government securities
외국타점예금 due to foreign banks
외국통화선물 foreign currency futures
외국통화선물계약 foreign currency futures contracts
외국투자증권 foreign marketable securities
외국환 foreign exchange
외국환계정 foreign exchange account
외국환공인은행 authorized foreign exchange bank
외국환관리 foreign exchange control
외국환관리법 Foreign Exchange and Foreign Trade Control Law
외국환금융기관 financial institution for foreign exchange
외국환변동준비금 reserve for foreign exchange fluctuation
외국환브로커 foreign exchange broker
외국환상장 foreign exchange quotation
외국환선물 foreign exchange futures
외국환시장 foreign exchange market
외국환시장개입 foreign exchange market intervention
외국환시장조작 foreign exchange market operation
외국환어음 foreign bill of exchange; foreign exchange bill
외국환어음매수제도 system for purchase of foreign exchange bills
외국환예약 foreign exchange contract
외국환운영자금 fund for operation of foreign exchange
외국환유통신용장 negotiation credit
외국환율 foreign exchange rate
외국환은행 foreign exchange bank
외국환의 링크 exchange link
외국환자금증권 foreign exchange fund bill; Foreign Exchange Fund Securities
외국환자금특별회계 Foreign Exchange Fund Special Account
외국환전문은행 specialized foreign exchange bank
외국환조작 foreign exchange operation
외국환직접공제 direct financing tax credit
외국환차손 loss on foreign exchange
외국환차손익 foreign exchange gains and

losses
외국환취급지점 branch handling foreign exchange business
외국환투기 foreign exchange speculation
외국환포지션 foreign exchange position
외국환포지션표 foreign exchange position sheet
외국환환산율 foreign exchange conversion rate
외국환환산표 foreign exchange conversion table
외내거래 out-in transaction
외무부 Ministry of Foreign Affairs
외무원개발시대 agent development era
외무원대학 American College
외부감사 external audit
외부감사인 external auditor
외부거래 external transaction
외부경제 external economy
외부금융 external financing
외부부채 external liabilities
외부불경제 external diseconomy
외부수익률 external rate of return
외부위험 external hazard
외부유동성 external liquidity
외부자금 external fund
외부자본 external capital
외부자원 external resources
외부정합성 external consistency
외부증거 extrinsic evidence
외부평가 external valuation
외부화폐와 내부화폐 outside money inside money
외부환경 outside environment
외상거래 credit sales
외상거래가격 credit price
외상거래계정 credit account
외상거래채권 sales credit
외상구입 buying on credit; credit purchase; purchase on credit
외상매매 sale and purchase on credit
외상매입금 trade account payable
외상매출 sale on account
외상매출금 amount trade receivable; book credit; trade account receivable
외상매출금계정 charge account
외상매출금계정 account of credit sales
외상매출금원장 customers' ledger
외상매출금이나 대부금에 준하는 채권 claim similar to account receivable and loan
외상매출금회수 bill collection; collection of bill
외상보험 account receivable insurance
외상으로 판 상품 goods sold on credit
외상장부에서 on the books
외상적립기금 purchase payment fund
외상채권매입업무;팩터링 factoring
외상채권율 sales to accounts receivable
외상채권채무자 account debtor
외상채권회전율 sales to receivables
외상채권회전일수 number of days' purchases in accounts payable
외상채무 account payable
외상판매 credit sale
외상판매처 trade debtor
외생변수 exogenous variables
외생변화 exogenous change
외생수요 exogenous demand
외수 external demand; foreign demand
외압 external pressure; outside pressure
외외거래 out-out transaction
외외론 out-out loan
외자 foreign capital
외자계 기업 foreign affiliate
외자계 소비자금융 foreign capital consumer finance company
외자도입 intake of foreign capital
외자법 Foreign Investment Law
외자비율소멸정책 fade-out policy
외자수입 importation of foreign capital
외자유입 inflow of foreign capital; influx of foreign capital

외자흡수 foreign capital inducement
외주 order to outside manufacturer
외주가공비 processing expenses arising from outside manufacturer
외주제품 outside product
외채 external bond; external debt; external loan; foreign loan
외채디스카운트발행 bond issued at a discount
외채모집 flotation of external loan
외채발행대금 proceeds from external bond issuance
외채상환 redemption of external loan
외채이자 interest on external bond
외형과세 assessment by estimation on the basis of the size of business
외화 foreign currency
외화거래 foreign currency transactions
외화계정 foreign currency account
외화국채 government bond in foreign currency
외화기준 denominated in foreign currency
외화기준거래환산 translation of foreign currency transactions
외화기준계정항목을 환산함 conversion of items in foreign currencies
외화기준상장 exchange rate in foreign currency
외화기준외국채 foreign currency denominated bond
외화기준으로 foreign currency denominated
외화기준증권 foreign currency series securities
외화기준채권 claim in foreign currency; foreign currency-denominated bond
외화기준채무 debt in foreign currency
외화를 주고받지 않는 수입 non-draft import
외화를 주고받지 않는 수출 non-draft export
외화보유고 foreign currency holdings
외화어음 bill in foreign currency; foreign money bill
외화예금 foreign currency deposit; foreign currency deposits
외화예금계정 foreign currency deposit account
외화예금이자 interest on foreign currency deposits
외화예산 foreign exchange budget
외화예탁 foreign currency deposit with exchange bank
외화유입 foreign currency inflow
외화준비 external reserves; foreign currency reserves; foreign reserves
외화준비고 foreign exchange reserves; official foreign exchange reserves; sold and foreign exchange reserves
외화준비통계 statistics of foreign currency reserves
외화증권 foreign currency securities; securities in foreign currency
외화집중제도 foreign exchange centralization system; foreign exchange holding restriction system
외화징수외국환 foreign currency bill receivable
외화차입 foreign currency borrowing
외화채 foreign currency bond
외화통화유통 rate in foreign currency
외화표시부분을 환산함 translation of foreign currency statements
외화표시재무제표 foreign currency statements
외화할당권 right to obtain foreign money
외화할당제 foreign exchange allocation system
외화환산조정액 currency translation adjustments
외환법 foreign exchange law
외환보유고 overall balance of foreign exchange
외환차익 gains on foreign exchange
외환학설 theory of foreign exchange
외환환산손익 profit or loss on foreign exchange
요건 requirements
요구불 payable on demand
요구불계정 demand account

요구불어음 demand note
요구불예금 demand deposit
요구불채무 demand debt
요구수준 aspiration level
요물(要物)계약 contract in kind
요소가격 factor price
요소기술 factor technology
요소별 계산서 objective statement
요소별 원가 object cost
요소별 원가계산 electronic cost accounting
요소별의 objective
요소소득 factor income
요소수익률 factor return
요소원가 factor cost
요약 abstract
요약계정식 condensed account form
요약대차대조표 condensed balance sheet
요약보고식 condensed report form
요약손익계산서 condensed income statement
요요주식 yo-yo stock
요율단계변경 bracket creep
요율인상 rate hike
요율인하 rate cut
요인분석 attribution analysis
요주의명부 watch list
용선계약 affreightment; charter contract; charterparty
용수지역권 servitude for use of water
용역단위 service unit
용역생산고법 services output method
용역원가 service cost
용역제공 utility service
용인할 만한 수준 acceptable level
용지 land required for
용지비 land cost
용지품질조건 land quality terms
우대세제 special tax preferences
우대조치 favorable treatment
우대조치기간 free ride period
우량발행체 premium borrower; prime borrower; prime issuer
우량상품 blue chip stock
우량어음 prime bill; prime paper
우량의 premier
우량인 in good standing
우량주 blue chip; quality stock
우루과이라운드 Uruguay Round
우발거래 contingent transaction
우발경비 accidental cost
우발비용 contingent charge
우발사건회계 accounting for contingencies
우발사상 contingency
우발성 워런트 contingent warrant
우발손실 casual loss; contingent loss; loss contingency
우발손실준비금 special contingency reserve
우발신용스와프 contingent credit swap
우발이익 casual profit; contingent profit
우발자금 contingent fund
우발자산 contingent assets
우발적인 손익 windfall loss or gain
우발적인 위험 contingency risk
우발채무 contingent debt; contingent liabilities
우발채무적립금 contingent reserve
우선권 preferential right
우선권부 사채 prior bond
우선대부 senior loan
우선대출금리;프라임레이트 prime rate
우선매수권 preemption
우선배당 preference dividend; preferred dividend
우선배당부담배율 preferred dividend coverage ratio
우선성 priority
우선시키다 overriding
우선입찰자 preferred bidder
우선적인 보통주 preferred ordinary share
우선주 preferred equity; preferred stock
우선주배당금 dividend on preferred stock
우선주상환준비금 reserve for retirement of preferred stock
우선주식자본 preferred stock capital

우선주의 주주 preferred stockholder
우선주자본금 capital stock preferred
우선증권 senior securities
우선지불 preferential payment
우선지불채무 privileged debts
우선차압권 priority of attachment
우선채권 preferential bill
우선채권자 preferential creditor; preferred creditor; priority creditor
우선채무 preferred liability; senior debt
우선출자증권 preferred equity securities
우송료 mailing cost; postage
우송료선불 postage to be paid on delivery
우송료지불필 postage paid
우애조합 friendly society
우연손실보험 contingency insurance
우연오차 accident error
우월한 권리 paramount right
우위 edge down; precedence
우정관서 postal agencies
우편수표 postal check
우편예금이자 interest on postal savings
우편일수 mail days
우편저금 postal deposit; postal savings
우편저금법 Postal Savings Law
우편환 postal money order
우호적인 benign
우회무역 roundabout trade
우회생산 roundabout production
운동 interlocking
운송 transportation
운송료 transportation charges
운송보험 transport insurance; transportation insurance
운송비 carriage; shipping charge
운송비와 보험료를 포함해서 carriage and insurance paid to
운송비포함 carriage paid to
운송설비 transportation equipment
운송약관 transit clause
운송업 transportation business
운송업자 transportation company
운송용기기품선물 transportation equipment futures
운송용기기품업계 transportation equipment industry
운송인인도 free carrier
운송장가격 invoice amount
운송중 on passage
운송클레임 transportation claim
운영기본방침 basic administration policy
운영목표 intermediate target
운용 management
운용과 조달 사이의 기간차 maturity gap exposure
운용부분 cash value
운용실적 investment performance
운용이익 yield on investment
운용자산 invested assets; operating assets; working assets
운용자산액비례보수방식 compensation plans based on assets
운용잔고 working balance
운용장 position sheet
운임 cartage; fare
운임과 보험료 포함 cost; insurance and freight
운임보험 freight insurance
운임수입 freight receipts; freight revenue
운임유전스 freight usance
운임자금 circulating fund
운임전불 freight prepaid
운임착불 freight to collect
운임포함 cost and freight
운임환불제 deferred rebate system
운전비 running cost
운전비용 operating cost
운전시간법 working-hours method
운전자금 operating capital; operating fund; working capital; working fund
운전자금관리 working capital control
운전자본감소 deductions from working capital

운전자본구성 composition of working capital
운전자본매상률 sales to working capital
운전자본분석 working capital analysis
운전자본비율 working-capital ratio
운전자본상태 working capital position
운전자본운용 application of working capital
운전재고자산 working inventory
워런트계약서 warrant agreement
워런트대리인 warrant agent
워런트밸류 warrant value
워런트부 전환사채 convertible bond with warrant
워런트시장 warrant market
워런트채 bond with warrant; debenture with warrant; warrant bond
워런트패러티 warrant parity
원가 cost; initial cost
원가 및 비용 cost and expenses
원가(이윤) 가산방식 cost plus
원가; 조업도; 이익 관계 cost-volume-profit relationship
원가보험료·운임포함 가격 CIF price
원가가치 cost value
원가감사 cost audit
원가계산 cost accounting
원가계산 costing
원가계산기간 cost accounting period; costing period; cost accounting standards
원가계산단위 costing unit
원가계산서 cost card; cost statement
원가계산제도 cost accounting system
원가계산표 cost sheet
원가계정 cost account
원가관리 cost control
원가구성요소 components of cost
원가구조 cost structure
원가기간배분 periodic allocation of cost
원가기준 cost standard
원가기준법 cost plus method
원가단위 cost unit
원가대상 cost object
원가로 at cost
원가방식 interest capitalization method
원가배당 allocation of cost
원가배분 cost distribution
원가법 cost method; valuation at cost
원가보고서 cost report
원가분석 cost analysis
원가비교법 minimum cost rule
원가삭감 cost savings
원가산정 cost finding
원가시스템 cost system
원가요소 cost element
원가원장 cost ledger
원가율 cost rate
원가의식 cost consciousness
원가이하로 below cost
원가이하주의 cost-or-less principle
원가저감계획 cost-reduction programs
원가주의 cost principle; cost basis
원가차액 cost variance
원가차액계정 variance account
원가차액조정 adjustment of cost variance; apportionment of cost valuation; disposition of cost variance
원가차이분석 analysis of cost variances
원가회수 cost recovery
원가회수기간 recovery period
원가흡수 cost absorption
원계약 prime contract
원고 complainant; exchange rate in favor of won; plaintiff; strong won
원고 디플레 deflation caused by won appreciation
원고차익 exchange gain from the won appreciation
원금 principal amount
원금반제 amortization of principle
원금증가형 스와프 accreting swap
원기준 denominated in won
원기준외국채 foreign won denominated bond
원달러시프트 switch from won to dollars

원데이리저벌 one day reversal
원리 principal and interest
원리균등반제 equal monthly payments with interest
원리균등분할반제 level payment
원리균등불방식 equal payment method
원리균등불채 annuity bond
원리균등상환방식 annuity repayment method
원리반제액 interest and amortization
원리반제형모기지 repayment mortgage
원리주의 fundamentalism
원리지불 debt servicing; redemption and coupon payments; repayment of interest and principal
원리합계 interest included
원만한 소화 smooth absorption
원만한 유통 smooth trading operation
원문서 script
원보험 original insurance
원보험증서 original insurance policy
원본 original document
원본; 본인 principal
원본균등반제 principal-equal monthly payment
원본균등불방식 equal installment repayment method
원본금리를 완전분리함 complete stripping between interest and principal
원본만 principal only
원본보증 principal guaranteed
원본상환 redemption of principal; refund of principal
원본상환기간 amortization period
원본상환방법 principal amortization schedule
원본소유자이동 changes of owners of the principal
원본지불 principal payment
원본확실성 capital certainty
원부 original register
원산지증명 certificate of origin
원상회복;손해배상금 restitution
원수보험 direct insurance
원수보험료 direct premium
원수회사 direct insurer
원스톱파일링 one stop filing
원시기입 original entry
원시기입부 book of original entry
원시용장 prime letter of credit
원시자본 original capital
원시프트 shift to won
원신용장 master L/C; original credit; prime credit
원외계약 lobbying contract
원외운동 lobbying
원유가격연동형 사채 petrobond
원유선물옵션 crude oil futures option
원유오염배상책임보험 oil pollution liability insurance
원인 cause
원인채권 causal credit
원자력보험 unclear energy insurance
원자력손해배상책임보험 unclear energy liability insurance
원자력재산보험 nuclear energy property insurance
원자산 underlying assets
원자산의 underlying
원장 ledger
원장계 ledger clerk
원장계정 ledger account
원장대체 ledger transfer
원장마감 closing the ledger
원장에 옮겨 적다 post to the ledger
원장을 회복하기 위한 지출 expenditure incurred for the restoring to its original state
원장의 각 계정을 마감함 closing all accounts in the ledger
원장자산 ledger assets
원장잔고 balance on ledger; ledger balance
원장체결 closing of the ledger
원장페이지수 ledger folio
원재료 primary materials; raw and processed

materials
원재료구입보고서 material purchased report
원재료반환표 returned materials report
원재료수입보고서 material received report
원재료원장 stores ledger
원재료재고 raw material inventory
원저 depreciation in won
원적국주의; 본점감독주의 home country control
원조 assistance
원조금 aids
원조를 바라는 쪽 aid recipients
원조청원 aid prayer
원조하다 assist
원증권; 대상증권 underlying securities
원천 및 용도계산서 source and disposition statement
원천공제소득세 income tax withheld at source
원천과세 pay-as-you-earn; tax deducted at the source; taxation at the source; withholding tax
원천과세부담방식 tax absorption credit
원천분리과세 taxation on interest or capital gains separately withheld from other income
원천선택 withholding tax option
원천선택과세 optional assessment
원천세액공제 withholding tax credit
원천소득세 income tax collected at the source; withholding tax on income
원천예금 amount withheld
원천징수 withholding at the source
원천징수소득세 withholding income tax
원천징수와 납부 withholding and payment
원천징수의 대상이 되는 소득 scope of income subject to withholding income tax
원천징수의무자 withholding agent
원천징수제도 withholding tax system
원천징수표 withholding exemption certificate
원칙적인 납세지 general place of tax payment
원포장 original package
월가 Wall Street
월간고저 monthly high and low
월계표 monthly statement of account
월권행위 ultra vires activities
월드인덱스 world index
월말 end of the month; month-end
월말결산 monthly accounting
월말인도 month-end delivery
월보 monthly report
월부 monthly installment
월부투자계획 monthly investment plan
월부판매 installment sales; monthly installment sales
월부판매금융 financing for sales by installment payment
월스트리트저널 Wall Street Journal
월액균등지불 equal monthly payment
월중평균 monthly average
월차계산서 monthly statement
월차대차대조표 monthly balance sheet
월차손익계산서 monthly income statement
월차시산표 monthly trial balance
월차총평균법 monthly average method
월할계산 accounting by month
웨이브이론 Wave Theory
웨지 wedge
웨지포메이션 wedge formation
위기관리 crisis management
위로금 money in token of sympathy
위문금 solatium
위반 breach; contravention
위반행위 misconduct
위법대부 illegal lending
위법행위 illegal act
위성시장 satellite market
위약금 cancel money; forfeit; penalty
위약금액 penal sum
위약손실보상기금 Default Compensation Fund
위약손실보상기금특별위탁금 Special Deficit for the Default Compensation Fund
위약손실보상준비금운용 management of the

default compensation reserve
위약손실보상준비금을 적립함 accumulation of default compensation reserve
위약손실준비금;위약손실보상준비금 default compensation reserve
위약이자 penal interest
위원회 committee
위원회 백서 Commission's White Paper EC
위원회규칙 committee regulations
위임계약 contract of commission
위임장 letter of attorney; power of attorney
위임장;워런트 warrant
위임장경합 proxy contest
위임장근유 proxy solicitation
위임장쟁탈전 proxy fight
위임장투표 proxy vote
위임통지 notice of abandonment
위임하다 delegate
위장거래 disguised transaction
위장분실 false missing
위장자금 laundered money
위조 counterfeit; fabrication
위조수표 forged check
위조어음 forged bill
위조주 bogus stock
위조주권 forged stock
위조지폐 forged note; green goods
위조카드 counterfeit card
위크오더 week order
위크폼 weak form
위클리리저벌 weekly reversal
위탁 consignment; entrustment
위탁가공무역 processing deal
위탁거래 agency transaction
위탁계약 consignment contract
위탁계약서 commission of authority
위탁계정으로 on customer's account
위탁금 money in trust; trust money
위탁매매 consignment sales and purchases
위탁매매인 commission agent
위탁매매인;수수료 commission
위탁매입 buying on commission
위탁무역 trade on commission
위탁보증금비율 initial margin requirements
위탁분의 for customer's account
위탁수수료 brokerage commission; commission on consignment; consignment fee
위탁시의 지시사항 instructions at entrustment
위탁업무수수료 entrusted business commission
위탁연구 sponsored research
위탁인 consignor
위탁조항 abandonment clause
위탁증거금 consignment guarantee money
위탁증거금;차금;중간이윤 margin
위탁판매 best efforts selling; consignment sale; sale on commission; selling on a consignment basis
위탁판매계약 consignment sales contract
위탁판매미수금 account due on consignment -out
위탁판매수수료 commission to consignee
위탁판매수입 import on consignment
위탁판매수출 export on consignment
위탁품 consignment goods; product on consignment
위탁품송장 consignment invoice
위헌의 unconstitutional
위험 hazard; jeopardy; peril
위험기간 duration of risk
위험노출 risk exposure
위험변동 change of risk
위험부담인수 assumption of risk
위험분산 diffusion of risks
위험선택 selection of risk
위험선호자 risk lover
위험약관 perils clause
위험자본리스크 risk capital
위험자산 risk assets; risky assets
위험자산믹스 risky assets mix
위험자산비율 risk asset ratio

위험점 peril point
위험준비금 contingency fund
위험체증의 원리 principle of increasing risk
위험한정효과 effect of limiting risk
위험회피 risk aversion
위험회피;리스크헤지 risk hedge
윌리엄즈법 Williams Act
유가약인(有價約因) valuable consideration
유가증권 negotiable securities; securities; valuable papers
유가증권거래세 securities transaction tax; securities transfer tax; stock turnover tax
유가증권거래세법 securities transaction tax law
유가증권견본 specimen of certificates of the security
유가증권계정 securities account
유가증권계출서 registration statement
유가증권관리신탁 securities administration trust
유가증권관리책임자 person for handling securities
유가증권기입장 securities register
유가증권담보대부금 loan secured by securities
유가증권매각기입장 investment sold register
유가증권매각손 loss on securities sold
유가증권매각익 profit on securities sold
유가증권매매 buying and selling of securities; transaction in securities
유가증권매입 securities purchase
유가증권매입기입장 investment purchased register
유가증권매출집금 collection of securities by purchase
유가증권명세표 schedule of securities
유가증권법정평가법 statutory valuation method of securities
유가증권보고서 financial report; periodic securities report; securities report
유가증권상장신청서 application for listing of security
유가증권상품 designation of security
유가증권손익 security income and expense
유가증권신고서 securities registration statement
유가증권신고효력발생통지서 notice to inform of taking effect of securities registration statement
유가증권신탁 securities in trust
유가증권양도 transfer of securities
유가증권양도소득 income from transfer of securities
유가증권옵션 options based on securities
유가증권옵션거래 options trading on securities
유가증권원장 investment ledger; securities ledger
유가증권을 대차함 lending or borrowing of securities
유가증권을 조합함 combination of securities
유가증권의 범위 scope of securities
유가증권의 분류 classification of securities
유가증권이전세 tax for transfer of securities
유가증권인도표를 교부함 delivery of due bill
유가증권인수업법 securities underwriting business law
유가증권준비 securities reserve
유가증권지수선물거래 futures trading based on securities price index
유가증권취급자 securities handling clerk
유가증권취득가액 acquisition cost of securities
유가증권통지서 statement of notification of the specified issuance of securities
유가증권판매익 capital gain from sales of securities
유가증권평가 appraisal of securities; valuation of securities
유가증권평가법 appraisement method of securities
유가증권평가손 loss from revaluation of securities
유가증권평가익 gains from appreciation of

securities
유가하락 collapse in oil prices
유급휴가 compensated absence; vacation with pay
유급휴가회계 accounting for compensated absences
유기적인 자본구성 organic composition of capital
유니버설뱅킹 universal banking
유니버설보험 universal life insurance
유니크셀링프로포지션 unique selling proposition
유닛당 순자산가치 net asset value per unit
유닛링크보험 Unit Linked Life Insurance
유닛오브어카운트채 unit of account bond
유닛트러스트 unit trust
유담보 collateralized
유담보론 secured call loan
유담보익일물 collateralized overnight
유도목표 target level
유동담보 floating charge
유동담보결정화 crystallization of floating charge
유동보험증권 floating policy
유동부분 liquid part
유동부채 current liabilities; floating liability
유동부채비율 ratio of current liabilities to net worth
유동비율 current ratio; liquid ratio; working capital ratio
유동성 liquidity
유동성 배열 current-first order
유동성 배열법 current arrangement
유동성 비율 solvency ratio
유동성격차 liquidity differential
유동성결핍 reduced liquidity
유동성관리 liquidity management
유동성동기로 인한 매매 liquidity-motivated transactions
유동성딜레마 liquidity dilemma
유동성리스크 liquidity risk
유동성배열법 order of liquidity
유동성부족 liquidity scarcity
유동성분산 liquidity diversification
유동성분석 liquidity analysis
유동성비율 liquidity ratio
유동성상장주 liquidity-driven issue
유동성선호이론 liquidity preference theory
유동성압박 tightening of liquidity
유동성예금 liquid deposit
유동성위기 liquidity crisis
유동성위험 crisis of liquidity
유동성의 함정 liquidity trap
유동성이 낮은 상품 illiquid issues
유동성이 낮은 자산 illiquid assets
유동성조정필 liquidity adjusted
유동성준비금 liquid reserve
유동성지향상장 liquidity-driven market
유동성창출 liquidity creation
유동성포지션 liquidity position
유동성프리미엄 liquidity premium
유동성효과 liquidity effect
유동자본 circulating capital; floating capital; liquid capital
유동자산 circulating assets; current assets; floating assets; liquid assets
유동자산가설 liquid-asset hypothesis
유동자산비율 ratio of current assets to total deposits
유동자산회전기간 current-asset cycle
유동주 floating shares; floating stock
유동주식수 number of floating shares
유동주주 floating shareholder; liquidity index
유동채무 floating debt
유러금융시장 Eurocurrency banking market
유러기업어음 Eurocommercial paper
유러노트퍼실리티 Euronote facility
유러달러 Eurodollar
유러달러선물옵션 Eurodollar futures option
유러달러예금 Eurodollar deposit
유러달러예금금리선물 Eurodollar depositary interest futures

유러달러자금시장 Eurodollar market
유러달러정기예금 Eurodollar time deposit
유러대부시장 Eurocredit market
유러마크선물 Euromark futures
유러머니 Euromoney
유러시장 Euromarket
유러신디케이트론 Eurosyndicate loan
유러엔 Euroyen
유러엔금리 Euroyen interest rate
유러엔변동이부채 Euroyen floater
유러엔시장 Euroyen market
유러엔채발행 Euroyen bond issue
유러증권 Eurosecurity
유러채 Eurobond
유러채시장 Eurobond market; European bond market
유러통화시장 Eurocurrency market
유러통화신디케이트론시장 Eurocurrency syndicated loan market
유러트랙 Eurotrack
유러펀드채 Europound bond
유러피언옵션 European option
유러피언옵션거래소 European Options Exchange
유럽경제공동체 European Economic Community
유럽경제협력기구 Organization for European Economic Cooperation
유럽계산단위 European Unit of Account
유럽공동시장 European Common Market
유럽공동체 European Community
유럽방식 European term
유럽석탄철강공동체 European Coal and Steel Community
유럽시장의 어음교환소 Euroclear
유럽식 복리이율 annual compounding
유럽안보협력기구 Organization for Security and Cooperation in Europe
유럽연합 European Union
유럽예탁증권 European Depositary Receipts
유럽예탁증서 Curacao Depositary Receipts
유럽원자력공동체 European Atomic Energy Community
유럽위원회 European Commission
유럽의회 European Parliament
유럽자유무역연합 European Free Trade Association
유럽주식예탁증서 Continental Depositary Receipts
유럽지불동맹 European Payment Union
유럽타입 European type
유럽통화기금 European Monetary Fund
유럽통화단위 European Currency Unit
유럽통화제도 European Monetary System
유럽통화협력기금 European Monetary Cooperation Fund
유럽통화협정 European Monetary Agreement
유럽투자신탁기관 European Investment Trust
유럽투자은행 European Investment Bank
유럽펀드 European Fund
유력은행 prime bank
유로금리 interest rate on the Eurocurrecy market
유류분 legally secured portion
유리발행 interest bearing issuance
유리세라믹제품업계 glass and ceramics products industry
유리차이 favorable variance
유리한 조건 lucrative terms
유리한 투자 high grade investment
유발투자 induced investment
유배당회사평균배당금 average dividend of paying companies
유배주 dividend-paying stock
유보공제액 allowance for undistributed profits
유보금 retention money
유보금액 undistributed profits
유보사항 reservation; saving clause
유보소득에 대한 세 tax on undistributed profits
유보수익세 accumulated earning tax

유보이익 reserved profit; retained earnings; retained income
유보이익공제액 accumulated earnings credit
유보조건 under reserve
유보주식 reserved common stock
유사난수 pseudo-random numbers
유사물제작 imitation
유사품 similar goods
유사한 투자매체 similar investment media
유산관리 administration estate
유산관리인 administrator of bequest
유산관재장 letter of administration
유산분할 partition of the estate
유산상속 succession of property
유산소득 estate income
유상계약 onerous contract
유상소지인 holder for value
유상신탁 trust for value
유상증자 paid-in capital increase
유상취득 acquisition for value
유세상각 taxable depreciation
유어즈(팔았을 때) yours
유언부활 revival of will
유언신탁 testamentary trust
유언철회 revocation of will
유용한 정보 useful information
유이자부채 liability with interest
유인 inducement; invitation
유입 influx
유자격자 good and lawful men
유전스 usance
유전스레이트 usance rate
유족급부금 benefits for survivor
유족연금 survivor s annuity
유죄결정 conviction
유죄판결을 받은 자 convict
유지 maintenance
유지가격 support price
유지가능한 균형상장 sustainable equilibrium exchange rate
유지관리비용 administrative and maintenance expenses
유지비 maintenance cost
유지비;계약유지비 maintenance expense
유지자금 maintenance funds
유지준비금 maintenance reserve
유지증거금 maintenance margins
유지하다 sustain
유채발행필 주식 paid-in outstanding shares
유체동산 chose in possession
유출효과 spillover effect
유통 circulation
유통경로 distribution channel
유통계 카드 retail credit card
유통기구 distribution structure; marketing structure
유통문제 liquid stock
유통성이 없는 nonnegotiable
유통세 circulation tax
유통속도 velocity of circulation
유통시장 secondary market; trading market
유통시장에서의 채권딜링 secondary bond dealing
유통시장의 유동성 secondary market liquidity
유통시장조작 operation in the secondary market
유통시장형성 formation of secondary market
유통어음 negotiable bill
유통업계 distribution industry
유통증권 negotiable instrument; traded securities
유통증권법 Negotiable Instruments Act
유통혁명 distribution revolution
유통화폐 current money
유틸리티소비 utility consumption
유한내용연수자산 limited life assets
유한연금 limited annuity
유한차분 finite difference
유한책임 limited liability
유한책임보증회사 company limited by guarantee
유한책임조합 limited partnership
유한책임회사 limited company

유한회사 limited private company
유형고정자산 property; plant and equipment; tangible fixed assets; tangible property
유형고정자산명세표 schedule of tangible fixed assets
유형고정자산에서 공제함 deduction from property
유형상각자산 tangible depreciable property
유형자산 tangible assets
유형자산가치 tangible value
유효경쟁 effective competition; workable competition
유효구직자수 job application
유효기한 term of validity
유효수요 effective demand
유효수요의 원리 principle of effective demand
유효통계 efficient statistics
유효프론티어 efficient frontier
유효한 valid
유휴건물 unused buildings
유휴설비 idle equipment; idle plant; spare plant capacity; surplus equipment
유휴시설 idle facilities
유휴자산 idle assets
유휴토지 unused land
육상운송비 overland freight
육운업 land transportation industry
윤리 ethics
윤번제 rotational system
융자관행 lending practice
융자규제 loan restrictions; regulation of lending
융자리스크 loan risk
융자비율 loan-to-value ratio
융자신청 loan application
융자실행 extension of loan
융자잔고 balance of loans; outstanding balance of loan; outstanding loan
융자준칙 financing regulation
융자한도 loan limit
융통 accommodation
융통어음 accommodation bill; accommodation note; kite bill
융통어음발행인 accommodation marker
융통이서 accommodation endorsement
융통채 bonds issued for daily fund raising of the national treasury
은닉 concealment
은닉한 적립금 hidden reserves
은밀오퍼 confidential operation
은본위제 silver standard
은퇴급여준비금 reserve for retirement and severdance allowance
은행 **POS** bank point-of-sales
은행 bank
은행간 상장 inter-bank rate
은행간 스포트레이트 inter-bank spot rate
은행간 시장 interbank money market
은행간 예금 inter-bank deposit
은행간예금금리 interest rate on inter-bank deposit
은행간의 inter-bank
은행감사 audit of banks
은행거래약정서 banking transaction contract
은행거래일 banking day
은행거래정지 disposition by suspension of bank credit; suspension from bank account
은행거래정지처분 suspension of banking transaction
은행검사 bank examination
은행계 카드 credit cards issued by bank or its subsidiary
은행계신용카드 bank credit card
은행계좌 bank account
은행계증권회사 bank affiliated securities firm
은행공보 banking circular
은행공황 bank crisis
은행권 bank note; bank paper
은행규제 banking regulation
은행금융단 bankers syndicate
은행단 syndicate of banks; banking syndicate

은행대부 bank lending
은행데빗카드 bank debit card
은행딜러 bank dealer
은행면허 bank license
은행법 bank act; bank law
은행보증 bank guarantee
은행보험기금 bank insurance fund
은행부기 bank bookkeeping
은행부기회계기 bank bookkeeping machine
은행서비스 banking service
은행송금 bank remittance
은행수표 bank check; cashier's check; official check
은행신용장 bank letter of credit; banker's credit
은행어음 bank bill; bank draft
은행업무 bank activities; banking business
은행업선물 banks futures
은행예금 bank deposit; cash in bank; deposit due from bank; deposit due to bank
은행예금잔고 balance at the bank; bank balance
은행예금잔고증명서 certificate of bank balances
은행위임장 bank mandate
은행유동성 bank liquidity
은행유동성 liquidity of the banking system
은행융자 bank financing
은행융자한도 bank credit agreement
은행을 통한 증권금융 security credit by banks
은행의 어베이러빌러티 availability of bank
은행이율 bank rate
은행이자 bank interest
은행인수 bank acceptance
은행인수어음 banker's acceptance bill
은행인수어음할인 discount on banker's acceptances
은행자금포지션 bank fund position
은행자기자본규제 bank capital requirements
은행자동납부시스템 bank's automatic accounts transfer system
은행조사 audit on bank account
은행조회 bank reference
은행주의 banking principle
은행주주회사 bank holding company
은행주주회사법 Bank Holding Company Act
은행준비 bank reserve
은행증권간의 담장논쟁 issue of the wall between banking and security business
은행차입 bank debt; loan from banks; owing to bank
은행차입금 bank loans payable
은행차환 bank refinancing
은행채무 bank senior obligation
은행카드 bank card
은행포괄보증 banker's blanket bond
은행풀딜링 bank full dealing
은행할인료 bank discount rate
은행할인방법 bank discount method
은행휴업일 bank holiday
은환 silver exchange
음의 상환 negative amortisation
응낙 acknowledgment of order
응능원칙 ability to pay principle
응당일 corresponding day
응모 subscription
응모가격 subscription price
응모금액 amount subscribed
응모자이율 subscriber's yield
응모자이익 yield to subscriber
응익부담원칙 benefit principle
의견 opinion
의견거절 disclaimer of opinion
의견구분 scope of opinion
의견기초실(SEC) Office of Opinion and Review(SEC)
의견보류 denial of opinion
의결권 voting right
의결권다수결 majority of voting rights
의결권부 사채 bond with voting right; voting bond

의결권신탁 voting trust
의결권신탁증서 voting trust certificate
의결권이 없는 주 non-voting stock
의결권주식 voting stock
의결권행사 exercise of voting rights
의결방법 method of making a resolution
의뢰반송 requested return
의뢰서 requisition
의료급부 medical benefit
의료급부채무 health care obligation
의료법인 medical corporation
의료보건제도 health care plan
의료보험 insurance of medical expenses
의료비 medical costs; medical expenses
의료비공제 deduction for medical expenses; medical credit; medical expenses deduction
의료산업 medical industry
의무불이행 nonfeasance
의무위반 breach of duty
의사 intention; proceedings
의사결정 decision making
의사결정기관 decision-making body
의사결정지원시스템 decision support system
의사록 minutes
의사일정 agendum
의약품업계 pharmaceutical industry
의인화 이론 personification theory
의장 design
의장권 registered design; right of design
의장등록 registration of design
의제인도 constructive delivery
의제자본 fictitious capital
의제자본;수할자본 watered capital
의제자산 fictitious assets
의제증서 notional certificate
의제퇴거 constructive eviction
의존 dependence
의존도 degree of dependence
의존효과 dependence effect
이견포명 opinion expression
이관채권 transferred debt
이권 interest coupon; right and interest
이권양도 transfer of rights
이권획득 acquisition of concessions
이단계오퍼 two tier offer
이단자리스크 maverick risk
이더오어퍼실리티 either or facility
이동가중평균법 moving weighted average method
이동계속연금 portable pension
이동점포 mobile shop
이동평균 moving averag; moving equilibrium
이동평균법 moving average cost method; moving average method
이동평균수속 moving average convergence
이동평균지수 moving average index
이동평균치 moving average deviations
이득함수 pay-off function
이락기간 ex-interest period
이락채권 ex-interest bond
이론가격 theoretical price; theoretical valuation
이론가격산출 calculation of theoretical price
이론가치 theoretical value
이론금리 theoretical rates
이론상의 생산능력 theoretical capacity
이론상의 환매수익률; implied repo rate IRR
이론선물가격 theoretical future price
이론적 theoretical
이론적인 환상장 theoretical rate of exchange
이르게 하다; 이끌다 lead
이면계약 non-genuine agreement
이뮤니제이션펀드 immunization fund
이미 발생한 incurred
이미 발행한 상품 existing issue; seasoned issue
이미 발행한 채권 already-issued bond
이미 이행한 executed
이미디어트오어캔슬오더 immediate-or-cancel order
이벤트리스크 event risk
이보증(裏保證) guarantee in favor of the primary guarantor

ㅅ ㅇ

이부금융채 coupon bank debenture
이부상장 listing on the Second Section
이부채 coupon bearing bond
이분법 dichotomy
이분의 일 상각법 fifty percent depreciation
이분의 일 소유회사 fifty percent owned company
이분이승법 split taxation
이불기일 coupon payment date
이브닝세션 evening session
이사; 임원 director
이사장 president
이사회 Board of Governors
이사회결의 corporate resolution
이사회구성원 board member
이사회의사록 minutes of meeting of the board of directors
이산(離散)시간형 discrete time
이산변수형 discrete-variable
이상감모 abnormal shrinkage
이상결산 abnormal settlement of accounts
이상손실 unusual loss
이상손익항목 unusual profit or loss item
이상수익 abnormal returns
이상원가 abnormal cost
이상원가모델 abnormal growth model
이상위험준비금 contingency reserve; reverse for extraordinary casualties; unusual casualty reserve; unusual risks reserve
이상적인 밸런스 idle balance
이상표준원가 ideal standard cost
이상한 움직임 unusual movement
이상항목 abnormal item; extra item; unusual item
이서 backing; endorsement; indorsement
이서금지 prohibition of endorsement
이서금지어음 nonnegotiable bill
이서보증 guarantee by endorsement
이서양도 endorsement for transfer; transfer of endorsed note
이서양도어음 note endorsed; notes endorsed for payment
이서어음 endorsed bill; endorsed note; indorsed note; notes and bills endorsed
이서연속 succession of endorsement
이서의무 contingent liabilities on bill endorsed
이서인 endorser; indoser
이서채권 endorsed bond
이송신청기록 record on removal
이순위모기지론 second-lien mortgage loan
ECU 시장 ECU market
이연 deferred delivery
이연계약 carrying-over contract
이연계정 deferred account; deferred item
이연대변항목 deferred debit; deterred credit
이연법인세 income tax deferred
이연법인채무 deferred income tax liability
이연보수비용 deferred compensation
이연부채 deferred liabilities
이연비용 deferred charge; deferred expenses
이연비용계정 deferred charge account
이연상각 deferred depreciation
이연소득세채무 estimated future income taxes
이연수선비 deferred repairs
이연수익 deferred income; deferred revenue; income received but unearned
이연자산 deferred assets
이연자산상각 amortization of deferred assets
이연자산상각특례 exception to amortization of deferred charge
이연지불 deferred coupon
이연지출 deferred expenditure
이연채 bonds issued to substitute for government cash payment
이연채권 deferred bond
이용가능자본 available capital
이용가능자산 available assets
이용가능채권 available bond
이용원가 utilized cost
이월 carried forward
이월가액 carrying value
이월결손금 deficit carried forward; net loss

carried forward
이월결손액 amount of loss carried forward
이월계산표 post-closing trial balance
이월계정 brought forward account
이월기장 opening entry
이월비 over-carrying cost
이월상품계정 merchandise inventory account carried over
이월손익 loss and profit brought forward; profit and loss carried forward
이월외국세액공제 deduction of foreign corporation tax carried forward
이월을 허가받은 예산 approved expenses to be carried over to the following tear
이월이익잉여금 earned surplus carried forward to the following term; net earned surplus forwarded
이월잔고 balance brought forward
이월재해손실 casualty losses carried over
이월지분 carried interest
이월차손금 loss forwarded
이월평균단가불출법 month-end average method
이월평균단가지불법 method of average price at the close of the preceding month
이월하다 bring forward; carry forward
이유개시 rule to show cause
이윤분배신탁 profit sharing trust
이윤원리형 투자함수 investment function of profit principle type
이윤인플레이션 profit inflation
이윤증권 profit sharing securities
이율 earnings yield
이율격차 yield curve differential
이율곡선리스크 yield curve risk
이율곡선평준화 flattening of the yield curve; yield curve flattening
이율기간구조 term structure of yield
이율보증계약 guaranteed interest contract
이율비 yield rate
이율비차이 yield rate variance
이율상승 rise in yield
이율입찰 yield auction
이율저하 easing of yield
이율하락압력 pressure to cut interest rates
이의결정 decision on request for reinvestigation
이의신청 adverse claim; objection
이의심리청 reinvestigation organization
이의제기 request for reinvestigation
이익 investment return; profit
이익감 profit slide
이익감액 reduced profit
이익개선 pick-up of yield
이익개선스위치 yield improvement switch
이익격차 difference in yield; yield differential; yield spread
이익계정 profit account
이익곡선 profit curve
이익공헌도 profit contribution
이익관리 profit control
이익관리 profit management
이익구매 buying on an yield basis
이익구조 yield structure
이익금 profit margin of interest rate; rate spread
이익금대비배당률 ratio of earnings to dividends
이익금액 amount of profit
이익금확대 margin improvement
이익누적형 투신 contractual accumulation plan
이익도표 profit control chart; profit chart
이익률 margin ratio; profit ratio
이익률저하 slimmer profit margins
이익목표 earnings target
이익반환 profit commission
이익배당 distribution of profits
이익배당부 연금 participating annuity
이익배당세 tax on dividend
이익배당주 participating stock
이익배분 profit sharing
이익배분사채 profit sharing bond

이익배분제도 profit sharing system
이익보험 loss of profits insurance; profit insurance
이익분배금포함 cum-profit distribution
이익분배채 income share note
이익분배플랜 profit-sharing plan
이익성장률 profit growth rate
이익수준 yield standard
이익신장 profit growth
이익실현 income realization
이익에 반하는 공술 declaration against interest
이익에서 공제하는 항목 deductions
이익여잉금계산서 statement of retained earnings
이익요인 yield factor
이익유보 retention of earnings
이익을 자산화함 capitalization of interest
이익을 재투자함 plowing-back
이익의 공변동 co-movement of earnings
이익의 시계열변동 time series behavior of earnings
이익의 질 quality of earnings
이익이 변동하는 사업 business with fluctuating profit
이익이 평활화됨 smoothing of income
이익잉여금 accumulated earnings; earned surplus; earnings retained in business; reinvested earnings
이익잉여금계산금 earned surplus statement; statement of earned surplus
이익잉여금계산서 retained earnings statement
이익잉여금으로 대체함 addition to retained earnings
이익적립금 revenue reserves
이익적립금을 자본에 편입함 capitalization of accumulated earnings
이익준비금 earned reserve; earned surplus reserve; retained surplus
이익집단 special interests
이익참가사채 participating bond
이익처분 appropriation of profit; distribution of net profit
이익처분계정 appropriation account
이익처분부서 appropriation section
이익처분에 따른 주식상각 redemption of stock by distribution of net profit
이익평준화 income leveling
이익표 yield book
이익할당 profit quota
이익향상 yield enhancement
이입 import for manufacturing
이자 및 할인료 payment on interest and discount rate
이자계상정지 non-accrual
이자금융채 interest-bearing bank debenture
이자단위 minimum denomination on which interest is calculated
이자락 ex-interest
이자마진 interest margin
이자미불 accrual of interest
이자배당 dividend on interest
이자법 interest method
이자부 interest bearing
이자부 금융채 interest bearing bank debenture
이자부 어음 interest bill
이자부 채권 active bond
이자부 최고한도 maximum limit for interest rate
이자부국채 coupon-bearing government bond
이자부담 interest burden
이자부담배율 times interest earned; times interest earned ratio
이자부부채 interest-bearing debt
이자부증권 interest-bearing security
이자부채 interest-bearing bond
이자부채권의 원가 ex-interest for interest-bearing bond
이자부채권이율곡선 coupon curve
이자비용 interest cover; interest charge; interest cost
이자세 interest tax
이자소득 interest income

이자소득으로 귀속됨 real obtainer of interest income
이자율변화 interest rate change
이자율에 관한 리스크 interest-rate risk
이자율체계 system of interest rates
이자이론 theory of interest
이자일괄불 이자부금융채 debenture with lump-sum payment at maturity
이자자산화 interest capitalization
이자적립 accumulations
이자제한법 law concerning restrictions on the maximum interest rate; usury law
이자지불 coupon payment; interest outlay; interest payment
이자지불미스매치 payment mismatches
이자지불방법 interest payment method
이자클레임 interest claims
이자포함 cum-interest
이자표 coupon; cuttings
이자표가 떨어진 coupon off
이자표가 붙은 coupon on
이자표부 cum coupon
이전 relocation
이전가격세제 transfer pricing taxation system
이전가격조작 transfer pricing
이전가능한 alienable
이전경비 transfer expenditure
이전등기 registration of transfer
이전료 expenses incurred for having the user remove
이전보상금 compensation for transfer of property
이전소득 transfer income
이전수지 balance of transfer account
이전의 preceding
이전지출 transfer payment
이중가격 double price
이중경제 dual economy
이중경제구조 economic dualism
이중계산 double counting
이중계약주의 duplex system
이중계정거래 dual trading
이중과세 double taxation; duplicate taxation
이중과세방지조약 convention for the avoidance of double taxation
이중관세 double tariff
이중구조 dual structure
이중구조시장 two tier market
이중금리정책 dual interest policy
이중만기 double dated
이중바닥 double bottom
이중부채 double liability
이중분배 double distribution
이중성 duality
이중용량 dual capacity
이중운임제 dual rate system
이중위험 double jeopardy
이중은행제도 dual banking system
이중이자 double account interests
이중차압 double attachment; double seizure
이중천장 double peak
이중통화기준채 dual currency bond
이중환시장 dual exchange market
이질시장 heterogeneous market
이차계획서 quadratic programing
이차납세의무 secondary tax liability
이차보이콧 secondary boycott
이차부동산이전행위 secondary conveyance
이차부채 secondary liability; secondary rally
이차분매 secondary distribution
이차산업 secondary industry
이차온라인 second generation on-line system
이차유통자본 secondary liquidities
이차재원으로 급여를 지급함 salary from secondary source
이차저당 second mortgage
이차저당부 사채 second mortgage bond
이차적인 증거 secondary evidence
이차증권 secondary securities
이차차압 second-distress
이차초과액특약 second surplus treaty
이차트렌드 secondary trend

이차함수 quadratic function
이출(移出) export to an overseas territory
이출과세 taxation on shipment
이타주의 altruism
이탈 departure
이탈리아 **24** 오레종합주가지수 24 Ore Figure
이폭 profit margin
이표락 ex-coupon
이표채;이자부채권 coupon bond
이하 hereinafter
이하 **LIBOR** sub-LIBOR
이항분포 binomial distribution
이항분포모델 binomial model
이해 understanding
이해가 일치함 community of interest
이해관계가 없는 disinterested
이해관계자 interested party
이해대립 conflict of risk
이해충돌 conflict of interest
이해함수 particular interest
이행 fulfillment
이행보증 performance guarantee
이행보증보험 performance bond insurance
이행보증증권 performance bond
이행불능 impossibility of performance
이행증거금 performance guarantee deposit
익금불산입 exclusion from gross revenue
익금산입 inclusion in gross revenue
익금처분 distribution of surplus
익명의 anonymous
익명조합 anonymous association; secret partnership
익명참가 silent participation
익명참가베이스 silent base
익명참가자 silent partner
익스텔카드 extel card
익스퍼트시스템 expert system
익영업일인도 regular settlement
익월물 over month repurchase; over-month loan
익월인도 over-the-month delivery; value next month
익일물 overnight money
익일물레포 overnight repo
익일반제 overnight
익일반제콜 overnight call
익일반제콜금리 overnight call rate
익일인도 overnight delivery; value tomorrow
익일자금화 자금 next day fund
익일차입; 삼일후 반제 tomorrow-next
인가장 corporate charter
인간공학 human engineering
인간의 생명가치 human life value
인감 seal impression
인감신고 filing of a seal-impression
인감조회 verification of a seal impression
인감증명 certificate of a seal-impresstion
인건비 employment cost; personnel expenses
인건비율 ratio of personnel expenses
인격대표자 personal representatives
인계부채 assumed liability
인계자산을 과대평가함 overestimation of inherited assets
인계하다 assume
인과관계 causal relationship; causality
인과분석 causal analysis
인구구성변화 demographic change
인구동태통계 vital statistics
인구밀도 population density
인구통계 demographic statistics; population statistics
인근의 adjacent
인기 **50**문제 nifty fifty
인기가 높을 때 팔고 낮을 때 삼 trade against the trend
인기가 떨어진 물건 wall flower
인기주 active stock; favored stock; popular stock
인기증권 hot issue
인더머니 in the money
인더스트리얼뱅킹 industrial banking
인덱스옵션 index option

인덱스채 index linked bond
인덱스채권 index bond
인덱스파티시페이션 index participation
인덱스펀드 index fund
인덴처수탁인 indenture trustee
인도 delivery
인도가격 delivered price; delivery price
인도감시 monitoring of delivery
인도결제 delivery settlement
인도결제수량;결제건수 settlement volume
인도기준 delivery basis
인도리스크 settlement risk
인도불이행 non-delivery
인도일 date of delivery; delivery day; settlement day
인도장소 place of delivery
인도적격상품 deliverable issue
인도적격의 deliverable grade
인도적격채 deliverable bonds
인도조건 terms of delivery
인도최적채권 most deliverable bond
인도필 delivered
인도하다 bring over
인두세 capitation tax; head tax; poll tax
인디케이션방식 indication method
인디케이션오브인터레스트 indication of interest
인명계정 personal account
인명부 name list
인명원장 personal ledger
인베스터즈릴레이션즈 investors relations
인벤토리리세션 inventory recession
인보이스방식 invoice method
인사감사 personnel audit
인사관리 personnel management
인사방침 personnel policy
인사실(SEC) Office of Personnel(SEC)
인사이더 insider
인사이더거래 insider trading
인사이더정보 insider information
인사이드마켓 inside market
인세 royalty on a book
인쇄물 printed matter
인수 acceptance; honor
인수간사단 management group
인수거절 dishonor
인수계약서 underwriting agreement
인수계정 accounts to receive
인수계정대비재고자산비율 ratio of receivable to inventories
인수계정보험 accounts receivable insurance
인수계정회전율 turnover of receivables
인수과세 taxation at time of receipt from bonded area
인수단 syndicate; underwriting group
인수도 document against acceptance
인수를 위한 제시 presentation for acceptance
인수매출 sale on an underwriting basis
인수모집수수료 gross spread
인수방식 acceptance system
인수불 payment against acceptance
인수수수료 acceptance commission; underwriting commission; underwriting fee
인수어음 trade acceptances payable
인수업무 underwriting; underwriting business
인수업자 underwriter
인수업자간 계약 agreement among underwriters
인수업자의 할당액 underwriters' allocation
인수자 acceptor
인수조건부 신용장 acceptance credit
인수통지 acceptance notice; notice of acceptance
인수필 자본금 capital stock subscribed
인수필 환어음 bill accepted
인수한도 acceptance line
인수회사 underwriting company; underwriting firm
인식 knowledge
인식할 수 있는 identifiable assets
인신의 자유 personal liberty

인앤드풋딜러 in-and-put dealer
인원소멸 personnel reduction
인적 약관 personal covenant
인적과세 personal taxation
인적과세제외 personal exclusion from taxation
인적관할권 jurisdiction of the person
인적담보 personal security
인적상속재산 personal hereditament
인적소송 personal action
인적역무의 대가 remuneration for personal services
인적자본 human capital
인적자원 human resources
인적자원회계 human resources accounting
인적재산 personality
인적판결 personal judgment
인정사업연도 constructive taxable year
인정상여 constructive bonus
인정수입 constructive receipt
인증 authentication
인증등본 certified copy; exemplification
인증번호 authorization number
인증하다 adduce
인증행위 authentic act
인지 public acknowledgment; stamp
인지납부 tax payment by stamp
인지래그 recognition log
인지법 recognition method
인지세 documentary stamp tax; stamp duty; stamp tax
인지수입 stamp revenue
인지자의 수익 neighborhood benefits
인지적인 cognitive
인출 close of the market; close of the session; takedown
인출금계정 drawing account
인출플랜 withdrawal plan
인컴게인;배당소득 income gain
인컴기어링 income gearing
인컴워런트 income warrant
인컴인헨서 income enhancer
인컴펀드 income fund
인코텀스 Incoterms
인크리먼트카드 increment card
인터내셔널포트폴리오 international portfolio
인터레스트스키밍 interest skimming
인터뱅크 환거래 inter-bank exchange transaction
인터뱅크론 inter-bank loan
인터뱅크장 inter-bank market
인터컴즈 International Commercial Terms
인프라관련주 infrastructure stock
인프라비용 infrastructure cost
인프라사업 infrastructure work
인프라스트럭처 infrastructure
인프라정비 infrastructure improvement
인플레감응도 inflation sensitivity factor
인플레갭 inflation gap
인플레격차 inflation differential
인플레공급곡선 inflationary supply curve
인플레기대 inflationary expectation
인플레동향 behavior of inflation
인플레머니 inflationary money supply
인플레수요곡선 inflationary demand curve
인플레스파이럴 inflation spiral
인플레심리 inflation psychology
인플레압력 inflation pressure
인플레억제 control of inflation
인플레예비비 price contingency
인플레예측 inflation forecast; price outlook
인플레우려 inflation fear
인플레율 inflation rate
인플레율상승 pick-up of inflation rate
인플레이션 inflation
인플레이션헤징 hedging against inflation
인플레조정필 inflation adjusted
인플레지표 inflation indication
인플레헤지 inflation hedge
인플레헤지주 stock for inflation hedging
인플레회계 inflation accounting
인허가 official approval

일계매매 day trading; daylight trading
일계약 one contract
일계표 blotter; daily trial balance
일관생산 integrated production; process production
일관성 consistency
일관수송 through transportation
일관회계 throughout accounting
일괄경매;집단경쟁매매 group auction
일괄계약 contract in bulk
일괄구입 basket purchase; lump sum purchase
일괄기준 aggregate basis
일괄등록제도 self-registration
일괄등록필 증권 securities on the shelf
일괄매매 sale by bulk
일괄매매주문 all-or-none order
일괄매출 sale in gross
일괄매출; 블록오퍼 block offer
일괄모집 shelf offering
일괄반제 bullet repayment; repayment at one time
일괄반제론 bullet loan
일괄반제리스크 crisis at maturity
일괄비례배분방식 proportional method
일괄완제 pay-off
일괄운송 aggregated shipment
일괄원가 bunched cost
일괄전불 up front
일괄주문 blanket order
일괄지불 lump sum payment; single payment
일괄지불카드 non-installment card
일괄처리 batch processing
일년기준 one year rule
일년당 per annum
일년이 안 되는 해 fractional year
일년이내의 정기예금 time deposits available within one year
일당 daily allowance; per diem allowance
일드스와프 yield swap
일드커브 yield curve
일드커브스와프 yield curve swap
일람불 payable at sight
일람불상장 at sight rate; sight selling rate
일람불신용장 sight L/C
일람불약속어음 note at sight
일람불약속어음 sight note
일람불어음 at sight bill; demand bill; draft at sight; presentation bill; sight draft
일람불어음매입률 at sight buying rate
일람불환상장 sight rate
일람불환어음 sight bill
일람후 after sight
일람후 정기불환어음 time draft
일람후 지불 days after sight
일류기업 blue chip company
일류사채 prime corporate bonds
일류은행인수어음 prime bankers acceptance
일률급부연금 universal pension
일률적 uniform
일률적인 수수료 flat fee
일물일가(一物一價)의 법칙 law of indifference
일반가격 prevailing price
일반간접비 general indirect cost; general overhead
일반감사 general audit
일반경비 general expenses
일반경비율 ratio of general expenses to current income
일반경쟁입찰 open bidding; open tendering
일반고정자산자금 general fixed-assets fund
일반공공사업 general public work
일반공채자금 general binded-debt fund
일반관리비 administrative expense; general administrative cost
일반관리비 및 판매비 general administrative and selling expenses
일반관리비; 판매일반관리비 selling; general and administrative expenses
일반관리비예산 general administrative expenses budget
일반관리비차이 administrative expenses

variance
일반교서 state of the union message
일반구매력 general purchasing power
일반균형 general equilibrium
일반금지명령 common injunction
일반담보계약 general security agreement
일반대차대조표 general balance sheet
일반대체 general transfer
일반대출 conventional loan
일반대출금리 general lending rate
일반목적재무제표 general purpose financial statements
일반무역조건 general terms and conditions of trade
일반문언 general words
일반물가수준 general price level
일반물가수준회계 general price-level accounting
일반배상책임보험 general liability insurance
일반보조금 general grant
일반비 general cost
일반사업 general business
일반사업채 general corporate bond
일반소비재 general consumer goods
일반손익 general corporate revenues and expenses
일반승계인 general successor
일반시장 general market
일반영업활동비 general operating expenses
일반예금 ordinary deposit
일반우발채무준비금 general contingency reserve
일반유동성 general liquidity
일반인수 gearing acceptance
일반임금 prevailing wage
일반자금 general fund
일반자동차보험 basic automobile policy
일반자산 general public investment
일반재산세 general property tax
일반재원채 general obligation bond
일반적으로 사용되는 회계기준 generally accepted accounting principle
일반적인 리엔 general lien
일반적인 사회사 ordinary private company
일반적인 제삼자거래 arm's length transaction
일반적인 지불수단 general means of payment
일반정부부문 general government section
일반조건서 general conditions and terms of the contract
일반조정 general realignment
일반주택지 분양계획 general building scheme
일반차압금지재산 property generally prohibited from seizure
일반채권자 unsecured creditor
일반채무자 general creditor
일반통신사업자 common carrier
일반투자가 individual investor
일반항목 common counts
일반현금 general cash
일반화물 general cargo
일반회계 general account
일반회계세입세출내역 breakdown of revenue and expenditure of general account
일반회계세출 general account expenditure
일반회계원칙 general accounting principles
일반횡선수표 general crossed check
일방적인 거래 unilateral transaction
일방적인 기록 unilateral record
일변 interest per diem
일별주가지수 daily stock price index
일본국채유통시장 secondary market for Japanese government bonds
일본국채증권선물옵션거래 options trading on Japanese government bond futures
일본농림중앙금고 Norin Chukin Bank
일본보험의학회 Association of Life Insurance Medicine of Japan
일본손해보험대리업협회 Independent Insurance Agents of Japan
일본손해보험사업연구소 Non-Life Insurance Institute of Japan
일본손해보험요율산정회 oFire and Marine

Insurance Rating Association f Japan
일본손해보험협회 Marine and Fire Insurance Association of Japan
일본수출입은행 Export-Import Bank of Japan
일본엔통화선물 yen futures
일본은행 Bank of Japan
일본은행계정 accounts of the Bank of Japan
일본은행권 Bank of Japan note
일본은행권발행세 Bank of Japan note issue tax
일본은행금융 네트워크시스템 Bank of Japan financial network system
일본은행넷 BOJ net
일본은행대출 loan by the Bank of Japan
일본은행매출어음제도 Jsystem for sale of bills drawn by the Bank of apan
일본은행법 Bank of Japan Act
일본은행예금 deposit with the Bank of Japan
일본은행응모 subscription by Bank of Japan
일본은행재할인적격어음 commercial bill eligible for rediscounting with the Bank of Japan
일본은행총재 Governor of the Bank of Japan
일본은행협회연합회 Federal of Bankers Associations of Japan
일본전국지방은행협회 Regional Bank Association of Japan
일본정책은행 Development Bank of Japan
일본증권결제상황 settlement at Japan Securities Clearing Corporation
일본초장기국채증권선물 20 year Japanese government bond
일부보험 under insurance
일부불입채권 partly paid bond
일부상장 first section market; listing on the First Section
일부양도 partial assignment
일부위탁 partial abandonment
일부이서 partial endorsement
일부이행 partial performance
일부인도 partial delivery
일부인수 partial acceptance
일부준비제도 partial reserve system
일부증액반제 incidental increase payment
일부지급 partial payment; payment in part; payment on account
일부지불양로보험 single premium endowment insurance
일생의 권리 life interest
일수판매 sole agency
일수판매대리점 sole agent
일시금 money paid temporarily
일시금으로 in a lump sum
일시대부금 temporary loan
일시보류 temporary holding
일시불거치연금 single premium deferred annuities
일시불보험료 single premium
일시불생명보험 single pay life insurance
일시불연금 lump sum pension
일시불유가증권 non-amortizable securities
일시불입 payment in lump sum
일시불형 bullet
일시사용 temporary use
일시소득 occasional income
일시입체 temporary advance
일시적으로 하락할 때 구매함 bargain buying
일시적으로 하락할 때 매입함 buy on dip
일시적인 반등 brief rally; short lined rally; temporary rally
일시적인 자산대부 temporary loan on property
일시적인 현상 transitory phenomena
일시적인 호황 temporary boom
일시중단 temporary halt
일시지불 single payment annuity
일시차입금 temporary borrowing
일시차입어음 deficiency bill
일시투자 temporary investment
일어난 일; 사건 incidence
일은대출 Bank of Japan loans
일은신용 Bank of Japan credit
일인당 per capita incomes, per capita

일인당 국민총생산 per capita gross national product; GNP
일인당 상여 bonus paid per employee
일인당 생산 per capita product
일인당 세율 per capita rate
일인당 소득 per capita income
일인회사 one man company
일일계약 one day contract
일일당 per diem
일일잔고 daily balance
일일차트 daily chart
일일평균 daily average
일임신탁 discretionary trust
일임주문 discretionary order
일정기일이 있는 bearing date
일정기한지불 single order term
일정세율 fixed tax rate
일정이율 level yield
일정한 연속복리 constant continuously compounded
일주간지불 weekly payment
일주당 배당금 dividend per share
일주당 손실 loss per share
일주당 수치 per share data
일주당 순자산 book value per share; net asset per share; net asset worth per share
일주당 이익 earnings per share; profit per share; share earnings
일주당 이익변동 changes in earning per share
일주당 주주자본 stockholder's equity per share
일주주주 one share shareholder
일중고저치 intraday high and low
일차계정 primary account
일차부채 primary liability
일차분매 primary distributions
일차산업 primary industry
일차산품 primary goods
일차산품생산국기구 organizations of primary commodity producers
일차산품수출 primary industry product export
일차온라인 first generation on-line system
일차자본 primary capital
일차적인 부동산이동행위 primary advance
일차준비자산 primary reserve assets
일차초과액특약 first surplus treaty
일차평가 initial par value
일차화폐 primary money
일치 accordance; consensus
일치계수 coincident series
일치시키다 match
일치지수 coincident indicator
일치하는 accordant
일할계산 computation on a per diem basis
일할베이스 date count basis
일회불대부 single payment loan
일회성 고객 one shot customer
임검 official inspection
임계량 critical mass
임계치 critical point
임금 pay; salaries and wages
임금계정 labor account
임금공제 payroll deduction
임금급료지불부 pay-roll register
임금단위 wage unit
임금대장 payroll book
임금동결 pay-freeze; wage-freeze
임금물가 가이드라인 wage-price guideline
임금물가통제 wage-price control
임금상승률 rate of wage increase
임금상한설정 wage ceiling
임금생활자 wage-earner
임금세 payroll tax
임금세력설 power theory of wages
임금소득 wage income
임금수준 wage level
임금원장 wages ledger
임금인상 wage increase
임금인상률 ratio of wage-hikes
임금인플레이션 wage-push inflation
임금차이 wage variance
임금체계 wage structure; wage system

임금투쟁 wage-hike drive
임금하청대금지불보증증권 labor & material payment bond
임금협정 wage contract
임기 tenure of office
임대 let
임대가격 rental valu; value of lease
임대계약 lease contract
임대계약의 잔존기간 remaining period of the lease
임대료 및 사용료수입 rents and royalties
임대료 없이 rent-free
임대료수입 rent income
임대보증증권 lease bond
임대업 rental service
임대인 lessor
임대주택의 착공호수 rental starts
임료 ancient rent
임률 wage rate
임률차이 labor rate variance
임률표준 labor rate standard
임상요구 request for wage increase
임시가격설정 provisional rating
임시결의 extraordinary resolution
임시경비지출 extraordinary expenditure
임시계정 temporary account
임시금리조정법 Temporary Money Rates Adjustment Law
임시금지명령 temporary injunction
임시변동 temporary change
임시보고서 current report
임시비 contingent outlay; emergency funds; extra expenditure; extraordinary expenses
임시세리사 temporary tax accountant
임시소득 extraordinary income
임시소득 temporary income
임시소득특별공제 special deduction for occasional income
임시손익 unusual gains or losses
임시수선비 extraordinary repairs
임시의 provisional; temporary
임시의; 중간의 interim
임시이사회 special meeting of the Board of Governors
임시정지 temporary suspension
임시주권 scrip certificate
임시자산손실 property loss
임시지출 casual expenses
임시총회 extraordinary general meeting; special general meeting
임시필요에 따라 as occasion demands
임시회원대표 substitute member representative
임원급료 officer's salary
임원배상책임보험 directors and officers liability insurance
임원보수 compensation paid to directors; director's salaries and remuneration; executive salaries; officer's compensation; remuneration of officers
임원보수손금불산입 exclusion from expenses of remuneration of director
임원보장을 위한 옵션 executive compensation option
임원상여 bonus to directors
임원상여금 officer's bonus
임원선거세칙 bylaws for the election of officers
임원이 보상한 결손금 deficit covered by directors
임원채무면제 cancellation of debts of directors
임원퇴직금 officers retiring allowance
임원퇴직급여금 director's retirement allowance
임원해임 discharge of officers
임의감사 voluntary audit
임의규정 adoptive provisions
임의납세지 voluntary place of tax payment
임의법 adoptive act
임의보험 voluntary insurance
임의부동산대차권 tenancy at will
임의비용 discretionary expenses
임의상각 voluntary depreciation
임의상각법 voluntary depreciation method;

voluntary method of computing depreciation
임의상환 optional redemption
임의상환가능채권 callable securities
임의상환이익 yield to call
임의상환조항 call provision
임의상환채권 callable bond
임의상환채무 callable obligation
임의의 at one's own discretion
임의의;약인없이 voluntary
임의인도 free payment
임의재보험 facultative reinsurance
임의재보험협정 facultative reinsurance agreement
임의정리 voluntary liquidation
임의조합 voluntary partnership
임의준비금 optional reserve; voluntary reserve
임의중재 voluntary arbitration
임의편입액 voluntary additions
임의해산 voluntary dissolution; voluntary winding up
임의해약 optional cancellation
임의형 계속투자플랜 voluntary accumulation plan
임점검사 field examinations
임차권 right of lease
임차권이권 working interest
임차권평가 valuation of right of lease
임차보험 leasehold insurance
임차부동산 leasehold estate
임차수수료 rental agents' commissions
임차인 lessee; renter
임차지 leased land
임파워먼트 empowerment
임팩트론 impact loan
임퓨테이션방식 imputation method
임플라이드볼라틸리티 implied volatility
임플라이드선도금리 implied forward rates
임플라이드스프레드 implied spread
임플라이드일드 implied yield
입국세 landing tax
입금 money received; receipts of money
입금예정의 공백을 메우기 위해 받는 융자 bridge finance; interim loan
입금예측액 prospective cash receipts
입금전표 paying in slip; receipt slip
입금취소 charge back
입금통지 advice of credit
입금표 credit slip
입막음돈; 무마비 hush-money
입법부 legislative department; legislature
입수가능성 availability
입원비보험 hospital expense insurance
입장세 tax on admission
입증책임 burden of proof
입증할 수 있는 채권 provable debt
입찰 bidding
입찰공고 advertisement for bid
입찰기간 auction period; tender period
입찰발행 issue by tender
입찰보증보험 bid guarantee insurance
입찰보증서 tender bond
입찰보증증권 bid bond
입찰서 form of bid
입찰오퍼 tender operation
입찰인수;견적사양서 tender
입찰일 auction date
입찰자 bidder
입찰자에 대한 지시서 instruction to bidders
입찰총액 offering size
입체경비 reimbursed expenses
입체금 advance money; receivables from customers
입체지불 charges forward
입퇴료 secession from a corporation
입퇴비용을 보상함 compensation for moving expenses
입항비용 expenses of entering port
입항세 harbor dues; port dues
입회 attendance
입회권 common
입회금 entrance fee; initiation fee
입회금부담 burden of payment of entrance

fees
입회내 매매거래 on-hours trading
입회시 trading hour
입회시간 market hours; session period
입회심사 examination of entrance qualification
입회외 거래 trading outside the floor
입회외 분매취급료 fees for off-floor distribution
입회외 매매거래 off-hours trading
입회외 분매 off-floor distribution
입회외 분매취급정회원 regular member handling off-floor distribution
입회일수 trading days
입회장 arena
입회장거래 floor trading
입회장사무합리화시스템 Floor Order Routing and Execution System
입회장상품 floor issue
입회장에서 거래할 수 있는 회원 physical access member
입회장종업원 floor middleman
입회장회원 floor member
입회정지 suspension of transactions
입회후 상장 street price
잉여가치 surplus value
잉여금 surplus; surplus funds
잉여금거래 surplus transaction
잉여금결합계산서 statement of income and retained earnings
잉여금계산서 statement of surplus
잉여금계정 surplus account
잉여금구분 surplus section
잉여금구분의 원칙 principle of surplus section
잉여금부과 surplus charge
잉여금분석 surplus analysis
잉여금수정 surplus adjustment
잉여금조정 adjustment of surplus
잉여금조정서 reconciliation of surplus
잉여금처분 appropriation surplus
잉여금처분계산서 surplus appropriation statement
잉여익금 surplus profit
잉여인슈런스 surplus insurance
잉여적립금 surplus reserves

ㅈ

자가배달;자가인도 alongside delivery
자가보험 private insurance; self-insurance
자가보험기금 self-insurance fund
자가보험제도 self-insurance plan
자가보험준비금 reserve for self-insurance; self-insurance reserve
자가보험회사 captive insurance company
자가소비 self-consumption
자가영업소득 self-employment income
자가용자동차보험 private automobile policy
자가용자동차종합보험 special automobile policy
자가운용 internal investment management
자격을 빼앗다 disqualify
자격이 있는;관할권이 있는 competent
자격취득 acquisition of qualification
자국 nostro
자국내 onshore
자국통화 domestic currency; home currency
자국통화유통 rate in home currency
자국환매입외국환 home currency bill bought
자극책 stimulus package
자극하다 boosting
자금 등을 모아둠 earmark
자금 중의 자금 fund of funds
자금결제 fund settlement
자금계정 fund account
자금공급 supply of investible funds
자금과부족 financial surplus or deficit
자금관련스와프 fund swap
자금대차대조표 fund balance sheet
자금대체서비스 fund transfer service
자금력이 빈약함 poorly capitalized
자금부족 financial deficit; fund shortage; funding gap; shortage of funds
자금부채 fund obligation
자금세정 money laundering
자금수요 credit demand; demand for fund; fund demand
자금수지표 statement of cash flow
자금순환 money flow
자금순환계정 flow of fund accounts
자금순환분석 flow of funds analysis
자금여잉 financial surplus
자금예산 fund budget
자금용도 use of funds
자금운용 application of fund; fund management
자금운용부 Trust Fund Bureau
자금운용부 인수 subscription by the Trust Fund Bureau; underwriting by the Trust Fund Bureau
자금운용부 특별회계 Trust Fund Bureau Special Account
자금운용부예탁금 deposits with Trust Fund Bureau
자금운용부자금법 Government Trust Fund Law
자금운용수단 fund management method
자금운용표 application of funds statement;

cash flow statement; fund statement; statement of source and application of funds; statement of source and uses of funds
자금원 funding source; source of funds
자금의 원천과 용도 source and application of funds
자금이 딸림 tightness of money
자금이 크게 팽창한 overfunded
자금이동 movement of funds; transfer of fund
자금이전 fund transfer
자금인출 draw down
자금인출가능기간 drawdown period
자금인출가능기관 availability period
자금잉여금 fund surplus
자금재조달 refinancing; refunding
자금조달 financing; funding; raising of funds
자금조달력 fund raising capacity
자금조달방법 financing method
자금조달비용 financing cost
자금조달사이드 funding side
자금조달악화 tightened liquidity
자금조달액 amount raised
자금조달업무 fund raising business
자금조달코스트 cost of raising funds
자금조작 exchange funds operation
자금조정거래 exchange fund cover
자금조정법 financing adjustment law
자금조표 statement of cash receipts and disbursement
자금지분 fund equity
자금포지션 fund position
자금풀 pool of funds
자금풀법 pool of fund approach
자금협력 financial contribution
자금화 자금 good value
자금환급;자본보상 capital redemption
자금회계 fund accounting
자금회전율 turnover of funds
자금효율 leverage
자금흡수력 fund absorption
자기거래 transaction for members' account; principal transaction
자기거래증거금 clearing margin for proprietary account
자기계산에 따른 미결제약정 unsettled transactions on proprietary account
자기계정 own account
자기계정매매 proprietary trading
자기계정매매익 investment profit
자기계정으로 on one's own account; on one's proprietary account
자기금융 funds lent by members; self-finance
자기금융비율 self-finance ratio
자기매매 dealing; transaction on a dealer basis
자기부인 voluntary adjustment
자기분의 for one's proprietary account
자기사정 ones own convenience
자기생산에 관련된 고정자산 self-produced fixed assets
자기신고 self-assessment; self-return
자기신고납부제도 self-assessment system
자기앞수표 self-addressed check
자기에게 이익이 되는 공술 self-serving declaration
자기유동성 self-liquidity
자기융자 financing from brokers' own capital
자기의견 personal opinion
자기자본 net worth equity capital; own capital; own shares; shares lent by members
자기자본; 자본금; 출자금 equity capital
자기자본규제 capital requirement
자기자본규제비율 equity capital ratio
자기자본기준 capital adequacy standards
자기자본기준완화 reduced capital adequacy requirements
자기자본대비부채비율 ratio of net worth to total debt
자기자본대용 trading on equity
자기자본보완항목 Tier **2** capital
자기자본부가 equity at book value
자기자본비율 capital ratio; equity ratio; net

worth ratio; owner's equity to total assets; ratio of net worth to total capital
자기자본비율규제 capital adequacy requirements; regulatory capital adequacy
자기자본사이클 equity capital cycle
자기자본성장률 equity growth rate
자기자본시가 equity at market value; earnings on equity; net profit to net worth; percentage of profits available on net worth
자기자본이익률 ratio of profit to net worth; return on long-term liabilities plus equitycapital
자기자본장기자산율 long-term asset ratio to equity capital
자기자본충실 sound capitalisation
자기자본합계 total net worth
자기자본회전율 turnovers of net worth
자기제조에 관련된 재고자산 self-produced inventories
자기주 treasury stock
자기주권매입 issuer's own stock repurchase
자기주문 proprietary order
자기주식 common stock for treasury; reacquired share
자기주식소각 retirement of company's own stocks
자기주주매부상황보고서 report on the issuer's own stock repurchase
자기파산 voluntary bankruptcy
자기회전모델 auto-regressive model
자동갱신 automatic renewal
자동결제 automatic settlement
자동계속정기예금 automatic renewal time deposit
자동계좌이체 automatic account transfer
자동대체서비스 automatic transfer service
자동복원 automatic reinstatement
자동성 automaticity
자동안정장치 built-in stabilizer
자동어음교환 automated clearing
자동예금수납기 automated teller machine
자동이체대부 automatic premium loan
자동인가방식 automatic approval system
자동정지 automatic stay
자동집금(集金)서비스 automatic collection service
자동차론담보증권 car loan backed securities
자동차론채권 automobile receivables
자동차보험 automobile insurance; motor insurance
(일본)자동차보험요율산정회 automobile Insurance rating association ofjapan
자동차세 automobile tax; car tax
자동차손해배상책임보험 automobile liability insurance
자동차운전자 손해배상책임보험; 드라이버 보험 automobile drivers' liability insurance
자동차종합보험 package automobile policy
자동차중량세 automobile tonnage tax
자동차판매금융 automobile sales finance
자동차판매대수 auto sales
자력보증 financial guarantee
자력집행권 self-enforcement
자립회복 autonomous recovery
자매회사 sister company
자문위원회 advisory committee
자발적 항목 autonomous item
자발적이 아닌 involuntary
자발적인 실업 voluntary unemployment
자발적인 저축 voluntary saving
자발적인 조직 voluntary association
자본 capital
자본 대 산출고비율 capital-output ratio
자본가 capitalist
자본가계급 capitalist bracket
자본가동률 capital working rate
자본가치 capitalized value
자본감모준비 capital consumption allowance
자본감소 reduction of capital stocks
자본거래 capital transaction
자본거래자유화 liberalization of capital transactions

자본거출 capital contribution
자본결손 impaired capital
자본경영분리 separation between capital and administration
자본계수 capital coefficient
자본계정 capital account; capital stock account; stock account
자본계정보고서 statement of changes in stockholders' equity
자본계정지출 expenditure on capital accounts
자본고정부채비율 worth to fixed debt ratio
자본고정비율 net worth to fixed capital; worth to fixed ratio
자본고정자산비율 worth and fixed assets ratio
자본공급국 capital supplier nation
자본과세 capital levy
자본구성 capital composition; capital structure; equity structure; formal capitalization of reserves
자본구성비율 percentage of capital structure
자본금 capital stock
자본금계층별 증권회사 securities companies by size of capital
자본금명세표 schedule of capital
자본금편입액 amount credited to capital stock
자본금편입잉여금 capitalized surplus
자본금합계 total capital
자본금현재고 outstanding capital stock
자본도피 capital flight
자본등식 capital formula
자본배당 dividend from capital
자본변동 capital change
자본부담비율 capital and liabilities ratio
자본부채 capital liabilities
자본부채비율 net worth to debts; worth to debts ratio
자본분배 capital distribution
자본비용 capital cost
자본생산성 capital productivity; productivity of capital
자본설비 capital equipment
자본세 capital duty; capital stock tax; capital tax
자본소득 capital income
자본소비 capital consumption
자본소비를 조정함 capital consumption adjustment
자본수요 demand for capital
자본수유곡선 capital demand curve
자본수입 capital import; capital receipt
자본수정 adjustment of capital; capital adjustment
자본수지 capital account balance
자본수출 capital export; export of capital
자본수출국 country having deficit in cap transaction
자본스톡조정 capital stock adjustment
자본스톡조정원리 capital stock adjustment principle
자본시장 capital market
자본시장선 capital market line
자본액 amount of capital; capital sum
자본여잉금계산서 statement of capital surplus
자본연결 capital consolidation
자본예산 capital budget
자본유동부채비율 worth to current debt ratio
자본유입 capital inflow
자본유지 maintenance of capital
자본유출 capital outflow
자본유통 circulation of capital
자본의 최저한도 minimum surplus
자본이론 capital theory
자본이윤 capital profit
자본이익률 profit ratio of capital; profit ratio of net worth; ratio of net profit to capital; ratio of profit to capital; return of investment
자본이자 capital interest
자본이자세 capital interest tax

자본이전 capital transfer
자본이전수단 medium of capital transfer
자본자산; 자본재산 capital assets
자본자산가격모델; 자본자산평가모델 capital asset pricing model
자본자유화 capital liberalization
자본재 capital goods
자본재수출 capital goods export
자본절약산업 capital saving industry
자본절약을 위한 기술진보 capital saving technical progress
자본조정표 capital-reconciliation statement
자본주계정 proprietary account
자본주의 capitalism
자본주의시장경제 capitalism market economy
자본준비금 capital in excess of par or stated value
자본준비금 capital reserve; capital surplus
자본준비금편입액 excess over par
자본지출 capital disposition; capital expenditure; capital outlay
자본지출로 처리하는 개선 capital improvement
자본집약 capital intensity
자본집약성이 낮은 산업 low capital intensive industry
자본집약적인 상품 capital-intensive merchandise
자본집중 centralization of capital
자본참가 capital participation; equity participation
자본축적 accumulation of capital; capital accumulation
자본충실 capital adequacy
자본통제 capital control
자본투자 capital spending
자본편입 capitalization
자본포지션 capital position
자본하위회사 company of lower equity rank
자본한계효율표 schedule of the marginal efficiency of capital
자본형성 capital formation
자본형성; 자본수정 recapitalization
자본형성계정 capital formation account
자본회계 accounting for ownership equity
자본회복 capital recovery
자본회수 return of capital
자본회전율 capital turnover; turnover rate of capital
자사매각 divestiture of assets
자사제품 in-house product
자사주 company's own stock; corporation's own stock
자사주구매 share repurchase
자사주저가격구입권 incentive stock option
자사카드 own named cards; proper card; self-issue cards
자산 assets
자산가격 asset pool
자산가격평가모델 asset pricing model
자산가치 asset value
자산감가상각 depreciation on property
자산감정 appraisal of assets
자산개량 improvement of the property
자산갱신율 ratio of replacement of assets
자산거래 transaction in assets
자산거래에서 발생한 이득 gains derived from dealings in property
자산거품 asset bubble
자산격차 asset differentials; asset gap
자산결제 asset selection
자산계상 asset capitalization
자산계획 estate planning
자산과 부채 assets and liabilities
자산과 부채계산서 statement of assets and liabilities
자산과 부채의 미스매치 mismatch between assets and liabilities
자산과 지분 asset allocation and equities
자산관리 asset-management
자산교환 exchange of property
자산교환세법상의 특전 tax benefit for

exchange of property
자산구성 asset mix; asset structure
자산구성비율 percentage of each classification of assets to total assets
자산기반 capital base
자산기준 asset basis
자산내용연수 asset life
자산내용연수지침 asset period guidelines
자산담보율 asset coverage
자산담보증권 asset backed securities; asset-backed bond
자산대장 asset register
자산동결 asset freeze
자산매각 asset sales; liquidation of the assets
자산매각손 loss on sale of property
자산매각익 portfolio gains
자산매입 asset acquisition
자산보유 holding of assets
자산부채종합관리 asset and liability management
자산부채증감법 net worth method
자산분배 asset allocation; asset distribution
자산분배법 asset allocation technique
자산분산 asset diversification
자산상실비 loss on property destroyed
자산상황 actual state of property
자산선택 portfolio selection
자산선택이론 theory of portfolio selection
자산선호이론 theory of asset preference
자산세 tax on property
자산소득 asset income; income from assets
자산소득의 세대합산과세 family taxation of assets income
자산소유 possession of property
자산소유비용 cost of carry
자산손실 loss of property; loss on assets
자산수익률 asset return
자산시프트 asset shift
자산악화 asset deterioration
자산양도 transfer of assets; transfer of property
자산양도익 gains from the transfer of property
자산운용 asset management
자산운용자 money manager
자산운용투자 portfolio investment
자산유출 asset outflow
자산을 전속적으로 이용함 exclusive use of property
자산의 소실 extinguishment of property
자산의 질 asset quality
자산이체 asset reshuffling
자산임대 lease of property
자산재평가 asset revaluation
자산재평가법 assets revaluation law
자산재평가세 asset revaluation tax; assets revaluation tax; tax on the write-up
자산제거 scrapping of property
자산조사 means test
자산주 income stock
자산준비금 asset reserves
자산증권화 asset securitization
자산처분 disposition of assets
자산청산에 따른 손실 loss from liquidation of properties
자산취득 acquirement of properties
자산취득가액 acquisition cos of assets; acquisition cos of property
자산취득원가 cost of assets
자산클래스 asset class
자산클래스타겟 asset class target
자산평가 valuation of assets
자산평가감 asset write down
자산평가론 theory of asset valuation
자산평가손 loss from valuation of property; loss on property revaluation
자산평가손익 profit or loss resulting from valuation of assets
자산평가익 profit from valuation of assets
자산평가절하 asset devaluation
자산평가준비금 asset valuation reserve
자산평가환 revaluation of assets

자산폐기손 loss on property abandoned
자산화 단위 capitalization unit
자산화이익 capitalized interest
자산화폐 assets money
자산활용 asset utilization
자산활용률 asset-utilization ratios
자산회계 asset accounting
자산회전율 asset turnover ratio
자산효과 assets effect
자산효율 asset efficiency
자서 sign manual
자선기부 charitable donation
자선기부금 charities and donations
자세히 조사함 detailed check; due diligence
자손사고보험 self-sustained personal accident insurance
자스닥 JASDAQ
자신에 대한 증거 self-regarding evidence
자신에게 불리한 증거 self-disserving evidence
자연감 natural attrition
자연경계 natural boundary
자연권 natural rights
자연대수 natural logarithm
자연발화 spontaneous combustion
자연법 law of nature; natural law
자연보험료 natural premium
자연실업률 natural rate of unemployment
자연영업연도 natural business year
자연이자율 natural rate of interest
자연인 natural person
자연자본 natural capital
자연적 지지 natural support
자연적인 자유 natural liberty
자연적인 추정 natural presumption
자연증식계정 accrual account
자연증식자산 accrued assets
자연채무 moral obligation
자영 self-management
자영업자 individual proprietor
자영업자 퇴직연금 Keogh Plan
자영업자연금 self-employed pension
자영업자퇴직연금 self-employed retirement annuity
자영의 self-employed
자원 resources
자원개발 tapping of resources
자원배분 resource allocation
자원집중 concentration of resources
자유 liberty
자유가격 free price
자유경제 free economy
자유금리 deregulated interest rate
자유금리상품 deregulated interest rate product
자유무역지대 free trade zone
자유반제시스템 free payment system
자유변동상장제 free floating exchange rates system
자유보유의 freehold
자유보유재산 freehold property
자유시장; 제삼시장 free market
자유시장경제 free market economy
자유오퍼 free offer
자유요율 free rate
자유원계정 free won account
자유원예금 free won deposit
자유자본 free capital
자유재량 discretion
자유준비 free reserves
자유화율 liberalization rate
자율반등 autonomously strong; technical rebound
자재평가 valuation of goods
자정에서 자정까지의 24시간 calendar day
자주관세 autonomous tariff
자주규제 self-regulations; self-restraint
자주규제계획 voluntary restraint program
자주규제금리 self-restraint interest
자주규제기관 self-regulatory organization; self-restraint agency
자주납부 voluntary tax payment
자주점유 hostile possession

자치 autonomy; home rule
자필압인의무 obligation of signature and seal
자행유전스 own usance
자행인수 own bill
자회사 offshoot; subsidiary
자회사대부금 loan to subsidiary
자회사선수금 advance from controlled companies
자회사수익연동주식 tracking stock
자회사주식투자 stock investment in subsidiary
작도법 visual curve-fitting method
작업 work
작업능률 operation efficiency
작업비 operation expenses
작업손실 loss of work
작업시간 working hours
작업시간차이 labor time variance
작업일수 working days
작업장 workshop
작업전표 job slip
작업조건 working condition
작업표 production card
작업효율 labor efficiency
작은 가게 slightly firmer
잔고 amount outstanding
잔고계정 balance account
잔고부족 insufficient funds
잔고시산표 trial balance of balances
잔고식 balance form
잔고장 balance book
잔고조정식 reconciling type
잔고조회 inquiry for the balances
잔고증명서 balance certificate
잔무정리 winding-up of pending affairs
잔액인수; 스탠드바이인수 standby agreement
잔액인수발행 stand-by underwriting
잔여기간 time to expiration
잔여리스크 residual risk
잔여배분 residual share
잔여부분 residue
잔여분석 residual analysis
잔여순이익 residual net income
잔여원가 residual cost
잔여이익 residual benefit; residual income; residual profits
잔여재산 residual assets; residual property; residuary estate
잔여재산분배 distribution of residual property
잔여재산분여 distribution of residual assets
잔여재산여분 share of the residual property
잔여지분 residual equity; residual interest
잔여지출 residuary outlay
잔여청구권 residual claim
잔여클래스 residual class
잔여표준편차 residual standard deviation
잔존 remainder
잔존가격 remainder price; residual value; salvage prices
잔존가액 scrap value
잔존계정 old account
잔존기간 remaining period; time to maturity
잔존내용연수 remaining useful life
잔존물대위 subrogation arising out of salvage
잔존보험금액 sum insured left
잔존원본 outstanding balances; outstanding principal
잔존원본액 outstanding principal amount; principal outstanding
잔존율 residual ratio
잔존캐리 remaining carry
잔지보상금 compensation for residual land
잔차수익률 residual return
잔채 balances
잔채방식 charge on the declining balance
잔품 goods left
잔품; 팔다 남은 물건 frozen stock
잠재가격 shadow price
잠재고객 potential customer
잠재성장률 potential growth
잠재수요 latent demand; potential demand
잠재실업 latent unemployment

잠재워런트 latent warrant
잠재이익 profit potential
잠재적인 존재 potential existence
잠재적인 콜옵션 latent call option
잠정세율 provisional tariff; rate of temporary duty; temporary tariff rate
잠정예산 provisional budget; tentative budget
잠정입찰일 tentative auction date
잠정청산인 provisional liquidator
잠정합의 tentative agreement
잡계정 sundry account
잡비 general merchandise; miscellaneous expenses; petty expenses; sundries; unclassified expenses
잡비내역장 petty expense analysis book
잡소득 miscellaneous income
잡손 casualty loss; miscellaneous losses
잡손공제 casually loss deduction; deduction for casualty losses
잡손실을 이월공제함 carry over of casualty loss
잡손익 petty loss and profit
잡수익 miscellaneous revenue
잡수입 miscellaneous receipts; sundry income; sundry receipts
잡익 miscellaneous gains
잡자산 miscellaneous assets
잡종세 miscellaneous local taxes
잡칙 miscellaneous provision
잡화 sundry goods
장기 long-run
장기공급곡선 long-run supply curve
장기공사를 인도함 delivery of long-term contract work
장기구입 long-term buying
장기국채 long-term government bond
장기국채선물거래 10 year government bond futures
장기균형 long-run equilibrium
장기금리 long-term interest rate
장기금융 long-term finance
장기금융상품에 투자함 investment in long-term financial instruments
장기금융시장 long-term money market
장기기채 longest remaining life bonds
장기대부금 long-term loan; long-term loan receivable
장기보유자산 property held for a long time
장기보유전략 buy and hold strategy
장기부채 캐시플로비율 cash flow ratio to long-term liabilities
장기부채순고정자산 net tangible asset ratio to long-term debt
장기부채의 당기반제액 current maturity of long-term debt
장기부채자기자본율 equity capital ratio to long-term capital
장기사업 long-term business
장기선도거래 long-dated forwards
장기신용 long-term credit
장기신용금융기관 financial institutions for long-term credit
장기신용은행 long-term credit bank
장기양도소득 long-term capital gains
장기어음 long-dated bill; long-term bill
장기연기채권 long-term suspended claims
장기외화기준채권 long-term accounts receivable in foreign currency
장기외화기준채무 long-term accounts payable in foreign currency
장기이율 long-term yield
장기임대계약예금 deposit on long-term leases
장기임대차계약 long-term-lease
장기자금 long-term fund
장기자본 long-term capital
장기자본거래 long-term capital transaction
장기자본수지 long-term capital balance
장기저하 secular decline
장기전불세금 accumulated income tax prepayment
장기종합보험 long-term comprehensive insurance

장기지불능력 long-term solvency
장기차입금 long-term borrowing; long-term loan payable
장기차입반제액 reductions in long-term debt
장기차입에서의 자금증가 proceeds from long-term debt
장기채 long-dated issue; long-term bond
장기채무 funded debt; long-term debt; long-term liabilities; non-current liabilities
장기채무증가 long-term debt assumed
장기채이자 interest on funded debt
장기채차환예정증권 bond anticipation notes
장기청부공사 long-term contract
장기투자 long-term investment
장기트렌드 long-run trend
장기파동 long waves
장기프라임레이트 long-term prime rate
장기현물기간 long cash period
장기화한 prolonged
장기환 long exchange
장기환예약 long-term forward exchange agreement
장내 inside the room
장단기이율격차축소 curve flattening
장단이율격차평준화 flattening of curve
장래가치 future value
장래권 executory interest
장래의 고유리스크 future specific risk
장래이자율 forward interest rate
장래자금흐름 future cash flows
장려 incentive
장려효과 incentive effect
장문식 감사보고서 detailed audit report; long-form audit report
장문식 보고서 long-form report
장벽 barrier
장부가격 book value; book-value
장부가격감소 decrease in book value
장부가격방식 book value method
장부가격이율 book yield
장부가격주식구입제도 book value stock purchase plan
장부계 book-keeper
장부기입 book entry
장부기재가격 stated value
장부방식 account method
장부상의 구주 1주의 가격 book value per old stock
장부상의 자산가격 asset book value; book value of assets; carrying amount
장부상의 채권가격 book value of bond
장부서류를 정리하고 보존함 maintenance of books and records
장부에 계상되지 않은 손실 book loss
장부외자산 asset out of books; assets off the book; non-concealed assets
장부외채무 liabilities off the book
장부원가 recorded cost
장부잔고 book balance
장부정리 adjustment of accounts
장부화폐 book money
장소에 어울리지 않는 사람 outsider
장애 impediment
장애보상 disablement benefit
장애인공제 credit for handicapped person; deduction for physically handicapped person
장애자공제 exemption for handicapped person; physically handicapped person allowance
장외거래 outside dealing; over-the-counter transaction; trading on the over-the-counter market
장외거래상품 OTC firm
장외거래시장 third market
장외거래점 bucket shop
장외관리상품 over-the-counter managed issues
장외금리옵션 OTC interest rate option
장외등록기업 OTC company
장외등록상품 issues listed on the over-the-counter market

장외매매고 volume of over-the-counter transaction
장외매매이율 over-the-counter sales yield
장외상품시황자동정보시스템 National Association of Securities Dealers Automated Quotations
장외선물거래 off-exchange futures transactions
장외시세 quotation of over-the-counter issue
장외시장 curb market; off-board market; over-the-counter market
장외옵션 OTC option; over-the-counter option
장외주 over-the-counter stock
장외중매인 street broker
장외증거금주식 OTC margin stock
장외증권 unlisted securities
장외통화옵션 over-the-counter currency option
장외표시 indication at a store counter
장중기금리 long and medium-term interest rate
장치; 설비 device
장표관리 forms control
재갱정 re-correction
재건계획 reorganization scheme
재건계획결정 decision of a reorganization scheme
재결서 written decision
재고관리 inventory management
재고금융 inventory financing
재고단위 inventory unit
재고량 volume of inventories
재고변동 inventory change
재고비용 carrying cost
재고손 inventory loss
재고순환 inventory cycles
재고예산 inventory budget
재고율 inventory ration; inventory sales ratio; inventory shipments ratio; stock-to-sales ratio
재고자산 inventory; inventory assets; inventory capital
재고자산가격변동계정 inventory fluctuation account
재고자산감사 inventory audit
재고자산계산법 inventory method
재고자산계정 inventory accounts
재고자산보관 storage of inventories
재고자산에 적용되는 자산기준 property basis applicable to inventories
재고자산의 범위 composition of inventory
재고자산의 시가 market value of inventory
재고자산이익 inventory profit
재고자산증감 inventory variation
재고자산취득가액 acquisition cost of inventory
재고자산평가 inventory valuation
재고자산평가 valuation of inventory
재고자산평가방법 cost flow assumption; inventory valuation method
재고자산평가준비금 inventory reserve; inventory valuation- reserves
재고자산평가하락 decline in prices of inventories
재고자산회계 accounting for inventories; inventory accounting
재고자산회전기간 average age of inventory
재고자산회전율 inventory turnover
재고정리 inventory control
재고정리자산매상률 sales to inventories
재고정리자산회전일수 number of days' sales in inventories
재고조사법 retail inventory method
재고조정 inventory adjustment
재고조회 checking inventory
재고증명서 inventory certificate
재고지수 inventory indexes
재고채권 bond inventory
재고투자 inventory investment
재고평가액 inventory value
재고평가조정 inventory valuation adjustment

재고표 inventory sheet; inventory tag
재고품 clearance goods; stock ill the inventory; stock in trade
재고품대장; 주식대장 stock book
재고회전율 stock turnover
재공매 re-auction
재교섭 renegotitation
재난사무용 자산 business assets suffering from disaster
재단 foundation
재단저당 foundation collateral
재단채권 superior obligation
재담보설정 rehypothecation
재대부 further advance
재량대출 discretionary loan
재량원가 discretionary cost
재량행위 discretional act
재료 raw material
재료가격차이 material price variance
재료구입고 material purchased
재료구입장 stores purchase book
재료명세서 bill of material
재료분개장 material distribution sheet
재료비 material cost
재료비차액; 실질적인 차이 material variance
재료사양서 material specification
재료수량차이 material quantity variance; material usage variance
재료예산 material cost budget
재료원자 material ledger
재료재고고 material inventory
재료표준가격 material price standard
재료표준소비량 standard quantity of materials consumed
재리스 re-leasing
재무 financial affairs
재무감사 financial audit
재무개황 financial review
재무건전성 financial strength
재무계획 financial planning
재무고문 financial advisor
재무관리 financial management
재무국 local finance bureau
재무내용 financial condition
재무내용개시 financial disclosure
재무담당경영자협회 Financial Executive Institute
재무담당임원 chief financial officer
재무대리인 fiscal agency
재무대리인 fiscal agent
재무대리인계약 fiscal agent agreement
재무레버리지 capital leverage
재무레버리지 financial gearing
재무레버리지 financial leverage
재무레버리지비율 financial leverage ratio
재무리스크 financial risk
재무면의 증익효과 financial leverage effect
재무면의 증익효과도 degree of financial leverage
재무목표 financial target
재무밸런스 financial balance
재무보고 financial reporting
재무보고서상의 주주자본 reported equity
재무보고회계 financial reporting accounting
재무부 Department of Treasury
재무부 Ministry of Finance
재무부 중기증권 T-note
재무부 증권 Ministry of Finance Securities
재무부 통지 Notification of the Ministry of Finance
재무부단기증권시장 Treasury bill market
재무부령 Finance Ministry Ordinance
재무부발행증권 Treasury Bill issued
재무부예탁금 deposit by the Ministry of Finance
재무부원안 budget draft by Ministry of Finance
재무부장 treasurer
재무부장기증권 treasury bond
재무부조세국채증권계정 treasury tax and loan note accounts
재무부중기저축채권 treasury savings notes
재무부중기증권 treasury note

재무부증권 Finance Ministry note; treasury bonds; treasury financing bills
재무부증권; 단기증권 treasury bill
재무부증권시장 treasury securities market
재무부증권이율 Treasury yield
재무부채무증서 Treasury Certificate of Indebtedness
재무부청문절차규칙 Regulations of Procedures of Hearings by the Ministry of Finance
재무부투자채권 Treasury Bonds Investment Series
재무분석 financial analysis
재무비율 accounting ratio; financial ratio
재무상의 상승효과 financial synergy
재무상의 슬랙 financial slack
재무상품 treasury product
재무수익 financial revenue
재무예산 financial budget
재무정책 fiscal agenda
재무제표 financial statement
재무제표각주 explanatory notes to the financial statements; notes of financial statements; notes to the financial statement
재무제표감사 financial statement audit
재무제표규칙 regulations of financial statements
재무제표를 작성함 preparing the financial statements
재무제표리뷰 review of financial statements
재무제표부속명세표 schedules of financial statements
재무제표분석 analysis of financial statement; financial statement analysis
재무제표적요서 abstract of financial statements
재무제한조항 restrictive financial covenant
재무지표 financial measurement
재무지표; 재무수치 financial variables
재무처리 management of property
재무체질 financial structure
재무컨설턴트 financial consultant
재무코스트 financial cost
재무플로 financial flow
재무활동 financing activities
재무활동으로 인한 캐시플로 cash flow from financial activities
재무회계 financial accommodation; financial accounting
재무회계기준심의회 Financial Accounting Standards Board
재무회계기준자문위원회 Financial Accounting Standards Advisory Council
재무회계재단 Financial Accounting Foundation
재물손괴 property damage
재반대심문 re-cross-examination
재배부원가 redistributed cost
재벌 financial clique; zaibatsu
재보험 reinsurance
재보험거래 reinsurance transaction
재보험계약 reinsurance agreement
재보험금 reinsurance recovery
재보험레버리지 reinsurance leverage
재보험료 ceded premium; reinsurance premium
재보험브로커 reinsurance broker
재보험수수료 reinsurance commission
재보험조항 reinsurance clause
재보험특약 reinsurance treaty
재보험특약서 treaty wording
재보험풀 pooling arrangement
재보험회계 reinsurance accounting
재분류 reclassification
재분배 redistribution
재산 belongings; property
재산검사 inspection of property
재산관리명령 receiving order
재산구 property ward
재산권 property right
재산매각익 profit on assets sold
재산목록 general inventory; list of property; statement of assets
재산보유비용 carrying charge
재산분여 distribution of property

재산소득 property income
재산양도 conveyance of estate
재산에 부속되는 권리 appurtenance
재산원장 property ledger
재산을 무상으로 사용함 gratuitous use of property
재산이전금지법 disabling statutes
재산조사 audit on property
재산증가 accretion
재산증여 donation of property
재산차압 levy of attachment
재산처분능력 disposing capacity
재산평가 valuation of property
재산평가익 income from appreciation of assets
재생산 reproduction
재생산원가 reproduction cost
재생산표식 schema of reproduction
재생원재료 reclaimed materials
재수정기입 readjusting entry
재수출 re-export
재심 new trial
재심리 rehearing
재야내각 shadow cabinet
재연 resurgence
재원 financial resources; source of revenue
재인도 second deliverance
재일외은 foreign banks in Japan
재임 tenure of the office
재전환 reconversion
재정 government finance
재정가격결정이론 arbitrate pricing theory
재정개혁 fiscal reform
재정거래 arbitrage business; arbitrage operation; arbitrage transaction
재정거래와 관련된 현물포지션 positions established with index arbitrages
재정거래자 arbitrageur
재정경직화 fiscal inflexibility
재정규모 scale of central and local public finance
재정금융정책 fiscal and monetary policy
재정기회 arbitrage opportunity; arbitrage possibility
재정긴축정책 tight fiscal policy
재정데이터 arbitage date
재정력지수 index of financial condition
재정마진 arbitrage margin
재정목표 fiscal target
재정민주주의 financial democracy
재정방식 pension financing method
재정법 finance law; Public Finance Law
재정본질 fiscal structure
재정상 긴급처분 emergent financial disposition
재정상장 arbitrated rate
재정상태 financial conditions; financial position; financial status
재정상태계산서; 대차대조표 statement of financial condition
재정상태변동표 statement of changes in financial position
재정수지 budget balance; fiscal balance
재정예견 fiscal outlook
재정인플레이션 fiscal inflation
재정자극 fiscal boost
재정자극책 fiscal stimulus package
재정자금대비민간수지 receipt and payment of treasury accounts with the public
재정적자 budget deficit; deficit of fiscal balance; fiscal deficit; public sectors deficit
재정정책 fiscal policy
재정제도심의회 Finance System Council
재정제한 crunch
재정준비 fiscal reserve
재정지출 fiscal expenditure
재정지출계획 spending program
재정지출을 충당하기 위한 국채 bonds used to finance government expenditure
재정착각 fiscal illusion
재정통합 fiscal consolidation
재정투융자 fiscal investment and loan; treasury investments and loans

재정투융자계획 Financial Investment and Loan Program
재정투자 fiscal investment
재정팽창억제 fiscal drug
재정포지션 arbitrage position
재정핍박 fiscal tightness
재정환상장 arbitrated exchange rate
재정환율 arbitrated rate of exchange
재정흑자 fiscal surplus
재조달가치 prevailing value
재조정 realignment
재조정교섭 realignment negotiation
재지정 reassessment of section
재직기한 length of service; term of office
재직사망보험부 퇴직금적립제도 Superannuation Plan
재직증명 certificate of incumbency
재출발 fresh start
재취득가격 current replacement cost
재취득리스크 replacement risk
재취득비율 repurchase rate
재측정 remeasurement
재테크 financial engineering; zai-tech
재투자 reinvestment
재투자리스크 reinvestment risk
재투자이율 reinvestment rate
재투자이익 earnings reinvested
재판 adjudication
재판; 전매 resale
재판가격 resale price
재판가격유지 resale price maintenance
재판매가격기준법 resale price method
재판절차 legal procedure
재판청구권 right of access to courts
재평가 reassessment; rebalance
재평가; 재검토 reappraisal
재평가익 revaluation profit
재평가잉여금 appreciation surplus; revaluation surplus; surplus from revaluation
재평가적립금 appraisal surplus; revaluation surplus reserve
재평가적립금을 자본편입함 capitalization of revaluation surplus reserve
재평가차액 revaluation excess
재할인 rediscount
재할인금리 rediscount rate
재할인정책 rediscount policy
재해감면법 law relating to tax reduction and postponement of collection for disaster victims
재해로 인한 소실 loss arising from casualty
재해보험 casualty insurance
재해손실 loss resulting from casualty
재해손실금 loss due to disaster
재해손실이월 carry forward of casualty loss
재해준비금 reserve for accidents
재향군인관리국 Veterans Administration
재형저축 worker's property accumulation savings
재확인 double check
쟁점사항 matter in issue
쟁점에 달한 at issue
저가 basement
저가격 lower in quotation
저가격시장 lower end of the market
저가법 lower-of-cost-or-market method
저가법에 따른 평가 valuation by lower of cost or market method
저가재 lower order goods
저가주 fancy stocks; penny stock
저가주의 lower-of-cost-or-market value basis
저감; 감소 decrement
저감하다 erode
저고정가격 lower closing quotation
저금리론 low interest loan
저금리예상 anticipation of low interest rate
저금리자산 cheap money
저당계약 impignorative contract
저당권 hypothec
저당권; 모기지 mortgage
저당권부 사채 secured bond
저당권설정 establishment of hypothec;

settlement of mortgage
저당권설정등기 register of settlement of mortgage
저당권설정약관 mortgage clause
저당권설정자 mortgage debtor; mortgagor
저당권소멸 extinction of hypothec
저당권자 mortgagee
저당금융회사 mortgage company
저당론 mortgage loan
저당론금리 mortgage rate
저당물 pawn
저당보험 mortgage insurance
저당부 모기지증서 collateralized mortgage obligations
저당신용조합 Mortgage Credit Association
저당신용채 mortgage credit bond; mortgage debenture
저당약관 insecurity clause
저당우선권 priority of mortgage
저당은행 mortgage bank
저당을 되찾음 redemption of pledge
저당이 될 수 있는 동산 mortgageable chattels
저당자산 pledged assets
저당잡힘 impignoration
저당증권 mortgage note; mortgage securities
저당증서류 mortgage documents
저당차입금 mortgage payable
저대원가 absolute cost
저배주 low dividend stock
저비용 low cost
저성장 low growth; slower growth
저성장산업 low growth industries
저소득국 low income countries
저속상장 stagnant market
저수준 low level
저액면주식 low par issue
저액양도 transfer at low price
저위주 low grade stocks; low price stock
저작권 copyright
저작권사용료 royalty of the copyright
저작권평가 valuation of copyright
저장경비 storage costs
저장원재료 material in storage
저장품 inventories of merchandise and supplies
저장품 stored goods
저장품관리 storage management
저점이탈 turning upward
저조업도원가 idle capacity cost
저축계정 saving account
저축금융기관 thrift bank; thrift institution
저축금융업계 thrift industry
저축대부조합 savings-and-loan association
저축동향조사 family saving survey
저축률 savings rate; savings ratio
저축성향 propensity to save
저축예금 savings deposit
저축은행 savings bank
저축제도 thrift and savings plans
저축주 savings share
저축채권 savings bond; savings debenture; savings note
저축투자소득결정론 savings-investment theory of income determination
저축투자이자율결정론 savings-investment theory of interest-rate determination
저축함수 saving function
저축형 보험 cash value insurance
저하시키다 deteriorate
저하율 decreasing rate
저항선 resistance line
적격급부 relevant benefit
적격기관투자가 qualified institutional investor
적격담보 eligible security
적격성 eligibility
적격유가증권 eligible securities
적격인 qualified
적격인도 good delivery
적격증권 qualified securities
적격채권 qualified bond
적격퇴직연금 approved retirement annuity; approved superannuation fund; qualified

pension plan
적격퇴직연금계약 qualified pension contract; approved pension contract; approved retirement annuity contract
적격퇴직연금적립금 approved pension funds; qualified pension funds
적격퇴직연금제도 approved retirement annuity plan; qualified pension system
적격투자 eligible investment
적격투자가 accredited investor
적격투자액 qualified investment
적극신탁 active trust
적극예산 expansionary budget
적극재산 positive property
적극재정; 팽창재정 positive financial policy
적극적인 딜러 active dealer
적극적인 매입 active buying
적극적인 운용 active management; aggressive portfolio
적극적인 조정정책 positive adjustment policies
적극적인 확인 positive confirmation
적극조건 positive condition
적극투자이론 active investment management theory
적기 apt time
적당한 가격의 modestly-priced
적대적인 매수 hostile acquisition; hostile takeover
적대적인 매수를 고려하는 주식취득자 raider
적립금 accumulated fund; reserve; reserve fund
적립금반려 surplus reserves transferred to income
적립금반환 reversal of surplus
적립금편입 additions to reserves
적립금회계 reserve accounting
적립방식 funding method
적립이월 provision for surplus
적립자산 accumulated assets
적립정기예금 installment time deposit
적립플랜 accumulation plan
적립한도액 allowed limit of accumulation
적법계약 legal contract
적법의 lawful
적법절차 due process of law
적법한 legal
적법한 통지 legal notice
적선하증권 red B/L
적성상하한계수익률 optimal threshold return
적송인 sender; shipper
적송품 shipment
적시개시정보전달시스템 Timely Disclosure Network
적시정보개시 timely disclosure
적요 abridgment
적용내용연수 applicable useful life
적용법정내용연수 applicable statutory useful life
적용순서 order of application
적용원가 applied cost
적용제외 contracted out
적용제외범위 exemption regime
적용제외증권 exempted securities
적용하는 정당한 이유 justifiable reason to apply
적용할 수 있는 applicable
적은 주 scarce stock
적자 deficit, in red
적자경영 loss making operations
적자국채 deficit-covering bond
적자금융 deficit-covering finance; finance for deficit
적자기입 red-ink entry
적자보전 filing up of a deficit; making up of a deficit
적자소멸 deficit reduction
적자예산 deficit budget; unbalanced budget
적자융자 deficit financing; financing for deficit-covering
적자의 in red ink
적자임에도 배당함 dividend payment despite

deficit
적자잔액 red-balance
적자재정 deficit finance
적자전락 newly deficit; turn to red figures
적자지속 continued deficit
적자축소 reduced losses
적재목록 manifest
적재비용 loading charges
적재한 선박의 이름을 알지 못함 vessel unknown
적절하게 성장하는 growing at a moderate speed
적절한 이익 adequate profit
적정교환비 social and entertainment expenses provided in lump sum
적정베이시스 equilibrium basis
적정성장률 warranted rate of growth
적정외화준비고 optimum foreign exchange reserves
적정유동성 adequate liquidity
적정이율 appropriate interest rate
적정임금 fair wage
적채기준 issuance guidelines; issue standards; requirements for issuing bonds
적취비율 trade sharing
적하가격신고서 valuation form
적합범위 relevant range
적합성 conformity
적합하지 않은 ineligible
적환선하증권 transshipment bill of lading
전가성이론 shiftability theory
전가하다 pass on
전개 deployment
전개를 기다림 waiting for further development
전광정보판 broad tape
전구성원이 공유함 tenancy in common
전국기업단기경제관측 short-term economic survey of all businesses
전국시가지가격지수 index of urban land prices
전국신용보증협회연합회 National Federation of Credit Guarantee Corporations
전국신용조합본부 National Credit Union Administration
전국은행계정 banking accounts of all banks
전국은행대출약정평균금리 average contracted interest rates on loans and discounts of all banks
전국은행신탁계정 trust accounts of all banks
전국중앙치 national median
전국증권거래소협의회 National Conference of Stock Exchanges
전국평균 national averages
전국평균기금 national reserve fund
전권 plenipotentiary
전기 previous term
전기가스공업 electric power and gas industry
전기가스세 electricity and gas tax
전기대비 quarter-on-quarter
전기세 electricity tax
전기손익금 profit or loss brought forward from previous business term
전기손익수정 correction of prior years earnings; prior period adjustment
전기수정항목 correction of prior periods
전기업계 electric industry
전기이월손실 loss brought forward from the previous term
전기이월이익금 retained earnings at the beginning of a period; surplus brought forward from the previous term
전기이월이익잉여금 surplus at the beginning of the period
전기이월차손금 deficit at the beginning of a period
전기제품선물 electric appliances futures
전기제품업계 electric appliances industry
전기통신사업 telecommunication business
전기통신사업자 telecommunication carriers
전기통신시장 telecommunication market
전날 종가보다 싼 거래 downtick

전년 preceding year; previous year
전년대비변화율 year-to-year percentage change
전년도 preceding fiscal year
전년동기 corresponding period of last year
전달 과정에서 발생한 차이 errors in posting
전당포 pawn-shop
전대제도 putting-out system
전대차 under lease
전도금 advanced money; down payment; imprest cash
전략 strategy
전략리스크 strategic risk
전략분야 strategic field
전략산업 strategic industries
전략적인 의사결정 strategic decision
전략적인 제휴 strategic alliance
전략적인 파트너 strategic partner
전력가스주 utilities stock
전력개발주식회사 Electric Power Development Co., Ltd.
전력비 electric power expense; power expense
전력채 electric power bonds; utilities bond
전망 near time prospect
전매 public monopoly
전매과세 monopoly assessment; taxation on government monopoly
전매납부금 state monopoly payment
전매이익 monopoly profit
전매장 sellers over
(신용거래나 선물거래에서) 전매나 환매를 마치고 거래관계를 청산함 evening up
전몰자 유족 war bereaved
전무이사 senior managing director; senior managing governor
전문가 Fed watcher FRB; professionals
전문보험회사 monoline insurance company
전문상품취급업자 special product firm
전문용어 technical terms
전문적으로 artificially
전문적인 상장 professional's market
전문적인 증권회사 boutique
전문직업인배상책임보험 professional liability insurance
전문품 specialty goods
전문화; 특화 specialization
전미교직원보험퇴직연금조합 Teachers' Insurance Annuity Association of America
전미기업재무담당자협회 NACT
전미선물협회 National Futures Association
전미증권분석가연합회 Financial Analysts Federation
전미증권업자협회 Securities Industry Association
전미증권업협회 분쟁처리규칙 Code of Procedure for Handling Trade Practice Complain
전미증권업협회통일관습규칙 Uniform Practice Code
전반자산 general corporate assets
전반적인 시황 undertone
전방차분 forward difference
전방통합 forward integration
전부원가 absorption cost; full cost; total cost
전부원가계산 absorption costing; full costing; total costing
전부차압 grand distress
전불금반환보증 refundment guarantee
전불금반환보증증권 refund bond
전불보험료 insurance prepaid
전불식 할부판매금융 finance for prepaid installment sales
전불여비 travel advances
전불자산 prepaid asset
전불지대 forehand rent
전불한 사망보험금 accelerated benefits
전사업연도 preceding taxable year; prior taxable year
전세보증금; 거래보증금 deposit with landlord
전속관할권 exclusive jurisdiction
전속외무원제도 career agency system
전속중개자 tied-agent

전손 total loss
전손만의 담보 total loss only
전수수익 income in advance
전수이자계정 deferred interest account
전수익금 unearned revenue
전술적인 자산배분 tactical asset allocation
전신거래환 reverse telegraphic transfer
전신매상장 telegraphic transfer buying rate; telegraphic transfer selling rate
전신송금 electronic fund transfer; cable transfer; wire transfer
전신신용장 cable credit
전신환 telegraphic transfer
전액보험 full insurance
전액불입 fully paid-up; payment in full
전액불입필 주식 full paid capital stock
전액영수서 receipt in full
전액정화준비제도 total reserve system
전액지불 full payment
전액출자한 자회사 fully owned subsidiary
전영업양도 transfer of the whole business
전용 exclusive use
전용의 single purpose
전용주택 exclusive-occupation house
전원일치로 unanimous
전월 preceding month; previous mouth
전위험담보 against all risks
전일대비변동률분포 distribution of single day advances and declines
전일로 앞당기다 revert to the previous day
전일부 pre-date
전일부 수표 antedated check
전일부로 하다 predate
전일부의 antedating
전일종가 last close price; previous close price
전자거래시장 electronic trading market
전자공학 electronic engineering
전자금융 electronic banking
전자산합동방식 portfolio method
전자상거래 electronic commerce
전자시장 electronic market
전자주문전달시스템 electronic order transfer system
전자화폐 electronic money
전장 morning session; morning trading session
전쟁약관 war clause
전쟁위험 war perils
전적 change in employment
전조 preceding article
전종목지수 **FT** Actuaries All-share Index FT
전통시장 traditional market
전통적인 상품시장 conventional commodity market
전페이지 preceding page
전표 chit; slip; ticket; voucher
전표대조 vouching
전표식 부기 slip bookkeeping
전표식회계법 slip system of accounting
전표제도 slip system
전표지불제도 chit system
전화가입권 right of telephone; telephone subscription right
전화를 통한 거래권유 cold call
전화보급률 penetration of phones
전화부스 telephone booth
전화요금 telephone rates
전화주문 order by telephone
전화확인 verification by telephone
전환 디스카운트 conversion discount
전환가격 conversion price
전환가격방식 conversion price formula
전환가격을 넘는 금액 premium over conversion value
전환가정법 if-converted method
전환가치 conversion value
전환대리인 conversion agent
전환모기지 convertible mortgage
전환비율 conversion parity; conversion ratio
전환사채 convertible bond; mezzanine money
전환사채이율 convertible bond index
전환우선주 convertible preferred stock
전환일 conversion date

전환자산 convertible assets
전환점 turning point
전환조건 conversion conditions
전환주식 convertible stock
전환증권 convertible securities
전환청구 demand for conversion
전환청구기간 conversion period
전환프리미엄 conversion premium
전회규칙 front-foot rule
절대명령 rule absolute
절대소유가설 absolute income hypothesis
절대수준 absolute level
절대오차 absolute error
절대우위 absolute advantage
절대적 고정자산 absolute fixed capital
절대적 양도 absolute conveyance
절대적 퍼포먼스 absolute performance
절대적인 absolute
절대적인 부동산보유권 fee simple absolute
절대전손 absolute total loss
절대주의 absolutism
절대차액 absolute difference
절대치 absolute value
절대확률 absolute probability
절대확산모델 amortizing diffusion model
절도범 thief
절상; 재평가; 평가절상 revaluation
절세 tax saving
절세거래 tax oriented transaction
절점 node
절차감사 procedural audit
절차법 adjective law
절차수권서 authority to pay
절차이행 fulfillment of procedures
절차중지예고 caveat
절충방식 compromise method
절하 devaluation
절하리스크 devaluation risk
절하하다 devalue
절호의 매장 attractive trading opportunity
점용권평가 valuation of occupancy right
점유 possession
점유자 occupant
점유적인 리엔 possessory lien
점유채무자 debtor in possession
점유하다 perception
점유한 seized
점유합동 unity of possession
점진적인 국유화 creeping nationalization
점탄력성 point elasticity
점포종합보험 storekeepers' comprehensive insurance
점포휴업보험 store business interruption insurance
점프과정 jump process
접수로 인한 손실 expropriation loss
정관변경 amendment of articles of corporation
정규가 아닌 상장 back door listing
정규감사절차 normal auditing procedures
정규권 regular interest
정규방정식 normal equation
정규부기의 원칙 principle of orderly system of bookkeeping
정규분포 normal distribution
정규절차 normal procedure
정규확률분포 normal probability distribution
정기간행물 periodicals
정기감사 periodic audit
정기거래 periodical transaction; time bargains; time transaction
정기대부 time loan
정기보험 term insurance
정기생명보험 term life insurance
정기선물 term repo; term RP
정기수익 periodical return
정기시장 terminal market
정기실지재고 periodic actual inventory
정기예금 fixed deposit; installment savings; term deposits; time deposit; time saving
정기예금계정 time deposit account
정기예금금리 interest rate on time deposit

정기예금담보대출금리 interest rate on loans secured by time deposit
정기예금증서 certificate of time deposit; time deposit certificate
정기재고조사 periodic inventory
정기적금 periodical deposits
정기주주총회 regular general meeting of shareholders
정기총회 regular general meeting
정기콜시장 period call market
정당방위 self-defense
정당성 validity
정당하다고 인정하다 validate
정당한 권한이 있는 기관 legal organ
정당한 보상 just compensation
정당한 주의 due care
정당한 지대(地代) rent reasonably fixed
정당행위 justifiable act
정당화 justification
정독 perusal
정량분석 quantitative analysis
정량적인 어셋앨로케이션 quantitative asset allocation
정령(政令) government ordinance
정례이사회 regular meeting of the Board of Governors
정리; 해결 strengthening
정리기입 adjustment entry
정리사채 adjustment bond; reorganization bond
정리신탁공사 Resolution Trust Corporation
정리포스트 post for stocks to be delisted
정리후 시산표 adjusted trial balance
정밀기계 precision machinery
정밀기계업계 precision instruments industry
정밀기술 precision technology
정박료 groundage
정방행렬 square matrix
정보가치 information value
정보감사 information audit
정보검색 information retrieval
정보경제학 information economics
정보고속도로 information highway
정보공개전의 증권거래 gun jumping
정보공해 information pollution
정보기술 information technology
정보누설 tip
정보동기로 인한 거래자 information-motivated trader
정보동기에 따른 매매 information-motivated transaction
정보리스크 information risk
정보벤더 information vendors
정보산업 information industry
정보서비스 information service; value line
정보시스템 information system
정보시스템관리실(SEC) Office of Information System Management(SEC)
정보시스템사업 information system business
정보제공자 common informer
정보지수 information ratio
정보화사회 information society
정보회계 information accounting
정부가 재화와 서비스를 구입함 purchase of goods and services by government
정부간 무역 government to government trade
정부간의 inter-government
정부감사 government audit
정부개발원조 Official Development Assistance
정부개입 government intervention
정부거래 government transaction
정부경상여잉 government current surplus
정부계 기간채권 bond issued by government related agency
정부계 기관 government agency
정부계 기관증권 securities issued by government related agency
정부계 기관채권 government agency bond
정부계정 government account
정부관계예금 government related deposit
정부구입 government purchases

정부금융기관 government financial agency
정부기관증권 government agency securities
정부기업 government enterprise
정부단기증권 finance bill; short-term government securities
정부당좌예금 government current deposit
정부무역 government trade
정부보조금 government grant; government subsidy
정부보증공영기업증권 government-guaranteed public corporation bond
정부보증채 government guaranteed bond; government guaranteed bonds; government obligation; state guaranteed debt
정부브로커 government broker
정부이전수지 government transfers
정부자금 government fund
정부저당금고 Government National Mortgage Association
정부저축 government saving
정부저축증권 government saving certificate
정부조달 government procurement; public procurement
정부증권 government securities
정부증권상환 redemption of government securities
정부지출 government expenditure
정부지폐 government note
정부차관 government credit
정부채무 national government debts
정부통화 currency note
정산 settlement of debt
정산표 work sheet
정산표방식 worksheet method
정상배부율 normal burden rate
정상상각 normal depreciation
정상상태 stationary state
정상원가 normal cost
정상이윤 normal profit
정상이익 normal return
정상잔고 normal balances
정상재 normal goods
정상재고 running stock
정상재고고 normal stock
정상적인 상업순환 normal operating cycle
정상표준원가 normal standard cost
정상환상장 normal rate of exchange
정서가 불안정한; 걱정하는 hung up
정성분석 qualitative analysis
정성정보 qualitative information
정수배 multiple
정시감사 regular audit
정시불 payment at regular fixed times
정시불사용료 royalty to be paid every fixed time
정시상환 redemption at fixed date; scheduled repayment
정식계약 formal contract
정식맨데이트 official mandate
정식본권 definitive bond
정식편입액 formula additions
정신적인 충격 nervous shock
정액 fixed amount
정액감가상각법 straight-line depreciation
정액과세 fixed amount taxation
정액법 constant dollar plan; fixed amount method; fixed installment method
정액법에 준거한 방법 manner similar to straight line depreciation method
정액보수실비지불계약 cost plus fixed fee contract
정액보험 fixed return insurance
정액상각법 straight line amortization
정액연금 fixed annuity; fixed rate annuity; level annuity
정액전도자금 imprest fund
정액전도제 imprest system
정액지불변동이부채 level pay floating rate note
정액청부계약 lump sum contract
정액회비 fixed-amount membership fee

정율감가상각법 declining balance depreciation, fixed percentage depreciation
정율감세 fixed rate tax reduction
정율법 constant percentage method; declining balance method
정율보수 fixed fee
정율보조금 percentage grant
정율상각 diminishing balance depreciation
정율상각법 percentage on diminishing value plan
정율성장모델 constant-growth rate model
정율성장평가모델 constant-growth rate valuation model
정율편입 fixed-rate transfer
정율회비 fixed-rate membership fee
정의 definition
정의 레버리지효과 positive leverage effect
정의 분포도 positive covariance
정의 상관관계 positive correlation
정의 이율곡선 positive yield curve
정적균형 static equilibrium
정정 revision
정정매출 corrective selling
정정상장 corrective market
정족수를 채우지 못했다고 인정하여 유회하다 count out
정지 suspension
정지시효 suspension of prescription
정지조건 condition precedent
정지조건부 옵션 knock-out option
정지조건부 옵션거래 knock-out option trading
정책금리 key rate; official interest rate; policy rate
정책금리인상 hike in official rate
정책방해 hindrance to business
정책수단을 할당함 policy assignment
정책적인 감가상각 policy depreciation
정책포지션 policy state
정책협조 policy coordination
정체산업 stagnant industry
정치단체 political corporation
정치리스크 political risk
정치안정지수 political system stability index
정치위기 political crisis
정치적인 책임 political accountability
정치적인 혼란 political turmoil
정크본드 junk bond
정크채 junk issue
정탄성 분산모델 constant elasticity of variance model
정태리스크 static risk
정태분석 static analysis
정태비율 static ratio
정태통계 static statistics
정학모델 static model
정학승수 static multiplier
정형무역조건 trade terms
정형화이외거래기간 odd date
정화 specie money
정화준비(正貨準備) specie reserve
정확성 accuracy
정확한 가치 precise value
정황증거 circumstantial evidence
정회원 regular member
제 1 거부권 first refusal
제 1 권 first exchange
제 1 순위 모기지 first lien mortgage
제 1 순위 모기지론 first mortgage loan
제 1 순위 저당권부 사채 first mortgage bond
제 1 심 first instance
제 1 심관할권 original jurisdiction
제 1 저당 first mortgage
제 2 지방은행 member bank of the Second Association of Regional Banks; member banks of the Second Association of Regional Banks
제 3 구역 third sect
제 3 세계 Third World
제 3 세계 각국 third world countries
제 3 섹터 quasi public corporation
제 3 채무자 garnishee
제각손익 profit or loss from retirement of

fixed assets
제거가액 retirement price
제거단위 retirement unit
제거비 retirement cost
제거비용 removal expenses
제거손실 loss on retirement of fixed assets
제거자산 scrapped property
제거하다 subduct
제거회계 retirement accounting
제경비 overhead
제너럴모기지 general mortgage
제너럴모기지사채 general mortgage bond
제너럴크레디트 general credit
제네릭스와프 generic swap
제도공준 institutional postulate
제도금융 financing by public institutions for implementing policies
제도상의 institutional
제도상의 요인 institutional factor
제도신용거래 organized margin transactions
제도연구 institutional approach
제도학파 institutional school
제도회계 institutional accounting
제로베타포트폴리오 zero-beta portfolio
제로섬게임 zero-sum game
제로코스트옵션 zero-cost option
제로코스트옵션거래 zero-cost option trading
제로코스트칼라 zero-cost collar
제로쿠폰 T-노트 zero-coupon T-note
제로쿠폰채 zero-coupon bond; zero-coupon issue
제로쿠폰커브 zero-coupon curve
제로펄스틱 zero-plus tick
제명 expulsion; expulsion from membership
제명회원 lame duck
제삼자 third party
제삼자가 발행한 어음 note issued by a third person
제삼자납부 및 대위 tax payment and subrogation by third party
제삼자리스크 third-party risk
제삼자배상개별보험 comprehensive general liability insurance
제삼자배상책임보험 third party liability insurance
제삼자배상특약보험 third party liability cover
제삼자신용보상 third-party credit support
제삼자의 개입 intermediation of a third party
제삼자의 권원 outstanding title
제삼자지불약관 loss payable clause
제삼자할당 allocation of new shares to a third party
제삼자할당주 stock allotted to third persons
제시 presentation
제시기간 time of presentation
제시은행 presenting bank
제시지연 late presentation
제시하지 않는 특약수표 memorandum-check
제안하다 propound
제약 constraint
제외 ruling out
제외위험 excepted risks
제외조항; 면책조항 exclusion clause
제외하고는 with the exception of
J-NET 시장 J-NET
제일수익자원칙 primary benefit rule
제일우선주 prior preferred stock
제일우선주식 first preferred stock
제작중인 물건 goods in process; products in progress; work in progress
제작중인 물건의 원장 goods in process ledger; work in process ledger
제작중인 물건의 이월고 inventory of work in process at the beginning of period
제잡비 sundry expenses
제재관세 punitive tariff
제정법 status law
제정법상의 양도 statutory assignment
제조간접비 factory expenses; factory overhead; manufacturing burden
제조간접비배부 overhead allocation

제조간접비배부계정 applied manufacturing expenses account
제조간접비배부액 applied factory burden
제조간접비예산 manufacturing expenses budget
제조간접비원장 manufacturing expenses ledger
제조경비 manufacturing expenses; production expenses
제조공정 manufacturing process
제조과세 manufacturing taxation
제조능률차이 production efficiency variance
제조물책임 product liability
제조물책임보험 product liability insurance
제조보고서 production statement
제조부문 manufacturing department; production department
제조부문비 producing departments cost
제조부문이 없는 개발메이커 fabless
제조비 on cost
제조비예산 cost of production budget
제조설비 production equipment
제조업고용자수 manufacturing payroll
제조예산 production budget
제조요소의 factoral
제조원가 cost of manufactured goods; cost of production; fabricating cost; output cost
제조원가계산 manufacturing cost accounting; manufacturing costing
제조원가명세표 schedule of the cost of goods manufactured
제조원가보고서 factory cost report; manufacturing statement; statement of production cost
제조자리스크 manufacturer's risks
제조지도서 manufacture order; production order; work order
제조차이 production variance
제조허가 manufacturing license
제지; 억제 restraint
제출; 신청 offer
제출연기 extension of time to file
제출일 filing date
제출하다 file
제품 manufactured goods; product
제품가격 product price
제품계정 finished products account
제품군 product group
제품금융 finished product ledger
제품기준 product standards
제품라이프사이클 product life-cycle
제품믹스 product mix
제품별 원가계산 cost accounting by product
제품보증 product warranties
제품보증준비금 reserve for after-care of products
제품소지액 finished products on hand
제품원가 cost of finished goods; product cost
제품원가계산표 product cost accounting
제품원장 finished goods ledger
제품재고액 finished products inventory
제품포트폴리오매니지먼트 product portfolio management
제한 limitation
제한기간 restricted period
제한납세의무 limited tax liability
제한납세의무자 taxpayer with limited tax liability
제한법화 limited legal tender
제한부 계정 restricted account
제한부 부동산권 estate upon limitation
제한부 잉여금 restricted surplus
제한부동산권 base free
제한상환청구권부 론 limited recourse loan
제한세율 limited tax rate
제한외발행세 tax on excess issue
제한요인 limitational factor
제한적인 교환성 limited convertibility
제한적인 보증 limited guarantee
제한적인 재산권 qualified property
제한조치 sanction
제한조항 restrictive provision

제한주 restricted stock
제한주식 restricted share
제휴 collaboration
제휴그룹 affiliated group
제휴론 affiliated loan; tie-up loan
제휴론에 따른 모기지조건 introduced mortgage business
제휴자사카드 private label card
제휴카드 affiliated card; co-branded card
조건 condition; terms and conditions
조건; 단서 proviso
조건개요서 term sheet
조건교섭 negotiation on terms and conditions
조건부 conditional; with a proviso
조건부 계약 conditional contract
조건부 구조 tied aid
조건부 국고보조금 conditional subsidy from the national treasury
조건부 날인증서 escrow
조건부 매매 conditional sales
조건부 부동산권 estate upon condition
조건부 서하증권 claused bill of lading
조건부 승인 conditional approval
조건부 유동성 conditional liquidity
조건부 융자 conditional loan; tied loan
조건부 인수 conditional acceptance
조건부 회귀분석 conditional regression analysis
조건인수 qualified acceptance
조기등록 acceleration of registration
조기반제 early repayment
조기상각 accelerated redemption
조기상환 early redemption; pre-maturity redemption
조기상환리스크 call risk; prepayment risk
조기상환예상 prepayment projection
조기상환옵션 early redemption option
조기상환일 call date
조기상환하다 redeem before maturity
조기완제 full repayment before maturity
조달가격 acquisition cost price
조달금리 borrowing rate; borrowing rate
조달비 procurement cost
조달비용 cost of borrowing
조달코스트 funding cost
조달코스트삭감 reduced borrowing costs
조례 municipal bylaws; municipal law; ordinance by local government
조립보험 erection insurance
조미료 sweetener
조변환 rebalancing
조별법 group method
조별상각 group depreciation
조별원가 class cost
조별원가계산 class cost system
조사 examination by reference
조사데이터 survey data
조사비 research expenditure
조사자료 materials for investigation
조사후 소득 income after tax audit
조상상환이익 yield-to-call
조성금 grant in aid
조세 tax
조세 및 인지수입 tax and stamp revenues
조세감면 reduction or exemption of tax
조세거래 tax transaction
조세계정 tax accountant
조세공채계정 treasury tax and loan account
조세구조 tax structure
조세국가 tax state
조세귀착 tax incidence
조세를 전가함 shifting of tax burden
조세면제 exemption of taxes
조세범 tax criminal
조세법률관계 legal relationship in tax
조세부담 burden of tax; incidence of taxation; tax burden
조세부담경감 tax relief
조세부담율 tax burden ratio
조세부담자 ratepayer
조세사정 tax assessment
조세선취특권 tax lien

조세수탁금 tax collected
조세예납 prepayment of tax
조세우선권 priority of taxes
조세원칙 principle of taxation
조세의 수익자부담원칙 compensation principle of taxation
조세의 중립성 neutrality of taxation
조세정책 tax policy
조세조약 tax convention; tax treaty
조세준비증권 tax anticipation bill
조세징수 collection of rates
조세채권 tax claims
조세채권상당이율 equivalent taxable yield
조세채무 tax liabilities
조세채무관계설 theory of liabilities taxation
조세체계 system of taxation
조세특별조치 special taxation measures
조세특별조치법 Special Taxation Measures Law
조세피난처 tax paradise
조세환부청구권 claim for tax refunds
조세회피 tax avoidance
조세흡수 tax absorption
조악화 adulteration
조약 treaty
조약의정서; 프로토콜 protocol
조언의견 advisory opinion
조언적인 advisory
조업단축 curtailed operation; curtailment of operation; output reduction; reduction of operation
조업도 operating rate; operation capacity; production level; rate of output
조업도 차이 volume variance; volume indicator; operation variance; production volume budget; utilization variance
조업률 activity level; operation ratio
조업일수 operated days
조업정지 plant outages
조위금; 부조금 condolence money
조이익률 gross margin rate; gross profit margin rate
조이익증감 changes in gross margin
조이익총계 aggregate gross margin
조인트리드 joint lead
조자본스톡 net capital stock
조작 manipulation
조작목표 operating target
조작변수 operating variable
조정 compilation; conciliation; reconciliation
조정가능고정상장 adjustable peg system
조정가능이부어음 adjustable rate notes
조정계정 reconciliation account
조정금리저당론 adjustable rate mortgage loan
조정기준 adjusted basis
조정보험료 adjustment premium
조정세액 tax amount settled
조정소득금액 adjusted income
조정압력 adjustment pressure
조정인플레이션 adjustment inflation
조정증권 adjustment securities
조정지수 adjustment factor
조정패턴 consolidation pattern
조정필 adjusted
조정항목 adjustment item; reconciliation item
조정후 배당증가율 adjusted dividend increase
조정후 양도소득 adjusted capital gain
조정후 **EPS** 증가율 adjusted EPS increase
조정후 중앙은행통화스톡 adjusted central bank money stock
조직감사 organization audit
조직개혁 organizational changes
조직계획 organization planning
조직단위 organizational unit
조직편제시간 setup time
조직형태 organization form
조치; 대책 countermeasure
조합 reference; society; tally
조합원 associate
조합원 선취득권 lien of partners
조합원자격유지 maintenance of membership

조합재산 partnership assets; partnership property
조합정관 articles of partnership
조합증표 union label
조항 article; claus; stipulation
조회 checking; collation; inquiry
조회계정 adjustment account
조회목적 verification purpose
조회적합률 matching ratio
조회처은행 reference bank
조회표 comparison slip
조회필 기호 check mark
존속실체 surviving entity
존속회사 surviving company
졸업조항 graduation clause
졸업채 exit bond
종가 ad valorem; final value; last price
(거래소의) 종가 closing price
종가가 전일의 종가보다 비쌈 close up
종가가 전일의 종가보다 쌈 close down
종가보관료 ad valorem storage
종가세 ad valorem duty; ad valorem tax
종가세율 ad valorem tariff
종가월중평균 monthly closing average
종가지정주문 market on close
종교법인 religious corporation
종량보관료 specific storage
종량세 specific duty; specific tax
종량세율 specific tariff
종료 wrapping-up
종사하다 engage in
종속 dependency
종신건강보험 permanent health insurance
종신고용 lifetime employment
종신보험 permanent life insurance; whole life insurance
종신연금 life annuity; perpetual annuity; straight life annuity
종신연금보험 life annuity insurance
종업원 employee
종업원급부제도 employee benefit plan
종업원급여수당 employees bonus and allowance
종업원복지급여제도 employee welfare benefit plan
종업원에 대한 채무 account owed to employees
종업원연금기금적립금 employees pension fund
종업원연금제도 employee pension benefit plan
종업원예금 deposit from employees
종업원자사주구입권 qualifying stock option
종업원조합 employees union; workers union
종업원주식구입계획 employee stock purchase plan
종업원지주제도 employee stock ownership plan
종업원퇴직급여금 employees retirement allowance
종업원퇴직급여준비금 reserve for employees retirement allowance
종업원퇴직소득보증법 Employee Retirement Income Security Act of 1974
종이홍수 paper credit
종장거래 at-closing price transaction
종장무렵 at the close of the market
종합감가상각 composite depreciation
종합거래정보시스템 composite quotation system
종합경기지수 composite index
종합계정; 요약 summary
종합계좌 multiple purpose bank account
종합과세 comprehensive income taxation; general taxation; taxation on aggregate income; taxation upon total income; total taxation
종합내용연수 composite useful life
종합배상책임보험 comprehensive general liability insurance coverage part
종합보세지역 comprehensive bonded area
종합보험 comprehensive insurance
종합분개장 summary journal

종합상각자산 composite depreciation assets
종합세율 synthesis tax rate
종합소득세 consolidated income tax
종합수지 overall balance
종합수지흑자 favorable balance of overall
종합원가계산 process cost system
종합의견 comprehensive opinion
종합이율 total return
종합주가지수 broad based stock index; composite stock price index
종합주가표 composite stock price tables
종합주식티커 consolidated stock ticker
종합증권회사 national full line firm
종합지고 overall position
종합지수 general index
종합테이프 consolidated tape
종합효과세율 effective aggregate tax rate; overall effective tax rate
죄를 면하게 하다 exculpate
주가 market price of stock; market value per share; share price; stock price
주가가 천정부지로 치솟음 topless
주가규제 regulation of stock Prices
주가동향 fluctuation of stock prices; price movement of stocks; share price performance
주가분석 stock price analysis
주가상승 rise on stock price
주가수익률 earnings multiplier; per share earning ratio; price earnings multiple
주가수준 share price level
주가수준분포 distribution of stock prices
주가수준이 높은 주 heavy share
주가순자산배율 price book-value ratio
주가안정조작 operations for stabilizing the stock market price
주가정보 stock quotations
주가조작 stock price manipulation
주가지수 **FT** Stock Index FT; stock price index
주가지수선물 stock price index futures
주가지수선물거래 futures trading based on the stock price index; stock price index futures trading
주가지수선물거래특별참가자 special participant in stock price index futures trading
주가지수선물계약 stock price index futures contract
주가지수선물옵션 options on stock index futures
주가지수연동채권 bond linked to stock price index
주가지수옵션 options on stock price index
주가지수옵션거래 option trading based on the stock price index
주가지수재정거래 stock price index arbitrage transaction
주가지수콜옵션 stock price index call option
주가지수풋옵션 stock price index put option
주가폭락 falling off
주가하락 erosion in stock price; falling in stock price
주간사 lead manager
주거 dwelling house
주거비 housing expenses
주거수당 housing allowance
주계국 National Accounting Office
주관적인 판단 subjective judgment
주관적인 확률 subjective probability
주권 sovereign power; sovereignty; stock certificate
주권 등의 보관 및 대체에 관한 법률 Law Concerning Central Securities Depository and Book-Entry Transfer
주권견본 specimen of stock certificate
주권교부 withdrawl of stock certificates
주권교체 replacement of stock certificates
주권국 sovereign state
주권대체 book-entry transfer of stock certificates
주권리스크 sovereign risk

주권명의변경 transfer of a share-certificate
주권명의변경정지 transfer books closed
주권명의변경정지해제 transfer books open
주권선물거래 futures trading based on stocks
주권양도위임장 stock power
주권양도증 stock receipt
주권양식 form of stock certificate
주권예탁 deposit of stock certificates
주권옵션거래특별참가자 special participant in equity options trading
주권이 있는 주식 certificated share
주권자 sovereign
주권제권판결 judgment of exclusion on shareholders rights
주금불입명령 balance order
주기 cycle
주내지점설치 state branching
주도권; 헤게모니 hegemony
주도주 leaders
주력부문 core business division
주력은행 major relationship bank
주류 mainstream
주류심의회 council on alcoholic beverages
주말효과 weekend effect
주면허조직 state-chartered association
주목할 만한 noteworthy
주무대신 competent minister
주무부령 ordinance of competent minister
주문 order
주문기록부 order book
주문부거래 order book trading
주문불이행 order-filling cost
주문상대 order negotiation
주문서; 매입위탁서 indent
주문엔트리 order entry
주문유효기간 effective period of order
주문의 불균형 imbalance of orders
주문이 쇄도함 rush order
주문잔액 backlog of orders
주문접수시간 order-taking hours
주문중개업자 introducing firm
주문집행 execution of order, filling of orders
주문집행확인서 exchange ticket
주민세 inhabitant tax; resident tax
주민세특별징수 special collection of inhabitants tax
주법 state law
주법은행 state bank
주법은행이 연방준비제도에 가맹함 Federal Reserve membership of state banks
주법인세 state franchise tax
주변상품 off-the-run issue
주보험국 state insurance department
주사무소; 본사 main office
주석 annotation; chief; explanatory note; head
주소 place of abode
주소득세 state income tax
주소득자 main income earner
주소이서 indorsement of address
주순환 major cycles
주시선물 stock futures
주식 등의 지속적인 거래 continuous transaction of securities
주식거래 stock dealing
주식거래소 stock exchange
주식거래소공보 stock exchange daily official list
주식거래소대부 stock exchange loan
주식거래소회원권 stock exchange seat
주식거래소휴일 stock exchange holiday
주식거래손실준비금 reserve for stock dealing losses
주식거래실적 actual results of recent stock transactions
주식거래원 broker agent
주식결제예비금 contango
주식계정 share account
주식공개 equity flotation
주식공개매부 tender offer
주식공개매입 takeover bid
주식공개화 going public
주식공모 public offering of stock

주식공황 stock exchange panic; stock market crash
주식교부청구 demand for withdrawal of stock certificates
주식교환 exchange of shares; share exchange
주식구분 classification of shares
주식구입계획 stock purchase plan
주식구입선택권 stock option plan
주식구조상품 structured equity product
주식담보금융 stock collateral loan
주식대장 share ledger; stock ledger
주식등급 classes of stocks
주식딜러 equity securities dealer
주식리스크추정 stock risk estimation
주식리스크프리미엄 equity risk premium
주식매각익 profit from sales of stocks
주식매매손실준비금 stock trading transaction loss reserve
주식매수; 주식구입에 의한 매수;주식취득 stock acquisition
주식매수권증서 option warrants
주식매입선택권; 스톡옵션 stock option
주식매입옵션 stock purchase option
주식매집에 따른 소득 income from collection of securities by purchase
주식매취권부 사채 bond with stock purchase warrant
주식매취청구권 appraisal rights of shareholder
주식명 stock name
주식모집개시 subscription book open
주식모집마감 subscription book closed
주식미니투자 stock mini-investment
주식발행 issue of shares
주식발행비용 cost of issuing stocks; stock issuing expenses
주식발행차금 stock premium
주식배당 dividend on stock; stock dividend
주식배당락 ex-stock-dividends
주식배당락에 관계되는 증가신주 new shares issued through stock-dividends
주식병합 reverse split of stocks; stock consolidation
주식보관인 custodian
주식보상제도 stock compensation plan
주식보유율 share holding ratio
주식부족 scarcity of stock
주식분포 distribution of shares
주식분포상황 distribution of ownership of shares
주식분할 share split-up; split-ups of stocks
주식분해 stock split-up
주식불입잉여금 paid-in capital in excess of par
주식붐 equity boom
주식브로커 share broker
주식비율 interlocking stockholding; stock rating
주식사무대행기관 share-handling service agent
주식상각 retirement of shares
주식상장표시판 ticker
주식상환 stock redemption
주식상환채 equity redemption bond
주식선물거래 stock futures transaction
주식소각 cancellation of shares
주식소멸회사 defunct company
주식소유와 관련있는 배당 dividend from stocks owned
주식수 number of shareholders
주식스와프 stock swap
주식시가발행 issue of shares at market price
주식시가총액 total market capitalizatioin
주식시장 equity market; stock market
주식시장의 변동 stock market fluctuation
주식신용거래나 상품선물거래에서 성립된 판매주문 writing
주식신청금 application money for stock
주식신청서 application form for stock; subscription blank
주식심볼 stock symbol
주식액면 par
주식약어 stock abbreviation

주식양도 assignment of stock
주식양도제한 restriction on transfer of shares
주식어음계정 share draft account
주식옵션 equity options
주식옵션거래 equity options trading
주식워런트 equity warrant
주식원장 stock register
주식을 매각하다 divest
주식을 발행함 issuance of stock
주식을 시가발행함 increase in capital at the market price
주식을 통한 자금조달 equity financing
주식을 통한 자본조달액 amount raised by stock
주식응모 stock subscription; subscription for shares
주식의 종류 class of the stock
주식이율 stock yield
주식인수 subscription for stock
주식인수계정 subscription's receivable account
주식자금조달 financing for stocks; security financing; stock funding
주식자본 share capital
주식장외시황발표제도 OTC stock quotation exchange system
주식전환대부 convertible loan
주식제정거래 stock arbitrage
주식중매인 stock broker
주식지분 equity stake
주식지분가치 stock equity value
주식청산소 stock exchange clearing house
주식취급 share handling
주식취득 acquisition of stock
주식취득을 위한 차입금 money borrowed to purchase stocks
주식콜옵션 equity call option
주식투기 speculation in stocks; stock speculation
주식투신 stock trust
주식투자 equity investment; investment in stocks; stock investment
주식투자가 equity investor
주식투자신탁 stock investment trust
주식트렌드 price trend on stocks
주식파생상품 equity derivatives
주식펀드 equity fund
주식편입률 equity weighting
주식편입상황 stock portfolio
주식평가 appraisal of shares; stock valuation
주식평가개요 stock valuation summary
주식평가손 equity write-off
주식평가환 revaluation of stocks
주식풋옵션 equity put option
주식할당 allotment of share
주식할당증 allotment certificate
주식할당증서 share allotment certificate
주식할당통지 share allotment letter
주식합병 share consolidation; share split-down
주식해외매출 international equity placement
주식환매 equity repurchase; stock buy-back
주식환매계획 stock repurchase plan
주식회사 joint stock company; company limited; company limited by shares
주식회사의 재평가적립금을 자본편입함 capitalization of revaluation reserve of joint stock company
주요 대주(貸主) ultimate lender
주요거래 main customer
주요계정 main account; principal account
주요국 major nations
주요기업단기경제관측 short-term economic survey of principal enterprises
주요딜러 responsible and recognized dealer
주요부분 stating part
주요사실 fact in issue; ultimate fact
주요산업 major industry
주요상품 major commodity
주요원인 efficient cause; key factor
주요원재료 main materials
주요은행 major banks
주요이용자 primary user
주요인 prime factor

주요장부 head book; main books; principal books
주요제조지도서 principal production order
주요주주 major stockholders; majority of stockholders
주요채무자 primary obligor
주요트렌드 major trend
주요한 원재료 major raw materials
주원인 proximate cause
주의 care; diligence; prudence
주의의무 duty of care
주임변호인 leading counsel
주임애널리스트 lead analyst
주임회계사 accountant in charge
주임회계사실(SEC) Office of Chief Accountant(SEC)
주장의 요점 points
주재감사인 resident auditor
주재원사무소 representative office
주재원사무소; 연락사무소 liaison office
주정부증권 state government securities
주정부채권 state government bond; state government bond and debenture
주제(州際)통상 Interstate Commerce
주제(州際)통상위원회 Interstate Commerce Commission
주제품 major product; prime product; principal products
주조가격 mint price
주주 equity holder; shareholder; stockholder
주주가 소송함 shareholder litigation
주주결의 shareholders' resolution
주주계정 shareholder's account
주주구조 ownership structure
주주권 shareholder's right; stockholder's right
주주권리 shareholder's rights
주주대표소송 shareholders' representative suit
주주를 위한 연차보고서 annual report to stockholders
주주명부 shareholders' list; list of shareholders
주주명부상의 주주 holder of record
주주안정공작 stable stockholder operation
주주에 의한 임의청산 member's voluntary winding-up
주주에게로 회귀함 return to shareholder
주주우선배정 privileged allocation of issuance to stockholders
주주원장 shareholders' ledger
주주의결권 voting right of stockholder
주주이해 interest of shareholder
주주자본 owner's capital; shareholders' equity; stockholder's equity
주주자본배당률 ratio of dividends to shareholders' equity
주주자본이익률 return on common stockholders' equity; accounting return on equity; return on equity; return on equity capital; return on net worth
주주중시경영 shareholders-oriented management
주주지분 shareholder's interest; stock equity; stockholder's equity
주주지분계산서 statement of stockholders' equity; statement of stockholders' net worth
주주지분상환 refundment of stockholders' equity
주주총회 general meeting of shareholders; general meeting of stockholders; shareholders' meeting; stockholder's meeting
주주총회결의 decision of a general meeting of stockholders
주주총회소집통지 proxy statement
주주할당 allotment to shareholders; issues to shareholders; offering to shareholder; rights offering
주주할당발행증자 rights issue
주주행동주의 shareholder activism
주지불 principal paying
주지불대리인 principal paying agent

주차결산 weekly accounting
주채 state bond
주체회사 principal company
주택건축착공수 housing starts
주택관련주 housing stocks
주택금융 housing loan
주택금융회사 housing loan corporation
주택도시정비공단 Housing and Urban Development Corporation
주택론금리공제 mortgage interest deduction
주택론보험 housing loan guarantee
주택론사업 mortgage business
주택론채무 housing loan claim
주택모기지 home mortgage
주택시장 housing market
주택신용 housing credit
주택용 부동산시장 residential property market
주택용 토지 land for residence
주택저당세액공제 mortgage credit
주택저축공제 deduction for housing savings; housing savings tax credit
주택종합보험 householders' comprehensive insurance
주택착공허가건수 housing permits; new permits
주택취득특별공제 special credit for acquisition of dwelling house
주택투자 residential investment
주택판매호조 robust home sales
주택화재보험 fire insurance on dwelling houses
죽은 차익 mortality profit
준갱생 quasi-reorganization
준거법 applicable law; governing law; proper law
준거법조항 governing clause
준계약 implied contract; quasi contract
준고정비 semi-fixed cost
준금반언(準禁反言) quasi estoppel
준금치산자 quasi incompetent person
준변동비 semi-variable charge
준변동비항목 semi-variable expenses
준변동원가 semi-variable cost
준비금 allowance
준비금계정 allowance account; provision account; reserve account
준비금의 타당성 reserve adequacy
준비금이월 addition to reserve
준비서면 brief; case
준비시간 make-ready time
준비예금제도 reserve deposit requirement system
준비은행 reserve bank
준비잉여금 reserved surplus
준비자본 reserve capital
준비자산 reserve assets
준비제도 reserve system
준비통화 reserve currency
준비포지션 reserve position
준비필 재산 property reserved
준사법권력 quasi judicial power
준소비대차 quasi loan for consumption
준수 compliance
준수상황 state of observance
준수테스트 compliance test
준수하다 abide by
준용규정 provisions of mutatis mutandis application
준인플레이션 semi-inflation
준정부기관 quasi-government agency
준주식 quasi equity
준지역권 quasi easement
준차입 quasi-loan
준채무 quasi-debt obligations
준통화 near money; quasi currency
준화폐 quasi money
준확정신고 quasi final return
준회원 quasi member
줄이다 abate
중가 middle rate; mid-market level
중가격품 mid-range product
중가산금 heavy additional charge imposed

중가산세 heavy penalty tax
중간감사 semi-annual audit
중간감사보고서 semi-annual audit report
중간값 mean price
중간결산 interim closing; interim results; semi-annual closing of accounts; settlement for the first half of the year
중간계산서 interim statement
중간계정 interim account
중간기 결산 six month closing of accounts
중간기술 middle range technology
중간래그 intermediate lag
중간매상 interim sales
중간발행 issue at intermediate price
중간배당 interim dividend
중간보고 interim report; interim return
중간보고서 interim return form
중간세율 intermediate tariff
중간수치 average exchange rate
중간신고 interim tax return
중간재 intermediate goods
중간재무제표 interim financial statements
중간제품 intermediate product
중간지불이자 interim interest payment
중간치 mean value
중개 introducing; mediation
중개규정 mediation regulations
중개기관 intermediary agents
중개대리인 middleman
중개료 mark-downs; mark-ups
중개수수료 intermediation fee
중개업자 broker
중개은행 intermediary bank
중개인 concession hunter
중개인차환예금 agent replacement deposit
중개자 intermediary
중개증거금 agency margin
중견기업 middle-sized companies
중견주 middle-sized stock
중계가공무역 intermediate improvement trade
중고자산 used property
중고자산사용가능기간 usable period of used property
중고자산의 견적내용연수 estimated useful life of used property
중과실 gross negligence
중국인민보험공사 People's Insurance Company of China
중급회계학 intermediate accounting
중기국채선물거래 5 year government bond futures
중기국채펀드 medium-term government bond fund; medium-term government securities funds
중기금융자산 medium-term financial assets
중기길트채 medium gilt
중기대부 medium-term loan
중기론 intermediate-term loan
중기물 mid-maturities
중기예상 intermediate term market outlook
중기유러채 Euronote
중기이자부 국채 medium-term coupon-bearing government bonds; medium-term fixed rate government bond
중기일본국채 5-year Japanese government bond
중기자금조달 medium-term funding
중기전망 medium-term outlook
중기증권 intermediate securities
중기채 medium-term bond
중기채입찰 note auctions
중기트란시 intermediate tranche
중노동 hard labor
중단 disruption
중단클레임 suspension of work claims
중대한 부실표현 material misrepresentation
중대한 영향 material impact
중도재료비 material in process
중도전환계약 convertible contract
중도해약 cancellation before maturity; cancellation of a contract
중도환금 redemption before maturity

중량용적증명서 certificate of weight and measurement
중립국선증명서 sea letter
중립선증명서 sea brief
중립성 neutrality
중립적인 균형 neutral equilibrium
중립화폐정책 neutral money principle
중매인 floor broker; jobber
중매행위 jobbing
중미공동시장 Central American Common Market
중미기구 Organization of Central American States
중미상품거래소 Mid-America Commodity Exchange
중복 duplication
중복계정 overlapping account
중복보험 double insurance
중복보험의 순위주의약관 American clause
중복상장 double listing
중복상장기업 multiply listed company
중복채무 overlapping debt
중세 heavy taxation
중소기업 small and medium-sized enterprises
중소기업구조개선준비금 reserve for improvement of structure of small-and medium-sized enterprise
중소기업근대화시책 small- and medium-sized enterprise modernization activities
중소기업금융기관 financial institutions for small business
중소기업금융기관계정 principal accounts of financial institution for small-business
중소기업의 근대화 modernization of smaller enterprise
중심경향 central tendency
중심레이트 central party
중심상장; 중심레이트 central rate
중앙시장 central market
중앙은행 central bank
중앙은행권 central bank note
중앙은행할인율 central bank rate
중앙정부 central government
중앙치 median
중요부문 crown jewel
중요사실 material fact
중요성 materiality
중요성 원칙 materiality principle
중요성의 원칙 principle of materiality
중요하지 않은 쟁점 immaterial issue
중요하지 않은 증거 immaterial evidence
중요한 금액 significant amount
중요한 변수 material alternation
중요한 부분 integral part
중요한 업무 important part of business
중요한 요소 important factor
중요한 자회사 significant subsidiaries
중요한 증거 material evidence
중장기파이낸스 term financing
중장기협조융자 syndicated term loan
중재 arbitration
중재; 재정거래; 차익매매 arbitrage
중재소 arbitrage house
중재업자 arbitrage trader
중재인 arbitrator
중재인선정기관 appointing authority
중재재정 arbitration award
중재절차 arbitration proceeding
중재조항 arbitration clause
중전(重電)상품 heavy electrical stocks
중핵 core
중핵사업 core business
중형주 medium-sized stock
즉매 spot sale
즉매하다 sell on the spot
즉시 thereupon
즉시 또는 취소주문 fill-or-kill order
즉시 이용가능한 자금 immediately available fund
즉시개시연금 immediate annuity
즉시그로스결제 real time gross settlement

즉시상환가능한 채권 callable debt
즉시속행 fresh pursuit
즉시지불 prompt payment
즉시집행 fill or kill
즉일인도 cash delivery
증가(增價) price appreciation
증가담보 additional collateral
증가상각 additional deposit
증가소득세 increased income tax
증가수익 incremental return
증가운전자본 increasing working capital
증가자본 additional capital
증감대조식 self-balancing type
증감법 increase and decrease method
증개축론 home improvement loan
증개축적립금 additions and betterment reserve
증거 evidence
증거금 more margin
증거금거래 margin transaction
증거금계정; 신용거래구좌 margin account
증거금구분 division of margin
증거금규칙 margin rule
증거금기준액 standard of price for margin calculation
증거금내부규제 house margin rule
증거금부족 margin deficiency
증거금부채 margin debt
증거금분리 segregation of margin
증거금소요액 required margin
증거금시스템 margin system
증거금에 대한 권리행사 exercise of claim on clearing margin
증거금예탁 deposit of margin
증거금율 margin rate
증거금인출 withdrawl of deposited margin
증거금제도 margin money system
증거금코스트 margin cost
증거금특례 special rule relating to margin
증거기준 authorization criteria
증거사실 evidentiary facts
증거서류 documentary evidence; evidenced document
증거서류; 첨부서류 exhibit
증거요약 summing-up
증거의 무게 weight of evidence
증권감독원 Securities Supervisory Board
증권거래 securities trading
증권거래감사위원회 Securities and Exchange Surveillance Commission; Securities Exchange Surveillance Commission
증권거래법 Securities and Exchange Law
증권거래법시행령 Cabinet Order of the Securities and Exchange Law
증권거래세법 securities business tax law
증권거래소 securities exchange
증권거래소 준회원 allied members
증권거래소시장 market of a stock exchange
증권거래소에 상장된 유가증권 marketable securities listed on a securities exchange
증권거래소의 회원 local dealers
증권거래손실준비금 reserve for loss securities transactions
증권거래심의회 securities exchange commission
증권거래업자협회 trade associations
증권거래책임준비금 reserve for liability for security transactions; reserve for losses from securities transactions
증권거래침체 poor securities trading
증권경제일지 diary on securities market
증권고유리스크 security-specific risk
증권관리 securities management
증권규칙 securities regulations
증권금융 securities financing; securities loan; security credit
증권금융회사 securities finance company
증권납부 tax payment by securities
증권담보론 secured loan on securities
증권딜러 securities dealer
증권리스크 security risk curve
증권매리 marrying transaction
증권매매익 trading profit

증권발행 securities issuance
증권발행수수료 policy fee
증권발행시장 primary securities market
증권법의 진실 truth in securities act
증권보유수요 demand to hold securities
증권분석 analysis of securities; securities analysis
증권분석전문가 security analyst
증권브로커 securities broker
증권선물거래 securities futures
증권시장 securities market
증권시장개혁법안 Securities Market Reform Act
증권시장선 securities market line
증권시장안정화법안 Securities Market Stabilization Act
증권업 securities business
증권업계 securities industry
증권업자의 대리인으로서 거래소에 나와 거래하는 사람; floor representative
증권외무원 registered representative
증권위탁납부 request payment by securities
증권이율 securities yield
증권이율곡선 security yield curve
증권인수업자수수료 underwriting contract
증권임차 stock lending
증권자본 securities capital
증권중개회사를 통해서 by measurement
증권클리어링 securities clearing
증권통계연보 annual securities statistics
증권투자 securities investment
증권투자가보험법 Securities Investor Protection Act of 1970
증권투자가보호회사 securities investor protection corporation
증권투자상담 securities investment advisory service
증권투자신탁 investment trust on securities; securities investment trust
증권투자신탁 및 증권투자법인에 관한 법률 Law Concerning Seciruties Investment Trust and Securities Investment Companies
증권투자신탁을 부분해약함 partial correlation of securities investment trust
증권투자신탁협회 Investment Trust Association of Japan
증권투자위원회 Securities and Investments Board
증권특별계정 special account for inward portfolio investment
증권포함익 unrealized gains in securities
증권행정 securities administration
증권화 securitization
증권화 자산 securitized assets
증권화된 자산 securtised asset
증권화법 securitisation law
증권화시장 securitisation market
증권회사 securities company; securities firm
증권회사가 판매를 위해 보유한 채권 securities inventory
증권회사딜러 securities house dealer
증명 attestation
증명서 certificate
증명증인 attested witness
증명하다 attest; prove
증배 dividend increase; increase in dividend
증분분석 incremental analysis
증분수익률 incremental rate of return
증분원가 incremental cost; incremental profit
증서가 발행된 증권 materialized securities
증서교부 withdrawl of certificate
증서대부 loan on deeds
증서를 발행하지 않음 dematerialization
증서발행을 수반하지 않는 증권 dematerialized securities
증서발행을 수반하지 않음 dematerialized
증서배당 scrip dividend
증서번호 certificate number
증서보유자 certificate holder
증서사항 matter in deed
증서의 문면 face of instrument
증서의 설명부분 recital

증설적립금 reserve for additions
증세 increased tax; tax increase
증수 increase of revenue
증식보험 increased value insurance
증언 testimony
증언기록 deposition
증언을 증거로 보전함 perpetuating testimony
증언하다 testify
증여 donation; gift
증여세 donation tax; gift tax
증여세과세가격 taxable value of gift tax
증여세면제 exemption of gift tax
증여세율 tax rate of gift tax
증여잉여금 donated surplus
증여재산 donated property
증여주 donated stock
증익 increased earnings; profit increase
증인심문 examination of witness
증자 additional equity; amount added to capital; capital increase
증자 increase in capital stock
증자권리락 ex-rights of capital increase
증자권리부 주식 stock cum rights
증자로 취득한 주식 stock acquired by capital increase
증자신주매수권 stock right
증자압박 potential over-supply produced by new issues
증지징수 tax collection by stamp
지가 land price
지가공시제도 government appraisal of land price
지가제도(持家制度) one's own house system
지구외무원 home service agent
지급 supply
지급개시연령 pensionable age
지급주문 immediate order
지나친 행위 overshoot
지니메이 Ginnie Mae; GNMA
지니메이채 Government National Mortgage Association debenture
지니메이패스스루증권 GNMA pass-through securities
지니지수 Gini coefficient
지대(地代)부담 rent charge
지대봉사 rent service
지대위양 transfer of land tax
지대표(地代表) rent roll
지도 direction
지도금지어음 non-order bill
지도력 leadership personality
지도식 또는 소지인불식 payable to order
지도식 이서 endorsement to order
지도인도 delivery to order
지도인식 선하증권 order B/L
지도적인 판례 leading case
지도증권 bill to order
GDP 신장률 growth rate GDP
지명경쟁입찰 selective bid; selective tendering
지명권 power of appointment
지명도 rate of awareness
지명입찰 designated bind; private tender
지명채권 claim payable to a specific person
지명하다 nominate
지목 land category
지목변환계 declaration of change of land category
지방거래소 regional exchange
지방공공단체 municipal corporation
지방공공단체의 채무조정 adjustment of the debts of a municipality
지방공공단체채권펀드 municipal bond fund
지방공공재 local public goods
지방교부금 central government transfers to local governments
지방교부세 local grant tax
지방교부세교부금 distribution of local allocation tax
지방기업 local company
지방배포세 local distribution tax
지방분여세 local allocation tax; partial tax

transfer to local government
지방분포 prefectural location
지방사무소 regional office
지방세 local expenditure; local tax; prefectural inhabitants tax
지방세납세 local tax payment
지방세법 Local Tax Law
지방세연체금 arrears of local tax
지방소비세 local consumption tax
지방양여세 local transfer tax
지방업자 regionals
지방은행 local bank; regional bank
지방은행카드 regional bank card
지방자치 local autonomy
지방자치체 local authorities; local government; local public entity
지방재정 local finance; local public finance
지방재정법 Local Public Finance Law
지방증권거래소 local stock exchange
지방채 local authority bond; local bond; local government bond; municipal bond; municipal note; prefectural bond; regional government bond
지방채공모 public offering of municipal bond
지방채선물 municipal futures
지방채이자 municipal bond interest
지방채증권 municipal securities
지배관계 controlling relationship
지배소유분 controlling stake
지배시장 control market
지배주 control stock
지배주주소유분 controlling equity
지배집중도 degree of concentration of control
지배회사 controlling company
지분; 이해관계; 이권 interest
지분계정 equity account
지분법 equity method
지분이익 equity income
지분주 shareholdings
지분주식 equity share
지분증권 equity instrument
지분지수 equity index
지분체증모기지 growing equity mortgage
지분풀링 pooling of interests
지분풀링방식 pooling of interest method
지분환급 refunding of equity
지불 disbursement
지불거절 under protest
지불거절선언 declaration of non-payment
지불거절수표 rejected check
지불고 amount paid
지불금액 paid amount
지불기일 payment date
지불기일연기서면 letter of license
지불기일이 도래한 payable
지불기일이 온 보험료 premium due
지불기일현재의 신주가격 price of new stocks on the day to be paid in
지불기입장 payment book
지불기한 due date for payment; term of payment
지불능력 ability to pay; solvency
지불능력과세설 faculty theory of taxation
지불능력기준 ability to pay basis
지불능력이 있는 solvent
지불능력평가 evaluation of solvency
지불대리인 paying agent
지불률 payment rate
지불명령 order to pay
지불명세 payment statement
지불보증 certification of payment
지불보증은행 certifying bank
지불불능 failure to pay
지불불능으로 인한 대손 bad debt caused by insolvency
지불불능판결 decree of insolvency
지불불능행위 act of insolvency
지불불능회사 insolvent corporation
지불수수료 charge and commission; del credere commission
지불순환 disbursement cycle
지불시기 time of payment

지불신용장 payment credit
지불약속어음 note payable
지불어음 acceptance payable; bill payable; draft payable; notes and bills payable
지불어음기입장 note payable register; notes payable book
지불여력 margins of solvency
지불워런트 대리인계약서 paying & warrant agency agreement
지불유예 grace of payment; postponement of payment
지불유예기간 days of grace; moratorium period
지불은행 paying bank
지불이자과세공제 tax deduction of interest payment
지불인 payer
지불인도 delivery against payment
지불인수수표 certified check
지불일 payment day
지불임대료 rent payable
지불장부 cash disbursement book
지불전표 debit slip
지불전표기입장 payable register; voucher payable register
지불정지 payment stop; suspension of payment
지불정지; 모라토리엄 moratorium
지불정지통지 stop payment order; stop-payment order
지불제시 presentation for payment
지불제시기간 presentation period for payment
지불조건 conditions for payment; payment terms
지불조서 payment record
지불준비계정계약 payment account agreement; proceeds account agreement
지불준비금 reserve for outstanding claims
지불준비율 reserve rate; reserve ratio
지불준비율정책 reserve requirement policy
지불준비제도 reserve requirements system
지불지 place of payment
지불지도 payment order
지불지정어음 domiciled bill
지불채무 notes and accounts payable; trade payables
지불초과 unfavorable balance
지불카드 debit card
지불통지서 note of payment
지불필 계정 account paid
지불필 수표 paid check; cancelled check
지불항목 items of payment
지불해야 할 owing
지불협정 payment agreement
지사제도 branch system
지상권 surface right
지상권설정 settlement of superficies
지소(地所) demises
지속 continuation
지속가능한 개발 sustainable development
지속계약 continuing contract
지속계정 continuing account
지속기업 going concern
지속기업가치 going concern value; going value
지속비 continuing expenditure
지속사업 continuing operations
지속사업부문의 이익 income from continuing operations
지속성장률 sustainable growth rate
지속약관 continuation clause
지속재고 continuous inventory
지속적으로 운영되는 사업 business continuously carried on
지속적인 경제성장 sustained economic expansion
지속적인 매매 continuous buying and selling
지속적인 재보험 continuous reinsurance cover
지속패턴 continuation pattern
지속회계감사 continuous audit
지수 index
지수거래 index transaction
지수곡선 exponential curve

지수리스크 index risk
지수링크채 index linked products
지수보유 index holding
지수분포 exponential distribution
지수옵션 TOPIX index option TOPIX
지수용 상장주식 listed stocks used in the computation of indices
지수재정거래 index arbitrage trading
지수재정거래자 index arbitrager
지수화 indexation
지시 instruction
지시를 취소함 cancellation of designation
지시신탁 directory trust
지시적인 법률 directory statute
지식공학 knowledge engineering
지식산업 knowledge industry
지식집약산업 knowledge intensive industry
지역간 대체 transfers between geographic areas
지역개발 regional development
지역경제 regional economy
지역경제학 regional economics
지역권 easement; servitude
지역권설정 settlement of easement
지역권자 easement holder; servitude holder
지역내 무역 interregional trade
지역법 local law
지역별 관리 geographic control
지역연관분석 interregional analysis
지역재투자 community reinvestment
지역정책 regional policy
지역주의 regionalism
지역카르텔 regional cartel
지연 lagging
지연결제 delaying settlement
지연손해금 delinquent charge; last fee; late payment charge; penalty charge
지연이자 interest arrears; interest for arrears
지연주식 lagging stock
지원책 aid package; rescue package
지위재 positional goods
지입자본 brought-in capital
지적 acreage
지적소유권 intellectual property right
지점 branch; branch office
지점계정 branch account
지점상호간 손실 inter-branch loss
지점상호간 이익 inter-branch profit
지점상호계정 inter-branch account
지점원장 branch ledger
지점은행제도 branch banking system
지점회계 accounting for branch office; branch accounting
지정 appointment
지정가격대응 matching of bids and offers
지정가격순위 precedence of bids and offers
지정가격주문 leave order; limit order
지정거래 designated trading
지정거래소 designated exchange
지정계좌 designated account
지정권자 appointor
지정금전신탁 designated money in trust
지정기부금 donation to designated organization
지정도시 designated city
지정명의인 designated nominee
지정상속분 specified portion
지정상품 appointed goods; designated stock
지정수표 check to order
지정예금 designated deposit
지정인지불어음 bill payable to order
지정입찰 approved tender
지정입찰자 approved bidder
지정통계 designated statistics
지정통화 designated currency
지정하청업자 nominated subcontractor
지조(地租) land tax
지조부가세 surtax on land tax
지주매입협정 buy-out arrangement
지주비율 ratio of shareholding
지주제도실시회사 companies with employee stock ownership plan
지주회사 holding company

지지선 support level
지진보험 earthquake insurance
지참인 bearer
지참인불 payable to bearer
지참인지불수표 check to bearer
지참인지불어음 bill payable to bearer
지참인지불증권 instrument payable to bearer
지체 delay
지체클레임 delay claims
지출 cash disbursed; expenditure; outgo; outlay
지출 spending
지출가능자금 expendable fund
지출부담준비금 reserve for encumbrance
지출삭감 expenditure curtailment
지출세 expenditure tax
지출소비 outlay expiration
지출원가 outlay cost
지출율 expenditure rate
지출전표제도 voucher system
지출증대 spending increase
G 5 Group of 5
지폐 paper currency
지표 indicator
지표가 되는 지수 reference index
지표상품 bellwether issue
지표상품이율 benchmark yield
지표증권 benchmark securities
지하경제 underground economy
지하자금 underground money
지행계수 lagging series
지행지수 lagging indicator
직각분포 rectangular distribution
직간접비율 ratio of direct and indirect taxes
직거래 direct deal
직권 competence; official power
직권남용죄 oppression
직근원인 immediate cause
직능급 wages on job evaluation
직무 duty
직무급 pay according to function
직무분석 job analysis
직무집행과정 course of employment
직물 spot
직물가격 underlying value
직물거래 spot dealing; spot operation; pot trading; spot transaction
직물레이트 actual exchange rate
직물보유고 actual balance
직물상장과 선물상장의 가격차 spread between spot rate and futures rate
직물선물스프레드 spot-forward spread
직물위치 spot position
직별업자 trade contractor
직선법 straight line method
직업감사인 professional auditor
직업상의 규범 professional discipline
직업윤리 professional ethics
직업회계사 professional accountant
직전사업연도 immediately proceeding business year
직전의 immediately proceeding
직접개입 direct intervention
직접거래 direct transaction
직접경비 direct expense; direct overhead
직접공격 direct attack
직접국세 direct national tax
직접금융 direct financing; direct loan
직접금융형 리스 direct financing lease
직접노동 direct labor
직접노무비 direct labor cost
직접매출페이퍼 direct issue paper
직접모집 direct placement
직접법 direct method
직접부문 direct department
직접상각 direct method of depreciation
직접세 direct tax
직접손해 proximate damage
직접예금 direct deposit
직접원가배부법 prime cost method
직접원조 direct aid
직접이율 income yield; simple yield
직접이익 current yield; direct yield

직접이해관계 direct interest
직접인식 personal knowledge
직접임금 productive wages
직접자본 direct capital
직접재료비 direct material cost
직접정산법 direct pricing
직접증거 direct evidence
직접증권 primary securities
직접참가방식단체연금계약 immediate participation guarantee contract
직접참가예탁관리계약 direct rated deposit administration contract
직접투자 direct investment; direct or equity investment
직접투자규제 foreign direct investment regulation
직접투자총액(계약베이시스) Investment contracts
직접평가 direct valuation
직접표시 direct presentation
직접행사 direct exercise
직접환거래 direct dealing
직접환재정 direct exchange arbitrage
직판 direct selling
진동이론 oscillation theory
진부화 자산 obsolete assets; obsolete property
진부화 자산상각 depreciation on obsolete assets
진사(생명보험을 계약할 때 피보험인의 건강 상태를 조사함) medical examination
진성대부법 truth in lending
진실성의 원칙 principle of truth
진실하며 공정한 의견 true and fair view
진실하며 공정함 true and fair
진입장벽 barriers to entry
진정한 authentic
진정한 원가 bona fide cost
진정한 준비금 true reserve
진행감사 progressive audit
진화 evolution
질권 right of pledge
질권계좌 pledge account
질권등기 registration of the right of pledge
질권목적 object of pledge
질권설정 establishment of the right of pledge
질권설정자 pledgor
질로 도피함 flight to quality
질멜비율 Zillmer quota
질멜식 책임준비금 Zillmerized reserve
질문검사권 authority to inquire and inspect
질병급부 sickness benefit
질서있는 수출 orderly export marketing
질적실질성의 원칙 qualitative substantiality test
질적인 경제정책 qualitative economic policy
질적인 금융통제 qualitative credit control
질적인 요인 qualitative parameters
짐을 옮겨 실음 transshipment
집계계정 summary account
집계의 문제 aggregation problem
집계표 summary sheet
집단소송 class action
집단적용면제 block exemption
집약척도 summary measure
집중경제 centralized economy
집중도 degree of concentration
집중배제; 분권 decentralization
집중분석 convergence analysis
집중적으로 거래되는 주 highly traded stock
집중투자 concentrated investment; intensive investment
집중효과 concentration effect
집합법인 corporation aggregate
집합이론 aggregate theory
집행 laps
집행관리 executive officer
집행권 executive power
집행기간 term of execution
집행기관 executive organ
집행기일 date of execution
집행위원회 executive committee
집행절차 executive proceedings

집행정지 suspension of execution
집행채권자 execution creditor
집행채무자 executive debtor
집행처분 executive measure
징계처분 disciplinary action
징벌 discipline
징벌적인 손해배상 punitive damages
징세 tax collection
징세권 taxing power
징세기구 tax collection system
징세비용 cost of tax collection
징세상의 편의 convenience of tax collection
징수 collecting tax
징수경비 collection charge
징수권 power of collection
징수권소멸시효 status of limitation on collection
징수료 collection fee
징수명령 order for collection
징수비용 collection expenses
징수순위 precedence of customer's order
징수액 collected amount
징수액계산서 accounting sheet of collected amount
징수어음 collection bill
징수업자 collecting agent
징수유예 postponement of tax collection
징수율 rate of charge
징수은행 collection bank
징수조치 collection measure
징수촉탁 entrust of collection
징수표준율 standard rate of charge
징수하다 collect
징조 signs
찌꺼기; 토막 scrap

ㅊ

차가 rented house
차가권 rented house right
차고료 warehouse charges
차관공여 loan extension
차관반제 replacement of loan
차관수령 loan received
차금거래 speculating for difference; speculation for margin
차금결제 net settlement
차금계정 debt account
차기(借記)통지서 debit advice
차기결산 next closing of account
차기계정 ensuing account
차기대통령 president-ELECT
차기이월 balance carried forward to the next term
차기이월고 amount carried forward
차기이월이익금 surplus profit carried forward to the following term
차기이월차손금 loss carried forward to the following term
차등세율 graded tariff
차량보험 automobile physical damage insurance
차변 debit; debit side
차변계정 debit account; debtor account
차변메모 debit memorandum
차변승인 debit authorization
차변잔고 debit balance; debtor balance
차변표 debit note
차별 discrimination
차별가격 discriminative price
차별관세 discriminating duty
차별세율 discriminative tariff
차별요인 discriminant
차별화 differentiation
차분분석 differential analysis
차손금 loss from difference of price
차손금을 되돌림 loss carry back
차순위보험금수취인 contingent beneficiary
차압 attachment; distress; seizure
차압금지재산 property not subject to seizure
차압금지채권 exemptions
차압대상재산 property subject to seizure
차압명령 order for attachment of property
차압명장 warrant of attachment
차압물건 attached goods; seized goods
차압물건매각 distress sale
차압서 document of seizure
차압선착순주의 principle of priority to first seizure
차압유예 suspension of seizure
차압인 seizor
차압재산환가 conversion into cash of seized property
차압조서 record of seizure
차압지소등기 register of cancellation of attachment
차압통지서 notice of seizure
차압하다 distrain
차압해제 release of seizure

차액; 잔고 balance
차액계정 differential account
차액수입 take out
차액식 remainder type
차액원가 differential cost
차액원가계산 differential costing
차용개념 adopted concept
차용증권 IOU
차원 dimension
차이 difference; discrepancy; variance
차입계약 debt agreement
차입계정 borrowing arrangement
차입금 borrowed money; borrowing; debt loan; loan payable
차입금계정 borrowing account
차입금금리 interest rate on borrowing
차입금상환 loan redemption
차입금으로 취득한 주식 stock acquired by borrowed money
차입금이자 interest on borrowed
차입금잔고 loan outstanding
차입반제보증 guarantee of repayment
차입보증금 guaranty money deposited
차입수요 borrowing demand
차입예약 standby arrangement
차입유가증권 borrowed securities; pledged security; securities borrowed
차입으로 자금을 조달함 debt financing
차입이자를 자산계상함 capitalization of interest cost
차입자 borrower
차입자금 borrowing fund
차입자본 borrowed capital; loan capital
차입자의 신용도 borrower's credit worthiness
차입잔고를 일괄지불함 balloon payment
차입주식 borrowed share, borrowed stock
차입주잔주;차주잔고 short interest
차입초과 overborrowing
차입코스트 borrowing cost
차입필요액 borrowing requirements
차입한도 borrowing facility
차입한도 borrowing limit
차입한도액 debt ceiling
차주잔고 balance of stock loans
차지계약갱신 및 변경 renewal or change of the lease
차지권 lease tenant right
차지권; 대차권 tenant right
차지권가격 fair leasehold value
차지권비율 ratio of leasehold to land value
차지권설정 establishment of leasehold
차지권을 부여하는 계약 leasehold
차지권의 기간이 경과함 lapse of the leasehold
차지권자 leaseholder
차지권취득원가 acquisition cost of leasehold
차지권평가 valuation of leasehold
차지인 lease-holder, tenant
차터파티 charter party B/L / B/L
차트 chart
차트분석 chart analysis; chart reading
차트패턴 chart pattern
차티스트 chartist
차환발행 conversion issue; refinance of redemption; refinancing issue
차환예탁금 replacement deposit
차환정책 funding policy
차환증권 refunding securities
차환채 refinancing bond; refunding bonds
착공호수전체 total starts
착불 freight collect
착실한 신장 steady rise
착지거래 Chakuchi transaction; transaction with delayed settlement
착취 exploitation
착하 arrival of shipment
참가 participation
참가금 participation fee
참가방식 participation method
참가보험 participating insurance
참가비용 cost of entry
참가우선주식 participating preferred stock

참가융자 participation loan
참가인수 act of honor
참가자 participant
참가주 participation stock
참가증권 participation certificate
참가지불 payment supra
참가차압 participation in seizure
참고기간 reference period
참고상장권 reference range; reference zone
참고수치 pro forma amount
참고이율 reference yield
참고통계 reference statistics
참여은행 participating bank
참여지분 participating interests
참조서류 reference document
창고료 warehouse fee
창고운송관련업 warehousing and harbor transportation service industry
창공법 blue sky law
창구 window
창구지도 window guidance
창립 creation
창립사무소 organization office
창립위원 organization committee
창립자 founder; organizer
창립준비비 preopening expenses
창립총회 inaugural meeting; organization meeting
창업비 formation expenses; initial expenses; organization expenses; promotion expenses
창업비상각 amortization of initial expenses
창업자이익 founder's profit; promoter's profits
채 **ECU** bond ECU
채 **NTT** bond NTT
채권 active debt
채권 bond and debenture; claim receivable; debenture; fixed income debt; receivables
채권가격 bond price
채권가격모델 bond pricing model
채권가격지표 bond price index
채권거래손실준비금 reserve for bond dealing losses
채권계정 bond account; debenture account
채권구매오퍼 bond buying operation
채권구입 bond purchase
채권국 creditor country
채권권리자 bond creditor
채권담보 finance receivables as collateral; security for obligation
채권대차 bond lending
채권대차거래 bond loan transaction
채권대차시장 bond lending market
채권등급을 매김 bond rating
채권딜러 bond dealer
채권매매이율 yield of bond transaction
채권매입 debt factoring
채권발행 bond issuance; bond issue; issuance of bond
채권발행비용 bond issue costs
채권발행은행 bond issuing bank
채권발행차금상각 discount bond amortization
채권발행차입금 bonded debt
채권법 law of obligations
채권변제 liquidation of claim; settlement of claim
채권보관대체결제제도 book-entry system for bond
채권보유 bond holding
채권보유자 debenture holder
채권보전 preservative attachment
채권보전화재보험 fire-insurance for mortgagee interest
채권보증 guarantee of debt
채권보증자회의 noteholders meeting
채권보합 bond cross holding
채권분석가 bond analyst
채권브로커 bond broker
채권상각특별계정 special bad debts reserve
채권상각특별계정소멸 write-off from special bad debts reserve
채권상각특별계정제거 liquidation of special bad debts

채권상승액 bond premium
채권상응이율 equivalent bond yield
채권상장상승 rally in the bond market
채권상황 bond redemption
채권선물 bond futures
채권선물거래 bond futures transaction
채권선물거래제도요강 procedures for bond futures trading
채권선물옵션 government bond futures option
채권선택옵션 bond selection option
채권설정 sales of bond
채권속성 bond attribute
채권손실커버리지 loan loss coverage
채권수요 bond demand
채권수탁자 bond trustee
채권순위 order of credit
채권스와프 bond swap; swap of bond
채권시장 bond market; debt capital market
채권시장균형 bond market equilibrium
채권신고 filing of claims
채권신탁증서 bond trust indenture
채권양도 assignment of claim; assignment of receivable; cession of a credit
채권에 대한 데디케이트포트폴리오 dedicated bond portfolio
채권옵션 bond option
채권원가 ex-coupon price of bond
채권은행 bank creditor
채권을 대량으로 발행함 large scale bond issue
채권을 지불할 수 있을 만한 능력 sufficient solvency to settle the credit in full
채권응모 bond subscription
채권의 등급을 매김 bond credit rating
채권의 등급을 매김 rating of bond
채권의 임의상환조항 bond call provision
채권의 표면이자율 coupon rate
채권이연계정 unamortized discount on debenture accounts
채권이율 bond return; bond yield
채권이익 yield on bond
채권인수 bond underwriting
채권인수업자 bond underwriter
채권입체거래 bond switching
채권자 creditor; obligee
채권자구제수속 receivership
채권자대위권 subrogation right of obligee
채권자에 의한 임의청산 creditor's voluntary winding-up
채권자지분 creditor's equity
채권자회의 creditors' meeting
채권장외옵션 bond option at over-the-counter
채권전이 bond transfer
채권전환 bond conversion
채권절차 process of garnishment
채권주식조합 bond stock mixes
채권지수 bond index
채권지표상품 benchmark bond; fixed income benchmark
채권차압인 garnisher
채권차압통지 garnishment
채권차환 bond refunding
채권채무 debts and credits
채권채무계약 receivable and payable contract
채권펀드 bond fund
채권평균만기 duration of bond
채권포트폴리오 bond portfolio; receivable from portfolio
채권풀 receivables pool
채권할인 bond discount
채권현선거래 bond transaction with repurchase agreement
채권확정판결 judgment of definite liabilities
채권환산이율 bond equivalent yield
채권회수 collection of claim; debt collection; recovery of credits
채널라인 channel line
채무 indebtedness; obligation
채무; 부채 debt
채무가 있는 stand in debt
채무공제 deduction of liabilities
채무과다 over-indebtedness

채무국 debtor country
채무레버레지 debt leverage
채무매입계약 note purchase agreement
채무면제 acquittal of debt; debt relief; discharge of debt; exemption of debt; forgiveness of debt; release from debts; waiver of obligation
채무면제익 gains from forgiveness of debt; income arising as a result of exemption of debts; income from discharge of indebtedness
채무미이행분 unperformed part of obligation
채무반제 debt retirement; repayment of liabilities
채무반제능력 debt coverage
채무반제부담 servicing burden
채무반제비율 debt service ratio
채무반제연기 repayment moratorium
채무보류 long-term postponement of credit
채무보증 guarantee facility; guaranty of liabilities
채무부담날인채무증서 single bill; single bond
채무불이행 default of obligation
채무불이행 예측지표 predictors of default
채무불이행 프리미엄 default risk premium
채무불이행리스크 default risk
채무불이행에 따른 청산 insolvent liquidation
채무비율증대 growing leverage
채무삭감 debt reduction
채무상환 amortization
채무상환계획 amortization schedule
채무상환비 government debt redemption cost
채무상환적립금 surplus appropriated for redemption fund
채무소멸 expiration of obligation
채무수단 debt instrument
채무스와프 liability swap
채무양도 cession of an obligation
채무완제 acquittance
채무의 상호성 mutuality of obligation
채무의 채권화 debt bond swap
채무이행 performance of obligations
채무인계 succession of liabilities
채무인수 debt assumption
채무자 debtor; obligor
채무자 및 파산재단 debtor and estate
채무자예금 debtor's deposit
채무자의 반제불능 insolvency of debtors
채무자의 위험 obligor risk
채무잔고 debt balance
채무정리계획 scheme of arrangement
채무정리증서 deed of arrangement
채무조정 adjustment of debts
채무증권 debt securities
채무증권발행차금 premium on debt
채무증권시장 debt securities market
채무증서 bill of debt; certificate of indebtedness; evidences of indebtedness
채무증서대부 Schuldschein Darlehen
채무초과 excess of debt; insolvency; liabilities exceeding assets
채무해약 repurchases of bond
채산라인 profitable line of business
채산수준 break-even line
채산주 income share
채용 adoption
책상조사 office audit
책임 blame; responsibility
책임단위 accountability unit
책임서열 hierarchy of responsibilities
책임소재 liability for damage
책임원가계산 responsibility costing
책임이행 discharge of reponsibility
책임있는 accountable
책임자 accountable person
책임준비금 liability reserve; loss reserves; policy reserve
책임준비금증가액 inside build-up
책임한도액 total maximum liability
책임회계 responsibility accounting
처분 disposal; disposition
처분가격 disposal price

처분가치 disposal value; salvage value
처분매수 buy-in
처분매출 selling out
처분비용 cost of disposal
처분수입 proceeds from disposals
처분에 대한 이의 objection to discipline; objection to disposition
처분일 disposal date
처분청산계산서 statement of realization and liquidation
처분필 이익잉여금 appropriated earned surplus; appropriated surplus
처짐; 늘어짐 sag
척도분석 scale analysis
천연과실 natural fruits
천연자원감모상각비 depletion of natural resources
천이확률행렬 transition matrix
천재자금 natural disaster relief loans
천재지변 natural diaster
천정권 vicinity of the upper limit
철강업계 iron and steel industry
철거자산 removed assets
철도인도 free on rail
철도채 railroad bonds
철수 withdrawl
철수; 반환 repossession
철회 revocation
철회하다 abandon
철회할 수 없는 irrevocable
첨부명세서대로 as per specifications attached
첨부서류 accompanying document; appendix; attached document
첫 천정 first peak
청구 request
청구 즉시 on call
청구권 right of claim
청구명세서 bill of particulars
청구불이행 non-claim
청구서 invoice book
청구서; 법안 bill
청구액 amount billed; amount claimed
청구원인분할 splining a cause of action
청구취지신청 prayer
청부공사 contract work
청부공사미수금 contract work account receivable
청부대금거치금 premium in addition to the original contract price
청부인 independent contractor
청부제도 contract system; contract work system
청산 clearing; closing out
청산가격 clearing price
청산가치 break-up value; liquidation value
청산거래 clearing contract; clearing transaction
청산계정 liquidation accounts; settled account
청산기관 clearing agency; clearing organization
청산기능 clearing function
청산대차대조표 liquidation balance sheet
청산매매 one time trading
청산명령 winding-up order
청산배당 liquidation dividend
청산사무 liquidation affairs; liquidation matter
청산사무소 liquidation office
청산사유 liquidation event
청산서 statement of liquidations
청산소득 income at liquidation; liquidation income
청산소득세 liquidation tax
청산소득에 대한 법인세예납 prepayment of tax on liquidation income
청산손익 liquidation profit and loss
청산수속 liquidation proceedings
청산우선권 liquidation preference
청산인 liquidating partner; liquidator
청산잉여금 surplus at liquidation
청산절차 clearing procedure
청산절차중인 법인 corporation under liquidation
청산중인 법인 corporation in the course of liquidation

청산지수 settlement index; settlement index
청산치 liquidation price
청산하다 settle
청산한 법인 liquidated corporation
청산협정 clearing agreement
청산확정신고 liquidation final return
청산확정신고서 final return of liquidation
청산회사 clearing corporation; liquidated company; liquidation company
청산회원 clearing member
청색신고 blue form return
청색신고를 할 수 있는 법인 corporation qualifying for filing a blue return
청색신고법인 corporation filing a blue return
청색신고승인 approval of filing a blue return
청색신고승인취소 revocation of approval to filing blue return
청색신고자 blue return taxpayer; taxpayer filing a blue return
청색신고제도 blue return system
청색신고취소 cancellation of filing a blue return
청색신고특별공제 special deduction for blue return
청색신고회 Blue Return Association
청원 petition
청원권 right of petition
체감원가 degressive cost
체감원가법 diminishing balance method
체감잔고법 reducing balance method
체납 delinquency
체납독촉수수료 charge for demand for tax in arrears
체납세 back tax; delinquent tax
체납임차금 back rent
체납자 delinquent taxpayer
체납처분 disposition for failure to pay; procedure for collection of tax delinquency
체선료; 하차유치료 demurrage
체인뱅킹 chain banking
체인지오버 change over
체제구축; 조정 adjustment
체증비 progressive cost
체크개런티카드 check guarantee card
체크라이터 check writer
체화 backlog
체화금융 financing for carrying unsold inventories; stockpile financing
체화융자 loan for carrying unsold inventory
초감 first check
초과공급 excess supply
초과대부 overdrawn
초과대출 overdrawing
초과대출계정 overdrawn account
초과매출 overselling
초과발행이자 overdraft interest
초과배부 overabsorption
초과보험 over insurance
초과부담 excess burden
초과사용시간 over-used hours
초과상각 depreciation in excess of the limit; excessive depreciation deduction
초과서비스 excessive service
초과세율 tax rate higher than standard
초과소득 excess income
초과손해보험 stop loss coverage
초과손해액 excess of loss
초과손해액특약재보험 excess of loss treaty reinsurance
초과손해재보험 excess of loss reinsurance; spread toss reinsurance; stop loss reinsurance
초과수요 excess demand
초과액특약재보험 surplus treaty reinsurance
초과의 overrun
초과이윤 excess profits; excess profits tax
초과이윤공제 excess profits credit
초과이익 above-normal earning
초과인출경제 overdraft economy
초과준비 excess reserves
초과증거금 excess margin
초과지불 excess disbursement; excess payment

초과차압 excessive seizure
초과펀드 excess fund
초국적기업 transnational corporation
초기상각 initial depreciation
초기설정 initial establishment
초기증거금비율 initial margin requirement
초기투입자금 seed money
초년도수수료 first year commission
초본 abstract of register
초연도특별상각 initial special depreciation
초인플레이션 hyper inflation
초일류은행 prime name bank
초장기 super long-run
초장기국채 super-long government bonds
초장기국채선물 20 year government bond futures
초토작전 scorched earth defense
초회금 amount of the first payment
초회준비금 initial reserve
촉진세제 special incentive measures
촉진클레임 acceleration claims
촌수 degree of consanguinity
총(總) gross of
총감마수치 total gamma
총거래 gross transaction
총계 aggregate; grand total; total sum
총계로 all totaled; in all
총계의 combined
총계정원장 general ledger
총계정원장계정 general ledger account
총공급량 aggregate supply
총공급함수 aggregate supply function
총과실 gross loss
총괄예산 summary budget
총괄운임 lump sum freight
총괄표 summary of statistics
총노말포트폴리오 aggregate normal
총대리인 universal agent
총대리점 general agent
총대리점제도 general agency system
총델타치 total delta
총로치 total roh
총매상고 gross sales; total sales
총매상원가 gross cost of merchandise sold
총매입계약 total buying contract
총매출계약 total selling contract
총무부 Ministry of Public Management home; Affairs; Posts and Telecommunications
총무처; 사무국 secretariat
총무청 Management & Coordination Agency
총무청 통계과 Statistics Bureau of the Management and Coordination Agency
총발행필 주식수 total of shares outstanding; total stocks issued
총보험료 gross premium
총부채자기자본비율 equity capital ratio to total liabilities
총부채자기자본율 equity capital ratio to total debt
총비용곡선 total cost curve
총상품매매차익 gross merchandise margin
총생산 gross product; total production
총생산고 total turnover
총선거 general election
총세액 amount of tax payment
총세타수치 total theta
총소득 gross income
총소득금액 total net income
총수득액 amount of income
총수요 aggregate demand
총수요기능 aggregate demand function
총수익 gross earnings; gross gains; gross revenue; total earnings
총수익률 total rate of return
총수입 total receipts
총시장가액 total market value
총시장델타치 total market delta
총액 aggregate amount; gross amount
총액 중의 부족액 deficit in aggregate amount
총액규제 aggregate limit
총액베이스 gross base
총액예산주의 principle of gross budget

accounting
총액주의 gross amount principle
총액티브리스크 aggregate active risk
총영업이폭 gross operating spread
총예금 total deposit
총운용포트폴리오 aggregate managed portfolio
총운전자본 gross working capital
총운전자본 및 순운전자본회전율 turnover of gross and net working capital
총원가 gross cost
총이익 gross profit; gross profit method
총이익률 gross profit ratio
총이익분석 gross profit analysis
총이익테스트 gross profit test
총자본 gross capital; total liabilities and net worth
총자본경상이익률 ratio of ordinary profits to total capital
총자본수익률 profit rate of total liabilities and net worth; total capital profit ratio
총자본순이익률 rate of earnings on total capital
총자본회전율 turnover of total capital; turnover ratio of total liabilities and net worth
총자산 gross assets; total assets
총자산매상률 sales to total assets
총자산상각률 rate of depreciation of total assets
총자산수익률 return on assets
총자산이익률 return on total assets
총자산장부가액 total book value of assets
총자산회전율 total asset turnover ratio
총장기자금 total capitalization
총장부가격 gross book value
총재 governor
총준비 total reserves
총지출 gross expenditure; gross output
총채무 gross debt
총출자금액 all amounts invested in capital
총칙 general provisions
총캐퍼수치 total kappa
총통화공급고 total money supply
총투자 gross investment
총평균 aggregate average
총평균법 periodic average method; progressive average inventory method
총화법지수 index number by aggregative method
총회 general assembly; general meeting
총회의 결정 decision of the general meeting
총회정족수 quorum for a general meeting
최고가격 maximum price
최고가격선출법 highest-in first-out method
최고가입찰자 top bidder
최고경영책임자 chief executive officer
최고고문 supreme advisor
최고발행액제한제도 maximum limit system
최고법원 Supreme Court
최고서 notification
최고세율 top tax rate
최고수준 maximum level
최고액 ceiling price
최고업무책임자 chief operating officer; chief operating officer
최고최저세율제 maximum and minimum tariff system
최근수준 recent standards
최대목표 primary objective
최대생산능력 maximum capacity
최대선의 utmost good faith
최대손실추정치 maximum loan estimates
최대우도법 maximum likelihood method
최대재고량 maximum inventory
최대피영향국 most seriously affected countries
최량증거 best evidence
최빈치; 최빈값 mode
최선노력원칙 best efforts basis
최소변동단위 minimum fluctuation unit
최소부채 minimum liability
최소이윤 minimum profit
최소제곱법 least-squares method
최소치 minimum value
최소한계비용 minimum marginal cost

최염가저당 cheapest-to-deliver
최염가저당채권 cheapest-to-deliver bond
최우선 first priority
최우선인수권 right of first refusal
최유리조업도 maximam operating ratio
최저거래단위 round lot
최저경매가격 upset price
최저과세 minimum tax
최저권면단위 minimum denomination
최저대출비율 minimum lending rate
최저리스지불액 minimum lease payment
최저면세소득 minimum exempt income
최저목표수익률 hurdle rate
최저보증금 minimum guarantee
최저시세까지 내려감 bottoming out
최저시세로 떨어짐 touching the bottom
최저연간이익 minimum annual return
최저요율 minimum rate
최저운임 minimum freight
최저유동성비율 minimum liquidity ratio
최저의 희생 minimum sacrifice
최저이율 minimum rate of interest
최저이폭 minimum margin
최저임금 minimum wage
최저입찰가격 minimum bid
최저자본 basic capital
최저자본금 minimum capital requirements
최저자본금제도 minimum capital system
최저재고 minimum inventory; minimum stock
최저적립기준 minimum funding standard
최저점 descending tops
최저주문량 minimum quantity
최저증거금율 minimum margin requirement
최저지불액 minimum payment
최저추가채무 additional minimum liability
최저한도지불의무액 fixed amount minimum payment
최저한수입업무 minimum access
최적관세이론 theory of optimum tariff
최적규모 optimal scale; option seller
최적분배 optimum distribution
최적생산량 optimum output
최적성기준 optimality criterion
최적성장률 optimum rate of growth
최적성장모델 optimal growth model
최적이자율 optimum rate of interest
최적자본구성 optimal capital structure
최적자원배분 optimum allocation of resources
최적재고량 optimum inventory
최적조건 optimal condition
최적조업도 optimum capacity
최적조업도와 최유리조업도 optimal operating ratio maximal operating ratio
최적채권포트폴리오 optimal bond portfolio
최적통화지역 optimum currency
최적포트폴리오 optimal portfolio
최적폴리시믹스 optimal policy mix
최적헤지수단 optimal hedge instrument
최적화 optimization
최종가치 terminal value
최종거래일 final trading day; last day of trading
최종거래일에 속하는 월 month to which the last trading day pertains
최종결과 end result; filing accounts
최종결제 final cash settlement
최종구입원가법 last cost method; last purchase method; most recent purchase method
최종국면 final phase
최종기입부 book of final entry
최종대주 lender of last resort
최종목표 end goal; policy objective
(거래소의) 최종 분위기 closing tone
최종상속인 last heir
최종생산물 final products
최종설립취지서 final prospectus
최종수요 final demand
최종수요자 end-user
최종수익률 final rate of return
최종수익자 final beneficiary
최종이익 final yield

ㅈ ㅊ ㅋ

최종잔고방식 final balance method
최종적으로 확정한 재무제표 finally settled financial statements
최종지표 macroeconomic indicators
최종투자가 retail investor
최종투자이익 final yield on investment
최종특별시세 final bid-asked quotation
최종회의 closing meeting
최첨단 leading edge
최초인도 initial delivery
최초취득자 first purchaser
최혜국대우 most favored nation treatment
최혜국조항 most favored nation clause
최후의 대주(貸主) last resort lender
최후통첩 ultimatum
추가 및 생략 additions and omissions
추가기입 post entry
추가문서 addenda
추가발행 added float
추가비용 additional charge; additional expenses; extra cost
추가사례금 refresher
추가상장 additional listing
추가설정 additional establishment; additional issue
추가소유 adding to holdings
추가수익 remargin
추가이익 additional margin
추가자본준비금 additional paid-in capital
추가조항 additional conditions
추가증거금 maintenance call; margin call
추가증액 overlay
추가지불 pay-up
추가출자 additional investment
추가특별예금제도 supplementary special deposits scheme
추가형 open-end type
추가형 투자신탁 additional-type investment trust
추계과세 taxation by estimate
추계를 통한 갱정 determination by estimate
추량차이 physical variance
추리 inference
추방 relegation
추보서류 supplementary document
추선상환증권 securities called by lot
추세 trend
추세분석 trend analysis
추이 **TOPIX** trends TOPIX
추적가능원가 traceable cost
추정 presumption
추정량차이 quantity variance
추정상속인 heir presumptive
추정샘플링 estimation sampling
추정신탁; 복귀신탁 resulting trust
추정오차 estimation error
추정의 putative
추정증거 presumptive evidence
추정치표준오차 standard error of estimate
추징처분 punishment on penalty tax
추천장 letter of recommendation
추천주 recommended stock
추첨 drawing of number
추첨상환 redemption by drawing; redemption by lottery; redemption by the number of drawing
추첨포함 cum-drawing
축선 axis; moderation
축소재생산 reproduction on a diminishing scale
축소하다 narrow
축적 accumulated capital
축적예산 bottom-up budget
출고표 material requisition; material requisition note
출금전표 disbursement slip; payment slip
출금통지 advice of debit
출납부 cash-book
출납부; 장부 account book
출납전표 cash slips
출소기한 limitation of actions
출신주 home state

출원권 application right
출원권취득 acquisition of the application right
출입금지 off limit
출자 capital subscription; equity contribution; investment
출자 IMF subscription IMF
출자; 거출국채 subscription/contribution government bond
출자가 equity partner
출자금 investment in capital
출자금불입 payment of capital contribution
출자법 law concerning restrictions on the acceptance of subscription; deposit and interest rate; etc.; law of subscription
출자비율 equity position
출자사원 partner
출자액 amount invested; amount of investment
출자예금 share deposits
출자의무자 contributory
출자자 equity participant; financier; investor
출자증권 subscription certificate
출장여비 traveling expenses for business
출처 source
출판권 publishing right
출판법 press law
출하지도서 ship order
출하지수 shipments index
출항수수료 clearance fee
출현 emergency
충당 appropriation
충당금 money earmarked
충당순위 priority order of application
충돌 collision
충동구매 impulse buying
충분한 보상 full compensation
충분한 보호 adequate protection
충실 enrichment
충족 sufficiency
취급 interpretation
취급비 handling cost; handling expenses
취급수수료 lifting charges
취득 acquisition
취득가격 acquisition value
취득시 환산표 translation method at historical rates
취득시효 acquisitive prescription; positive prescription
취득원가 acquisition cost; historical cost; original cost
취득원가기준 historical cost basis
취득원가법 acquisition cost method; method of historical cost; original cost method
취득원가조정 acquisition adjustment; acquisition cost adjustment
취득원가주의 acquisition cost theory
취득원가주의재무제표 historical cost financial statements
취득원가주의회계 current cost accounting; historical cost accounting
취득일 acquisition date; date of acquisition
취득일 이전의 유보이익 pre-acquisition profit
취득잉여금 acquired surplus
취득자산 property acquired
취득잔고비례법 cost depletion method
취리히의 난쟁이; 스위스금융계의 실력자 gnomes of Zurich
취소가능신용장revocable L/C
취소권 annulment right
취소불가능한 위임 irrevocable commitment
취소불능보증 non-cancellable guarantee
취소불능신용장 irrevocable L/C
취소소송 revocation suit
취소신고서 statement of withdrawal
취소주문 cancel order
취소하다 annul; countermand; revoke
취소할 때까지 유효한 주문 good-till-canceled orders
취소할 수 없는 허가 irrevocable license
취소할 수 있는 권원 defeasible title
취약성 sign of fragility; vulnerability

취약한 vulnerable
취업규제 work rules
취업불능소득보상보험 disability income insurance
취지; 요령 gist
취직촉진수당 allowance for promotion of employment
측량 surveying
측정계약 measurement contract
측정기준 measurement principles
측정방법 measurement method
측정일 measurement date
층별의 stratified
치과치료비보험 dental expense insurance
치료비보험 physician's expense insurance
치외법권 extraterritoriality
칙령으로 허가된 회계사 chartered accountant
친회사 parent company
침몰 sinking
침묵 silence
침묵에 의한 by silence
침투가격 penetration price
침하; 후퇴 dip
침해 transgression
칭하다 referred to as

ㅋ

카드 integrated circuit card IC
카드가맹점 card merchant
카드갱신 card renewal
카드결제 pay by card
카드도난보험 credit card burglary insurance
카드론 card loan
카드범죄 card criminal fraud
카드쇼핑 card shopping
카드시스템 card system
카드식 기장법 card system of bookkeeping
카드식별코드 card discrimination code
카드위조 card counterfeiting
카드유효기한 expiration date of the credit card
카드재발행 card replacement
카드표준화 card standardization
카드회사 card issuer
카드회원 card member
카르텔 cartel
카르텔관세 cartel tariffs
카운터파트레이팅 counterparty rating
카운터파트리스크 counterparty risk; exposure to counterpary
카탈로그판매 catalog sales
카터본드 Carter bond
카테고리킬러 category killer
칵테일스와프;복합스와프 cocktail swap
칼라 collar
칼라스와프 collared swap
캐나다달러장기국채 Canadian-dollar long-term bond
캐리인컴 carry income
캐시; 현금 cash
캐시매니지먼트빌 cash management bills; cash-management bills
캐시매니지먼트서비스 cash management service
캐시플로 cash flow
캐시플로 대 유동부채 cash flow to current liabilities
캐시플로계약 cash forward contract
캐시플로리턴 cash flow return
캐시플로배율 price cashflow ratio
캐시플로부담배율 cash flow coverage ratio
캐시플로비율 cash flow ratio
캐시플로에 영향을 받지 않는 항목 items not affecting cash flows
캐시플로예측 cash flow projection
캐시플로위기 cash flow crisis
캐시플로의 여력 cushion of cash flow
캐시플로이율 cash flow interest
캐시플로해석 interpretation of cash flows
캐싱 cash advance
캐피탈게인; 매매이익 capital gain
캐피탈게인과세 capital gain taxation; taxation on capital gain
캐피탈게인세 capital gain tax
캐피탈게인에서 공제함 exclusion from capital gain
캐피탈게인펀드 capital gain fund
캐피탈기어링 capital gearing

캐피탈로스 capital loss
캐피탈론 capital loan
캐피탈리스 capital lease
캐피탈리스크 capital risk
캐피탈플로 capital flow
캐핑 capping
캔슬드오더 canceled order
캔슬러블스와프 cancelable swap
캔자스시티상품거래소 Kansas City Board of Trade
캘린더스프레드 calendar spread
캘린더스프레드거래 calendar spread transaction
캡 & 플로어 cap and floor
캡론 cap loan
캡부론 capped loan
캡부채 capped floating rate note
캡스와프 capped swap
커런시컨버전채 currency conversion bond
커런트어섬션종신보험 current-assumption whole life insurance
커런트익스포저 current exposure
커머디티스와프 commodity swap
커머디티풀 commodity pool
커머디티플로법 commodity flow method
커머셜유니온 Commercial Union Assurance Co
커먼갭 common gap
커뮤니티크레디트 community credit
커미션제 commission system
커미트먼트베이스 commitment base
커버거래 exchange cover
커버드스트래들 covered straddle
커버드옵션 covered option
커버드워런트 covered warrant
커버드콜 covered call
커버드콜옵션 covered call option
커버드포지션 covered position
커버딜링 cover dealing
커브 J curve J
커브효과 J curve effect J
커스텀인덱스 custom index
커스텀퍼포먼스스탠다드 customized performance standards
컨벤셔널방식 conventional auction; conventional method
컨설팅세일즈 consulting sales
컨소시엄뱅크 consortium bank
컨트리익스포저 country exposure
컨트리펀드 country fund
컨퍼밍하우스 confirming house
컴비네이션 combination
컴워런트 cum warrant
컴포지트프라이스 composite price
컴퓨터감사 computer audit
컴퓨터센터 computer center
컴퓨터화 computerization
케이스스터디 case study
케인스학파 Keynesian
케인스혁명 Keynesian revolution
케인즈경제학 Keynesian economics
케인즈효과 Keynes effect
코레스계약 correspondent agreement
코레스계정 correspondent account
코레스관계 correspondent relation
코레스비용 correspondent charge
코레스은행 correspondent bank
코메르츠은행 Commerzbank
코메르츠지수 Commerzbank-Index
코스모모델 comprehensive system model
코스트삭감 cost reduction
코스트푸시인플레이션 cost-push inflation
코어홀딩 core holding
코콤(COCOM; 대공산권 수출통제위원회) Coordinating Committee for Multilateral Strategic Export Controls
콘글로머리트; 거대복합기업 conglomerate
콘도르스프레드거래 condor type spread transaction
콘드라티에프파(주기) Kondratieff wave
콘솔공채 consolidated annuities; Consols
콘솔리데이션론 consolidation loan

콘솔시장 console market
콘허그순환 corn hog cycle
콜; 소집하다 call
콜금리 call money rate; call rate; per-diem rate for call loan
콜러블론 callable loan
콜러블스와프 callable swap
콜러블스왑션 callable swaption
콜레이쇼백스프레드거래 call ratio back spread transaction
콜론; 단자; 당좌차입금 call loan
콜론이자 interest on call loans
콜머니 call money
콜머니이자 interest on call money
콜스왑션 call swaption
콜스프레드 call spread
콜시장 call market
콜시장평균잔고 call market average outstanding
콜어음시장 call and bill market
콜옵션 call option
콜옵션가치범위 within limits on value of call option
콜옵션계약 call option contract
콜옵션부 채권 call bond
콜옵션의 옵션료 call option premium; call premium
콜옵션평가 valuation of call option
콜옵션평가와 배당 call option valuation and dividend
콜워런트 call warrant
콜트리거 call trigger
쿠션채 cushion bond
쿠폰금리 coupon interest
쿠폰만의 통화스와프 coupon-only currency swap
쿠폰세일 coupon sale
쿠폰수입 coupon income
쿠폰스와프 coupon swap
쿠폰재투자수입 income by coupon reinvestment
쿠폰지불기간 coupon payment period
쿠폰패스 coupon pass
쿨링오프 cooling-off
쿨링오프기간 cooling-off period
쿼트리포터 quote reporter
퀄리파이드비즈니스유니트 qualified business unit
퀵단말 QUICK-terminal
크게 깎은 가격 knock-down price
크라우드거래 crowd trading
크라우딩아웃; 구축 crowding out
크라우딩아웃효과; 구축효과 crowding out effect
크레디스위스지수 Credit Suisse Index Generals
크레디트디폴트스와프 credit default swap
크레디트링크채 credit-linked note
크레디트스왑 credit swap
크레디트스코어링 credit scoring
크레디트옵션 credit option
크레디트이용권 right of credit availability
크레디트트란시 credit tranche
크레디트퍼실리티;신용편의 credit facility
크레디트히스토리 credit history
크로스거래 cross trading
크로스디폴트 cross default
크로스디폴트조항 cross default clause
크로스레이트 cross rate
크로스마진 cross margin
크로스매매 cross
크로스보더 cross border
크로스섹셔널평가법 cross-sectional valuation approach
크로스오더 cross order
크로스재정 cross arbitration
크로스헤지 cross hedge
크롤링페그; 단계적인 평가변동방식 crawling peg
크리티컬패스메소드 critical path method
크리티컬패스회계 criteria path accounting
크리핑디플레이션 creeping deflation

크리핑인플레이션; 잠행성 인플레이션 creeping inflation
크림스키밍 cream skimming
큰 기관투자가 large institutional investors
큰 벌이 killing
큰 변화가 없는 virtually unchanged
큰; 주요한 major
클로즈드기간 closed period
클리어링펀드; 결제기금 clearing fund
클리어밴드 clear band
클린 clean bill of lading B/L
클린론; 무담보론 clean loan
클린신용장 clean letter of credit
클린오피니언 clean opinion
클린플로트; 자유변동시세제도 clean float
키스톤채권 keystone bond funds
킥백 kick back
킹스턴체제 Kingston Regime

ㅌ

타겟리턴 target return
타겟발행 target issue
타겟존; 목표상장권 target zone
타기업비교 cross sectional analysis
타당성조사 feasibility study
타당성확인 validation
타발환 inward exchange
타보험조항 other insurance clause
타사주식교환가능채권 exchangeable bond
타소불수표 out town check
타소불어음 out town bill
타소인도 out town delivery
타이밍스와프 timing swap
타이밍옵션 timing option
타인자본 debt capital; outside capital
타인자본회전율 turnover ratio of total liabilities
타임디케이 time decay
타임래그 time lag
타임바이어스 time bias
타임스팬 time span
타임옵션 time option
타임카드 time card
타임필터 time filter
타행인수 bill of others
타협 compromise
타회계 other accounting
탁월한 prominent
탄력관세 elastic tariff
탄력성 낙관 elasticity optimism
탄력성 비관 elasticity pessimism
탄력성 어프로치 elasticity approach
탄력예상 flexible budget
탄력적인 수요 elastic demand
탄력조항 elasticity clause
탈공업화 deindustrialization
탈공업화 사회 post industrial society
탈세 tax dodging; tax evasion
탈세방조범 accessory to tax evasion
탈세자 tax dodger; tax evader
탈은행 disintermediation of bank
탈퇴 withdrawl of membership
탈퇴신청 application for withdrawal
탈퇴회원 withdrawing member
탈환; 회복 recapture
탑승자상해보험 automobile passengers' personal accident insurance
태도 attitude
태도측정 measure of value
태평양보험회의 Pacific Insurance Conference
태평양지역경제협력기구 Organization of Pacific Economic Cooperation
태환권발행세 tax on bank note system
태환준비 convertible reserve
태환지폐 convertible note
태환통화 convertible currency
택스레버리지리스 tax leverage lease
택스리스 tax lease
택스스와프 tax swap
택스컷백 tax cutback
택스플레이션 taxflation

택지 premises
택지개발세 land development tax
택지조성비 development cost of residential site
택지평가 valuation of residential site
탠덤통화 tandem currencies
탭발행 tap issue
탭빌 tap bills
탭채 bond on tap; tap stock
탭채로 발행하다 issue on a tap basis
터널 속의 뱀 snake in the tunnel
터미네이션데이트 termination date
턴키 turnkey
턴키계약 turnkey contract
텀론 term loan
텀스와프 term swap
텀채권 term receivable
텀페더럴펀드 term federal fund
텀페드 term fed
텀페드펀드레이트 term fed fund rate
테이크아웃론 takeout loan
테일 tail
테일헤지 tail hedge
테크니컬트레이딩 technical trading
텐더가격 tender price
텐더빌 tender bill
텐더옵션 tender option
텐더패널 tender panel
텔러 teller
텔레폰론 telephone loan
텔레폰마켓 telephone market
텔레폰뱅킹 telephone banking
템퍼러리본드 temporary bond
템포럴법 temporal method
토런스시스템 Torrens System
토론토공업주지수 Toronto Industrial Index
토론토선물거래소 Toronto Futures Exchange
토론토증권거래소 Toronto Stock Exchange
토빈의 **q** Tobin's q
토의보고서 issues paper
토지 land; land lot
토지가격세 land value tax
토지개량 land improvement; land reform
토지개량비 land improvement expenses
토지개량사업 land improvement enterprise
토지건물 land and building
토지계정 land account
토지과세대장 land tax register book
토지대금모기지 purchase money mortgage
토지대장 land ledger; terrier
토지등기 land registration
토지등기소 land registry
토지배분제도 allotment system
토지보유 land tenure
토지보유자 land tenant
토지부담 encumbrance; land charges
토지세법 Land Value Tax Law
토지세제 land taxation
토지소유 land ownership
토지소유자 land proprietor; landowner
토지수용 condemnation of land; eminent domain; land expropriation
토지수용권 land expropriation right; right of eminent domain
토지수용법 land expropriation law
토지신탁 land trust
토지에 대한 후순위권리 junior encumbrance
토지점유 possession of land
토지조성비 ground-making expenses
토착자본 indigenous capital
토킨펀드 tokkin
토탈리턴스와프 total return swap
톤세 tonnage due
톤세 납부서 note for payment of tonnage dues
톤틴연금 tontines
톱다운형 예측 top-down forecasting
톱다운형 투자 top-down investment
톱리버설데이 top-reversal day
톱버티컬컴비네이션 top vertical combination
톱스 trust obligation participating securities TOPS
톱스트래들 top straddle

통계가정이론 statistical decision theory
통계모델 statistical model
통계분석 statistical analysis
통계오차 statistical error
통계용어 statistical terminology
통계이론 statistical theory
통계처리 statistical procedure
통계척도 statistical measure
통계총괄표 key statistics
통계학 statistics
통고처분 notification procedure
통과 passage
통과무역 transit trade
통과선하증권 through B/L
통관 customs clearance
통관베이스 customs basis
통관용 송장 customs invoice
통관절차 customs procedures
통괄계정 controlling account
통괄국세사찰관 chief investigator
통괄국세조사관 chief examiner
통괄국세징수관 chief revenue officer
통괄하다 preside over
통달 directive
통산 integration
통상결산 general closing
통상결제 ordinary payment
통상비용 ordinary charges; regular fee
통상사용시간 normal and average use hours
통상손해 ordinary tosses
통상약관 usual covenants
통상양도증서 ordinary conveyance
통상어음 ordinary bill
통상외국세액공제 ordinary foreign tax credit
통상운영 ordinary and normal recurring operations
통상인도 regular delivery; regular way of delivery
통상정관 articles of association
통상조약 treaty of commerce
통상조항 commerce clause
통상주의 ordinary care
통상총회 ordinary general meeting
통상해산 common liquidation
통상형 모기지론 conventional mortgage loan
통상확대법 trade expansion act
통신비 communication charges
통신업계 communications industry
통신판매 mail order
통일경리기준 uniform accounting regulations
통일관습규칙 uniform practice code
통일보험법 Uniform Life Insurance Act
통일상사법전 Uniform Commercial Code
통일상표 unified brand
통일양식 prescribed format
통일원가계산 uniform cost accounting
통일원가계산제도 uniform cost accounting system
통일적인 운용 unified operation
통일증권법 Uniform Securities Act
통일회계기준 uniform accounting standards
통일회계제도 uniform accounting system
통장 passbook
통장저축예금계좌 passbook savings account
통제경제 controlled economy
통제무역 controlled trade
통제예산 control budget
통제회계 accounting for control
통지를 받고 빚을 갚음 advice and pay
통지보험 declaration policy
통지예금 deposit at notice; notice deposit; savings at call
통지은행 advising bank; notifying bank
통지전표 advice slip
통지지불 advice payment
통치경제 integrated economy
통치행위 sovereign act
통합 integrity
통합시황정보시스템 consolidated quotation system
통행권 way
통행료 toll

통행세 passengers tax; toll charges
통화 currency
통화가치 currency value
통화가치저하 depreciation of currency
통화가치하락 currency depreciation
통화간 채무교환거래 cross currency swap
통화감독관사무소(SEC) Office of the Comptroller of the Currency
통화개혁 monetary reform
통화공급량 money supply
통화관리 monetary control; monetary management
통화금융정책 monetary and financial policy
통화단위 currency unit; monetary unit
통화당국 monetary authority
통화동맹 monetary union
통화등귀 currency appreciation
통화디플레이션 currency deflation
통화바스켓 currency basket; exchange rate basket
통화방위 protecting the currency
통화변동 currency fluctuation
통화보상 currency indemnity
통화불안 monetary instability
통화블록 currency bloc; monetary bloc
통화상품 currency commodity
통화선물 currency futures
통화선물가격동향 currency futures price movement
통화선물거래 currency futures trading
통화성 금융자산 monetary financial assets
통화성 예금 currency deposit
통화성 예저금 demand deposits
통화스와프 currency swap
통화스와프채 currency swap bond
통화스톡 money stock
통화승수 money multiplier
통화안정 monetary stability
통화옵션거래 currency option trading
통화위기 currency crisis
통화위험 monetary crisis
통화유통고 currency in circulation
통화인플레 currency inflation
통화재팽창 reflation
통화절상 currency upvaluation
통화절하 currency devaluation
통화제예금 transferable deposits
통화조정 currency adjustment
통화주의 currency principle; monetarism
통화주의자 monetarist
통화준비 monetary reserve
통화체계 currency system
통화총량 monetary aggregate
통화침투설의 trickle down
통화팽창 expansion of currency
통화협정 agreement on commerce; monetary agreement
통화환산 currency conversion
퇴거명령 eviction order
퇴거시킴 eviction
퇴직관련급부 retirement related benefits
퇴직금 retirement pay
퇴직금공제계약 mutual aid contract for retirement allowance
퇴직금을 일괄지급함 retirement allowance in a lump sum
퇴직금적립금 superannuation reserve
퇴직금제도 retirement plan
퇴직금중간정산지급 payment of retirement allowance for termination
퇴직급부 termination benefit
퇴직급여 retirement allowance
퇴직급여규정 retirement allowance regulations
퇴직급여예비금 accrued severance indemnities
퇴직급여적립금 reserve for pension fund
퇴직급여준비금 accrued employees retirement benefit
퇴직급여준비금 employees retirement benefit
퇴직급여준비금편입한도액 allowed limit of retirement allowance reserve

퇴직소득 retirement income
퇴직소득공제 allowed retirement income deduction; deduction for retirement income
퇴직소득부 보험 retirement income policy
퇴직소득신고서 return form for retirement income
퇴직수당 severance benefit; terminal pay allowance
퇴직수당으로 처리하는 일시금 lump sum payment regarded as retirement allowance
퇴직연금 retirement annuity; retirement pension
퇴직연금과세 taxation on retirement annuity; taxation on retirement pension
퇴직연금부금 premium payment of a retirement annuity
퇴직연금수취인 beneficiary of the retirement annuity
퇴직연금업무 retirement annuity business
퇴직연금적립금 reserve for retirement annuity
퇴직연금적립금 retirement annuity reserve
퇴직연령 age of retirement
퇴직일시금 retirement lump sum grants
퇴직후 급부 postretirement benefit
투기 speculation
투기거래 speculation transaction; speculative transaction
투기계정을 정리함 liquidation of speculative accounts
투기구매; 매점매석 speculative buying
투기구입 speculator buying
투기꾼 speculative buyers
투기동기 speculative motive
투기리스크 speculative risk
투기매입 bull speculation
투기시장 speculative market
투기열 craze for speculation; speculative enthusiasm
투기이윤 speculative gain
투기자 speculators
투기자금 speculative money
투기적인 등급 speculative grade
투기적인 채권 speculative grade bond
투기전 deal between speculators; speculative dealing
투기전에서 손해를 봄 taking a bath
투기주 cats and dogs stock; speculative stock
투기행위 taking a flier
투매 selling off; shaking-out; slaughter sale
투매; 출혈판매 distress selling
투매; 헐값으로 팔기 sacrifice sale
투명성이 있는 transparent
투신상표 portfolio of investment trust
투신편입주식 shares held by investment trusts
투웨이마켓 two way market
투융자 investment and loan
투입 infusion
투입계수 input coefficient
투입산출분석 input-output analysis
투입산출표 input-output table
투자가를 위한 세미나 investor briefings
투자가별 공사채매매상황 bond transaction by investor types
투자가보호 protection of investors
투자가의 견해 investor perceptions
투자가의 관심 investor interest
투자가의 구매 investor buying
투자가치 investment value
투자결정 investment decision
투자경기 investment boom
투자계정부문 investment account
투자계획 investment program
투자계획기간분석 horizon analysis
투자고문 investment advisor
투자고문법 investment advisory law
투자고문업 advisory service
투자고문업계 investment advisory industry
투자고문회사 investment management company
투자곡선 investment curve

투자공제 investment credit
투자관리국(SEC) Division of Investment Management(SEC)
투자관리자와 고객의 관계 manager-client relations
투자기간 investment holding period; investment period
투자기관경합시스템 competitive market maker system
투자기회 investment opportunities
투자달러 investment dollar
투자대상기업 investment grade corporate
투자를 위한 자금수요 demand for investing fund
투자리스크 investment risk
투자마찰 Investment friction
투자매 investment buying
투자매각 liquidation of investments
투자매니저 investment manager
투자매니저구성 investment manager structure
투자메리트 investment merit
투자목적확인서 investment letter
투자목표 investment objectives
투자법인에 출자하는 단위 unit of investment securities
투자부동산 investment property; investment real estate
투자분석 investment analysis
투자분석가 investment analyst
투자분쟁해결국제센터 International Center for Settlement of Investment Disputes
투자상품 investment products
투자선택개괄 investment selection summary
투자성과 investment result
투자성향 investment propensity; propensity to invest
투자세액공제 investment tax credit
투자소득 investment income
투자수요 investment demand
투자수익; 투자수익률 return on investment
투자수익률 market rate of return, ROI
투자수익을 예측함 prediction of investment return
투자승수 investment multiplier
투자승인리스트 approved list of investment
투자승인액 investment approvals
투자시장 investment market
투자신탁 investment fund; investment trust
투자신탁설정 sales of investment trusts
투자신탁수익증권 beneficiary certificate of investment trust
투자신탁운용상황 distribution of net assets of investment trusts
투자신탁위탁업무 management business of investment trust
투자신탁위탁회사 investment trust management company
투자신탁유가증권 securities held for investment trust
투자신탁의 유가증권보험 securities ownership by investment trusts
투자신탁판매회사 securities investment trust sales company
투자업 investment business
투자연기 deferment of investment; postponement of investment
투자연도별 방식 investment year method
투자예산 investment budget
투자운용 investment management
투자원천운용표 where got and where gone statement
투자위원회 investment committee
투자유가증권 investment in securities; investment securities
투자유가증권거래 investment securities transaction
투자유가증권수익 investment securities gains
투자유가증권시장 investment securities markets
투자유가증권포트폴리오 investment securities portfolio

투자유연성 investment flexibility
투자유인 inducement to invest
투자율 investment rate
투자은행 investment bank
투자은행가 merchant banker
투자은행금융기관 Investment Banking Financing Company
투자은행업법 investment banking business
투자의 이중성 dual character of investment
투자이익률 rate of return on invested capital; rate of return on investment
투자자금 investment capital
투자자보호 protection of investor
투자자산 investment assets
투자자회사 investment vehicle
투자재 Investment goods
투자재평가적립금 investment revaluation reserve
투자적격 investment grade
투자적격대상 legal investment
투자적격레이팅 investment grade rate
투자적격채 investment grade securities
투자적격채권 investment grade bond
투자전략 investment strategy
투자정보원 investment information sources
투자정책 investment policy
투자주 investment stock
투자주총회 general meeting of investors
투자증권 investment security
투자지출 investment expenditure
투자처 investment choice
투자척도 investment criteria; measure of investment
투자철학 investment philosophy
투자카운셀러 investment counselor
투자클럽 investment club
투자통화 investment currency
투자판단 investment judgment
투자포트폴리오 investment portfolio
투자한계효율 marginal efficiency of investment
투자함수 investment function
투자해제 disinvestment
투자허가리스트 authorized investment list
투자환경 investment climate; investment environment
투자활동 investing activities
투자활동으로 인한 캐시플로 cash flow from investing activities
투자회사 investment company; unit investment trust company
투자회수 investment recovery
투표 ballot; voting
투하자본 invested capital
트기자금 speculative fund
트라이앵글리버설패턴 triangle reversal patterns
트란시방식 tranche issue
트랜스퍼메카니즘 transfer mechanism
트랜스퍼문제 transfer problem
트럼프세 playing cards tax
트레이더 trader
트레이드티켓 trade ticket
트레이딩목적유가증권 trading securities
트레이딩스탬프 trading stamp
트레이딩풀 trading pool
트레이트오프 trade off
트렌드라인 trend line
트렌드채널 trend channel
트렌드플라워 trend follower
트리거가격 trigger price
트리구조 tree structure
트리티쇼핑 treaty shopping
트리플크로스오버법 triple crossover method
트리플톱 triple top
트윈카드 twin-card
특권 및 면제 privileges and immunities
특권남용 breach of privilege
특권료 option money
특례 special rule; special treatment
특례공채 Special Deficit-Financing Bonds
특례공채법 Special Deficit-Financing Bond

Law
특례참여자 exceptional participant
특례취급 interpretation for special rule
특무원장 special ledger
특별가입금 special admission fee
특별감사 special audit
특별감세국채 special tax reduction bond
특별결의 special resolution
특별결제 special payment
특별계정에 산입된 보조금 subsidy charged to the special account
특별계정잔고 balance of the amount charged to special account
특별공제 special deduction
특별과징금 special assessment
특별교환 special exchange
특별구 special ward
특별구민세 special ward inhabitants tax
특별국세조사관 special examiner
특별국세징수관 special revenue officer
특별대량구매 special bid
특별대부계정금리 special loan account interest rate
특별대출금리 special advances rate
특별대행구매 specialist block purchases
특별매개기관 special intermediary institution
특별목적세채권 special tax bond
특별목적트러스트 special purpose trust
특별목적회사 special purpose company
특별배당 bonus dividend; dividend extra; extra dividend; plum; special dividend
특별배당주 bonus stock
특별법 special law
특별부담금 Special Dues
특별비 special expenses
특별비용 special charges
특별상각 extraordinary depreciation; special depreciation
특별상각률 ratio of special depreciation deduction
특별상각부족액 shortage of special depreciation
특별상각준비금 reserve for special depreciation; special depreciation reserve
특별상각한도액 maximum special depreciation allowance
특별소득세 special income tax
특별손실 extraordinary loss
특별손익 extraordinary profit and loss; extraordinary gain or loss; special profit and loss
특별손익전 이익 earnings before extraordinary items
특별손익항목 extraordinary item; extraordinary profit and loss item
특별수선비 special repair expenses
특별시 county borough
특별신용거래 special margin transaction
특별약관 special clause
특별예금제도 special deposit scheme
특별요율 special rate
특별요율적용;편차 deviation
특별원 special won
특별위원회 special committee
특별위험 special risks
특별은행계정업자 special bank account firm
특별이익 extraordinary gain
특별이해관계자 special interest party
특별인출권 Special Drawing Rights
특별인출권보유액 holdings of Special Drawing Rights
특별인출권이자 interest on Special Drawing Rights
특별적립금 special reserve
특별적립잉여금 assigned surplus; special surplus fund
특별조건서 special conditions of the contract
특별증거금요건 special margin requirement
특별지방교부세 special local grant tax
특별지방소비세 special local consumption tax
특별지출조건부 매상할인 sales rebate with special payment terms

특별징수 special collection
특별징수의무자 special collecting agent
특별참가자 special participant
특별참가자예탁금 special participant deposit
특별참가자참가금 special participant participation fee
특별채 special bond
특별청산 special clearance
특별청산승인 approval of special liquidation
특별청산에 동의함 agreement of special liquidation
특별청산지수 special quotation
특별토지보유세 special landholding tax
특별톤세 special tonnage due
특별편익설 special benefit theory of taxation
특별한 감가상각방법 special methods of computing depreciation
특별한 경제적 이익 special economic benefit
특별한 상각방법 special depreciation method
특별한 평가법 special valuation method
특별항목 special item
특별회계 special account
특별회계 Special Accounts
특별회원 special member
특별회의 special membership fee
특성선 characteristic line
특성선의 정의 definition of characteristic line
특손 special loss
특수관계인 associated person
특수구조스와프 tailored swap transactions
특수법인 juridical person in a public law
특수분개장 special journal
특수생산요소이론 specific productive factors
특수수익 peculiar benefits
특수용도면세 nontaxable-goods for special use
특수원가조사 special cost studies
특수채 specific bonds
특수회사 special corporation
특약리베이트 loyalty rebate
특약의료기구 Preferred Providers Organization
특약이 없는 계약 open contract
특약일거래 seller's option transaction
특약일결제거래 special day delivery transaction
특약재보험 treaty reinsurance
특약조항; 약인 covenant
특약지불조건부 구입할부 purchase rebate with special payment terms
특약판매 selective selling
특유재산 separate property
특정거래 specified day transaction
특정거래계정 special trading accounts
특정거래손익 special trading income or loss
특정금전신탁 specified money in trust
특정기간인도 broken term
특정기부금 specified donation
특정기일인도 odd date or broken date delivery
특정담보 fixed charge; specific charge
특정당좌예금 specified current account
특정리엔 particular lien
특정목적재무제표 special purpose financial statement
특정사업의 용지매수 land purchase for specified business
특정사원 holders of preferred equity securities
특정설비폐기세액공제 scrapping of equipment tax credit
특정수입고 restricted receipts
특정용도면제 tax exemption for specific use
특정위험 named peril
특정의 ill specie
특정의료법인 specified medical corporation
특정의료법인의 특별세율 reduced tax rate on specified medical corporation
특정이자 specified interest
특정이행 specific performance
특정자본의 유동화에 관한 법률 Law on Securitization of Specified Assets
특정자산 specified assets
특정재원채 limited obligation bond, revenue bond

특정전문투자신탁 specialized fund
특정제조지도서 special production order
특정주 specified stock
특정준비금 reserve for special purpose
특정지역 포트폴리오 regional portfolio
특정지역지점설치 limited branching
특정질병보장보험 specified disease insurance
특정퇴직금공제단체 mutual aid organization for specific retirement allowance
특정합병 직후의 자본 capital immediately after the specified merger
특정현물출자 specified investment in kind
특정현물출자로 취득한 자산 property acquired by the specified investment in kind
특정현물출자증권 securities acquired by the specified investment in kind
특정횡선수표 special crossed check
특주의 tailor made
특징 characteristics; features
특허 patent
특허국 Patent Bureau
특허권 patent right
특허권계정 patent account
특허권교환계약 cross license contract
특허권사용료 royalty of patent right
특허권자 patentee
특허권침해 patent infringement; infringement of patent right
특허권평가 valuation of patent right
특허료 patent fee
특허법 patent law
특허변리사 patent attorney
특허보유지 charter-land
특허분쟁 patent dispute
특허유효기간 patent period
특허증 letters patent
특허출원중 patent applied for; patent pending
특허품 patented article
특허회사 chartered company
특혜관세 preferential duty; preferential tariff
특혜적인 preferential
특화계수 location quotient
티켓판매금융 ticket sale finance
T 규칙초과증거금 Regulations T exces
T-본드입찰최저가 stop-out price of T-bond
T-Bond 선물거래 T-Bond Futures
T-Bond 선물옵션 T-bond futures option
TED 스프레드 Treasury Eurodollar spread
T자형 계정 skeleton form account; T form account
T형 계정 T-account method
TSE 이사장 president of TSE
T+3 4영업일인도
T+7 8영업일인도
틱 tick
틱테스트룰 tick-test rule

ㅍ

파견사원 detached employees
파괴처분 destructive disposition
파급경로 transmission mechanism
파급권 recourse right
파급급여 back pay
파급불배당금 back dividend
파급수정 catch-up adjustments
파급효과 knock-on effect; multiplied effect; repercussion effect
파급효과클레임 impact claims
파기반송 reversed and remanded
파는 값 selling price
파는 권리 selling right
파는 자의 시장 sellers' market
파는 쪽 bargainer; seller
파동조정 rolling readjustment
파동함수 wave function
파라메트릭방법 parametric method
파레토 상수 Pareto's constant
파리거래소 Paris bourse
파리종합주가지수 French Institute Index
파리클럽 Paris Club
파리패스조항 pari passu clause
파면책채권 undischargeable claim
파벌 clique
파산 bankruptcy
파산감사관 comptroller in bankruptcy
파산고지 bankruptcy notice
파산관리 case administration
파산관재 administration in bankruptcy
파산관재인 administrator in bankruptcy; bankruptcy administrator; bankruptcy trustee; receiver; receiver in bankruptcy; trustee in bankruptcy
파산규칙 bankruptcy rules
파산기업 bankrupt equity
파산명령 adjudication order
파산법 bankruptcy law
파산법원 bankruptcy court
파산선고 declaration of bankruptcy; adjudication of bankruptcy
파산신청 bankruptcy filing; petition in bankruptcy
파산심리인 referee in bankruptcy
파산예기 contemplation of bankruptcy
파산우선지불 preferential payment in bankruptcy
파산원인 cause of bankruptcy
파산자 insolvent debtor; bankrupt
파산자 재산차압명령 warrant in bankruptcy
파산재단 bankrupt's estate
파산절차 bankruptcy proceedings; insolvency proceedings
파산채권 claim in bankruptcy
파산채무자 bankruptcy debtor
파산청산인 accountant in bankruptcy
파산행위 act of bankruptcy
파생거래 derivative transaction
파생상품 contingent claim; derivative product
파생상품시장 derivative market

파생상품포트폴리오 derivative portfolio
파생소득 derived income
파생소송 derivative suit
파생예금 derivative deposit
파생적인 contingent
파생증권 derivative security
파생취득 derivative income
파생패스스루증권시장 derivative pass-through securities market
파손 breakage
파쉐계산식 Paasche formula
파업폭동부담보조항 free from strikers; riots and civil commotion clause
파열 burst
파울 **B/L** foul B/L
파이낸셜뉴스지수옵션 Financial News index option
파이낸셜타임즈공업주가지수 Financial Times Index of Industrial Ordinary Shares; Financial Times Index of Industrial Sensitive World Commodity Prices
파이낸셜타임즈주가지수 FT Industrial Ordinary Stock Index
파이낸셜플래너 financial planner
파이낸스리스 finance lease; financing lease
파이낸스중개 financial arrangement
파인더 finder
파일드 par yield
파일럿플랜트 pilot plant
파일링 filing
파탄금융기관 failed financial institution
파탄기업 failing company
파트너십 partnership
파트너십계약 partnership agreement
파티서페이션계약 participation agreement
파포워드 par forward
팍스아메리카나 Pax Americana
판결 decree
판결등록 entry of judgment
판결부활 revival of judgment
판결채권이 상쇄됨 judgment set-off
판결채권자 judgment creditor
판결채무자 judgment debtor
판결파기 reversal of judgment
판권등록 registration of copyright
판권침해 infringement of copyright
판례 judicial definition
판례법 case law
판로 sales network
판로개척 development of distribution channel
판매가; 입찰가격 bid price
판매가레이트 asked rate
판매간접비 selling overhead
판매경로 marketing channel
판매계약 selling agreement
판매관리비 sales and general administrative expense; selling and administrative expenses
판매금액 sales amount
판매금융 sales finance
판매금융회사 sales finance company
판매기간 subscription period
판매단 selling group
판매단계약서 selling group agreement
판매력 sales force
판매방법 sales method
판매보증증권 sale bond
판매비 distribution cost; marketing cost; selling expense
판매비용 selling charges
판매비차이 selling expense variance
판매수량 quantity sold
판매수수료 load charges; placement commission; sales commission; selling concession
판매순환 selling cycle
판매시점정보관리 point of sales
판매예약 selling contract
판매오파 selling offer; selling operations
판매옵션 written option
판매용 상품 goods for sale
판매용 토지 real estate held for sale
판매운임 freight out

판매원가 cost of sales
판매원전도금 advance made to salesmen
판매자 vendor
판매자가 부르는 가격 asked quotation
판매자독점 seller's monopoly
판매자회사 sales subsidiary
판매장부표 sales record
판매적성품질 good merchantable quality
판매촉진 sales promotion
판매촉진비 sales promotion expense
판매할인 sales discount
판매형 리스 sales type lease
판매환 selling exchange
판매회계 sales accounting
판사 judge
판정의 기초가 되는 주주 basic stockholder
팔기로 예정하고 아직 결제하지 않은 상품 short positions
팔다 offer for sale
팔다 남은 unsold
팔행식 정산표 eight column work sheet
패니메이; 저당증권 Fannie Mae
패럴렐마켓 parallel market
패리티가치 parity value
패리티계산 parity account
패리티그리드 parity grid
패리티지수 parity index
패리티직선 parity line
패밀리펀드 family fund
패스스루 pass-through
패스스루비율 pass-through rate
패스스루증권 pass-through securities
패시브손실 passive loss
패시브파트너 passive partner
패자의 게임 losers game
패키지딜 package deal contract
패키지리스 package lease
패키지폴리시 package policy
패킹크레디트 packing credit
패턴인식 pattern recognition
패턴정보처리 pattern information processing
팩맨디펜스 Pac-man defense
팩터리스크 factor risk
팩터베타 factor beta
팩터수수료 factorage
팩트북 fact book
팬라인 fan line
팬이론 fan theory
퍼센티지리스 percentage lease
퍼스널체크 personal check
퍼스트디맨드본드 first demand bond
퍼시픽증권거래소 Pacific Stock Exchange
퍼실리티요금 facilities fee
퍼지이론 fuzzy theory
퍼포먼스비례보수체계 performance-based fee system
퍼포먼스증거금 performance margin
퍼포먼스측정 performance measurement
퍼포먼스특성 performance attribution
퍼포먼스펀드 performance fund
펀드 **LBO** fund LBO
펀드 대 미달러율 cable
펀드기준변동이부채 sterling floaters
펀드매니저 fund manager
펀드멘털분석 fundamental analysis
펀드멘털즈가 악화됨 fundamentals deterioration
펀드베타수치를 비교함 comparison of beta values of funds
펀드블록 pound bloc
펀드스와프레이트 sterling swap rate
펀드스테이트먼트 funds statement
펀드앤드트러스트 fund and trust
펀드위기 pound crisis
펀드잔고 sterling balance
펀드통화선물 sterling currency futures
펀드트러스트 fund trust
펄프제지업계 pulp and paper industry
펄하버파일 pearl harbor file
펌뱅킹 firm banking
페넌트 pennant
페르시아만협력회의 Gulf Cooperation Council

페세타 peseta
페이드아웃방식 fade-out formula
페이먼트인카인드 우선주 payment-in-kind preferred stock
페이스루채권 pay-through bond
페이오프다이어그램 pay-off diagram
페이오프행렬 pay-off matrix
페이퍼리스트레이딩 paperless trading
페이퍼컴퍼니 paper company; shell corporation
편도 one way
편도함수 partial derivative
편도헤지 one sided hedge
편무계약 unilateral contract
편의 convenience
편의공작물 accommodation works
편익관세 beneficial duty
편입률 weighting ratio
편재 maldistribution
편탄력성 partial elasticity
편향된 biased
평가 appraisal; parity
평가가격 estimated value
평가가치 assessed valuation
평가감 write-down
평가감후 가격 written down value
평가계정 negative account; valuation account
평가과목 valuation item
평가기관 rating agency
평가기준 appraisal standard; numeraire; valuation basis
평가모델 valuation modeling
평가방법변경 change in valuation method
평가방법을 선정함 selection of valuation method
평가법 appraisal method
평가사정 appraisement
평가성 준비금 valuation reserve
평가손 appraisal loss; loss resulted from valuation; valuation loss
평가손익 appraisal profit or loss; profit or loss from valuation
평가시기 term for evaluation
평가액 amount appraised; amount assessed; appraisal value; assessment; valuation
평가원칙 valuation principle
평가이상 above par
평가익 appraisal profit; profit accrued from valuation; valuation profit
평가익의 익금불산입 exclusion of profit accrued from valuation profit
평가인 appraiser
평가일 valuation date
평가조정 parity adjustment
평가증 write-up
평가차액 variance of the estimate
평가특성 valuation characteristics
평가필 보험 valued policy
평가하기 어려운 매매 scale trading
평가하다 assess
평결 verdict
평균 가격을 낮추다 average down
평균 가격을 올리다 average up
평균가격 averaging
평균가격가중 price weighted
평균가격가중지수 price weighted index
평균개인세율 personal average tax rate
평균결제 settlement of balance
평균공제 balancing adjustment
평균과세 average taxation
평균금리 average interest rate
평균금리캡 average interest rate cap
평균매가대금 average trading value
평균매출 selling on balance
평균발행고 average issued
평균발행잔고 average balance outstanding
평균배당금 average dividend paid
평균배당률 average rate of dividend
평균법 average method
평균법인세율 corporate average tax rate
평균변동율 average volatility
평균부채기간 average maturity of debts

평균상환연한 average term to maturity
평균생산기간 average period of production
평균세율 average tax rate
평균소득 average income
평균소비성향 average propensity to consume
평균소비자물가지수 average consumer price index
평균수익 average earnings
평균스폿레이트옵션 average spot rate option
평균신장률 average growth rate
평균실제노동시간 actuarial hours
평균여명 expectation of life
평균원가 average cost
평균원가법 average cost method
평균이율 average yield
평균이익 average profit
평균자본연령 vintage of capital
평균자본코스트 average cost of capital
평균잔고 average of daily figures; average outstanding
평균잔존연수 average life
평균잔존연한이익 yield for average life
평균재고 average inventory
평균절대편차 average absolute deviation
평균절대편차 mean absolute deviation
평균제곱오차 mean squared error
평균주가 stock price average
평균주가채용문제 issue used in the average
평균주가채용주 stock used in the average
평균준비율 average provision rate
평균지불기일 equaled time of payment
평균차 mean difference
평균채무코스트 average cost of debt
평균투자수익 average return on investment
평균편차 mean deviation
평균표준보수월액 average index monthly earnings
평균품질 fair average quality
평균행사가격옵션 average strike price option
평균회귀 mean reversion
평균회귀과정 mean reverting process
평균회수기간 average collection
평년도 full year
평생교육 life-long education
평의회 board of trustees, council
평준거출 level contribution
평준보험료 level premium
평준상장 parity quotation
평준적립방식 level annual premium method
평준화준비금 equalization reserve
평판 reputation
평행거래 parallel transaction
평행기채 parallel issue
평행본위제도 parallel standard
평행수입 parallel import
평행이동 parallel shift
평형개입 central bank intervention
평형부기 position bookkeeping
평형으로 회귀함 return to equilibrium
평활법 smoothing method
폐기물 mortality; waste
폐기법 retirement method
폐쇄 closure
폐쇄매각 private sale
폐쇄시장 closed market
폐쇄식 closed-end type
폐쇄식 담보 closed-end mortgage
폐쇄식 담보부사채 closed-end mortgage bond
폐쇄식 신탁 closed-end trust
폐쇄형 듀얼펀드 closed-end dual fund
폐쇄형 펀드 closed-end fund
폐업 discontinuance of business
폐잔설비 discarded equipment; scrap equipment
폐정 rising of the court
폐지 abolition; abrogation
폐지부문 discontinued operations
폐지부문의 이익 income from discontinued operations
포괄담보설정방식 blanket system
포괄보험계약 blanket policy

포괄보험증서 open policy; open price
포괄손익계산서 all-inclusive income statement
포괄수유자 universal legatee
포괄수출신용방식 umbrella export credit facility
포괄예산 comprehensive budget
포괄예정보험 open insurance
포괄유증 universal legacy
포괄이익 comprehensive income
포괄재산 floating property
포괄저당권 blanket mortgage
포괄저당권부 채권 blanket bond
포괄적인 권한 general authority
포괄주의 all-inclusive basis; all-inclusive concept; all-inclusive principle
포괄주의원칙 principal of all-inclusiveness
포괄주의이익약관 all-inclusive income concept
포괄통상법안 comprehensive trade bill
포괄표준계약서 umbrella master agreement
포렉스클럽 forex club
포뮬러타이밍 formula timing
포뮬러투자 formula investing
포뮬러펀드 formula fund
포뮬러플랜 formula plan
포스트케인시안 post Keynesian
POS 시스템 point of sales system
포워드캘린더 forward calendar
포이즌분포 Poisson distribution
포이즌필 poison pills
포인트앤드피규어 point and figure
포인트앤드피규어법 point and figure method
포인트앤드피규어차트 point and figure chart
포장명세서 packing list
포장비 baling charges; packing and wrapping expenses; packing charge
포지션감마 position gamma
포지션델타 position delta
포지션리스크 position risk
포지션매매 position trading
포지션세타 position theta
포지션조정 position adjustment
포지션지도 position instruction
포지션트레이더 position trader
포지티브정보 positive credit file
포지티브캐리 positive carry
포트폴리오 world market portfolio
포트폴리오가격결정법 portfolio pricing methodology
포트폴리오가치 portfolio value
포트폴리오거래 portfolio trade
포트폴리오관리 portfolio management
포트폴리오리스크모델 portfolio risk model
포트폴리오매니저 portfolio manager
포트폴리오모니터링 portfolio monitoring
포트폴리오믹스 portfolio mix
포트폴리오밸런스어프로치 portfolio balance approach
포트폴리오보험 portfolio insurance
포트폴리오분산투자 portfolio diversification
포트폴리오분석 portfolio analysis
포트폴리오뷰 portfolio view
포트폴리오수법 portfolio approach
포트폴리오수익패턴 pattern of portfolio return
포트폴리오수정 portfolio revision
포트폴리오엔지니어 portfolio engineers
포트폴리오옵티마이저 portfolio optimizer
포트폴리오의 특성선 portfolio characteristic line
포트폴리오이론 portfolio theory
포트폴리오이율 portfolio's yield
포트폴리오재편 portfolio restructuring
포트폴리오최적화 portfolio optimization
포함손 embedded loss
포함손익 unrealised profits and losses
포함익 embedded profit
포함자산주 asset-backed stock
포합판매 tie-in sale
포획나포부담보조항 free from capture and seizure clause

폭락 collapse; sharp drop
폭발적인 신장 explosive growth
폴리시믹스 policy mix
폴리시어셋믹스 policy asset mix
폴리시어셋앨로케이션 policy asset allocation
표견상의 권리 color
표류물 flotsam
표류믹스 drifting mix
표면금리 nominal interest rate; nominal rate
표면상의 대리 apparent agency
표면예금 nominal deposit; nominal gross deposit
표면이율 nominal coupon
표명 representation
표본단위 sampling unit
표본분포 sampling distribution
표본조사 sampling survey
표본추출오차 sampling error
표본평균 sample mean
표시를 통한 매매 sale by description
표시부채 stated liabilities
표시에 의한 by representation
표시원가 scheduled cost
표시작업 representation work
표식원장 tabular ledger
표제 heading
표준 benchmark; criteria
표준 **EPS** base EPS
표준가격권 benchmark rate
표준금리 standard interest rate
표준기계시간 standard machine time
표준노무비 standard labor cost
표준물 standardized bonds
표준바스켓방식 standard basket; standard currency basket system
표준배부율 standard burden rate
표준산업분류 standard industrial classification
표준상관계수 standard correlation
표준상품 standard issue
표준생산량 standard-run quantity
표준서식 standard documentation
표준세율 standard tax rate
표준손료 standard depletion expenses
표준수수료 standard commission
표준약관 standard clause
표준오차 standard error
표준원가 standard cost
표준원가계산 standard cost accounting
표준원가계산제도 standard-cost system
표준은달러 standard silver dollar
표준이익 standard profit
표준일 standard date
표준재료비 standard material cost
표준재무제표 standardized financial statements
표준저당권자 지불약관 union mortgage clause
표준제조간접비 standard manufacturing expense
표준주 barometer stock; standard stocks
표준책임준비금평가법 Standard Valuation Law
표준치 standard values
표준크로스디폴트조항 standard cross default provision
표준품매매 sale on standard
표준하체보험계약 insurance of substandard lives
표준화 standardization
표준화 볼라틸리티 standardized volatility
표준 **EPS** normalized EPS
표창제도 commendation system
푸시풀 push pull
푸터블스와프 puttable swap
푸터블스왑션 puttable swaption
푸터블워런트 puttable warrant
푸터블채권 puttable bond
풀링에 따른 증권화 securitization by pooling
풀링회계 pooling accounting
풀뱅킹서비스 full banking service
풀오브파이낸싱 pool of financing
풀잔고 pool balance
풀전략 pull strategy

풀조작 pool operation
풀코스트원칙 full cost principle
풀쿠폰본드 full coupon bond
풀특정거래 specified pool trade
풀펀드 pooled fund
풀헤지 full hedge
풀협정 pool agreement
품절 all gone; all sold; outright sales
품질관리 quality control
품질기준 quality standards
품질이 같은 of like grade and quality
풋가격선 put-value line
풋내기의 lay
풋다이어그램 put diagram
풋레이쇼백스프레딩 put ratio back spread trading
풋보유자 put holder
풋스왑션 put swaption
풋앤드콜 put and call
풋옵션 put option
풋워런트 put warrant
풋콜레이쇼 put-call ratio
풋콜인도 option delivery
풋콜조합옵션 option combination
풍수해보험 windstorm and flood insurance
퓨어캡 pure cap
프라이머리딜러 primary dealer
프라이베이트리스크 private risk
프라이베이트뱅킹 private banking
프라이베이트패스스루 private passthrough
프라이스리더 price leader
프라이스메이커 price maker
프라이스필터 price filter
프라임네임 **CD** prime name CD
프라임레이트 prime interest rate; short-term prime rate
프랑스 **AGEF** 지수 AGEF Index
프랑스 **CAC** 공업주가지수 CAC General Index
프런트엔드피 front-end fee
프런팅 fronting
프레디맥 Freddie Mac
프레비드계약 prebid agreement
프레페이드카드 prepaid card
프로그램매각 program trading
프로그램예산 program budgeting
프로덕션론 production loan
프로덕트사이클론 product cycle theory
프로라타조항 pro-rata clause
프로비저널섬; **PS** 단가 provisional sum
프로세스이노베이션 process innovation
프로젝트론 project loan
프로젝트리스크 project risk
프로젝트파이낸스 project finance
프로텍티브풋 protection put
프로텍티브풋 거래 protective put trading
프로포마인보이스 pro-forma invoice
프로포절레터 proposal letter
프로포절방식 proposal method
프로핏센터 profit center
프리기간 free period
프리라이더 free rider
프리라이딩; 달러로 신주를 일부 유지함 free riding
프리론 free loan
프리미엄발행 premium issue
프리미엄시가방식 premium quotation system
프리미엄증권 premium securities
프리미엄채 premium bond
프리미엄환원 returning of premium
프리캐시로 free cash flow
프리파이낸셜펀드 free financial fund
프린시펄멤버 principal member
프린지뱅킹 fringe banking
플라스틱머니;신용카드 plastic money
플라워본드 flower bond
플라자합의 Plaza Accord
플랜수익자 plan beneficiaries
플랫론 flat loan
플랫마켓 flat market
플랫커브 flat curve
플러스틱 plus-tick

플레인딜 plain deal
플레인바닐라 plain vanilla
플레인바닐라변동이자부채 plain vanilla floater
플레인바닐라스와프 plain vanilla swap
플레징 pledging
플로다이아그램 flow diagram
플로스루법 flow through method
플로어드스와프 floored swap
플로어트레이더; 룸트레이더 floor trader
플로차트 flow chart
플로터스와프 super floater swap
플로트예금 deposit float
플로팅베이시스 floating basis
플리트계약자 fleet insured
플립플롭채권 flip-flop FRN
피고인 accused
피난 parking
피드백 feedback
피라미드형 관리방식 pyramid management method
피라미딩과정 pyramiding process
피매수회사 acquired company
피발송은행 receiving bank
피보나치수열 Fibonacci sequence
피보좌인 quasi-incompetent person
피보험물 insured property
피보험위험 insured peril; perils insured against
피보험이익 insurable interest
피보험자 assured; insured
피상속인의 소득 income in respect of a decedents
피셔효과 Fisher effect
피어리뷰 peer review
PO 증권 principal-only securities
피이서인 endorsee
피임명자 appointee
피지배회사 controlled company
피크로드 peak load
피통괄계정 controlled account
피트 pit
피트리포터 pit reporter
피트브로커 pit broker
피플미터 people meter
피합병법인 corporation amalgamated
피합병회사 predecessor company; transferor corporation
피합병회사로부터 승계한 결손금 net operating loss assumed from a transfer of corporation
피해사업용 자산의 손실 loss from damaged business assets
피해자 aggrieved party
피해자산 damaged property
필기시험 written examination
필라델피아플랜 Philadelphia plan
필립스곡선 Phillips curve
필수가구 necessary household furniture
필수조건 cause sine qua non; essential condition; mandatory clause
필요경비 necessary expense
필요경비에 해당하는 손실 loss qualifying for necessary expenses
필요당사자 necessary party
필요물 estovers
필요성원칙 principle of need
필요요건 requisite
필요자본계수 required capital coefficient
필요증거금법 margin required method
필요한 세무수속 necessary tax procedure
필요한 증거서류 necessary documentary evidence
필요한 평가방법을 선정함 selection of a necessary appraisal method

ㅎ

하강 descending; drop; fall; moving downward
하강곡선 descending curve
하강국면 downswing phase; downward phase of the business cycle
하강선 downhill course
하기결산 settlement of accounts for the latter half; settlement of accounts for the latter half
하도지시서 delivery order
하드랜딩 hard landing
하드론 hard loan
하드웨어시장 hardware market
하락 downfall
하락기조상장 falling market
하락삼각형 descending triangle; descending triangle pattern
하락순위 ranking of declines
하락시세 bear market
하락전환패턴 bearish reversal patterns
하락촉진 big push in the downward move
하락하다 decline
하루 이자 daily rate
하루 중에 intraday
하리키리스와프 harakiri swap
하반기 latter half; second half of the year
하우스빌 house bill
하우스에이전시 house agency
하우징리뉴얼프로그램 housing renewal program
하위사채 subordinated bond; subordinated debenture
하위성 무담보사채 subordinated unsecured debenture
하위열후 junior subordinated
하위주 subordinated stock
하위증권 junior issue
하위채권 subordinated debt
하위채권자 subordinated creditor
하위트란시 junior tranche
하위페이먼트인카인드채 subordinated payment-in-kind bond
하이리스크하이리턴 high-risk high-return
하이브리드상품 hybrid instrument
하이브리드트레이딩시스템 hybrid trading system
하이쿠폰채 high-coupon bond
하이테크상품개발자 rocket scientist
하이테크주 technology shares
하이테크주식 high-tech stock
하이테크주펀드 technology fund
하이파워드머니 high powered money
하인(荷印) shipping marks
하인수업자 sub-underwriter
하자가 있는 권원 defective title
하자드함수 hazard function
하자보수보증증권 maintenance bond
하주위험부담 owner's risk
하청 subcontract
하청공장 subcontract factory
하청업자 subcontractor

하치지시선 support line
하한금리 floor rate
하향수정 downward revision
하향수정함 making a downward revision
하향제한스트래들 bottom straddle
하향탄력성 downside potential
학교법인 incorporated school
학생종합보험 student comprehensive insurance
학습곡선 learning curve
한가한 시간 idle time
한계 threshold
한계가치 marginal value
한계가치곡선 marginal value curve
한계공제제도 marginal deduction system
한계기업 marginal firm
한계단위원가 marginal unit cost
한계대부선 revolving line of credit
한계분석 marginal analysis
한계비용 cost at the margin; marginal cost
한계비용곡선 marginal cost curve
한계비율 marginal ratio
한계생산 marginal production
한계생산비 marginal cost of production
한계생산성 marginal productivity
한계세율 marginal tax rate
한계소비성향 marginal propensity to consume
한계손익계산 marginal income statement
한계수요 marginal demand
한계수익 marginal returns
한계수익률 marginal rate of return
한계수입 marginal revenue
한계수입성향 marginal propensity to import
한계순적합도 marginal net suitability
한계신용 marginal credit
한계예대율 marginal loan-deposit ratio
한계요소 marginal factor
한계원가계산 marginal costing
한계원리 marginal principle
한계이론 marginal theory
한계이익 marginal balance; marginal income; marginal profit
한계이익도표 profit volume graph
한계이익률 marginal income ratio; marginal profit ratio
한계자본계수 marginal capital coefficient
한계자본지출 marginal capital expenditure
한계저축성향 marginal propensity to save
한계조건 marginal condition
한계편익 marginal benefit
한계효용 marginal utility
한계효율 marginal efficiency
한도를 넘은 차용 outstanding debt
한도초과발행상품 over-issue
한산 thin
한산시장 inactive market; narrow market
한산한 거래; 소액매매 low turnover
한산한; 활발하지 않은 inactive
한월(限月) contract month
한월간 스프레드거래 intercontract month spread trading
한은(韓銀) 인수 underwriting by the Bank of Korea
한정감사 limited audit
한정감사보고서 qualified audit certificate
한정개월간 스프레드거래 spread trading between contract months
한정매출 restrict sales
한정모집 limited offering
한정보고서 qualified report
한정사항; 적격성; 면채사항 qualification
한정상속 qualified acceptance heritage; qualified inheritance
한정의견 limited opinion; qualified opinion
한정의견감사보고서 qualified auditor's report
한정의견증명서 qualified certificate
한정이서 qualified endorsement
한정적인 판로 limited distribution
한정조항; 부작위약관 restrictive covenant
한정준비금 qualifying reserve
(계약의) 한쪽 당사자 counterparty

할당 allotment
할당량 quota
할당비용 assignment expense
할당서 allotment letter
할당예산원장 allotment ledger
할당장 letter of allotment
할당적립방식 allocated funding instrument
할당채권 assigned accounts receivable
할부 installment
할부가격 total payment of installments; face of note
할부구매 installment purchase
할부구입알선 third party sales credit
할부구입알선업 third party credit
할부기준 installment basis; installment method
할부매상미실현익 unrealized gross profit on installment sales
할부매상익 realized gross profit on installment sales
할부미불금 installment payable
할부수수료 charge for installment payment
할부외상금 installment receivable
할부채권 installment credit
할부카드 multiple payment credit card
할부판매 time sales
할부판매법 installment plan
할부판매손익 profit or loss from installment sales
할부판매전용어음 special bills for installment sales credit
할인 discounting
할인가격 discount value
할인계수 discount factor
할인국채 discount government bond
할인금융채 discount bank debenture
할인기간대응할부 accrual of discount
할인단기국채 treasury bills
할인료 discount expenses
할인발행 discount issue
할인발행된 issued at a discount
할인보증계정 per contra noted discounted account
할인상사 discount house
할인수수료 discount commission
할인수익 discounted cash flow
할인수취계정 account receivable discounted
할인시장 discount market
할인어음 discounted bill; note discounted; note received discounted; notes and bills discounted; sold bill
할인어음계정 bill discounted account
할인어음기입장 discount register
할인어음원장 discount ledger
할인율 discount charge; discount rate
할인율의 리스크구조 risk structure of discount rate
할인은행 discount bank
할인이익 discount yield
할인일수 days to run
할인적격어음 eligible bill
할인정책 discount policy
할인주 bargain stock
할인준비금 reserve for discount
할인창구 discount window
할인채 discount bond
할인채상환익 profit on redemption of discount bond
할인함수 discount function
할인효과 effect of discount
할증보험료 additional premium; extra premium
할증상각 additional depreciation deduction; extra depreciation
할증상각률 additional depreciation ratio
할증수당 additional allowance
할증운임 additional freight
할증임금 extra wage
함리스워런트채 harmless warrant
합계 sum total; total
합계시산표 trial balance of totals
합계잔고시산표 trial balance of totals and balances

합계전기 summary posting
합동 combine; trust joint
합동검사 joint inspection
합동계정 combined account
합동공모채계정 pooled publicly traded bond account
합동보통주 및 공모채계정 pooled common stock and publicly traded bond account
합동보통주계정 pooled common stock account
합동부동산계정 pooled real property account
합동사모채계정 pooled private placement bond account
합동사채 joint bond
합동운용신탁 joint trust
합동운용펀드 commingled fund
합동운용형 펀드 collective investment fund
합리원칙 rule of reason
합리적이고 상당한 원인 reasonable and probable cause
합리적인 rationalized; reasonable
합리적인 구조 rational structure
합리적인 의문 reasonable doubt
합리화를 계획하다 rationalize
합명회사 unlimited partnership
합병 amalgamation; joint investment
합병; 혼동 merger
합병계약서 contract of merger
합병과 매수 merger and acquisition
합병과정 amalgamation process
합병교부금 amount of money delivered due to merger
합병교부주식 delivered stock due to merger
합병법인 transferee corporation
합병비율 merger ratio
합병사업연도 accounting period in case of merger
합병사업연도 taxable year of merger
합병손익계산서 combined income statement
합병시의 장부가격으로 인수함 succession of book value in the case of merger
합병에 따른 청산소득 liquidation income due to merger
합병으로 소멸한 회사 corporation ceased to exist after merger
합병으로 취득한 고정자산 fixed assets acquired through merger
합병으로 취득한 재고자산 inventories acquired by merger
합병으로 취득한 주식 stock acquired by merger
합병을 통한 해산; 소멸 dissolution and extinction due to merger
합병잉여금 amalgamation surplus
합병절차 amalgamation procedures
합병조건 merger terms
합병차손 loss from amalgamation; loss from merger
합병차익 profit form amalgamation; profit from consolidation; profit from merger; surplus from merged company
합병촉진세액공제 promoting mergers tax credit
합병확정신고 filing of final return of merger
합병확정신고서 final return of merger
합병회계 merger accounting
합병회사 amalgamated company
합산 aggregation
합산과세 unitary tax; unitary taxation
합산비율 combined ratio
합성 synthesis
합성변동금리 synthetic floating rate
합성스와프 synthetic swap
합성어셋 synthetic asset
합성자산 synthetic assets
합성지수펀드 synthetic index fund
합성통화 synthetic currency
합성포지션 synthetic position
합성포트폴리오 synthetic portfolio
합성현물재정거래 synthetic cash arbitrage transaction
합유 joint right

합유부동산권 joint tenancy
합유채권 joint obligation
합의관할 agreement jurisdiction
합의관할법원 agreement jurisdictional court
합의명령 agreed order
합의사실기재서 statement of facts
합의사실진술서 agreed statement of facts
합의에 따른 국제분업 international agreed specialization
합의하에 이율을 내림 agreed cut
합의확인서 letter of intent
합작투자 Joint venture
핫머니시장 hot money market
항; 단락 paragraph
항공기보험 aircraft hull insurance; aviation hull insurance
항공기파이낸스 aircraft financing
항공보험 aviation insurance
항공요금 air fare
항공운송업 air transport industry; air transportation industry
항공운임 airway freight
항공화물운송장 airway bill
항구적인 시설 permanent establishment; permanent facility
항만료 port charges
항만세 in-port duty
항목 item
항변하다 assent claims
항상 운영함 day-to-day management
항상단가 standing cost
항상달러 constant dollars
항상달러베이스 constant dollar base
항상비용 standing charge
항상제수(恒常除數) constant divisor
항해보험 voyage policy
항해에 견디는 seaworthy
항행가능한 navigable
항행방해죄 obstruction of navigation
해결하다 strengthen
해난구조 salvage
해당하는 concerned
해당하다 fall under
해머링마켓; 값을 몹시 깎는 시장 hammering the market
해방 emancipation
해방담보 open mortgage
해사검사인 marine surveyor
해사고용감독관 shipping commissioners
해사법 maritime law
해사법규 sea law
해사사건법원 Instance Court
해사선취특권 maritime lien
해사심판소 Naval Court
해사의 maritime
해사재판소 maritime court
해사저당 maritime hypothecation
해사채 maritime bonds
해산 dissolution; winding up
해산법 winding-up Act
해산에 따른 청산소득 liquidation income from dissolution
해상 및 운송보험 marine and transport insurance
해상고유의 위험 perils of the sea
해상대물운송계약 affreightment contract
해상보험 marine insurance
해상보험계정 marine insurance account
해상선하증권 marine bill of landing
해상위험 dangers of navigation; marine perils; maritime perils; sea peril
해석 construction
해석전손(全損); 추정전손(全損) constructive total loss
해석조항 interpretation clause
해손인협회 Association of Average Adjusters
해약 cancellation; rescission
해약가능한 cancelable
해약권 right of cancellation
해약금 cancellation money
해약기일 canceling date
해약률 surrender ratio

해약반려금 return premium for cancellation; surrender value
해약반환금 cash surrender value
해약불가능한 noncancellable
해약사유 termination events
해약수수료 redemption fee
해약예고 notice to quit
해약이유 trigger event
해약조항 termination provisions
해약청구 cancellation request
해외거래 overseas transaction
해외경제협력기금 Overseas Economic Cooperation Fund
해외계정거래 external transactions account
해외관계회사 overseas affiliated firm
해외근무수당 foreign service allowance
해외금리 interest rate abroad; overseas interest rate
해외금융선물거래소 foreign financial futures exchange
해외금융자회사 overseas finance subsidiary
해외기술거래 overseas technical service transaction
해외기채분 overseas flotation
해외민간투자공사 Overseas Private Investment Corporation
해외법정준비금 overseas legal reserves
해외법정준비금편입 provision for overseas legal reserves
해외부채 overseas liabilities
해외사업 foreign operations; overseas business
해외사업법인 overseas undertaking corporation
해외상장 overseas listing; quotation on overseas markets; rate in overseas market
해외생산능력 overseas production capacity
해외생산비율 overseas production ratio
해외시장개척준비금 overseas market development reserve; reserve for development of overseas market
해외여행상해보험 overseas travel accident insurance
해외원조 development assistance
해외원천소득 foreign source income
해외자본 foreign assets
해외자산 offshore assets; overseas assets
해외전보수신인 cable address
해외주요시장 overseas major market
해외증권발행 overseas securities financing
해외지점 foreign branch
해외지점계정 foreign branch account
해외직접투자 foreign direct investment
해외투자 foreign investment; investment abroad; investment overseas
해외투자보고서 overseas investment report
해외투자손실준비금 reserve for overseas investment loss
해외투자손실준비금편입 provision for reserve for overseas investments
해외투자손실준비금환수 reversal of reserve for overseas investments
해운 marine transportation; maritime traffic; shipping
해운수입 shipping receipts
해운시장 shipping market
해운업 marine transportation industry
해제조건 condition subsequent
해제조건부 매매 sale and return
해제조항 defeasance clause
해체 disintegration
해체비 demolition expenses
해협 narrow seas
핵심시장 core market
핵심주 core stock
행내교환 in-house exchange
행동규범 code of conduct
행동이론 behavioral theory
행렬부기 matrix bookkeeping
행렬승수 matrix multiplier
행방이 정해지지 않은 idle money
행사가격 exercise price

행사금리 strike rate
행상인 itinerant merchants
행위 action
행위능력 capacity; legal capacity
행위세 act tax
행위에 바탕을 둔 ex facto
행위지 venue
행정개혁 administrative reform; reform of the administrative structure
행정구제 administrative remedy
행정권 administrative power
행정명령 administrative order
행정서비스실(SEC) Office of Administrative Service(SEC)
행정소송 administrative litigation
행정소송심판관실(SEC) Office of Administrative Law Judges(SEC)
행정재량 administrative discretion
행정쟁소 administrative dispute
행정조치 regulatory action
행정지도 administrative guidance
행정직원 administrative officer
행정처분 administrative disposition
행정해석 administrative interpretation
행정행위 administrative act
허가 admission; license
허용률 tolerable rate
허용면세율 tolerable deviation rate
허용변동폭내 개입 intramarginal intervention
허용수준 tolerance level
허용오차 permissible error
허용원가 allowed cost
허용차; 공차 tolerance
허용하다 allow
허용한도 tolerance limit
허용한도액 allowable maximum amount
허용할 수 없는 inadmissible
허위보고 false report
허위상품표시 false trade description
허위신고 false return
허위의 simulated
허위진술 false statement
허위표시 false representation
헌터보험 hunters' insurance
험프드커브 humped curve
헤드앤드숄더 head and shoulder
헤비유저 heavy users
헤저 hedger
헤지 hedge
헤지거래 hedge trading; hedge transaction
헤지계산대행서 hedge account representation letter
헤지구매 hedge buying
헤지기간 hedge period
헤지기능 hedging function
헤지드포트폴리오 hedged portfolio
헤지비율 hedge ratio
헤지상품 hedge instrument
헤지수단 hedging vehicle; means for hedging
헤지수법 hedging technique
헤지스킴 hedging scheme
헤지이익 hedge gains
헤지조작 hedge operation
헤지증거금 hedge margin
헤지채 hedged bond
헤지코스트 hedging cost
헤지펀드 hedge fund
헤지포지션 hedged position
헤지회계 hedge accounting
헤지회계처리 hedge accounting treatment
헤징; 연계매매 hedging
헬스케어 health care
헬오어하이워터조항 hell or high water clause
혁신; 갱정 innovation
혁신적인 innovative
현가법 present value method
현가율 present value rate
현금 및 현금등가물 cash and cash equivalents
현금가격 cash price
현금감사 cash audit
현금결제 cash settlement
현금계산서 cash statement

현금공개매부 cash tender offer
현금공여 cash contribution
현금과부족 cash over and short
현금과부족계정 cash over and short account
현금관리 cash control; cash management
현금구매 cash purchase
현금구입 bought for cash
현금기록 cash records
현금대부 cash loan
현금대비일개월부채비율 ratio of cash to thirty-day debts
현금매매 cash sale
현금매상장 cash buying rate; cash selling rate
현금반송 cash remittance
현금배당 cash dividend
현금배당결의액 cash dividend declared
현금부족액 deficit in cash
현금부채 cash liabilities
현금분개장 cash journal
현금비율 cash ratio
현금상태 cash position
현금상환 cash redemption
현금송장 cash letters
현금수납장 cash receipt book; cash receipt journal
현금수령 cash receipt
현금수수 payment and receipt of cash
현금수입 cash earnings; cash income; money income
현금신용장 cash letter of credit
현금에 부착함 suction to cash
현금예금 cash and deposits; cash deposit
현금예금계정 cash and deposits banks accounts
현금예금자산 cash and deposits with banks
현금유동부채비율 cash to current liabilities ratio
현금자본 cash capital
현금자산 cash assets
현금자산가치 cash asset value
현금잔고 cash balance
현금주의 cash basis
현금주의회계 cash basis accounting
현금준비 reserve cash
현금준비고 cash reserves
현금지불 cash and carry; cash disbursement; cash payment; pay down; payment by cash
현금지불거래 cash and carry trade
현금지불기 cash dispenser
현금지불방식 cash and carry system
현금지불비용 out-of-pocket cost
현금지불장 cash payment journal; disbursement book; paid cash book
현금지불주의 pay-as-you-go
현금지출 cash outlays
현금지출비 out-of-pocket expense
현금청구 claim to cash
현금출납계 cashier
현금출납과 cashier's department
현금출납장 cash book
현금출자 investment in money
현금카드 cash card
현금통화 cash currency
현금판매 sale for cash
현금할인 cash discount
현금항목 cash items
현금화 enactment
현금화; 청산 liquidation
현금화하다 liquidate
현금환가가치 actual cash value
현금회수 cash collection
현대자본주의 comtemporary capitalism
현대포트폴리오이론 modern portfolio theory
현명한 투자가 smart money
현물 actuals
현물가격 spot price; spot value
현물거래 cash trading
현물거래; 당일거래 cash transactions
현물급여 truck system
현물급여 wage in kind
현물납부 tax payment in kind
현물대당 cash matching

현물로 in-kind
현물바스켓 cash basket
현물배당 dividend in kind
현물배당주 pay-in-kind bond
현물상장 spot quotation; spot rate
현물상장; 직물환상장 spot exchange rate
현물상품 cash issue; straight cash vehicles
현물선도거래 cash forward transaction
현물승수 cash multiplier
현물시장 cash market; spot market; underlying market
현물옵션 cash option
현물인도 actual delivery; actual delivery of stock sold; spot delivery
현물주 cash equity; cash stock; underlying share
현물증권 physical security
현물지급 allowance in kind
현물지수 cash index
현물채권 cash bond
현물출자 investment in kind; issuance of capital stock for non-cash assets
현물출자가 될 수 있는 경제적 가치 economic value qualifying for investment in kind
현물출자로 취득한 고정자산 fixed assets acquired as contribution in kind to capital
현물출자를 과대평가함 overestimation of investment in kind
현물출자설 investment in kind theory of merger
현물출자취득주 stock acquired by the investment in kind
현물환 spot exchange
현상분석 present data analysis
현선매매 repos
현선시장 repo market
현시선호 revealed preference
현실거래 actual receipt of stock purchased
현실금액 amount realized
현실성장률 actual rate of growth
현실의 actual
현실인도 physical delivery
현실적인 이유 pragmatic reasons
현실적인 지침 practicable guidance
현실전손 actual total loss
현실점유 possession in deed
현실주의적인 결정 pragmatic decisions
현실표준원가 actually expected standard cost
현예금 cash equivalent
현예금회전율 sales to cash
현장감사 field inspection; site audit
현장감사인 field inspector
현장인도가격 loco price
현재 소유한 vested in possession
현재가격 present price
현재가격표 table of the present value
현재가치 current value; present value; present worth; real-time price
현재가치로 환원하다; 디스카운트 discount
현재가치회계 present value accounting
현재고 amount on hand; balance of stores
현재수량; 재고 amount in hand
현재원가 current cost; present cost
현재의 주가수준 current level of stock price
현재재 present goods
현재치 current amount
현재품 stock in hand
현저하게 unreasonably
현주 spot share
현지생산공장 local production factory
현지일관생산 full scale local production
현지조달율 local content ratio
현지코스트 local cost
현지통화 local currency
현직 incumbency
현직자기금 active life fund
현품주문 order stock; unfilled orders
현행시장가액 current market value
현행이자율 current interest rate
현행절도죄 open theft
현행프리미엄 current premium value

현회계연도 current fiscal year
혐의 suspicion
협동조합 cooperative association; cooperative society
협박 threat
협박; 긴축 tightening
협약 pact
협의 conference
협의발행 negotiated sale
협의사항 agenda
협의인수 negotiated underwriting
협정 accord
협정가격 agreed price; contract price; price agreed upon; stipulated price
협정관세 conventional tariff
협정무역 trade by agreement
협정보험가액 agreed insured value
협정요율 tariff by agreement
협정임금 contractual wage
협조가격하락 coordinated cut
협조개입 concerned intervention; coordinated intervention; joint intervention
협조융자; 신디케이트론 syndicated loan
협조행동 concerned activities
협회 association
협회도난불도착담보약관 institute theft; pilferage and non-delivery clauses
협회약관 institute clauses
협회전쟁위기담보약관 institute war clauses
협회파업폭동담보약관 institute strikes; riots and civil commotion clauses
협회화물약관 Institute Cargo Clauses
형법 Criminal Code
형사상의 penal
형사소송 criminal suit
형식 form
형식적인 formal
형평법상의 리엔 equitable lien
형평법상의 모기지 equitable mortgage
형평법상의 양도 equitable assignment
형평법상의 채무 equitable obligation
호가 bid and ask; bid and asked price; bid and offer; quote
호가단위 tick size
호가를 주지함 announcement of bids and offers
호가상황 bid and offer situation
호가스프레드 bid ask spread; bid-offer spread
호가주도형 quoted driven
호경기 economic boom
호경기시대 prosperous days
호성적 good results
호순환 virtuous cycle
호이율 good yield
호재 favorable factor; favorable news; good news
호재료 strong incentive
호적 family-register
호전 upturn
호출게시판 annunciator board
호출장 summons
호프만의 법칙 Hoffmann's law
호혜관세 reciprocal duty
호환성이 있는 compatible
호황 boom
호황시장 active market
혼동 confusion
혼란 disarray
혼성관세 mixed tariff
혼성농업 mixed farming
혼성보관 commingled custody
혼성의; 엇갈린 mixed
혼성자본주의체제 mixed capitalist economy
혼성저당 mixed collateral
혼합 hybrid
혼합거래 mixed transaction
혼합경제 mixed economy
혼합계약 mixed contract
혼합계정 mixed account
혼합보험 mixed insurance; mixed policy
혼합신탁 hybrid trust
혼합잉여금 mixed surplus
혼합자산 mixed assets

혼합재고정리 mixed inventory
혼합재산 mixed property
혼합주식 hybrid stocks
혼합준비금 mixed reserve
혼합증여 mixed gift
혼합차이 mixed variance
혼합캡 hybrid cap
혼합투자계정 commingled investment account
혼합형 hybrid model
홀세일뱅크 wholesale bank
홈메이드인플레 home made inflation
홈뱅킹 home banking
홈에퀴티론 home equity loan
홍콩달러 Hong Kong dollar
홍콩예탁증권 Hong Kong depositary receipts
홍콩은행간 오퍼레이트 Hong Kong inter-bank offered rate
홍콩한센지수 Hang Seng Index
화공업계 chemicals industry
화물 freight
화물관리인 supercargo
화물수입 freight earnings
화물운송면장 transire
화물운임 freight rates, freight tariff
화물해상보험 cargo insurance; marine cargo insurance
화물해상보험증권 marine cargo policy
화의 bankruptcy and composition
화재로 인해 발생한 비용 expenses incurred for the fire
화재보험 fire insurance
화재보험금 fire insurance proceeds
화재보험료 fire insurance premium
화재보험약관 fire clause
화재보험증권 fire policy
화재상호보험 fire mutual insurance
화재손실 fire loss
화재손실미결산계정 fire loss suspense account
화재손해보험 fire and casualty insurance
화폐가치변동회계 accounting for changing prices
화폐가치일정공준 stable dollar assumption
화폐개량설 quantity theory of money
화폐베일이론 money veil theory
화폐분석 monetary analysis; money analysis
화폐성장모델 monetary growth model
화폐수요 demand for money
화폐수요함수 demand function for money
화폐승수 monetary multiplier
화폐유통속도 velocity of circulation of money
화폐의 구매력 purchasing power of money
화폐의 대외가치 external purchasing power of money
화폐의 한계효용 marginal utility of money
화폐이자율 monetary interest rate
화폐자본 monetary capital; money capital
화폐자본유지 maintenance of financial capital
화폐적인 어프로치; 모네터리어프로치 monetary approach
화폐제도 monetary system
화폐환각 money illusion
화폐환상 monetary illusion
화해 concord
화환신용장 documentary credit; documentary letter of credit
화환어음 documentary bill
확대 enlarged European Communities EC
확대 **EC** expanded EC
확대경로 expansion path
확대경제 expansive economy
확대되는 격차 widening gap
확대상장변동 wider margin
확대신용공여제도 extended fund facility
확대종업원지주제도 broader employee stock ownership
확대주간사 expanded lead manager
확률계열 stochastic sequence
확률곡선 probability curve
확률론 theory of probability
확률모델 probability model; stochastic model
확률분석 probability distribution

확률비례 probability-proportional-to-size
확률시뮬레이션 stochastic simulation
확률예측 probabilistic forecasting
확률이 높은 probable
확률적 특성선 probabilistic characteristic lines
확률적인 stochastic
확률프로세스 stochastic process
확률해석 stochastic calculus
확산변환모델 displaced diffusion model
확신인관계 quasi-fiduciary relationship
확신적인 입증 convincing proof
확실성 자산 certain assets
확실히 회수할 수 있는 good and collectible
확실히 회수할 수 있는 대금 good debt
확약 affirmation
확약; 전액인수 firm commitment
확인 confirmation
확인서류 confirmation document
확인수수료 confirmation fee
확인은행 confirming bank
확인의 proven
확인장 confirmation letter
확인지불 pay on application
확인청구 confirmation request
확인통지서 confirmation note
확인필 신용장 confirmed letter of credit
확인하다 declaratory
확인하다(액수를) affirm
확인해야 할 곳 referable name
확장 extension
확장급부 extended benefit
확장담보특약 extended coverage
확정 lock-in
확정가격 firm price
확정가격제시 firm offer
확정거출제도 defined contribution plan
확정거출형 연금플랜 defined contribution annuity plan
확정결산 definite settlement of accounts
확정계약 firm contract
확정계정 account rendered; account stated; liquidated account
확정권리 vested interest
확정급부 defined benefit; specified benefit
확정급부채무 vested benefit obligation
확정급부형 연금플랜 defined benefit plan
확정기일 fixed maturity
확정기일 상환채 fixed payment bond
확정매호수치 firm bid
확정배당 guaranteed dividend
확정보험 definite insurance
확정보험증권 definite policy
확정부채 direct liabilities
확정소득증권 fixed income securities
확정손실신고서 final return of loss
확정신고 final return; final tax return
확정신고에 따른 납부 final payment
확정신고에 따른 환부 refund by final return
확정연금 annuity certain
확정이부채 fixed coupon bond
확정이익 fixed gain
확정이자 fixed interest
확정이자부 자산 fixed income assets
확정이자부 채권 fixed interest-bearing bond
확정일부 date proved by notary; fixed date
확정일불 payable on a fixed date
확정일인도 fixed date delivery
확정일지불어음 bill payable at a fixed date
확정자본금 stated capital
확정잔여권 vested remainder
확정주문 firm order
확정차액 fixed difference
확정채무 fixed obligations; liquidated debt
확정한 결산 final settlement of accounts
환가능계정 transferable account
환가불능자산 unrealizable assets
환가처분 conversion into cash; tax sale
환개입 exchange intervention
환거래 exchange dealing; foreign exchange transaction; transfer transactions
환결제 exchange settlement
환결제청산 exchange clearing

환경 circumstances
환경감사 environmental audit
환경데이터 environmental data
환경보호 environmental protection
환경부 Ministry of the Environment
환경세 environmental tax
환경오염배상책임보험 environmental impairment liability insurance
환경파괴 destruction of environment
환경평가 environmental assessment
환관리 exchange control
환구입 buying exchange
환금성 상품 cashable goods
환금성이 높은 available
환금판매 realization sales
환급 carry back
환급수수료 return commission
환급프리미엄 premium on redemption
환기입 transfer entry
환끝환산차금 inter-office exchange adjustment account
환당좌대 export account
환당좌대이자 interest on overdrafts for export bills
환당좌대출 overdrafts for export bills
환덤핑 exchange dumping
환동향 currency movement
환딜러 exchange cambiste; exchange dealer
환류 channeling back; recycling
환리스크 foreign exchange risk; forex risk
환매가; 재취득가격 repurchase price
환매결제 short covering
환매권 rights of repurchase
환매를 조건으로 매각함 sales under agreement to repurchase
환매리 exchange marry
환매리이익 exchange marriage profit
환매의무 repurchase obligation
환매입 bill bought
환매조건부 거래 repurchase agreement
환매조건부 매각어음 discount on bills sold on condition of repurchase
환매조건부 매출오퍼레이션 selling operation under repurchase agreement
환매청구권 repurchase right
환매출 bill sold
환번호 transfer number
환변동 exchange fluctuation
환변동보험 exchange risk insurance
환변동손실준비금 reserve for loss from fluctuation of foreign exchange rate
환변동준비금 exchange fluctuation reserve
환변동폭 width of currency movements
환보유고 exchange position; position
환보유고조정조작 exchange risk cover
환부가산금 additional amount to refundment
환부금 repayment money
환부금의 익금불산입 exclusion of refund from gross revenue
환부금지불통지서 notification of payment of refund
환부금충당 appropriation of refund
환부금충당통지서 notification of appropriation of refund
환부법인세 refunded corporation tax
환부세 refund tax
환부신청서 refund claim
환부청구 claim for a refund; making a claim for a refund
환부청구권시효 status of limitation on refund claim
환불세 tax rebate
환불세급부 drawback allowance
환브로커 exchange broker
환산 commutation
환산계수테이블 table of price factors
환상장권 exchange rate band
환선물계약 foreign currency forward
환송명령 mandate on remission
환수급안정성 stability of the foreign exchange market
환수수료 charges for remittance

환수취인 remittee
환승 switch
환심리설 psychological theory of exchange
환안정기금 exchange stabilization fund
환어음 bill of exchange; draft bill of exchange
환어음업자 cambist
환어음제시 presentment of bill of exchange
환업무 exchange business
환예약 exchange contract; exchange reservation
환원장 transfer ledger
환율 exchange rate
환율문언 exchange clause
환율변동에 따른 손실 loss from foreign exchange rate fluctuation
환율정책 exchange rate policy
환은행 exchange bank
환은행이 환보유고를 조정하기 위해 다른 은행과 조건이 일치할 때 하는 거래 exchange cover rate
환이익 transfer profit
환인수상장 accepting rate of exchange
환자금조정거래 exchange fund cover operation
환자유화 liberalization of exchange control
환재정 arbitration of exchange
환재정거래 exchange arbitrage transaction
환저금계좌 transfer savings account
환전 exchange of money
환전상 money changer
환전소 money exchange
환전표 transfer slip
환조작 exchange manipulation; exchange operation
환조정의 소득효과 income effect of exchange adjustments
환지처분 substitution of land lot
환지처분에 따른 양도 transfer of property due to the delivery of substitute property
환차손 exchange loss; foreign currency translation gain or loss; loss from fluctuation of foreign exchange rate; loss incurred from exchange rate
환차손익 exchange loss and profit
환차익 exchange gain; exchange profit
환청산협정 exchange clearing agreement
환태평양 Pacific basin
환태평양경제문화권 Pacific Economic and Cultural Enclave
환태평양지역 Pacific Basin
환투기 exchange speculation
환평가 exchange parity; par value of exchange rate
환평형계정 exchange equalization account
환평형기금 exchange equalization fund
환평형조작 exchange equalization operation
환프리미엄 exchange premium
환헤지 currency hedging
환환산수정 effect of exchange rate changes
환환산조정 translation adjustments
환환산차손익 exchange gain or loss
환환산차액 translation gains and losses
활기가 없는 lackluster
활기를 잃다 languish
활동계정 active account; working account
활동률 activity rates
활동영역 domain
활동잔고 active balance
활동회계 activity accounting
활용 abuse
활황 buoyant market; gather steam
활황시장 brisk market
황금률 golden rule
황금분할 golden section
회계 accounting
회계 SEC accounting SEC
회계감사 accountant's inspection; accounting audit; auditing
회계감사실시발표 Accounting and Auditing Enforcement Release
회계감사업무 accountancy service
회계감사인 independent auditor

회계거래 accounting transactions
회계검사관 controller
회계검사원 General Accounting Office
회계공리 accounting axiom
회계공준 accounting postulate
회계과 accounting division; accounting section
회계관리 accounting control
회계규정 accounting regulation
회계기 accounting machine; tabulating machine
회계기간 fiscal period
회계기록 accounting records
회계기준 accounting base; accounting standards
회계기준부서회 Accounting Standard Division
회계기준서 Statement of Accounting Standard
회계기준심의회 Accounting Standard Board
회계단위 accounting unit
회계단일원칙 principle of unified accounting
회계담당자 accountable officer
회계등식 accounting identity
회계매뉴얼 accounting manual
회계모델 accounting model
회계목적 accounting objectives
회계방침 accounting policy
회계방침변경에 따른 누적영향액 cumulative effect of accounting change
회계법 public account law
회계법규에 따른 규제 accounting based on legal requirements
회계베타 accounting beta
회계베타수치 accounting beta value
회계보고 accounting report
회계사 accountant
회계사무소 accounting firm
회계사무처리 accounting data process
회계사보 junior accountant
회계사보조 assistant certified public accountant
회계사사무소 accountant's office
회계사상 accountable event
회계사업 accounting profession
회계사책임 accountant's responsibility
회계상의 가정 assumption of accounting
회계상의 문제점 accounting issues
회계상의 보고서 accountant's report
회계상의 인식 accounting recognition
회계수정처리 accounting adjustment
회계실무 accounting practice
회계실무권고서 recommended accounting practices
회계실체 accounting entity
회계연구공보 Accounting Research Bulletin
회계연도 accounting year; financial year; fiscal year
회계연도를 공준함 postulate of accounting period
회계연속통보 SEC Accounting Releases SEC
회계연속통첩 Accounting Series Release
회계용어 accounting terminology
회계용어공보 Accounting Terminology Bulletin
회계워런트 accountable warrant
회계원칙 accounting convention; accounting principle
회계원칙변경 changes in accounting principles
회계원칙심의회 Accounting Principles Board
회계이론 accounting theory
회계이익 accounting earnings; accounting rate of return
회계일 account day
회계자기자본이익률 accounting ratio of profits to net worth
회계자료 accounting data
회계장부 accounting book; books of account; financial books
회계장표 set of accounts
회계절차 accounting procedures
회계절차규정 manual of accounting procedure
회계절차위원회 Committee on Accounting Procedure
회계제도 accounting system

회계조직 accounting information system; accounting organization; system of accounts
회계주임 chief accountant
회계주임; 경리담당자 paymaster
회계증거 accounting evidence
회계직능 accounting function
회계집무규정 manual of accounting instructions
회계처리 accounting treatment
회계통칙 accounting rules
회계통화 accounting currency
회계평가 accounting valuation
회계학 accountancy
회귀 regression
회귀계수 regression coefficient
회귀기대 regressive expectations
회귀모델 regression model
회귀방정식 regression equation
회귀분석 regression analysis
회귀분석법 regression analysis method
회기 session
회람판 circular letter
회복권 right of resumption
회복불가능한 침해 irreparable injury
회비 club dues; membership fee
회사 company
회사간 계정 inter-company account
회사간 이익 inter-company profit
회사간 제거 inter-company elimination
회사갱생 corporate reorganization; reorganization of corporation
회사갱생법 company rehabilitation law; corporation reorganization law
회사갱생절차관재인 equity receiver
회사기록을 검사함 inspection of corporate record
회사대리인 company representative
회사등기소 registrar of companies
회사레포트 corporation report
회사를 흡수합병함 merger of corporation
회사명의회원 membership in the capacity of a corporation
회사법 companies act; company law; corporation law
회사분할 corporate separation; partition of corporation
회사상호간 대차소법 elimination of intercompany indebtedness
회사상호간 손실 inter-company loss
회사상호간 이익소법 elimination of intercompany profits
회사상호간 지분소법 elimination of intercompany ownership
회사설립등기 registration of incorporation
회사설립면허 certificate of incorporation
회사설립수속 incorporation procedures
회사설립전 이익 profit prior to incorporation
회사설립취지서 prospectus of promotion
회사설립허가서 charter provision
회사신용을 유지하기 위한 배당 fictitious dividend
회사정관 articles of incorporation
회사정리; 채무정리 arrangement
회사정산인 liquidator of a corporation
회사조직 company organization
회사중역 corporate executive
회사창립기념 anniversary of the foundation of a corporation
회사특권 corporate franchise
회사행위 corporate action
회사형 신탁 corporate-type investment trust
회수 collection
회수가능가치 recovery value
회수가능원가 recovery cost
회수가능지출 recovery expenditure
회수가능한 collectible; recoverable
회수규제 regulation of debt collection
회수기간 collection period; collection term; payback period
회수기간법 pay back method
회수기술 collection management technique

회수기준 collection basis
회수기한도래기준 due date coming basis
회수를 마친 원가 absorbed cost
회수불능 frozen credit
회수불능원가 irrecoverable cost; sunk cost
회수순환 collection cycle
회수업무 collection practices
회수업자 debt collector
회수에 문제가 있는 대부 substandard loan
회수율 collection rate; percentage of debt collection
회원가입 admission to membership; membership admission
회원가입신청 application for membership
회원가입일 day of admission
회원가입절차 affiliation procedure
회원권 seat
회원대표자 member representative
회원명부 list of members
회원법 law of member firms
회원복권 restoration of suspended membership
회원비즈니스 membership business
회원사내 상당금액 amount matched within each member
회원신임금 membership guarantee deposit
회원에 대한 권고 recommendation to a member
회원외이사 non-member governor
회원이사 member governor
회원제조직 membership organization
회원조직법인 membership corporation
회원종류 categories of members
회원증권회사 member securities company
회원증서 membership certificate; membership equity
회원지분양수인 transferee of membership equity
회원처분 discipline on members; disposition of a member
회원총회 general assembly meeting of members
회원출자금 contribution to the equity capital
회원탈퇴 withdrawl from membership
회원표식 member's mark
회원회사 member firm; member organization
회의비 convention expense
회전기간 turnover period
회전무역 revolving trade
회전신용장 revolving letter of credit
회전신용장; 리볼빙크레디트 revolving credit
회전어음 endorsed bills exchanged between two parties
회전율 turnover rate; turnover ratio
회전자금 revolving fund
회피 aversion
회피가능원가 avoidable cost; escapable cost
회피불가능원가 unavoidable cost
회피불능비용 inescapable cost
회피하다 evade
회화 dialogue
회화통각검사; TAT thematic apperception test
횡단분석 cross-sectional analysis
횡령 embezzlement
횡령; 환산 conversion
횡선수표 crossed check
효과 effect
효과가 높은 high-leveraged
효력발생통지서 notice to inform of taking effect
효력이 없는 법률행위 void transaction
효력이 없는 쿠폰 invalid coupon
효용이론 utility theory
효용지표 utility indicator
효용함수 utility function
효율성 operational efficiency
효율적인 시장 efficient market
효율적인 시장 가설 efficient market hypothesis
효율적인 포트폴리오 efficient portfolio
후견 guardianship
후견인 conservator; curator

후계자 successor
후기 latter half of the year
후기배당 dividend for the second half
후발발전도상국 least less developed countries
후발사상 post-balance sheet event; subsequent events
후발사상리뷰 subsequent review
후방차분근사치 backward difference
후방차분지불인 backward difference approximation
후방통합 backward integration
후배주 deferred share; deferred stock
후보자신고제도 entry system of a candidate
후비용 after cost
후생경제학 welfare economics
후생노동성 Ministry of Health; Labour and Welfare
후생연금 welfare pension
후생연금보험 welfare pension insurance
후순위 subordination
후순위담보 junior security
후순위선취특권부 사채 junior lien bond
후순위저당 junior mortgage
후순위채권 junior bond
후순위채권자 junior creditor
후순위청구권 secondary claim
후일부의 dating backward
후일불신용장 deferred payment credit
후입선출기준 last-in first-out basis
후입선출매가환원법 lifo adaptation of retail method
후입선출법 last-in first-out method
후입선출법준비금 LIFO reserve
후장 afternoon session; afternoon trading session
후진국 backward countries
후퇴 pulling-back
훈계; 경고 admonition
훼손된 수표 mutilated check
휴가수당 vacation pay
휴대전화사무 cellular operation
휴면구좌 sleeping account
휴면회원 sleeping member
휴식하다; 잔여 rest
휴업기간중의 고정비를 보상함 compensation for fixed costs during the suspension of business
휴지계정 dormant account
휴지잔고 dormant balance
휴회 recess
흑백논리 disjunctive allegation
흑자 in black; positive figure
흑자국 surplus country
흑자재정 surplus finance
흑자전환 recovery from deficit
흡수적 접근방법 absorption approach
흡수합병 consolidation take-over; purchase acquisition
흡수합병된 회사 absorbed corporation
흥미 appetite
흥행권 playright
흥행수입 box office revenue
희귀주 rare stock
희망적; 낙관적 bullish
희박화 dilution
희박화 방지조항 anti-dilution clause
희박화율 dilution factor
희석필 fully diluted
희소자원 scarce resources
희소통화조항 scarce currency clause
히스토그램법 histogram method
히스토리컬데이터 historical data
히스토리컬베타 historical beta

기타

1/5상각법 20% depreciation method
100선물옵션 S&P 100 spot option S&P
100종 주가지수 FT-SE 100 FT-SE
100퍼센트 자회사 totally-held subsidiary
10년 이부채권 10-year coupon-bearing government bonds
10년간 비교재무제표 ten years comparative financial summary
10라인특약 10 line treaty
120종 주가지수 SBF 120 SBF
1940년의 투자회사법 Investment Company Act of 1940
1959년 생명보험회사소득세법 Life Income Tax Act of 1959
1970년의 개정투자회사법 Investment Company Amendments Act of 1970
1983년 증권법 Securities Act of 1983
1년의 12분의 1; 역월 calendar month
24시간거래 24 hours trading
24시간거래시장 round-the-clock market
25 옵션 25 Option
2달러 브로커 2 dollar broker
2위군; 후발주자 second tier
360일 베이시스 360 day basis
3개월 이동평균 three-month moving average
3일후 결제 skip-day settlement
40종 주가지수 CAC 40 CAC
4계지불지급일 quarter-days
4반기 quarter
4반기 리펀딩 quarterly refunding
4반기 베이스의 실질성장률 quarterly real growth rate
4반기보고서 quarterly reports
4반기이익 quarterly earnings
4반기입찰 quarterly auction
4일후 인도 triple settlement
50%상각법 replacement method
500종 주가지수 P 500 Stock Price Index S&P
5년 할인국채 5-year discount government bonds
60년 상환룰 60-year redemption rule
~와 대비하여 versus
~을 제외하고는 except for
~일 현재 as at